AF856361

Study Guide

Intermediate Accounting

Ninth Edition

THOMSON
SOUTH-WESTERN

Australia · Canada · Mexico · Singapore · Spain · United Kingdom · United States

Study Guide

Intermediate Accounting

Ninth Edition

Loren A. Nikolai

Ernst & Young Professor, School of Accountancy

University of Missouri – Columbia

John D. Bazley

Professor, School of Accountancy

University of Denver

Prepared by

Natalie M. Krawitz, CPA

University of Missouri – System

Theodora A. Arthur, CPA

Harry C. Winfrey CPA Firm

Loren A. Nikolai, Ph.D., CPA

University of Missouri – Columbia

THOMSON

SOUTH-WESTERN

Australia · Canada · Mexico · Singapore · Spain · United Kingdom · United States

THOMSON

SOUTH-WESTERN

Study Guide To Accompany Intermediate Accounting

Loren A. Nikolai and John D. Bazley

Editor-in-Chief:
Jack W. Calhoun

Team Leader:
Melissa S. Acuña

Acquisitions Editor:
Sharon Oblinger

Developmental Editor:
Erin McGraw

Marketing Manager:
Keith Chassé

Production Editor:
Amy A. Brooks

Manufacturing Coordinator:
Doug Wilke

Printer:
Globus
Minster, Ohio

Design Project Manager:
Casey Gilbertson

Cover Designer:
Casey Gilbertson

ISBN: 0-324-18293-7

Printed in the United States of America
1 2 3 4 5 05 04 03 02

For more information contact South-Western, 5191 Natorp Boulevard, Mason, Ohio 45040.
Or you can visit our Internet site at: http://www.swcollege.com

PREFACE

The purpose of this **Study Guide** is to help you master terms, concepts, and practices introduced in **INTERMEDIATE ACCOUNTING** (ninth edition), by Nikolai and Bazley and to give you a means of testing this mastery.

Each chapter of the **Study Guide** corresponds to a text chapter and contains a list of Chapter Objectives, a Synopsis (summary) of the chapter, numerous Self-Evaluation Exercises (with answers), and a three-part Post Test (with answers). The appropriate sequence to follow in your learning is to read the chapter in the text, work any assigned material in the text, and then turn to the **Study Guide** and use it to reinforce and test your understanding of the chapter's key concepts. Each component of the **Study Guide** chapters and its intended use is discussed below.

Chapter Objectives: This list highlights what you should expect to know after you have carefully studied the material in each chapter. The objectives help define and clarify the important skills introduced in the chapter. By the time you have completed your study of the chapter and the exercises in the guide, you should be able to demonstrate to yourself and your instructor a thorough mastery of each objective.

Synopsis: This is a summary of the key points in each section of the chapter. You may use it as a preview (before you read the text chapter) or as a review (after you have read the chapter) and in studying for exams. It cannot, however, be used in place of the text.

Self-Evaluation Exercises: After you feel you have a good grasp of the chapter's content, you should evaluate your progress by means of these exercises. Answering each question will reinforce your knowledge of the chapter and help you assess your strengths and weaknesses. As you check your answers to the exercises in the answer key that follows the section, be sure to refer to the text whenever you find an incorrect response. Read over the corresponding text pages until you know why your answer was incorrect and are sure you could complete a similar exercise on one of your class examinations.

Post Test: This set of practice examinations consists of a number of true/false and multiple-choice questions and three or more accounting problems. As soon as you feel that you understand the chapter (and can complete each Chapter Objective), set aside some time to take the Post Test in a place where you will not be interrupted. Keep track of the time you needed to finish the test; this will help you plan your time when confronted in class with a "for real" exam. Answer each question thoroughly and carefully. Then check your answers in the answer key at the end of the **Study Guide** chapter and correct any question or problem you missed. Again, take a few minutes to review those parts of the text chapter that gave you trouble on the Post Test. There are few more frustrating experiences than missing a practice question . . . and then missing it again when it really counts!

Also included at the end of the **Study Guide** are Check Figures of key answers for the end-of-chapter exercises and problems in the main textbook. These are designed to help you check your work as you solve the exercises and problems.

When you have completed the **Study Guide** chapter and reviewed any topics presented in the chapter that gave you trouble on the Self-Evaluation Exercises and Post Test, you should be ready to pass any test your instructor might give. Remember, however, that the mastery of accounting concepts and principles is essentially the mastery of a number of creative and critical thinking skills and their application to different financial situations. While it is useful to be able to define important accounting terms--to know the "language of accounting"--such knowledge is largely wasted unless you can apply these terms and concepts. This means being able to work accounting problems of all types. The problems in your text and in this **Study Guide** will provide you with a great deal of practice. Therefore, they should be your main focus as you go through each chapter. Pay special attention to them, work them out fully, correct mistakes, and then "fix" each problem in your mind before going on. You may even want to try your hand at creating some of your own practice problems, taking those that appear in the text or **Study Guide** and changing the numbers or conditions to produce new problems. This will accomplish two important objectives. It will help you improve your problem-solving skills, and it will get you into the habit of thinking creatively in your application of basic accounting tools. The way you are judged in this course and, for many of you, in your business career will ultimately depend on how successfully you master both of these aspects of accounting.

We wish to express our appreciation to our spouses, children, and friends who provided us with moral support and understanding during the production process.

Natalie M. Krawitz
Theodora A. Arthur
Loren A. Nikolai

CONTENTS

1

THE ENVIRONMENT OF FINANCIAL REPORTING

CHAPTER OBJECTIVES

After careful study of this chapter, you will be able to:

1. Understand capital markets and decision making.
2. Know what is included in financial reporting.
3. Explain generally accepted accounting principles (GAAP) and the sources of GAAP.
4. Identify the types of pronouncements issued by the FASB.
5. Understand how the Financial Accounting Standards Board (FASB) operates.
6. Describe the relationship between the Securities and Exchange Commission (SEC) and the FASB.
7. Use ethical models for decision making about ethical dilemmas.
8. Understand creative and critical thinking.

SYNOPSIS

Accounting Information

1. Accounting, the "language of business," has been described as the process of identifying, measuring, recording, and communicating economic information to permit informed judgments and decisions by users of information. Accounting provides a link between the economic activities of a company and decision makers who are interested in the company. These decision makers who use accounting information can be divided into two major groups: external users (such as investors) and internal users (the company's management). Because of their different relationships to the company, the two groups have somewhat dissimilar information needs.

2. External users include, for example, actual and potential investors in stocks and bonds, creditors, employees, taxing and regulatory authorities, financial analysts, and the general public. Investors need accounting information on a timely basis for three basic decisions: the buy, hold, and sell decisions. Creditors need timely information for decisions on extending and continuing credit. Published financial statements are a primary source of information for investment and credit decisions, which should be continuously reevaluated.

3. In capital markets, investors exchange capital for the stocks and bonds of companies. Exchanges between investors themselves are made in secondary markets, such as the New York and American Stock Exchanges and NASDAQ. Companies deal directly with investors in primary markets, by borrowing from lending institutions or issuing capital stock or bonds. Primary markets include both public offerings and private placements. Public offerings involve advertising and sales of stocks or bonds to the general public, while in private placements, advertising and sales are directed to a limited number of institutions, such as insurance companies and pension funds, or employees.

4. Internal users are the company's managers. Managers may request any information that the accounting system can provide, in any format, to use in short-term and long-term planning and control.

5. Financial accounting is the information accumulation, processing, and communication system designed to satisfy the investment and credit decision-making information needs of external users. Financial accounting information is presented in published financial statements.

6. Financial reporting is the process of communicating financial accounting information about a company to external users, primarily through the company's annual report. The annual report includes at least three major financial statements: the balance sheet, income statement, and statement of cash flows. Many companies also include a statement of changes in stockholders' equity as a fourth major financial statement. In addition, notes, sometimes with supporting schedules, further explain financial statement information. Most financial statements are audited by an independent certified public accountant, who expresses an opinion as to the fairness, in accordance with generally accepted accounting principles, of the financial statements and accompanying notes.

7. Managerial accounting is the information accumulation, processing, and communication system designed to meet the decision-making information needs of internal users. The format for internal reports is determined by the company. The system is constrained by the need for information and the cost of providing that information.

8. A company's management is often evaluated and rewarded based on financial reports. Agency theory, which suggests that agents do not always act in the best interest of their principals, implies that basing management's compensation on company performance is an effective way to align the interests of management and the company.

Generally Accepted Accounting Principles

9. In its audited financial statements, a company must follow generally accepted accounting principles (GAAP), the guidelines, procedures, and practices required for recording and reporting accounting information. GAAP define accepted accounting practices and standards of reporting at a particular time. They have evolved over many years, with the involvement of different policy-making bodies.

10. There is no single document including all of the standards for accounting, although the FASB Financial Accounting Research System (FARS) includes most accounting standards in its electronic data base. Sources of generally accepted accounting principles, in descending order of importance, are:

    (a) Pronouncements of authoritative bodies: the Financial Accounting Standards Board (FASB), the Accounting Principles Board (APB), the Committee on Accounting Procedure (CAP) of the American Institute of Certified Public Accountants (AICPA), and the Securities and Exchange Commission (SEC). Included are FASB Statements of Financial Accounting Standards and Interpretations, APB Opinions, CAP (AICPA) Accounting Research Bulletins, SEC Regulation S-X and SEC Financial Reporting Releases.

    (b) Pronouncements issued by bodies of expert accountants after exposure for public comment, including FASB Technical Bulletins, AICPA Industry Audit and Accounting Guides, and AICPA Statements of Position.

    (c) Pronouncements issued by bodies of expert accountants without exposure for public comment, including FASB Emerging Issues Task Force Consensus Positions and AICPA Practice Bulletins.

    (d) Widely accepted practices and pronouncements of practices prevalent in a particular industry or applied to specific circumstances, such as AICPA Accounting Interpretations, FASB Q's and A's, and AICPA Accounting Trends and Techniques.

    (e) Other accounting literature, including FASB Statements of Financial Accounting Concepts, APB Statements, AICPA Issue Papers, AICPA Technical Practice Aids, and accounting texts and articles.

The Establishment of Accounting Standards

11. From 1938 to 1959 the Committee on Accounting Procedure (CAP) of the AICPA issued 51 Accounting Research Bulletins, which are still part of GAAP unless specifically superseded or amended. The CAP had no enforcement authority.

12. Because of criticism of the processes of formulating accounting principles, the AICPA replaced the CAP with the Accounting Principles Board in 1959. The 17 to 21 members of the APB were part-time volunteers. From 1959 to 1973 the APB issued 31 Opinions, many based on Accounting Research Studies. Unless amended or rescinded, APB Opinions are also still part of GAAP.

13. Development of accounting principles by the APB was criticized, with that criticism centered on three factors: (a) lack of independence of members of the APB from their business, governmental, or academic employers, (b) over-representation of public accounting firms and the AICPA on the APB, and (c) slow response time in solving problems. The structure of the Financial Accounting Standards Board (FASB), which replaced the APB in 1973, was designed to meet these criticisms. The parent Financial Accounting Foundation (FAF) is governed by sixteen trustees appointed from the membership of nine specified organizations. The FAF appoints the seven members of the FASB, raises funds for the operation of the FASB, and provides general oversight. FASB appointees are full-time, fully paid members, representing a wide cross-section of interests. The FAF, in addition, appoints members of the Financial Accounting Standards Advisory Council (FASAC), which advises the FASB.

14. The FASB issues several types of pronouncements, including Statements of Financial Accounting Standards, Interpretations, Technical Bulletins, and Statements of Financial Accounting Concepts. Before issuing a statement of concepts or standards, the FASB usually completes a multistage process designed to develop accounting standards efficiently and with due process, in a public forum. The process includes research leading to a Discussion Memorandum or Invitation to Comment, public hearings, issuance of an Exposure Draft, more public hearings, modification of the Exposure Draft, and a vote (simple-majority) of the Board resulting in a Statement. Because accounting policy decisions are complex and part of a broader social system, input from interested parties is important. Negotiation and compromise are often necessary during the development of fair, acceptable standards.

15. The Securities and Exchange Commission has the legal authority to prescribe accounting principles and reporting practices for all companies issuing publicly traded securities. The SEC has usually allowed accounting principles to be formulated in the private sector, and has stated that standards set by the FASB are considered to have substantial authoritative support. However, the commission has occasionally exerted pressure on the CAP, APB, and FASB. In addition, the SEC administers the extensive disclosure requirements of the Securities Act of 1933 and the Securities Exchange Act of 1934. The 1934 Act requires companies to file a number of reports, which are available to users on the Internet in the SEC's Electronic Data Gathering, Analysis, and Retrieval System (EDGAR).

16. The American Institute of Certified Public Accountants is the professional organization for all certified public accountants in the U.S. The AICPA issues numerous publications, including Industry Audit Guides, Industry Accounting Guides, Statements of Position, Practice Bulletins, Issue Papers, and Accounting Trends and Techniques.

17. The FASB Emerging Issues Task Force (EITF) identifies significant emerging accounting issues and develops consensus positions on accounting for these issues.

18. The Cost Accounting Standards Board (CASB), a congressional agency, is charged with setting standards of accounting for negotiated federal contracts and subcontracts exceeding $500,000.

19. The Internal Revenue Service (IRS) administers the provisions of the Internal Revenue Code. These provisions do not always reflect the goals of financial accounting. However, they do at times influence the choice of accounting methods and procedures.

20. The American Accounting Association (AAA) is an organization comprised primarily of academic and practicing accountants. The AAA attempts to influence the development of formal accounting pronouncements through education and persuasion.

21. The International Accounting Standards Committee (IASB) has as its goals to develop and promote the use of global accounting standards, and to bring national accounting standards into agreement with international standards. The IASB has 12 full-time members (and 2 part-time members) from various countries. It issues International Accounting Standards. To do so, its operating procedures include study of the topic, issuance of an Exposure Draft, evaluation of comments, and consideration of a revised draft. If approved by at least 8 members of the IASB, the International Accounting Standard is issued. The FASB is working with the IASC to harmonize accounting standards. However, financial statements prepared according to international standards may not comply with U.S. GAAP.

22. The Governmental Accounting Standards Board (GASB) operates under the auspices of the Financial Accounting Foundation. It establishes accounting standards for certain state and local governmental entities.

23. The G4+1 is a group of standard-setting boards that strives to influence the development and harmonization of useful, high quality accounting standards for international capital markets.

24. Several professional associations also influence the development of accounting standards. The Financial Executives Institute (FEI) is composed mainly of high-level financial executives. The Institute of Management Accountants (IMA) emphasizes managerial and cost accountancy. The Association for Investment Management and Research (AIMR) is made up of financial analysts. Each of the three organizations provides input to the FASB through the FAF and the public hearings process.

Ethics in the Accounting Environment

25. In their professional roles, accountants are often faced with ethical dilemmas (ethical conflicts). The AICPA Code of Professional Conduct (CPC) includes six basic principles: members should (a) exercise sensitive professional and moral judgments in carrying out their responsibilities; (b) serve the public interest, honor the public trust, and demonstrate commitment to professionalism; (c) perform professional responsibilities with the highest sense of integrity; (d) maintain objectivity, be free from conflicts of interest, and be independent in fact and appearance; (e) observe due care in practice, and (f) follow CPC principles in determining the scope and nature of services to be provided.

26. The CPC provides guidelines for practicing accountants, but does not present a structured approach to resolving ethical dilemmas. Three basic approaches to moral reasoning have been identified by the noted ethicist Velasquez: (a) the utilitarian model, emphasizing the greatest good for the greatest number; (b) the rights model, emphasizing individual moral rights; and (c) the justice model, emphasizing the fair distribution of benefits and burdens. Velasquez combines the three approaches in a system for moral reasoning.

27. Because of the important role of accounting in society, accountants must maintain high ethical standards.

Creative and Critical Thinking in Accounting

28. The global business environment is continually becoming more complex, with new products, services, and methods of production, distribution, and communication. To establish and maintain accounting systems which meet the needs of users, accountants must be both creative and critical thinkers. Creative thinking involves the use of imagination and insight to solve problems by finding new relationships (ideas) among items of information. Critical thinking involves the logical analysis of issues, using inductive or deductive reasoning to test new relationships (ideas) to determine their effectiveness.

SELF-EVALUATION EXERCISES

Supply the words necessary to complete each of the following items.

Accounting Information

AI-1. The two major groups of decision makers using accounting information are ______________ and _____________ users.

AI-2. External users include __________ in stocks and bonds, __________ such as suppliers and lending institutions, employees, taxing and regulatory authorities, financial analysts, and the __________ _________.

AI-3. Investors need accounting information for three basic decisions: the _______, ___________, and _________________ decisions.

AI-4. Investors may buy stocks and bonds in ______________ ___________ such as the New York Stock Exchange.

AI-5. The balance sheet, income statement, and statement of cash flows are included in a company's _____________ _________, which also includes explanatory ______________, sometimes with supporting schedules.

AI-6. In addition to a balance sheet, income statement, and statement of cash flows, many companies present a ________________ ________ ___________ _______ ______________ _____________ as a major financial statement.

AI-7. A company's managers are _________ users of accounting information.

AI-8. ____________________ ______________ is the information accumulation, processing, and communication system designed to meet the decision-making information needs of internal users.

AI-9. Agency theory suggests that agents may not always act in the

________ ______________ of their principals.

Generally Accepted Accounting Principles

GA-1. With the involvement of various policy-making bodies, the guidelines, procedures, and practices required for recording and reporting accounting information have evolved into the current ____________ ____________ ____________ ____________.

GA-2. The sources of generally accepted accounting principles are:

(1) Pronouncements of authoritative bodies including:

the ____________ ______________ ____________ ________

the ______________ __________ ________, the Committee

on Accounting Procedure of the ____________ ______________

___ ______________ ________ ____________, and the

__________ ____ __________ ______________.

(2) Pronouncements issued by expert accounting bodies, after public

exposure, include the ______________ ______________

____________ ________ Technical Bulletins, and the

______________ ______________ ___ ____________

__________ ______________ Industry Audit and Accounting Guides, and Statements of Position.

(3) Pronouncements of bodies of expert accountants issued without exposure for

public comment, such as FASB Emerging Issues Task Force ____________

____________ and AICPA ____________ ______________.

(4) Accounting practices which are ______________ __________ and pronouncements of practices prevalent in a particular industry.

(5) Other accounting literature, including FASB Statements of Financial

Accounting Concepts, APB Statements, AICPA ________ ________ and

__________ ____________ _____, and accounting ________ and ______.

The Establishment of Accounting Standards

EA-1. Accounting Research Bulletins were issued from 1938 to 1959 by the

____________ ___ ________________ ______________ of the AICPA.

EA-2. Part-time volunteers made up the _______________ __________________ ____________, successor to the CAP.

EA-3. The Financial Accounting Foundation appoints the seven full-time members of the _____________ _________________ _____________ ________.

EA-4. Pronouncements issued by the FASB include _______________ ______ ________________ ________________ ________________.

Interpretations, Technical Bulletins, and _______________ _____ __________________ __________________ _____________________.

EA-5. The multistage process used by the FASB to develop accounting standards includes research leading to a Discussion Memorandum, ___________ ______________, issuance of an ______________ ___________, more public hearings, modification of the Exposure Draft, and a vote of the Board.

EA-6. Congress gave legal authority to prescribe accounting principles to the ______________ _____ ______________ _______________.

EA-7. The group charged with setting accounting standards for negotiated federal contracts and subcontracts exceeding $500,000 is the

________ __________________ _________________ ________.

EA-8. The American Accounting Association, an organization of academicians and practicing accountants, influences development of accounting pronouncements through ____________ and ___________.

EA-9. The professional accountancy groups of about 104 countries are members of the _____________ _____________ ______________ ______________.

EA-10. Accounting standards for certain state and local governmental entities are established by the ___________ _________________ ______________ ______________.

EA-11. The G4+1 attempts to influence accounting standards for ____________________ ___________ _____________.

Ethics in the Accounting Environment

EE-1. Six basic principles to guide accountants in the resolution of ethical dilemmas are included in the AICPA ________ ____ ________________ ___________.

EE-2. The ethicist Velasquez identified three basic approaches to moral reasoning: the _____________, _________, and __________ models.

Creative and Critical Thinking

CC-1. In the complex global business environment, accountants may need to use both the imagination and insight of __________ __________ and the logical analysis of __________ __________ to solve problems.

ANSWERS TO SELF-EVALUATION EXERCISES

AI-1. external, internal; AI-2. investors, creditors, general public; AI-3. buy, hold, sell; AI-4. secondary markets (or capital markets); AI-5. annual report, notes; AI-6. statement of changes in stockholders' equity; AI-7. internal; AI-8. managerial accounting; AI-9. best interests; GA-1. generally accepted accounting principles; GA-2. (1) Financial Accounting Standards Board, Accounting Principles Board, American Institute of Certified Public Accountants, Securities and Exchange Commission; (2) Financial Accounting Standards Board, American Institute of Certified Public Accountants; (3) <u>Consensus Positions</u>, <u>Practice Bulletins</u>, (4) widely accepted; (5) <u>Issue Papers</u>, <u>Technical Practice Aids</u>, texts, articles; EA-1. Committee on Accounting Procedure; EA-2. Accounting Principles Board; EA-3. Financial Accounting Standards Board; EA-4. <u>Statements of Financial Accounting Standards</u>, <u>Statements of Financial Accounting Concepts</u>; EA-5. public hearings, Exposure Draft; EA-6. Securities and Exchange Commission; EA-7. Cost Accounting Standards Board; EA-8. education, persuasion; EA-9. International Accounting Standards Committee; EA-10. Governmental Accounting Standards Board; EA-11. international capital markets; EE-1. <u>Code of Professional Conduct</u>; EE-2. utilitarian, rights, justice; CC-1. creative thinking, critical thinking.

POST TEST

Part A Circle T if the statement is true and F if it is false.

T F 1. Consensus Positions of the FASB Emerging Issues Task Force are preliminary discussions of accounting issues and are not considered to be part of GAAP.

T F 2. Financial accounting is the information accumulation, processing, and communication system designed to meet the decision-making information needs of internal users.

T F 3. The three basic decisions of investors are the buy, hold, and sell decisions.

T F 4. APB Opinions and AICPA Accounting Research Bulletins are sources of generally accepted accounting principles.

T F 5. One goal of the FASB is to bring generally accepted principles into conformity with tax laws.

T F 6. The AICPA Code of Professional Conduct provides a structured system for accountants to use in the resolution of ethical conflicts.

T F 7. The International Accounting Standards Committee, with members from about 104 countries, often uses compromise while promoting the adoption of sound, comparable accounting standards internationally.

T F 8. The utilitarian model, an approach to moral reasoning, emphasizes the greatest good for the greatest number.

T F 9. Managerial accounting is the information system primarily designed to meet the needs of investment analysts.

T F 10. The New York Stock Exchange, the largest stock exchange in the U.S., is designated as the primary market, while the American Stock Exchange is a secondary market.

T F 11. The SEC, which has the authority to prescribe accounting principles, has to date usually allowed principles to be formulated in the private sector.

T F 12. Accounting literature, such as texts and articles, is considered to be a source of GAAP.

T F 13. The Cost Accounting Standards Board establishes rules for federal contracts for negotiated amounts greater than $500,000.

T F 14. The Accounting Research Bulletins issued by the AICPA's Committee on Accounting Procedure were rescinded by the Accounting Principles Board in 1959.

T F 15. The Financial Accounting Standards Board appoints the seven members of the Financial Accounting Standards Advisory Council, which oversees the Financial Accounting Foundation.

T F 16. The Accounting Principles Board was criticized for lack of independence, over-representation by public accounting firms and the AICPA, and slow response time.

T F 17. Shortly after its formation in 1973, the FASB issued a summary of GAAP, which serves as the authoritative standard for accounting principles.

T F 18. Agency theory implies that it is effective for a company to base management compensation on company performance.

T F 19. An independent auditor expresses an opinion on the fairness, in accordance with GAAP, of a company's financial statements and accompanying notes.

T F 20. The FASB restricts public input during the development of new accounting standards in order to enhance efficiency and preserve the Board's independence.

T F 21. Financial statements prepared according to international (IASC) standards are automatically considered to be in compliance with U.S. GAAP.

T F 22. Many companies present a statement of changes in stockholders' equity as a major financial statement, in addition to a balance sheet, income statement, and statement of cash flows.

T F 23. The SEC requires companies to file certain reports electronically and makes these reports available to users via its Electronic Data Gathering, Analysis and Retrieval System.

T F 24. The FASB's Financial Accounting Research System is an electronic data base which includes most accounting standards.

Part B Select the one <u>best</u> answer, and place its letter in the space provided.

____ 1. External users of a company's reports do <u>not</u> include (a) union representatives; (b) shop foremen; (c) company controllers; (d) bank loan officers.

____ 2. Sources of generally accepted accounting principles do <u>not</u> include (a) widely accepted practices; (b) SEC regulations; (c) AICPA <u>Accounting Research Bulletins</u>; (d) formal pronouncements of the American Accounting Association.

____ 3. Which of the following statements about the AICPA Code of Professional Conduct (CPC) is true? (a) the CPC provides accountants with step-by-step procedures for resolving ethical conflicts; (b) the CPC recognizes that, given the factual nature of accounting, accountants seldom face ethical dilemmas in their profession; (c) the CPC requires that accountants give priority to their responsibilities toward their clients when ethical conflicts arise; (d) the CPC requires that accountants be independent in appearance, as well as fact.

____ 4. The Committee on Accounting Procedure (a) had no authority to enforce its pronouncements; (b) raises funds for the operation of the FASB; (c) is a Congressional group with the authority to oversee accounting practices; (d) issued 31 Opinions between 1959 and 1973.

____ 5. The Accounting Principles Board was criticized for (a) its lack of independence; (b) the complexity of its pronouncements; (c) its failure to represent accounting practitioners and their professional organizations; (d) all of the above.

_____ 6. Which of the following statements describing approaches to moral reasoning is true? (a) the utilitarian model and the rights model both emphasize the fair distribution of benefits and burdens; (b) the justice model is based on service in the public interest and a commitment to professionalism; (c) the utilitarian model stresses the greatest good for the greatest number; (d) the utilitarian, rights, and justice models are all based on the six basic principles of the AICPA Code of Professional Conduct.

_____ 7. Which of the following statements regarding the FASB is true?
(a) pronouncements issued by the FASB include Statements of Financial Accounting Concepts, Statements of Financial Accounting Standards, Interpretations, and Technical Bulletins; (b) Members of the FASB are appointed by the Financial Accounting Foundation, which also provides general oversight; (c) the seven FASB appointees are full-time members, representing a wide cross-section of interests; (d) all of the above.

_____ 8. In primary markets, (a) investors make exchanges with other investors; (b) companies borrow from lending institutions or issue capital stocks or bonds; (c) U.S. companies operate under regulations established by the International Accounting Standards Committee; (d) managerial accounting statements are the primary source of information for investors making the buy, hold, and sell decisions.

_____ 9. Financial accounting information is (a) prepared to meet the decision-making information needs of internal users; (b) presented in published financial statements; (c) published in the format prescribed in SEC Financial Reporting Releases; (d) seldom useful in the decision making of investors in primary markets.

_____ 10. The Financial Accounting Foundation (a) exercises general oversight over the FASB; (b) consists of seven full-time members appointed by the FASB; (c) issues Opinions which are considered to be a source of GAAP; (d) is governed by the 16-member FASAC.

Part C   Solve each of the following short problems.

1. Each of the organizations listed below has been a source of generally accepted accounting principles. Following the list is a series of descriptive statements. Match each descriptive statement with an organization by placing the appropriate letter in the space provided.

   a. Committee on Accounting Procedure
   b. Accounting Principles Board
   c. Financial Accounting Standards Board
   d. Securities and Exchange Commission
   e. American Institute of Certified Public Accountants

   _____ 1. Recognizing that accounting is part of a broad social system, this organization attempts to develop standards fairly, with due process, in a public forum.

   _____ 2. This AICPA organization, which had no enforcement authority, issued Accounting Research Bulletins.

   _____ 3. The 17 to 21 members of this group, working part-time, issued Opinions.

   _____ 4. This organization has seldom used its congressional authority to prescribe accounting principles and practice.

   _____ 5. The 7 full-time members of this group issue several types of pronouncements, including Statements of Financial Accounting Concepts and Statements of Financial Accounting Standards.

   _____ 6. This group was criticized for lack of independence, over-representation of public accounting firms, and slow response time.

   _____ 7. This organization issues numerous publications, including Industry Audit Guides and Industry Accounting Guides.

   _____ 8. Members of this organization are appointed by the Financial Accounting Foundation, which raises funds and provides oversight.

   _____ 9. This organization administers the disclosure requirements of the Securities Act of 1933 and the Securities Exchange Act of 1934.

   _____ 10. This is the professional organization for certified public accountants in the United States.

2. Below is a list of words or terms. Following the list is a series of descriptive phrases. Match each word or term with its descriptive phrase by placing the appropriate letter in the space provided.

a. primary markets
b. internal users
c. justice model
d. annual report
e. accounting
f. financial accounting
g. AICPA Code of Professional Conduct
h. buy, hold, and sell
i. secondary markets
j. GAAP
k. FASB Financial Accounting Research System
l. creative thinking

_____ 1. a critical link between a company's economic activities and decision makers who are interested in the company.

_____ 2. the information accumulation, processing, and communication system designed to satisfy the investment and credit decision-making information needs of external users.

_____ 3. include both public offerings and private placements.

_____ 4. accepted accounting practices and standards of reporting at a particular time.

_____ 5. includes six basic principles for use as guidelines for ethical dilemmas by practicing accountants.

_____ 6. a company's management.

_____ 7. the three basic decisions of investors.

_____ 8. includes at least three major financial statement (balance sheet, income statement, and statement of cash flows), as well as notes, sometimes with supporting schedules.

_____ 9. emphasizes the fair distribution of benefits and burdens.

_____ 10. involves the use of imagination and insight to solve problems.

_____ 11. includes the New York Stock Exchange, the American Stock Exchange, and the National Association of Securities Dealers Automated Quotation System.

_____ 12. includes most accounting standards in its electronic data base.

3. Below is a list of organizations which have influenced the development of accounting standards. Following the list is a series of descriptive phrases. Match each organization with a phrase by placing the appropriate letter in the space provided.

a. Emerging Issues Task Force
b. Cost Accounting Standards
c. Internal Revenue Service
d. American Accounting Association
e. International Accounting Standards Board
f. Government Accounting Standards Board
g. Association for Investment Management and Research
h. Financial Executives Institute
i. American Institute of Certified Public Accountants
j. Financial Accounting Standards Board
k. Securities and Exchange Commission
l. Institute of Management Accountants

_____ 1. an association of financial analysts.

_____ 2. composed of 12 full-time (and 2 part-time) members from various countries.

_____ 3. identifies significant emerging accounting issues.

_____ 4. charged with developing accounting principles for negotiated federal contracts and subcontracts exceeding $500,000.

_____ 5. issues rules which sometimes conflict with the goals of financial accounting.

_____ 6. influences the development of accounting standards through education and persuasion.

_____ 7. establishes accounting standards for certain state and local government entities.

_____ 8. made up mainly of high-level financial executives.

_____ 9. formed the CAP and the APB.

_____ 10. emphasizes managerial and cost accountancy.

_____ 11. composed of seven full-time, fully paid members.

_____ 12. has the legal authority to prescribe accounting principles for publicly traded companies.

ANSWERS TO POST TEST

Part A

1. F	7. T	13. T	19. T
2. F	8. T	14. F	20. F
3. T	9. F	15. F	21. F
4. T	10. F	16. T	22. T
5. F	11. T	17. F	23. T
6. F	12. T	18. T	24. T

Part B

1. c	3. d	5. a	7. d	9. b
2. d	4. a	6. c	8. b	10. a

Part C

1.	1. c	6. b	2.	1. e	7. h	3.	1. g
	2. a	7. e		2. f	8. d		2. e
	3. b	8. c		3. a	9. c		3. a
	4. d	9. d		4. j	10. l		4. b
	5. c	10. e		5. g	11. i		5. c
				6. b	12. k		6. d

3. (continued): 7. f, 8. h, 9. i, 10. l, 11. j, 12. k

2

FINANCIAL REPORTING: ITS CONCEPTUAL FRAMEWORK

CHAPTER OBJECTIVES

After careful study of this chapter, you will be able to:

1. Explain the FASB conceptual framework.
2. Understand the relationship among the objectives of financial reporting.
3. Identify the general objective of financial reporting.
4. Describe the three specific objectives of financial reporting.
5. Discuss the types of useful information for investment and credit decision making.
6. Explain the qualities of useful accounting information.
7. Understand the accounting assumptions and conventions that influence GAAP.
8. Define the elements of financial statements.

SYNOPSIS

FASB Conceptual Framework

1. The FASB has been charged with developing a conceptual framework of accounting theory and with establishing standards for financial accounting practice. The conceptual framework, which is intended to provide a theoretical foundation of interrelated objectives and concepts for consistent financial accounting standards, has been nearly completed. Seven Statements of Financial Accounting Concepts have been issued.

2. The FASB divided the conceptual framework activities into projects: (a) objectives of financial reporting, (b) qualitative characteristics of accounting information, (c) accounting projects (accounting elements, recognition, and measurement), (d) reporting projects (financial statements and financial reporting, income, and cash flow and liquidity). The first two Statements of Financial Accounting Concepts (objectives and qualitative characteristics) are discussed in this chapter.

Objectives of Financial Reporting

3. FASB Statement of Financial Accounting Concepts No. 1 deals with the objectives of financial reporting. These objectives relate to general-purpose financial reporting of companies. That is, they are to meet the needs of a variety of external, rather than internal, users.

4. Three broad objectives of financial reporting, which proceed from the more general to the more specific, are identified in the Statement:

   (a) The general objective is to provide information that is useful to present and potential investors, creditors, and other external users for decision making. Users are expected to have a reasonable understanding of business and economic activities, and to be willing to study the information carefully.

   (b) On a more specific level, the derived external user objective is to provide information useful in assessing the amounts, timing, and uncertainty of prospective cash flows to be received by external users. This information is important because individual and institutional decisions about outflows for investing and lending are made based on the potential for increasing their cash inflows.

   (c) The derived company objective is to provide information useful in assessing the amounts, timing, and uncertainty of prospective net cash inflows of the company. The company's investment activities take place within its operating cycle. In the operating cycle goods and services are acquired, their value is increased, they are sold, and the selling price is collected. The company's success in generating cash inflows affects investors' and creditors' cash flows through the market prices of the company's securities and the ability of the company to pay dividends and interest.

5. Additionally, three specific objectives are identified in FASB Statement of Financial Accounting Concepts No. 1:

(a) To provide information about a company's economic resources and the claims to those resources, i.e., its economic resources, obligations, and owners' equity.

(b) To provide information about a company's comprehensive income and its components.

(c) To provide information about a company's cash flows.

6. According to the Statement, information about comprehensive income and its components is the primary focus of financial reporting about a company's performance during a period. Comprehensive income should be measured with accrual accounting. That is, the financial effects of transactions, events, and circumstances having cash consequences should be reported in the period when they occur, rather than when cash is received or paid.

7. Management is responsible for the custody and use of company resources. Financial reporting should provide information about that stewardship responsibility.

8. Financial reporting should be based on full disclosure. That is, reports should include management explanations and interpretations of benefit to external users, as well as quantitative information.

Types of Useful Information

9. The FASB has identified five types of information related to the financial reporting objective to help external users assess the amounts, timing, and uncertainty of the future net cash inflows of the company. They are:

(a) Investors expect a return on the capital they invest. Before a company can provide a return on capital, the company must achieve a return of its capital. That is, the company's capital must be maintained or recovered.

(b) Risk is the uncertainty or unpredictability of a company's future results. In general, the greater the risk of an investment, the higher the rate of return expected by investors and the higher the interest charged by the creditors.

(c) Financial flexibility is the ability of a company to respond to unexpected needs and opportunities by changing the amounts and timing of cash flows.

(d) Liquidity relates to how quickly assets can be converted into cash, or liabilities can be paid.

(e) A company's operating capability is its ability to maintain a given physical level of operations.

Qualitative Characteristics of Useful Accounting Information

10. FASB Statement of Financial Accounting Concepts No. 2 specifies qualitative characteristics of accounting information, or "ingredients" that accounting information should possess in order to be most useful. The FASB hierarchy of qualitative characteristics is adapted in Exhibit 2-5 in the text.

11. The hierarchy shows two constraints to accounting information:

    (a) Cost-benefit: the benefit of information must be greater than its cost.

    (b) Materiality: the dollar amounts involved must be large enough to make a difference to decision makers. Since no quantitative guidelines were set by the FASB, materiality must be determined by judgment. However, the FASB suggested consideration of nature and relative size to separate material and immaterial items. In addition, the SEC, AICPA, and Big Five Audit Materiality Task Force have listed qualitative factors to consider when judging the materiality of a misstated item.

12. Understandability is a link between decision makers and the accounting information. Information should be understandable to broad classes of reasonably knowledgeable and diligent users.

13. Decision usefulness is the overall quality which accounting information must possess. The two primary qualities making accounting information useful are relevance and reliability.

14. Accounting information that can make a difference to decision makers is relevant. Relevance is closely linked to materiality: If an amount is large enough to affect the judgment of a reasonable person, that amount is material. If users have a need for information, that information is relevant. To be relevant, information must have (a) predictive value, or usefulness to decision makers in forecasting events more accurately; and/or (b) feedback value, or usefulness to decision makers in confirming or correcting prior expectations. In addition, relevant information must be timely.

15. Reliable information is reasonably free from error and bias and faithfully represents what it is intended to represent. To be reliable information must (a) be verifiable; (b) have representational faithfulness; and (c) be neutral. Information is verifiable (sometimes called objective) when it can be duplicated using the same measurement method. Verifiability is useful in reducing measurer bias. In auditing, verifiability is a primary concern when the independent accountant reviews the published financial statements of a company, i.e., performs the attest function. Accounting information has representational faithfulness when there is valid correspondence to the economic resources, obligations, transactions, and events it represents. A high degree of representational faithfulness is useful in reducing measurement bias. Neutral information is complete and free from intentional bias.

16. Comparability is a secondary characteristic of accounting information. Information is more useful if it can be compared with similar information from other companies (intercompany comparison) and with similar information from the same company over time (intracompany comparison). Comparability is closely linked to consistency, the use of unchanged accounting policies and procedures from period to period.

17. The hierarchy of qualitative characteristics in FASB Statement of Financial Accounting Concepts No. 2 does not rank the characteristics. All characteristics are required, to a minimum degree, in useful information. However, trade-offs between characteristics may be necessary.

Accounting Assumptions and Conventions

18. Certain assumptions and conventions have influenced the development of generally accepted accounting principles. The entity assumption distinguishes each business organization from its owners. For accounting purposes, the organization's financial records and reports are kept separate from those of the owners. Sometimes records from separate legal entities may be consolidated to more realistically report information about an overall economic entity.

19. Following the continuity (or going-concern) assumption, it is assumed that the company will continue to operate in the near future, unless substantial evidence to the contrary exists. This assumption underlies many accounting procedures. If, however, the company appears to be verging on bankruptcy, reports should be prepared on a liquidation basis.

20. The total profit or loss of a company cannot be determined precisely while the company continues to operate. However, timely information is needed by users. The period-of-time assumption enables a company to report the results of its activities after short time periods (primarily one year), rather than at the end of the company's existence. Historically, the calendar year was used as a reporting period. However, many companies now choose fiscal years based on their annual business cycles.

21. An economic activity or resource is initially measured by the exchange price (historical cost) of a transaction. Because the initial exchange price is reliable, verifiable, representationally faithful, and neutral, historical cost is usually retained as the value of an item until the item is removed from the accounting records. If a company were to recognize changes in the values of assets and liabilities, those changes would necessarily affect income. Understanding that historical cost is frequently criticized for lack of relevance, the FASB encourages companies to disclose supplemental current value information in their annual reports.

22. Under the monetary unit assumption accountants have traditionally treated the dollar, or other currency, as a stable unit of measure. However, values, as measured by a monetary unit, change over time for two reasons: (a) the real value of an item can change in relation to the real values of other goods and services, or (b) the purchasing power of the measuring unit (the dollar) can change. To enhance comparability, the FASB encourages companies to make supplemental disclosures relating to the impact of changing prices.

23. Realization is the process of converting non-cash resources or rights into cash or rights to cash. Recognition is the process of formally recording and reporting an item in the financial statements. To be recognized, an item must: (a) meet the definition of an element, (b) be measurable, (c) be relevant, and (d) be reliable. Revenues should be recognized when (a) realization has taken place and (b) the revenues have been earned. Companies most often recognize revenues at the point of sale, because this is usually when realization takes place, and when the earning process is substantially complete.

24. Occasionally companies recognize revenue before or after the point of sale to more accurately reflect the nature of their operations. In these cases revenue is not recognized at the same time it is realized.

    (a) Revenue may be recognized during production under the percentage-of-completion method for certain long-term construction contracts and the proportional performance method for certain long-term service contracts.

(b) When a fixed selling price exists and there is no limit to the amount that can be sold, revenue may be recognized at the end of production. This method might be used for certain valuable minerals or for farm products sold on the futures market.

(c) When collectibility is highly uncertain, recognition may be postponed using either the installment method or the cost-recovery method. Under the installment method, a portion of each receipt is recognized as revenue. Under the cost-recovery method, no revenue is recognized until the cost of the product has been recovered.

25. The matching principle states that expenses involved in obtaining a period's revenues should be related to (matched against) the revenues recognized during the period. Companies use three principles to match expenses to revenues: (a) association of cause and effect, (b) systematic and rational allocation, and (c) immediate recognition. Sales commissions and the product costs in cost of goods sold are recorded by associating cause and effect. Depreciation and amortization are recorded on the basis of systematic and rational allocation. Period costs (expenses related to a period of time), such as administrative salaries, are recognized immediately.

26. The convention of conservatism states that when alternative accounting valuations are equally possible, a company should select the alternative which is least likely to overstate assets and income in the current period. This convention counterbalances the normal optimism of management. However, conservatism has been criticized recently for distorting results in later periods, and for lack of neutrality. The FASB favors prudence, rather than excessive conservatism, in reporting information about business risks and uncertainties.

GAAP and Financial Statements

27. In the Conceptual Framework, the FASB identified four financial statements: the balance sheet, income statement, statement of cash flows, and statement of changes in equity. The elements of each statement are the broad classes of items comprising it. In practice, most companies prepare three primary financial statements, the balance sheet, income statement, and statement of cash flows, and present a schedule of changes in equity either as a separate statement or in a note to the financial statements.

28. The balance sheet (statement of financial position) summarizes the financial position of a company on a particular date. The three elements of the balance sheet are (a) assets, or economic resources; (b) liabilities, or economic obligations; and (c) equity, the owners' residual interest in a company's assets, after obligations have been deducted.

29. The income statement summarizes the results of a company's operations for a period of time. The four elements of an income statement are (a) revenues, increases in assets and/or decreases in liabilities due to the company's ongoing primary operations; (b) expenses, decreases in assets and/or increases in liabilities due to the company's ongoing primary operations; (c) gains, increases in the equity of the company not related to its primary operations or to investments by owners; (d) losses, decreases in the equity of the company not related to its primary operations or to distributions to owners.

30. The statement of cash flows summarizes a company's cash inflows and outflows for a period of time, and reconciles the company's beginning and ending cash balances as reported on the balance sheets. The three elements of the statement of cash flows are (a) operating cash flows, cash inflows and outflows from acquiring, selling, and delivering goods, and providing services; (b) investing cash flows, cash inflows and outflows from acquiring and selling investments, property, plant, and equipment, and intangibles, as well as from making and collecting on loans; and (c) financing cash flows, cash inflows and outflows from investments by and distributions to owners, as well as receipts from and distributions to creditors.

31. The statement of changes in equity (for a corporation generally called the statement of changes in stockholders' equity) summarizes the changes in a company's equity for a period of time and reconciles the equity items a company reports on its beginning and ending balance sheets. Two key elements of the statement of changes in equity are (a) investments by owners and (b) distributions to owners.

Model of Business Reporting

32. The AICPA Committee on Financial Reporting issued a report on the relevance and usefulness of reporting by companies. In addition, the committee developed a comprehensive model of business reporting, identifying an integrated range of information, broader than that included in the FASB's conceptual framework. Although the AICPA committee does not set standards, the model was developed to aid in the improvement of cost-effective business reports.

IASC Framework

33. The IASC Framework states that the objective of financial statements is to present information that is useful in making economic decisions. The Framework assumes that a company is a going concern using accrual accounting. The Framework identifies four qualitative characteristics of financial statements: understandability, relevance, reliability, and comparability. It identifies three constraints: timeliness, balance between benefit and cost, and balance between the qualitative characteristics.

34. The IASC Framework identifies the elements (e.g., assets, income) of the financial statements, and also discusses conceptual issues related to recognition and measurement of these elements. The Framework is designed to help the IASC develop international accounting standards.

SELF-EVALUATION EXERCISES

Supply the words necessary to complete each of the following items.

FASB Conceptual Framework

FCF-1. The FASB conceptual framework has been essentially completed, with the issuance of seven ____________ ____ ____________ ____________ ____________.

FCF-2. The conceptual framework was divided by the FASB into projects:

____________ of financial reporting, ______________

________________ of accounting information, ___________

projects, and ____________ projects.

Objectives of Financial Reporting

OFR-1. General-purpose financial statements are designed to meet the needs

of a variety of ___________ ______ .

OFR-2. The general objective of financial reporting is to provide

information that is _________ to external users for decision making.

OFR-3. The objective of providing information to investors and creditors about their prospective cash flows from a company is called the

__________ ___________ ______ objective.

OFR-4. Information useful in assessing the amounts, timing, and uncertainty of prospective cash inflows of a company is reported under the

_________ ____________ objective.

OFR-5. According to <u>FASB Statement of Financial Accounting Concepts No. 1</u>, the primary focus of financial reporting about a company's performance during a period is information about

______________ _________ and its components.

OFR-6. The financial effects of transactions, events, and circumstances having cash consequences are reported in the period when they occur

when _________ ____________ is used.

OFR-7. Financial reports should include information about management's

_____________ _______________ over company resources.

OFR-8. Management explanations and interpretations as well as quantitative

information, are included in financial reports under ______

____________.

Types of Useful Information

TUI-1. Before a company can provide investors with a return on capital, the

company must achieve a return _____________ its capital.

TUI-2. A company's ability to respond to unexpected needs and opportunities is its ____________ ____________.

TUI-3. A company's ability to maintain a given physical level of operations is its ____________ ____________.

Qualitative Characteristics of Useful Accounting Information

QC-1. The "ingredients" that accounting information must possess in order to be most useful are termed ____________ ______________ by the FASB.

QC-2. The two constraints to accounting information described in FASB Statement of Financial Accounting Concepts No. 2 are the ________-__________ and ______________ constraints.

QC-3. Accounting information should be understandable to broad classes of users who are reasonably ____________ and __________.

QC-4. The overall quality required of accounting information is _________ ___________.

QC-5. Information that users need for their decisions is __________ information.

QC-6. To be relevant, accounting information must have ___________ _______ and/or _________ _______, and must be ________.

QC-7. Reliable information must be verifiable and neutral, and must possess __________ _________.

QC-8. Verifiability is useful in reducing _________ _____, while a high degree of representational faithfulness is useful in reducing ____________ ______.

QC-9. Comparability, a secondary characteristic of accounting information, is closely linked to ______________, the use of unchanged accounting policies and procedures over time.

QC-10. Although all the qualitative characteristics are required to a minimum degree in useful accounting information, ________-______ between characteristics may be necessary.

Accounting Assumptions and Conventions

AAC-1. A business is distinguished from its owners for accounting purposes under the __________ assumption.

AAC-2. The continuity assumption underlies many accounting procedures. However, when a company is verging on bankruptcy, reports are prepared on a ________________ basis.

AAC-3. A business may report the results of its activities after short time periods under the ___________-_____-__________ assumption.

AAC-4. Although the calendar year has historically been used as a reporting period, many companies now use fiscal years based on their __________ _________.

AAC-5. Economic activities and resources are usually valued in the accounting records at the exchange price of their associated transactions under the _______________ __________ valuation method.

AAC-6. Recognition of changes in the values of a company's assets and liability would necessarily affect the company's ______________.

AAC-7. The effects of inflation on the measuring unit are ignored under the ________________-_________ assumption.

AAC-8. The conversion of non-cash resources or rights into cash or rights to cash is termed ____________________

AAC-9. The process of formally recording and reporting items in the financial statements is termed ______________.

AAC-10. Revenue is usually recognized, as well as realized, at the _________ _____ __________.

AAC-11. For certain long-term construction contracts revenue may be recognized during production under the _____________-___-______________ method.

AAC-12. Expenses involved in obtaining a period's revenues should be related to revenues recognized during the period, according to the ___________ principle.

AAC-13. Expenses that can be associated by cause and effect with the company's products are called __________ __________

AAC-14. Depreciation of property and equipment and amortization of intangibles are recorded on the basis of __________ _____ __________ allocation.

AAC-15. Costs related to a period of time are __________ __________.

AAC-16. Choice of the accounting valuation alternative least likely to overstate assets and income in the current period is justified by the convention of __________; however, the FASB favors __________ in reporting about business risks and uncertainties.

GAAP and Financial Statements

GF-1. The FASB identified four financial statements in its <u>Conceptual Framework</u>: the __________ __________, __________ __________, __________ _____ __________ __________, and __________ _____ __________ _____ __________.

GF-2. The three elements of the balance sheet are __________, __________, and __________.

GF-3. The results of a company's operations for a period are summarized in its __________ __________.

GF-4. Increases in equity not related to a company's primary operations or to investments by owners are called __________.

GF-5. The statement of cash flows summarizes a company's cash __________ and __________, and reconciles the company's beginning and ending __________ __________.

GF-6. Investments by owners and distributions to owners are the two elements of the __________ _____ __________ _____ __________.

IASC Framework

IF-1. The IASC Framework assumes that a company is a __________ __________ using __________ accounting.

IF-2. The IASC Framework identifies four qualitative characteristics of of financial statements: ______________, ____________, ____________, and ______________.

ANSWERS TO SELF-EVALUATION EXERCISES

FCF-1. Statements of Financial Accounting Concepts; FCF-2. objectives, qualitative characteristics, accounting, reporting; OFR-1. external users; OFR-2. useful; OFR-3. derived external user; OFR-4. derived company; OFR-5. comprehensive income; OFR-6. accrual accounting; OFR-7. stewardship responsibility; OFR-8. full disclosure; TUI-1. of; TUI-2. financial flexibility; TUI-3. operating capability; QC-1. qualitative characteristics; QC-2. cost-benefit, materiality; QC-3. knowledgeable, diligent; QC-4. decision usefulness; QC-5. relevant; QC-6. predictive value, feedback value, timely; QC-7. representational faithfulness; QC-8. measurer bias, measurement bias; QC-9. consistency; QC-10. trade-offs; AAC-1. entity; AAC-2. liquidation; AAC-3. period-of-time; AAC-4. business cycles; AAC-5. historical cost; AAC-6. income; AAC-7. monetary-unit; AAC-8. realization; AAC-9. recognition; AAC-10. point of sale; AAC-11. percentage-of-completion; AAC-12. matching; AAC-13. product costs; AAC-14. systematic and rational; AAC-15. period costs; AAC-16. conservatism, prudence; GF-1. balance sheet, income statement, statement of cash flows, statement of changes in equity; GF-2. assets, liabilities, equity; GF-3. income statement; GF-4. gains; GF-5. inflows, outflows, cash balances; GF-6. statement of changes in equity; IF-1. going concern, accrual; IF-2. understandability, relevance, reliability, comparability.

POST TEST

Part A Circle T if the statement is true and F if it is false.

T F 1. Liquidity is the ability of a company to respond to events by changing the amounts and timing of future cash flows.

T F 2. Verifiability is useful in reducing measurement bias.

T F 3. A company's operating capability is its ability to provide a return on capital to investors, regardless of the level of physical operations.

T F 4. Rather than strictly following the convention of conservatism, the FASB favors prudence in reporting accounting information.

T F 5. The entity assumption identifies a company with its owners for accounting purposes.

T F 6. Accountants presently assume that financial statements should not be tailored to meet the specific information needs of individual users.

T F 7. According to <u>FASB Statement of Financial Accounting Concepts No. 1</u>, the primary focus of financial reporting is on presentation of a company's resources and obligations at a point in time.

T F 8. Using accrual accounting, the financial effects of transactions, events, and circumstances having cash consequences are reported in the period when they occur.

T F 9. In <u>FASB Statement of Financial Accounting Concepts No. 2</u>, the FASB set the threshold for materiality at 5% of after-tax income.

T F 10. Timeliness, predictive value, and feedback value are components of the qualitative characteristic of relevance.

T F 11. In its hierarchy of qualitative characteristics of accounting information, the FASB ranks "reliability" as the most important characteristic.

T F 12. The historical cost principle is supported on the grounds of reliability and verifiability.

T F 13. According to the monetary unit assumption, the dollar (or other currency) is considered a stable unit of measure.

T F 14. Under the matching principle, expenses involved in obtaining a period's revenues are related to those revenues.

T F 15. Period costs should receive immediate recognition.

T F 16. In general, the greater the risk of an investment, the greater the rate of return expected by investors.

T F 17. Comparability is the primary concern of accountants performing the attest function in reviewing a company's financial statements.

T F 18. To be neutral, accounting information must be timely and must be prepared by an independent accountant.

T F 19. The IASC Framework discusses conceptual issues related to the recognition and measurement of the elements of the financial statements.

T F 20. When collectibility is highly uncertain, revenue should be recognized using the proportional-performance method.

T F 21. The AICPA Special Committee on Financial Reporting is a standard-setting body which issues requirements for the content of financial statements.

T F 22. Realization is the process of converting non-cash resources or rights into cash or rights to cash.

T F 23. The elements of the statement of cash flows are operating cash flows, investing cash flows, and financing cash flows.

T F 24. Following the qualitative characteristics of verifiability and objectivity, companies present only quantitative information in their financial reports.

Part B Select the one <u>best</u> answer, and place its letter in the space provided.

_____ 1. Which of the following is <u>not</u> one of the projects in the FASB conceptual framework? (a) qualitative characteristics of accounting information; (b) full disclosure and stewardship responsibility; (c) objectives of financial reporting; (d) accounting projects.

_____ 2. Which of the following is <u>not</u> a requirement for an item to be recognized in the accounting process? (a) the item must be relevant and reliable; (b) the item must be measurable; (c) the item must meet the definition of an element; (d) the item must meet cost-benefit and materiality constraints.

_____ 3. <u>General</u> objectives of financial reporting identified in <u>FASB Statement of Financial Accounting Concepts No. 1</u> do <u>not</u> include (a) providing information tailored to the unique needs of identified user groups; (b) providing information useful to external users for decision making; (c) providing information useful in assessing the amounts, timing, and uncertainty of cash flows to be received by external users; (d) providing information useful in assessing the amounts, timing, and uncertainty of prospective net cash inflows of the company.

_____ 4. <u>Specific</u> objectives identified in <u>FASB Statement of Financial Accounting Concepts No. 1</u> do <u>not</u> include providing information about a company's (a) comprehensive income and its components; (b) economic resources and the claims to those resources; (c) compliance with regulatory requirements; (d) cash flows.

_____ 5. According to <u>FASB Statement of Financial Accounting Concepts No. 1</u>, the primary focus of financial reporting about a company's financial performance is information on (a) resources and obligations; (b) comprehensive income and its components; (c) management's stewardship of resources; (d) cash flows, liquidity, and financial flexibility.

_____ 6. In the hierarchy of qualitative characteristics of accounting information, components of relevance do <u>not</u> include (a) predictive value; (b) decision usefulness; (c) feedback value; (d) timeliness.

_____ 7. Materiality is determined (a) by judgment; (b) by industry practice; (c) using quantitative guidelines issued by the FASB; (d) as a proportion of net income.

_____ 8. Realization is the (a) process of earning revenue as economic utility is added to goods produced; (b) recording of revenues in the accounting records; (c) matching of expenses incurred in earning revenues of the period to those revenues; (d) conversion of noncash resources or rights into cash or rights to cash.

_____ 9. Under the percentage-of-completion method, revenue is recognized (a) during production; (b) at the point of sale; (c) at the end of production; (d) as a portion of each receipt of cash.

_____ 10. The principles of matching expenses against revenues do not include (a) association of cause and effect; (b) systematic and rational allocation; (c) arbitrary assignment; (d) immediate recognition.

_____ 11. Which of the following statements about the income statement is correct? (a) a company must report comprehensive income on the face of its income statement; (b) the elements of the income statement include income from operations and distributions to owners; (c) the income statement summarizes the results of a company's operations for a period; (d) all of the above.

Part C Solve each of the following short problems.

1. Below is a list of accounting assumptions and conventions. Following the list is a series of descriptive phrases. Match each assumption and convention with its descriptive phrase by placing the appropriate letter in the space provided.

a. entity assumption
b. continuity assumption
c. period-of-time assumption
d. conservatism convention
e. monetary unit assumption
f. prudence
g. matching principle
h. historical cost
i. realization
j. recognition

_____ 1. Measures an economic activity or resource by the initial exchange price.

_____ 2. The basis for adjusting entries.

_____ 3. Relates expenses to revenues using (1) association of cause and effect, (2) systematic and rational allocation, and (3) immediate recognition.

_____ 4. Selects the accounting alternative least likely to overstate assets and income.

_____ 5. Should not be followed if the company appears to be verging on bankruptcy.

_____ 6. Traditional use of the dollar as a stable measuring unit.

_____ 7. Treats a company's resources, transactions, records, and reports as separate from those of its owners under this assumption.

_____ 8. Occasionally occurs before or after the point of sale to more accurately reflect a company's operations.

_____ 9. Conversion of noncash resources or rights into cash or rights to cash.

_____ 10. Favored by the FASB for those reporting about business risks and uncertainties.

2. Below is a list of phrases related to the recognition of revenue. Following the list is a series of descriptions. Match each description with the appropriate phrase or phrases to indicate the timing of revenue recognition.

a. point of sale
b. percentage-of-completion method
c. installment method
d. cost-recovery method
e. proportional performance
f. completion of production

_____ 1. Sidley Construction is building an office complex for the Granite Insurance Company over a three-year period.

_____ 2. Meteor Company mines a mineral in great demand. The price of the mineral is supported under international agreements.

_____ 3. The Appliance Store sells kitchen appliances for cash and on credit.

_____ 4. Sun Resorts signed a long-term contract to sell a large condominium development to Star Company. Soon afterward, Star fell behind in its payments to Sun. Ultimate collectibility is uncertain.

_____ 5. MA Software is working under a multi-year contract to develop a custom software system for Magna Corp.

3. Below is a list of the qualitative characteristics identified in FASB Statement of Financial Accounting Concepts No. 2. Following the list is a series of descriptive phrases. Match each characteristic with the appropriate phrase.

a. decision usefulness
b. relevance
c. reliability
d. predictive value
e. feedback value
f. timeliness
g. understandability
h. neutrality
i. verifiability
j. representational faithfulness
k. comparability
l. consistency

_____ 1. Enables users to confirm or correct prior expectations.

_____ 2. Reasonable freedom from error and bias, and reports what it is intended to show.

_____ 3. The quality of being needed by users.

_____ 4. Closely linked to consistency.

_____ 5. Completeness and freedom from intentional bias.

_____ 6. Capable of duplication using the same method.

_____ 7. The use of unchanged accounting policies and procedures from period to period.

_____ 8. The overall quality which accounting information must possess.

_____ 9. Helpfulness in correctly forecasting the outcome of events.

_____ 10. Promptness allowing usefulness to decision-makers.

_____ 11. Correspondence to the economic reality it represents.

_____ 12. Defined for users who are reasonably knowledgeable and willing to study the information with reasonable diligence.

ANSWERS TO POST TEST

Part A

1. F
2. F
3. F
4. T
5. F
6. T
7. F
8. T
9. F
10. T
11. F
12. T
13. T
14. T
15. T
16. T
17. F
18. F
19. T
20. F
21. F
22. T
23. T
24. F

Part B

1. b
2. d
3. a
4. c
5. b
6. b
7. a
8. d
9. a
10. c
11. c

Part C

1.
   1. h
   2. c
   3. g
   4. d
   5. b
   6. e
   7. a
   8. j
   9. i
   10. f
2.
   1. b
   2. f
   3. a
   4. c or d
   5. e
3.
   1. e
   2. c
   3. b
   4. k
   5. h
   6. i
   7. l
   8. a
   9. d
   10. f
   11. j
   12. g

3

THE BALANCE SHEET AND STATEMENT OF CHANGES IN STOCKHOLDERS' EQUITY

CHAPTER OBJECTIVES

After careful study of this chapter, you will be able to:

1. Understand the purposes of the balance sheet.
2. Define the elements of a balance sheet.
3. Explain how to measure the elements of a balance sheet.
4. Classify the assets of a balance sheet.
5. Classify the liabilities of a balance sheet.
6. Report the stockholders' equity of a balance sheet.
7. Prepare a statement of changes in stockholders' equity.
8. Understand the other disclosure issues for a balance sheet.
9. Describe the SEC integrated disclosures.
10. Explain the reporting techniques used in an annual report.

SYNOPSIS

Balance Sheet

1. A balance sheet, or statement of financial position, summarizes the financial position of a company at a particular date by reporting the economic resources (assets), the economic obligations (liabilities), stockholders' equity, and related information. It reports a company's resource structure (major classes and amounts of assets) and its financial structure (major classes and amounts of liabilities and equity). It is a detailed explanation of the basic accounting equation: Assets = Liabilities + Stockholders' Equity.

2. The balance sheet information helps external users (a) assess the company's liquidity, financial flexibility, and operating capability, and (b) evaluate its income-producing performance during the period. Liquidity is the speed with which the company's assets can be converted into cash or liabilities can be paid. Information about liquidity helps users evaluate the timing of cash flows. Financial flexibility is the ability of the company to generate sufficient net cash inflows from operations, from investors and creditors, or from selling of long-term assets. Information about financial flexibility is necessary for evaluating the uncertainty of future cash flows. Operating capability is the company's ability to maintain a given physical level of operations defined by either the volume of inventory produced or the productive capacity of the plant, property, and equipment. This is important in evaluating the amount of future cash flows.

3. A company's capital, its economic resources (assets) less its economic obligations (liabilities), is the same as its net assets or owners' equity. Information about a company's capital provides the basis for evaluating income-producing performance. By comparing beginning capital (owners' equity) with ending capital (owners' equity) the financial statement user can tell whether capital for the accounting period was decreased, maintained, or increased. To the extent capital is maintained, there is return of investment. This is capital maintenance. To the extent capital is increased, there is the potential for return on investment through dividends and/or market price appreciation on the stock. Capital can be defined as either (a) financial capital, the monetary value of the net assets contributed by stockholders plus the value of the increase in net assets resulting from earnings retained by the corporation, or (b) physical capital, a quantitative measure of the physical productive capacity of the corporation to provide goods or services.

4. Recognition is the process of formally recording and reporting an element in the financial statements. To be recognized, an item must (a) meet the definition of an element as specified in *FASB Statement of Concepts No. 6*, (b) be measurable, (c) be relevant, and (d) be reliable. Assets, liabilities, and stockholders' equity are the elements of a corporation's balance sheet. Assets are economic resources (a) acquired as a result of past transactions or events, (b) which will provide probable future economic benefit (service potential), (c) over which the company has control. Liabilities are (a) present economic obligations, (b) arising from past transactions or events, (c) which will be settled by probable future transfer of assets or performance of services. Stockholders' equity is the stockholders' residual interest in the assets of the corporation after all liabilities have been settled (that is, company assets minus liabilities). Therefore, stockholders' equity is determined by defining assets and liabilities.

5. Assets and liabilities must have a monetary value for balance sheet presentation. The FASB has identified five alternative valuation methods. (a) Historical cost is the exchange price of the asset at the time of the original transaction reduced by any recorded depreciation, amortization, or impairment to date. This valuation method is the most commonly used because of its high degree of reliability. Equipment used in manufacturing operations is recorded at historical cost. (b) Current cost (or current replacement cost) is the amount of cash necessary to obtain the same asset at the balance sheet date. When the market value of inventory is less than cost, it is recorded at current cost. (c) Current market value (or current exit value) is the amount of cash that could be obtained at the balance sheet date from selling the asset in an orderly liquidation. The market value of short-term investments at the balance sheet date is an example of current exit value. (d) Net realizable value (or expected exit value) is the amount of cash that may be realized as a result of a future sale of an asset or realization of cash. Accounts receivable is an example of an asset recorded at its net realizable value. (e) Present value is the net realizable value discounted to the balance sheet date. A Leased Asset Under Capital Lease is recorded in this manner.

6. Classifications of items on the balance sheet may vary from company to company. The common goal, however, is to facilitate analysis and to improve the usefulness of the information in predicting the amounts, timing, and uncertainty of future cash flows. A representative classification scheme would include three major sections, assets, liabilities and stockholders' equity, subdivided as follows:

   Assets: Current assets, Long-term investments, Property, plant, and equipment, Intangible assets, Other assets

   Liabilities: Current liabilities, Long-term liabilities, Other liabilities

   Stockholders' Equity: Contributed capital, Retained earnings, Accumulated other comprehensive income

   Exhibit 3-4 in the main text provides an excellent example of a classified balance sheet.

7. Current assets are cash and other assets that a company expects to convert into cash, sell, or consume within one year or the normal operating cycle, whichever is longer. An operating cycle, usually a year or less, is the average time taken by a company to spend cash for inventory, process and sell the inventory, and collect the cash from the sale. Current assets, usually presented in order of liquidity, include cash (and cash equivalents), temporary investments in marketable securities, receivables, inventories, and prepaid items. A company reports temporary investments in marketable securities at their market (fair) value; receivables at the net realizable value; inventories at the lower of their cost or market value; and prepaid items at historical cost, less any used up amount.

8. Current liabilities are obligations that a company expects to liquidate within 1 year or the operating cycle (if longer) through the use of current assets or the creation of other current liabilities. Accounts and short-term notes payable, wages payable, interest payable, the current portion of long-term debt, and deferred revenues (collections for goods and services not yet provided) are examples of current liabilities. Each is listed on the balance sheet at the amount owed (historical proceeds). Working capital is the difference between a company's current assets and its current liabilities. A company's working capital is a measure of the short-run liquidity of the company.

9. Long-term investments are investments that the company plans to hold for more than 1 year or its operating cycle, if longer. Examples are investments in equity securities (such as capital stock of another firm) and debt securities (such as bonds); land, buildings, and equipment held for future use (such as expansion); special cash funds held for future use; and non-current financial instruments such as stock options.

10. The property, plant, and equipment section of a company's balance sheet includes all tangible assets (fixed assets) used in operations such as land, buildings, machinery, furniture, and natural resources. Except for land, these assets are either depreciated, amortized (for leased assets), or depleted (for natural resource assets). For depreciable assets, a contra-asset account (such as accumulated depreciation) is deducted from the original asset cost in order to display both the historical cost and the book value (present undepreciated cost).

11. Intangible assets are noncurrent economic resources, such as patents, copyrights, trademarks, franchises, computer software costs, goodwill, and organization costs that are used in the operations but that have no physical existence. The value of this type of asset lies in the special right of the company to its use. These assets are recorded at historical cost. Intangible assets with finite useful lives (e.g., patents) are amortized over their useful lives, and disclosed on the balance sheet at book value. Intangible assets with indefinite lives (e.g., copyrights) and goodwill are not amortized but are reviewed for impairment at least annually. They are reported at their historical cost or, if impaired, at their lower fair value.

12. Most business assets will fit into one of the categories already described. Sometimes a balance sheet will have a section labeled "Other Assets" or "Deferred Charges" for assets that cannot be classified otherwise. Because of their vagueness such classifications, as well as "Other Liabilities," should rarely be used.

13. Long-term liabilities (noncurrent liabilities) are obligations that are <u>not</u> expected to require the use of current assets or <u>not</u> expected to create current liabilities within 1 year or the operating cycle, if longer. Examples are long-term notes payable, obligations under capital lease contracts, mortgages payable, accrued pension costs and bonds payable. Bonds (sometimes called debentures) are often sold for more than face value (at a premium) or less than face value (at a discount). On a balance sheet, bonds are reported at their book value. The book value is the face value of the bonds payable plus any unamortized premium or less any unamortized discount.

14. Assets and liabilities may also be further classified according to (a) their expected function in the central operations of the company (i.e., held for resale or used in production), (b) their financial flexibility (i.e., used in operations vs. held for investment) (c) the method of valuation (i.e., net realizable value vs. historical cost) or (d) the extent to which they result from usual or recurring activities vs. unusual or non-recurring activities (i.e. core vs. noncore). These subcategories are intended to enhance the external usefulness of the financial statement information.

15. The stockholders' equity section of a corporation's balance sheet consists of three main categories: contributed capital, retained earnings, and accumulated other comprehensive income. <u>Contributed capital</u> represents amounts owners have invested in the business. Contributed capital is separated into capital stock and additional paid-in capital. Capital stock reports the legal capital or par value of the stock, the minimum amount of stockholders' equity that a corporation may <u>not</u> distribute as dividends. Additional paid-in capital reports the difference between the par value and the market value when issued. Corporations may issue two types of capital stock, common and preferred, each of which has distinguishing characteristics. <u>Retained</u>

earnings represents the cumulative amount of undistributed past net income kept in the business for operating purposes or for purposes of expansion. Accumulated other comprehensive income (loss) includes (a) unrealized increases (gains) or decreases (losses) in the market (fair) value of investments in available-for-sale securities, (b) translation adjustments from converting the financial statements of a company's foreign operations into U.S. dollars, (c) certain gains and losses on "derivative" financial instruments, and (d) certain pension liability adjustments. Accumulated other comprehensive income (loss) is reported in stockholders' equity either in total or by listing each item. If reported in total, the detailed information must be disclosed in the notes to the financial statements. Miscellaneous items, such as donated or previously unrecorded assets, are reported at fair market value separately in stockholders' equity.

16. FASB Statement of Concepts No. 6 suggests that financial statements include information about (a) investments by owners, or increases in the equity from transfers to the company of assets and other valuable items by the owners, and (b) distribution to owners, or decreases in the equity from transfers by the company of assets and other valuable items to the owners. To disclose this information as well as the retained earnings changes, a statement of changes in stockholders' equity which discloses changes in all of the equity accounts is often presented as a financial statement. The statement of changes reconciles beginning balances of capital stock, additional paid-in capital, retained earnings and accumulated other comprehensive income to their ending balances by showing the changes in each item.

Related Disclosures

17. Since all of the relevant financial information pertaining to a company's activities cannot be disclosed directly in the body of the financial statements, a company may make additional disclosures in the notes to the financial statements. For example, APB Opinion No. 22 requires disclosure in a company's notes of information related to its accounting policies. This disclosure includes revenue recognition and asset allocation principles that involve: (a) a selection from existing alternatives, (b) principles peculiar to a specific industry, or (c) an innovative application of an accounting principle.

18. To improve the reporting of a company's risk, liquidity, and financial flexibility, FASB requires certain disclosures related to financial instruments. FASB Statement No. 107 requires the disclosure of the fair value of all its asset and liability financial instruments whether recognized or not on the balance sheet. The Statement also requires a company to disclose significant concentrations of credit risk due to these instruments. FASB Statement No. 133 requires a company to recognize all derivative financial instruments (e.g., futures, forwards, or swap contracts), as either assets or liabilities on the balance sheet at their fair value. A company must also disclose the types of derivative instruments, the objectives for holding and the strategies to achieve these objectives, and the risk management policy related to each type of instrument. These disclosures are usually in the notes to the financial statements.

19. A company discloses contingent liabilities (loss contingencies) in the notes to the financial statements if there is only a reasonable possibility that the loss may have been incurred or if the amount of the loss cannot be reasonably estimated. If it is probable that the loss has been incurred and if the amount can be reasonably estimated, an estimated loss from a loss contingency is accrued and reported directly on the balance sheet as a liability or a reduction of an asset. Gain contingencies are not reported in the financial statements and should be judiciously explained if disclosed in the notes.

20. Another common note to the financial statements describes a subsequent event, an important event that occurs between the balance sheet date and the date of issuance of the annual report. It provides evidence about conditions that did not exist on the balance sheet date. Subsequent events must be disclosed so that users may interpret the financial statements in light of the most recent company information. If a subsequent event provides information about conditions that existed on the balance sheet date and significantly affect the estimates used in the preparation of the financial statements, the company adjusts the statements themselves.

21. FASB Statement No. 57 requires that transactions between related parties be disclosed in the notes to a company's financial statements. This disclosure includes the nature of the relationship, a description of the transaction including the dollar amounts, and any amounts due to or from the related party at the balance sheet date.

22. Many users of financial statements are interested in evaluating trends of the company over time. For this reason, financial statements are usually prepared on a comparative basis by presenting information for the current and preceding year side by side. In addition, supplementary schedules often summarize some of the more critical accounting information for periods of up to 10 years.

23. Through the SEC's "integrated disclosures" provision, companies regulated by the SEC now satisfy certain Form 10-K disclosure requirements by reference to information included in the annual report. Therefore, these companies include (a) comparative balance sheets for two years and comparative income statements and statements of cash flows for three years; (b) a five-year summary of critical accounting information; (c) management's discussion and analysis (MD&A) of the company's financial condition, changes in financial condition, and results of operations; and (d) disclosures on common stock market prices and dividends. Each company's chief executive officer and chief financial officer both must "certify" that the company's annual report in the Form 10-K (or interim report within the company's Form 10-Q) is both complete and accurate.

24. The IASC sets international accounting standards for published financial statements that are similar to those in the United States. Under the International Accounting Standards, a balance sheet, statement of changes in equity, income statement, and statement of cash flows are required as well as related notes and explanatory materials. In general, classification of items and disclosures are similar to that required under U.S. GAAP. However, on the balance sheet, the liabilities and owners' equity sections are usually ordered differently. The "capital and reserves" section, which includes issued capital, reserves and accumulated profits (losses), is listed before non-current liabilities and current liabilities are listed last. The statement of changes in equity includes changes in share capital, share premium and reserves.

Reporting Techniques

25. Companies generally use one of three basic formats for balance sheet presentation: (a) the report form (the most common format) in which asset accounts are listed first and then liability and stockholders' equity accounts are listed in sequential order directly below assets, (b) the account form that lists asset accounts on the left-hand side and liability and stockholders' equity accounts on the right-hand side of the statement, and (c) the financial position form that first presents the amount of working capital, by listing current assets minus current liabilities. The remaining assets are added to working capital and the remaining liabilities are deducted to derive the residual stockholders' equity.

26. Balance sheets often show a single amount for a company's inventory and/or its total property, plant, and equipment. In such cases, to comply with generally accepted disclosure rules, a detailed listing of inventory by major category (raw material, and so forth) and of property, plant, and equipment (land, and so forth) must be presented in notes to the financial statements.

27. Supporting schedules (e.g., listing of equipment items) and parenthetical notations (e.g., method of valuation for an account) may be used to disclose required and/or optional supplementary information, in addition to notes (or footnotes).

SELF-EVALUATION EXERCISES

Supply the words necessary to complete each of the following items.

Balance Sheet

BS-1. The balance sheet discloses economic information at a particular

__________.

BS-2. Using the information on the balance sheet an investor can assess

the company's ____________, _______________ _______________, and

_____________ _______________.

BS-3. The ability of a company to generate sufficient net cash inflows in

order to adapt to change is the measure of its __________________

________________.

BS-4. The basis for evaluating the income-producing performance of a

company are beginning and ending ___________ _______________.

BS-5. The physical productive capacity of a corporation to provide goods

or services is a measure of _________________ capital.

BS-6. The elements of the balance sheet as defined by FASB Statement of

Concepts No. 6 are _________, ________________, and _____________

_______________.

BS-7. An item may be classified as an asset if it was acquired as a result

of a _________ transaction, and will provide probable ____________

_______________ over which the company has ____________________.

BS-8. An item may be classified as a liability if it is a present economic ____________, arising as a result of a __________ transaction, which will be settled in the ______________.

BS-9. Stockholders' equity is defined as _________ minus ____________.

BS-10. The valuation method which reports the exchange price at the time of the original transaction is __________ _________, while the method which reports the replacement cost of an asset at the balance sheet date is ____________ _________.

BS-11. The value of an asset that is equal to the amount of cash that may be realized as a result of a future sale is called the ______________ ____________ ___________ or _________ __________ _____________.

BS-12. Cash, accounts receivable, and temporary investments may all be classified as ____________ ___________.

BS-13. Current assets minus current liabilities is called ______________ ____________.

BS-14. If an item is expected to be held for investment purposes for longer than one year it is classified as a ____-________ ____________.

BS-15. Tangible assets that are used in operations and which will benefit more than one accounting period are classified as ______________, ____________, and ______________.

BS-16. Patents, copyrights, and trademarks are examples of _____________ __________.

BS-17. Obligations such as a twenty-year mortgage and bonds payable, due 2014, are examples of _____-_______ _________________.

BS-18. The stockholder's equity section of the balance sheet may be divided into categories of ___________ ____________, ______________ ____________, and _______________ _______ ______________ ____________.

BS-19. The purpose of a Statement of Changes in Stockholders' Equity is to provide information about (1) ________________ ____________ ________________, (2) ________________ _______ ___________, and changes in (3) ________________ ______________.

Other Related Disclosure Issues

RD-1. Important information not contained in the body of the financial statements is usually disclosed in the ______________ to the financial statements.

RD-2. Financial instruments such as contracts for loan commitments, collaterized mortgages, and put and call options on stocks require the disclosure of significant concentrations of ____________ ________________.

RD-3. An estimated loss from a loss contingency should be accrued and reported directly on the balance sheet as a liability or a reduction of an asset if the following two conditions are satisfied:

(1) ____

(2) ____

RD-4. So that users may interpret the statements in light of the most recent information available, disclosure of information related to significant ______________ events is required.

RD-5. Financial statements must be adjusted when a subsequent event satisfies the following two criteria:

a. ____

b. ____

RD-6. Transactions between related parties must be disclosed in the ________ _____ _____ ______________ ______________.

RD-7. Financial statements are prepared on a comparative basis to allow external users to evaluate ______________.

Reporting Techniques

RT-1. The balance sheet presentation most commonly used is the ______________ ________.

RT-2. Lists of property or methods of valuation that are not disclosed in the notes to the financial statements may be disclosed in ________ ________ or ________ ________.

ANSWERS TO SELF-EVALUATION EXERCISES

BS-1. date; BS-2. liquidity, financial flexibility, operating capability; BS-3. financial flexibility; BS-4. stockholders' equity; BS-5. physical; BS-6. assets, liabilities, stockholders' equity; BS-7. past, future benefits, control; BS-8. obligation, past, future; BS-9. assets, liabilities; BS-10. historical cost, current cost; BS-11. net realizable value, expected exit value; BS-12. current assets; BS-13. working capital; BS-14. long-term investment; BS-15. property, plant, equipment; BS-16. intangible assets; BS-17. long-term liabilities; BS-18. contributed capital, retained earnings, accumulated other comprehensive income; BS-19. investments by owners, distributions to owners, retained earnings; RD-1. notes; RD-2. credit, risk; RD-3. (1) It is probable that the loss has been incurred. (2) The amount can be reasonably estimated; RD-4. subsequent; RD-5. a. Existed on the balance sheet date, b. Significantly affects the estimates used in preparing the financial statements; RD-6. notes to the financial statements; RD-7. trends; RT-1. report form; RT-2. supporting schedules, parenthetical notations.

POST TEST

Part A Circle T if the statement is true and F if it is false.

T F 1. A reader may use balance sheet information to evaluate the company's liquidity but the balance sheet is not helpful in evaluating income-producing performance.

T F 2. Operating capability refers to the company's ability to maintain a given volume of production of inventory.

T F 3. Capital maintenance is necessary in order to guarantee a return on investment to stockholders.

T F 4. To be recognized as an element in the financial statements, an item need only be measurable and relevant.

T F 5. To be classified as an asset, a resource must first and foremost have service potential.

T F 6. According to the FASB, an obligation is a liability only if the company is bound by a legal responsibility to transfer assets or provide services.

T F 7. The present value of an asset is the amount of cash that would be required on the date of the balance sheet to obtain the same asset.

T F 8. While present-day balance sheets report most assets at their historical cost, more disclosure of current value may result from increased emphasis on reporting about liquidity, financial flexibility, and operating capability.

T F 9. Oil companies, like most other business entities, have an operating cycle of less than one year.

T F 10. Marketable securities are classified as current assets only if company management intends to convert them back into cash within the longer of one year or the company's normal operating cycle.

T F 11. Land that is being held to accommodate future expansion of the company's manufacturing plant is classified as a part of the property, plant, and equipment section of the balance sheet.

T F 12. Even though intangible assets with finite useful lives are often written off over time in the same manner as buildings and equipment, a contra account that includes the total amortized cost to date does not usually appear on the balance sheet.

T F 13. Whenever a balance sheet is prepared, the amount that should be presented as the current book value of a bond liability is the bond principal plus any related discount or less any related premium.

T F 14. The legal capital of a corporation is the amount which is legally available for distribution to stockholders as dividends.

T F 15. If a company has a million dollar balance in its Retained Earnings account, it could still have little or no cash in its bank account.

T F 16. Consistent with its emphasis on conservatism, the FASB requires the disclosure of <u>only</u> the historical cost associated with asset and liability financial instruments.

T F 17. Gain contingencies are not reported in the financial statements.

T F 18. Both International Accounting Standards and GAAP require assets to be listed in order of liquidity and liabilities to be listed in order of expected due date.

T F 19. No information may be included in the notes accompanying financial statements that is not presented in at least a condensed fashion in the body of the statements themselves.

T F 20. The FASB recommended format for the balance sheet is the account form.

T F 21. Under <u>FASB Statement No. 133</u>, the year-end fair value is the only disclosure required for derivative financial instruments.

<u>Part B</u> Select the one <u>best</u> answer, and place its letter in the space provided.

_____ 1. The purpose of the balance sheet is to help external users evaluate the company's: (a) liquidity, financial flexibility, operating capability, and financing activities; (b) liquidity, financial flexibility, operating capability, financing activities, and investing activities; (c) liquidity, financing activities, income-producing performance, and investing activities; (d) liquidity, financial flexibility, operating capability, and income-producing performance.

_____ 2. The ending balance sheet discloses: (a) the capital of the corporation at the beginning of the accounting period; (b) the results of the corporation's financing and investing activities during the accounting period; (c) the capital at the end of the accounting period; (d) changes in working capital accounts during the accounting period.

_____ 3. The elements of the balance sheet as identified by FASB Statement of Concepts No. 6 are (a) liquidity, financial flexibility, and operating capability; (b) assets, liabilities, and stockholders' equity; (c) financial capital, physical capital, and contributed capital; (d) current assets, property, plant, and equipment, current liabilities, long-term liabilities, and retained earnings.

_____ 4. A resource is classified as an asset when it is (a) a probable future economic benefit obtained and controlled by a particular company as a result of purchase, production, or investment; (b) a probable future economic benefit obtained as a result of past purchase, production, or investment; (c) a probable future economic benefit obtained and controlled by a particular company as a result of a past transaction; (d) a probable future economic benefit obtained as a result of a past transaction which involves legal rights and duties.

_____ 5. Because stockholders' equity is a residual interest (a) its value is determined independently of assets and liabilities; (b) its value is determined by stockholders' investments of economic resources; (c) its value is determined by the company's net assets; (d) its value is determined by the ultimate risks and uncertainties involved in the company's operations.

_____ 6. Accounts receivable on the balance sheet are valued at the amount estimated to be collectible. This is an example of the valuation alternative known as: (a) net realizable value; (b) current exit value; (c) present value; (d) current cost.

_____ 7. For a manufacturer of air conditioning units, the operating cycle represents the period of time: (a) between selling the product on credit and collecting cash from the customer; (b) between producing the product, selling it on credit, and collecting cash from the customer; (c) required to purchase raw material, produce the product, sell it on credit, and collect cash from the customer; (d) required to purchase raw material, produce the product, and sell it on credit.

_____ 8. Advance payment of premiums for 2 years of insurance coverage: (a) should not be classified as a current asset because the time period involved extends beyond 1 year; (b) may be included in the current asset section if the amount does not materially distort the current asset presentation; (c) meets all of the conceptual requirements for inclusion in the current asset section of the balance sheet; (d) should be included in the long-term investments section of the balance sheet.

_____ 9. The working capital of a company: (a) is rarely disclosed on the face of the balance sheet as a separate balance; (b) should be larger than the company's retained earnings balance; (c) is a primary measure used to evaluate the company's profitability; (d) is a legal measure related to the amount of stock the company has sold to those who have invested in the business.

_____ 10. A statement of changes in stockholders' equity: (a) is not required to be included as a basic part of a company's financial statements so long as the change in the various equity accounts is disclosed in some manner; (b) is required as an integral part of the statement of cash flows and usually appears on the face of the latter statement; (c) is designed primarily to link the balance sheet information with information in the income statement of the company; (d) is necessary only if the company has sold additional shares of stock since its last accounting period ended.

_____ 11. Which of the following accounting principles or methods is not required to be disclosed in a company's notes to its financial statements when complying with APB Opinion No. 22 on significant accounting policies? (a) use of the FIFO method to value inventories, where it represents a choice from among equally acceptable alternatives; (b) use of the net realizable value method to value inventory in the meat processing industry, a method not commonly used in other industries; (c) expensing all research and development costs as they are incurred, a method which must be followed by all reporting entities; (d) an unusual or innovative application of a normal accounting method within generally accepted accounting principles.

_____ 12. If a company sells 10,000 shares of $5 par value common stock for $15 a share, the result of this sale will appear on the company's balance sheet as a: (a) $150,000 increase in the Common Stock account; (b) $50,000 increase in the Common Stock account and a $100,000 increase in the Additional Paid-in Capital account; (c) $50,000 increase in the Common Stock account and a $100,000 increase in the Retained Earnings account; (d) $50,000 increase in the Common Stock account and a $100,000 increase in an item of other comprehensive income.

_____ 13. One of Tampa Bay Corporation's three manufacturing plants was totally destroyed by a fire on January 14, 2004. What effect should this event have on the corporation's 2003 financial statements that are to be released on March 1, 2004? (a) This event should have no effect on the financial statements or the accompanying notes, since the event occurred after December 31, 2003, which is the end of the company's accounting period; (b) The event should be included in the notes to the financial statements only if the event was not reported by the national news media; (c) The event should be included in the notes to the financial statements but the statements themselves should not be adjusted; (d) The event should be included in the notes to the financial statements and the statements should be adjusted.

Part C Solve each of the following short problems.

1. The balance sheet of the Longbow Company has the following major headings:

(A) Current assets
(B) Long-term investments
(C) Property, plant, and equipment
(D) Intangible assets
(E) Other assets
(F) Current liabilities
(G) Long-term liabilities
(H) Other liabilities
(I) Contributed capital
(J) Retained earnings
(K) Accumulated other comprehensive income (loss)

Below is a list of accounts. Using the letters A through K, indicate the section of the balance sheet in which each account belongs. Put parentheses around the letter used if the account is a contra account. If the account does not belong on the balance sheet, place an X in the space provided.

_____ 1. Trademarks

_____ 2. United States income taxes payable

_____ 3. Office supplies

_____ 4. Dividends payable

_____ 5. Goods in process

_____ 6. Bond sinking fund

_____ 7. Discount on bonds payable (bonds due in 7 years)

_____ 8. Preferred stock

_____ 9. Depreciation expense: building

_____ 10. Land on which factory is located

_____ 11. Current portion of long-term bonds payable

_____ 12. Unrealized increase in value of available-for-sale securities

_____ 13. Improvements on leased warehouse

_____ 14. Retained earnings restricted for plant expansion

_____ 15. Investment in Zee Company stock (for control purposes)

_____ 16. Mineral deposits

_____ 17. Unearned service revenue (to be earned within next 6 months)

_____ 18. Prepaid insurance

2. The balance sheet of the Junebug Company has the following sections:

(A) Current assets
(B) Long-term investments
(C) Property, plant, and equipment
(D) Intangible assets
(E) Other assets
(F) Current liabilities
(G) Long-term liabilities
(H) Other liabilities
(I) Contributed capital
(J) Retained earnings
(K) Accumulated other comprehensive income (loss)

Several items or events are listed below. Using the letters A through K, indicate which section of the balance sheet the item or event would affect. If the item or event will appear only in a note to the financial statements, place the letter N in the space provided. If the item will <u>not</u> appear in any manner on the financial statements, place an X in the space. If the item will appear as a contra account balance, place parentheses around the letter.

_____ 1. The company extends a 1-year warranty on all products sold.

_____ 2. Temporary investment of cash in marketable securities.

_____ 3. Company obtained a patent on a new production process.

_____ 4. Construction half completed on new manufacturing plant.

_____ 5. The government has filed suit against the company alleging violations of antitrust laws. There is a reasonable probability a loss may have been incurred.

_____ 6. A 10-year bond liability due in 6 months with no plan to refinance and no sinking fund on hand.

_____ 7. Portion of underground mineral resources expected to be mined and sold during the next 12 months.

_____ 8. Expected future value of services to be rendered to company by its chief management personnel.

_____ 9. Lease of a warehouse that is regarded as a capital lease.

_____ 10. Premium related to 30-year bond liability that is still 5 years from maturity date.

_____ 11. Net income from prior years that was kept in the business to finance expansion.

_____ 12. The company chooses to disclose the costs it incurred to issue certain bonds by carrying this amount under an asset classification of the balance sheet.

_____ 13. Income taxes have been deferred by using faster depreciation methods in tax returns than are used for financial reporting purposes.

_____ 14. Minimum pension liability adjustment.

_____ 15. An insurance policy held by the company to insure the life of its president has a large cash surrender value.

_____ 16. Preferred stock with a par value of $100 a share had been issued for $115 a share.

_____ 17. Contractual agreement requiring appropriation of prior earnings to be kept in the business.

_____ 18. Copyrights held on literary and musical works.

_____ 19. Mortgage related to new plant acquisition.

3. Financial information related to a company may appear in the following financial statements, or related notes, as discussed in this chapter:

A. Balance sheet
B. Statement of changes in stockholders' equity
C. Notes accompanying the financial statements

Various elements of financial information are listed below. By placing the appropriate letter in the space provided, indicate whether the information would most likely appear in one of the two financial statements listed above or in the accompanying notes. If none of the answer choices given above is applicable, place an X in the space provided. Two answer choices apply to a few items.

_____ 1. The specific amount of income earned by the company during the current period.

_____ 2. The amount of accounts receivable expected to be uncollectible.

_____ 3. Accounting methods used to depreciate buildings and equipment.

_____ 4. Commissions paid to sales personnel during the current period.

_____ 5. Face value of bonds sold 4 years ago that mature in 16 years.

_____ 6. Loss contingency related to a law suit filed against the company. It is probable that the loss has been incurred and the amount can be reasonably estimated.

_____ 7. Depreciation expense recorded by the company during the current period.

_____ 8. Proceeds from a sale of common stock during the current period.

_____ 9. Destruction of a major plant facility 1 month after the current accounting period closed. Destruction resulted from explosions and related fire.

_____ 10. Changes in the current assets (other than cash) and current liabilities involved in the operating cycle that affected cash flows differently from net income.

4. On January 1, 2004, the Ragtag Company had the following stockholders' equity balances:

Additional paid-in capital on common stock	$125,000
Common stock, $10 par	100,000
Retained earnings	340,000
Accumulated other comprehensive income	18,000

During 2004 the following events occurred and were properly recorded:

a. The company issued 1,000 shares of common stock for $30 per share.
b. The company earned net income of $75,000
c. The company invested in available-for-sale securities. At year-end the market value of the securities had decreased by $8,500.
d. The company paid a $1.50 per share dividend on the common stock outstanding at year-end.

Prepare a statement of changes in stockholders' equity that includes retained earnings for 2004.

ANSWERS TO POST TEST

Part A

1. F
2. T
3. T
4. F
5. T
6. F
7. F
8. T
9. F
10. T
11. F
12. T
13. F
14. F
15. T
16. F
17. T
18. F
19. F
20. F
21. F

Part B

1. d	6. a	10. a
2. c	7. c	11. c
3. b	8. b	12. b
4. c	9. a	13. c
5. c		

Part C

1.

1. D	7. G	13. C
2. F	8. I	14. J
3. A	9. X	15. B
4. F	10. C	16. C
5. A	11. F	17. F
6. B	12. K	18. A

2.

1. F	7. C	13. H
2. A	8. X	14. K
3. D	9. C and G	15. B
4. C	10. G	16. I
5. N	11. J	17. J
6. F	12. E	18. D
		19. G

3.

1. B	6. A
2. A	7. X
3. C	8. B
4. X	9. C
5. A	10. X

4.

Statement of Changes in Stockholders' Equity
For the Year Ended December 31, 2004

	Common Stock $10 par	Additional Paid-in Capital	Retained Earnings	Accumulated Other Comprehensive Income	Total
Balance, January 1, 2004	$100,000	$125,000	$340,000	$18,000	$583,000
Unrealized decrease in value of available-for-sale securities				(8,500)	(8,500)
Net income			75,000		75,000
Cash dividends paid			(16,500)		(16,500)
Common stock issued	10,000	20,000			30,000
Balance, December 31, 2004	$110,000	$145,000	$398,500	$ 9,500	$663,000

4

THE INCOME STATEMENT AND STATEMENT OF CASH FLOWS

CHAPTER OBJECTIVES

After careful study of this chapter, you will be able to:

1. Understand the concepts of income.
2. Explain the conceptual guidelines for reporting income.
3. Define the elements of an income statement.
4. Describe the major components of an income statement.
5. Compute income from continuing operations.
6. Report results from discontinued operations.
7. Identify extraordinary items.
8. Prepare a statement of retained earnings.
9. Report comprehensive income.
10. Explain the statement of cash flows.
11. Classify cash flows as operating, investing, or financing.

SYNOPSIS

Concepts of Income

1. The income statement summarizes the results of a company's operations for the period. It often is considered the most important financial statement for several reasons. First, the income statement enables absentee owners (stockholders) to evaluate the stewardship of management over invested capital. Second, past income is used to predict future earnings and net cash flows which, in turn, are useful in predicting future stock prices and current and future dividend payments. Finally, income information is used to predict the company's ability to generate cash from operations to meet interest payments and operating obligations.

2. Under the capital maintenance concept, income for a period is the amount that may be paid to stockholders during that period while leaving the company as well off at the end of the period as it was at the beginning. That is, capital must be maintained before a corporation earns income on that capital. In other words, income is the difference between the beginning and ending capital (or net asset) balances after adjustment for investments and disinvestments during the period. Accountants and economists could probably agree on the measurement of total income for the entire life of a company. However, for shorter time periods income is subject to dispute, because the values of a company's beginning and ending assets and liabilities may be measured in a variety of ways.

3. The transactional approach is currently used for income measurement. Under this approach, companies report assets and liabilities at their historical costs and do not record any change in value unless a transaction, event, or circumstance has provided reliable evidence of the change. The transactional approach uses the accrual basis. That is, a company records the impact of a change in the period in which the change occurs, rather than the period in which the company pays or receives the related cash. The accrual-based transactional approach matches efforts and accomplishments, so that reported income measures the company's earnings performance. Net income is measured by the equation:

   Net Income = Revenues - Expenses + Gains - Losses

4. Consistent with the transactional approach, the FASB has defined comprehensive income as the change in equity of a company during a period from transactions, other events, and circumstances relating to nonowner sources. It includes all changes in equity during a period except those resulting from investments by owners and distributions to owners.

Conceptual Reporting Guidelines

5. According to the FASB, the income statement should provide information on return on investment, risk, financial flexibility, and operating capability. Return on investment measures overall company performance. Investors desire a return on invested capital, which can only be provided after the company's capital is maintained. Risk is the uncertainty or unpredictability of the future results of a company. In general, the greater the risk, the higher the rate of return expected from an investment. Financial flexibility is the ability of a company to adapt to unexpected needs and opportunities. Operating capability refers to a company's ability to maintain a given physical level of operations.

6. Managers should not practice earnings management in reporting income statement information. That is, they should not enter into transactions or choose among generally accepted accounting principles for the purpose of artificially influencing reported net income.

7. The FASB has suggested types of information to be presented on the income statement and has established more specific guidelines on the reporting of such information. According to the FASB, components of net income may be more important than the total amount. Companies should report components separately when they are important for the assessment of future income.

8. The AICPA Special Committee on Financial Reporting issued guidelines for the reporting of income. The committee recommended that an income statement present two categories of earnings: core earnings and noncore earnings. In addition, the committee suggested increased detail on the income statement, improved interim reporting, and reporting of disaggregated information on an operating segment basis. The committee is not a standard-setting body, but the FASB has implemented some of its recommendations and is considering others.

Elements of the Income Statement

9. In FASB Statement of Concepts No. 6, the FASB defined the elements or "building blocks" of the income statement: revenues, expenses, gains, and losses.

10. Revenues are inflows of (or increases in) assets of a company or settlement of its liabilities (or a combination of both) during a period from delivering or producing goods, rendering services, or other activities that are the company's ongoing major or central operations. Revenues are a measurement of a company's accomplishments in operating activities and are a component of equity.

11. Most revenues result gradually from a combination of operating activities (a company's earning process). The earning process includes purchasing, producing, selling, delivering, administering, and collecting and paying cash. Revenues are usually not recognized (formally recorded and reported in a company's financial statements) until (a) realization has taken place, and (b) the revenues have been earned; that is, when the earning process is complete or essentially complete. Realization means the process of converting noncash resources into cash or rights to cash, and encompasses two terms: Realized refers to the actual exchange of noncash resources into cash or near cash. Realizable describes noncash resources that are readily convertible into known amounts of cash or claims to cash. A company usually recognizes revenue under the accrual method at the time goods are sold or services are rendered. Alternative recognition methods, used in exceptional cases, include the (a) percentage-of-completion method, used for certain long-term construction contracts; (b) proportional-performance method, used for certain long-term service contracts; (c) installment method, used when collectibility is very uncertain; and (d) cost-recovery method, used when collectibility is extremely uncertain. (a) and (b) advance revenue recognition while (c) and (d) defer recognition.

12. Expenses are outflows of (or decreases in) assets or incurrences of liabilities (or a combination of both) during a period from delivering or producing goods, rendering services, or carrying out other activities that are the company's ongoing major or central operations. Expenses are a measurement of a company's efforts or sacrifices during operating activities, and are components of (decreases in) equity.

13. For income determination, companies recognize and match expenses against revenues using three principles: (a) association of cause and effect (for example, costs of products sold, delivery costs, and sales commissions), (b) systematic and rational allocation (for example, depreciation, amortization, and allocated prepaid costs), and (c) immediate recognition (for example, management salaries and most selling and administrative costs).

14. Gains are increases in a company's equity (net assets) from peripheral or incidental transactions of the company and from all other events and circumstances affecting the company during a period, except those that result from revenues or investments by owners.

15. Losses are decreases in a company's equity (net assets) from peripheral or incidental transactions of the company and from all other events and circumstances affecting the company during a period, except those that result from expenses or distributions to owners.

16. Revenues and expenses differ from gains and losses in several ways: (a) Revenues and expenses are associated with a company's major operating activities, while gains and losses are identified with peripheral or incidental activities or events and circumstances, many beyond the control of the company. (b) Revenues and expenses are reported at "gross" amounts, while gains and losses are reported "net." (c) Revenues are generally recognized when realized. In contrast, some gains are recognized when realizable; that is, when recorded assets are readily convertible into known amounts of cash based on interchangeable units and quoted prices available in an active market.

17. The distinctions between revenues and gains, and expenses and losses depend on the nature and circumstances of the company. However, in general, gains and losses are classified into three categories; (a) exchange transactions; (b) changes in value while items are held; and (c) nonreciprocal transfers between a company and nonowners.

Income Statement Content

18. The major components of a company's income statement are (a) income from continuing operations; (b) results from discontinued operations; (c) extraordinary items; (d) cumulative effects of changes in accounting principles; (e) net income; and (f) earnings per share.

19. Some accountants and external users have advocated the current operating performance concept, under which only normal, ordinary, recurring results of current operations are included in net income. Unusual and nonrecurring items are reported in the retained earnings statement under this concept.

20. Under the all-inclusive concept, all items increasing or decreasing stockholders' equity during the period (except dividends and capital transactions) are included in net income. The FASB supports the all-inclusive concept of net income and suggested that a company's financial statements should present both net income and comprehensive income for the period. Net income is a measure of performance for the period. Comprehensive income is a broad measure of the effects of transactions and other events and circumstances on the company.

An all-inclusive income statement, taken from Exhibit 4-2 in the text, is shown as follows:

BANNER CORPORATION
Income Statement
For Year Ended December 31, 2004

Sales revenue		$150,000
Less: Sales returns and allowances	$ 4,000	
Sales discounts taken	2,300	(6,300)
Net sales		$143,700
Cost of goods sold		(86,000)
Gross profit		$ 57,700
Operating expenses		
Selling expenses	$10,200	
General and administrative expenses	16,000	
Depreciation expense	7,800	
Total operating expenses		(34,000)
Operating income		$ 23,700
Other items		
Interest revenue	$ 1,800	
Dividend revenue	600	
Loss on sale of equipment	(4,000)	
Interest expense	(2,100)	(3,700)
Pretax income from continuing operations		$ 20,000
Income tax expense		(6,000)
Income from continuing operations		$ 14,000
Results from discontinued operations		
Income from operations of discontinued component A (net of $1,950 income taxes)	$ 4,550	
Loss on disposal of component A (net of $3,150 income tax credit)	(7,350)	(2,800)
Income before extraordinary items		$ 11,200
Extraordinary loss from explosion (net of $750 income tax credit)		(1,750)
Cumulative effect on prior years' income of change in depreciation method (net of $600 income taxes)		1,400
Net income		$ 10,850

Components of Income	Earnings per Common Share (5,000 shares)
Income from continuing operations	$2.80
Results from discontinued operations	(0.56)
Extraordinary loss from explosion	(0.35)
Cumulative effect on prior years' income of change in depreciation method	0.28
Net income	$2.17

Income from Continuing Operations

21. Income from continuing operations summarizes a company's income from usual and recurring operating activities. It includes sales revenues (net of returns, allowances, and discounts), cost of goods sold, operating expenses, other items, and income tax expense related to continuing operations. The computation of cost of goods sold (or cost of goods manufactured for a manufacturing company) is usually shown in a supporting schedule, not on the face of the income statement. Operating expenses are usually classified according to functional categories, such as selling expenses, and general and administrative expenses. Alternatively, expenses may be classified as variable (changing in direct proportion to changes in volume) or fixed (not affected by changes in volume). Other items include recurring revenues and expenses not directly related to the company's primary operations (for example, dividend revenue and interest revenue and expense), material gains and losses from sales of assets that are not classified as results of discontinued operations, and material gains and losses that are not classified as extraordinary.

22. Tax regulations frequently differ from accounting principles. Consequently taxable income often is not the same as the pretax financial income reported on a corporation's income statement, and income tax expense (based on pretax financial income) may be more or less than the actual tax liability (based on taxable income). Interperiod tax allocation involves the allocation of a company's income tax expense to various accounting periods because of temporary (timing) differences between taxable income and pretax financial income. The temporary difference between income tax expense and the actual tax liability is reported as a deferred tax liability or asset. Intraperiod tax allocation involves the allocation of a company's total income tax expense to the various components of net income, retained earnings, and other comprehensive income, if any. The purpose of intraperiod tax allocation is to report the after-tax impact of the components on net income.

23. Two basic formats--single-step and multiple-step--are used in the income statement to report income from continuing operations. Under the pure single-step format, a company classifies its items as either revenues or expenses. Total expenses are then deducted from total revenues in a single computation to determine income from continuing operations. In the multiple-step format, several subtotals are presented. For example, cost of goods sold is typically deducted from net sales to compute the gross profit or gross margin on sales, from which operating expenses are deducted to determine operating income. The net total of other items is then added or deducted, resulting in pretax income from continuing operations. Related income tax expense is subtracted to determine income from continuing operations. (See the Banner Corporation income statement shown on the previous page.)

Results from Discontinued Operations

24. FASB Statement No. 144 addressed the reporting by a company of the sale of a component of its operations. A component of a company involves operations and cash flows that can be clearly distinguished, operationally and for financial reporting purposes, from the rest of the company. A component may be, for instance, a subsidiary, an operating segment (e.g., division), or an asset group. A company reports information about a discontinued component in a section of its income statement called results from discontinued operations when: (1) the operations and cash flows of the component have been eliminated, and (2) the company will have no significant involvement in the operations of the component after the disposal.

25. The results of discontinued operations section, included on the company's income statement directly after its income from continuing operations, reports (1) the operating income (loss) of the discontinued component for the period, and (2) the gain (loss) from its sale. The income (or loss) from discontinued operations and the loss (or gain) from the sale of the component are reported net of income tax. That is, the related income taxes are deducted directly from each item, and only the after-tax amount is included in the computation of net income.

26. A company may take some time to plan and complete the sale of a component of its operations. The company classifies this component as held for sale when all of six specified criteria are met. A company classifying a component as held for sale records and reports the component at the lower of (1) book value (book value of assets minus book value of liabilities) or (2) fair value less any costs to sell. If the fair value (less any costs to sell) is less than the book value, the company records a loss and decreases the book value of the assets of the component. The company reports the loss (after taxes) in the results of discontinued operations section of its income statement. It reports the assets and liabilities in the respective asset and liability sections of its ending balance sheet, as discussed in Chapter 3.

Extraordinary Items

27. APB Opinion No. 30 addressed the reporting of extraordinary items. In the Opinion, an event or transaction is defined as extraordinary if it is both unusual in nature and infrequent in occurrence. The environment in which a company operates is a primary consideration in using judgment to determine whether an item is extraordinary. Examples of events that are treated as extraordinary items, provided that they are both unusual and infrequent for the particular company, include natural disasters, expropriations by a foreign government, and newly enacted prohibitions. Material gains and losses from extraordinary items are reported, net of taxes, in a separate section of a company's income statement after results of discontinued operations (if any). Individual extraordinary gains and losses should be disclosed in the income statement or notes.

28. An event or transaction is "unusual" if it is highly abnormal and unrelated to, or only incidentally related to, the company's ordinary activities, taking into account the environment of the company. An event or transaction is "infrequent" if it would not reasonably be expected to recur in the foreseeable future, taking into account the environment of the company.

29. Material gains and losses from events or transactions that are either unusual in nature or infrequent in occurrence but not both are reported as a separate component of income from continuing operations. Such items are not shown net of income taxes. Examples include (a) write-downs or write-offs of receivables, inventories, equipment leased to others, or intangible assets; (b) gains or losses from exchanges or translation of foreign currencies; (c) gains or losses from the sale or abandonment of property, plant, or equipment; (d) the effects of strikes, (e) the adjustment of accruals on long-term contracts, and (f) the effects of a terrorist attack.

Effects of Accounting Changes

30. Accounting changes may be classified into four categories: (1) a change in an accounting principle; (2) a change in an accounting estimate; (3) a correction of an error; and (4) a change in the reporting entity.

31. A change in accounting principle occurs when a company changes from one generally accepted accounting principle to another for use in its financial reports. A principle, once adopted, should be used consistently, unless a change results in more informative financial statements. The burden of justifying a change is on the company.

32. In most instances a company reports a material change in accounting principle by including the cumulative effect of the change on prior years' earnings as a component of net income for the year in which the change is made. This cumulative effect is shown, net of taxes, after any extraordinary items and before net income. The new principle is applied normally in the year of the change.

33. Changes in accounting estimates, which result frequently from new information or events, are accounted for in the current year, and in future years if affected. A note to the financial statements discloses the effects of a material change in estimate on income before extraordinary items, net income, and earnings per share.

Earnings Per Share

34. Earnings per share ratios are often used in financial analysis to predict future earnings and dividends and to determine the attractiveness of the company's common stock. The authors recommend the use of an earnings per share schedule showing earnings per share amounts net of tax for net income and each of its major components. The number of common shares used in the calculations should also be disclosed. (Earnings per share is discussed in Chapter 16.)

Related Issues

35. Recognizing limitations of the income statement, the FASB requires or encourages companies to make additional disclosures in notes or supplemental schedules to help external users in their decision making.

36. Although many accounting requirements and much of the content of the income statement are similar under U.S. and international accounting standards, differences exist, leading to a lack of comparability. The current IASC project of eliminating alternative accounting treatments should bring IASC standards closer to U.S. standards.

Statement of Retained Earnings

37. The statement of retained earnings is a schedule linking a company's balance sheet and its income statement. Retained earnings, a major component of stockholders' equity, is the total amount of company earnings that has not been paid out as dividends. In the schedule, net income is added to, and dividends are deducted from, the beginning retained earnings balance to arrive at ending retained earnings. When prior period adjustments occur, they are reported as adjustments to beginning retained earnings. Prior period adjustments include corrections of material errors in the financial statements of earlier periods.

38. The statement of retained earnings may be presented as a separate schedule or included in a statement of changes in stockholders' equity. The authors do not recommend presenting the statement of retained earnings on the face of the income statement.

Comprehensive Income

39. A company's <u>comprehensive income</u> consists of net income and <u>other comprehensive income</u>. Other comprehensive income includes (a) any unrealized increase (gain) or decrease (loss) in the market (fair) value of a company's investments in available-for-sale securities; (b) any change in the excess of a company's additional pension liability over its unrecognized prior service cost; (c) certain gains or losses on "derivative" financial instruments; and (d) any translation adjustment from converting the financial statements of foreign operations into U.S. dollars.

40. A company may report comprehensive income: (a) on the face of its income statement, (b) in a separate statement of comprehensive income, or (c) in its statement of changes in stockholders' equity. If a company chooses (c) the statement must be included as a <u>major</u> financial statement in the annual report. Disclosure of earnings per share on the company's comprehensive income is not required.

Statement of Cash Flows

41. <u>FASB Statement No. 95</u> requires that a company present a statement of cash flows for the accounting period, with its income statement and balance sheet. The statement of cash flows reports on the company's cash inflows and cash outflows, and reconciles the beginning and ending cash balances. It includes three major sections, showing the net change in cash from <u>operating</u>, <u>investing</u>, and <u>financing</u> activities. This reconciliation <u>articulates</u> the statement of cash flows with the balance sheet.

42. External users need information to assess a company's liquidity, financial flexibility, and operating capability. The statement of cash flows, used with the other financial statements, aids external users in assessing a company's (a) ability to generate positive future cash flows, (b) ability to meet its obligations and pay dividends, (c) need for external funding, (d) net income in relation to its associated cash receipts and payments, and (e) cash and noncash investing and financing transactions for the period.

43. Operating activities include the transactions and events related to the earning process. The most common operating cash inflows are collections from customers and interest and dividends received. The most common operating cash outflows are payments to suppliers and employees, and payments of interest and taxes. The section showing <u>Net Cash Flow From Operating Activities</u> is most often prepared by the <u>indirect method</u>. Using this method, net income is listed first. Then adjustments are made to convert net income to net cash provided by (or used in) operations. The FASB encourages the use of the <u>direct method</u>, in which operating cash outflows are deducted from operating cash inflows to determine the net cash provided by (or used in) operating activities.

44. The <u>Cash Flows From Investing Activities</u> section includes all cash inflows and outflows from the company's investment transactions. The most common cash inflows from investing activities are receipts from sales of investments in stocks and bonds, and receipts from sales of property, plant, and equipment. The most common outflows from investing activities are payments for investments in stocks and bonds, and payments for investments in property, plant, and equipment.

45. The <u>Cash Flows From Financing Activities</u> section includes all cash inflows and outflows from the company's financing transactions. The most common cash inflows from financing activities are receipts from the issuance of stocks and debt securities. The most common cash outflows from financing activities are payments of dividends, and payments to reacquire stock and to retire debt securities.

46. The net cash amounts provided by (used in) the operating, investing, and financing sections are summed to determine the net increase or decrease in cash of the company for the period. The net change in cash is added to the beginning cash balance to arrive at the ending cash balance, which is the same amount reported on the company's year-end balance sheet.

SELF-EVALUATION EXERCISES

Supply the words necessary to complete each of the following items.

Concepts of Income

CI-1. Income for a period is the amount that stockholders may be paid while leaving the company as well off at the end of the period as it was at the beginning,

according to the ________ __________ concept.

CI-2. Changes in values of assets and liabilities are not recorded unless a transaction, event, or circumstance has provided verifiable

evidence of the change under the _________________ __________.

CI-3. The transactional approach uses the _________ basis, in which changes in value of assets and liabilities are recorded in the period when the changes occur, rather than when cash is paid or collected.

CI-4. The FASB defines ________________ _________ as the change in a company's equity during a period from transactions and other events and circumstances from nonowner sources.

Conceptual Reporting Guidelines

CG-1. According to the FASB, a company's income statement should provide

information on return on investment, ________, financial

flexibility and _____________ ________________.

CG-2. A company's ability to adapt to unexpected needs and opportunities

is its _________ ____________.

CG-3. A company's ability to maintain a given physical level of operations

is its ____________ ____________.

CG-4. According to the FASB, <u>total</u> net income may be less important than

_____________ of net income.

CG-5. The AICPA Special Committee on Financial Reporting discussed two categories of earnings: _______ earnings and _________ earnings.

Elements of the Income Statement

EI-1. In FASB Statement of Concepts No. 6, the FASB defined four elements of the income statement: ________, ____________, _______, and _________.

EI-2. Most revenues result from a gradual combination of operating activities, otherwise known as the ________ _________.

EI-3. Revenues are usually not ___________ until the earning process is complete or virtually complete, and an exchange has taken place.

EI-4. Expenses are outflows of assets and/or incurrences of liabilities associated with the company's ongoing __________ or ___________ operations.

EI-5. Using association of cause and effect, systematic and rational allocation, or immediate recognition, expenses are recognized and __________ against revenues.

EI-6. Increases in net assets from peripheral or incidental activities of the company are _________.

EI-7. Decreases in net assets from peripheral or incidental activities of the company are _________.

EI-8. Revenues are generally recognized when ___________; in contrast, some gains are recognized when ______________.

EI-9. Generally, gains and losses are classified into three categories: ____________ transactions, changes in value while items are ______, and ________________ transfers between a company and nonowners.

Income Statement Content

ISC-1. The major components of the income statement are income from

_____________ _____________, results from _____________

_____________, _____________ _______, cumulative effects

of ________ ___ _________ __________, _____

_____________, and _________ _____ ________.

ISC-2. Only normal, recurring operating activities are included in net

income under the _______ _________ _____________ concept of income advocated by some accountants.

ISC-3. All transactions affecting stockholders' equity during the period, except dividends and capital transactions, should be included in net

income according to the _____-__________ concept of income.

Income from Continuing Operations

ICO-1. Operating expenses are usually classified according to ____________ categories.

ICO-2. Deferred income taxes arise as a result of _____________ (timing) differences between financial and taxable income.

ICO-3. Temporary differences between pretax financial income and

taxable income are allocated across time periods using _____________ tax allocation.

ICO-4. The total income tax expense of a period is allocated to the components

of net income and retained earnings using ____________ tax allocation.

ICO-5. Under the _______-_______ format for income from continuing operations, total expenses are deducted from total revenues in a single computation.

ICO-6. Using the multiple-step format, cost of goods sold is typically

deducted from net sales to arrive at ________ ___________. Then

operating expenses are deducted to determine ____________ ___________.

Results from Discontinued Operations

RDO-1. Operations and cash flows that can be clearly distinguished operationally and for

financial reporting purposes comprise a _______________ of a company.

RDO-2. The results from discontinued operations section of a company's income statement includes the ________ ________ or ________ of a discontinued component, and the ______ or ______ from the component's sale.

RDO-3. The income or loss from discontinued operations and the gain or loss on the sale of a component are reported _____ of income taxes.

RDO-4. When all six specified criteria are met during the process of selling a component, the company classifies the component as ________ _____ ________.

RDO-5. A company reports a component held for sale at the lower of ________ ________ or _____ _______ less any costs to sell.

Extraordinary Items

EX-1. To be extraordinary, an item must be both ___________ _______ ___________ and ______________ ______ ______________.

EX-2. An event or transaction is ____________ if it is highly abnormal and unrelated to, or only incidentally related to, the entity's ordinary activities.

EX-3. An event or transaction is _______________ if it would not reasonably be expected to recur in the foreseeable future.

EX-4. A primary consideration in determining whether an item is extraordinary is the _______________ in which the company operates.

EX-5. Material results of events or transactions that are either unusual in nature or infrequent in occurrence, but not both, are shown as a separate component of _________ ______ ____________ __________.

Accounting Changes

AC-1. A change in accounting principle takes place when a company changes from one ___________ _________ _____________ ___________ to another.

AC-2. A material change in accounting principle is in most instances reported by including the cumulative effect of the change (net of tax) on ________ periods' earnings as a component of ______ _________ in the period of the change.

AC-3. A change in accounting estimate is accounted for in the _________ year, and in ___________ years affected.

Statement of Retained Earnings

SRE-1. The statement of retained earnings is a schedule linking the

________ ______ and the _________ __________.

SRE-2. The correction of a previous material error is reported on the

statement of retained earnings as a ________ ________ _____________.

Comprehensive Income

CIN-1. Comprehensive income consists of net income and ________________

_________________ ________.

CIN-2. Other comprehensive income includes any unrealized gain or loss in the market value of a company's investments in available-for-sale

______________.

Statement of Cash Flows

SCF-1. The statement of cash flows reports on a company's cash _________

and ________, and reconciles the beginning and ending _______ ____________.

SCF-2. The three major sections of the statement of cash flows show the net

change in cash from ___________, ___________, and ___________ activities.

SCF-3. The FASB encourages the use of the _________ method to present net cash flows from operating activities.

SCF-4. Operating activities include the transactions and events related to

the __________ ___________.

SCF-5. Receipts from sales of property, plant, and equipment are included in the

Cash Flows From _____________ Activities section of the statement of cash flows.

SCF-6. Payments to reacquire stock are reported in the Cash Flows From

_____________ Activities section of the statement of cash flows.

ANSWERS TO SELF-EVALUATION EXERCISES

CI-1. capital maintenance; CI-2. transactional approach; CI-3. accrual; CI-4. comprehensive income; CG-1. risk, operating capability; CG-2. financial flexibility; CG-3. operating capability; CG-4. components; CG-5. core, noncore; EI-1. revenues, expenses, gains, losses; EI-2. earning process; EI-3. recognized; EI-4. major, central; EI-5. matched; EI-6. gains; EI-7. losses; EI-8. realized, realizable; EI-9. exchange, held, nonreciprocal; ISC-1. continuing operations, discontinued operations, extraordinary items, changes in accounting principles, net income, earnings per share; ISC-2. current operating performance; ISC-3. all-inclusive; ICO-1. functional; ICO-2. temporary; ICO-3. interperiod; ICO-4. intraperiod; ICO-5. single-step; ICO-6. gross profit, operating income; RDO-1. component; RDO-2. operating income, loss, gain, loss; RDO-3. net; RDO-4. held for sale; RDO-5. book value, fair value; EX-1. unusual in nature, infrequent in occurrence; EX-2. unusual; EX-3. infrequent; EX-4. environment; EX-5. income from continuing operations; AC-1. generally accepted accounting principle; AC-2. prior, net income; AC-3. current, future; SRE-1. balance sheet, income statement; SRE-2. prior period adjustment; CIN-1. other comprehensive income; CIN-2. securities; SCF-1. inflows, outflows, cash balances; SCF-2. operating, investing, financing; SCF-3. direct; SCF-4. earning process; SCF-5. Investing; SCF-6. Financing.

POST TEST

Part A Circle T if the statement is true and F if it is false.

T F 1. Expenses include decreases in net assets from peripheral or incidental transactions of a company.

T F 2. The current operating performance concept is now generally accepted for income statement reporting.

T F 3. Revenues and expenses are reported at "gross" amounts.

T F 4. The current operating income or loss of a discontinued segment is included in income from continuing operations on the income statement.

T F 5. Material gains and losses from transactions or events that are either unusual in nature or infrequent in occurrence, but not both, are reported as a separate component of income from continuing operations.

T F 6. A company's comprehensive income consists of net income and other comprehensive income.

T F 7. A material change in accounting principle is in most instances reported as a prior period adjustment.

T F 8. A major unforeseen strike is an example of an extraordinary item.

T F 9. Deferred income taxes are allocated across accounting periods as the differences between financial and taxable income reverse.

T F 10. Under the capital maintenance concept, income for a period is the difference between beginning and ending capital balances after adjustments for investments and disinvestments during the period.

T F 11. Under the transactional approach, assets and liabilities are carried at historical cost unless a transaction, event, or circumstance provides reliable evidence of a change in value.

T F 12. Use of the transactional approach is justified by the qualitative characteristic of relevance.

T F 13. As required by FASB Statement No. 144, the sale of a component of a company is reported as an extraordinary item.

T F 14. Revenues are usually recognized when realization has taken place and the revenues have been earned.

T F 15. Under the current operating performance concept, unusual and nonrecurring items are disclosed in the statement of retained earnings.

T F 16. A company's operating capability is its ability to adapt to unexpected needs and opportunities.

T F 17. According to the FASB, the components of net income may be more important than the total amount.

T F 18. Amortization expense is matched against revenues using association of cause and effect.

T F 19. The cost-recovery method is used for certain long-term service contracts when collectibility is uncertain.

T F 20. One way that revenues and gains differ is that some gains are recognized when realizable.

T F 21. The results from discontinued operations section of a company's income statement reports the operating income or loss from any discontinued component, while any gain or loss from the sale of a component is included in income from continuing operations.

T F 22. Prior period adjustments include corrections of material errors in the financial statements of prior periods.

T F 23. The three major sections of the statement of cash flows report the net change in cash from operating, investing, and financing activities.

T F 24. The FASB encourages the use of the indirect method to report net cash flows from operations on the statement of cash flows.

Part B Select the one best answer, and place its letter in the space provided.

____ 1. Which of the following is not a pervasive principle for matching expenses against revenues? (a) association of cause and effect; (b) systematic and rational allocation; (c) immediate recognition; (d) arbitrary assignment.

____ 2. A material change in accounting principle is in most instances reported (a) as a prior period adjustment on the face of the income statement; (b) by including the cumulative effect of the change on prior periods' earnings as a component of net income in the period of the change; (c) by including the cumulative effect of the change on prior periods' earnings in current income from continuing operations; (d) as an extraordinary item.

____ 3. The major components of the income statement do not include (a) prior period adjustments; (b) extraordinary items; (c) net income; and (d) cumulative effects of changes in accounting principles.

____ 4. Income from continuing operations does not include (a) net sales revenues; (b) cost of goods sold; (c) operating expenses; (d) current results of discontinued operations.

____ 5. Which of the following is not a reason that the income statement has become the predominant financial statement? (a) the income statement is useful to stockholders in evaluating the stewardship of management over invested capital; (b) the income statement summarizes the financing and investing activities of the firm; (c) past income may be used to predict future stock prices and dividends; (d) income information is useful for predicting future cash from operations.

____ 6. The operating income or loss for the period of a discontinued component is reported on the income statement (a) as an item of income from continuing operations; (b) as an extraordinary item; (c) net of tax, in a separate section; (d) as a prior period adjustment to retained earnings.

____ 7. The AICPA Special Committee on Financial Reporting recommended that (a) the income statement report only core earnings; (b) increased detail be reported on the income statement; (c) disaggregation of industry information on the income statement be minimized; (d) its pronouncements be considered generally accepted accounting principles by the FASB.

____ 8. Using the transactional approach, (a) a change in value is recorded when a transaction, event, or circumstance provides verifiable evidence of the change; (b) assets and liabilities are carried at current value; (c) net income equals revenues minus expenses plus investments by owners minus payments to owners; (d) all of the above.

____ 9. Which of the following statements regarding gains and losses is incorrect? (a) some gains are recognized when realizable; (b) gains and losses are reported at net, rather than gross, amounts; (c) gains and losses are not associated with the entity's major operating activities; (d) gains and losses are disclosed directly in the retained earnings statement under the all-inclusive concept.

_____ 10. Under the capital maintenance concept (a) income always is determined using historical cost measurements; (b) income includes dividends and capital transactions; (c) income is the difference between the beginning and ending net asset balances, after adjustments for investments and disinvestments; (d) income is the amount that may be paid to stockholders during a period without impairing the entity's operating capability.

_____ 11. Alternative revenue recognition methods, used in exceptional cases, include (a) the realization method, used when noncash resources are converted into rights to cash; (b) the proportional-performance method for certain long-term construction contracts; (c) the installment method, used when collectibility is very uncertain; (d) association of cause and effect, systematic and rational allocation, and immediate recognition.

_____ 12. Expenses (a) are a measurement of a company's efforts or sacrifices; (b) are components of (decreases in) equity; (c) include incurrences of liabilities; (d) are (include) all of the above.

_____ 13. Which of the following statements regarding comprehensive income is <u>incorrect</u>? (a) a company may report comprehensive income either on the income statement preceding net income or in a footnote to the financial statements; (b) the FASB does not require disclosure of a company's earnings per share on comprehensive income; (c) any change in the excess of a company's additional pension liability over its unrecognized prior service cost is a component of other comprehensive income; (d) comprehensive income includes all changes in the equity of a company, except those resulting from investments by owners and distributions to owners.

Part C Solve each of the following short problems.

1. The list below includes components of the income statement, the statement of retained earnings and statement of comprehensive income.

   a. Income from continuing operations
   b. Results from discontinued operations
   c. Extraordinary items
   d. Cumulative effects of changes in accounting principles
   e. Earnings per share
   f. Statement of retained earnings
   g. Other comprehensive income

   Show where each of the following items would be most appropriately reported by placing one letter in the space provided.

_____ 1. crop loss of farming corporation due to flooding of Missouri River bottomland.

_____ 2. effect on prior periods' earnings of changing from straight-line to sum-of-the-years' digits method of depreciation.

_____ 3. service revenues of computer equipment company.

_____ 4. dividends declared during the current period.

_____ 5. current operating income of a subsidiary which was sold at end of current period.

_____ 6. cost of goods manufactured.

_____ 7. correction of a material computational error in prior year's financial statements.

_____ 8. beginning retained earnings balance.

_____ 9. item presented on the face of the income statement, usually directly below net income.

_____ 10. gain from the sale of the net assets of an operating segment.

_____ 11. cost of goods sold.

_____ 12. income tax related to continuing operations.

_____ 13. net income.

_____ 14. recording of bad debts expense.

_____ 15. financial effects of a natural disaster.

_____ 16. unrealized decrease in value of available-for-sale securities.

_____ 17. sudden expropriation of assets by a foreign country.

2. Below is a list of terms related to the income statement. Following the list is a series of descriptive phrases. Match each term with its descriptive phrase by placing the appropriate letter in the space provided.

a. accrual basis
b. return on investment
c. realization
d. comprehensive income
e. single-step format
f. losses
g. component
h. operating capability
i. extraordinary item
j. transactional approach
k. earning process
l. stewardship
m. other items
n. proportional-performance method
o. other comprehensive income

_____ 1. can only be provided after maintenance of the entity's capital

_____ 2. the entity's ability to maintain a given physical level of operations

_____ 3. decreases in equity from peripheral or incidental transactions

_____ 4. includes net income

_____ 5. carries assets and liabilities at historical cost until a transaction, event, or circumstance provides verifiable evidence of change

_____ 6. records the financial impact of transactions in the period of occurrence

_____ 7. unusual in nature and infrequent in occurrence

_____ 8. deducts total expenses from total revenues

_____ 9. the process of converting noncash resources into cash or rights to cash

_____ 10. involves operations and cash flows that can be clearly distinguished, operationally and for financial reporting purposes

_____ 11. management's responsibility for invested capital

_____ 12. includes purchasing, producing, selling, delivering, collecting, and paying

_____ 13. a component, with net income, of comprehensive income

_____ 14. used for recognition of revenue from certain long-term service contracts

_____ 15. recurring revenues and expenses not directly related to a company's primary operations

3. Below are selected pretax account balances of the Port Company on December 31, 2004. Prepare a multiple-step income statement for the year. Include a separate schedule for cost of goods sold.

Purchases (net)	$25,000
Merchandise inventory, 1/1/04	4,000
Extraordinary gain	13,000
Income from operations of discontinued component	2,000
Loss on disposal of discontinued component	5,000
Sales (net)	60,000
Other items (revenues)	6,000
Operating expenses	7,000
Cumulative effect on prior periods' income of change in depreciation method (increase in earnings)	4,000

Merchandise inventory at 12/31/04 is $4,000. Five thousand shares of stock have been outstanding for the entire year. The income tax rate is 30%. Round all calculations to the nearest dollar.

4. On December 31, 2004 at the end of its first year of operations, Troup Company shows the following account balances:

Revenues	$90,000
Expenses	68,000
Unrealized increase in value of available-for-sale securities	2,000

The income tax rate is 30% on all items of income.

Required: (a) Prepare a 2004 income statement, which includes comprehensive income (ignore earnings per share).

(b) Instead, prepare (1) a 2004 income statement (ignore earnings per share) and (2) a 2004 statement of comprehensive income.

5. Below is information about the Sierra Company for 2004:

Cash balance, January 1, 2004	$ 4,100
Payment for purchase of land	45,000
Proceeds from issuance of bonds	50,000
Payments to suppliers and employees	30,000
Increase in accounts receivable (net)	1,000
Collections from customers	72,000
Increase in deferred income taxes	300
Bond discount amortization	500
Payments of income taxes	7,000
Depreciation expense	15,000
Proceeds from sale of building	30,000
Interest and dividends collected	1,000
Decrease in advances from customers	1,200
Increase in accounts payable	1,500
Decrease in salaries payable	600
Payments of interest	4,000
Increase in inventories	2,500
Payment of dividends	2,000
Net income	20,000

Required: (a) Prepare a 2004 statement of cash flows for the Sierra Company, using the indirect method to report the net cash flow from operating activities.

(b) Prepare the operating cash flows section of the statement, using the direct method.

ANSWERS TO POST TEST

Part A

1. F	7. F	13. F	19. F
2. F	8. F	14. T	20. T
3. T	9. T	15. T	21. F
4. F	10. T	16. F	22. T
5. T	11. T	17. T	23. T
6. T	12. F	18. F	24. F

Part B

1. d	4. d	7. b	10. c
2. b	5. b	8. a	11. c
3. a	6. c	9. d	12. d
			13. a

Part C

1.

1. a	6. a	11. a	16. g
2. d	7. f	12. a	17. c
3. a	8. f	13. f	
4. f	9. e	14. a	
5. b	10. b	15. c	

2.

1. b	5. j	9. c	13. o
2. h	6. a	10. g	14. n
3. f	7. i	11. l	15. m
4. d	8. e	12. k	

3.

PORT COMPANY
Income Statement
For Year Ended December 31, 2004

Sales (net)		$60,000
Cost of goods sold (Schedule 1)		(25,000)
Gross profit		$35,000
Operating expenses		(7,000)
Operating income		$28,000
Other items		6,000
Pretax income from continuing operations		$34,000
Income tax expense		(10,200)
Income from continuing operations		$23,800
Results from discontinued operations		
Income from operations of discontinued component (net of $600 income taxes)	$ 1,400	
Loss on disposal of discontinued component (net of $1,500 income tax credit)	(3,500)	(2,100)
Income before extraordinary items		$21,700
Extraordinary gain (net of $3,900 income taxes)		9,100
Cumulative effect on prior years' income of change in depreciation method (net of $1,200 income taxes)		2,800
Net income		$33,600

Components of Income	Earnings Per Share (5,000 shares)
Income from continuing operations	$4.76
Results from discontinued operations	(0.42)
Extraordinary gain	1.82
Cumulative effect on prior years' income of change in depreciation method	0.56
Net income	$6.72

Schedule 1: Cost of Goods Sold
For Year Ended December 31, 2004

Inventory, 1/1/04	$ 4,000
Purchases (net)	25,000
Cost of goods available for sale	$29,000
Less: Inventory, 12/31/04	(4,000)
Cost of goods sold	$25,000

4. (a)

TROUP COMPANY
Income Statement
For Year Ended December 31, 2004

Revenues	$90,000
Expenses	(68,000)
Income before income taxes	$22,000
Income tax expense	(6,600)
Net income	$15,400
Other comprehensive income	
Unrealized increase in value of available-for-sale securities (net of $600 income taxes)	1,400
Comprehensive Income	$16,800

(b) (1)

TROUP COMPANY
Income Statement
For Year Ended December 31, 2004

Revenues	$90,000
Expenses	(68,000)
Income before income taxes	$22,000
Income tax expense	(6,600)
Net income	$15,400

(b) (2)

TROUP COMPANY
Statement of Comprehensive Income
For Year Ended December 31, 2004

Net income	$15,400
Other comprehensive income	
Unrealized increase in value of available-for-sale securities (net of $600 income taxes)	1,400
Comprehensive Income	$16,800

5. (a)

SIERRA COMPANY
Statement of Cash Flows
For Year Ended December 31, 2004

Net Cash Flow From Operating Activities		
Net income	$ 20,000	
Adjustments for differences between income flows and cash flows from operating activities:		
Add: Depreciation expense	15,000	
Bond discount amortization	500	
Increase in accounts payable	1,500	
Increase in deferred income taxes	300	
Less: Increase in accounts receivable (net)	(1,000)	
Increase in inventories	(2,500)	
Decrease in salaries payable	(600)	
Decrease in advances from customers	(1,200)	
Net cash provided by operating activities		$32,000
Cash Flows From Investing Activities		
Payment for purchase of land	$(45,000)	
Proceeds from sale of building	30,000	
Net cash used for investing activities		(15,000)
Cash Flows From Financing Activities		
Payment of dividends	$ (2,000)	
Proceeds from issuance of bonds	50,000	
Net cash provided by financing activities		48,000
Net Increase in Cash		$ 65,000
Cash, January 1, 2004		4,100
Cash, December 31, 2004		$ 69,100

5. (b)

Cash Flows From Operating Activities		
Cash Inflows:		
Collections from customers	$ 72,000	
Interest and dividends collected	1,000	
Cash inflows from operating activities		$ 73,000
Cash Outflows:		
Payments to suppliers and employees	$ 30,000	
Payments of interest	4,000	
Payments of income taxes	7,000	
Cash outflows for operating activities		(41,000)
Net cash provided by operating activities		$ 32,000

5

ADDITIONAL ASPECTS OF FINANCIAL REPORTING AND FINANCIAL ANALYSIS

CHAPTER OBJECTIVES

After careful study of this chapter, you will be able to:

1. Describe an auditor's report.
2. Explain the disclosures in management's discussion and analysis.
3. Understand the meaning of an operating segment.
4. Describe the disclosures in a segment report.
5. Explain interim reporting.
6. Prepare an interim report.
7. Understand intracompany and intercompany comparisons (Appendix).
8. Prepare horizontal and vertical percentage analyses (Appendix).
9. Perform ratio analysis (Appendix).

SYNOPSIS

Financial Statements and Market Efficiency

1. General purpose financial statements designed to meet the needs of external users are published in a company's annual report, which also includes accompanying notes, an auditor's report, the management report, and management's discussion and analysis. In addition, companies prepare interim reports for accounting periods of less than one year.

2. The efficient markets hypothesis presumes that the prices of securities traded in the capital markets fully reflect all publicly available information, and that these prices adjust to new information almost immediately in an unbiased manner. Full disclosure of financial information helps to prevent unscrupulous use of insider information and aids in the efficient operation of capital markets.

Auditor's Report (Opinion), Audit Committee, and Management's Report

3. Most published financial statements are audited by an independent certified public accountant. In an audit, the accountant conducts an examination and expresses an opinion concerning the fairness of the financial statements in conformity with generally accepted accounting principles. An unqualified opinion states that the financial statements present the information fairly in accordance with generally accepted accounting principles (GAAP), in all material respects. A qualified opinion states that, except for the effects of the qualified item, the financial statements present the information fairly, in conformity with GAAP. An adverse opinion states that the financial statements do not present the information fairly, in conformity with GAAP. A disclaimer states that the auditor does not express an opinion.

4. An unqualified opinion contains three paragraphs. The introductory paragraph lists the financial statements audited, states that management is responsible for the statements, and asserts that the auditor is responsible for expressing an opinion on the statements. The scope paragraph describes the auditor's activity, stating that the auditor has examined the financial statements in accordance with generally accepted auditing standards and has performed appropriate tests to evaluate the reasonableness of the information. The opinion paragraph tells the auditor's opinion.

5. Many companies have an audit committee, with oversight over the financial reporting process. Such a committee is usually composed of "outside directors" rather than company management, to help maintain auditor independence. Usually the audit committee of a company oversees internal control, helps to select accounting policies, helps to select the auditor, reviews the audit plan, reviews suggestions by auditors about weaknesses in internal control, reviews the financial statements and audit report, and acts as the liaison between the auditor and management.

6. The preparation and presentation of a company's financial statements are the responsibility of its management. Many companies include a management report in their annual reports, acknowledging management's responsibility and discussing internal control and the roles of the audit committee and the independent auditor.

7. The Securities and Exchange Commission requires a management's discussion and analysis (MD&A) in a company's Form 10-K annual report. SEC Regulation S-K provides general guidelines and specific instructions for MD&A requirements. Disclosures required by the AICPA about existing risks and uncertainties are also often included in a company's MD&A. Many companies include the MD&A in their annual reports. The MD&A is a "forward-looking" narrative analysis and discussion by management, providing information about the company's liquidity, capital resources, and results of operations, as well as other information needed for an understanding of the company's financial condition and changes in financial condition.

Segment Reporting

8. Financial statements prepared by a company on a "consolidated" basis aggregate the accounting results of various legal segments. Disaggregation of segment financial information improves the predictive value and feedback value of financial statement information. FASB Statement No. 131 requires that the financial statements of a company include certain disaggregated information about its operating segments.

9. An operating segment is a company component (a) that operates to earn revenues and incur expenses, (b) whose operating results are regularly reviewed by the company's chief operating officer, and (c) for which financial information is available. That is, the identification of operating segments for financial reporting is based on the "management approach," the way a company's management organizes the company's segments. Financial information must be provided about each reportable segment - each operating segment that satisfies at least one of the following tests:

   (a) Revenue Test. Its reported revenues (including sales to external customers and intersegment sales) are 10% or more of the combined revenues of all of the company's reported operating segments.

   (b) Profit Test. The absolute amount of its profit or loss is 10% or more of the combined reported profits of all industry segments that did not report a loss.

   (c) Asset Test. Its segment assets are 10% or more of the combined assets of all operating segments.

10. Enough reportable segments must be disclosed so that their combined revenues are at least 75% of total company revenues (excluding intersegment sales).

11. A company must disclose general information about how it is organized and about the types of products and services from which each reportable segment earns its revenues. In addition, for each reportable segment the company must disclose:

   (a) Information about profit (or loss): The company must report a measure of the profit (loss) for each reportable segment, and must also disclose the segment's revenues, interest revenue and interest expense, and depreciation, depletion, and amortization expense.

   (b) Information about assets: The company must report a measure of the total assets of each reportable segment, as well as the total related capital expenditures.

   (c) Reconciliations: The company must reconcile the segments' revenues, profits, and assets to its respective total revenues, pretax income from continuing operations, and total assets.

Furthermore, on a company-wide basis, the company must disclose its revenue from external customers for each product and service, information about its geographic areas (e.g., revenues and long-level assets) and revenues from major customers.

12. The intent of disaggregated disclosures is to help users better understand a company's performance, better assess its likely future cash flows, and make more informed judgments. There are some comparability issues, however, related to differences between companies as to their operations, transfer pricing policies, and expense allocation procedures.

Interim Financial Reports

13. Interim financial statements, intended to improve the timeliness of accounting information, are reports for periods of less than one year. Interim reports are issued by all publicly held companies. APB Opinion No. 28 set out guidelines for the presentation of interim information. According to the Opinion, each interim period is considered primarily an integral part of an annual period.

14. The generally accepted accounting principles used in preparation of a company's annual report are used, with some modifications, for interim periods. Revenues are recognized during an interim period in the same manner as during an annual period. Seasonal variations in revenue are disclosed. Expenses that can be associated directly with or allocated to interim product or service revenues are matched against those revenues. In general, the same inventory pricing method (e.g., FIFO, LIFO) is used for interim as for annual reports. Expenses that are not directly associated with product sales or services are matched against revenues using a variety of bases: (a) expenses identified with the operating activities of more than one interim period are allocated among the interim periods based on an estimate of time expired, benefit received, or activity associated with the periods, and (b) expenses identified only with activities of the current interim period are allocated to that period. Gains and losses which occur during an interim period and which would not be deferred at year-end are recognized in the interim period of occurrence.

15. Income taxes for each interim period are computed using an estimate of the effective tax rate on annual income from continuing operations. The amount of income taxes applied to each interim period is the income tax computed on year-to-date income from continuing operations minus the related income taxes reported in previous interim periods of the year. Where an established pattern of seasonal losses offset by income in later periods exists, the resulting income tax credit is recognized in the loss period.

16. Material extraordinary items and results of discontinued operations are reported, net of taxes, in the interim period during which they occur. The cumulative effects of changes in accounting principles, net of income taxes, are reported in the first interim period, regardless of when they occur. Materiality is determined in relation to estimated income for the entire year.

17. Earnings per share is computed for each interim period presented. Care is needed in reporting comparative interim earnings per share, because differences arising from the short time periods may make prediction of annual earnings per share difficult.

18. According to APB guidelines, publicly held companies presenting interim reports must at a minimum disclose (a) sales or gross revenues, income taxes, extraordinary items (net of tax), the cumulative effects of changes in accounting principles, and net income; (b) earnings per share; (c) seasonal revenues, costs, and expenses; (d) significant changes in estimates of income taxes; (e) results of discontinued operations and material unusual or infrequent items; (f) contingent items; (g) changes in accounting principles or estimates; and (h) significant changes in financial position (i.e., cash flows). When a company reports the above information on a quarterly basis, it must also provide current year-to-date information and comparable data from the previous year. When an interim condensed balance sheet and cash flow data are not presented, significant changes in liquid assets, working capital, long-term liabilities, and stockholders' equity are disclosed.

SEC Reports

19. The Securities and Exchange Commission (SEC) has the legal authority to prescribe accounting principles and reporting practices for companies issuing publicly traded securities. The Office of the Chief Accountant provides the SEC with advice on accounting and auditing. The Chief Accountant is responsible for Regulation S-X, which governs the form and content of financial statements filed with the SEC. The Chief Accountant also has authority over the Financial Reporting Releases which prescribe accounting principles for regulated companies. The Division of Corporation Finance assists in the establishment of reporting standards (except those applying to financial statements) and is responsible for reviewing financial reports submitted to the SEC by regulated companies.

20. Two of the required SEC reports, Form 10-K and Form 10-Q, are important to accountants. Form 10-K is the most common SEC annual report form. It requires two types of information: (1) information which must also be reported in annual reports to stockholders and which may be included in Form 10-K simply by reference to the company's published annual report, such as the financial statements, notes, and MD&A; and (2) information which is required only in SEC reports. This second type of information is considered to be of interest primarily to a limited and sophisticated group of users (e.g., security analysts) and includes items such as directors and officers, executive compensation, and legal proceedings.

21. Form 10-Q contains disclosures similar to those in Form 10-K, but on a quarterly and year-to-date basis. The financial statement disclosures included are similar to those in a company's published quarterly report. However, Form 10-Q disclosures may be more extensive because the SEC requires presentation of comparative interim income statements. Companies must file both Form 10-K and Form 10-Q electronically.

22. International accounting standards differ from U.S. accounting standards for both segment reporting and interim reporting. Segment reporting is required under international standards, but reportable segments are identified differently than under U.S. standards. Under international standards, reportable segments include both business segments and geographic segments. International and U.S. standards require a company to make similar segment disclosures but there are some differences in measurement and reporting requirements. International standards provide guidance for what to include in an interim report, but do not specify which companies must publish them or how frequently. Public companies, however, are encouraged to provide at least half-year reports. If a company issues an interim report, under international standards it is required to include a condensed balance sheet, income statement, cash flow statement, statement of changes in equity, and selected explanatory notes.

Appendix: Financial Analysis Comparisons

23. In intracompany comparison, a company's current financial performance and condition are compared with the company's past results. Evidence of trends is an important factor in such comparisons. Consistency over time of information prepared for use in such comparisons is critical.

24. In intercompany comparison, a company's performance is compared with that of competitors, with the industry as a whole, or with the results in related industries. Comparability of the information used across companies, as well as consistency over time, is of concern in such comparisons.

Percentage Analyses

25. The three types of percentage analysis used on financial information are horizontal analysis, vertical analysis, and ratio analysis. In horizontal analysis, changes in a company's operating results and financial position over time are shown in percentages as well as dollars. Comparisons may be made with the preceding year or with a base year. Care must be used in computing and interpreting percentage changes under horizontal analysis. No percentage change may be validly expressed if the base year amount is negative or zero. No vertical addition or subtraction of percentages can be made, because the percentages may have been developed from different bases. When base amounts are small, a relatively small dollar change may produce a high percentage change.

26. In vertical analysis, monetary relationships between items on the financial statements of a period are shown in percentages as well as dollars. When vertical analysis is used with the income statement, net sales are usually expressed as 100% and all other components are expressed accordingly. On the balance sheet, total assets represent 100%; on the retained earnings statement, beginning retained earnings is 100%; and on the statement of cash flows, the increase in cash is usually expressed as 100%. Vertical analysis is helpful in identifying trends or changes in relationships between items over time. Common-size statements are financial statements shown only in percentages.

Ratio Analysis

27. Ratios computed by dividing one or more financial statement items by another related item or items are frequently used to evaluate the return, risk, financial flexibility, liquidity, and operating capability of a company. Ratios may be used for comparisons between companies or for analysis of a single company's results over time. Many "benchmark" ratios are routinely computed for companies and industries by financial analysts. The primary standard ratios may be classified into five groups: (a) stockholder profitability ratios, (b) company profitability ratios, (c) liquidity ratios, (d) activity ratios, and (e) stability ratios.

28. Stockholder profitability ratios indicate how effectively a company has been meeting the profit objectives of its owners.

    (a) Earnings per share, probably the most frequently cited ratio in financial analysis, shows the amount of earnings attributable to each share of common stock.

$$\text{Earnings per Share} = \frac{\text{Net Income - Preferred Dividends}}{\text{Average Common Shares Outstanding}}$$

(b) The <u>price/earnings ratio</u> is used by actual and potential investors to evaluate the attractiveness of an investment in a company's stock. The ratio may indicate the growth potential perceived by investors for a company. Comparisons should be made between "similar" companies.

$$\text{Price/Earnings} = \frac{\text{Market Price per Common Share}}{\text{Earnings per Share}}$$

(c) The <u>dividend yield ratio</u> indicates the rate of return actually received by stockholders. The sum of the dividend yield and the percentage change in the market price of the stock held during the period often is considered the stockholder's total return on investment.

$$\text{Dividend Yield} = \frac{\text{Dividends per Common Share}}{\text{Market Price per Common Share}}$$

29. <u>Company profitability ratios</u> indicate how effectively a company has met its overall profit (return) objectives, particularly in relation to the resources invested.

(a) <u>Profit margin</u> commonly is used to evaluate a company's efficiency in controlling costs and expenses in relation to sales. A weakness of the ratio is that it does not take into consideration the amount of investment used to generate the sales and income.

$$\text{Profit Margin} = \frac{\text{Net Income}}{\text{Net Sales}}$$

(b) <u>Return on total assets</u> indicates how efficiently the company uses its economic resources. When intercompany comparisons are made, the age of assets should be considered. The return on aging assets increases as depreciation lowers asset book values. Furthermore, assets purchased at high prices in a period of inflation will show a lower return.

$$\text{Return on Total Assets} = \frac{\text{Net Income + Interest Expense (net of tax)}}{\text{Average Total Assets}}$$

(c) <u>Return on stockholders' equity</u> shows the residual return on the owners' equity. Comparison of this ratio with the return on total assets indicates the degree of financial <u>leverage</u>. However, this ratio, like the return on total assets ratio, does not take into account the current value of the capital invested.

$$\text{Return on Stockholders' Equity} = \frac{\text{Net Income}}{\text{Average Stockholders' Equity}}$$

30. <u>Liquidity ratios</u> indicate a company's ability to meet its currently maturing financial obligations. These ratios generally involve components of the company's working capital.

(a) The <u>current ratio</u> (or <u>working capital ratio</u>) probably is the most commonly used indicator of short-run liquidity. Too <u>low</u> a ratio indicates liquidity problems. A current ratio too <u>high</u> for the industry may indicate inefficient management of current assets.

$$\text{Current Ratio} = \frac{\text{Current Assets}}{\text{Current Liabilities}}$$

(b) The acid-test ratio (or quick ratio) is a more severe test of a company's short-term debt-paying ability. Only the current assets which may be easily converted into cash are used in the calculation. These quick assets usually consist of cash, temporary investments, accounts receivable, and short-term notes receivable.

$$\text{Acid-Test Ratio} = \frac{\text{Quick Assets}}{\text{Current Liabilities}}$$

31. Activity ratios are used to evaluate the liquidity of certain current assets and to indicate the efficiency of the company in using its short-term economic resources.

(a) The inventory turnover ratio shows the number of times the inventory was "turned over" or sold during the period. Generally, the higher this ratio the more effective the company is in its operations, the smaller the amount of investment tied up in inventories, and the shorter the operating cycle needed to replenish cash. However, too high a ratio may indicate sales lost because of insufficient inventory.

$$\text{Inventory Turnover} = \frac{\text{Cost of Goods Sold}}{\text{Average Inventory}}$$

(b) The receivables turnover ratio indicates the company's efficiency in collecting receivables and converting them to cash. Generally, a high receivables turnover ratio suggests that the company has few resources tied up in receivables, collects these resources at a fast pace, and has few uncollectible accounts.

$$\text{Receivables Turnover} = \frac{\text{Net Credit Sales}}{\text{Average Net Receivables}}$$

(c) The payables turnover ratio reflects the company's time lag between purchasing inventory and making cash payments. Too high a payables turnover ratio may indicate that the company is making payments too quickly and losing the credit advantages of accounts payable. A payables turnover ratio lower than average for the industry may indicate financial difficulties.

$$\text{Payables Turnover} = \frac{\text{Cost of Goods Sold}}{\text{Average Accounts Payable}}$$

32. Stability ratios indicate the long-run solvency and stability of the company. They give evidence of the safety or risk of investments in the company by long-term bondholders and stockholders.

(a) The debt ratio shows the percentage of total assets contributed by creditors. Subtracting this ratio from 100% yields the equity ratio - the percentage of total assets contributed by stockholders. In general, creditors prefer a lower debt ratio, while stockholders prefer a higher debt ratio, up to a point. Favorable "trading on the equity" occurs when a company borrows money from creditors at an interest rate, net of taxes, lower than the return the company earns from operations. However, a highly leveraged company is usually considered a more risky investment.

$$\text{Debt Ratio} = \frac{\text{Total Liabilities}}{\text{Total Assets}}$$

(b) The times interest earned ratio (or interest coverage ratio) shows the ability of the company to cover its interest obligations through its annual earnings. It measures the safety of creditors' investments in the company, particularly over the long term.

$$\text{Times Interest Earned} = \frac{\text{Pretax Operating Income}}{\text{Interest Expense}}$$

(c) Book value per common share shows the net assets per share of stock. Book value is of limited use as an indicator of a company's financial stability because (1) the sale value of assets is not important to a going concern; (2) book value is based on assets recorded primarily at historical cost and does not reflect true liquidation value; and (3) book value has no direct relationship to market value per share.

$$\text{Book Value per Common Share} = \frac{\text{Common Stockholders' Equity}}{\text{Outstanding Common Shares}}$$

33. Cash flow ratios may be useful in understanding relationships and trends among cash flows. Users should be aware, however, that cash flow from operations may vary more than accrual income due to the timing of cash flows, and that management may be able to influence that timing.

(a) The ratio of Cash Flow From Operations (CFO) to Sales indicates the proportion of each sales dollar available for investing and financing activities.

$$\text{Cash Flow From Operations to Sales} = \frac{\text{Cash Flow From Operations}}{\text{Sales}}$$

(b) The ratio of CFO to Net Income relates accrual income to cash flows.

$$\text{Cash Flow From Operations to Net Income} = \frac{\text{Cash Flow From Operations}}{\text{Net Income}}$$

(c) CFO per Share may be computed by users, although its disclosure by companies is expressly prohibited.

$$\text{Cash Flow From Operations per Share} = \frac{\text{Cash Flow From Operations}}{\text{Average Shares of C/S Outstanding}}$$

(d) The ratio of CFO to Debt Maturing in the Next Year indicates the ability of a company to make principal payments.

$$\text{Cash Flow From Operations to Maturing Debt} = \frac{\text{Cash Flow From Operations}}{\text{Debt Maturing Next Year}}$$

SELF-EVALUATION EXERCISES

Supply the words necessary to complete each of the following items.

Financial Statements and Market Efficiency

FS-1. A company's annual report includes ____________ ______________ and accompanying notes, an auditor's report, the ______________ __________, and management's discussion and analysis.

FS-2. For accounting periods of less than a year, many companies prepare

____________ ____________.

FS-3. The ____________ ____________ ____________ presumes that the prices of securities traded in capital markets adjust to publicly available information almost instantaneously.

Auditor's Report (Opinion), Audit Committee, and Management's Report

AR-1. An unqualified opinion expressed by an ____________

____________ states that financial statements present information

fairly in accordance with ____________ ____________

____________ ____________, in all ____________ respects.

AR-2. An unqualified opinion contains three paragraphs: the

____________, ____________, and ____________ paragraphs.

AR-3. Responsibility for oversight over the financial reporting process is

held by the ____________ ____________ in many companies.

AR-4. The preparation and presentation of a company's financial statements

are the responsibility of its ____________.

AR-5. A management's discussion and analysis is required by the ____________

______ ____________ ____________ in a company's Form 10-K annual report.

Segment Reporting

S-1. Consolidated financial statements present the ____________ information of various legal entities.

S-2. An operating segment is a company component that operates to earn

____________ and incur ____________ whose operating results are

reviewed by the company's ____________ ____________ ____________,

and for which ____________ ____________ is available.

S-3. A segment is reportable if it satisfies the ____________ test,

the ____________ test, or the ____________ test.

S-4. For each reportable segment a company must disclose information about __________ or _______, information about ___________, and _________________.

S-5. A company must disclose information on geographic areas and on revenue from _____________ _____________ and ___________ ____________________.

Interim Financial Reports

I-1. All publicly held companies issue ____________ _______, reports for periods of less than one year.

I-2. Each interim period is considered an __________ __________ of an annual period.

I-3. Interim reports disclose _______________ variations in revenues.

I-4. Interim period income taxes are computed using the estimated effective rate on ______________ income from continuing operations.

I-5. A tax credit is recognized in an interim loss period when an _______________ pattern of seasonal losses offset by income in later periods exists.

I-6. Material extraordinary items and __________ ____ ________________ ______________ are disclosed, net of taxes, in the interim period of occurrence.

SEC Reports

SR-1. Regulation S-X and Financial Reporting Releases are the responsibility of the SEC's ________ _______________.

SR-2. The most common SEC annual report form is __________ _______.

SR-3. The SEC requires presentation of comparative interim income statements in _______ ______.

SR-4. Companies file Form 10-K and Form 10-Q ____________.

Appendix: Financial Analysis Comparisons

F-1. A company's performance is evaluated over time in ______________ comparison, while the company's performance is compared with that of competitors in ________________ comparison.

F-2. In intercompany comparisons, two characteristics are important:

________________ of the information across companies, as well as

______________ over time.

Appendix: Percentage Analyses

PA-1. Horizontal analysis, vertical analysis, and ratio analysis are the

three types of ______________ ________________ used on financial information.

PA-2. Changes in a company's financial results and position over time are

expressed as percentages, as well as dollars, with _______________ analysis.

PA-3. Relationships on the financial statements of one period are expressed as

percentages, as well as dollars, with _______________ analysis.

PA-4. Statements which are expressed only in percentages are

________________-_________ statements.

Appendix: Ratio Analysis

R-1. The primary ratios used in financial analysis may be classified into

five groups: ______________ _______________ ratios, ____________

______________ ratios, ____________ ratios, _____________ ratios,

and _____________ ratios.

R-2. The ratio which shows earnings attributed to each share of common

stock is ___________ ______ __________.

R-3. The ratio which shows the rate of return actually received by

investors is the ______________ ________.

R-4. The ratio which indicates the company's efficiency in controlling costs relative to sales and which is computed by dividing sales into net income is the

___________ ___________.

R-5. An indicator of short-run liquidity is the ____________ ratio, or working capital ratio.

R-6. The ratio which indicates the company's efficiency in collecting

receivables is the ______________ ____________.

R-7. A company's time lag between purchasing inventory and making cash payments is reflected in the __________ __________ ratio.

R-8. The stability ratio which shows the net assets (valued primarily at historical cost) per share of stock is the __________ __________ per share.

R-9. Cash flow from operations may vary more than accrual income due to the __________ of cash flows.

R-10. Cash flow from operations divided by net income relates cash flows to income on the __________ basis.

ANSWERS TO SELF-EVALUATION EXERCISES

FS-1. financial statements, management report; FS-2. interim reports; FS-3. efficient markets hypothesis; AR-1. independent auditor, generally accepted accounting principles, material; AR-2. introductory, scope, opinion; AR-3. audit committee; AR-4. management; AR-5. Securities and Exchange Commission; S-1. aggregated; S-2. revenues, expenses, chief operating officer, financial information; S-3. revenue, profit, asset; S-4. profit, loss, assets, reconciliations; S-5. external customers, major customers; I-1. interim reports; I-2. integral part; I-3. seasonal; I-4. annual; I-5. established; I-6. results of discontinued operations; SR-1. Chief Accountant; SR-2. Form 10-K; SR-3. Form 10-Q; SR-4. electronically; F-1. intracompany, intercompany; F-2. comparability, consistency; PA-1. percentage analysis; PA-2. horizontal; PA-3. vertical; PA-4. common-size; R-1. stockholder profitability, company profitability, liquidity, activity, stability; R-2. earnings per share; R-3. dividend yield; R-4. profit margin; R-5. current; R-6. receivables turnover; R-7. payables turnover; R-8. book value; R-9. timing; R-10. accrual.

POST TEST

Part A Circle T if the statement is true and F if it is false.

T F 1. A qualified opinion by an auditor states that the financial statements as a whole do not present the information fairly, in conformity with GAAP.

T F 2. A company must provide certain disaggregated information about an operating segment only if it satisfies all three of the following tests: the revenue test, the profit test, and the asset test.

T F 3. Expenses identified with the operating activities of more than one interim period are allocated among those periods.

T F 4. Materiality for an interim period is determined in relation to income for the entire year.

T F 5. Publicly traded companies are required to disclose CFO per share, as well as earnings per share, on the face of the income statement.

T F 6. For the purpose of determining whether an operating segment is reportable, intersegment sales are included in the segment's revenues.

T F 7. On a company-wide basis a company must disclose information about its geographic areas and about revenues from major customers.

T F 8. With horizontal analysis, relationships on the financial statements of one period are expressed as percentages, as well as dollars.

T F 9. A current ratio too low for the industry may indicate liquidity problems.

T F 10. A company's financial statements are the responsibility of its management.

T F 11. An unqualified opinion contains five paragraphs: the introductory, materiality, scope, opinion, and disclaimer paragraphs.

T F 12. The current ratio, computed by dividing current assets by current liabilities, is the most commonly used indicator of short-run liquidity.

T F 13. Publicly traded companies presenting interim financial statements should treat the interim period primarily as a separate reporting period, rather than as an integral part of an annual period.

T F 14. Common-size statements are financial statements expressed only in percentages.

T F 15. The timing of cash flows may cause cash flows from operations to vary more than accrual income.

T F 16. The efficient markets hypothesis presumes that the market price of a company's securities will eventually adjust to all events affecting the company.

T F 17. The audit committee of a company is usually composed of "outside directors," rather than management.

T F 18. Financial statements are prepared on a consolidated basis in order to include disaggregation of segment financial information.

T F 19. When a company is required to report disaggregated information about its operating segments, enough reportable segments must be disclosed so that their combined revenues make up at least 75% of total company revenues.

T F 20. In intracompany comparison, a company's current financial performance is compared with the company's past results.

T F 21. In general, a low inventory turnover ratio indicates effective operations and a short operating cycle.

T F 22. The SEC requires a management's discussion and analysis in a company's Form 10-K annual report.

Part B Select the one <u>best</u> answer, and place its letter in the space provided.

____ 1. Minimum interim disclosures by a publicly held company include (a) sales or gross revenues; (b) earnings per share; (c) significant changes in estimates of income taxes; (d) contingent items; (e) all of the above.

____ 2. Which of the following facts would <u>not</u> make an operating segment reportable? (a) the segment's revenues, including intersegment sales, are 20% of the total company's revenues; (b) the segment's profit is $50,000, while the company's profit is $430,000; (c) 75% of the segment's revenues are earned from one unaffiliated customer; (d) the segment's identifiable assets are 11% of the company's assets.

____ 3. The times interest earned ratio (a) measures the safety of creditors' investments in a company; (b) shows the net assets per share of a company's stock; (c) relates accrual income to cash flows; (d) is the most commonly used indicator of short-run liquidity.

____ 4. Information about which of the following is required in a company's financial statements under <u>FASB Statement No. 131</u>? (a) types of products and services from which each reportable segment earns its revenue; (b) revenue from external customers for each product and service; (c) information about geographic areas; (d) revenues from major customers; (e) all of the above.

____ 5. For each reportable operating segment a company must disclose (a) total assets and total related capital expenditures; (b) interest revenue and interest expense; (c) profit or loss; (d) all of the above.

____ 6. Which of the following ratios indicates the rate of return actually received by shareholders? (a) profit margin; (b) return on stockholders' equity; (c) dividend yield ratio; (d) current ratio.

____ 7. Which of the following ratios is a commonly used indicator of short-run liquidity? (a) inventory turnover; (b) price/earnings; (c) profit margin; (d) current.

____ 8. Horizontal analysis (a) is a type of ratio analysis; (b) expresses monetary relationships between items on the financial statements of a period as percentages as well as dollars; (c) may be useful in evaluating trends in a company's operating results and financial position over time; (d) uses financial statements expressed only in percentages.

____ 9. Interim financial statements (a) are issued by all publicly held companies; (b) need not disclose seasonal variations in revenue; (c) may recognize a tax credit resulting from a seasonal loss only in the period when the credit is realized; (d) do not report extraordinary items and the effects of changes in accounting principles.

____ 10. The SEC (a) reviews the audited information of all corporations; (b) requires the presentation of comparative interim income statements on Form 10-Q; (c) requires that publicly traded companies file interim financial information on Form 10-K; (d) requires that a company include a management's discussion and analysis in any published financial statements.

_____ 11. An unqualified audit opinion (a) is usually expressed by a company's audit committee; (b) describes the auditor's activity in the scope paragraph; (c) accepts the auditor's responsibility for the financial statements presented; (d) is identical to a qualified opinion except that it does not include an opinion paragraph.

Part C Solve each of the following short problems.

1. Financial information about the Multi-Products Company is presented below:

	Total	Segment A	Segment B	Segment C	Segment D
Sales	$ 500,000	$344,000	$100,000	$36,000	$20,000
Assets	1,000,000	420,000	400,000	90,000	90,000
Profit (loss)	50,000	(10,000)	48,000	5,500	6,500
Intersegment sales	60,000	-0-	55,000	2,000	3,000

Determine which segments are reportable and indicate why.

2. Which of the following statements regarding segment reporting are correct? (a) determination of whether an operating segment is reportable is made on the basis of materiality; (b) a company's financial statements are disaggregated using the "management approach" rather than classified by products, geography, legal entity, or type of customer; (c) all separate departments of a company are considered to be operating segments; (d) a company must report enough segments to include information about a substantial portion of its total operations; (e) disaggregation of financial reports is intended to improve the reliability, but not the predictive value or the feedback value, of a company's financial reports.

3. Condensed statements of the Katy Corporation and other selected data are presented below.

Balance Sheet
December 31, 2004

Current assets		
Cash	$ 65,000	
Marketable securities	30,000	
Accounts receivable (net)	100,000	
Merchandise inventory	165,000	
Total current assets		$360,000
Plant assets (net)		450,000
Total assets		$810,000
Current liabilities	$200,000	
Long-term liabilities	210,000	$410,000
Common stock, $10 par	$300,000	
Retained earnings	100,000	400,000
Total liabilities and stockholders' equity		$810,000

Income Statement
For Year Ended December 31, 2004

Net sales (all credit sales)	$1,100,000
Cost of goods sold	(800,000)
Gross profit on sales	$ 300,000
Operating expenses	(150,000)
Net operating income	$ 150,000
Interest expense	(25,000)
Income before income taxes	$ 125,000
Income tax (40%)	(50,000)
Income before extraordinary items	$ 75,000
Uninsured extraordinary flood loss (net of tax)	(20,000)
Net income	$ 55,000

Selected data from the balance sheet at the end of the preceding year: Accounts receivable (net), $120,000; merchandise inventory, $145,000; total assets, $700,000; total stockholders' equity, $350,000; total common stock, $300,000. The average accounts payable amount during the year was $20,000.

Compute the following ratios or amounts:

(1) Current ratio

(2) Acid-test ratio

(3) Inventory turnover

(4) Receivables turnover

(5) Debt ratio and equity ratio

(6) Return on total assets

(7) Return on stockholders' equity

(8) Earnings per share

(9) Payables turnover

4. Which of the following statements related to the SEC is correct?

(a) The SEC requires a management's discussion and analysis in a company's Form 10-K annual report.
(b) The management's discussion and analysis is a narrative analysis and discussion which provides information, for example, on the company's liquidity, capital resources, and results of operations.
(c) The SEC requires that each regulated company file a financial reporting release summarizing its financial statements.
(d) Form 10-K, which contains only information included in a company's published financial statements, may be completed by reference to those statements.
(e) Comparative interim income statements are included in Form 10-Q.
(f) The Division of Corporation Finance establishes reporting standards for financial statements.
(g) The Chief Accountant, who is responsible for Regulation S-X, has authority over the Financial Reporting Releases.
(h) Form 10-Q disclosures may be more extensive than those in a company's published quarterly report.
(i) The SEC has the legal authority to prescribe accounting principles and reporting practices.
(j) The SEC requires companies to file Form 10-K and Form 10-Q electronically.

ANSWERS TO POST TEST

Part A

1. F	5. F	9. T	13. F	18. F
2. F	6. T	10. T	14. T	19. T
3. T	7. T	11. F	15. T	20. T
4. T	8. F	12. T	16. F	21. F
			17. T	22. T

Part B

1. e	4. e	7. d	9. a	11. b
2. c	5. d	8. c	10. b	
3. a	6. c			

Part C

1. Segments A, B, and D are reportable.
Segments A and B meet the revenue test.*
Segments B and D meet the profit test.
Segments A and B meet the asset test.

*Intersegment sales are included in sales for the revenue test.

2. Correct statements: a, b, d

3. (1) Current Ratio $= \dfrac{\text{Current Assets}}{\text{Current Liabilities}} = \dfrac{\$360,000}{\$200,000} = 1.80:1$

(2) Acid-Test Ratio $= \dfrac{\text{Quick Assets}}{\text{Current Liabilities}}$

$$= \frac{\$65,000 + \$30,000 + \$100,000}{\$200,000} = \frac{\$195,000}{\$200,000} = 0.98:1$$

(3) Inventory Turnover $= \dfrac{\text{Cost of Goods Sold}}{\text{Average Inventory}}$

$$= \frac{\$800,000}{(\$145,000 + \$165,000) \div 2} = \frac{\$800,000}{\$155,000} = 5.16$$

(4) Receivables Turnover $= \dfrac{\text{Net Credit Sales}}{\text{Average Net Receivables}}$

$$= \frac{\$1,100,000}{(\$120,000 + \$100,000) \div 2}$$

$$= \frac{\$1,100,000}{\$110,000} = 10$$

(5) Debt Ratio $= \dfrac{\text{Total Liabilities}}{\text{Total Assets}} = \dfrac{\$410,000}{\$810,000} = 51\%$

Equity Ratio = 100% - Debt Ratio = 49%

(6) Return on Total Assets $= \dfrac{\text{Net Income}^{(a)} + \text{Interest Expense (net of tax)}}{\text{Average Total Assets}}$

$$= \frac{\$75,000 + [\$25,000 \times (100\% - 40\%)]}{(\$700,000 + \$810,000) \div 2} = \frac{\$90,000}{\$755,000} = 11.9\%$$

(a) excluding extraordinary items

(7) Return on Stockholders' Equity $= \dfrac{\text{Net Income}^{(a)}}{\text{Average Stockholders' Equity}}$

$$= \frac{\$75,000}{(\$350,000 + \$400,000) \div 2} = \frac{\$75,000}{\$375,000} = 20\%$$

(a) excluding extraordinary items

(8) Earnings Per Share $= \dfrac{\text{Net Income - Preferred Dividends}}{\text{Average Common Shares Outstanding}}$

$$= \frac{\$55,000 - 0}{\$300,000 \div \$10} = \frac{\$55,000}{\$30,000} = \$1.83$$

(9) Payables Turnover $= \dfrac{\text{Cost of Goods Sold}}{\text{Average Accounts Payable}}$

$$= \frac{\$800,000}{\$20,000} = 40$$

4. Correct statements: a, b, e, g, h, i, j

6

CASH AND RECEIVABLES

CHAPTER OBJECTIVES

After careful study of this chapter, you will be able to:

1. Understand the importance of cash management.
2. Prepare a bank reconciliation.
3. Discuss revenue recognition when the right of return exists.
4. Understand the credit policies related to accounts receivable.
5. Explain the gross and net methods to account for cash discounts.
6. Estimate and record bad debts using a percentage of sales.
7. Estimate and record bad debts using an aging analysis.
8. Explain pledging, assignment, and factoring of accounts receivable.
9. Account for short-term notes receivable.
10. Prepare a proof of cash (Appendix).

SYNOPSIS

Cash

1. Investors, long-term creditors and short-term creditors are interested in the ability of a company to pay its operating expenses, dividends, and interest and to repay its current debts. The existence of cash and other liquid assets which may be quickly converted into cash to pay current debts is important to these users of financial statements.

2. In the current asset section of a company's balance sheet, "cash" is the resource on hand available to pay current obligations. "Cash" cannot be subject to any contractual restrictions that prevent using it to pay current debts. Items properly included in the measurement of cash on hand are coins, currency, checking accounts, savings accounts, negotiable checks, and bank drafts. Items which should not be included are certificates of deposit, bank overdrafts, postdated checks, travel advances, and postage stamps. Certificates of deposit (CDs), which are normally classified as temporary investments, are short-term investments issued by banks that allow a company to invest idle cash for short periods.

3. Most companies use the title Cash and Cash Equivalents on their balance sheet in place of Cash. This category includes cash as well as securities that are defined as "cash equivalents" because of their liquidity and low risk. Examples of cash equivalents are commercial paper, treasury bills, and money market funds.

4. Efficient cash management is very important to every company. Proper cash management requires the investment of idle funds. However, a company must estimate the timing of cash inflows and outflows to ensure the availability of cash to meet its needs prior to embarking on a short-term investment program.

5. Cash planning systems consist of those methods and procedures, such as cash budgets, adopted to ensure that a company has adequate cash available to meet maturing obligations and that it invests any unused or excess cash. Cash control systems are the methods and procedures adopted to ensure the safeguarding of the company's funds.

6. Internal control, which forms the basis for cash control systems, has the following four objectives: (a) to safeguard a company's assets, (b) to produce accurate and reliable accounting data, (c) to promote a company's operational efficiency, and (d) to encourage adherence to the company's prescribed managerial policies. Particular internal control procedures should be established only if the benefits of the procedures exceed their costs.

7. Cash control systems can be subdivided into control over cash receipts and control over cash payments. Key elements in a cash receipts internal control system are (a) an immediate counting of receipts by the person opening the mail or the salesperson using the cash register, (b) a daily recording of all cash receipts in the accounting records, and (c) daily deposit of all cash receipts. Key elements in a cash payments internal control system include (a) making all payments by check so that a record of the expenditures exists, (b) authorizing and signing checks only after the proposed expenditures have been verified and approved, and (c) reconciling the bank statement cash balance with the general ledger cash balance on a periodic basis.

8. A petty cash system is a cash fund established to allow a company to pay for small amounts that might be impractical or impossible to pay by check. An employee is appointed petty cash custodian, and the fund is established at an amount estimated to be enough to cover small expenditures over a short period of time. The entry to record the establishment of the fund is:

Petty Cash	500	
Cash		500

The petty cash account is neither debited nor credited again unless the fund size is to be increased or decreased. As money is paid from the fund, the custodian prepares a prenumbered voucher to document the expenditure but no journal entries are made until the fund is reimbursed. At the time of reimbursement, appropriate expense accounts are debited and the general ledger cash account is credited as follows:

Office Supplies Expense	120	
Postage Expense	150	
Cash		370

Any difference between the original petty cash fund balance and the sum of the actual cash plus petty cash vouchers is debited or credited to a Cash Short and Over account when the reimbursement entry above is made. The company reports a debit balance as a miscellaneous expense and a credit balance as a miscellaneous revenue.

9. A company prepares a monthly bank reconciliation in order to analyze and reconcile the differences between the cash balance on the monthly bank statement and the company's accounting record of the proper cash balance. The reconciliation starts from two different amounts--the cash balance on the books and the bank statement balance--and adjusts each of these balances to one common amount, the adjusted cash balance. Most of the discrepancy is usually due to timing differences such as deposits in transit, outstanding checks, bank service charges, and direct deposits made by the bank. However, the reconciliation may also disclose errors made by the bank or the company.

10. The following procedures should be followed in preparing a bank reconciliation: (1) compare the deposits listed on the company's records with the deposits on the bank statement; (2) compare the checks listed in the company's records with the checks shown on the bank statement; (3) identify any deposits or charges made directly by the bank that are not included in the company's records; (4) determine the effect of any errors; (5) complete the bank reconciliation. After the company completes the reconciliation, it makes adjusting entries to correct errors made by the company, and to record items previously unrecorded on its books such as bank service charges, collections made by the bank, and NSF (not sufficient funds) checks.

11. Electronic funds transfers (EFT), the use of computer systems to transfer funds between parties without the use of checks, is increasingly being used by banks to process the large number of cash transactions generated by large companies. Because fewer physical source documents (in the form of checks) are available to substantiate such transactions, the importance of internal controls, such as bank reconciliations, is even greater.

12. Banks may require a portion of any amount loaned to remain on deposit with the bank for the duration of the loan period. These required deposits are called compensating balances. These deposits reduce the cash available to the company and increase the effective interest rate the company pays to borrow the funds. The Securities and Exchange Commission (SEC) requires that companies report compensating balances separately on the balance sheet if the compensating balances are legally restricted. If they are not legally restricted, they are disclosed in the notes to the financial statements.

Receivables

13. Receivables consist of various claims against customers and others arising from the operations of a company. Most of a company's receivables are trade receivables that arise from selling products or rendering services to customers. Most trade receivables are recorded at their maturity value, rather than present value, because the short collection period (usually 60 days or less) makes the difference between the two values negligible. Most trade receivables are in the form of accounts receivable, which are nonwritten promises by customers to pay the amount due within a specified time period (typically 30 days).

14. Nontrade receivables are claims that are not related to selling products or rendering services. A company keeps these receivables separate from trade receivables both in the accounting records and also in its financial statements. Examples of nontrade receivables are deposits with utilities, advances to subsidiary companies, deposits made to guarantee performance, declared dividends to be received and accrued interest on investments, and loans made by nonfinancial companies.

15. While sales on credit increase revenue, they also result in bad debt losses from nonpayment by some customers. To minimize expenses and losses related to credit sales, companies should establish a credit department and effective internal controls over sales information and cash inflows from receivables.

16. A company recognizes revenue from credit sales when realization has occurred and the revenue is earned. When the right of return exists, as in book publishing, FASB Statement No. 48 identifies six criteria that must be satisfied to recognize revenue at the time of sale: (a) the sales price is fixed or determinable at the date of sale; (b) the buyer has paid or will pay the seller and there is no contingency; (c) the buyer's obligation to the seller is not affected by theft or damage to the product; (d) the buyer has an economic substance apart from the seller; (e) the seller does not have significant future obligations related to resale by the buyer; and (f) the seller can reasonably estimate the amount of future returns.

17. Sellers offer cash (sales) discounts on credit sales to induce buyers to pay more promptly and to reduce the risk of nonpayment by customers. A buyer should take advantage of any cash discount with a higher effective interest rate than its borrowing rate. Cash discounts are recognized for financial accounting purposes. They may be accounted for by one of two methods by the seller:

    (a) Gross price method: The selling company records the receivable at the gross sales price with no accounting recognition of the available cash discount until it is actually taken. When the customer takes the discount, it is debited to the Sales Discounts Taken account. This account is deducted from sales on the income statement to determine net sales.

(b) Net Price Method: The selling company records the receivable at the sales price less the available cash discount (the net price). Subsequently, if the customer does not take the discount, the company credits the difference between the amount paid (the gross price) and the amount originally recorded (the net price) to the Sales Discounts not Taken account. This account is reported as interest revenue in the Other Items section of the income statement.

While the gross price method lacks conceptual validity, most companies use it because the cash discount is usually immaterial and the record keeping less complicated. For a numerical example, refer to Exhibit 6-2 of the text.

18. A sales allowance is a reduction in price to compensate the customer for defective goods which are retained by the customer. A sales return occurs when the customer returns defective or non-defective goods and receives credit. If sales returns and allowances are estimated at the time of sale, the amount is debited to Sales Returns and Allowances and credited to Allowance for Sales Returns and Allowances. This allowance account is a contra account to Accounts Receivable and decreases the carrying value of Accounts Receivable on the balance sheet. However, since sales returns and allowances are usually immaterial, a company normally records them at the time they occur and discloses them on the income statement as a deduction from sales revenue.

Uncollectible Accounts

19. Companies that sell on credit must maintain a balance between maximizing revenue and minimizing bad debt risks. When a reasonable credit policy has been established, the seller will normally experience some degree of nonpayment by customers. A company may account for bad debt losses, which decrease the value of Accounts Receivable, by either of two procedures: (a) in the year of the sale based upon an estimate of the amount of uncollectible accounts, the estimated bad debts method, or (b) when it determines that a specific customer account is uncollectible, the direct write-off method.

20. FASB Statement No. 5 requires bad debt losses that are material to be estimated and included in the current financial statements if (a) sufficient evidence exists at the balance sheet date that some receivables will not be collected and, (b) the amount can be reasonably estimated. The journal entry involves a debit to Bad Debt Expense and a credit to Allowance for Doubtful Accounts. Bad Debt Expense is usually classified as an operating expense on the income statement. Allowance for Doubtful Accounts is a contra account to Accounts Receivable and, as such, is disclosed on the balance sheet. The difference between Accounts Receivable and the Allowance account is the net realizable value of the receivables.

21. Under the estimated bad debts method, a company may estimate bad debts using techniques that emphasize either the income statement or the balance sheet. Under the income statement approach, a rate for estimating bad debt expense (percentage of sales) is established by determining the historical relationship between actual bad debts incurred and net credit sales (although total sales may be used). This relationship is expressed as a percentage which is then applied to net credit sales in the current year to determine Bad Debt Expense for the current period. The existing balance in the Allowance for Doubtful Accounts is disregarded in calculating and recording the bad debt expense. The focus is on correctly estimating the expense. This procedure is simple to apply and results in a matching of expenses with sales in the current period.

22. Under the balance sheet approach, a company may estimate bad debt expense as a percentage of outstanding accounts receivable or based on an aging of accounts receivable. When estimating bad debt expense as a percentage of outstanding accounts receivable, a rate determined from the historical relationship between accounts receivable and bad debts is applied to currently outstanding accounts receivable to determine the estimated uncollectible accounts. When using an aging schedule, accounts receivable are categorized according to the length of time outstanding (e.g., 60 days, 120 days, 240 days) and then historically determined bad debt percentages are applied to each category. These are summed to determine the total estimated uncollectible accounts. Under both balance sheet approaches, a company compares the amount of estimated uncollectible accounts receivable with the existing balance in the Allowance for Doubtful Accounts. The entry to record bad debt expense is the amount necessary to bring the Allowance account balance up to the required ending balance. The balance sheet approaches provide useful credit information and result in reporting the best estimate of the net realizable value of accounts receivable.

23. A company may also use the "receivables turnover" (net credit sales) average net accounts receivable) along with the aging schedule to determine how efficiently it collects its accounts receivables.

24. If a company changes its estimated percentage of bad debts during the current accounting period, APB Opinion No. 20 requires the company to record the effects of this change in the current and future periods with no restatement of prior-year amounts. Such changes are considered to be changes in estimates.

25. Under the estimated bad debts methods, a company uses the valuation account, Allowance for Doubtful Accounts, since the actual accounts which will ultimately become uncollectible are not known at the time the estimate is made. Therefore, when the company determines that a specific account is uncollectible, it is written off by debiting the Allowance account and crediting Accounts Receivable. The write-off entry does not change either total current assets or the net realizable value of the accounts receivable. The income statement is also unaffected by this entry.

26. If a company later collects an account which had previously been written off, it reinstates the account in accounts receivable before recording the cash receipt. This process provides a better record of the customer's credit history. If the company is using either of the estimated bad debts methods, the reinstatement entry involves a debit to Accounts Receivable and a credit to Allowance for Doubtful Accounts for the amount of cash received. The cash collection is then recorded in the usual manner. If the company is using the direct write-off method (discussed in the next item), the reinstatement entry debits Accounts Receivable and credits Bad Debt Expense.

27. When using the direct write-off method, a company records bad debts as an expense during the period in which it determines that a specific receivable account is uncollectible. The journal entry debits Bad Debt Expense and credits Accounts Receivable. However, this method violates the matching principle and is not allowed under generally accepted accounting principles unless bad debt losses are immaterial.

Cash Flow From Accounts Receivable

28. Rather than waiting for customer payments in order to receive cash from accounts receivable, a company may speed up the cash flow by one of three processes:

(a) using the receivables as collateral for a loan (<u>pledging</u>). The company retains both risks and benefits of ownership and is responsible for routine collection and administration;

(b) contracting with a finance company to receive cash advances on specific customer accounts and to make repayment as the receivables are collected by the borrowing company (<u>assigning</u>). The company retains credit activities and because the accounts are assigned with recourse, the risk of ownership is retained; or

(c) selling the receivable (without recourse) to a bank or finance company which assumes credit and collection activities, as well as risk of ownership (<u>factoring</u>).

29. <u>FASB Statement No. 140</u> requires that a company (transferor) record the transfer of accounts receivable in which it surrenders control over the receivables to another company (the transferee) as a sale when <u>all</u> three of the following conditions are met: (a) the transferred assets (e.g. accounts receivable) have been isolated from the transferor (the company); (b) the transferee (the other company) has the right to sell the accounts receivable; and (c) the company has no agreement that entitles and obligates it to repurchase the receivables before maturity. Upon completion of the transfer of accounts receivable, the transferor continues to report on its balance sheet any retained interest in the accounts receivable. If the transfer is a sale, the company records the proceeds, eliminates the receivables, and records a gain or loss. If the transfer is not deemed a sale, the company records the proceeds of the transfer as a secured borrowing with a pledge of collateral.

30. Credit card sales involving a national credit card company result in an account receivable in the name of the card-issuing company. The value of this account receivable is reduced by credit card fees owed by the seller to the credit card company for the use of its credit department. The seller reports Credit Card Expense as an operating expense on the income statement. When credit cards are affiliated with banks, any credit card sales receipts may be deposited directly into its checking account. Such transactions are recorded as Cash Sales. An agreement between a retail company and a national credit card company is in essence a factoring agreement.

31. While factoring and assignment agreements are formally entered in the accounting records, pledge agreements are not. However, the assignor company should disclose the existence of factoring, pledging, or assignment agreements related to accounts receivable either parenthetically or in the notes to its financial statements. Such information is important in evaluating a company's liquidity and financial flexibility. The disclosure should include important conditions and terms related to the agreements. In addition, receivables which are assigned, should be reported on the balance sheet separately from unassigned receivables.

Notes Receivable

32. A note receivable is an unconditional written agreement to collect a specified sum of money on a specified date. In addition, it is a negotiable instrument, and usually involves an agreement to receive interest on the principal amount of the note.

33. A company records short-term notes with a stated interest rate (interest-bearing notes) at face value and subsequent interest revenue in the usual fashion. It records most short-term notes without a stated interest rate (non-interest-bearing notes) at their maturity value unless the interest is readily determinable and the company wishes to recognize interest. However, recording a non-interest-bearing note at its present value and recognizing interest revenue as it is earned is conceptually better.

34. A company may wish to obtain cash from a customer's note prior to its maturity date by discounting the note at a bank. The bank deducts the amount of interest discount it wishes to earn on the transaction from the maturity value of the note and remits the net amount to the company. In order to account for a discounted note each of the following items must be determined: (1) face value of note, (2) interest to maturity (face value x interest rate x interest period), (3) maturity value of note (face value + interest to maturity), (4) discount (maturity value of note x discount rate x discount period), (5) proceeds (maturity value - discount), (6) accrued interest revenue (face value x interest rate x period of time note is held by company), (7) book value of note (face value + accrued interest revenue), (8) gain or loss on sale of note (proceeds - book value). On the date of the discount, the company makes journal entries to accrue interest revenue and to record the proceeds received, any gain or loss on the transfer of the note, and the contingent liability. Most discounting is done on a with recourse basis which means that the company agrees to pay the bank the maturity value of the note at its maturity date if the maker of the note fails to do so.

35. When a note is discounted on a recourse basis, the company discounting the note is contingently liable on the note until the maker of the note pays it in full at its maturity date. FASB Statement No. 5 requires disclosure of this contingent liability in the financial statements if the contingency exists at the balance sheet date. The discounted note is recorded in a separate account, Notes Receivable Discounted. This may appear on the face of the balance sheet as a deduction from Notes Receivable. Alternatively, a company may report notes receivable net of the discounted note and disclose the contingent liability in a note to the financial statements.

36. FASB Statement No. 133 requires a company to recognize as assets any derivative financial instruments that involve rights of the company based on their fair value. In addition a company must disclose derivative instruments it holds, including types, objectives, and strategies, to improve the reporting of the company's risk, liquidity, and financial flexibility.

Appendix: Proof of Cash

37. To test a company's internal control over cash and provide additional evidence of the accuracy of the cash balance, an auditor may prepare a more comprehensive form of bank reconciliation which is called a proof of cash. This reconciliation reconciles a company's information with that of the bank for four items: balances at the beginning of the month, receipts for the month, payments for the month, and the balances at the end of the month.

SELF-EVALUATION EXERCISES

Supply the words, symbols, or amounts necessary to complete each of the following items.

Cash

C-1. Negotiable checks and bank drafts are examples of ____________

____________ which would be classified as __________ on the balance sheet.

C-2. To be classified under "Cash" on the balance sheet the asset must be

available to pay ____________ ____________.

C-3. Because of their liquidity, securities such as commercial paper and treasury bills may be reported on the balance sheet in the current asset category titled

Cash and ____________ ____________.

C-4. Short-term investments sold by banks that allow a company to invest

idle cash for short periods of time are called ____________ ______

____________.

C-5. Identify four objectives of a system of internal control.

(1)

(2)

(3)

(4)

C-6. A major component of a cash planning system is the ____________

____________.

C-7. A cash control system must provide control over ____________

____________ and ____________ ____________.

C-8. An account established to accumulate differences between the original balance in a petty cash fund and the actual cash plus petty cash vouchers on hand is called

a(n) ____________ ____________ __________ ____________ account.

C-9. A bank reconciliation reveals differences between the cash balance on the bank statement and the cash balance on the depositor's records which are due to

____________ ____________ and to ____________.

C-10. To facilitate the execution of large numbers of cash payments or receipts and reduce the paperwork involved, increasingly banks are using

__________ __________ __________.

C-11. A bank loans a company $100,000 but requires that $10,000 of the loan remain on deposit with the bank. The $10,000 is known as a __________

__________.

Receivables

R-1. Claims that arise from selling products or rendering services to customers are classified as __________ __________.

R-2. Nonwritten promises by customers to pay a specified amount due within a specified period of time are __________ __________.

R-3. Deposits with utilities, employee travel advances, and declared dividends are examples of __________ __________.

R-4. Having a credit department and using prenumbered sales invoices improves a company's __________ __________ related to credit sales.

R-5. To speed up payment on accounts receivable, sellers offer __________

__________.

R-6. If a company makes a credit sale of a product with a list price of $3,000 and the terms of sale are 2/10, n/30, the debit to accounts receivable to record this sale will likely be for $__________ if the gross price method is used.

R-7. If a customer receives a reduction in price because the item purchased was defective, the reduction is called a __________ __________.

R-8. Four items which may decrease the value of Accounts Receivable are

__________ __________ __________ __________, __________ __________,

__________ __________ __________, and __________ __________.

Uncollectible Accounts

UA-1. When bad debts are recorded as an expense in the period in which an account is deemed uncollectible, the __________ __________-__________ method of accounting is used.

UA-2. FASB Statement No. 5 requires that material estimated losses, such as bad debts, be accrued and reported in the body of the financial statements if what two conditions are met?

(1) ____

____

(2) ____

UA-3. The estimated bad debts method determines the historical relationship between actual bad debts incurred and either __________ or __________ __________.

UA-4. Under the balance sheet approaches to estimating bad debts, the recorded amount of bad debt expense is dependent on the required ending balance in the

__________ ______ __________ __________ account.

UA-5. The method of revising the balance in a company's Allowance for Doubtful Accounts account that requires an analysis of the amount of time each balance has been outstanding is called __________ the accounts receivable.

UA-6. Under the balance sheet approach, Accounts Receivable is valued at its __________ __________ __________.

UA-7. Under the estimated bad debts method the entry to write off an account which has been determined to be uncollectible consists of a debit to __________ ______ __________ __________ and a credit to __________ __________.

UA-8. The entry to write off an account receivable balance under the estimated bad debts method causes ____________________ in a company's total current assets.
(an increase, a decrease, no change)

UA-9. To determine the efficiency of accounts receivable collections, companies use an aging schedule and also calculate the __________ __________.

Generating Immediate Cash

GC-1. The process of selling a company's accounts receivable to a finance company is called __________ the receivables.

GC-2. If the buyer of a company's accounts receivable agrees to assume all future bad debt risks, the receivables are said to be sold without ______________.

GC-3. When accounts receivable are used as collateral for a loan, the accounts have been ____________________.

GC-4. If a cash advance has been obtained in exchange for accounts receivable and the loan may be offset against an asset on the balance sheet, the receivables have been ______________.

Notes Receivable

NR-1. Notes receivable differ from accounts receivable in that the agreement is ______________ and the date the sum of money is due is ______________.

NR-2. Short-term interest-bearing notes receivable are recorded at their _________ ______.

NR-3. When a bank discounts a note receivable, the bank discount percentage is applied against the note's ______________ __________.

NR-4. A note receivable discounted on a recourse basis is a ___________ ______________ to the company that discounted the note.

Appendix

PC-1. An auditor might prepare a comprehensive form of bank reconciliation known as a(n) _________ _______ ___________.

ANSWERS TO SELF-EVALUATION EXERCISES

C-1. liquid assets, cash; C-2. current obligations; C-3. cash equivalents; C-4. certificates of deposit; C-5. (1) safeguard assets, (2) produce accurate and reliable accounting data, (3) promote operational efficiency, (4) encourage adherence to prescribed managerial policies; C-6. cash budget; C-7. cash receipts, cash payments; C-8. cash short and over; C-9. timing differences, errors; C-10. electronic funds transfer; C-11. compensating balance; R-1. trade receivables; R-2. accounts receivable; R-3. nontrade receivables; R-4. internal control; R-5. cash discounts; R-6. $3,000; R-7. sales allowance; R-8. sales returns and allowances, bad debts, credit card fees, sales discounts; UA-1. direct write-off; UA-2. (1) it is probable that an asset has been impaired or a liability incurred as of the balance sheet date, (2) the amount of loss can be reasonably estimated; UA-3. sales, accounts receivable; UA-4. Allowance for Doubtful Accounts;

UA-5. aging; UA-6. net realizable value; UA-7. Allowance for Doubtful Accounts, Accounts Receivable; UA-8. no change; UA-9. receivables turnover; GC-1. factoring; GC-2. recourse; GC-3. pledged; GC-4. assigned; NR-1. written, specified; NR-2. face value; NR-3. maturity value; NR-4. contingent liability; PC-1. proof of cash.

POST TEST

Part A Circle T if the statement is true and F if it is false.

T F 1. Cash included in a sinking fund would ordinarily be classified under the cash heading on the balance sheet.

T F 2. The measurement of cash on hand classified as a current asset includes postage stamps.

T F 3. Proper cash management by a company requires the investment of idle funds on hand.

T F 4. Cash control systems are employed to ensure the safeguarding of an organization's funds.

T F 5. A cash budget would probably be an integral part of a company's cash planning system.

T F 6. In deciding whether to adopt an internal control procedure, a key requirement is that the cost of the control must equal the benefit derived from it.

T F 7. The Petty Cash account is debited and the general Cash account is credited whenever the petty cash fund is reimbursed.

T F 8. The Bartow Corporation borrowed money from a bank which required the loan agreement to include a compensating balance requirement. If the interest rate charged on the loan was 10%, the compensating balance will cause the effective interest rate to be more than 10%.

T F 9. If neither companies with bank accounts nor the banks made any accounting errors, the companies would not need to prepare bank reconciliations.

T F 10. Electronic funds transfers reduce the amount of paperwork in the accounting system, thus simplifying the internal control requirements relating to cash.

T F 11. Since the existence of a written promise to pay provides strong legal evidence to support collection, it is not necessary to provide a bad debt estimate on notes receivable.

T F 12. The adjusting journal entry to record estimated bad debts under the allowance method involves a debit to Bad Debts Expense and credits to the accounts of customers whose balances are believed to be uncollectible.

T F 13. At the date of sale most trade accounts receivable are recorded at their maturity value.

T F 14. The collection period for most trade receivables is 60 days or less.

T F 15. If a credit sale is made with terms of 2/10, n/30, the customer is given a 10% discount if the bill is paid in less than 30 days.

T F 16. If the seller grants a cash discount to credit customers, it is acceptable accounting practice to record both the sale and the receivable net of the available cash discount.

T F 17. When sales returns and allowances are not material to a company's financial statements, they are usually not accounted for in the statements on an estimated basis.

T F 18. The direct write-off method of accounting for bad debts is widely used by companies that sell on credit.

T F 19. If the proportion of credit sales to total sales varies from period to period, a company should base its bad debt loss estimate on total sales rather than credit sales.

T F 20. Basing a bad debt loss estimate on the relationship between actual losses and the accounts receivable total does not precisely match a company's current expenses with current revenues.

T F 21. A bad debt adjusting entry that is developed from an aging of accounts receivable must take into consideration the preadjustment balance in the allowance for doubtful accounts.

T F 22. When accounts receivable are factored, ownership of the receivables is transferred to the party acting as the factor.

T F 23. When a company pledges its accounts receivable to a bank, the bank takes title to the receivables at the time of the pledging.

T F 24. Assigned accounts receivable should be disclosed separately from unassigned accounts receivable on the borrowing company's balance sheet.

T F 25. An agreement to allow for credit card sales between a retail company and a national credit card company is essentially a pledge agreement.

T F 26. The term "non-interest-bearing note" is a misnomer because all notes do in fact contain an interest element.

T F 27. FASB Statement No. 5 requires that the contingent liability from discounted notes receivable be disclosed in a company's financial statements, even if the possibility of default by the maker of the note is remote.

T F 28. Travel advances to sales personnel are properly classified as trade accounts receivable.

T F 29. Accounts receivable discounted with a recourse provision are always accounted for as factored receivables.

T F 30. FASB Statement No. 133 requires a company to recognize derivative financial instruments as liabilities on the balance sheet.

Part B Select the one best answer, and place its letter in the space provided.

____ 1. The measurement of cash on hand classified as a current asset would include each of the following, except (a) bank drafts; (b) negotiable checks; (c) certificates of deposit; (d) unrestricted funds on deposit with a bank.

____ 2. Good internal control over cash is not provided if (a) the assistant controller prepares the cash budget; (b) small freight bills are paid out of cash from the petty cash fund rather than by check; (c) payment of a bill is delayed until after the bill has been verified and approved; (d) the deposit of several checks is delayed for a few days while the proper accounts to be credited are identified.

____ 3. Which of the following accounts could logically be debited in recording the entry related to the replenishment of the petty cash fund, when prior to reimbursement the total of petty cash vouchers and cash on hand exceeded the original fund balance? (a) Miscellaneous Expense; (b) Petty Cash; (c) Accounts Payable; (d) Cash Short and Over.

____ 4. After completing a bank reconciliation, for which of the following items would an adjusting entry be unnecessary? (a) interest collected by the bank on a note receivable; (b) customer's check returned for lack of funds; (c) bank service charge; (d) deposit in transit.

____ 5. An auditor is preparing a proof of cash. Which of the following reconciliations would not be included, assuming that the reconciliation was prepared for the month ending November 30? (a) reconciliation of the bank and book balance as of October 31; (b) reconciliation of the payments recorded by the bank with payments recorded in the books during November; (c) reconciliation of the bank and book balance as of November 30; (d) reconciliation of the receipts recorded by the bank with the receipts recorded in the books during October.

____ 6. A $1,000 credit purchase by Sapada Corporation involved credit terms of 1/10, n/30. If Sapada pays the full $1,000, what effective interest rate has it paid on this transaction by not taking advantage of the cash discount? (a) 36%; (b) 18%; (c) 10%; (d) 0%.

____ 7. Use of the direct write-off method in accounting for bad debts would in most instances violate which of the following accounting principles? (a) objectivity; (b) consistency; (c) materiality; (d) matching.

____ 8. The method of estimating bad debts which most closely matches current expenses with current revenues is one which obtains the estimate from: (a) a percentage of total sales; (b) a percentage of total credit sales; (c) a percentage of accounts receivable; (d) an aging of accounts receivable.

____ 9. A company determined that $10,600 of existing accounts receivable may not be collected by aging its accounts receivable. At this date, the Allowance for Doubtful Accounts account had a credit balance of $1,200. Based on this information, an adjusting journal entry should involve a debit to Bad Debt Expense for: (a) $11,800; (b) $10,600; (c) $9,400; (d) $1,200.

_____ 10. Wright Corporation had total sales in the current year of $700,000 and credit sales of $650,000. The Accounts Receivable balance was $400,000 at the balance sheet date and the Allowance for Doubtful Accounts had a debit balance of $28,000 before adjusting entries. Bad Debt Expense is estimated as 4% of credit sales. The adjusting entry to record estimated bad debt expense would include a (a) $54,000 debit to Bad Debt Expense; (b) $54,000 credit to Bad Debt Expense; (c) $26,000 debit to Bad Debt Expense; (d) $26,000 credit to Bad Debt Expense.

_____ 11. BRD Associates had credit sales of $500,000 in the current year, an ending accounts receivable balance of $350,000, and a $17,000 preadjustment credit balance in Allowance for Doubtful Accounts. Bad debts are estimated as 5% of outstanding accounts receivable. The adjusting entry to record bad debt expense for the year would include a (a) $500 debit to Bad Debt Expense; (b) $500 credit to Bad Debt Expense; (c) $500 credit to Allowance for Doubtful Accounts; (d) $17,500 debit to Bad Debt Expense.

_____ 12. Jacobs Company follows the procedure of estimating its bad debts from credit sales. Recently, the company evaluated all of its trade accounts receivable balances and wrote off $16,000 worth of accounts that were considered to be uncollectible. Just prior to this write off, the Allowance for Doubtful Accounts account had a credit balance of $82,000. The effect of this write off on the financial statements was to: (a) increase company expenses by $16,000; (b) increase company expenses by $66,000; (c) decrease total current assets by $16,000; (d) leave the balance of total current assets unchanged.

_____ 13. The equity that a company has in trade accounts receivable that it has assigned should be disclosed in its financial statements as a: (a) separate component of the stockholders' equity section of the balance sheet; (b) contra asset account; (c) current liability; (d) current asset.

_____ 14. Kenneth Corporation received a note from a credit customer on June 15. The note, which had a face value of $10,000 at 8% interest and was due in 45 days, was discounted at a local bank 15 days after it was received. If the bank's discount percentage was 9%, how much cash did Kenneth Corporation receive from the bank? (a) $9,887.50; (b) $9,966.67; (c) $10,024.25; (d) $10,112.50.

_____ 15. To recognize revenue at the time of sale where the right of return exists, each of the following criteria must be satisfied <u>except</u>: (a) the conditions under which future damage to the goods affects the sales price are articulated at the date of sale; (b) the amount of future returns can be estimated; (c) the sales price is fixed or determinable at the date of sale; (d) there is no contingency on the sale.

Part C Solve each of the following short problems.

1. You are in the process of preparing a reconciliation of the Bart Company's bank balance as of June 30. A framework for the reconciliation has been provided. In addition, seven items which will be a part of the completed reconciliation have been described. You are to complete the reconciliation by placing the number of each listed item with the corresponding dollar amount on the appropriate lines in the reconciliation where that item should appear.

   (1) June bank service charge - $60;
   (2) deposit of Cart Company credited in error by bank to Bart's account - $3,000;
   (3) NSF check of Rex Company deposited in June by Bart Company and returned by the bank with the June bank statement - $300;
   (4) check written in May by Bart Company which is still outstanding at June 30 - $500;
   (5) deposit made by Bart Company on June 30 which was not received by the bank until early July - $1,500;
   (6) loan made by bank to Bart Company was added to Bart's account in June by the bank, but Bart's accountant failed to record the loan proceeds in the company's accounting records - $6,000;
   (7) check written in June for $57 was recorded in the books as if it were written for $75.

June 30 balance per bank statement		$30,400
Add:	______	______
	______	______
	______	______
Deduct:	______	______
	______	______
	______	______
Adjusted cash balance		$______
June 30 balance per company records		$22,742
Add:	______	______
	______	______
	______	______
Deduct:	______	______
	______	______
	______	______
Adjusted cash balance		$______

2. The Argon Company has a petty cash fund with an imprest balance of $150. On December 31, vouchers in the petty cash box indicate that the following expenditures from the fund were made: postage stamps, $40; taxi fare for employees who worked late, $23.50; pens, pencils, paperclips, etc., $21.30; donations made to charitable organizations, $18; and miscellaneous expenditures, $9.50. Remaining currency and coin in the petty cash box totaled $36.50. Prepare the necessary journal entry to reimburse the fund on December 31.

3. The December 31, 2003 balance sheet of the Tampa Corporation included the following information pertaining to accounts receivable:

Trade Accounts Receivable	$420,000	
Less: Allowance for Doubtful Accounts	(21,500)	$398,500

During 2004, the following transactions occurred:

a.	New sales on account	$973,000
b.	Collections from past credit sales	847,000
c.	Accounts receivable written off as uncollectible	28,500
d.	Collections of accounts previously written off as uncollectible	900
e.	Recorded bad debt expense estimate using an aging analysis which indicates an Allowance for Doubtful Accounts balance of $24,900 is needed	

Required: (1) Prepare summary journal entries to record each of the above facts.

(a)

(b)

(c)

(d)

(e)

(2) Calculate the net realizable value of accounts receivable that will appear on Tampa's December 31, 2004 balance sheet.

(3) Calculate the receivables turnover for 2004. Assume that new sales on account during 2004 are net of discounts.

4. In the space below, prepare journal entries to record the following transactions related to notes receivable of the Kendra Company.

March 1	Received a $3,000, 12%, 90-day note from R. Trax in settlement of an open account receivable balance from this customer.
March 4	Sold merchandise on credit and accepted a $6,000, 10%, 60-day note from the customer, T. Little.
March 31	Discounted the Trax note at the bank. The bank charged a discount percentage of 13%. Kendra records its contingent liability on discounted notes in an appropriate account.
May 3	Received payment from T. Little on his note.
May 30	Since R. Trax did not pay his note at maturity, the bank collected the necessary proceeds plus a $15 protest fee from Kendra.

March 1

March 4

March 31

May 3

May 30

ANSWERS TO POST TEST

Part A

1. F	7. F	13. T	19. F	25. F
2. F	8. T	14. T	20. T	26. T
3. T	9. F	15. F	21. T	27. T
4. T	10. F	16. T	22. T	28. F
5. T	11. F	17. T	23. F	29. F
6. F	12. F	18. F	24. T	30. F

Part B

1. c	4. d	7. d	10. c	13. d
2. d	5. d	8. b	11. a	14. c
3. a	6. b	9. c	12. d	15. a

Part C

1.

June 30 balance per bank statement		$30,400
Add:	5	1,500
Deduct:	2	(3,000)
	4	(500)
Adjusted cash balance		$28,400
June 30 balance per company records		$22,742
Add:	6	6,000
	7	18
Deduct:	1	(60)
	3	(300)
Adjusted cash balance		$28,400

2.	Dec. 31		Postage Expense	40.00	
			Transportation Expense	23.50	
			Office Supplies Expense	21.30	
			Charitable Contributions Expense	18.00	
			Miscellaneous Expense	9.50	
			Cash Short and Over	1.20	
			Cash		113.50

3.	(1)	(a)	Accounts Receivable	973,000	
			Sales		973,000
		(b)	Cash	847,000	
			Accounts Receivable		847,000
		(c)	Allowance for Doubtful Accounts	28,500	
			Accounts Receivable		28,500
		(d)	Accounts Receivable	900	
			Allowance for Doubtful Accounts		900
			Cash	900	
			Accounts Receivable		900
		(e)	Bad Debts Expense	31,000	
			Allowance for Doubtful Accounts		31,000

$24,900 needed as a credit balance in the allowance account plus the $6,100 debit balance in the allowance account prior to adjustment

(2)

$420,000	Balance at December 31, 2003
973,000	Credit sales in 2004
(847,000)	Collections of accounts receivable in 2004
(28,500)	Accounts written off as uncollectible in 2004
$517,500	Receivables balance at December 31, 2004
(24,900)	Allowance for Doubtful Accounts balance at December 31, 2004
$492,600	Net realizable value of receivables at December 31, 2004

(3)

$$\frac{\text{Net Credit Sales}}{\text{Average Net Accounts Receivable}} = \frac{\$973,000}{\frac{(\$398,500 + \$492,600)}{2}} = 2.184$$

4.

Date	Account	Debit	Credit
March 1	Notes Receivable	3,000.00	
	Accounts Receivable		3,000.00
March 4	Notes Receivable	6,000.00	
	Sales		6,000.00
March 31	Cash	3,023.05	
	Interest Expense	66.95	
	Notes Receivable Discounted		3,000.00
	Interest Revenue		90.00

Market value of note = $3,000 + ($3,000 x 0.12 x 90/360) = $3,090.00

Bank charge = $3,090.00 x 0.13 x 60/360 = $66.95

Date	Account	Debit	Credit
May 3	Cash ($6,000 + ($6,000 x 0.10 x 60/360))	6,100.00	
	Interest Revenue		100.00
	Notes Receivable		6,000.00
May 30	Notes Receivable Dishonored	3,105.00	
	Notes Receivable Discounted	3,000.00	
	Notes Receivable		3,000.00
	Cash		3,105.00

7

INVENTORIES: COST MEASUREMENT AND FLOW ASSUMPTIONS

CHAPTER OBJECTIVES

After careful study of this chapter, you will be able to:

1. Describe how inventory accounts are classified.
2. Explain the uses of the perpetual and periodic inventory systems.
3. Identify how inventory quantities are determined.
4. Determine the cost of inventory.
5. Compute ending inventory and cost of goods sold under specific identification, FIFO, average cost, and LIFO.
6. Explain the conceptual issues regarding alternative inventory cost flow assumptions.
7. Understand dollar value LIFO.
8. Explain additional LIFO issues.
9. Understand inventory disclosures.
10. Record foreign currency transactions involving inventory (Appendix).

SYNOPSIS

Classifications of Inventory

1. Inventories are the assets of a company which are (1) held for sale in the ordinary course of business, (2) in the process of production for sale, or (3) held for use in the production of goods or services to be made available for sale. A merchandising company needs only one type of inventory account, usually called merchandise inventory. Inventories of a manufacturing concern normally include raw materials, goods in process, and finished goods.

2. Raw materials inventory includes the tangible goods acquired by a manufacturing concern for direct use in the production process. Incidental supplies which do not actually become a physical part of the finished product are normally recorded in a separate factory supplies, manufacturing supplies, or indirect materials account.

3. Goods (or work) in process inventory consists of the raw materials, direct labor, and manufacturing (factory) overhead costs for those products which are partially completed at the end of a period. Direct labor is the cost of the labor used directly in manufacturing the product. Manufacturing overhead includes variable costs, such as supplies and some indirect labor, and fixed costs, such as insurance, utilities, and depreciation on production assets.

4. Finished goods inventory includes the completed manufactured products awaiting sale and contains the same cost components as the goods in process inventory.

Perpetual and Periodic Inventory Systems

5. A perpetual inventory system provides for a continuous record of the physical quantities in the inventory. Such a system is essential to maintain effective planning and control by management over inventory and to avoid stockouts. A perpetual inventory system may keep track of units only or can be maintained for both costs and units. Comprehensive perpetual systems are increasingly common with the availability of sophisticated computer systems.

   A company using a perpetual inventory system should make a physical count of the ending inventory at least once a year to verify the accuracy of the accounting records. A difference between the physical count and the inventory account balance requires an adjusting entry to bring the perpetual records into agreement with the physical count.

6. A company using the periodic inventory system does not maintain a continuous record of the physical quantities (or costs) of inventory on hand. Therefore, the company will not be able to determine its inventory accurately until it takes a physical inventory at the end of the period. At that time, the cost of goods sold, in terms of either units or costs, is represented by the following equation:

   Beginning Inventory + Purchases (net) - Ending Inventory = Goods Sold

   A company with a periodic system typically debits the costs of inventory acquisitions to a temporary Purchases account. In both the perpetual and periodic systems, companies usually maintain separate accounts for purchases returns and allowances, purchases discounts, and freight-in. Net purchases are determined as follows:

Net Purchases = Purchases + Freight-in - Purchases Returns and Allowances - Purchases Discounts Taken

Items To Be Included in Inventory

7. Economic control at the balance sheet date, and not legal ownership or physical possession, determines what items a company includes in its ending inventory. Frequently, some inventory is in transit to the company or its customers at the balance sheet date. If the goods are shipped FOB (free on board) shipping point, control of (and legal title to) the goods is transferred to the buyer at the shipping point. Therefore, the goods in transit should be included in the buyer's inventory. If the goods are shipped FOB destination, the legal title to the goods is transferred to the buyer on delivery. Therefore, the goods remain under the control and legal ownership of the seller while in transit and should be retained in the seller's inventory.

8. Goods which are to be picked up by the buyer and are segregated from the seller's other inventory are considered to be under the control of the buyer. Such goods should be reported as inventory by the buyer, not by the seller.

9. Goods delivered by a consignor are included in the consignor's inventory because economic control (and ownership) are retained by the consignor until the goods are sold by the consignee. The consignee will not include in its inventory any goods held on consignment.

Determination of Inventory Costs

10. Inventory cost includes costs directly or indirectly incurred in bringing the inventory to its existing condition and location. The cost of purchased inventory includes the purchase price (net of purchases discounts), normal transportation, insurance, storage, applicable taxes, and similar items. Selling costs, which are not associated with bringing the inventory to its existing condition and location, are never included in inventory.

11. Because of cost/benefit considerations, some costs (for example, the costs of a purchasing department) are usually recognized when incurred, rather than attached to inventory. According to FASB Statement No. 34, interest costs are not included in the cost of inventory that is routinely manufactured.

12. Material manufacturing costs which are related directly or indirectly to the production of inventory are costs of inventory. Variable manufacturing overhead is related directly and is always included in inventory. The allocation of fixed manufacturing overhead is difficult and may be somewhat arbitrary: the costs incurred must be traceable to the benefits. Materiality is also a consideration in deciding whether to include costs in inventory.

13. For internal reporting, most manufacturing companies use a standard-cost system in which unit costs are based on budgeted standards for the period. Valuation of inventory at standard costs is acceptable for financial reporting only if the company adjusts the standard costs for cost variances occurring during the period.

14. With <u>variable costing</u> (<u>direct costing</u>), ending inventory includes <u>only</u> variable production costs, such as direct materials, direct labor, and variable manufacturing overhead. Fixed overhead costs, which do not vary with changes in production levels, are expensed when incurred under variable costing. With <u>absorption costing</u> (<u>full costing</u>) the cost of the inventory includes allocated fixed manufacturing overhead, as well as the direct costs. Variable costing <u>is not</u> generally accepted for external financial reporting; absorption costing <u>is</u> generally accepted.

15. <u>Purchases discounts</u> available for prompt payment are accounted for by the gross price method or the net price method. A company using the <u>gross price method</u> records purchases at gross prices and records discounts only when they are taken. A company using the <u>net price method</u> records purchases at net prices and records discounts only when they are <u>not taken</u>. The net price method always records the correct inventory cost, invoice price less all available discounts, while the gross price method records the correct cost only when all discounts are taken or when an adjustment removes discounts lost from the inventory. Purchases discounts lost are a financing expense for the period and do not increase the economic benefit to be received from the inventory. Purchases discounts taken under the gross price method should not be considered income. According to the revenue recognition principle a company must sell goods or services before recognizing income.

16. Purchases discounts are not the same as <u>trade discounts</u>, amounts which are subtracted before arriving at the invoice price.

Cost Flow Assumptions

17. A company allocates the cost of goods available for sale between the cost of goods sold and the ending inventory by means of a <u>cost flow assumption</u>. Most companies use a first-in, first-out method for the physical management of inventory. However, the <u>physical flow</u> of goods does <u>not</u> need to match the <u>assumed flow of costs</u> used for financial statements. The specific identification; first-in, first-out (FIFO); average cost; and last-in, first-out (LIFO) methods all match historical cost with revenue, and all are considered generally accepted accounting principles.

18. A company using the <u>specific identification</u> cost flow assumption identifies each inventory unit as sold or remaining in the ending inventory, and includes the actual costs of those units in cost of goods sold and ending inventory, respectively. This method is appropriate when each inventory unit is unique, but specific identification may be impractical or prohibitively expensive for high-volume inventories, and may permit management to manipulate profits by arbitrarily selling high-cost or low-cost identical inventory items.

19. A company using the <u>FIFO</u> cost flow assumption allocates costs in the order in which they are incurred. That is, the first input costs incurred are the first to be transferred to cost of goods sold or to goods in process, then to finished goods and cost of goods sold. The ending inventory is assigned the most recent costs incurred. With FIFO, the ending inventory and cost of goods sold are the same under the perpetual and periodic systems.

20. A company using the <u>average cost</u> assumption considers that all the costs and units are commingled and does not identify individual costs and units. Under a <u>periodic</u> inventory system, the average cost method is known as the <u>weighted average</u> method. The average cost per unit using the weighted average method is the cost of goods available for sale divided by the number of units available for sale. Under a <u>perpetual</u> inventory system, the average cost method is known as a <u>moving average</u> method, because a new weighted average cost must be calculated after <u>each</u> purchase.

21. A company using the <u>LIFO</u> cost flow assumption assumes that the most recent costs incurred are the first to be transferred out or sold, so the earliest costs incurred are assigned to the ending inventory. With LIFO, the cost of goods sold and the ending inventory usually differ between the perpetual method and the periodic method.

Evaluation of Inventory Cost Flow Assumptions

22. Different cost of goods sold and inventory values usually result from different cost flow assumptions. During periods of rising prices, FIFO produces lower cost of goods sold, higher ending inventory, and higher gross profit (and income) than LIFO because FIFO includes the oldest and lowest costs in cost of goods sold. The opposite results are produced during periods of falling prices. Results from the average cost assumption fall between the FIFO and LIFO extremes.

23. A <u>holding gain (inventory profit)</u> is the difference between the historical cost and the higher replacement cost of items sold. Since LIFO matches the most recent costs (closer to replacement costs) with revenues, it excludes some of the holding gains from net income. Consequently, net income, which reflects earnings after capital has been maintained, is a better measure of the company's increase in wealth. In contrast, FIFO includes all the holding gains in income.

24. In periods of rising costs, LIFO results in the lowest gross profit (and income) and, consequently, reduces income taxes. Federal tax regulations permit the use of LIFO for income tax purposes only if it is also used in the company's financial statements (the LIFO conformity rule).

25. "Uniform capitalization rules" in the Tax Reform Act of 1986 require companies to include certain costs (such as purchasing, warehousing, and distribution costs) in inventory, rather than expensing these costs as incurred. Since such costs often should be expensed for financial reporting, inventory is frequently reported at different amounts for financial and income tax purposes.

26. In a period of inflation, a <u>LIFO liquidation profit</u> results when a company sells more units than it purchases and thus includes the lower costs of inventory acquired in previous periods in cost of goods sold in the current period. The lowering of cost of goods sold results in an unrealistically high gross profit. The company then reports higher income, which has no economic substance, and pays higher income taxes. This is contrary to what usually happens under LIFO during an era of inflation, when current period purchases raise the cost of goods sold and decrease net income. Companies reporting to the SEC must disclose the amount of LIFO liquidation profit.

27. Under the LIFO method, the timing of a company's inventory purchases affects gross profit (and income). Consequently, profits may be deliberately manipulated by delaying or increasing inventory purchases. The FIFO and average cost methods are not so susceptible to income manipulation. The influence on income of the purchasing activities of a company using LIFO is inconsistent with the revenue recognition principle.

28. In a period of rising prices the LIFO method may result in an inventory valuation which is lower than current costs and is not <u>relevant</u> for users. When prices are changing, evaluation of assets, current assets, working capital, and financial ratios which include inventory are affected so that comparability between companies using LIFO and those using FIFO is reduced. Comparability is also impaired among companies using LIFO, because inventory valuation is affected by the date on which LIFO was adopted.

29. The value of the ending inventory on the balance sheet of a company using the FIFO method is usually relevant because it includes the most recent costs.

30. The average cost method produces the same cost in a particular period for identical units with the same utility. However, because the average is continually affected by the costs incurred in previous periods, it reflects neither the actual costs paid for the units sold nor the actual costs for inventory held.

31. The selection of an inventory cost flow assumption by management should in most cases be based on the expectation of future cost changes. If rising prices are expected, LIFO should generally be used as a better measure of gross profit (and income). Although financial accounting principles should not be chosen on the basis of income tax accounting, companies often choose LIFO during times when rising prices are expected and FIFO during times when falling prices are expected, in order to pay lower income taxes.

Dollar-Value LIFO

32. <u>Dollar-value LIFO</u>, a variation of the LIFO method, keeps track of inventory costs according to dollar-value layers rather than physical units. Using dollar-value LIFO, inventory may be grouped into pools which are similar as to types of material or use. Use of inventory pools eliminates LIFO liquidations due to fluctuations in the quantities of similar inventory items. The dollar-value LIFO method simplifies recordkeeping, which may become very complicated under ordinary LIFO. The following steps are used in the dollar-value LIFO calculations:

Step 1. Value the total ending inventory at current-year costs.

Step 2. Convert (roll back) the ending inventory cost to base-year costs by applying the base-year conversion index:

$$\text{Ending Inventory at Base-Year Costs} = \text{Ending Inventory at Current-Year Costs} \times \frac{\text{Base-Year Cost Index}}{\text{Current Cost Index}}$$

Step 3. Compute the change in inventory level (physical quantity) by comparing the ending inventory and beginning inventory valued at base-year costs.

Step 4. If there is an <u>increase</u> in inventory at base-year costs, use the following formula to convert the base-year increase to current-year costs:

$$\text{Layer Increase at Current-Year Costs} = \text{Increase at Base-Year Costs} \times \frac{\text{Current Cost Index}}{\text{Base-Year Cost Index}}$$

The ending inventory cost is the dollar-value LIFO cost at the beginning of the year <u>plus</u> the layer increase at current-year costs.

Step 5. If there is a decrease in the inventory level at base-year costs, each of the most recently added LIFO layers (or parts of layers) must be converted to cost as follows:

$$\text{Decrease at Costs of Most Recently Added Layer} = \text{Decrease at Base-Year Costs} \times \frac{\text{Cost Index of Most Recently Added Layer}}{\text{Base-Year Cost Index}}$$

The ending inventory cost is the dollar-value LIFO cost at the beginning of the period minus the decrease at the cost of the most recently added layer. If more than one layer is liquidated, the base-year costs must be converted to the costs of as many layers as is necessary to eliminate the total decrease.

33. A price index is a general index prepared by an external organization, while a cost index is internally generated. A company may develop its own cost index by comparing the current cost per unit to the base year cost per unit. Two methods, the double-extension method and the link-chain method, are used in practice.

Additional LIFO Considerations

34. When a company uses LIFO for taxes but another method for internal management, a valuation adjustment is made to convert the internally reported ending inventory to LIFO for external reporting. This adjustment also affects the cost of goods sold. Typically, the valuation adjustment is not part of the company's formal accounting system, but is reported on the balance sheet or in the notes.

35. According to APB Opinion No. 28, the effect of a temporary LIFO inventory liquidation which will not exist at year-end should not be included in interim financial statements. A liquidation which is expected to last beyond the end of the year should, however, be included.

36. When a company changes to LIFO from another inventory method, usually the effect of the change on prior periods is not determinable and only the effect of the change on the results of current operations is disclosed. A change from LIFO is disclosed by retroactively restating the results of prior periods.

37. International accounting standards for inventories are generally the same as U.S. standards. However, international standards specify FIFO and weighted average as "benchmark" methods, and specify LIFO as an acceptable alternative because LIFO is generally not allowed in most countries.

Appendix: Foreign Currency Transactions Involving Inventory

38. Frequently, inventory transactions of U.S. companies with customers and suppliers in other countries are expressed in foreign currencies. The U.S. company records the transaction as converted into U.S. dollars at the exchange rate on the day of the transaction. When the date of payment differs from the transaction date, an exchange gain or loss may result from a change in the exchange rate.

39. An exchange <u>gain</u> occurs when the exchange rate declines between the date a payable is recorded and the date of cash payment, and when the exchange rate increases between the date a receivable is recorded and the date of cash receipt. An exchange <u>loss</u> occurs when the exchange rate increases between the date a payable is recorded and the date of cash payment, and when the exchange rate declines between the date a receivable is recorded and the date of cash receipt.

SELF-EVALUATION EXERCISES

Supply the words, symbols, or amounts necessary to complete each of the following items.

Classifications of Inventory

CI-1. The three common inventory accounts of a manufacturing company are:

(1)

(2)

(3)

CI-2. The cost of lumber used to build a table is an example of __________ materials, while the cost of lubrication supplies to operate the saw is an example of ______________ materials.

CI-3. The cost of workers who build the table is an example of __________ labor, while the cost of workers who clean the work area is an example of ___________ labor.

CI-4. The cost of direct materials, direct labor, and allocated factory overhead for partially completed production at the end of the year is included in ____________ ____ ___________ inventory at the end of the period, while the cost of completed goods is included in _____________ __________ inventory.

Perpetual and Periodic Inventory Systems

PP-1. A company that keeps a continuous record of its inventory receipts, returns, and shipments uses a __________ inventory system. A company that <u>cannot</u> determine cost of goods sold until the end of the accounting period uses the ____________ inventory system.

PP-2. A company using a periodic inventory system normally debits inventory acquisitions to a temporary _______________ account.

Items to Be Included in Inventory

II-1. The basic criterion for including items in inventory is

____________ ____________.

II-2. Legal title to goods is transferred to a buyer on delivery when the goods are sold ______ ____________.

II-3. Goods to be sold on consignment are included in the ____________'s inventory.

Determination of Inventory Cost

DIC-1. Inventory cost includes costs directly or indirectly incurred in bringing an article to its existing __________ and ____________.

DIC-2. Selling costs __________ (are/are not) included in inventory.

DIC-3. Purchasing department costs are usually recognized when __________.

DIC-4. ____________ manufacturing overhead is always included in inventory.

DIC-5. Material fixed manufacturing overhead costs which are __________ to inventory production are allocated to the cost of inventory.

DIC-6. Unit costs are based on budgeted standards in a __________-______ system.

DIC-7. Fixed overhead costs are expensed as incurred when ____________ costing is used.

DIC-8. Allocated fixed manufacturing overhead, in addition to direct costs, is included in the cost of inventory under ____________ costing.

DIC-9. Two accounting methods used to record a purchases discount are:

(1)

(2)

DIC-10. Indicate by a check mark whether or not each of the following material items should be included in the ending inventory for Kent Company.

	Do Not Include	Include
(1) Kent Co. shipped a product (FOB shipping point) which was in transit at year end.		
(2) Kent Co. shipped a product (FOB destination) which was in transit at year end.		
(3) Kent Co. purchased merchandise (FOB shipping point) which was in transit at year end.		
(4) Kent Co. purchased merchandise (FOB destination) which was in transit at year end.		
(5) Kent Co. paid a $2,000 transportation charge for inventory it owned at year end.		
(6) Kent Co. paid $500 insurance (during transit) for inventory it owned at year end.		
(7) Kent Co. paid $400 freight charges on a product Kent sold. The product was in transit (FOB shipping point) at year end to Lake Co.		
(8) Kent Co. delivered on a consignment basis a product with a cost of $1,000 to Akron Co. Akron Co. held the inventory at year end.		
(9) Kent Co. spent $15,000 on sales commissions during the year.		
(10) Kent Co. inadvertently failed to pay the invoice for a purchase within the discount period. Should Kent Co. include the purchases discount lost in inventory if the goods are still owned at year end?		

Cost Flow Assumptions

CFA-1. The assumed flow of inventory costs used in financial accounting does not necessarily match the ____________ ________ of goods.

CFA-2. List the different cost flow assumptions available for determining cost of goods sold and ending inventory (including alternative systems of applying):

(1)	(5)
(2)	(6)
(3)	(7)
(4)	(8)

CFA-3. Each inventory unit is identified, and its actual cost is included in cost of goods sold or ending inventory when the ____________ __________________ cost flow assumption is used.

CFA-4. Costs are allocated in the order in which they are incurred under the _______ cost flow assumption.

CFA-5. Inventory costs are commingled under the __________ cost flow assumption.

CFA-6. The most recent costs incurred are assumed to be the first transferred out or sold under the _______ cost flow assumption.

CFA-7. The Gas-A-Haul Company was organized on January 1 of the current year to buy and resell a new chemical additive designed to extend the mileage of gasoline. The following inventory transactions occurred during the first year of operations, in the sequence listed:

	Units	Unit Cost	Total	Units Sold
Purchase No. 1	5,000	$10	$ 50,000	
Sales				1,000
Purchase No. 2	2,000	11	22,000	
Sales				2,200
Purchase No. 3	3,000	12	36,000	
Total	10,000		$108,000	3,200

Units available	10,000
Units sold	(3,200)
Ending inventory	6,800

Determine the amounts for each of the following cost flow assumptions:

	Ending Inventory	Cost of Goods Sold
(1) FIFO, periodic		
(2) FIFO, perpetual		
(3) LIFO, perpetual		
(4) LIFO, periodic		
(5) Weighted average, periodic		
(6) Moving average, perpetual		

Show your computations in good form below and on the next page.

Evaluation of Inventory Cost Flow Assumptions

EIC-1. In periods of rising prices and increasing inventory levels, the ______ (LIFO or FIFO) inventory method would produce lower net income and the ______ (LIFO or FIFO) method would produce higher net income.

EIC-2. The difference between the historical cost and the replacement cost of an item sold is a __________ ________ or ________.

EIC-3. For income tax purposes, the use of the _______ cost flow assumption is permitted only if it is also used in the company's financial statements.

EIC-4. For income tax purposes, certain costs are included in inventory, rather than expensed, under the "__________ ________________ ________" of the Tax Reform Act of 1986.

EIC-5. When, during a period of inflation, a company using LIFO sells more units than it purchases, a _______ ________________ ___________ results.

EIC-6. The effect on income when a company using LIFO purchases inventory is _______________ (consistent/inconsistent) with the revenue recognition principle.

EIC-7. In a particular period, the same cost is produced for identical inventory units with the same utility using the __________ cost method.

Dollar-Value LIFO

DVL-1. A variation of the LIFO inventory method that applies cost indexes to current cost values for inventory valuation is the ________ - __________ ________ inventory system.

DVL-2. The general principle underlying the dollar-value LIFO method is that the inventory is initially valued at ___________-________ cost which is "rolled back" to the cost of the ________ year. A comparison of the beginning and ending inventory at ________-year cost indicates whether a real increase or decrease in inventory level has occurred.

DVL-3. With dollar-value LIFO, a ____________ index refers to an internally generated index that is specific to the company's particular inventory, while a

__________ index is a more general index prepared by an external organization such as a governmental body.

Additional LIFO Considerations

ALC-1. The effect of a temporary LIFO inventory liquidation is not included

in ___________ financial statements.

ALC-2. Retroactive restatement of the results of prior periods is made to disclose a

change ________ (to, from) LIFO ________ (to, from) another inventory method.

ALC-3. In most countries the use of LIFO is not allowed. Consequently,

international standards specify ______________ and _____________

______________ as "benchmark" inventory methods, with LIFO specified as an acceptable alternative.

Appendix: Foreign Currency Transactions Involving Inventory

FCT-1. A change in the exchange rate between the date of a transaction expressed in a

foreign currency and the payment date may result in an _____________ ________ or

________.

FCT-2. When the exchange rate increases between the date a payable is

recorded and the date of cash payment, an exchange ________ occurs.

ANSWERS TO SELF-EVALUATION EXERCISES

CI-1. (1) raw materials inventory, (2) goods in process inventory, (3) finished goods inventory; CI-2. direct, indirect; CI-3. direct, indirect; CI-4. goods in process, finished goods; PP-1. perpetual, periodic; PP-2. purchases; II-1. economic control; II-2. FOB destination; II-3. consignor; DIC-1. condition, location; DIC-2. are not; DIC-3. incurred; DIC-4. variable; DIC-5. traceable; DIC-6. standard-cost; DIC-7. variable; DIC-8. absorption; DIC-9. (1) gross price method, (2) net price method;

DIC-10.

	Do Not Include	Include
(1)	X	
(2)		X
(3)		X
(4)	X	
(5)		X
(6)		X
(7)	X	
(8)		X
(9)	X	
(10)	X	

CFA-1. physical flow; CFA-2. (1) LIFO, periodic, (2) LIFO, perpetual, (3) FIFO, periodic, (4) FIFO, perpetual, (5) weighted average, periodic, (6) moving average, perpetual, (7) specific identification, (8) dollar value LIFO; CFA-3. specific identification; CFA-4. FIFO; CFA-5. average; CFA-6. LIFO;

CFA-7.

	Ending Inventory	Cost of Goods Sold
(1) FIFO, periodic	$76,000	$32,000
(2) FIFO, perpetual	76,000	32,000
(3) LIFO, perpetual	74,000	34,000
(4) LIFO, periodic	69,800	38,200
(5) Weighted average, periodic	73,440	34,560
(6) Moving average, perpetual	75,274	32,726

Computations:	Cost of Goods Sold	Ending Inventory
FIFO, perpetual	1,000 x $10 = $10,000	*1,800 x $10 = $18,000
	2,200 x 10 = 22,000	2,000 x 11 = 22,000
Total	3,200 $32,000	3,000 x 12 = 36,000
		6,800 $76,000

*(5,000 - 1,000 - 2,200) = 1,800 units

	Cost of Goods Sold	Ending Inventory
FIFO, periodic	3,200 x $10 = $32,000	1,800 x $10 = $18,000
		2,000 x 11 = 22,000
		3,000 x 12 = 36,000
		6,800 $76,000

Computations:	Cost of Goods Sold	Ending Inventory
LIFO, perpetual	1,000 x $10 = $10,000	*3,800 x $10 = $38,000
	2,000 x 11 = 22,000	3,000 x 12 = 36,000
	200 x 10 = 2,000	6,800 $74,000
	3,200 $34,000	

*(5,000 - 1,000 - 200) = 3,800

LIFO, periodic	3,000 x $12 = $36,000 200 x 11 = 2,200 3,200 $38,200	5,000 x $10 = $50,000 *1,800 x 11 = 19,800 6,800 $69,800

*(2,000 - 200) = 1,800

Weighted average	3,200 x $10.80* = $34,560	6,800 x $10.80 = $73,440

*$108,000 / 10,000 = $10.80

Moving average	1,000 x $10 2,200 x 10.33* = 3,200	$10,000 22,726 $32,726	$108,000 - $32,726, or 6,800 x $11.0697** = $75,274

*Unsold amount of first purchase	4,000 x $10 =	$40,000
Amount of second purchase	2,000 x 11 =	22,000
Total available after second purchase	6,000	$62,000

$62,000 / 6,000 = $10.33 (moving average cost per unit)

Cost available after last sale ($62,000 - $22,726) =	$39,274
Add cost of purchases (3,000 x $12) =	36,000
Total costs after purchase No. 3	$75,274

**New average cost $75,274 / 6,800 = $11.0697

EIC-1. LIFO, FIFO; EIC-2. holding gain, loss; EIC-3. LIFO; EIC-4. uniform capitalization rules; EIC-5. LIFO liquidation profit; EIC-6. inconsistent; EIC-7. average; DVL-1. dollar-value LIFO; DVL-2. current-year, base, base; DVL-3. cost, price; ALC-1. interim; ALC-2. from, to; ALC-3. FIFO, weighted average; FCT-1. exchange gain, loss; FCT-2. loss.

POST TEST

Part A Circle T if the statement is true and F if it is false.

T F 1. One advantage of a perpetual inventory system is that a physical inventory does not need to be taken at year end, because a continuous record of inventory transactions is provided in the accounting records.

T F 2. The balance of the Merchandise Inventory account on a mid-period trial balance for a company that uses a periodic inventory system is the beginning merchandise inventory.

T F 3. The finished goods inventory reported on the financial statements of a manufacturing company includes applied factory overhead.

T F 4. Companies interested in determining income after capital has been maintained would be more likely to use the FIFO rather than the LIFO inventory method.

T F 5. The company receiving consigned goods is called the consignor.

T F 6. Valuation of inventory using standard costs is acceptable for financial reporting unless the costs have been adjusted for variances occurring during the period.

T F 7. Goods under the economic control of a company are included in inventory, even if the goods are in transit.

T F 8. A company that uses the gross price method records purchases discounts in its accounting system only if the discounts are not taken.

T F 9. The Purchases Discounts Lost account is treated as a financial expense for the period if the net price method is used.

T F 10. The inventory of a manufacturing company normally includes raw materials, goods in process, and finished goods.

T F 11. The specific identification method is a practical inventory method which is useful in preventing manipulation of profits.

T F 12. If the FIFO cost flow assumption is used, the ending inventory consists of the latest costs incurred.

T F 13. FIFO periodic and FIFO perpetual usually result in different ending inventory values.

T F 14. A new weighted average cost is calculated after each purchase if the moving average method is used.

T F 15. The LIFO perpetual and LIFO periodic methods may result in different ending inventory values if LIFO layers are liquidated and replaced by year end.

T F 16. Selling, ordering, and handling costs are considered product costs and are included in inventory for financial reporting.

T F 17. When the FIFO cost flow assumption is used, holding gains are included in net income.

T F 18. Incidental supplies used in the production process are normally included in the raw materials inventory of a manufacturing concern.

T F 19. Selling costs and indirect labor are examples of variable manufacturing overhead costs.

T F 20. International standards specify LIFO as the "benchmark" inventory method.

T F 21. The FIFO and average cost methods are more susceptible to income manipulation than the LIFO method.

T F 22. Dollar-value LIFO simplifies LIFO recordkeeping and eliminates LIFO liquidations resulting from fluctuations in the numbers of similar inventory items.

T F 23. Consistent with the revenue recognition principle, purchasing activities may be a major component of the income of a company using the LIFO method.

Part B Select the one best answer, and place its letter in the space provided.

____ 1. Which one of the following is true for periodic inventory but not true for perpetual? (a) a physical inventory count should be made at least once a year; (b) the Merchandise Inventory account in the year-end trial balance represents ending inventory; (c) the Inventory account in the year-end trial balance represents beginning inventory; (d) material freight-in costs should be treated as an inventory cost.

____ 2. Which one of the following should not be included in the ending inventory of the Dayton Company? (a) Dayton goods in transit to Kent Company shipped FOB Kent factory; (b) goods in transit to Dayton Company that were shipped FOB shipping point; (c) goods sold by the Dayton Company and segregated in Dayton's warehouse while awaiting pickup by the Kent Company; (d) inventory shipped by Dayton Company on consignment basis and held by the consignee at the balance sheet date.

____ 3. Which one of the following items appropriately describes the inventory cost for a manufacturing company based on generally accepted accounting principles? (a) include direct materials, direct labor, and variable factory overhead; (b) include direct materials, direct labor, variable factory overhead, and allocated fixed factory overhead; (c) include direct materials and direct labor costs, but exclude all overhead cost from inventory; (d) include direct materials, direct labor, variable factory overhead, allocated factory overhead, and variable selling expenses.

____ 4. Purchases discounts lost should be treated as: (a) financing expense; (b) reduction of cost of inventory; (c) addition to cost of ending inventory; (d) adjustment to cost of goods sold.

____ 5. Under the gross price method (a) purchases discounts taken increase the economic benefit expected from the inventory; (b) the correct inventory cost is recorded regardless of whether purchases discounts are taken; (c) purchases discounts are recorded only when not taken; (d) inventory purchases are recorded at gross prices and discounts are recorded when taken.

____ 6. In a period of decreasing prices, which cost flow assumption will result in the lowest income? (a) FIFO periodic; (b) weighted average; (c) dollar value LIFO; (d) LIFO perpetual.

____ 7. Which one of the following inventory methods is least susceptible to profit manipulation by management? (a) FIFO; (b) LIFO perpetual; (c) LIFO periodic; (d) dollar-value LIFO.

____ 8. Fixed factory costs are treated as period expenses with the use of: (a) full costing; (b) absorption costing; (c) standard costs; (d) variable costing.

_____ 9. Which of the following statements concerning foreign currency transactions is true? (a) an exchange gain occurs when the exchange rate increases between the date a payable is recorded and the date of cash payment; (b) an exchange loss occurs when the exchange rate declines between the date a receivable is recorded and the date of cash receipt; (c) an exchange gain occurs when the exchange rate declines between the date a receivable is recorded and the date of cash receipt; (d) an exchange loss occurs when the exchange rate declines between the date a payable is recorded and the date of cash payment.

Part C Solve each of the following short problems.

1. The Toledo Merchandising Company started business on August 1 of the current year. The following purchases were made during August on the dates indicated:

August 10	6,000	units at $5	$30,000
August 20	4,000	units at $6	24,000
August 25	3,000	units at $8	24,000
	13,000		$78,000

Sales were made on the following dates:

August 22	4,000 units
August 27	3,000 units

Determine the cost of ending inventory based on each of the following methods of inventory valuation.

(1) Weighted Average Periodic

(4) LIFO Periodic

(2) FIFO Periodic

(5) LIFO Perpetual

(3) FIFO Perpetual

2. The Miami Company adopted the dollar-value LIFO method of pricing ending inventory on December 31, 2002. The cost index for each of the indicated years is listed below along with the ending inventory valued <u>at current costs</u>. Compute the ending inventory based on the dollar-value LIFO method, taking into consideration the cost index at the end of the particular year.

End of	Ending Inventory at Current Cost	Cost Index at End of Year	Ending Inventory
2002	$40,000	100	$________
2003	46,200	105	$________
2004	47,300	110	$________
2005	55,200	120	$________

3. The Glenn Co. began manufacturing a single product in 2004. At the end of the year a trial balance included the following account balances:

Raw materials purchases	$ 75,000
Factory wages	100,000
Purchases discounts	3,000
Freight charges on raw materials purchased	1,500
Sales salaries	10,000
Storage	4,000
Interest expense	1,000
Insurance on inventory	1,200
Salary--company president	30,000

During the year $60,000 of raw materials were used in production, 51,000 units were completed, and 40,000 units, with an inventory value of $116,000, were sold. On December 31, 4,000 units remained out on consignment.

Required: Determine the year end balances of Glenn's Inventory accounts:

Raw Materials
Goods in Progress
Finished Goods

ANSWERS TO POST TEST

Part A

1. F
2. T
3. T
4. F
5. F
6. F
7. T
8. T
9. T
10. T
11. F
12. T
13. F
14. T
15. T
16. F
17. T
18. F
19. F
20. F
21. F
22. T
23. F

Part B

1. c	4. a	7. a
2. c	5. d	8. d
3. b	6. a	9. b

Part C

1. Answers: / Computations:

Answers	Computations
(1) $36,000 ($6.00 x 6,000)	$\frac{\$78,000}{13,000}$ = $6.00 Average cost
(2) $42,000	3,000 x $6 = $18,000 3,000 x $8 = 24,000 $42,000
(3) $42,000	FIFO periodic and FIFO perpetual always produce the same ending inventory.
(4) $30,000	6,000 x $5 = $30,000
(5) $30,000	*6,000 x $5 = $30,000

*Note: The August 22 sale was made up of 4,000 units purchased on August 20.

---

2. 2002 $\underline{\underline{\$40,000}}$ $\$40,000 \times \frac{100}{100} = \$40,000$ Ending inventory at cost

---

2003 = $\underline{\underline{\$44,200}}$ $\$46,200 \times \frac{100}{105} = \$44,000$ Ending inventory at base-year cost

(40,000)	Beginning inventory at base-year cost
$ 4,000	Increased layer at base-year cost
x 1.05	Year-end index
$ 4,200	Additional LIFO layer at cost

Inventory Cost:

Base-Year Cost		Cost
$40,000	x 100 =	$40,000
4,000	x 105 =	4,200
$44,000		$44,200

2004 $\underline{\underline{\$43,150}}$ $\$47,300 \times \frac{100}{110} = \$43,000$ Ending inventory at base-year cost

Inventory Cost

Base-Year Cost		Cost
$40,000	x 100 =	$40,000
3,000	x 105 =	3,150
$41,000		$43,150

2005 = $\underline{\underline{\$46,750}}$ $\$55,200 \times \frac{100}{120} = \$46,000$ Ending inventory at base-year cost

(43,000)	Beginning inventory at base-year cost
$ 3,000	Increased layer at base-year cost
x 1.20	Year-end index
$ 3,600	Additional LIFO layer at cost

Inventory Cost:

Base-Year Cost		Cost
$40,000	x 100 =	$40,000
3,000	x 105 =	3,150
3,000	x 120 =	3,600
$46,000		$46,750

---

3. Raw Materials: [$75,000 - $3,000 + $1,500 - $60,000] $ 13,500
Goods in Process: $ 17,300
Finished Goods $ 31,900

Goods in Process plus Finished Goods:
$60,000 + $100,000 + $4,000 + $1,200 = $165,200
Finished Goods:
$116,000) 40,000 = $2.90/unit
(51,000 - 40,000) x $2.90 = $ 31,900
Goods in Process: $165,200 - ($116,000 + $31,900) = $ 17,300

2. 2002 $40,000 $\quad \$40,000 \times \frac{100}{100} = \$40,000$ Ending inventory at cost

---

2003 = $44,200 $\quad \$46,200 \times \frac{100}{105} = \$44,000$ Ending inventory at base-year cost

$44,000	Ending inventory at base-year cost
(40,000)	Beginning inventory at base-year cost
$ 4,000	Increased layer at base-year cost
x 1.05	Year-end index
$ 4,200	Additional LIFO layer at cost

Inventory Cost:

Base-Year Cost		Cost
$40,000	x 100 =	$40,000
4,000	x 105 =	4,200
$44,000		$44,200

2004 $43,150 $\quad \$47,300 \times \frac{100}{110} = \$43,000$ Ending inventory at base-year cost

Inventory Cost

Base-Year Cost		Cost
$40,000	x 100 =	$40,000
3,000	x 105 =	3,150
$41,000		$43,150

2005 = $46,750 $\quad \$55,200 \times \frac{100}{120} = \$46,000$ Ending inventory at base-year cost

$46,000	Ending inventory at base-year cost
(43,000)	Beginning inventory at base-year cost
$ 3,000	Increased layer at base-year cost
x 1.20	Year-end index
$ 3,600	Additional LIFO layer at cost

Inventory Cost:

Base-Year Cost		Cost
$40,000	x 100 =	$40,000
3,000	x 105 =	3,150
3,000	x 120 =	3,600
$46,000		$46,750

---

3. Raw Materials: [$75,000 - $3,000 + $1,500 - $60,000] $
13,500
Goods in Process: $ 17,300
Finished Goods $ 31,900

Goods in Process plus Finished Goods:
$60,000 + $100,000 + $4,000 + $1,200 = $165,200
Finished Goods:
$116,000) 40,000 = $2.90/unit
(51,000 - 40,000) x $2.90 = $ 31,900
Goods in Process: $165,200 - ($116,000 + $31,900) = $
17,300

8

INVENTORIES: SPECIAL VALUATION ISSUES

CHAPTER OBJECTIVES

After careful study of this chapter, you will be able to:

1. Understand the lower of cost or market method.
2. Explain the conceptual issues regarding the lower of cost or market method.
3. Understand purchase obligations and product financing arrangements.
4. Explain the valuation of inventory above cost.
5. Use the gross profit method.
6. Understand the retail inventory method.
7. Explain the conceptual issues regarding the retail inventory method.
8. Understand the dollar-value LIFO retail method.
9. Understand the effects of inventory errors on the financial statements.

SYNOPSIS

Lower of Cost or Market

1. The lower of cost or market (LCM) rule requires that a company recognize a decline in its inventory's utility as a loss of the period, and that the company write down its ending inventory to the market value. This rule is consistent with the conservatism convention.

2. Market value is defined as the current replacement cost of inventory (not the current selling price) by purchase or manufacture, with upper and lower constraints imposed. Market value cannot be higher than the ceiling constraint or lower than the floor constraint. Ceiling constraint: The market value cannot be greater than the net realizable value (estimated selling price in the ordinary course of business, less reasonably predictable costs of completion and disposal). Floor constraint: The market value cannot be less than the net realizable value reduced by a normal profit margin (normal markup). The ceiling ensures that a write-down will cover all expected losses currently and prevents the recognition of further losses in the future. The floor prevents the recognition of excessive losses currently, and excessive profits in the future.

3. To apply the LCM method, a company (1) calculates and ranks the current replacement cost, ceiling, and floor and selects the middle amount as the market value; (2) compares the selected market value to cost and uses the lower of the two amounts; (3) reports inventory at the lower value on its balance sheet and reports any loss on its income statement. The example below illustrates the calculation of LCM:

Case	Current Replacement Cost	Net Realizable Value (Ceiling)	Net Realizable Value Less a Normal Markup (Floor)	Market (Constrained by Ceiling and Floor)	Cost	Lower of Cost or Market Inventory Value	Loss
1.	$4.00	$6.00	$3.00	$4.00	$5.00	$4.00	$1.00
2.	7.00	6.00	3.00	6.00	5.00	5.00	0
3.	3.00	6.00	4.00	4.00	5.00	4.00	1.00
4.	3.00	6.00	4.00	4.00	2.00	2.00	0
5.	7.00	6.00	3.00	6.00	8.00	6.00	2.00

Case 1. Replacement cost is used because it is between the ceiling and floor and is less than cost.

Case 2. Cost is used because it is less than the ceiling, which is between replacement cost and the floor.

Case 3. The floor is used because it is between replacement cost and the ceiling, and is less than cost.

Case 4. Cost is used because it is less than the floor, which is between replacement cost and the ceiling.

Case 5. The ceiling is used because it is between replacement cost and the floor, and is less than cost.

4. The LCM method implicitly assumes that selling (exit) prices parallel replacement costs (entry prices) within the ceiling and floor constraints. The method uses three different concepts for the loss recognized during a period and for the profit recognized in the future periods of sale. Consequently, the application of accounting principles may be inconsistent, and treatment of inventory may not be in accord with the conservatism convention.

5. A company may apply the LCM rule to individual inventory items, categories of inventory, or total inventory. The method which most clearly reflects periodic income should be used. The acceptability of three alternative methods for the same economic events does not follow the qualitative characteristic of comparability. However, differences resulting from the alternatives are often immaterial. Applying LCM to each individual item is the most common inventory method because it is required for income taxes and results in the most conservative inventory values. Once a company writes down its inventory to market, it does not write the inventory back up to cost, even if there is a subsequent recovery in the utility of the inventory.

6. Two alternative accounting methods are acceptable for recording a write-down of inventory to market value. The direct method records the write-down directly in the inventory and cost of goods sold accounts. The allowance method uses a separate inventory valuation account and a loss account. Although these methods produce the same net results, the allowance method is more desirable because it clearly identifies the effects of the write-down on the company's cost of goods sold. The following journal entries illustrate the allowance method:

Income Summary	XX	
Inventory		XX
To close beginning inventory.		
Inventory	XX	
Income Summary		XX
To record ending inventory.		
Loss Due to Market Valuation	XX	
Allowance to Reduce Inventory to Market		XX
To record inventory at market.		

7. According to APB Opinion No. 28, an interim period market decline which appears unlikely to reverse should be recognized in the period of decline. If the decline does reverse in a later interim period, a company should recognize a loss recovery and increase the inventory value by the amount of the recovery up to the original cost. However, a temporary market decline that is expected to reverse by the end of the annual period should be ignored for interim statements.

8. The theoretical criticisms of LCM include the following: (a) A holding loss due to a decline in the utility of the inventory is recognized; however, a comparable holding gain due to an increase in the utility of the inventory is not recognized, and (b) the revenue recognition principle is violated because a loss is recognized before the earning process is complete and before an exchange transaction has occurred. However, it can be argued that modification of the revenue recognition principle is justified because an economic event that results in a reduction of the company's stockholders' equity has occurred.

9. When a company recognizes an inventory loss in the period of market decline, its income in a future period will be higher than if the inventory value had remained at cost. That is, the loss is transferred from the period of sale to the period of decline.

10. Throughout the world the lower of cost or market method is used widely. Market is commonly defined as net realizable value and generally is applied to individual items. Also, a reversal of a write-down is allowed.

Purchase Obligations and Product Financing Arrangements

11. Normally, a company does not record purchase obligations in its accounts because neither an asset nor a liability is created by placing an order. However, a company discloses unconditional (noncancelable) purchase obligations made at a definite price in a note to its financial statements. A company records a loss on an unconditional purchase obligation made at a fixed price if the current market price (replacement cost) is lower than the fixed price. Recognition of the loss is in accordance with the conservatism convention and with *FASB Statement No. 5*, which requires that a company record a contingent loss if the loss is probable and can be reasonably estimated.

12. Product financing arrangements are sometimes used to finance the cost of inventory. The company "sells" the inventory, typically without delivery, while agreeing to repurchase the inventory (or a substantially identical item) at specified prices over specified periods. According to *FASB Statement No. 49*, the company does not record such "sales" proceeds as sales revenue. Instead, the company records the proceeds as a liability, and retains the inventory at cost.

Valuation Above Cost

13. According to *Accounting Research Bulletin No. 43*, a company may value its inventory above cost at the market price in certain circumstances. The inventory (such as precious metals, or agricultural or mineral products) must be made up of interchangeable units and must be saleable at the quoted market price. Valuation above cost violates the conservatism convention and the usual application of revenue recognition principles.

Gross Profit Method

14. A company uses the gross profit method to estimate the cost of its inventory by applying a gross profit rate based on its income statements of previous periods to the net sales of the current period. The gross profit method may be used, for example, for internal financial statements, for published interim financial statements when the method is disclosed, for estimation by auditors, to estimate casualty losses, or to estimate the cost of inventory from incomplete records. The method involves four steps: (1) Calculate the historical gross profit rate by dividing the gross profit (net sales minus cost of goods sold) of the prior period(s) by the net sales of the prior period(s). (2) Estimate current gross profit by multiplying the historical gross profit rate by net sales for the period. (3) Subtract the estimated gross profit from the actual net sales to determine the estimated cost of goods sold. (4) Subtract the estimated cost of goods sold from the actual cost of goods available for sale to determine the estimated cost of the ending inventory.

15. Gross profit may be expressed as a percent of cost of goods sold, instead of as a percent of sales. The general relationship between the two measures can be stated as follows:

$$\text{Gross Profit to Net Sales Ratio} = \frac{\text{Gross Profit to Cost of Goods Sold Ratio}}{1 + \text{Gross Profit to Cost of Goods Sold Ratio}}$$

16. The following example illustrates the application of the gross profit method:

Given Information:

Historical gross profit rate (on net sales)	30%
Net sales for the current year	$100,000
Cost of goods available for sale	90,000

Estimation of Ending Inventory:

Cost of goods available for sale		$ 90,000
Less: Estimated cost of goods sold:		
Net sales	$100,000	
Gross profit rate	0.30	
Estimated gross profit	$ 30,000	
Cost of goods sold ($100,000 - $30,000)		(70,000)
Estimated cost of ending inventory		$ 20,000

17. The relevance of estimates computed using the gross profit method depends on the accuracy of the gross profit percentage. That accuracy may be enhanced by adjustments for (a) known changes in the relationship between gross profit and net sales; (b) varying gross profit rates in different types of inventory; or (c) period-to-period fluctuations in the gross profit rate.

Retail Inventory Method

18. A company using the retail inventory method determines the cost of its ending inventory by applying current-period estimates of the profit percentage. The retail inventory method enables ending inventory to be determined without a physical inventory, simplifies record-keeping procedures, and facilitates computation of the ending inventory because reference to actual purchase documents is not required. The method is acceptable for income tax purposes as well as under generally accepted accounting principles. The retail method requires that the company value inventory items at cost and retail in order to determine the cost-to-retail ratio. The company then uses the cost-to-retail ratio to convert the retail value of ending inventory to approximate cost.

19. The following terms are used in the retail inventory method:

(a) Markup (mark-on) - the original markup from cost to the first selling price.

(b) Additional markup - an increase in the selling price above the original selling price.

(c) Markup cancellation - a reduction in the selling price after an additional markup. The markup cancellation cannot be greater than the additional markup.

(d) Net markups - total additional markups less total markup cancellations.

(e) Markdown - a decrease in the selling price below the original selling price.

(f) Markdown cancellation - an increase in the selling price after a markdown. The markdown cancellation cannot be greater than the markdown.

(g) Net markdown - total markdowns less total markdown cancellations.

20. A company may use the retail inventory method with the FIFO, average, and LIFO cost flow assumptions, and the company can use the lower of cost or market rule with each. The specific items included in the cost and retail calculations are discussed below. Notice below that the methods differ in the calculation of the cost-to-retail ratio, but that the net markup and net markdown always are added and subtracted to compute the retail value of the ending inventory, and that markups and markdowns are only recorded at retail.

(a) FIFO

	Ratio	Cost	Retail
Purchases		$40,000	$57,000
Add net markups			2,000
Subtract net markdowns			(5,000)
Cost-to-retail ratio ($40,000/$54,000)	0.74	$40,000	$54,000

Note: Exclude beginning inventory in computing the cost-to-retail ratio. Include net markups and net markdowns. Account for the FIFO layer by applying the cost ratio of beginning inventory to the retail value of beginning inventory.

(b) Average cost

	Ratio	Cost	Retail
Beginning inventory		$20,000	$26,000
Purchases		40,000	57,000
		$60,000	$83,000
Add net markups			2,000
Subtract net markdowns			(5,000)
Cost-to-retail ratio ($60,000/$80,000)	0.75	$60,000	$80,000

Note: Include net markups and net markdowns in the computation of the cost-to-retail ratio. Add beginning inventory to purchases. Determine ending inventory by applying the cost ratio to the retail value of ending inventory.

(c) LIFO

	Ratio	Cost	Retail
Beginning inventory cost-to-retail ratio ($20,000/$26,000)	0.769	$20,000	$26,000
Purchases		$40,000	$57,000
Add net markups			2,000
Subtract net markdowns			(5,000)
Cost-to-retail ratio ($40,000/$54,000)	0.74	$40,000	$54,000

Note: Calculate separate cost-to-retail ratios for beginning inventory and purchases. Include net markups and net markdowns in the computation of the cost-to-retail ratio for purchases. Account for LIFO retail layers by applying the appropriate cost-to-retail ratio to each layer of ending inventory and LIFO layers sold.

(d) Lower of average cost or market

Beginning inventory		$20,000	$26,000
Purchases		40,000	57,000
Add net markups		______	2,000
Cost-to-retail ratio ($60,000/$85,000)	0.706	$60,000	$85,000

Note: The retail inventory method is commonly used with the lower of average cost or market cost flow assumption (conventional retail method). Unless markups and markdowns do not exist simultaneously or all marked-down items have been sold, this method results in an inventory value (less than cost) which only approximates the lower of cost or market.

Include beginning inventory and net markups in the computation of the cost-to-retail ratio. Exclude net markdowns. Compute ending inventory by applying the cost ratio to the retail value of inventory.

21. A company using the retail inventory method makes adjustments for certain inventory activities. It subtracts purchase returns and allowances from both the cost and retail values of purchases which have been recorded at retail. It subtracts sales returns and allowances from sales at retail to determine net sales. However, it does not subtract sales discounts, which are considered financing items. For interim statements, a company subtracts employee discounts and estimated normal inventory shrinkage to determine estimated inventory at retail.

22. Two assumptions underlie the retail inventory method. The first assumption is that a company's markup is uniform for all inventory items, or that the proportions of items with different markups are the same in ending inventory and goods available for sale. The second assumption is that the company's cost-to-retail ratio is constant over the period or that changes in retail prices parallel changes in purchases.

23. The lower of cost or market method of the retail inventory method usually produces an inventory value that is less than cost but only approximates the lower of cost or market. The method is completely accurate only if either markups and markdowns do not exist at the same time as all of the marked down items have been sold.

Dollar-Value LIFO Retail Method

24. The dollar-value LIFO retail method is a combination of the dollar-value LIFO method and the retail LIFO method. The cost-to-retail ratio is determined as in the LIFO retail method. That is, net markups and net markdowns are included in calculating the ratio and a separate ratio is used for beginning inventory. The dollar-value LIFO retail method consists of the following steps:

    Step 1. Compute the ending inventory at retail by taking a physical inventory or by adding the beginning inventory, purchases, and markups and subtracting the sales and markdowns.

Step 2. Convert the retail ending inventory to base-year retail prices by applying the base year conversion index:

$$\text{Ending Inventory at Base-Year Retail Prices} = \text{Ending Inventory at Retail} \times \frac{\text{Base-Year Price Index}}{\text{Current-Year Price Index}}$$

The conversion index used in the above formula is based on a price index rather than a cost index (used in the dollar-value LIFO method). A price index is computed using retail prices.

Step 3. Compare beginning inventory at retail in base-year prices with ending inventory at retail in base-year prices to determine the change (increase or decrease) in inventory at retail in base-year prices.

Step 4. Convert the increase or decrease in inventory at retail in base-year prices to current-year retail prices as follows:

Increase in inventory level:

The increase in inventory level at retail in base-year prices for the layer added in the current year is converted to current-year retail prices with the appropriate conversion index:

$$\text{Layer Increase at Current-Year Retail Prices} = \text{Increase at Base-Year Retail Prices} \times \frac{\text{Current-Year Price Index}}{\text{Base-Year Price Index}}$$

Decrease in inventory level:

The decrease in inventory at retail in base-year prices for a layer decrease is converted to appropriate retail prices using the appropriate conversion index:

$$\text{Decrease at Retail Prices of Most Recently Added Layer} = \text{Decrease at Base-Year Retail Prices} \times \frac{\text{Price Index of Most Recently Added Layer}}{\text{Base-Year Price Index}}$$

When the decrease affects more than one layer of inventory, the price index appropriate for each layer must be used.

Step 5. Convert the increase (decrease) at current-year retail prices to cost using the appropriate cost-to-retail ratio for the year each layer was added.

Step 6. Compute ending inventory by adding (subtracting) the increase (decrease) at cost to the beginning inventory at cost.

Effects of Inventory Errors

25. Errors made by a company in the valuation of its inventory and the recording of its purchases can result in errors on the company's balance sheet and income statement for current and succeeding years. Each error must be analyzed carefully to determine the appropriate correction. Examples of common errors and their effects are given in the text. When a company discovers a material error from a prior period, it makes the correction as a prior period adjustment.

Summary of Inventory Issues

26. Exhibit 8-15 in the text provides a summary of the inventory issues discussed in Chapters 7 and 8.

SELF-EVALUATION EXERCISES

Supply the words or amounts necessary to complete each of the following items.

Lower of Cost or Market

LCM-1. The lower of cost or market rule recognizes the decline in the ____________ of a company's inventory.

LCM-2. The lower of cost or market rule is consistent with the ___________ convention.

LCM-3. The ceiling constraint in the lower of cost or market rule is the _____ _______________ value, and the floor constraint is net realizable value less _____________ ___________.

LCM-4. The ceiling ensures that a write-down of inventory will cover all expected losses in the _______________ period, and prevents the recognition of expected losses in the ______________.

LCM-5. The lower of cost or market method implicitly assumes that selling prices parallel ________________ ________.

LCM-6. The lower of cost or market rule may be applied to:

(1)

(2)

(3)

LCM-7. The most conservative inventory valuation will result from applying the lower of cost or market to each _________________ _________.

LCM-8. The two acceptable methods for recording a loss in the utility of the inventory for lower of cost or market are the __________ method and the _______________ method.

LCM-9. An interim period market decline which appears unlikely to ________ is recognized in the period of decline, while a ____________ market decline is ignored for interim statements.

LCM-10. The Springfield Company follows the practice of valuing inventory at the lower of cost or market on an item-by-item basis. The normal profit is $1.00 per unit. What is the value of inventory if the LCM rule is applied to each of the following items?

Item	Quantity	Unit Cost	Current Replacement Cost	Net Realizable Value	Answer
(1)	1,000	$4.00	$3.00	$2.50	$_________
(2)	2,000	5.00	2.50	4.00	_________
(3)	1,000	3.00	3.50	4.00	_________
(4)	4,000	5.50	5.00	6.75	_________
Total					_________

LCM-11. When the lower of cost or market rule is applied, holding losses _______ (are/are not) recognized, while holding gains ______ (are/are not) recognized.

Purchase Obligations and Product Financing Arrangements

PO-1. If the current market price of an unconditional purchase obligation made at a fixed price is lower than the fixed price, a ________ is recorded.

PO-2. According to <u>FASB Statement No. 49</u> the "sales" proceeds from a product financing agreement should be recorded as a ______________.

Valuation Above Cost

VAC-1. Inventory such as agricultural and mineral products may sometimes be valued above cost, at the _________ ________.

Gross Profit Method

GPM-1. The gross profit method is used to __________ the cost of inventory.

GPM-2. The gross profit percentage can be stated as a percentage of ______ or a percentage of _________ ______ _________ ____________.

GPM-3. A 50% gross profit to cost of goods sold ratio can be converted to a ____% gross profit to sales ratio.

GPM-4. The following three modifications enhance the accuracy of the gross profit method:

(1)

(2)

(3)

GPM-5. Determine the estimated ending inventory with use of the gross-profit method assuming the following facts:

Sales (net)	$200,000
Gross profit percent on sales	40%
Beginning inventory at cost	$ 40,000
Purchases (net)	$115,000

Compute answer here:

Retail Inventory Method

RIM-1. With the retail inventory method, the cost of ending inventory is based on current-period estimates of the _________ _____________.

RIM-2. With the retail inventory method, the retail value of the ending inventory is converted to approximate cost using the ______-___-_________ ratio.

RIM-3. When the retail inventory method is used, a reduction of the selling price to the original selling price after there has been an additional markup, is called a _________ _____________.

RIM-4. When the retail inventory method is used, an increase of the selling price to the original selling price after there has been a markdown is called a

__________ ______________.

RIM-5. Following are four cost flow assumptions for applying the retail inventory method:

FIFO
Average
LIFO
Lower of average cost or market

Match these cost-flow assumptions to the following descriptions of computing the cost-to-retail ratio for the retail-inventory method.

(1) Include the beginning inventory and the net markups; however, exclude the net markdowns. ____________________

(2) Include the beginning inventory, net markups, and net markdowns. Apply the cost-to-retail ratio to the ending inventory at retail. ________________

(3) Exclude the beginning inventory; however, include the net markups and the net markdowns. Apply the cost-to-retail ratio to the ending inventory, assuming the beginning inventory is sold. ________________

(4) Exclude the beginning inventory; however include the net markups and the net markdowns. Apply the cost-to-retail ratio to the additional layer added this period. ________________

Dollar-Value LIFO Retail Method

DVLR-1. What two methods can be used to determine the ending inventory at retail when the dollar-value LIFO retail method is used?

1.

2.

DVLR-2. The formula to convert the ending inventory at retail to base year retail prices is:

DVLR-3. The Stow Company had a beginning inventory of $40,000 at base-year retail prices and an ending inventory of $60,000 at base-year retail prices. The base-year price index for beginning inventory was 100 and the current-year price index is 150.

(a) Compute the LIFO layer increase (at current-year retail prices).

(b) Compute the cost of the increased layer if the cost-to-retail ratio for the current year was 0.70.

Effects of Inventory Errors

EIE-1. The correction of a material error from a prior period is made

as a ________ __________ ________________.

ANSWERS TO SELF-EVALUATION EXERCISES

LCM-1. utility; LCM-2. conservatism; LCM-3. net realizable, normal profit; LCM-4. current, future; LCM-5. replacement costs; LCM-6. (1) individual inventory items, (2) categories of inventory, (3) total inventory; LCM-7. individual item; LCM-8. direct, allowance; LCM-9. reverse, temporary; LCM-10. (1) $2.50--Market cannot be higher than ceiling limit ($2,500). (2) $3.00--Market cannot be lower than floor ($6,000). (3) $3.00--Cost is lower than market ($3,000). (4) $5.50--Market cannot be below $5.75 floor limit ($6.75 - $1.00); therefore cost of $5.50 is lower ($22,000); total inventory value = $33,500; LCM-11. are, are not; PO-1. loss; PO-2. liability; VAC-1. market price; GPM-1. estimate; GPM-2. sales, cost of goods sold; GPM-3. 33-1/3; GPM-4. (1) Adjust gross profit for <u>known</u> changes in the relationship between net sales and gross profit. (2) Use gross profit per type of inventory rather than companywide. (3) Base the average gross profit rate on several past periods, rather than only on the most recent period;

GPM-5.

Beginning inventory		$ 40,000
Net purchases		115,000
Cost of goods available for sale		$155,000
Less: Estimated cost of goods sold:		
Net sales	$200,000	
Gross profit rate	0.40	
Estimated gross profit	$ 80,000	
Cost of goods sold ($200,000 - $80,000)		(120,000)
Estimated cost of ending inventory		$ 35,000

RIM-1. profit percentage; RIM-2. cost-to-retail; RIM-3. markup cancellation; RIM-4. markdown cancellation; RIM-5. (1) lower of average cost or market, (2) average, (3) FIFO, (4) LIFO; DVLR-1. (1) physical inventory, (2) adding beginning inventory, purchases, and markups, and subtracting sales and markdowns; DVLR-2. Ending inventory at base-year retail prices = Ending inventory at retail x (Base-year price index/Current-year price index); DVLR-3. (a) $20,000 x (150/100) = $30,000, (b) $30,000 x 0.70 = $21,000; EIE-1. prior period adjustment.

POST TEST

Part A Circle T if the statement is true and F if it is false.

T F 1. The term "market" in lower of cost or market is defined as the selling price at year end.

T F 2. The ceiling limit (net realizable value) under the LCM rule is the selling price in the normal course of business less predictable costs of completion and disposal.

T F 3. Valuing inventory at a value lower than the floor would result in an excessive loss in the year of a writedown and an excessive profit in a subsequent period of sale.

T F 4. A temporary decline in the utility of inventory due to the lower of cost or market rule is ignored in interim-period financial statements if the decline is expected to reverse by the end of the annual period.

T F 5. A company must recognize a loss in the financial statements when the year-end market price is below a fixed price for a cancelable purchase commitment.

T F 6. Disclosure in the notes to the financial statements, rather than the accrual of losses, is preferred for purchase commitment losses on noncancelable purchase commitments if the current market price is less than the fixed contract price.

T F 7. The retail inventory method is a generally accepted accounting principle for external financial statements but is not acceptable in applying the provisions of the Internal Revenue Code.

T F 8. If net markups are excluded in computing the cost-to-retail ratio, the ratio will be higher than if they are included.

T F 9. A company using the retail inventory method for interim financial statements subtracts employee discounts and estimated normal inventory shrinkage to compute ending inventory at retail.

T F 10. The cost-to-retail ratio for the dollar-value retail LIFO method is computed in the same manner as used for the LIFO retail method.

T F 11. Applying the lower of cost or market value rule to the inventory on a category-by-category basis will usually result in the most conservative inventory valuation of the three acceptable methods.

T F 12. If a market decline occurs in an interim period and is considered permanent, it should be ignored because the market price will normally increase in a subsequent annual period.

T F 13. It is acceptable to write inventory up to original cost if a recovery in utility occurs in an annual period subsequent to the lower of cost or market writedown.

T F 14. If ending inventory is understated (but purchases are recorded correctly), income will be overstated in the current year.

T F 15. According to FASB Statement No. 49, the proceeds received under a product financing arrangement are recorded as sales revenue.

T F 16. When the retail inventory method is used, and the lower of cost or market rule is applied with the average cost flow assumption, net markups and markdowns are included in, but beginning inventory is excluded from, the computation of the cost-to-retail ratio.

T F 17. A separate inventory valuation account and a loss account are used under the allowance method to record a write-down of inventory to market value.

T F 18. A company using the LCM method recognizes holding losses, but does not recognize comparable holding gains.

T F 19. A contingent loss is recorded if the loss is probable and can be reasonably estimated.

T F 20. The gross profit method of estimating the cost of inventory is accepted for internal reporting and for interim reports when the method is disclosed.

T F 21. An assumption underlying the retail inventory method is that either the company's markup is uniform for all inventory items or that the proportions of items with different markups are the same in ending inventory and goods available for sale.

Part B Select the one best answer, and place its letter in the space provided.

_____ 1. The term "market" in lower of cost or market refers to (a) market price at time of purchase; (b) selling price by the retailer; (c) selling price by the retailer less normal profit; (d) current replacement cost.

_____ 2. The lower limit in the lower of cost or market is (a) selling price; (b) selling price less costs of disposal; (c) net realizable value less normal profit margin; (d) selling price less normal profit.

_____ 3. The lower of cost or market rule may be applied to (a) individual inventory items; (b) categories of inventory; (c) total inventory; (d) all of these.

_____ 4. If a company has a noncancelable purchase commitment at a fixed price: (a) the company must recognize a gain in the period if the current market price is greater than the fixed price; (b) the company must recognize an expected loss in the period if the current market price is less than the fixed price; (c) the company must disclose a loss in a note to the financial statements rather than recognize the loss when the current market price is less than the fixed contract price; (d) no disclosure or accounting entry is necessary to record the expected gain or loss on noncancelable fixed-price contracts.

_____ 5. Stating inventory at an amount in excess of cost is a violation of: (a) the conservatism convention but not the revenue recognition principle; (b) the revenue recognition principle but not the conservatism convention; (c) both the conservatism convention and the revenue recognition principle; (d) neither the conservatism convention nor the revenue recognition principle.

____ 6. The gross profit method may be used (a) to estimate the amount of an inventory theft; (b) to estimate the amount of the loss of inventory from flood or fire; (c) by auditors to estimate the value of inventory; (d) to determine the inventory value for interim financial statements; (e) all of the above.

____ 7. Which of the following would <u>not</u> have an effect on the cost-to-retail ratio if the lower of average cost or market rule is applied to the retail-inventory method? (a) markdown; (b) markup cancellation; (c) additional markup; (d) markup.

____ 8. The Givens Company had beginning inventory of $2,250 at cost and $2,500 at retail; purchases of $15,000 at cost and $20,000 at retail; retail sales of $18,000; markups of $1,000 and markdowns of $500. The cost of ending inventory using average cost under the retail method is: (a) $3,750; (b) $17,250; (c) $3,860; (d) $2,000.

____ 9. Using the information given in Question 8, except that purchases at cost were $14,965, the cost of the Givens Company's ending inventory applying the retail method and the FIFO cost flow assumption is (a) $3,750; (b) $3,650; (c) $3,850; (d) $3,375.

____ 10. The accountants at the Piper Company neglected to record a $10,000 credit purchase in the Purchases account. However, ending inventory is reported at the correct value. As a result, which of the following statements is correct? (a) in the current year income is correct, and in the succeeding year accounts payable are understated; (b) in the current year accounts payable are understated, and in the succeeding year retained earnings is overstated; (c) in the current year cost of goods sold is overstated, and in the succeeding year accounts payable are overstated; (d) in the current year income is understated, and in the succeeding year ending inventory is overstated.

<u>Part C</u> Solve each of the following short problems.

1. The Hollywood Company, which uses the retail inventory method, had a beginning inventory of $9,000 at cost and a $12,000 retail value. The following data pertains for the year.

	At Cost	At Retail
Markdowns (net)		$ 8,000
Markups (net)		6,000
Purchases	$69,000	85,000
Sales		60,000

Determine the ending inventory using:

(a) Lower of average cost or market Answer __________

1. (b) FIFO Answer ____________

(c) LIFO Answer ____________

(d) Average cost Answer ____________

2. The Peoria Company computed the following information for its inventory by applying the lower of cost or market method on a unit-by-unit basis.

	Inventory Cost	At Market*	LCM Allowance
January 1, 2004	$ 8,000	$ 8,400	-0-
December 31, 2004	11,000	7,000	$4,000
December 31, 2005	12,000	10,000	2,000

*Assume market has passed the ceiling and floor test.

(a) Prepare each of the following entries at December 31, 2004, if the allowance method is used.

Close beginning inventory:

Record ending inventory:

Record reduction of inventory to market:

(b) Prepare each of the following entries at December 31, 2005, if the allowance method is used.

Close beginning inventory:

Record ending inventory:

Record reduction of inventory to market:

3. On January 1, 2004 the Skidaway Company adopted the dollar-value LIFO retail inventory method. The price index was 100 on January 1, 2004 and 105 on December 31, 2004. Information from the company's records is shown below:

	Cost	Retail
Inventory 1/1/04	$30,000	$ 42,000
Purchases	90,480	120,000
Net markups		2,000
Net markdowns		6,000
Sales		95,000

Compute the cost of the Skidaway Company's inventory on December 31, 2004.

ANSWERS TO POST TEST

Part A

1. F	6. F	11. F	16. F
2. T	7. F	12. F	17. T
3. T	8. T	13. F	18. T
4. T	9. T	14. F	19. T
5. F	10. T	15. F	20. T
			21. T

Part B

1. d	4. b	7. a	10. b
2. c	5. c	8. a	
3. d	6. e	9. b	

Part C

1. (a) Lower of average cost or market

	Cost	Retail
Beginning inventory	\$ 9,000	\$ 12,000
Purchases	69,000	85,000
Net markups		6,000
	\$78,000	\$103,000
Cost-to-retail ratio: $\frac{\$78,000}{\$103,000} = 0.7573$		
Net markdowns		(8,000)
Goods available for sale	\$78,000	\$ 95,000
Less: Sales		(60,000)
Ending inventory at retail		\$ 35,000
Ending inventory at lower of cost or market (0.7573 x \$35,000)	\$26,506	

(b) FIFO

	Cost	Retail
Purchases	\$69,000	\$ 85,000
Net markups		6,000
Net markdowns		(8,000)
	\$69,000	\$ 83,000
Cost-to-retail ratio: $\frac{\$69,000}{\$83,000} = 0.8313$		
Beginning inventory	9,000	12,000
Goods available for sale	\$78,000	\$ 95,000
Less: Sales		(60,000)
Ending inventory at retail		\$ 35,000
Ending inventory at FIFO cost (0.8313 x \$35,000)	\$29,096	

1. (continued)

(c) LIFO

	Cost	Retail
Beginning inventory	$ 9,000	$12,000
Cost-to-retail ratio: $\frac{\$9,000}{\$12,000} = 0.75$		
(for beginning inventory layer)		
Purchases	$69,000	$85,000
Net markups		6,000
Net markdowns		(8,000)
Total purchases	$69,000	$83,000
Cost-to-retail ratio: $\frac{\$69,000}{\$83,000} = 0.8313$		
Goods available for sale	$78,000	$95,000
Less: Sales		(60,000)
Ending inventory at retail		$35,000
Ending inventory at LIFO cost:		
$12,000 x 0.75 (beginning inventory layer)	$ 9,000	
$23,000 x 0.8313	19,120	
Total	$28,120	

(d) Average cost

	Cost	Retail
Beginning inventory	$ 9,000	$12,000
Purchases	69,000	85,000
Net markups		6,000
Net markdowns		(8,000)
Goods available for sale	$78,000	$95,000
Cost-to-retail ratio: $\frac{\$78,000}{\$95,000} = 0.8211$		
Less: Sales		(60,000)
Ending inventory at retail		$35,000
Ending inventory at average cost (0.8211 x $35,000) =	$28,739	

2. (a)

2004				
Dec.	31	Income Summary	8,000	
		Inventory		8,000
		Inventory	11,000	
		Income Summary		11,000
		Loss Due to Market Valuation	4,000	
		Allowance to Reduce Inventory to Market		4,000

(b) 2005

Dec.	31	Income Summary	11,000	
		Inventory		11,000
		Inventory	12,000	
		Income Summary		12,000
		Allowance to Reduce Inventory to Market	2,000	
		Gain Due to Market Valuation		2,000

3. Ending inventory at retail:

Beginning inventory	$ 42,000
Purchases	120,000
Markups	2,000
Markdowns	(6,000)
Sales	(95,000)
	$ 63,000

Ending inventory at base-year retail prices:

100/105 x $63,000 = $60,000

Increase in inventory at retail in base-year prices:

$60,000 - $42,000 = $18,000

Layer increase in inventory at retail base-year prices converted to current-year prices:

105/100 x $18,000 = $18,900

Increase at current-year retail prices converted to cost:

$18,900 x 0.78* = $14,742

Ending inventory at cost:

$30,000 + $14,742 = $44,742

*90,480/(120,000 + 2,000 - 6,000)

9

PROPERTY, PLANT, AND EQUIPMENT: ACQUISITION AND DISPOSAL

CHAPTER OBJECTIVES

After careful study of this chapter, you will be able to:

1. Identify the characteristics of property, plant, and equipment.
2. Record the acquisition of property, plant, and equipment.
3. Determine the cost of assets acquired by the exchange of other assets.
4. Compute the cost of a self-constructed asset, including interest capitalization.
5. Record costs subsequent to acquisition.
6. Record the disposal of property, plant, and equipment.
7. Understand the disclosures of property, plant, and equipment.
8. Explain the accounting for oil and gas properties (Appendix).

SYNOPSIS

Characteristics of Property, Plant, and Equipment

1. Assets categorized by a company as property, plant, and equipment must (a) be held for use in the business and not for investment, (b) have an expected life of more than one year, and (c) be tangible in nature. Sometimes these assets are referred to as plant assets, fixed assets, or operational assets.

2. A company initially records assets included in the property, plant, and equipment category at their acquisition cost (historical cost). The company then allocates the cost of the assets, other than land, as an expense to the periods in which it consumes the assets and receives the benefits in order to comply with the matching principle. This process is called depreciation. The major types of assets that a company classifies as property, plant, and equipment are land, buildings, equipment, machinery, furniture and fixtures, leasehold improvements, and natural resources (also called wasting assets).

Acquisition

3. The cost of a company's property, plant, and equipment is the cash outlay or its equivalent that is necessary to acquire the asset and put it in operating condition. This cost includes the contract price (less any available discounts), freight, assembly, installation, and testing costs. A company capitalizes the costs incurred to obtain the benefits of the asset when it records them as an asset.

4. The recorded value of land includes (a) the contract price, (b) the costs of closing the transaction and obtaining title (such as commissions, options, legal fees, title search, insurance, and past due taxes), (c) the costs of surveys, and (d) the costs of preparing the land for its particular use (such as the cost of removing an old building) if such improvements have an indefinite life. The costs of land improvements that have a limited life (such as sidewalks) are separately capitalized and depreciated if the company is responsible for maintaining them. If the local government has the responsibility for maintaining such improvements, then the company adds the costs to the cost of the land. Because land has an unlimited economic life and its residual value is unlikely to be less than its acquisition cost, a company generally does not depreciate it.

5. Land acquired for future use or as an investment should not be classified as property, plant, and equipment. A company may capitalize interest related to the purchase of such land only if the land is undergoing activities to ready it for future use. Property taxes and insurance on land which is not being developed for sale or lease to others, however, may be capitalized or expensed regardless of whether the land is acquired for future use or as an investment. Once the land is used in operations, both interest and property taxes must be expensed.

6. The recorded cost of buildings includes (a) the contract price, (b) the costs of remodeling and reconditioning, (c) the costs of excavation for the specific building, (d) architectural costs and the costs of building permits, (e) certain capitalized interest costs, and (f) unanticipated costs resulting from the condition of the land. A company should expense unanticipated construction costs (such as a strike or fire). The cost to raze an old building that is already owned is an element of the gain or loss on retirement of the old building and is not capitalized. A company may expense or capitalize any costs of property taxes and insurance during construction.

7. Improvements made by a lessee to leased property normally revert to the lessor at the end of the lease. In this case, the lessee capitalizes the costs of leasehold improvements and amortizes them over their economic life or the life of the lease, whichever is shorter.

8. When a company acquires several dissimilar assets categorized as property, plant, and equipment for a lump-sum purchase price, it allocates the price paid to the individual assets purchased. The allocation basis is the relative fair value of the individual assets and is calculated as follows: (Fair Value of Individual Asset/Fair Value of Assets Acquired in Lump Sum Purchase) x Total Cost. The company records (capitalizes) the allocated cost of each asset.

9. When a company acquires property, plant, and equipment on a deferred payment basis (e.g., issuance of bonds or notes or assumption of a mortgage), it records the asset at its fair value or the fair value of the liability on the transaction date, whichever is more reliable. If neither is determinable, the asset is recorded at the present value of the deferred payments using the stated rate. If the stated rate is materially different from the market rate, the market rate is used.

10. A company may also acquire assets categorized as property, plant, and equipment by issuing securities such as common stock. In this case the recorded cost is either the fair value of the assets obtained, or the fair value of the securities issued, whichever is more reliable.

11. When a company acquires an asset through a nonreciprocal transfer (donation), it records the asset at its fair value rather than its cost which would be zero. In this case, cost provides an inadequate method of accounting for the asset and for subsequent relevant income measurement. A donation by a governmental unit is credited to a donated capital account; a donation by a non-governmental unit is credited as a gain and reported in the other items section of the income statement.

12. Under AICPA Statement of Position No. 98-5, a company is required to expense the costs of start-up activities as incurred. A company may incur one-time start-up costs associated with opening a new facility, introducing a new product or service, conducting business in a new territory, conducting business with a new class of customers, initiating a new process in an existing facility, or beginning a new operation. Organization costs are considered start-up costs.

13. In contrast to U.S. standards, international accounting standards allow a company to write up the value of its property, plant, and equipment to fair value. The increase is credited to stockholders' equity as a “revaluation" surplus.

14. Under APB Opinion No. 29, a nonmonetary exchange is a reciprocal transfer between a company and another entity which results in the acquisition of nonmonetary assets or services or the satisfaction of liabilities by surrendering other nonmonetary assets or services or incurring other obligations. Nonmonetary exchanges may be accompanied by the payment and/or receipt of small amounts of boot (monetary consideration). The

general principle is that the cost of a nonmonetary asset acquired in exchange for another nonmonetary asset is the fair value of the asset surrendered. A gain or loss is recognized on the exchange as the difference between the fair value of the asset surrendered and its book value.

15. Productive assets are assets that a company holds for or uses in the production of goods and services. Similar productive assets are of the same general type, perform the same function, and are used in the same line of business. If the assets do not meet the criteria just cited for similar productive assets, they are dissimilar productive assets. Nonmonetary productive asset exchanges are summarized in Exhibit 9-2 in the text.

16. To determine the cost of dissimilar productive assets acquired through a nonmonetary exchange the following equation is used:

    Cost = Fair Value of Asset Surrendered
    (unless the fair value of the asset received is more evident)

    If boot accompanies the exchange, the cost is determined as follows:

    Cost of Asset Acquired = Fair Value of Asset Surrendered + Boot Paid or - Boot Received

    Whether or not boot is involved in the exchange, all gains and losses on dissimilar productive assets are recognized in full because the earnings process is considered complete. The Gain (Loss) is determined as follows:

    Gain (Loss) = Fair Value of Asset Surrendered - Book Value of Asset Surrendered

17. A monetary exchange of similar productive assets occurs when the boot is equal to or greater than 25% of the total value of the exchange. In this case, both parties record the exchange at fair value. For similar productive assets acquired through a nonmonetary exchange (boot is <25% of total value) between two companies that are using the assets in the same line of business, both parties to the exchange recognize all losses in full whether or not boot is involved. If fair value of the asset surrendered is less than the book value of the asset surrendered, cost and the loss (if there is one) are determined as follows:

    Cost of Asset Acquired = Fair Value of Asset Surrendered + Boot Paid or - Boot Received

    Loss = Fair Value of Asset Surrendered - Book Value of Asset Surrendered

    Because the earning process is not essentially completed by a nonmonetary exchange of similar productive assets, a company does not recognize gains unless boot is received. When the boot received is less than 25% of the total value, the earnings process is considered complete to the extent that boot is received, and the company recognizes a partial gain. Therefore, if boot is received, and the fair value of the asset surrendered is greater than the book value of the asset surrendered, cost and gain are determined as follows:

    Cost of Asset Acquired = Book Value of Asset Surrendered + Boot Paid

    or

$$\text{Cost of Asset Acquired} = \text{Book Value of Asset Surrendered} + \text{Gain Recognized} - \text{Boot Received}$$

$$\text{Gain} = \frac{\text{Boot}}{\text{Boot} + \text{Fair Value of Asset Acquired}} \times (\text{Fair Value of Asset Surrendered} - \text{Book Value of Asset Surrendered})$$

If there is no boot, or boot is paid and the fair value of the asset surrendered is greater than the book value of the asset surrendered, a company does not recognize gains because the earnings process is not complete. Cost is determined as follows:

Cost of Asset Acquired = Book Value of Asset Surrendered

<u>or</u>

Cost of Asset Acquired = Book Value of Asset Surrendered + Boot Paid

Self-Construction

18. <u>FASB Statement No. 34</u> specifies the treatment of interest incurred during the self-construction of assets. If a company constructs an asset for either its own use or as a discrete project for sale or lease to others, interest <u>must</u> be capitalized. A company <u>must not</u> capitalize interest on (a) routinely manufactured inventories, (b) assets in use or ready for use, or (c) assets not used in the earnings activities of the company. A company determines the <u>amount of interest</u> to be capitalized for a qualifying asset by multiplying either the interest rate incurred on the specific borrowing or a weighted average interest rate on all other borrowings times the average cumulative expenditures for the qualifying asset during the capitalization period. The total interest cost capitalized each period may not exceed the interest cost incurred during the period. The <u>capitalization period</u> begins when (a) expenditures for the asset have been made, (b) activities that are necessary to get the asset ready for its intended use are in progress, and (c) interest cost is being incurred. The capitalization period ends when the asset is (a) substantially complete and (b) ready for its intended use.

19. International accounting standards state that expensing all costs is the "benchmark," but that capitalization of interest for a qualifying asset is an allowable alternative.

20. The cost of <u>self-constructed assets</u> (items of property, plant, and equipment constructed by a company for use in its own production process) should include all direct costs of materials, labor, engineering, and variable manufacturing overhead. The cost of the self-constructed asset should also include: (a) interest costs incurred during the period of self-construction on the average cumulative invested costs during the period; (b) fixed manufacturing overhead costs: either an allocated portion of total fixed overhead, particularly appropriate when the company is operating at full capacity; the incremental fixed overhead actually incurred, particularly appropriate when the company is operating with excess capacity; or no amount of fixed overhead, if the overhead does not change; and (c) recognition of a loss and a write down of the asset to the fair value if construction cost materially exceeds the fair value of the asset. However, if the asset is constructed at a cost below the asset's normal purchase price, the company should not recognize any profit.

Costs Subsequent to Acquisition

21. A cost which increases the future economic benefits of the asset above those originally expected is a capital expenditure and should be capitalized to an asset account. A cost that is incurred to maintain existing benefits and does not increase the economic benefits is an operating expenditure and should be expensed.

22. Additions to already existing assets (e.g., a new wing to a building) represent new assets and are capitalized. Improvements (or betterments) and replacements (or renewals) involve the substitution of new or better assets for old ones. Because the economic benefits to be derived from the asset are increased, a company should capitalize the costs by one of the following methods depending on the circumstances: (a) The Substitution Method (when the book value of the old asset is known): the book value of the old asset is removed from the accounts and the new asset is recorded; (b) Reduce Accumulated Depreciation (when the service life of the asset has been extended): the specific Accumulated Depreciation account is debited with the costs of improvements or replacements on the grounds that service potential that has been written off has been restored; or (c) Increase the Asset Account (when benefits are increased above those originally expected): the specific asset account is debited directly with the new costs on the grounds that an addition has been made to the service potential of the asset.

23. The costs of rearranging or relocating are capitalized and expensed over the periods expected to benefit, or expensed immediately if the difference is immaterial.

24. A company expenses, in the period incurred, routine repair and maintenance costs which are incurred to maintain the operating condition of an asset. However, in order to prevent distortion of interim financial statements, a company may estimate annual repair and maintenance expense and then record an equal amount as an expense each quarter. The company records the difference between the actual expense and the prorated portion in an Allowance for Repairs account (an addition to or offset from property, plant, and equipment) which would have a zero balance at the end of the year.

Disposal and Disclosure of Property, Plant, and Equipment

25. A company may dispose of property, plant, and equipment by sale, involuntary conversion, abandonment, or exchange. When recording the disposal, depreciation expense up to the date of the disposal must be recorded first. Then the asset account is credited and the accumulated depreciation account is debited to remove these accounts from the records. Any gain or loss on the disposal is recognized and is usually included as an element of ordinary income in the income statement.

26. APB Opinion No. 12 requires a company to disclose the balances of its major classes of depreciable assets by nature or by function.

27. A company may acquire an asset (e.g., power plant, mine) that creates an obligation related to the retirement of the asset because of the significant costs related to closure. FASB Statement No. 13 requires a company to record the fair value of a liability for the obligation, usually when the asset is acquired. The company records (credits) the fair value of the liability at acquisition and increases (debits) the asset. Then the company increases the liability (and recognizes accretion expense) each year it uses the asset. Upon retirement, the company eliminates the estimated liability when it pays the actual retirement costs, and records a gain/loss if necessary.

Appendix: Oil and Gas Properties

28. Two alternative methods of accounting for the cost of oil and gas properties are used: (a) the successful-efforts method which capitalizes the costs associated with successful wells and expenses the costs associated with unsuccessful (or dry) wells, and (b) the full-cost method which capitalizes the costs associated with successful and unsuccessful wells. The costs associated with unsuccessful wells are carried forward to future periods as the cost of oil and gas reserves and subsequently amortized. The proponents of the successful-efforts method assert that there must be a direct cause-effect relationship for a cost to be associated with an asset, while the proponents of full cost assert that the costs associated with dry wells are necessary for the discovery of reserves.

SELF-EVALUATION EXERCISES

Supply the words or amounts necessary to complete each of the following items.

Characteristics and Acquisition

A-1. To qualify for inclusion in the property, plant, and equipment section of the balance sheet, an asset must (1) ________________

____,

(2) ____, and

(3) ____.

A-2. The allocation of the cost of depreciable assets over the periods benefiting from the use of the assets is an example of the __________ principle.

A-3. A company initially records property, plant, and equipment assets at their __________ ________.

A-4. Costs recorded as assets have been ____________.

A-5. Costs incurred to remove an existing building from a recently acquired piece of property in order to construct a new building should be debited to the

__________ account.

A-6. Zeebo Company acquired a building and the equipment therein for a lump sum of \$150,000. If the building has a fair market value of \$105,000 and the equipment has a fair value of \$70,000, Zeebo should debit the building account for

\$________ and the equipment account for \$________.

A-7. Argon Company acquired a piece of land by giving the seller $15,000 in cash and a $65,000 interest-bearing note. Over the life of the note the buyer will pay interest of $24,000. To record this acquisition, Argon should debit the land account for $________.

A-8. Any monetary consideration included in an exchange of assets is referred to by <u>APB Opinion No. 29</u> as __________.

A-9. Aye Company exchanged a piece of land it owned for a similar parcel owned by Bee Company. <u>APB Opinion No. 29</u> labels this transaction a __________ __________ __________ __________.

A-10. In a nonmonetary exchange of dissimilar assets involving no exchange of boot, the recorded cost of the asset acquired is equal to the ________ ________ ____ _____ _______ ______________.

A-11. When a similar productive asset is acquired through a nonmonetary exchange, a company does not recognize a gain unless __________ ______ ______________.

A-12. When a company acquires an asset through donation, it should record the acquired asset at its __________ __________.

A-13. Under international accounting standards, a company may write up the value of property by crediting the increase to stockholders' equity as a ____________________ ____________________.

Costs Subsequent to Acquisition

CS-1. Costs incurred subsequent to acquisition which increase the economic benefits of an asset are ______________ ______________ and costs which maintain existing benefits are ______________ ______________.

CS-2. The ABC Corporation is expanding its manufacturing plant. The cost of the expansion should be ______________.

CS-3. If a company improves an already existing asset so that its service potential is restored, the company would probably record the cost by debiting the related __________ ________________ account.

Self Construction

SC-1. Interest incurred during the routine manufacture of inventories

_______ (is/is not) capitalized.

SC-2. The cost of self-constructed assets includes all _______ _______ of materials, labor, and engineering, as well as _____________ manufacturing overhead.

Disposal and Disclosure of Property, Plant and Equipment

DD-1. Before a company may record the disposal of a fixed asset, it must bring the accounts relating to the asset up to date by recording the appropriate amount of _____________.

DD-2. A company should include any gain or loss recognized on the disposal of property, plant, and equipment on the income statement as an element of ____________ ____________.

DD-3. A company may disclose the balances of the major classes of depreciable assets in the financial statements by _____________ or _________________.

Appendix: Oil and Gas Properties

OG-1. In accounting for oil and gas properties, if the costs associated with dry wells are capitalized the company is using the _____-__________ method.

OG-2. If a company expenses the costs associated with dry wells, the method of accounting being used is the ________________-__________ method.

ANSWERS TO SELF-EVALUATION EXERCISES

A-1. (1) be held for use rather than investment, (2) have an expected life of more than one year, (3) be tangible in nature; A-2. matching; A-3. historical cost; A-4. capitalized; A-5. land; A-6. $90,000, $60,000; A-7. $80,000; A-8. boot; A-9. similar productive asset exchange; A-10. fair value of the asset surrendered; A-11. boot is received; A-12. fair value; A-13. revaluation surplus; CS-1. capital expenditures, operating expenditures; CS-2. capitalized; CS-3. accumulated depreciation; SC-1. is not; SC-2. direct costs, variable; DD-1. depreciation; DD-2. ordinary income; DD-3. nature, function; OG-1. full-cost; OG-2. successful-efforts.

POST TEST

Part A Circle T if the statement is true and F if it is false.

T F 1. A company expenses the cost of all assets classified as property, plant, and equipment over the periods in which the assets are consumed and the benefits are received.

T F 2. Conceptually, in determining the costs of an asset which are to be capitalized, cash discounts available rather than cash discounts taken should be deducted from the asset's contract price.

T F 3. When purchasing land, a company immediately expenses rather than capitalizes the closing costs and costs of obtaining title because they do not extend the useful life of the asset.

T F 4. A company may capitalize interest related to the purchase of land held as an investment if the land is being readied for some future use.

T F 5. A company should capitalize unanticipated costs of constructing a building, such as labor strikes or storm damage, as part of the total cost of the building.

T F 6. A company should include the costs of razing an old building that is already owned in order to construct a new building in the gain or loss on the old building rather than in the cost of the new building.

T F 7. Improvements with a 10-year life made to a building leased under a 5-year nonrenewable lease are capitalized and amortized over 10 years by the lessee.

T F 8. If a company acquires two assets in a lump-sum purchase, it should capitalize each asset at its fair value.

T F 9. An asset acquired by a deferred payment plan may be recorded at the present value of the deferred payments, which is determined by discounting the payments at an appropriate rate of interest.

T F 10. When a company receives a building donated by a governmental unit, the asset is debited at its fair value and the credit is recorded as a gain to recognize the increased earnings to the company.

T F 11. If an exchange of property involves dissimilar productive assets, a company must recognize a loss in full on the exchange but gains only to the extent that boot is involved.

T F 12. The primary reason for deferring a gain on the exchange of similar productive assets is that the earning process has not yet been completed with respect to these assets.

T F 13. If a company is operating at full capacity, it is logical to allocate a portion of total fixed overhead to self-constructed assets produced during the period.

T F 14. A company must capitalize one-time start-up costs associated with beginning a new operation.

T F 15. Once a company purchases an asset and capitalizes its original costs, all subsequent expenditures which are related to the asset are expensed.

T F 16. Under generally accepted accounting principles, the degree of materiality determines if relocation costs are capitalized or expensed immediately.

T F 17. The rationale for debiting the cost of improvements to a specific asset's Accumulated Depreciation account is that improvements to the asset restore the asset's service potential.

T F 18. Under generally accepted accounting principles, when accounting for the cost of oil and gas properties, the costs associated with both successful and unsuccessful wells may be capitalized.

Part B Select the one best answer, and place its letter in the space provided.

____ 1. Davpas Company acquired an asset by issuing 100 shares of its $100 par value preferred stock to the seller. The company last sold shares of its preferred stock 2 years ago at a price of $130 a share. While no current market value for the asset obtained is readily available, an independent appraisal placed its value at $12,000. Davpas should record this asset at: (a) $12,000; (b) $10,000; (c) $13,000; (d) a zero book value until such time as transaction-based market value is available.

____ 2. Panda Company exchanged a machine worth $1,000 and having a book value of $1,300 for a similar machine with a fair value of $790. Panda Company also received $210 cash as part of the exchange. In recording this transaction, Panda should recognize: (a) neither a gain nor a loss; (b) a loss of $63; (c) a loss of $300; (d) a gain of $57.

____ 3. Land donated to the Blarney Corporation by Mecklenburg County should be recorded in Blarney's accounting records at: (a) Mecklenburg County's book value; (b) historical cost; (c) fair value on the date of the donation; (d) its tax assessment value which is 80% of fair value.

____ 4. During 2004, Reamer Inc. built a new building to house its corporate offices. The contract cost of the building was $350,000 including excavation costs of $37,000 and architectural costs of $42,000. The demolition costs to raze an old building on the site that Reamer already owned was $47,000. During the construction phase, the company also incurred $12,000 of unanticipated labor costs due to an electrical workers strike. The capitalized cost of the building will be recorded at (a) $350,000; (b) $397,000; (c) $362,000; (d) $409,000

____ 5. The Repco Company incurred costs of $3 million in 2004 drilling oil wells. Thirty percent of the drilling resulted in oil being found. The rest of the drilling was unsuccessful. If Repco uses the full-cost method of accounting, the Oil and Gas Properties will be valued on the 2004 ending balance sheet at (a) $3,000,000; (b) $2,100,000; (c) $900,000; (d) $1,500,000.

____ 6. In constructing a warehouse for its own use, Rightway Company incurred material costs of $25,000, direct labor costs of $60,000, and interest on funds borrowed for construction of $7,200. Rightway's fixed overhead rate is 40% of direct labor. An outside contractor had bid $115,000 to build the warehouse. The capitalized cost of the warehouse should be (a) $116,200; (b) $116,000; (c) $109,000; (d) $92,200.

_____ 7. On June 30, Hilltop, Inc. purchased new equipment by making a down payment of $12,000 and issuing a $25,000 five-year note with a stated (and fair) interest rate of 12%. The acquisition would be recorded by a debit to Equipment for (a) $25,000; (b) $37,000; (c) $54,058; (d) $44,059.

_____ 8. Fairdown Co. acquired land, buildings, and equipment for a lump sum price of $210,000. At the time of acquisition, the land was appraised at $80,000, the buildings at $100,000, and the equipment at $60,000. The cost that should be assigned to the equipment is (a) $70,000; (b) $60,000; (c) $52,500; (d) $80,000.

Part C Solve each of the following short problems.

1. Costs incurred by Jeremy Corporation that relate to its property, plant, and equipment assets might be recorded in one of the five following classes of accounts:

a. a land account
b. a building account
c. an equipment account
d. an accumulated depreciation account
e. an expense account

For each of the costs identified below, indicate the type of account in which the cost should be recorded by placing the appropriate letter (a through e) in the space provided.

_____ (1) cost of overhauling certain equipment, thereby extending its depreciable life by 4 years

_____ (2) property taxes paid on land used in the business

_____ (3) cost of raw material used in testing new equipment prior to using the equipment in production operations

_____ (4) cost to paint and recarpet an old building recently acquired by Jeremy

_____ (5) labor costs to install new equipment

_____ (6) addition of safety devices to existing equipment with no effect on the useful life of the equipment

_____ (7) cost of title search related to land acquisition

_____ (8) cost of changing fan belts and lubricating existing equipment

_____ (9) cost of an addition to the manufacturing plant that will be used to store spare equipment parts

_____ (10) delinquent taxes owed by the former owner of land and paid by Jeremy in the process of acquiring the land

_____ (11) one-time costs associated with opening its new warehouse.

2. Alpha Corporation exchanged a piece of equipment with an original cost of $30,000 for a similar piece of equipment owned by Beta Corporation. Beta's equipment originally cost $20,000. Below you will find three independent sets of assumptions related to this exchange. In the spaces provided, show for each corporation the journal entries required to record the exchange given the additional information.

(a) Alpha's equipment had a book value of $15,000, and Beta's had a book value of $8,000. At the exchange date both assets had a fair value of $12,000. No boot was involved in the transaction.

Alpha Corporation:

Beta Corporation:

(b) Alpha's equipment had a book value of $16,000 and a fair value of $12,000. Beta's equipment had a book value of $8,000 and a fair value of $14,000. Alpha paid Beta $3,000 cash in addition.

Alpha Corporation:

Beta Corporation:

(c) Alpha's equipment had book value of $14,000 and a fair value of $12,000. Beta's equipment had a book value of $8,000 and a fair value of $10,000. Beta paid Alpha $2,000 in cash.

Alpha Corporation:

Beta Corporation:

3. Kitterman Corporation spent $3.5 million in 2004 drilling oil wells in west Texas. Sixty-five (65) percent of the drilling was successful resulting in oil being found for commercial purposes and thirty-five (35) percent resulted in dry wells.

(a) Determine the drilling expense that the company should recognize under:

1. The successful-efforts method

2. The full-cost method

(b) Determine the value of the asset Oil and Gas Properties on the December 31, 2004 balance sheet under:

1. The successful-efforts method

2. The full-cost method

ANSWERS TO POST TEST

Part A

1. F
2. T
3. F
4. T
5. F
6. T
7. F
8. F
9. T
10. F
11. F
12. T
13. T
14. F
15. F
16. T
17. T
18. T

Part B

1. a
2. c
3. c
4. a
5. a
6. a
7. b
8. c

Part C

1. (1) d (2) e (3) c (4) b (5) c (6) c (7) a (8) e (9) b (10) a (11) e

2.	(a)	Alpha:	Equipment (new)	12,000	
			Accumulated Depreciation: Equipment	15,000	
			Loss on Exchange of Equipment	3,000	
			Equipment (old)		30,000
		Beta:	Equipment (new)	8,000	
			Accumulated Depreciation: Equipment	12,000	
			Equipment (old)		20,000
	(b)	Alpha:	Equipment (new)	15,000	
			Accumulated Depreciation: Equipment	14,000	
			Loss on Exchange of Equipment	4,000	
			Equipment (old)		30,000
			Cash		3,000
		Beta:	Cash	3,000	
			Equipment (new)	6,200	
			Accumulated Depreciation: Equipment	12,000	
			Gain on Exchange of Equipment		1,200
			Equipment (old)		20,000
	(c)	Alpha:	Equipment (new)	10,000	
			Accumulated Depreciation: Equipment	16,000	
			Cash	2,000	
			Loss on Exchange of Equipment	2,000	
			Equipment (old)		30,000
		Beta:	Equipment (new)	10,000	
			Accumulated Depreciation: Equipment	12,000	
			Equipment (old)		20,000
			Cash		2,000

3. (a) 1. $1,225,000 (0.35 x $3,500,000)

 2. -0-

 (b) 1. $2,275,000 (0.65 x $3,500,000)

 2. $3,500,000

10

DEPRECIATION AND DEPLETION

CHAPTER OBJECTIVES

After careful study of this chapter, you will be able to:

1. Identify the factors involved in depreciation.
2. Explain the alternative methods of cost allocation, including activity- and time-based methods.
3. Record depreciation.
4. Explain the conceptual issues regarding depreciation methods.
5. Understand the disclosure of depreciation.
6. Understand additional depreciation methods, including group and composite methods.
7. Compute depreciation for partial periods.
8. Explain the impairment of noncurrent assets.
9. Understand depreciation for income tax purposes.
10. Explain changes and corrections of depreciation.
11. Understand and record depletion.

SYNOPSIS

Terms and Factors Involved in Depreciation

1. Depreciation is the process of allocating, in a systematic and rational manner, the total cost of an asset held for more than one year as an expense to each period benefited by the asset. The total expense or depreciation base (depreciable cost) involved is the difference between the purchase price and the estimated residual value. Depreciation is not an attempt to reflect the market value of an asset. Land, which generally has an unlimited life and a future selling price higher than its cost, is not depreciated.

2. The term depreciation describes the allocation of the cost of tangible assets, such as property, plant, and equipment. The term depletion describes the allocation of the cost of natural resource assets, such as oil, gas, minerals, and timber. The term amortization describes the allocation of the cost of intangible assets, such as patents and copyrights. "Amortization" is also sometimes used as a synonym for "depreciation" and "depletion."

3. A company considers four factors in computing a periodic depreciation charge: (a) asset cost, (b) service life, (c) residual value, and (d) method of cost allocation.

4. The cost of an asset includes all the acquisition costs required to obtain the benefits expected from the asset. These acquisition costs include the contract price, freight, assembly, installation, and testing costs.

5. Service life is a measure of the number of units of service expected from an asset before its disposal. A company may make this measurement in units of time or units of activity or output. Service life is limited by (a) physical causes, including wear and tear from use, deterioration from the passage of time, and damage and destruction, and (b) functional causes, through obsolescence and inadequacy.

6. The residual value (salvage value) of an asset is the net amount that can be expected to be obtained from the disposition of the asset at the end of its service life. Because the residual value is difficult to estimate, it is often ignored or recorded at a standard percentage of cost. Such treatments of the residual value are acceptable unless the effects are material. Sometimes a company expects an obligation related to the retirement of an asset at the end of its life. In this case, at the time of acquisition the company computes the present value of the obligation and records this amount both as an increase in the cost of the asset and as an obligation.

Methods of Cost Allocation

7. As a general principle, cost allocation methods must be "systematic and rational." To be systematic, a method must be determined by a formula and must not be arbitrary. To be rational, a method must relate each period's depreciation expense to the benefits generated in that period.

8. In practice companies use either <u>activity</u> (or use) methods or <u>time-based</u> methods. Activity methods are appropriate when an asset's service life is affected primarily by the amount of usage, rather than by the passage of time. The measure of activity is usually hours worked or units of output. The depreciation rate is determined by dividing the asset's depreciable cost by an estimate of the asset's lifetime activity. Depreciation for the period is computed by multiplying this rate by the period's activity level. Companies seldom use activity methods for depreciation, however, because of the difficulties of estimation and the cost of measuring and recording the activity level of each asset each period. In contrast, depletion (discussed later) is normally recorded using an activity method.

9. Time-based methods are appropriate when an asset's service life is affected primarily by the passage of time, rather than by the amount of usage. Time-based methods may be divided into two general categories: the <u>straight-line</u> method and the <u>accelerated</u> methods. The straight-line method allocates a constant depreciation charge to each period of the asset's life. It is appropriate when the benefits from the asset are expected to remain approximately constant over the periods of use.

10. <u>Accelerated</u> (declining-charge) methods are appropriate when the benefits from the asset are expected to decline over each period of use. The selection of a particular declining depreciation method is basically arbitrary, since generally a specific declining depreciation method cannot be matched against the expected pattern of declining revenue. Accelerated methods include the <u>sum-of-the-years'-digits</u> method and <u>declining-balance</u> methods.

11. A company using the sum-of-the-years'-digits method computes the depreciation charge by multiplying the asset's depreciation base (cost less residual value) by a declining fraction. The denominator of that fraction is the sum of the digits of the asset's estimated life. The numerator is determined by taking those digits in reverse order. For example, the fraction used for first-year depreciation of an asset with a five-year life is:

$$5/(1 + 2 + 3 + 4 + 5) = 5/15$$

12. A company using a declining-balance method applies a <u>constant</u> depreciation rate to the <u>book value</u> of the asset at the beginning of the period, <u>ignoring</u> residual value. Periodic depreciation under this method declines because the book value, rather than the depreciation base, is used. The highest rate allowed for both income tax and financial reporting is twice the straight-line rate. To depreciate the asset accurately to its residual value, most companies change from the declining-balance method to the straight-line method during the life of the asset.

13. Depreciation on <u>merchandising</u> assets and on assets used for <u>selling, general</u>, and <u>administrative</u> functions is expensed currently. However, depreciation charges are not always expensed immediately. A company initially capitalizes depreciation on its <u>manufacturing</u> assets as part of the cost of the inventory produced through an increase to its Goods in Process inventory account. When inventory is sold the company reports this depreciation on the income statement as part of the cost of goods sold. The company carries depreciation on unsold units as part of the inventory asset value on its balance sheet.

Conceptual Evaluation of Depreciation Methods

14. The choice of a depreciation method can have a significant impact on a company's reported income and assets, although its total income over the life of the asset will be unaffected. In selecting a depreciation method, a company should make an attempt to match total costs (including expected repair and maintenance costs) associated with the asset with the benefits expected from that asset. A company should also consider the effect of changing prices and the risk associated with the cash flows from the asset. Depreciation is not a measurement of the value of an asset, and is not recorded to fund the replacement of an asset.

15. Rate of return on total assets (net income divided by assets) is a ratio commonly used in financial analysis. As a company records depreciation on an asset, the asset's book value is lowered and the company's rate of return is raised. Consequently, comparisons between companies with different asset ages and within one company over time are difficult.

Disclosure of Depreciation

16. APB Opinion No. 12 requires a company to make the following disclosures related to its depreciation: (a) depreciation expense for the period, (b) balances of major classes of depreciable assets, by nature or function, at the balance sheet date, (c) accumulated depreciation, either by major classes of depreciable assets or in total, at the balance sheet date, and (d) a general description of the method or methods used in computing depreciation with respect to the major classes of depreciable assets.

17. International accounting standards for depreciation are very similar to U.S. standards. However, international standards require a company to use "systematic" depreciation and to review the estimated useful lives and depreciation method periodically. The company must disclose the accumulated depreciation for each class of assets.

Additional Depreciation Methods

18. A company using group depreciation capitalizes the cost of a group of homogeneous (similar) assets in a single asset account and depreciates the cost as a single asset. The company bases the group depreciation rate on the average life of the group assets and applies the rate each period to the balance in the group account. It accumulates depreciation in a single contra-asset account. The company records the retirement of an individual asset by a credit to the asset for the asset's original cost and a debit to accumulated depreciation for the difference between the retirement proceeds and original cost. It does not record a gain or loss on the assets until all assets in the group have been retired. Then the company recognizes a total net gain or loss on the group.

19. A company may use composite depreciation with heterogeneous (dissimilar) assets which have somewhat similar characteristics or purposes. It applies composite depreciation in the same way as group depreciation. Both group and composite depreciation simplify a company's record keeping, particularly for large numbers of low-cost items. However, the methods may mask faulty estimates and defer gains and losses beyond the period of occurrence.

20. Retirement and replacement methods recognize depreciation expense only when an asset is retired or replaced. A company using the retirement method expenses the cost of the old asset (less residual value) when the asset is retired. A company using the replacement method expenses the cost of the new asset (less residual value of the old asset) when it is acquired. Neither method matches expenses with revenues in each period of the asset's life. However, retirement and replacement methods are sometimes used by railroads and public utilities.

21. Under the inventory (appraisal) system, typically used with large numbers of similar low-cost items, a company determines the depreciation cost by multiplying the number of units at year-end by the replacement cost. As in a periodic inventory system, this method depends on a physical count at the end of the period. The method tends to lack reliability and is not a systematic and rational allocation of costs.

Depreciation for Partial Periods

22. Companies commonly use three alternatives to compute depreciation on assets purchased or sold during the year:

    (a) Depreciation may be computed to the nearest whole month, considering assets purchased on or before the 15th of the month as owned for the whole month, and assets purchased after the 15th as not owned during the month.

    (b) Depreciation may be computed to the nearest whole year, considering assets purchased during the first six months as owned for the whole year, and assets purchased during the last six months as not owned during the year.

    (c) One-half year's depreciation may be charged on all assets purchased or sold during the year.

Impairment of Noncurrent Assets

23. FASB Statement No. 144 requires that a company review its property, plant, and equipment for impairment when events or changes in circumstances indicate that the book value of these assets may not be recoverable. To test for impairment, a company compares the total expected cash flows (undiscounted) of an asset with the asset's book value. If future net cash flows are lower than book value, the company recognizes an impairment loss. For this comparison the company groups assets at the lowest level at which identifiable cash flows are largely independent of the cash flows of other groups of assets.

24. The impairment loss is the difference between the asset's book value and its lower fair value, which may be measured by the present value method. The discount rate used is the rate of return that the company requires for similar investments with similar risks. The company includes the impairment loss in income from continuing operations on the income statement and reports the new lower book value on the company's ending balance sheet.

25. Disclosures regarding a write-down include: a description of the impaired asset and the circumstances of the impairment, the amount of the loss, the method of determining fair value, the income statement caption which includes the loss, and the operating segment affected, if applicable.

26. Financial reporting is enhanced by the requirements of FASB Statement No. 144: a company recognizes an impairment loss when it occurs, and the company reports its productive assets at their fair values. However, dissenters criticize the use of fair value as a departure from transaction-based historical cost and point out that a current write-down will ensure future profits.

27. International standards for the impairment of assets are similar to U.S. standards. However, international standards use an asset's selling price to measure the impairment loss, and also allow impairment losses to be reversed.

Depreciation and Income Tax

28. The purpose of income-tax depreciation methods is to stimulate capital investment through rapid capital-cost recovery. In contrast, accounting depreciation is used in the determination of accounting income, whose purpose is to fairly represent the results of the company's activities for a period. The use of different depreciation methods for income tax reporting and financial reporting is acceptable and common.

29. For assets purchased before 1981, the methods described earlier are required for income tax reporting. For assets purchased in the years 1981 through 1986, the Accelerated Cost Recovery System (ACRS) is used. MACRS (Modified ACRS) rules apply to assets purchased in 1987 and later. MACRS depreciation differs from depreciation for financial reporting in three major ways: (a) the MACRS mandated tax life is usually shorter than the economic life of the asset, (b) MACRS accelerates cost recovery (except for buildings), and (c) MACRS ignores residual value. Each difference lowers income taxes payable in the early years of the asset's life. However, over the asset's total life, the sum of total depreciation and the gain or loss on disposal will be equal under income tax and financial reporting.

30. MACRS specifies lives (recovery periods) to be used for classes of assets. The following methods are specified:

Method	MACRS Life (in Years)
Double-declining balance	3, 5, 7, 10
150% declining balance	15, 20
Straight-line	27½, 39

One-half year's depreciation is recorded in the year of acquisition and in the last year of the MACRS life. Residual value is not considered under MACRS. The IRS has published tables to simplify the MACRS calculations; these tables are illustrated in Exhibit 10-12 of the main text.

31. Companies may use the straight-line method over the mandated life as an alternative to MACRS for income tax reporting.

Changes and Corrections of Depreciation

32. APB Opinion No. 20 specifies how a company makes accounting changes. The treatment of depreciation changes is as follows:

    (a) A change in the depreciation method for a currently owned asset is accounted for by a cumulative-effect change on prior years' income.

(b) Use of a new depreciation method for a newly acquired asset is disclosed in the notes to the company's financial statements.

(c) A change in an estimate of the residual value or service life of a currently owned asset is accounted for prospectively, allocating the undepreciated cost over the new remaining life, considering the new residual value.

(d) An error in prior depreciation is accounted for as a prior period adjustment to correct the company's previous financial statements, and an adjustment of the accumulated depreciation and retained earnings balances in the company's current period financial statements.

Depletion of Natural Resources

33. Depletion, the allocation of the depletable cost of the consumption of a natural resource (wasting asset) to the periods when benefits are received, is normally recorded on the basis of an activity method. The total number of units expected to be extracted is the activity measure. A company determines depletion by multiplying actual production for the period by the unit depletion rate:

$$\text{Unit Depletion Rate} = (\text{Cost} - \text{Residual Value})/\text{Units}$$

When additional capital expenditures are made or estimates are revised, the company calculates a new depletion rate.

34. Tangible assets, such as buildings, whose useful life is dependent on the life of the natural resource, are depreciated over the shorter of the life of the resource (using the same activity method) or the life of the asset itself.

35. For income tax purposes, a company may use percentage depletion (statutory depletion) instead of the cost depletion described above. Under percentage depletion, a stated percentage of gross income may be deducted as depletion expense. Percentage depletion over the life of the asset may exceed the cost of the asset less the expected residual value. Percentage depletion is not acceptable for financial reporting.

SELF-EVALUATION EXERCISES

Supply the words necessary to complete each of the following items.

Terms and Factors Involved in Depreciation

TF-1. Depreciation allocates the difference between the purchase price and the residual value of an asset in a ________________ and ____________ manner to the periods benefited.

TF-2. Depreciation is the allocation of the cost of ______________ assets.

TF-3. Depletion is the allocation of the cost of ______________ ____________ assets.

TF-4. Amortization is the allocation of the cost of __________________ assets.

TF-5. A company considers four factors in computing periodic depreciation: ________ __________, ____________ ________, ________________ ________, and __________ _____ ______ _________________.

TF-6. Units of time or units of activity or output may be used to measure ____________ _______.

TF-7. The net amount expected to be obtained in the final disposition of an asset is the ______________ ___________.

TF-8. The present value of an expected obligation related to the retirement of a depreciable asset is recorded as an increase in the ________ of the asset and as an _________________.

Methods of Cost Allocation

MC-1. A cost allocation method must be determined by formula, and must not be arbitrary in order to be ____________.

MC-2. A cost allocation method must relate each depreciation charge to the benefits received from the asset in that period in order to be ____________.

MC-3. When a company determines an asset's service life more by the amount of usage than by the passage of time, an ____________ method of depreciation is appropriate.

MC-4. The straight-line method and the accelerated methods are the two categories of ________-___________ methods.

MC-5. A company allocates a constant depreciation charge to each period of the asset's life using the _____________-_________ method.

MC-6. When a company expects the benefits received from an asset to decrease over the asset's life, an ____________ method of depreciation is appropriate.

MC-7. Depreciation expense is computed by multiplying an asset's depreciable cost by a declining fraction when the _____-______ ______-________-____________ method is used.

MC-8. A constant depreciation rate is applied to the beginning book value of an asset when _____________-_____________ methods are used.

MC-9. Depreciation on manufacturing assets is included in the cost of inventory produced and enters the income statement as part of the _________ ________ ___________ __________.

Conceptual Evaluation of Depreciation Methods

CE-1. A depreciation method should ________ the total costs of an asset with the benefits expected from that asset.

CE-2. A ratio computed by dividing net income by assets is called the _________ _____ _____________.

Additional Depreciation Methods

AD-1. Homogeneous or similar assets are capitalized in a single asset account and depreciated as a single asset when ________ depreciation is used.

AD-2. Heterogeneous assets are capitalized in a single asset account and depreciated as a single asset when ______________________ depreciation is used.

AD-3. A company charges the cost (less residual value) of an old asset to expense when it retires the asset under the ______________ method.

AD-4. The cost of a new asset, less the residual value of the old asset, is charged to expense when the new asset is acquired under the _____________ method.

AD-5. The depreciation cost under the _____________ _________ is determined by multiplying the number of units at year-end by the replacement cost.

Depreciation for Partial Periods

DPP-1. The three common alternatives for computing depreciation on assets purchased or sold during the year are:

(1) ______________________________

(2) ______________________________

(3) ______________________________

Impairment of Noncurrent Assets

IN-1. When the future cash flows expected from equipment are lower than the equipment's book value, an impairment loss is __________.

IN-2. The fair value of an impaired asset may be measured by the __________ __________ method.

IN-3. An impairment loss is included on the income statement in __________ ________ ______________ ______________.

Depreciation and Income Tax

DI-1. The asset life mandated under MACRS for income tax reporting is usually __________ than the asset's economic life.

DI-2. MACRS specifies lives, or __________ ______________, to be used for classes of assets.

DI-3. For assets with recovery periods of 3, 5, 7, or 10 years MACRS specifies the use of the __________-______________ ____________ method.

DI-4. As an alternative to MACRS, the __________-______ method over the mandated life may be used for income tax reporting.

Changes and Corrections of Depreciation

CC-1. For a change in the depreciation method used for currently owned assets, a ______________-__________ change is used.

CC-2. The use of a new depreciation method for a newly acquired asset is disclosed in the ________ to the financial statements.

CC-3. A change in an estimate of the residual value or service life of an asset is accounted for ______________.

CC-4. For the correction of an error in the depreciation of previous periods, a company uses a ________ __________ ______________.

Depletion of Natural Resources

DN-1. Depletion is normally recorded on the basis of an __________ method.

DN-2. When a company makes additional capital expenditures for development of a natural resource asset, it must calculate a new depletion _______.

DN-3. Depletion over the life of an asset may exceed the asset's cost less expected residual value under the ____________ ____________ method allowed for income tax purposes.

ANSWERS TO SELF-EVALUATION EXERCISES

TF-1. systematic, rational; TF-2. tangible; TF-3. natural resource; TF-4. intangible; TF-5. asset cost, service life, residual value, method of cost allocation; TF-6. service life; TF-7. residual value; TF-8. cost, obligation; MC-1. systematic; MC-2. rational; MC-3. activity; MC-4. time-based; MC-5. straight-line; MC-6. accelerated; MC-7. sum-of-the-years'-digits; MC-8. declining-balance; MC-9. cost of goods sold; CE-1. match; CE-2. rate of return; AD-1. group; AD-2. composite; AD-3. retirement; AD-4. replacement; AD-5. inventory system; DPP-1. (1) Compute depreciation to the nearest whole month. (2) Compute depreciation to the nearest whole year. (3) Charge one-half year's depreciation on all assets purchased or sold during the year; IN-1. recognized; IN-2. present value; IN-3. income from continuing operations; DI-1. shorter; DI-2. recovery periods; DI-3. double-declining balance; DI-4. straight-line; CC-1. cumulative-effect; CC-2. notes; CC-3. prospectively; CC-4. prior period adjustment; DN-1 activity; DN-2. rate; DN-3. percentage depletion.

POST TEST

Part A Circle T if the statement is true and F if it is false.

T F 1. The straight-line method of depreciation is appropriate when benefits to be received from an asset are expected to remain constant over the asset's service life.

T F 2. The sum-of-the-years'-digits method of depreciation ignores residual value.

T F 3. The choice of depreciation method will have no effect on total income over the life of an asset.

T F 4. As accumulated depreciation increases, the rate of return on assets rises.

T F 5. Composite depreciation is appropriate only for homogeneous or similar assets.

T F 6. For financial reporting, depletion is normally charged on the basis of an activity method.

T F 7. Over an asset's total life, the sum of total depreciation and gain or loss on disposal will be equal under tax and financial reporting.

T F 8. MACRS specifies use of the double-declining balance method for assets with a life (recovery period) of 15 years.

T F 9. A change in an estimate of residual value or service life of a currently owned asset should be accounted for by a cumulative-effect change.

T F 10. Percentage depletion is not acceptable for financial reporting.

T F 11. The term "depletion" describes the amortization of intangible assets.

T F 12. The purposes of depreciation for financial reporting and income tax reporting are the same.

T F 13. According to generally accepted accounting principles, one-half year's depreciation must be taken on assets purchased or sold during the year.

T F 14. An asset's service life may be limited by functional causes long before the asset has physically deteriorated.

T F 15. Under the inventory method, typically used with individual, high-cost items, the cost of a new asset is expensed when the asset is acquired.

T F 16. The unit depletion rate of a natural resource equals the cost of the asset, net of residual value, divided by the estimated number of units of the resource.

T F 17. Land, which is assumed to have an unlimited life, is not depreciated.

T F 18. The net residual value of a wasting asset may be negative because of extensive reclamation costs.

T F 19. Depreciation, depletion, and amortization are recorded to reflect the market value of owned assets.

T F 20. International accounting standards require a company to disclose accumulated depreciation for each class of assets.

T F 21. When evaluating the impairment of an asset, a company compares the total discounted cash flows expected from the asset with the asset's book value.

Part B Select the one best answer, and place its letter in the space provided.

_____ 1. The Osage Company uses the sum-of-the-years'-digits method of depreciation and computes depreciation to the nearest whole year. What amount should Osage record for second-year depreciation of a chain saw (purchased in April) costing $500, with an expected life of 5 years and an expected residual value of $50? (a) $120; (b) $150; (c) $100; (d) $132.

_____ 2. Which of the following depreciation-related disclosures is not required under APB Opinion No. 12? (a) depreciation expense for the period; (b) accumulated depreciation, either by major classes of assets or in total; (c) a general description of the depreciation method or methods used; (d) disclosure in the notes to the financial statements of straight-line depreciation if a declining-balance method was used.

_____ 3. Which of the following is not a way in which MACRS differs from depreciation for financial reporting? (a) MACRS uses shorter asset lives; (b) MACRS increases income in the early years of the asset's life; (c) MACRS accelerates cost recovery; (d) MACRS ignores residual value.

_____ 4. The Pommel Company uses the double-declining balance method of depreciation and charges one-half year's depreciation on assets purchased. What amount should Pommel record for first-year depreciation of an asset with a list price of $500, delivery charges of $80, an estimated life of 5 years, and an expected residual value of $100? (a) $192; (b) $96; (c) $116; (d) $232.

_____ 5. The factors involved in computing periodic depreciation charges do not include (a) asset cost; (b) service life; (c) current value; (d) residual value.

_____ 6. The depreciable cost of an asset does not include (a) maintenance costs; (b) acquisition cost; (c) installation costs; (d) costs of preparation for use.

_____ 7. On March 1 the Bing Company purchased an asset for $500 plus $50 freight and $100 installation. The expected life of the asset is 5 years. Expected salvage value is $100. Maximum allowable first-year depreciation is (a) $260; (b) $220; (c) $200; (d) $110.

_____ 8. The straight-line method of depreciation is an example of (a) an activity method; (b) a declining-charge method; (c) a time-based method; (d) an accelerated method.

_____ 9. Company A and Company B each purchased a $50,000 asset with an expected life of 10 years on January 1, 2002. Company A uses the straight-line method, and Company B uses the double-declining balance method. Each company had net income of $40,000 in 2004. Which of the following statements is true? (a) Company A's method is appropriate for an asset whose benefits are expected to decline over the periods of use; (b) Company B's 2004 rate of return on its asset is higher than Company A's; (c) Company A and Company B have the same rate of return; (d) Company B uses an activity method of depreciation.

_____ 10. Which of the following methods is in use when a number of homogeneous or similar assets are capitalized in a single asset account and depreciated as a single asset? (a) composite method; (b) retirement method; (c) activity method; (d) group method.

____ 11. Depreciation on manufacturing assets (a) is initially capitalized in the Goods in Process account; (b) enters the income statement as a component of the cost of goods sold; (c) is carried on the balance sheet as a component of the value of unsold inventory; (d) all of the above.

____ 12. The inventory (appraisal) system (a) recognizes the expense of an asset when the asset is retired; (b) determines the depreciation cost by multiplying the number of units at year-end by the replacement cost; (c) is a perpetual inventory system; (d) results in a systematic and rational allocation of costs.

____ 13. Which of the following statements regarding impaired assets is true? (a) an impairment loss is included in income from continuing operations on the income statement; (b) a company reviews a productive asset for impairment when events or circumstances indicate that the asset's book value is overstated; (c) after an impairment loss is recognized, the productive asset is reported at its fair value; (d) the fair value of an impaired asset may be measured by the present value method; (e) all of the above.

____ 14. The Level Company uses group depreciation for its 25 delivery vans. The company purchased the vans, each with an estimated life of four years and an estimated residual value of $5,000, for $25,000 per van. At the beginning of the second year Level sold three vans, for $10,000 each. What is the balance in Level's accumulated depreciation account for the group at the end of the second year? (a) $190,000; (b) $205,000; (c) $250,000; (d) $291,250.

Part C Solve each of the following short problems.

1. Below is a list of depreciation-related terms. Following is a list of ten descriptive phrases. Match each term with its descriptive phrase by placing the appropriate letter in the space provided.

a. depletion	g. rate of return
b. service life	h. group depreciation method
c. systematic	i. Modified Accelerated Cost Recovery System
d. activity methods	j. percentage depletion
e. time-based methods	k. impairment loss
f. accelerated methods	l. depreciation base

____ 1. include straight-line and accelerated methods.

____ 2. a measure of the number of units of service expected from an asset before its disposal.

____ 3. the difference between a productive asset's future net cash flows and its higher book value.

____ 4. over the life of an asset may exceed the asset's cost less expected residual value.

____ 5. the difference between the purchase price and the estimated residual value of a depreciable asset.

____ 6. determined by formula, and not arbitrary.

_____ 7. required for income tax reporting for assets purchased in 1987 and later.

_____ 8. appropriate when benefits from an asset are expected to decline over the periods of use.

_____ 9. net income divided by assets.

_____ 10. capitalizes and depreciates homogeneous or similar assets as a single asset.

_____ 11. appropriate when an asset's service life is determined by usage.

_____ 12. allocation of the acquisition cost of assets such as oil, gas, minerals, and timber.

2. The Trimble Company purchased a machine costing $400,000 on January 1, 2004. Estimated service life is 10 years or 20,000 hours. Estimated production is 600,000 units. Estimated residual value is $50,000. In 2004 the company used the machine for 2,000 hours to produce 75,000 units. The company computes depreciation to the nearest whole year.

Calculate 2004 depreciation using each of the following methods:

1. straight-line
2. double-declining balance
3. sum-of-the-years'-digits
4. hours worked
5. units of output

3. Mineral Mountain Mining Company purchased land on January 1, 2004 for $13,000,000. The Company expects to produce 600,000 tons of ore over a 5-year period. After completing mining operations, the Company expects to sell the land for $1,000,000.

In 2004, the Company constructed buildings at a cost of $1,000,000. The buildings have an estimated physical life of 20 years. They will be used by Mineral Mountain Mining only for mining operations. The expected residual value of the buildings is $250,000.

150,000 tons of ore were produced in 2004.

(a) Determine Mineral Mountain Mining's depletion for 2004.

(b) Determine Mineral Mountain Mining's depreciation on buildings for 2004 (use activity method).

ANSWERS TO POST TEST

Part A

1. T
2. F
3. T
4. T
5. F
6. T
7. T
8. F
9. F
10. T
11. F
12. F
13. F
14. T
15. F
16. T
17. T
18. T
19. F
20. T
21. F

Part B

1. a
2. d
3. b
4. c
5. c
6. a
7. a
8. c
9. b
10. d
11. d
12. b
13. e
14. c

Part C

1. 1. e
   2. b
   3. k
   4. j
   5. l
   6. c
   7. i
   8. f
   9. g
   10. h
   11. d
   12. a

2. 1. $35,000 [($400,000 - $50,000)/10]
   2. $80,000 [$400,000 x 0.20]
   3. $63,636 [($400,000 - $50,000) x 10/55]
   4. $35,000 [($400,000 - $50,000)/20,000 = $17.50; $17.50 x 2,000 = $35,000]
   5. $43,750 [($400,000 - $50,000)/600,000 = $0.5833; $0.5833 x 75,000 = $43,750]

3. (a) $3,000,000 {[($13,000,000 - $1,000,000)/600,000] x 150,000}
   (b) $187,500 [($1,000,000 - $250,000) x (150,000/600,000)]

11

INTANGIBLES

CHAPTER OBJECTIVES

After careful study of this chapter, you will be able to:

1. Explain the accounting alternatives for intangible assets.
2. Record the amortization or impairment of intangibles.
3. Identify research and development costs.
4. Explain the conceptual issues for research and development costs.
5. Account for identifiable intangible assets including patents, copyrights, franchises, computer software costs, and trademarks and tradenames.
6. Account for unidentifiable intangibles, including internally developed and purchased goodwill.
7. Understand goodwill amortization.
8. Understand the disclosure of intangibles.
9. Explain the conceptual issues regarding intangibles.
10. Estimate the value of goodwill (Appendix).

SYNOPSIS

Nature of and Accounting for Intangible Assets

1. Intangible assets, which generally result from legal or contractual rights, do not have a physical substance. Like tangible noncurrent assets, intangible assets are held for use rather than investment; have an expected life of more than one year; are valuable because of their ability to generate revenue for their owners; and are expensed in the periods when their benefits are received if the assets have finite lives. Four additional characteristics of intangible assets distinguish them from tangible assets:

   (a) There is generally a higher degree of uncertainty regarding the future benefits of intangibles.

   (b) The value of intangibles is subject to wider fluctuations because it may depend considerably on competitive conditions.

   (c) Intangibles may have value only to a particular company.

   (d) Goodwill and intangible assets with indefinite lives are not expensed.

2. Accounting for intangible assets follows some of the general principles used for tangible assets. Both are initially recorded at cost. Some intangibles are amortized, while others are not but are reviewed for impairment. Intangible assets that are amortized are reported on a company's balance sheet at their book values (cost - accumulated amortization). Amortization follows the same principles as depreciation. Similar principles apply to both intangible and tangible assets in regard to determining the acquisition cost, impairment, and disposal.

3. Companies may classify intangible assets as either purchased or internally developed, and as either identifiable or unidentifiable. Accounting for the costs of intangibles is discussed in FASB Statement No. 142:

   (a) Companies capitalize the costs of purchased identifiable intangibles (for example, purchased patents).

   (b) Companies capitalize the costs of purchased unidentifiable intangibles. (Goodwill, the major unidentifiable intangible, will be discussed later.)

   (c) Companies capitalize certain costs associated with internally developed identifiable intangibles (for example, the legal and related costs of establishing the rights associated with a patent). However, according to FASB Statement No. 2, research and development costs are an exception to the general rule of capitalization and must be expensed. (Research and development costs will be discussed later.)

   (d) Companies expense the costs of internally developed unidentifiable intangibles (such as employee training and product design) as incurred.

4. Intangible assets (other than goodwill, which we discuss later) are classified into two categories: (a) intangible assets with a finite (limited) life, and (b) intangible assets with an indefinite life.

5. Intangible assets with a finite life are amortized. An intangible asset with a finite life (e.g., patent) is amortized over its useful life. The amount of an intangible asset to be amortized is the cost less the residual value. A company selects the amortization method based on the expected pattern of benefits. If the company cannot determine the expected pattern, then it uses the straight-line method. The entry to record the amortization includes a debit to Goods in Process (or an operating expense) and a credit to Accumulated Amortization. If an intangible asset with a finite life becomes impaired, a company must write down the asset to its fair value.

6. Intangible assets with an indefinite life are reviewed for impairment. Some identifiable intangible assets (e.g., trademarks) have a potentially indefinite life. These intangible assets are not amortized (unless they are determined to have a useful life that is finite), but are reviewed at least annually for impairment. To review an intangible asset for impairment, a company estimates the fair value of the asset. The asset is impaired if its fair value is less than its carrying value. In this case, the company debits a Loss account and credits the intangible asset account.

Research and Development Costs

7. FASB Statement No. 2 requires that a company expense all research and development (R&D) costs as incurred, although R&D costs often benefit future periods. The requirement to expense R&D costs was based primarily on the belief that uniform treatment of R&D costs enhances comparability and eliminates the possibility of income manipulation. In addition, the problems of reliably determining the amount to capitalize and the amortization period are avoided.

8. "Research" and "development" are broadly defined in FASB Statement No. 2. To help with application of those definitions, Exhibit 11-2 in the text presents examples of activities included in and excluded from R&D. A company capitalizes or expenses the costs of activities excluded from R&D according to the normal accounting criteria. A company includes the following costs of R&D activities in R&D costs and expenses them as incurred: (a) materials, equipment, and facilities, (b) personnel, (c) intangibles purchased from others, (d) contract services--the cost of services performed by others in connection with the company's R&D activities, and (e) a reasonable allocation of indirect costs, not including general and administrative costs unless they are clearly related to R&D.

9. A company includes the costs of any materials, equipment, facilities, and intangibles which are purchased from others and have no alternative future uses (even if only in other R&D projects) in R&D expense as incurred. For items which do have alternative future uses, normal accrual procedures are followed.

10. In formulating FASB Statement No. 2, the Board considered four methods of accounting for R&D costs: (a) expensing all costs as incurred, (b) capitalizing all costs when incurred and amortizing them over the periods benefitted, (c) capitalizing some costs and expensing other costs, (d) accumulating all costs in a special category until the existence of future benefits is determined. Because of the problems of determining the amount to capitalize and the period of amortization, Alternatives 2 through 4 are difficult to implement with reliability. Although Alternative 1 (immediate expensing) is not perfect conceptually, that alternative was chosen by the FASB because it is easy to implement and it is likely to lead to greater comparability between companies.

11. International accounting standards require research project costs to be expensed, but allow the capitalization of development costs.

Identifiable Intangible Assets

12. Identifiable intangible assets are those intangibles which can be purchased or sold separately from the other assets of the company. Because R&D and operating costs are expensed, a company capitalizes only certain costs of internally developed identifiable intangibles. For example, a company capitalizes the direct legal costs of applying for and registering an internally developed trademark, while it expenses all the indirect costs as incurred. In contrast, if a company purchases an identifiable intangible asset, it capitalizes the cost on the same basis as for a tangible asset by including all necessary costs.

13. A patent is an exclusive right granted by the federal government giving the owner control of the manufacture, sale, or other use of an invention for 20 years from the date of filing. The value of a patent lies in the competitive advantage it gives to the company. If that competitive advantage is expected to last less than 20 years, the company amortizes the patent over its shorter useful life. A company normally capitalizes the legal costs of successfully defending a patent against infringement. However, some companies expense the legal costs as incurred, because of uncertainty over the outcome of an infringement case. In any case, if an infringement lawsuit is lost, all legal expenses, as well as the remaining book value of the patent, are expensed.

14. A copyright is a grant by the federal government covering the right to publish, sell, or otherwise control literary or artistic products for the life of the author plus 70 years. A company amortizes the cost of a copyright over its useful life, on either a straight-line or an activity basis.

15. A franchise is an agreement in which, for a fee, one party (the franchisor) gives another party (the franchisee) rights to perform certain functions or to sell certain products or services. The franchisee capitalizes the initial franchise cost paid and amortizes it over the useful life of the franchise, unless the franchise is granted in perpetivity (in which case it would be tested for impairment at least annually.) The franchisee expenses the continuing franchise fees paid for services in subsequent years according to normal matching criteria.

16. FASB Statement No. 86 divides the costs of computer software developed to be sold, leased, or otherwise marketed into three categories:

    (a) A company treats software production costs (such as costs of design, coding, and testing) as research and development expenses until the technological feasibility of the product is established. Technological feasibility is established either on the date of completion of detail program design or on completion of a working model. A company capitalizes the software production costs incurred between the time of technological feasibility and the time when the product is available for general release and amortizes them over the expected life of the product, typically a relatively short period, such as five years. After the date of general release, the company expenses all software production costs as incurred. Amortization expense for capitalized software costs is the greater of (1) the ratio of current gross revenues from the software to estimated total (current and future) revenues from the software multiplied by the cost of the asset, or (2) straight-line expense. If the net realizable value of the software is less than the book value, the software is written down to the lower value, and a loss is recognized.

(b) A company records the unit costs of producing the software (such as the disk and duplication costs) as inventory and expenses them as cost of goods sold when the related revenue is recognized.

(c) A company expenses maintenance and customer support costs which arise after the software is released, as incurred.

Note that the discussion above applies to software developed for external use. As a result of FASB Statement No. 86, companies expense most computer software costs. Since the amount capitalized depends on the company's programming process, the costs capitalized may vary significantly from company to company.

17. AICPA Statement of Position No. 98-1 discusses accounting for the costs incurred in developing internal-use software. A company expenses costs incurred in the preliminary stage of development. A company capitalizes costs after the preliminary stage has been completed, management has authorized and committed to funding the project, and it is probable that the project will be completed and that the software will be used for the intended function. Capitalized costs include external direct costs of materials and services, payroll and payroll-related costs for the time employees spend on the project, and interest costs. A company amortizes the capitalized costs by the straight-line method over the estimated useful life of the software.

18. Leases (leaseholds) are actually intangible assets to the lessee, because they give the lessee the right to use property rather than ownership of the property. However, lessees normally include capitalized leases in property, plant, and equipment, rather than report them as intangible assets. Lessees normally include leasehold improvements, also intangible assets, as a separate item in property, plant, and equipment.

19. Registration of a trademark or tradename with the U.S. Patent Office gives a company the right to exclusive use of a name, symbol, or other devices used for product identification. Registration lasts for 20 years and is renewable indefinitely if the trademark or tradename is used continuously. Therefore, they typically are not amortized, but are reviewed for impairment at least annually.

20. Deferred charges (or other "noncurrent assets") is a common, catch-all category on the balance sheet. Most deferred charges should be placed in other balance sheet categories. Companies amortize all deferred charges over their expected economic lives.

21. Organization costs incurred in forming a corporation include legal fees, stock certificate costs, underwriting fees, accounting fees, and promotional fees. AICPA Statement of Position No. 98-5 requires that the costs of start-up activities, including organization costs, be expensed as incurred.

Unidentifiable Intangibles

22. Many intangibles essential to the performance of the company (such as superiority of employees and advantageous geographical location) do not appear on the balance sheet. Such internally developed intangibles are categorized as goodwill. Goodwill is distinguished by two characteristics: (a) Intangibles included are considered unidentifiable because they are not separable from the identified and recorded assets, and (b) Measurement of these unidentifiable intangibles is very difficult, and less reliable than measurement of identifiable intangibles. Companies expense internally developed goodwill as incurred.

23. Goodwill is recorded by the acquiring company when it purchases a company (or a significant part of a company). The purchase transaction establishes a reliable valuation. Purchased goodwill is defined as the difference between the purchase price (market value) of the acquired company as a whole and the fair value of its identifiable net assets (assets - liabilities). That difference is the price paid for the unidentifiable intangibles that were internally developed by the acquired company. The value recorded for goodwill is determined by the price paid in the purchase transaction. As required by FASB Statement No. 141, companies capitalize purchased goodwill.

24. Goodwill is never amortized. A company must review its goodwill for impairment at least annually at the reporting unit (i.e., operating segment) level. The company reviews its goodwill for impairment whenever events or changed circumstances occur that make it likely that the fair value of the goodwill has been reduced below its carrying value.

25. A company reviews its goodwill for impairment using a two-step approach. First, the company compares the fair value of the reporting unit with its book value (including goodwill). Second, if the fair value is less than the book value, the company must measure the amount of the impairment loss, if any.

26. The amount of the impairment loss is the difference between the carrying value of the goodwill and the lower implied fair value of the goodwill (i.e., the implied value is the excess "purchase price" over the amounts assigned to the identifiable assets and liabilities). The entry to record the loss includes a debit to Impairment Loss and a credit to Goodwill.

27. Negative goodwill arises when the price paid for a company is less than the fair value of the net assets acquired. Negative goodwill is not separately recorded. FASB Statement No. 141 requires that the acquiring company allocate the negative amount to proportionately reduce the cost of the noncurrent assets acquired (except certain assets). If noncurrent assets are reduced to zero, the acquiring company records and reports any remaining amount as an extraordinary gain.

Disclosure of Intangibles

28. FASB Statement No. 142 requires a company to disclose certain information about its intangible assets, including:

    (a) In the period it acquires intangible assets: (1) the cost (separated into assets subject to amortization, not subject to amortization, and goodwill); (2) for assets subject to amortization, the residual value and amortization period; and (3) the cost of any R&D acquired and written off (and where reported on its income statement).

    (b) In each period for which it presents a balance sheet: (1) for amortized intangibles, the cost, accumulated amortization, amortization expense, and estimated amortization expense for the next 5 years; (2) for non-amortized intangibles, the total cost and cost of each major intangible asset class; (3) for goodwill, the amount acquired, amount of any recognized impairment loss, and amount included in the disposal of a reporting unit; and (4) for any intangible asset impairment, the reason, the amount of the impairment loss, and the method of determining the fair value.

Conceptual Evaluation and International Differences

29. Several aspects of accounting for intangibles appear to be inconsistent. First, the requirement that a company expense any purchased R&D costs in an acquisition of another company is inconsistent with the general rule that items purchased are assets. Second, purchased goodwill is recorded as an asset, while internally developed goodwill is expensed. Third, some intangible assets are amortized while other intangible assets are not.

30. International accounting standards require that goodwill be amortized over a maximum period of 20 years, unless there is evidence of a longer life. Also, international accounting standards allow intangible assets to be revalued upward, and allow some internally generated intangibles to be recorded as assets.

Appendix: Estimating the Value of Goodwill

31. From an income perspective, goodwill may be defined as the value attached to a company's ability to earn a higher than normal rate of return (an excess rate of return) on the market value of its identifiable net assets.

32. During purchase negotiations, the price offered for a company is typically much greater than the book value of its net assets. Three factors can account for that difference: (a) Identifiable net assets are generally listed on the balance sheet at their historical costs, which may differ greatly from their current fair values; (b) Identifiable intangibles may be unrecorded or undervalued; and (c) Unidentifiable intangibles (goodwill) may exist.

33. Six steps may be used in estimating the value of the goodwill of a company considered for possible acquisition: (a) estimating the average future annual earnings from the identifiable net assets, (b) estimating the rate (or rates) of return that should be earned by the company on its identifiable net assets, (c) estimating the current fair value of the identifiable net assets, (d) computing the estimated excess annual earnings, (e) estimating the expected life of the excess annual earnings, and (f) computing the present value of the estimated excess annual earnings. In addition, the total value of the company considered for purchase may be computed, and sensitivity analysis may be performed on the estimates. Sensitivity analysis involves calculating the change in the estimated value of the company under consideration resulting from changes in values of the items used in the estimates. Thus, management may be provided with both a value based on best estimates and a range of values in case those estimates are in error.

34. Estimating the average future annual earnings from the identifiable net assets is very difficult. An alternative is to base the prediction of future earnings on the earnings of recent years, with adjustments for nonrecurring items and for operating and competitive changes that can be predicted reliably.

35. The rate of return that a company should earn on its identifiable net assets is influenced by the risk of the investment and by available alternative investments. Published average rates of return on book value are available, but the published rates may need adjustments for the use of the fair value of assets. The effects of the company's accounting methods must also be considered.

36. Because accounting records are based on historical cost, the book value of a company's net assets is likely to differ from the current fair value. For example, the book value of property, plant, and equipment commonly needs significant adjustments to approximate current fair value. When the LIFO inventory method is used in a period of rising prices, the inventory book value is lower than fair value.

37. The estimated excess annual earnings are calculated by multiplying the normal rate of return by the fair value of the net identifiable assets and subtracting this amount from the estimated average future annual earnings.

38. The excess annual earnings attributable to goodwill existing at the time of purchase have a limited life, which must be estimated.

39. The present value of the estimated excess annual earnings is usually computed by discounting the earnings at the normal rate of return for their estimated life. As an alternative, a higher discount rate may be used to reflect higher risk.

40. Knowledge of goodwill is an important element in the negotiation process to determine the actual purchase price of a company being considered for acquisition. The amount paid for goodwill, however, is determined solely by the parties involved and is not defined by GAAP.

SELF-EVALUATION EXERCISES

Supply the words necessary to complete each of the following items.

Nature of and Accounting for Intangible Assets

NA-1. Intangible assets generally result from ____________ or ________________ rights.

NA-2. Both tangible and intangible assets are initially recorded at ______________.

NA-3. The costs of purchased identifiable intangible assets are ______________________.

NA-4. The costs of internally developed unidentifiable intangibles are _____________.

NA-5. A capitalized intangible asset with a finite life is amortized over its ____________ __________.

NA-6. The amortization method for an intangible asset with a finite life is selected based on the asset's ___________ _______ _______________.

NA-7. At least annually, a company reviews assets with indefinite lives for __________________.

Research and Development Costs

RD-1. *FASB Statement No. 2* requires that all research and development costs be __________ ________ ______________.

RD-2. According to the FASB, uniform expensing of research and development costs enhances ____________________.

RD-3. The costs of any research and development materials, equipment, facilities, and intangibles which are purchased from others and have no ____________ __________ ________ should be included in R&D expense as incurred.

Identifiable Intangible Assets

II-1. A ____________ granted by the federal government gives the owner control of the use of an invention for ________ years.

II-2. A ____________ granted by the federal government gives the owner control of literary or artistic products for the life of the author plus 70 years.

II-3. A company may obtain the right to exclusive use of a name or symbol by registering a ____________ or ________________.

II-4. Rights to perform certain functions or to sell certain products or services are conveyed under a _____________ agreement.

II-5. According to *AICPA Statement of Position No. 98-5* the costs of start-up activities, including organization costs, are ____________ ______ ________________.

II-6. The design, coding, and testing of software developed to be marketed are treated as research and development expenses until the ____________ _____________ of the product is established.

II-7. After the date of general release of software developed for external use all software production costs are ____________ _____ ________________.

II-8. Maintenance and customer support costs for externally released software are ____________ ______ _______________.

II-9. Costs incurred in the preliminary stages of development of internal-use software are ______________ _____ ______________.

II-10. Although capital leases are actually intangible assets to the lessee, they are normally included in __________, ________, ____ ____________.

II-11. Deferred charges, which are often placed in a catch-all category on the balance sheet, should be amortized over their ____________ ________________ __________.

Unidentifiable Intangibles

UI-1. Superior employees and advantageous geographical location are examples of __________________ _______________ goodwill.

UI-2. The difference between the purchase price of an acquired company as a whole and the fair value of its identifiable net assets is ___________ ___________.

UI-3. At least annually a company must review its goodwill for ____________.

UI-4. When the price paid for a company is less than the fair value of the company's net assets, _____________ ______________ exists.

Disclosure of Intangibles

DI-1. FASB Statement No. 142 requires the following disclosures on a company's balance sheet regarding amortized intangibles: ______, _____________ _____________, _____________ expense, and estimated amortization expense for the next 5 years.

Conceptual Evaluation and International Differences

CE-1. Purchased goodwill is recorded as an _________ , while internally developed goodwill is _______________.

CE-2. International accounting standards _______ (allow, do not allow) intangible assets to be revalued upward.

Appendix: Estimating the Value of Goodwill

EV-1. Goodwill may be defined from an income perspective as the value resulting from a company's ability to ______________________ ______________________ on ______________________.

EV-2. When estimating the value of goodwill a range of values, in addition to the best estimate, may be computed using ______________ ________.

EV-3. The amount paid for goodwill ________ (is, is not) defined by GAAP.

ANSWERS TO SELF-EVALUATION EXERCISES

NA-1. legal, contractual; NA-2. cost; NA-3. capitalized; NA-4. expensed; NA-5. useful life; NA-6. pattern of benefits; NA-7. impairment; RD-1. expensed as incurred; RD-2. comparability; RD-3. alternative future uses; II-1. patent, 20; II-2. copyright; II-3. tradename, trademark; II-4. franchise; II-5. expensed as incurred; II-6. technological feasibility; II-7. expensed as incurred; II-8. expensed as incurred; II-9. expensed as incurred; II-10. property, plant, and equipment; II-11. expected economic lives; UI-1. internally developed; UI-2. purchased goodwill; UI-3. impairment; UI-4. negative goodwill; DI-1. cost, accumulated amortization, amortization; CE-1. asset, expensed; CE-2. allow; EV-1. earn a higher than normal rate of return, the market value of its identifiable net assets; EV-2. sensitivity analysis; EV-3. is not.

POST TEST

Part A Circle T if the statement is true and F if it is false.

T F 1. Similar principles for determination of acquisition costs, impairment, and disposal apply to both tangible and intangible assets.

T F 2. Companies capitalize the costs of purchased identifiable intangible assets.

T F 3. Companies capitalize the costs of purchased unidentifiable intangible assets.

T F 4. Companies capitalize the costs of internally developed unidentifiable intangible assets.

T F 5. In general companies capitalize the costs associated with internally developed identifiable intangible assets.

T F 6. Intangible assets with an indefinite life are reviewed at least annually for impairment.

T F 7. FASB Statement No. 2 requires companies to capitalize all research and development costs.

T F 8. The value of capitalized goodwill is determined by the purchase price of the acquired company.

T F 9. A company includes the cost of purchased R&D materials and intangibles with no alternative future uses in research and development expense on the current income statement.

T F 10. Intangible assets with an indefinite life are amortized using the straight-line method over a period not to exceed 20 years.

T F 11. A company records negative goodwill on the balance sheet as a noncurrent liability.

T F 12. The amount recorded for purchased goodwill is determined reliably by statistical techniques.

T F 13. A company capitalizes the costs incurred in developing an invention at the time it is granted a patent.

T F 14. Intangible assets which appear to have an indefinite life are expensed when they are acquired.

T F 15. The straight-line method is always used for the amortization of capitalized intangibles.

T F 16. Up until the time a software product is released for sale, all production costs are capitalized, to be amortized over the expected life of the product.

T F 17. Like tangible assets, intangibles are initially recorded at cost.

T F 18. When estimating the value of goodwill, the product of the normal rate of return and the fair value of the net identifiable assets is subtracted from the estimated average future annual earnings to calculate the estimated excess annual earnings.

T F 19. The unit costs of producing software for general release are recorded as inventory.

T F 20. A franchisee capitalizes continuing franchise fees and amortizes the fees over the useful life of the franchise.

T F 21. When an infringement lawsuit is lost by the company owning a patent, all legal fees and the remaining book value of the patent are expensed.

T F 22. An impairment loss on an intangible asset with a finite life is amortized over the useful life of the asset.

T F 23. International accounting standards require that development costs be expensed.

Part B Select the one <u>best</u> answer, and place its letter in the space provided.

_____ 1. Which of the following is <u>not</u> a characteristic distinguishing intangible assets from tangible assets? (a) the value of intangibles fluctuates less from competitive conditions; (b) there is generally greater uncertainty regarding expected future benefits of intangibles; (c) intangibles may have value only to a particular company; (d) goodwill and intangible assets with indefinite lives are not expensed.

_____ 2. Which of the following methods of accounting for research and development costs is required in <u>FASB Statement No. 2</u>? (a) capitalizing all costs as incurred; (b) capitalizing some costs and expensing other costs; (c) accumulating all costs until the existence of future benefits is determined; (d) expensing all costs as incurred.

_____ 3. Which of the following statements about goodwill is <u>not</u> correct? (a) components may include superiority of employees and advantageous geographical position; (b) companies capitalize purchased goodwill but expense the costs of internally developed goodwill as they are incurred; (c) internally developed goodwill is periodically evaluated and capitalized; (d) measurement of goodwill is less reliable than measurement of identifiable intangibles.

_____ 4. Which of the following statements is <u>not</u> correct? (a) international accounting standards allow the capitalization of development costs; (b) international accounting standards require that goodwill be amortized over a maximum period of 40 years; (c) international accounting standards allow intangible assets to be revalued upward; (d) international accounting standards allow some internally generated intangibles to be recorded as assets.

_____ 5. Which of the following is <u>not</u> an advantage of the policy of expensing all research and development costs as incurred? (a) expensing enhances comparability; (b) expensing lessens the possibility of income manipulation; (c) expensing avoids the problem of estimating the amortization period; (d) expensing appropriately matches the research and development costs to revenues produced.

_____ 6. Which of the following costs of research and development activities should <u>not</u> be expensed? (a) costs of intangibles purchased from others; (b) costs of contract services; (c) costs of externally purchased assets with alternative future uses; (d) a reasonable allocation of indirect costs.

_____ 7. Which of the following may be a component of a company's goodwill? (a) the value of leasehold improvements; (b) the value of the company's trademark; (c) the value of the company's inventory; (d) the value of a favorable location.

_____ 8. Which of the following costs should a company expense as incurred? (a) the costs of purchased identifiable intangible assets; (b) the costs of internally developed unidentifiable intangible assets; (c) the costs of purchased unidentifiable intangible assets; (d) the costs, other than R&D costs, associated with internally developed identifiable intangible assets.

_____ 9. Capitalized intangible assets (a) are amortized if the assets appear to have potentially indefinite lives; (b) are always amortized using the straight-line method; (c) considered impaired if their carrying values are less than their fair values; (d) are reviewed for impairment, rather than amortized, if their useful lives appear to be indefinite.

_____ 10. Which of the following statements related to computer software costs is correct? (a) production costs of software developed for sale are included in R&D expenses until the technological feasibility of the product is established; (b) costs incurred during the preliminary stage of development of software intended for internal use are capitalized; (c) production costs of software developed for sale incurred between the times of technological feasibility and general release are expensed; (d) after the date of technological feasibility all software production costs of software developed for sale are expensed as incurred.

Part C Solve each of the following short problems.

1. The Grimes Company was organized on January 1, 2004. At December 31, 2004, the company had the following intangible assets on its balance sheet:

(1)	Patent (purchased January 1, 2004)	$28,900
(2)	Copyright (purchased July 1, 2004) with an estimated useful life of 10 years	20,000
(3)	Trademark (purchased January 1, 2004) with an indefinite life	6,400
(4)	Goodwill (acquired January 2, 2004 with purchase of the Golden Company)	9,600
(5)	Initial franchise fee paid (payment made January 1, 2004 to cover 5-year franchise period)	8,500

The company spent $45,000 on research and development during 2004, including $20,000 for a machine, purchased on January 1, which will be used in various research and development projects over the next 5 years. The company uses the maximum allowable amortization periods. Prepare journal entries to record amortization and depreciation expense for 2004.

2. According to generally accepted accounting principles, some costs associated with intangible assets are initially capitalized, while other costs are expensed as incurred. Indicate how each of the costs listed below should be recorded by placing a C (capitalized) or an E (expensed) in the space provided.

_____ 1. cost of a machine purchased for temporary use in research and development, then subsequent use in production of a product.

_____ 2. unit costs of producing software.

_____ 3. cost of goodwill recorded on purchase of a subsidiary.

_____ 4. costs of development of a product now in production.

_____ 5. costs of design, coding, and testing of software developed for sale during the period prior to technological feasibility.

_____ 6. cost of a purchased patent.

_____ 7. cost of initial franchise fee paid by franchisee.

_____ 8. underwriting costs and accounting fees incurred during organization of the corporation.

_____ 9. cost of employee training and product design.

_____ 10. payments for contract services related to R&D.

_____ 11. legal fees paid for unsuccessful attempt to defend a patent against infringement.

_____ 12. software production costs after the date of general release.

_____ 13. costs associated with internal development of goodwill.

_____ 14. legal costs of applying for an internally developed trademark.

_____ 15. payments of continuing franchise fees by franchisee.

3. Investors are considering the purchase of the Wizard Company. They have compiled the following data about Wizard:

Book value of net assets	$ 975,000
Fair value of recorded net assets	1,050,000
Fair value of internally developed (unrecorded) patent	10,000
Fair value of fully depreciated buildings	200,000
Average annual earnings	120,800
Industry average earnings	100,800
Present value factor for annuity of 10 periods at 10%: 6.144567	

(1) It is estimated that excess earnings will continue for 10 years. The investors are willing to pay the current market price of identifiable net assets plus goodwill equal to the present value at 10% of excess earnings. Compute (a) the purchase price, and (b) goodwill.

(2) It is assumed that the Wizard Company will earn $120,800 in perpetuity, and that the normal industry return is 8% of identifiable net assets. Compute (a) the purchase price, and (b) goodwill.

ANSWERS TO POST TEST

Part A

1. T
2. T
3. T
4. F
5. T
6. T
7. F
8. T
9. T
10. F
11. F
12. F
13. F
14. F
15. F
16. F
17. T
18. T
19. T
20. F
21. T
22. F
23. F

Part B

1. a
2. d
3. c
4. b
5. d
6. c
7. d
8. b
9. d
10. a

Part C

1. Amortization Expense 5,145

Amortization Expense	5,145	
Patent ($28,900 ÷ 20)		1,445
Copyright ($20,000 ÷ 10)		2,000
Initial Franchise Fee ($8,500 ÷ 5)		1,700
To record amortization of intangible assets.		
Depreciation Expense	4,000	
Accumulated Depreciation - Machinery		4,000
To record depreciation of machine with alternative future uses.		

The trademark and the goodwill are not amortized. Instead, they are reviewed for impairment at least annually.

2.

1. C	5. E	9. E	13. E
2. E	6. C	10. E	14. C
3. C	7. C	11. E	15. E
4. E	8. E	12. E	

3. (1) (a) $1,382,891 [$1,050,000 + $10,000 + $200,000 + ($20,000 x 6.144567)]
   (b) $122,891 [$1,382,891 - ($1,050,000 + $10,000 + $200,000)]
   (2) (a) $1,510,000 [$120,800/0.08]
   (b) $250,000 [$1,510,000 - ($1,050,000 + $10,000 + $200,000)]

12

CURRENT LIABILITIES AND CONTINGENCIES

CHAPTER OBJECTIVES

After careful study of this chapter, you will be able to:

1. Explain the characteristics of a liability.
2. Define current liabilities.
3. Account for compensated absences.
4. Understand and record payroll taxes and deductions.
5. Record property taxes.
6. Account for warranty costs.
7. Explain the terms "probable," "reasonably possible," and "remote" related to contingencies.
8. Record and report a loss contingency.
9. Disclose a gain contingency.

SYNOPSIS

Conceptual Overview of Liabilities

1. In its Conceptual Framework, the FASB defined liabilities as probable future sacrifices of economic benefits arising from present obligations of a company to transfer assets or provide services to other entities in the future as a result of past transactions or events.

2. Liabilities include both legal and nonlegal (but not illegal) obligations. Legal liabilities, such as accounts payable, notes payable, and sales taxes payable, arise from contractual transactions. Consequently, the company is legally required to pay cash or provide goods or services. With nonlegal liabilities (accounting liabilities) payments are expected as part of the company's normal operations, even though they are not legally required.

3. There are three essential characteristics of a liability for a company:

   (a) A liability involves a present obligation that will be settled by a probable future transfer or use of assets at a specified or determinable date, on occurrence of a specified event, or on demand.

   (b) The obligated company is left little or no discretion to avoid the future sacrifice.

   (c) The transaction or other event obligating the company has already happened.

4. Two other points are made about liabilities:

   (a) The obligated company does not need to know the identity of the recipient to record a liability, as long as a transfer of assets to settle an existing obligation is probable.

   (b) If the company has a duty or responsibility to pay cash, transfer assets, or provide services, the obligation need not be legally enforceable to qualify as a liability.

Nature and Definition of Current Liabilities

5. Current liabilities are obligations whose liquidation is expected to require the use of existing current assets or the creation of other current liabilities within one year or an operating cycle, whichever is longer. An operating cycle is the time normally required for a company to convert cash into inventory, sell the inventory, and collect the resulting receivables.

6. Information about liquidity (how quickly a liability can be paid, or its nearness to cash) is important to users because in part the prediction of future cash flows is based on the nearness to cash of liabilities and assets. The FASB discussed alternative methods of reporting liquidity and examined useful liquidity ratios. The AICPA Special Committee on Financial Reporting stated that a company should identify internal and external sources of liquidity and significant unused sources of liquid assets in its MD&A.

7. <u>Financial flexibility</u> refers to a company's ability to use its financial resources to adapt to change. Financial flexibility primarily involves the management of cash and other resources. In addition, it includes the potential to create new current and long-term liabilities, to restructure existing debt, and to manage debt in other ways.

8. The primary types of current liabilities are classified into three groups in the text: (a) current liabilities having a contractual amount; (b) current liabilities whose amounts depend on operations; and (c) current liabilities requiring amounts to be estimated.

9. Conceptually, a company should record all liabilities at the present value of the future outlays they will require, and should disclose the liabilities in a way that provides useful information about their liquidity. However, most current liabilities are measured, recorded, and reported at their maturity or face value. Usually the difference between maturity value and present value is not material.

Current Liabilities Having a Contractual Amount

10. Because of the terms of contracts or the existence of laws, the amount and maturity of some current liabilities are known with reasonable certainty. Examples include trade accounts payable, notes payable, currently maturing portions of long-term debt, dividends payable, advances and refundable deposits, accrued liabilities, and unearned items.

11. <u>Trade accounts payable</u> arise from the purchase of inventory, supplies, or services on an open charge-account basis. The amount to be recorded is based on the invoice received from the creditor. Theoretically, a company should record a liability net of any cash discount. However, in practice, companies record liabilities in two ways: using the <u>gross price method</u> (at the invoice price) or using the <u>net price method</u> (at the invoice price less the cash discount). Care must be taken that end-of-year purchases and liabilities are recorded in the proper accounting period, when economic control of (and legal title to) the goods passes.

12. A <u>note payable</u>, which may be either long-term or short-term, is an unconditional written agreement to pay a sum of money to the bearer on a specific date. Notes arise out of either trade situations (the purchase of goods or services on credit) or bank borrowings. The interest for a note payable may be either stated or implied in different ways. When a note is <u>interest bearing</u>, the principal amount (face value) recorded is the present value of the liability. The company records interest expense over the life of the note by applying the stated interest rate to the face value. When a note is <u>non-interest-bearing</u>, it is made out for the maturity value and discounted, and the borrower receives less than the face amount. The company systematically recognizes the difference between the face amount and the amount received (the interest element or <u>discount</u>) as interest expense over the life of the note. The company shows the discount currently remaining on its balance sheet as a contra account to Notes Payable in order to report the net amount of the current liquidation value.

13. The <u>currently maturing portion of long-term debt</u> includes (a) any long-term debt whose retirement will require the use of current assets in the following year, and (b) the currently maturing installments of serial bonds.

14. <u>Dividends payable</u> in cash, property, or scrip are current liabilities when declared by the board of directors if there is an intention to distribute the dividends within one year or operating cycle. However, companies do <u>not</u> report two types of dividends as current liabilities: (a) <u>stock dividends</u> to be issued (payable in the corporation's

own stock), which are reported as an element of stockholders' equity, and (b) undeclared dividends in arrears on cumulative preferred stock, which are not reported as liabilities until they are formally declared by the board of directors (although they are disclosed in the notes to the financial statements).

15. Advances and refundable deposits are required by many companies (for example, utilities) to guarantee payment for equipment or future services provided to customers. Since these payments are either refundable or later offset against trade accounts receivable, they are liabilities.

16. Accrued liabilities, most of which are current liabilities, represent obligations that accumulate systematically over time. Often, for convenience, companies record these liabilities and their associated expenses at the end of the period. Accounting for several specific types of accrued liabilities is discussed in the chapter:

    (a) Employees' compensated absences include vacation, holiday, illness, or other personal activities for which employees are paid. A company recognizes an expense and accrues a liability for such absences if all of the following conditions are met: (1) the company's obligation to compensate for future absences is related to past services by the employee; (2) the obligation relates to rights that vest or accumulate; (3) payment of compensation is probable; and (4) the amount can be reasonably estimated. A vested right exists when an employer has an obligation to make payment to an employee. Accumulated rights can be carried forward by the employee to future periods if they are not used in the period when earned.

    The most common compensated absence is vacation time, which a company recognizes as an expense and accrues as a liability, allowing for the vacation rights not expected to be exercised. Sick pay is treated differently than vacation pay. If the sick pay benefits unused at the end of the period are vested, the company recognizes an expense and records an accrued liability. If sick pay benefits accumulate, but do not vest, recognition and accrual are optional.

    (b) FASB Statement No. 47 requires specified disclosures in the notes to the financial statements regarding certain unconditional purchase obligations (a type of "off-balance-sheet financing"), regardless of whether the obligations and related assets are reported on the balance sheet. Such obligations require future transfers of funds for fixed or minimum amounts or quantities of goods or services at fixed or minimum prices.

    (c) FASB Statement No. 107 requires a company to disclose the fair value of all its financial instruments, either in the body of the financial statements or in the notes. FASB Statement No. 133 requires a company to recognize as liabilities any "derivative" financial instruments that are obligations and to disclose information about all its derivative instruments.

    (d) In a product financing arrangement (a type of "off-balance-sheet financing"), a company "sells" inventory and agrees to repurchase it at a specified price. The company keeps the inventory on its balance sheet and does not record such a transaction as a sale. However, it records a liability for the proceeds received. When a company has another entity purchase products on its behalf, the company records the asset and related liability.

17. Unearned items (sometimes called deferred revenues) are amounts which a company has collected in advance but has not earned or recorded as revenues. Unearned items should be properly classified as current or long-term liabilities. Examples include advance

collections of interest, rent, subscriptions, or tickets. Such items are current unless more than one year (or one operating cycle, if longer) is required in the earning process, or if noncurrent assets primarily are used to earn the revenue.

Current Liabilities Whose Amounts Depend on Operations

18. A sales tax is levied on the transfer of tangible personal property and on certain services. A seller collects sales tax from the customer and remits it to the proper governmental authority, usually monthly. Typically, the amount collected is recorded as a current liability until paid. Some businesses, however, include sales taxes in the price of merchandise and credit the Sales account for the sum of the sales amount and sales taxes payable. In this case the company must make an adjusting entry when the remittance is due, to reduce the Sales account and create a current liability for sales taxes payable.

19. A use tax is levied by a state or local government on the buyer of merchandise purchased for the buyer's own use or consumption, when goods are bought in a nonsales-tax area. A use tax is a liability of the buyer, who must file a use tax return and remit the tax.

20. Payroll taxes are paid by both the company (employer) and employee. Taxes withheld from employees' pay include federal and state (and sometimes local) income taxes payable by the employee, and the employee's social security (Federal Insurance Contribution Act or F.I.C.A.) taxes. Such withholdings are current liabilities of the employer until remitted. In addition, the employer must also pay taxes based on payroll, including employer's social security and unemployment insurance taxes. Employer payroll taxes are an expense and a liability. Voluntary payroll deductions may also be made, through contractual agreement between individual employees and their employer. Examples include deductions for insurance, union dues, and retirement annuities.

21. F.I.C.A. taxes consist of two items: the tax used for paying federal old-age, survivor, and disability insurance, and the tax used for paying federal hospital insurance (Medicare) benefits. In 2002, the F.I.C.A. tax rate was 15.30% on the first $84,900 earned by the employee and 2.90% on any additional amount. One-half of F.I.C.A. taxes is paid by the employer and one-half by the employee. Congress has changed the F.I.C.A. tax rates and wage base repeatedly.

22. Typical payroll journal entries using an assumed F.I.C.A. rate of 16% (8% on the employer and 8% on the employee) follow:

    (a) To record salaries and employee withholding items:

Salaries Expense	10,000	
F.I.C.A. Taxes Payable		800
Employee Federal Income Taxes Withholding Payable		730
Employee State Income Taxes Withholding Payable		300
Employee Insurance Premium Withholding Payable		100
Cash		8,070

(b) To record employer payroll taxes:

Payroll Taxes Expense	1,150	
F.I.C.A. Taxes Payable		800
Federal Unemployment Taxes Payable		80
State Unemployment Taxes Payable		270

23. Companies are subject to federal, state, and sometimes foreign income taxes. Companies report the various payables resulting from payroll as current liabilities. The journal entry to accrue income taxes payable is a debit to Income Tax Expense and a credit to Income Taxes Payable, a current liability. If prepayment of taxes is required, the company debits Prepaid Income Taxes and makes an adjustment to the expense, liability, and prepaid accounts when the actual liability for taxes is determined.

24. Bonuses may be given to certain employees, particularly officers and managers, as incentives. As additional salaries, bonuses are an operating expense of the corporation and are deductible in computing taxable income. A company records a bonus obligation as an expense and a current liability when it has been earned by the employee and is pending payment. Typically, bonus plans base the bonus amount on either (a) the corporation's income after deducting income taxes but before deducting the bonus, or (b) the corporation's net income after deducting both income taxes and the bonus. In both cases, the bonus is computed using two simple simultaneous equations, and income tax cannot be determined until the bonus has been calculated.

Current Liabilities Requiring Amounts to Be Estimated

25. Property taxes are assessed by local (and some state) governments on the value of property as of a given date. They become a legal liability on the date, specified by law, when a lien arises against the property. The Committee on Accounting Procedure recommended equal monthly accrual of property taxes. A company calculates the estimated property tax accrued by applying the estimated rate to the assessed valuation. Any difference between actual and estimated property taxes is, according to APB Opinion No. 20, accounted for prospectively.

26. Product warranties require the seller, for a specified period of time after the sale, to correct deficiencies in the quality, quantity, or performance of merchandise, or replace items, or refund the selling price. Theoretically, the matching principle requires that companies estimate and record warranty expense and warranty obligation in the period of the sale. However, in practice other methods are also used to account for warranty costs:

    (1) The expense warranty accrual method is the theoretically correct method. A company using this method recognizes estimated warranty expense and warranty liability in the period of sale, with the warranty liability divided into current and long-term portions. Typical journal entries for the expense warranty accrual method follow:

        (a) To record sales for the period:

Cash or Accounts Receivable	10,000,000	
Sales		10,000,000

(b) To recognize warranty expense associated with sales for the period:

Warranty Expense	250,000	
Estimated Liability Under Warranties		250,000

(c) To record payment or incurrence of warranty costs:

Estimated Liability Under Warranties	50,000	
Cash (or other assets)		50,000

(2) Many companies sell "service contracts," which require customers to make fixed payments for future services. Even when there is no separate service contract, the sales price may have two components - the price of the product and the price of an implied warranty. The sales warranty accrual method separates accounting for these two components even when no separate service contract is involved. Typical journal entries for the sales warranty accrual method follow:

(a) To record sales of products and warranties for the period:

Cash or Accounts Receivable	10,000,000	
Sales		9,750,000
Unearned Warranty Revenue		250,000

(b) To recognize warranty expense:

Warranty Expense	50,000	
Cash (or other assets)		50,000

(c) To recognize warranty revenue in an amount equal to warranty costs incurred:

Unearned Warranty Revenue	50,000	
Warranty Revenue		50,000

Note that a cost recovery approach to revenue recognition is used, with a company assuming that revenue from an implied warranty contract equals the estimated warranty costs.

(3) Under the modified cash basis, a company records warranty costs as an expense during the period when warranty expenditures are made. This method is required for income tax reporting. It is also often used for financial reporting, although it is conceptually unsound because it violates the matching principle.

27. Many companies offer premiums, such as toys, for product purchases, or cash coupons reducing or refunding purchase prices. A company matches the costs of such sales incentives as expenses against revenues in the period of the sale. At the end of the period, estimates of outstanding offers that will be redeemed within the next year (or operating cycle, if longer) are reported as current liabilities.

28. Direct-response advertising is advertising that is expected to produce sales resulting from customers' specific responses to the advertising. The specific responses must be documented, for example, by coded coupons or coded order forms. A company capitalizes the following costs of direct-response advertising and amortizes them as advertising

expense over the period of expected benefits, if the company provides evidence (e.g., historical patterns) that they will result in future net revenues: (a) incremental direct costs of transactions with independent third parties; and (b) payroll costs for employee activities directly related to the advertising. Costs of administration and occupancy are not capitalized.

Contingencies

29. According to FASB Statement No. 5, a contingency is an existing condition, situation, or set of circumstances involving uncertainty that will ultimately be resolved when one or more events occur or fail to occur. This definition has three primary characteristics: (a) an existing condition, (b) uncertainty as to the ultimate effect of this condition, and (c) the resolution of the uncertainty based on one or more future events.

30. The FASB used three terms describing the likelihood that a loss contingency will be confirmed: (a) probable - the future event (or events) is likely to occur, (b) reasonably possible - the chance of the future event occurring is more than remote but less than likely, (c) remote - the chance of the future event occurring is slight.

31. A company accrues an estimated loss from a loss contingency in its accounts and reports the loss in its financial statements as a reduction of income and as a liability (or reduction of an asset) if (a) it is probable that a loss has occurred, and that a future event or events will confirm the loss, and (b) the amount of the loss can be reasonably estimated. It is not necessary to know the exact payee or the exact date of payment. If the two conditions have not been met, but it is reasonably possible that a loss may have been incurred, the company must disclose that loss contingency in a note to its financial statements. Disclosure must indicate the nature of the contingency and give an estimate of the possible loss or range of loss, or state that such an estimate cannot be made. Certain contingencies where the possibility of loss is only remote are also disclosed in the notes to the financial statements.

32. Loss contingencies which companies usually accrue include uncollectible receivables, and obligations related to property taxes, product warranties, and premium offers. Loss contingencies which may be accrued if they meet the two conditions include the threat of expropriation of assets, pending or threatened litigation, actual or possible claims and assessments, guarantees of indebtedness of others, and agreements to repurchase receivables. Loss contingencies which are usually not accrued include uninsured risk of loss or damage from fire or other hazards, general or unspecified business risks, and risk of loss from catastrophes assumed by property and casualty insurance companies. Pending lawsuits should be analyzed to decide on accrual or note disclosure.

33. Following the convention of conservatism, and the revenue recognition criteria, gain contingencies usually are not accrued. Instead, they are disclosed in the notes to the company's financial statements.

34. In an executory contract (unexecuted contract), two parties agree to a future exchange of resources or services, but neither party has performed its responsibilities. A company discloses an executory contract with a likely material impact on future cash flows in a note to its financial statements.

Short-term Debt Expected to be Refinanced and Classification of Obligations That Are Callable by the Creditor

35. The classification of debt as short-term affects liquidity ratios such as current and acid-test ratios. In FASB Statement No. 6, the FASB issued guidelines on reporting short-term debt expected to be refinanced. Short-term obligations are excluded from a company's current liabilities if (a) the company intends to refinance on a long-term basis, and (b) the company has the ability to refinance. The ability to refinance must be demonstrated by either (a) the issue of long-term obligations or equity securities after the balance-sheet date but before issuance of the statements, or (b) a bona fide long-term financing agreement entered into before the balance sheet date.

36. FASB Statement No. 78 requires that a company classify the entire amount of a long-term obligation as a current liability if a violation of a provision of the debt agreement makes (or will make if the violation is not corrected) the liability callable within one year from the balance sheet date or within one operating cycle. This requirement does not conform to the definition of current liabilities. It classifies obligations as current when they are legally callable, even though liquidation may not be expected during the current period.

Financial Statement Presentation of Current Liabilities

37. The FASB has provided broad, rather than specific, guidelines for the presentation of assets and liabilities on the balance sheet. Reporting of assets and liabilities should highlight the company's liquidity and financial flexibility, and assets and liabilities measured by different attributes (e.g., historical cost, current cost, etc.) should be reported in separate categories. Most companies present current liabilities as the first classification under "Liabilities." Companies usually list current liabilities in order of the average length of maturities, or according to amount (largest to smallest), or in order of liquidation preference (the order of legal claims against assets).

38. A company includes a description of all significant accounting policies as an integral part of its financial statements. Any major issue of significance affecting the measurement or disclosure of current liabilities is included in the notes to the financial statements. Other notes and other supplemental information regarding current liabilities are included when necessary for full disclosure.

SELF-EVALUATION EXERCISES

Supply the words necessary to complete each of the following items.

Conceptual Overview of Liabilities

CO-1. Liabilities are defined as probable __________ ______________ of economic benefits arising from ____________ ______________ of a company to transfer assets or provide services to other entities in the future as a result of _______ transactions or events.

CO-2. Liabilities include both __________ and ______________ obligations.

CO-3. For a liability to be recorded, the identity of the recipient

_________ (must, need not) be known.

Nature and Definition of Current Liabilities

ND-1. A current liability is an obligation whose liquidation is expected to require the use of existing current assets or the creation of other current liabilities

within ________ ____________ or an ______________ ___________, whichever is

_____________.

ND-2. The time normally needed to convert cash into inventory, sell the inventory, and

collect the resulting receivables is an ___________ ___________.

ND-3. Liquidity is the _____________ ______ __________ of assets and liabilities.

ND-4. A company's ability to use its financial resources to adapt to

change is referred to as _____________ _________________.

ND-5. Conceptually, companies should record all liabilities at the

____________ __________ of the future outlays they will require.

Current Liabilities Having a Contractual Amount

CL-1. Open-charge purchases of inventory, supplies, or services result in

__________ ___________ _____________.

CL-2. In theory, a company should record trade accounts payable net of any

____________ _____________.

CL-3. A ______ _______________ is an unconditional written promise to pay a sum of money on a specified date.

CL-4. The difference between the face amount (maturity value) of a note with no interest stated and the amount the borrower actually receives is the

____________.

CL-5. Dividends payable in ________, _____________, or ____________ are usually current liabilities when declared.

CL-6. A company reports stock dividends to be issued as an element of

___________________ ___________.

CL-7. Obligations that accumulate systematically over time are ________

________.

CL-8. Vacations, holidays, and illnesses for which employees are paid are

examples of employees' ________ ________.

CL-9. Unconditional purchase obligations and product financing arrangements

are examples of ______-__________-________ financing.

CL-10. In a product financing arrangement, a company "sells" inventory with

an agreement to ________ the inventory at a specified price.

CL-11 Amounts which have been collected in advance, before they have been

earned, are ________ ________.

Current Liabilities Whose Amounts Depend on Operations

CLA-1. When goods are bought in a non-sales tax area, a state or local government

may levy a ______ ______ on the buyer of merchandise for personal use and consumption.

CLA-2. Payroll taxes are paid by both the ________ (________) and

________.

CLA-3. The FICA tax rate in 2002 was ________ on the first $84,900 earned

by the employee and ______ on any additional amount.

CLA-4. Many companies award incentive payments, or ________, to certain employees.

Current Liabilities Requiring Amounts to be Estimated

EC-1. Local (and some state) governments assess ________ ________ on the value of property as of a given date.

EC-2. A seller is required to correct certain deficiencies in merchandise for a

specified period after the sale under a ________ ________.

EC-3. Theoretically, warranty expense and warranty obligation should be estimated and

recorded in the period of the sale as required by the ________ principle.

EC-4. Estimated warranty expense and warranty liability are recognized in the period of the sale using the theoretically correct __________ ______________ ____________ __________.

EC-5. The sales warranty accrual method separates accounting for two components of the sales price - the price of the ____________ and the price of the implied ____________.

EC-6. Under the ____________ __________ __________, warranty costs are debited to expense as expenditures are made.

EC-7. If historical patterns indicate that employee activities directly related to direct-response advertising will result in future revenues, payroll costs for these activities may be ____________.

Contingencies

C-1. A company accrues an estimated loss from a loss contingency if (1) it is ____________ that the loss has occurred, and (2) the amount of the loss can be ____________ ______________.

C-2. If the conditions for accrual of a loss contingency have not been met but the loss contingency is ____________ ______________, the loss contingency is disclosed in a ___________ to the financial statements.

C-3. A company does not accrue a gain contingency, but discloses it instead in a ____________ ___ ____ ___________ ______________, following the convention of ______________.

C-4. An executory contract is disclosed in the notes to the financial statements if it is expected to have a __________ impact.

Short-Term Debt Expected to be Refinanced and Classification of Callable Obligations

S-1. Current and acid-test ratios are examples of ____________ ratios, which are affected by the classification of debt as short-term or long-term.

S-2. Short-term obligations expected to be refinanced must be reported as current liabilities unless the company (1) ________ to refinance on a ________-__________ basis, and (2) has the __________ to refinance.

S-3. When a violation of a debt agreement provision makes a long-term liability callable within one year or operating cycle, the entire amount of the obligation is classified as a ________ __________.

Financial Statement Presentation of Current Liabilities

FS-1. The FASB has stated that the reporting of assets and liabilities should highlight a company's ___________ and ___________ __________.

FS-2. Usually, current liabilities are listed on the balance sheet in order of the average length of ____________, according to ________, or in order of _____________ _________.

FS-3. A description of all ______________ ______________ policies is included as an integral part of the financial statements.

ANSWERS TO SELF-EVALUATION EXERCISES

CO-1. future sacrifices, present obligations, past; CO-2. legal, nonlegal; CO-3. need not; ND-1. one year, operating cycle, longer; ND-2. operating cycle; ND-3. nearness to cash; ND-4. financial flexibility; ND-5. present value; CL-1. trade accounts payable; CL-2. cash discount; CL-3. note payable; CL-4. discount; CL-5. cash, property, scrip; CL-6. stockholders' equity; CL-7. accrued liabilities; CL-8. compensated absences; CL-9. off-balance-sheet; CL-10. repurchase; CL-11. unearned items; CLA-1. use tax; CLA-2. company, employer, employee; CLA-3. 15.30%, 2.90%; CLA-4. bonuses; EC-1. property taxes; EC-2. product warranty; EC-3. matching; EC-4. expense warranty accrual method; EC-5. product, warranty; EC-6. modified cash basis; EC-7. capitalized; C-1. probable, reasonably estimated; C-2. reasonably possible, note; C-3. note to the financial statements, conservatism; C-4. material; S-1. liquidity; S-2. intends, long-term, ability; S-3. current liability; FS-1. liquidity, financial flexibility; FS-2. maturities, amount, liquidation preference; FS-3. significant accounting.

POST TEST

Part A Circle T if the statement is true and F if it is false.

T F 1. Accounts payable, notes payable, and sales tax payable are examples of nonlegal liabilities.

T F 2. A liability may not be recorded until the identity of the recipient is known.

T F 3. When a note is made out for its maturity value and discounted, no interest is stated, but the borrower receives less than the note's face amount.

T F 4. The term "financial flexibility" describes the nearness to cash of a company's assets and liabilities.

T F 5. Stock dividends declared but not yet issued are not reported as current liabilities.

T F 6. A company must recognize dividends in arrears on cumulative preferred stock as liabilities, regardless of whether they have been formally declared.

T F 7. The modified cash basis of accounting for warranty costs is a conceptually sound accounting method.

T F 8. A company may exclude short-term obligations from current liabilities if it can demonstrate the intent and the ability to refinance on a long-term basis.

T F 9. The interest element in a discounted note is recognized by the borrower at the inception of the note.

T F 10. Liabilities are recorded for obligations where payments are expected as part of a company's normal operations, even if payments are not legally required.

T F 11. An unconditional purchase obligation involves a current transfer of funds for a quantity of goods which will be specified at a future date.

T F 12. A use tax, levied by a state or local government when goods are sold in a nonsales tax area, is a liability of the buyer.

T F 13. Accrued liabilities and unearned revenues are examples of "off-balance sheet financing."

T F 14. All payroll taxes are an expense of the employer.

T F 15. According to generally accepted accounting principles, property taxes should be estimated and accrued monthly.

T F 16. A company capitalizes the costs of administration and occupancy related to direct-response advertising if the company has evidence that the costs will result in future net revenues.

T F 17. The principal amount recorded for an interest bearing note is the present value of the liability.

T F 18. A company must disclose unconditional purchase obligations only when it reports the obligations and related assets on the balance sheet.

T F 19. Obligations related to product warranties and premium offers are examples of loss contingencies which are usually accrued.

T F 20. Gain contingencies are not accrued.

T F 21. Conceptually, a company should record all liabilities at the present value of the future outlays that will be required.

T F 22. When an employer is obligated to make a payment to an employee, the employee's right to that payment is "vested."

Part B Select the one <u>best</u> answer, and place its letter in the space provided.

____ 1. Which of the following is <u>not</u> an essential characteristic of a liability? (a) a liability embodies a present obligation to be settled by a probable future transfer or use of assets; (b) the obligated company has little or no discretion to avoid the future sacrifice; (c) the obligation is legally enforceable; (d) the transaction or event obligating the company has already happened.

____ 2. Which of the following dividends are <u>not</u> reported as current liabilities when declared? (a) cash dividends; (b) stock dividends; (c) property dividends; (d) scrip dividends.

____ 3. Which of the following is an example of a nonlegal liability? (a) employee bonuses; (b) accounts payable; (c) notes payable; (d) sales tax payable.

____ 4. An operating cycle (a) is the time normally required to obtain financing and perform operations to ready inventory for sale; (b) is a concept which applies only to a manufacturing company; (c) is defined as one year under generally accepted accounting principles; (d) is the time normally required to convert cash into inventory, sell the inventory, and collect the resulting receivables.

____ 5. Which of the following loss contingencies is <u>not</u> usually accrued? (a) general business risks; (b) noncollectibility of receivables; (c) product warranty obligations; (d) premium offer obligations.

____ 6. Short-term debt expected to be refinanced may be classified as long-term (a) if there is an intent to refinance on a long-term basis; (b) only if long-term obligations are issued before the balance sheet date; (c) if off-balance-sheet financing has been obtained; (d) if there is an intent and the ability to refinance on a long-term basis.

____ 7. The modified cash basis of accounting for warranty costs (a) is seldom used for financial reporting; (b) is based on the matching concept; (c) is conceptually unsound; (d) requires warranty expense and warranty obligation to be estimated and recorded in the period of the sale.

____ 8. Trade accounts payable (a) should, theoretically, be recorded net of any cash discount; (b) are examples of liabilities which must be estimated and accrued; (c) do not include purchases on an open-charge basis; (d) are normally long-term liabilities.

_____ 9. Liquidity (a) refers to an entity's ability to use its financial resources to adapt to change; (b) describes the nearness to cash of a company's assets and liabilities; (c) involves the potential to create new current and long-term debt; (d) involves the potential to restructure existing debt.

_____ 10. Which of the following conditions defines a contingency? (a) a contingency is an existing condition, situation, or set of circumstances; (b) a contingency involves uncertainty; (c) the uncertainty related to a contingency will be resolved by one or more future events; (d) all of the above.

_____ 11. The Rarey Company has reasonably estimated the following probable costs for the compensated absences of its employees:

Vacation pay (vested)	$5,000
Vacation pay (accumulated but not vested)	$3,000
Sick pay (vested)	$4,000
Sick pay (accumulated but not vested)	$2,000

The costs are attributable to services which have already been rendered. In accordance with <u>FASB Statement No. 43</u> the minimum amount that Rarey must accrue as its liability for compensated absences is (a) $5,000; (b) $8,000; (c) $9,000; (d) $14,000; (e) $12,000.

Part C Solve each of the following short problems.

1. The Bitternut Company began operations on January 1, 2004. The company estimates that $0.06 of warranty costs will be incurred for each $1 of sales. In 2004, Bitternut's sales were $100,000, and payments arising out of warranty obligations were $4,000.

   (a) Prepare the December 31 journal entry for warranty expense using the modified cash basis.

   (b) Prepare the December 31 journal entries for warranty expense using the expense warranty accrual method.

(c) Prepare journal entries for the sales and warranties using the sales warranty accrual method.

2. On July 1, 2004, Bitternut issued a 4-year note at a face amount of $20,000. Proceeds of the note were $18,000. No interest was stated.

(a) Prepare journal entries to record the issuance of the note on July 1, and interest expense (using the straight-line method) at December 31, 2004.

(b) Show the balance-sheet presentation of the note at December 31, 2004.

3. The Tiller Company deducted the following amounts from employees' paychecks in August, 2004.

F.I.C.A.	$2,295
Federal income tax	2,121
State income tax	900
Union dues	100
Insurance premiums	300

Tiller pays state unemployment taxes of 5.4% and federal unemployment taxes of 0.8%. Employee paychecks totaled $24,284 in August. Record the payroll journal entries for August.

ANSWERS TO POST TEST

Part A

1. F
2. F
3. T
4. F
5. T
6. F
7. F
8. T
9. F
10. T
11. F
12. T
13. F
14. F
15. T
16. F
17. T
18. F
19. T
20. T
21. T
22. T

Part B

1. c
2. b
3. a
4. d
5. a
6. d
7. c
8. a
9. b
10. d
11. e

Part C

1.	(a)	Warranty Expense Cash To record payment of warranty costs.	4,000	 4,000
1.	(b)	Warranty Expense Estimated Liability Under Warranties To record warranty expense associated with sales for the period.	6,000	 6,000
		Estimated Liability Under Warranties Cash To record payment of warranty costs.	4,000	 4,000

	(c)	Cash (or Accounts Receivable)
		  Sales
		  Unearned Warranty Revenue
		To record sales of products and warranties.
			100,000	
				94,000
				6,000

		Warranty Expense Cash To record warranty expense incurred.	4,000	 4,000
		Unearned Warranty Revenue Warranty Revenue To record warranty revenue in an amount equal to warranty costs incurred.	4,000	 4,000
2.	(a)	Cash Discount on Note Payable Note Payable To record issuance on July 1 of a 4-year note at a face amount of $20,000.	18,000 2,000	 20,000
		Interest Expense [($2,000 ÷ 4) x 2] Discount on Note Payable To record interest on note.	250	 250
	(b)	Note Payable Less Discount on Note Payable	$20,000 (1,750)	 $18,250

3.	Salaries Expense	30,000	
	F.I.C.A. Taxes Payable		2,295
	Employee Federal Income Taxes Withholding Payable		2,121
	Employee State Income Taxes Withholding Payable		900
	Employee Insurance Premiums Withholding Payable		300
	Employee Union Dues Withholding Payable		100
	Cash		24,284
	To record salaries expense.		
	Payroll Taxes Expense	4,155	
	F.I.C.A. Taxes Payable		2,295
	Federal Unemployment Taxes Payable		240
	State Unemployment Taxes Payable		1,620
	To record payroll taxes expense.		

13

LONG-TERM LIABILITIES AND RECEIVABLES

CHAPTER OBJECTIVES

After careful study of this chapter, you will be able to:

1. Explain the reasons for issuing long-term liabilities.
2. Understand the characteristics of bonds payable.
3. Record the issuance of bonds.
4. Amortize discounts and premiums using the straight-line method.
5. Compute the selling price of bonds.
6. Amortize discounts and premiums using the effective interest method.
7. Explain extinguishment of liabilities.
8. Understand bonds with equity characteristics.
9. Account for long-term notes payable.
10. Understand the disclosure of long-term liabilities.
11. Account for long-term notes receivable, including impairment of a loan.
12. Understand troubled debt restructurings (Appendix).
13. Account for serial bonds (Appendix).

SYNOPSIS

Bonds Payable

1. Issuing long-term liabilities is one of the choices available to corporations to obtain financial resources. Companies prefer to issue debt rather than other types of securities for four basic reasons: (a) Debt financing may be the only available source of funds if the company is too risky to attract equity investments; (b) Debt financing may have a lower cost because of the lesser risk associated with debt investments; (c) Debt financing offers an income tax advantage because the interest payments to debt holders are a tax deductible expense for a corporation; (d) The voting privilege of stockholders is not shared with debt holders; and (e) Debt financing offers the opportunity for leverage.

2. Leverage (trading on the equity) refers to a company's use of borrowed funds to increase the return to stockholders. When a company invests borrowed funds, any excess of earnings over the interest to be paid to the debt holders increases the earnings per share of the stockholders.

3. (a) A bond is a type of note in which a company (the issuer) agrees to pay the holder (the lender) the face value at the maturity date and usually to pay periodic interest at a specified rate (the contract rate) on the face value.

   (b) The face (par) value is the amount the issuer agrees to pay at maturity. The face value of a corporate bond is generally $1,000.

   (c) The contract rate (stated, face, or nominal rate) is the annual rate at which the issuer agrees to pay periodic interest until maturity.

   (d) A bond certificate is a legal document which specifies the face value, the annual interest rate, the maturity date, and other characteristics of the bond issue.

   (e) The bond indenture is the contract between the issuing company and the bondholders which defines the rights of the bondholders. Included in the indenture are the characteristics of the bonds in the bond issue as well as any restrictions on the company's financial operations.

4. Companies may issue several types of bonds with different characteristics, such as: (a) debenture bonds which are not secured by specific property; (b) mortgage bonds which are secured by a lien against specific property of the company; (c) registered bonds which require registration of ownership with the company and notification to the company in the event of transfer of ownership for interest to be paid; (d) coupon bonds which are unregistered and which pay interest to the holder presenting a coupon to the company; (e) zero-coupon bonds (deep discount bonds) which pay interest only at maturity; (f) callable bonds which the bondholder can be required by the company to return before the maturity date for a predetermined price and interest to date; (g) convertible bonds which can be exchanged by bondholders for a predetermined number of shares; and (h) serial bonds which are issued at one time but which mature in installments at future dates.

5. The annual amount of interest to be paid on a bond is calculated by multiplying the stated annual rate times the face value. However, when the bonds are sold, the actual rate of interest that must be paid in order to sell the bonds may be different from the contract (stated) rate because of changing market conditions. This actual rate is also called the effective rate, or yield. Rather than change the stated rate which is printed on the bond certificate, the selling price of the bonds is altered to achieve

the demanded yield. If the yield and the contract rate are the same, the bonds are sold at par (their face value). If the yield demanded is greater than the contract rate, the selling price is less than the face value, and the bonds are sold at a discount. If the yield demanded is less than the contract rate, the selling price will be more than the face value, and the bonds are sold at a premium. For example, assume that on January 1, 2004, Nite Corporation sells bonds for $111,652.28 which have a face value of $100,000 and a contract interest rate of 10%. The bonds mature on December 31, 2011, and interest is paid semiannually. The selling price is determined by applying present value techniques to the future maturity value and future interest payments, using the yield rate, which in this case is 8%. The computations are as follows:

Present value of principal	
$100,000 x 0.533908[a]	$ 53,390.80
Present value of interest	
$5,000 x 11.652296[b]	58,261.48
	$111,652.28
Selling price	$111,652.28
Face value	(100,000.00)
Premium	$ 11,652.28

[a]From Present Value of 1 Table (n=16; i=0.04) in Appendix D.

[b]From Present Value of an Ordinary Annuity of 1 Table (n=16; i=0.04) in Appendix D.

The current market (selling) price is usually quoted as a percentage of the face value. For example, a $1,000 bond selling at 102 is selling for 102% of face value, or at $1,020 - that is, at a premium of $20; and a bond quoted at 96 is selling at 96% of face value, or $960 - that is, at a discount of $40.

Recording the Issuance of the Bonds

6. When bonds are sold, the company credits the face value of the bonds to a Bonds Payable account. If the company sells the bonds at a premium, it credits the premium to an account entitled Premium on Bonds Payable, an adjunct account which is shown as an addition to Bonds Payable on the balance sheet. If the company sells the bonds at a discount, it debits the discount to an account entitled Discount on Bonds Payable, a contra account which is shown as a deduction from Bonds Payable on the balance sheet. The book value (carrying value) of a bond issue is the face value plus any unamortized premium or minus any unamortized discount.

7. When the sale of bonds occurs between interest dates, the company usually collects from the investor the interest which has accrued from the last payment date to the date of sale, in addition to the selling price. The amount of accrued interest to be paid is calculated by multiplying the face value by the stated interest rate times the fraction of the year since the last payment date. The company usually credits this amount to Interest Expense on the issuance date. On the next interest payment date, the company pays the bondholders a full six months interest and debits the full amount to Interest Expense. The difference between these two entries is the interest expense that the company will report to date. By accounting for the interest expense and payment in

this manner, the company reduces errors, and where a computerized system is used, a single routine may be developed for recording and distributing all interest payments. Some companies account for the above transactions by crediting Interest Payable for the accrued interest paid at the time of issuance, and then debiting this account for the same amount on the interest payment date.

Amortizing Discounts and Premiums

8. To properly report interest cost, a company's Interest Expense account must reflect an amount based on the effective interest rate and the book value of the bonds. In order to do this, the company must amortize any premium or discount over the life of the bonds. APB Opinion No. 21 requires the use of the effective interest method of amortization but allows the use of the straight-line method when the interest expense which results is not materially different. When using the straight-line method, a company amortizes the premium or discount to interest expense in equal amounts each period by dividing the total discount or premium by the number of semiannual periods until maturity. If the bonds are sold at a discount, the recorded amount of interest expense (cash payment + discount amortization) will be higher than the cash paid, indicating that the effective interest rate is higher than the stated rate. If the bonds are sold at a premium, the recorded amount of interest expense (cash payment - premium amortization) will be lower than the cash paid, indicating that the effective interest rate is lower than the stated rate. For example, assuming straight-line amortization, the journal entry to record the semiannual payment of interest on the Nite Corporation bonds sold at a premium for $111,652.28, with a stated interest rate of 10% and an effective yield of 8%, would be as follows:

Interest Expense	4,271.73	
Premium on Bonds Payable ($11,652.28 ÷ 16)	728.27	
Cash ($100,000 x 0.10 x ½)		5,000

The straight-line method results in a constant interest expense per year.

9. When the effective interest method of amortization is used, the amount of discount or premium to be amortized is the difference between the amount of interest expense and the actual cash payment. The amount of annual interest expense is calculated by multiplying the effective interest rate (yield) times the book value of the bonds (if semiannual interest payments are made, one-half the yield is multiplied times the book value). The effective interest rate is equal to the discount rate which equates the present value of the face value of the bonds plus the present value of the future interest payments with the cash proceeds. Because the book value is the face value plus any unamortized premium or minus any unamortized discount, the book value changes with each successive premium or discount amortization and thus is equal to the present value of the remaining cash interest payments plus the present value of the future principal. This is consistent with the method of determining the issuance price of the bonds by discounting the future interest payments and the future principal using the effective interest rate. The effective interest method reflects the yield over the life of the bonds and results in a constant rate of interest each payment date although the amount of Interest Expense will vary. For example, if the premium on the Nite Corporation bonds yielding an effective annual interest rate of 8% were amortized using the effective interest method, the first two payments would be recorded as follows:

June 30, 2004

Interest Expense ($111,652.28 x 0.08 x ½)	4,466.09	
Premium on Bonds Payable ($5,000 - $4,466.09)	533.91	
Cash ($100,000 x 0.10 x ½)		5,000

December 31, 2004

Interest Expense [($111,652.28 - $533.91) x 0.08 x ½]	4,444.73	
Premium on Bonds Payable ($5,000 - $4,444.73)	555.27	
Cash ($100,000 x 0.10 x ½)		5,000

10. An amortization schedule which summarizes the discount or premium amortization, interest expense, and bond carrying value each period may be developed using either the effective interest method or the straight-line method. For example, assume Bay Corporation bonds were sold on January 1, 2004, for $97,502.25. The bonds have a face value of $100,000 and a stated interest rate of 10%. Interest is paid semiannually and the bonds mature on December 31, 2006. The effective interest rate (yield) is 11%. Following are examples of discount amortization schedules using the effective interest method and the straight line method.

BAY CORPORATION
Bond Interest Expense and Discount Amortization Schedule
Straight-Line Method

Date	Cash Credit[a]	Unamortized Discount Credit[b]	Interest Expense Debit[c]	Book Value of Bonds[d]
1/01/04				$ 97,502.25
6/30/04	$5,000	$416.29	$5,416.29	97,918.54
12/31/04	5,000	416.29	5,416.29	98,334.83
6/30/05	5,000	416.29	5,416.29	98,751.12
12/31/05	5,000	416.29	5,416.29	99,167.41
6/30/06	5,000	416.29	5,416.29	99,583.70
12/31/06	5,000	416.30[e]	5,416.30	100,000.00

[a]$100,000 (face value) x 0.10 (stated annual interest rate) x 1/2 (year)

[b][$100,000 - $97,502.25 (issue price)] ÷ 6 (semiannual periods until maturity)

[c]$5,000 + $416.29

[d]Previous book value + amount from footnote b

[e]Difference due to $0.01 rounding error

BAY CORPORATION
Bond Interest Expense and Discount Amortization Schedule
Effective Interest Method

Date	Cash Credit[a]	Interest Expense Debit[b]	Unamortized Discount Credit[c]	Book Value of Bonds[d]
1/01/04				$ 97,502.25
6/30/04	$5,000	$5,362.62	$362.62	97,864.87
12/31/04	5,000	5,382.57	382.57	98,247.44
6/30/05	5,000	5,403.61	403.61	98,651.05
12/31/05	5,000	5,425.81	425.81	99,076.85
6/30/06	5,000	5,449.23	449.23	99,526.08
12/31/06	5,000	5,473.92[e]	473.92	100,000.00

[a]$100,000 (face value) x 0.10 (stated annual interest rate) x 1/2 (year)

[b]Previous book value x 0.11 (effective interest rate) x 1/2 (year)

[c]Amount from footnote b - $5,000.00

[d]Previous book value + amount from footnote c

[e]Difference due to $0.01 rounding error

A comparison of the values in the two tables reinforces the idea that the interest expense using the straight-line method is a constant amount each period, while the interest expense using the effective interest method reflects a constant rate each period based on the remaining book value of the bonds.

11. APB Opinion No. 21 requires that a company defer any bond issue costs, such as legal fees, printing costs, or registration fees. Such costs are recorded in a separate account entitled Deferred Bond Issue Costs and classified as deferred charges on the balance sheet. A company amortizes these bond issue costs to interest expense over the life of the bonds, generally using the straight-line method. To record the amortization each period, a company debits Bond Interest Expense and credits Deferred Bond Issue Costs.

12. When a company issues bonds with interest payment dates (e.g., October 1 and April 1) that differ from the fiscal year (e.g., December 31), it must accrue interest and amortize a partial premium or discount at the end of the fiscal year in order to appropriately match expenses with revenues. A reversing entry is then made on January 1 so that the next entry to record semiannual interest expense can be made as usual.

13. Zero coupon bonds pay no interest each period. The selling price is the present value (based on yield) of the face value. A company debits the difference between the selling price and the face value to the discount account at issuance. Then it periodically recognizes interest expense, the yield times the book value of the bond at the beginning of the period, as a decrease in the discount account.

Extinguishment of Liabilities

14. Under FASB Statement No. 140, a liability is derecognized (extinguished) for financial reporting purposes under either of two conditions: (a) the debtor pays the creditor and is relieved of its obligation for the liability or (b) the debtor is released legally either judicially or by the creditor.

15. On the bond maturity date, the company repays the face value of the bonds to the bondholders. By this time, the book value equals the face value because any discount or premium has been completely amortized. When bonds are to be retired at maturity, the bonds are reclassified as a current liability on the balance sheet immediately before retirement. The entry to record the retirement includes a debit to Bonds Payable and a credit to Cash.

16. Bonds may be retired prior to the scheduled maturity date either as a result of a call provision, which allows the company to recall the debt issue at a prestated percentage of the face value, or by purchasing the bonds on the open market. If the debt is not replaced with another issue, the extinguishment is called a debt retirement; if the debt is replaced with another debt issue, this type of extinguishment is called a refunding.

17. The retirement or refunding of bonds prior to maturity usually results in either a gain or loss as measured by the difference between the current book value of the bonds (plus any unamortized bond issue costs) and the call price (or market price). Regardless of whether the extinguishment of debt is a retirement or a refunding, FASB Statement No. 145 requires that all debt extinguishments be accounted for in the same way. A company recognizes the gain or loss in the period of recall (the current period) and includes the gain or loss in its income from continuing operations for that period. For example, if Bay Corporation retires the bonds discussed earlier in #10 at the end of the second year on December 31, 2005 for $101,000, it would make the following journal entries to record the retirement after all straight-line amortization and interest expense entries are made.

Bonds Payable	100,000.00	
Loss on Bond Redemption	1,832.59[b]	
Discount on Bonds Payable		832.59[a]
Cash		101,000.00

[a]Original discount	$2,497.75	
Amortization on straight-line basis for 4 periods = 4 x $416.29	(1,665.16)	
Unamortized discount	$ 832.59	
[b]Call price (excluding interest)		$101,000.00
Less: Face Value	$100,000.00	
Unamortized discount	(832.59)	(99,167.41)
Loss on Bond Redemption		$ 1,832.59

18. In addition to retirement at or prior to maturity, a liability can be extinguished if the debtor is legally released from being the primary obligor for the debt either by law or by the creditor. This is referred to as defeasance. The debtor removes the liability from its records and reports a gain on the defeasance.

Bonds With Equity Characteristics

19. In order to increase the marketability of bonds, a company may issue bonds with detachable <u>stock warrants</u> (<u>stock rights</u>). The warrants (rights) represent the right of the investor to acquire a specified number of shares of common stock at a given price within a certain period of time. When the stock warrants are detached, the investor still retains the right to receive interest on the bonds. Because the warrants trade separately on the open market soon after issuance, a portion of the bond proceeds must be allocated to the stock warrants and accounted for as additional paid-in capital. The allocation is based on the relative fair value of the bonds and warrants, and the company determines the amount of allocation using the following formulas:

$$\text{Amount Assigned to Bonds} = \frac{\text{Market Value of Bonds Without Warrants}}{\text{Market Value of Bonds Without Warrants} + \text{Market Value of Warrants}} \times \text{Issuance Price}$$

$$\text{Amount Assigned to Warrants} = \frac{\text{Market Value of Warrants}}{\text{Market Value of Bonds Without Warrants} + \text{Market Value of Warrants}} \times \text{Issuance Price}$$

For example, assume $500,000 of 10% bonds are issued at par. Each bond carries 10 warrants and each warrant allows the holder to acquire one share of $8 par common stock for $20 per share. After issuance, the bonds are quoted at 98 ex rights and the warrants are quoted at $4 each.

$$\text{Value Assigned to Bonds} = \frac{\$980 \times 500}{(\$980 \times 500) + (\$4 \times 500 \times 10)} \times \$500{,}000$$

$$= \underline{\underline{\$480{,}392.16}}$$

$$\text{Value Assigned to Warrants} = \frac{\$4 \times 500 \times 10}{(\$980 \times 500) + (\$4 \times 500 \times 10)} \times \$500{,}000$$

$$= \underline{\underline{\$19{,}607.84}}$$

To record the issuance, the company records the following journal entry:

Cash	500,000.00	
Discount on Bonds Payable	19,607.84	
Bonds Payable		500,000.00
Common Stock Warrants		19,607.84

Each right has a value of $3.92 ($19,607.84 ÷ 5,000). If 200 warrants are later exercised, the appropriate journal entry would be:

Cash ($20 x 200)	4,000.00	
Common Stock Warrants ($3.92 x 200)	784.00	
Common Stock ($8 x 200)		1,600.00
Additional Paid-in Capital on Common Stock		3,184.00

Upon expiration of the remaining warrants, the company records the following journal entry:

Common Stock Warrants ($19,607.84 - $784.00)	18,823.84	
Additional Paid-in Capital from Expired Warrants		18,823.84

20. Convertible bonds are another form of debt which a company may issue and which allows creditors to ultimately become stockholders. The conversion feature, which usually allows the bonds to be sold at a lower interest rate and/or a higher price, enables the bondholder to exchange the bonds for a specified number of shares of common stock. It would appear that the issuance of convertible bonds would be accounted for in the same manner as bonds with detachable warrants by allocating a portion of the proceeds to the conversion feature. However, APB Opinion No. 14 specifies that the proceeds from the issuance of convertible debt be accounted for in the same manner as the issuance of nonconvertible debt because the conversion feature lacks reliable (verifiable) valuation. The conversion of the bonds into common stock may be accounted for by either of two methods. The book value method accounts for conversion to stockholders' equity (Common Stock and Additional Paid-in Capital) with no recognition of a gain or loss. The market value method records stockholders' equity at the market value of the shares issued on the date of conversion. Any loss that arises from a difference between the market value of the shares issued and the book value of the bonds on the conversion date is included in the company's income from continuing operations for the period.

21. After the initial issuance of its convertible bonds, a company may change the conversion privileges in order to induce conversion of these bonds into common stock. The changed terms may involve additional consideration such as a reduction of the original conversion price or the issuance of additional warrants. If such changes are effective for a limited period of time, the debtor company recognizes an expense equal to the excess of the fair value of the common stock (plus any other consideration) over the fair value of the common stock issuable under the original conversion terms. The expense is reported in the company's income from continuing operations.

Long-Term Notes Payable

22. A long-term note represents a future obligation to repay debt, and may or may not be backed by collateral. If the stated interest rate on a long-term note payable is equal to the fair interest rate at issuance, the issuer company records the note at its face value. It records subsequent payments of interest and accruals as debits to Interest Expense and credits to Cash or Interest Payable.

23. APB Opinion No. 21 provides guidelines to be used in accounting for long-term notes payable which are issued without a stated (or fair) interest rate. According to the Opinion, a company records a note at its present value and uses the effective interest method to record subsequent interest, regardless of the note's legal structure. The effective interest rate is the discount rate which equates the face value with the present value of the note. If a company issues a noninterest-bearing note for cash, the note is assumed to have a present value equal to the cash proceeds, and the appropriate interest rate is determined by comparing the cash proceeds with the face value. The company debits any difference between the proceeds and the face value to Discounts on Notes Payable which is then amortized to Interest Expense over the life of the note by the effective interest method (as discussed earlier). Discount on Notes

Payable is a contra account which is subtracted from the Notes Payable account on the company's balance sheet to determine the carrying value of the note.

24. In accounting for a note exchanged for cash and rights or privileges, such as the right to purchase goods from the borrower at less than prevailing prices, a company records the note at its present value at the time of issuance by discounting the maturity value using the borrower's incremental interest rate (the going market rate). The difference between the present value of the note and the cash proceeds is initially debited to Discount on Notes Payable and credited to Unearned Revenue. The discount is amortized to interest expense over the life of the note using the effective interest method. Revenue is recognized over the life of the contract using appropriate revenue recognition criteria.

25. When a note is exchanged solely for property, goods, or services in an external transaction, the stipulated rate of interest is presumed fair unless (a) no interest is stated; (b) the stated rate of interest is clearly unreasonable; or (c) the face value of the note is materially different from either the cash price of the property, goods, or services, or the fair value of the note at the date of the transaction. In any of these cases, the company records the note at the fair value of the note or fair value of the property, goods, or services, whichever is more reliable. If neither of the fair values is known, the present value of the note is determined by using the borrower's incremental interest rate to discount the future cash flows. Any difference between the value assigned to the property, goods, or services and the face value of the note is recorded as a discount and amortized to Interest Expense over the life of the note using the effective interest method.

Long-Term Notes Receivable

26. A company usually acquires a noninterest-bearing long-term note receivable in an exchange for property, goods, or services. The same generally accepted accounting principles apply to notes receivable and notes payable. The note receivable should be recorded at the fair value of the property, goods, or services or the fair value of the note, whichever is more reliable. If neither of these values is reliable, the note should be recorded at its present value using the borrower's incremental interest rate. The effective interest method is used to record interest revenue.

27. A loan (note receivable) is <u>impaired</u> if it is probable that the creditor will not be able to collect all amounts due according to the contractual terms of the loan agreement. The process of accounting for bad debt expense due to loan impairment used by financial institutions differs from the process used by retailers or manufacturers to account for bad debt expense due to other types of receivables. Because there is a delay in the recognition of bad debts by a financial institution, expenses are not matched against revenues in the period in which loans originate and receivables are not reported at their net realizable value at the end of that period.

28. <u>FASB Statement No. 114</u> requires companies to use a consistent method for valuing impaired loans and to measure the economic losses on such loans and include them in net income. The company must compute the present value of the expected future cash flows of the impaired loan using the effective interest rate on the loan. The effective interest rate is the original (contractual) interest rate on the loan (adjusted for any loan fees, discount, or premium). The difference between the present value and the recorded investment in the loan is debited to bad debt expense and credited to an allowance for doubtful notes account. After the write-down of the loan, the company recognizes interest revenue, the carrying value of the loan times the effective interest rate, each period as a reduction of the allowance account. Changes in the

amount or timing of the impaired loan's expected or actual cash flows require that the amount of impairment be recalculated. Any difference is recognized as an adjustment to bad debt expense and the allowance account.

29. The FASB has issued two Exposure Drafts that, if adopted, would have significant effects on how companies account for their liabilities. The first Exposure Draft would affect how a company accounts for the issuance of convertible bonds. At issuance, the company would have to allocate a portion of the proceeds to the conversion feature and treat this as additional paid-in capital, with the remaining portion treated as bonds payable. Upon conversion, the company would have to calculate a gain or loss based on the difference between the fair value of the bond component and the book value of the bonds payable.

30. The second Exposure Draft would affect how a company accounts for a guarantee of the debts of others. When a company issues such a guarantee, it would be required to record a liability for the fair value of the obligation and would be required to provide additional information in the notes to its financial statements.

Appendix 1: Troubled Debt Restructurings

31. FASB Statement No. 15 stipulates that a troubled debt restructuring occurs when a creditor, for economic or legal reasons related to a debtor's financial difficulties, grants a concession to a debtor that it would not otherwise consider. A troubled debt restructuring may include one or more of the following:

    (1) Modification of terms of the debt such as:

        a. Reduction of the stated interest rate for the remaining original life of the debt.

        b. Extension of the maturity date at a stated interest rate lower than the current market rate for new debt with similar risk.

        c. Reduction of the face amount or maturity amount of the debt.

        d. Reduction of accrued interest.

    (2) Issuance of an equity interest to satisfy the debt.

    (3) A transfer from the debtor to the creditor of receivables, real estate, or other assets to satisfy a debt.

32. In accounting by the debtor for a restructuring that involves only a modification of terms, two situations are possible depending on whether the carrying value of the liability is greater than or less than the total future cash payments specified by the new terms. If the undiscounted total future cash payments are greater than (or equal to) the carrying value of the liability, the debtor makes no adjustment to the carrying value and recognizes no gain on the restructuring. The debtor records the difference between the future cash payments (principal plus the stated interest) and the current carrying value as interest expense over the new remaining life of the liability using the effective interest method and an imputed interest rate.

33. If the future cash payments are less than the current carrying value of the liability, the debtor must make a downward adjustment of the carrying value of the liability. This adjustment equates the total future cash payments with the carrying value and results in a gain on the debt reduction. Each future cash payment reduces the carrying value of the liability, and no interest is recognized.

34. When a debtor exchanges an asset or an equity interest of lesser value to satisfy a liability, the debtor records the transfer at the fair value of the asset or equity interest transferred and recognizes a gain on the exchange. If the debtor exchanges an asset and its fair value is different from its carrying value, the debtor also records a gain or loss on the disposal.

35. If the troubled debt restructuring combines an asset (or equity) exchange with a modification of terms, the fair value of the asset (or equity) transferred is used first to reduce the debt. The debtor accounts for the remaining carrying value of the debt as a modification of terms as described earlier in #32.

36. FASB Statement No. 15 also requires disclosures by the debtor related to troubled debt restructuring, including a description of the principal terms of the settlement, any gain with related income tax effects in the aggregate and per share, the aggregate gain or loss on the transfer of assets, and related contingent payments.

37. Accounting by the creditor for a troubled debt restructuring that involves an equity or asset exchange is the "mirror image" of the accounting by the debtor. That is, the procedures as described in #32-35 above are the same if "receivable" is substituted for "liability," "revenue" is substituted for "expense," and "loss" is substituted for "gain."

38. Accounting by the creditor for a troubled debt restructuring that involves a modification of terms is not the mirror image of the accounting by the debtor. The creditor is required to recognize the fair value of the loan by discounting the total future cash flows specified by the new contractual terms to their present value. The original interest rate is used in the present value calculation. The creditor recognizes the difference between the present value of the future cash flows and the carrying value of the receivable as a loss.

Appendix 2: Serial Bonds

39. Bonds which contain provisions that require repayment of the face value in periodic installments over a number of years are called serial bonds. Serial bonds may sell at face value, at a premium, or at a discount. If serial bonds are sold at a premium or at a discount, a company can account for the amortization using either the bonds outstanding method or the effective interest method. The bonds outstanding method, which is similar to the straight-line method, accounts for each installment as if it were a separate issue and amortizes a fractional share of the premium or discount over the number of periods each installment is outstanding. This fractional share is calculated by multiplying the premium or discount times the following fraction:

$$\frac{\text{Face Value of Bonds Outstanding at the Beginning of Each Period}}{\text{Sum of the Face Values of the Bonds Outstanding at the Beginning of Each Period}}$$

For example, assume that on January 1, 2004, Tace Corporation issued $200,000 of serial bonds with a stated interest rate of 12% to be paid annually. The bonds sold at a premium of $12,000, and are to be repaid in four equal annual installments at the end of each year beginning on December 31, 2004. The following calculations are necessary to determine the premium amortization and interest expense:

	Bonds Outstanding at the Beginning of Each Period
1/01/04	$200,000
1/01/05	150,000
1/01/06	100,000
1/01/07	50,000
	$500,000 = Sum of Face Values of Bonds Outstanding at Beginning of Each Period

	Amortization of Premium	Interest Expense[a]
12/31/04	$\frac{\$200,000}{\$500,000}$ x $12,000 = $4,800	$19,200
12/31/05	$\frac{\$150,000}{\$500,000}$ x $12,000 = $3,600	14,400
12/31/06	$\frac{\$100,000}{\$500,000}$ x $12,000 = $2,400	9,600
12/31/07	$\frac{\$50,000}{\$500,000}$ x $12,000 = $1,200	4,800

[a](Face Value of Bonds Outstanding Beginning of Each Period x 0.12) - Amortization of Premium

40. When a company redeems serial bonds prior to their maturity date, it eliminates the amount of unamortized discount or premium associated with these bonds. In addition, the company recognizes the gain or loss arising from the early redemption in the current period. It calculates the gain or loss by comparing the book value of the bonds redeemed with the redemption price.

200,000 x 0.12 - 4,800

SELF-EVALUATION EXERCISES

Supply the words, symbols, or amounts necessary to answer each of the following items.

Bonds Payable

BP-1. If a company is too risky to attract equity investments, the company may choose to obtain financial resources by issuing Long-term liabilities.

BP-2. If a corporation uses borrowed funds to increase the return to stockholders, the corporation is trading on the equity.

BP-3. The face value of a corporate bond is generally $1000.

BP-4. The contractual agreement between the issuing corporation and the bondholder is called the bond indenture.

BP-5. The interest rate and payment dates, the maturity date, and any call provisions are stated on the bond certificate.

BP-6. Bonds which are secured by a lien against specific corporate assets are called mortgage bond; bonds which are unsecured are called debenture bond.

BP-7. Bonds which pay interest only at maturity are called zero-coupon bond; bonds which may be exchanged at a future date for common shares are called convertible bonds.

BP-8. To calculate the amount of annual interest to be paid on bonds, the face value is multiplied times the stated annual interest rate.

BP-9. The actual rate of interest that must be paid investors in order to sell bonds is called the effective rate or the yield.

BP-10. If the yield rate of interest and the contract (stated) rate are the same, the bonds will be issued at par; if the yield is greater than the contract rate the bonds will be issued at a discount; and if the yield is less than the contract rate the bonds will be issued at a premium.

BP-11. If a $1,000 bond is selling at 98, the price of the bond is $980 and the bond is selling at a discount of $20.

Recording the Issuance of the Bonds

RB-1. The account Premium on Bonds Payable is a(n) ________ (addition to, deduction from) Bonds Payable on the balance sheet; and Discounts on Bonds Payable is a(n) contra (addition, deduction).

RB-2. The Premium on Bonds Payable account is called an adjunct account; and the Discount on Bonds Payable is called a contra account.

RB-3. If a corporation has a balance in its Bonds Payable account of $100,000, and a balance in the Premium on Bonds Payable account of $1,755, the carrying value of the bonds is $101755

Amortizing Discounts and Premiums

AD-1. To account for interest expense related to bonds, the method of amortization required by APB Opinion No. 21, is the effective interest method, unless the results of using the straight-line method are not materially different.

AD-2. If the straight-line method of amortization is used, the Amount (amount, rate) of interest each year is constant; if the effective interest method is used, the rate (amount, rate) of interest is constant.

AD-3. When using the effective interest method, the amount of annual interest expense is calculated by multiplying the effective interest rate times the bonds' book value; the amount of premium or discount amortized is equal to the difference between the amount of interest expense and the actual cash payments.

AD-4. Legal fees, printing costs, and registration fees associated with a bond issuance are recorded in the account entitled Deferred Bond issue cost.

AD-5. The selling price of a zero coupon bond is the present value of the face value.

Extinguishment of Liabilities

EL-1. A corporation will repay the face value of the bonds to the bondholders on the maturity date.

EL-2. If a debt issue is retired and replaced with another issue, the extinguishment is termed a refunding.

EL-3. Gains or losses from the extinguishment of debt which are material are included on the income statement in Income from continuing operation.

EL-4. Under FASB Statement No. 140, the early extinguishment of debt that occurs when a debtor is released from the legal liability of the debt either by law or by the creditor is referred to as DEFEASANCE.

Bonds With Equity Characteristics

BEC-1. A stock right or stock warrant represents the right of an investor to acquire a specified number of shares of common stock at a given price within a certain time period.

BEC-2. The journal entry to record the issuance of bonds with detachable warrants must assign a portion of the proceeds to Bonds Payable and a portion to common stock warrant.

BEC-3. Proceeds from the issuance of convertible debt are accounted for in the same manner as the issuance of non convertible debts.

BEC-4. When convertible bonds are converted into common stock, a gain or loss may be recognized if the transaction is accounted for using the market value method.

Long-Term Notes Payable

LTNP-1. When a note having a stated and fair interest rate is exchanged solely for cash, the note is recorded at its fair value.

LTNP-2. When a noninterest-bearing note is issued for cash only, the present value of the note is assumed to equal the cash proceeds

LTNP-3. When a noninterest-bearing note is exchanged for cash, the difference between the face value of the note and the cash proceeds is debited to the account, Discount on notes payable

LTNP-4. The interest rate that is used to amortize the discount on a note is the rate that equates the face value with the present value.

LTNP-5. When a noninterest-bearing note is exchanged solely for property, goods, or services, the note should be recorded at either the

(1) fair value of property, goods & svcs or the

(2) fair value of the note, whichever is more reliable.

LTNP-6. If the value assigned to property, goods, or services exchanged for a note is less than the face value of the note, the difference is recorded as a discount.

Long-Term Notes Receivable

LTNR-1. The correct method for accounting for interest revenue on a note receivable is the effective interest method.

LTNR-2. If it is probable that the creditor will not be able to collect all amounts due according to the contractual terms of the loan, the loan is impaired.

Appendix 1: Troubled Debt Restructurings

DR-1. Where only a modification of terms is used to satisfy the troubled debt, if the value of the total future payments is less than the carrying value of the debt, the difference is treated by the debtor as a gain.

DR-2. If, in a troubled debt restructuring, the debt is partially satisfied by the transfer of an asset and partially by the modification of terms, the debt is first reduced by the fair value of the asset transferred

DR-3. If troubled debt is forgiven entirely by an asset or equity interest transferred, and the carrying value of the debt exceeds the fair value of the asset transferred, the difference is treated by the debtor as a gain or loss.

DR-4. In a troubled debt restructuring, where only a modification of terms is used, if the future cash receipts of the creditor are less than the current carrying value of the receivable, the difference is treated as a loss.

Appendix 2: Serial Bonds

SB-1. A premium or discount on serial bonds can be amortized using either the ____________ ____________ method or the ____________ ____________ method.

SB-2. On January 1, 2004, a corporation issued $100,000 of serial bonds with a stated interest rate of 14% to be paid annually. The bonds sold at a discount of $8,000 and are to be repaid in four annual installments at the end of each year beginning December 31, 2004. If the bonds outstanding method of amortizing the discount is used, the amount of discount to be amortized at the end of the first year will be $__________ and the amount of interest expense will be $__________.

SB-3. If serial bonds are redeemed prior to their maturity, a gain or loss on the early redemption is determined by comparing the ____________ ____________ of the redeemed bonds with their ____________ ____________.

ANSWERS TO SELF-EVALUATION EXERCISES

BP-1. long-term liabilities; BP-2. trading on the equity; BP-3. $1,000; BP-4. bond indenture; BP-5. bond certificate; BP-6. mortgage bonds, debenture bonds; BP-7. zero-coupon bonds, convertible bonds; BP-8. stated annual interest rate; BP-9. effective rate, yield; BP-10. par, discount, premium; BP-11. $980, discount, $20; RB-1. addition to, deduction; RB-2. adjunct, contra; RB-3. $101,755; AD-1. effective interest method; AD-2. amount, rate; AD-3. effective interest rate, book value, interest expense, cash payment; AD-4. Deferred Bond Issue Costs; AD-5. present value of the face value; EL-1. maturity; EL-2. refunding; EL-3. income from continuing operations; EL-4. defeasance; BEC-1. acquire a specified number of shares of common stock at a given price within a certain time period; BEC-2. Common Stock Warrants; BEC-3. nonconvertible debt; BEC-4. market value; LTNP-1. face value; LTNP-2. cash proceeds; LTNP-3. Discount on Notes Payable; LTNP-4. face value, present value; LTNP-5. (1) fair value of the property, goods, or services, (2) fair value of the note; LTNP-6. discount; LTNR-1. effective interest; LTNR-2. impaired; DR-1. gain; DR-2. fair value of the asset transferred; DR-3. gain, loss; DR-4. loss; SB-1. bonds outstanding, effective interest; SB-2. $3,200, $17,200; SB-3. book value, redemption price.

POST TEST

Part A Circle T if the statement is true and F if it is false.

T F 1. Bonds are an attractive way for corporations to finance their operations because the interest payments to bondholders are a tax deductible expense.

T F 2. Financing with debt allows corporations the possibility of increasing the rate of return to stockholders.

T F 3. Debenture bonds are secured by specific assets of the company.

T F 4. When coupon bonds are sold, the issuer of the bonds or the transfer agent must be notified of the change of ownership.

T F 5. A bond which has a contract rate of 10% and a yield of 12% is sold at a premium.

T F 6. The amount of interest that a bondholder will receive in a year is calculated by multiplying the price of the bond times the effective interest rate.

T F 7. When a bond with a face value of $1,000 is sold for $980, $1,000 is credited to Bonds Payable.

T F 8. When a bond is sold between interest dates, the buyer must usually pay the issuing company the interest which has accrued from the last payment date to the date of purchase.

T F 9. APB Opinion No. 21 allows the use of either the effective interest method or the straight-line method of premium or discount amortization because the differences which result are not material.

T F 10. When the effective interest method is used, the amount of interest expense each period is determined by multiplying the stated interest rate times the face value of the bonds.

T F 11. The straight-line method of amortization results in a constant amount of interest expense each period.

T F 12. Legal fees, printing costs, or registration fees associated with a bond issue should be expensed in the period when the bonds are issued.

T F 13. When bonds are retired at maturity, the face value equals the book value of the bonds on the retirement date.

T F 14. A call provision allows a company to recall a bond issue at a prestated price before the scheduled maturity date.

T F 15. Material gains and losses on the early extinguishment of debt are classified as extraordinary items.

T F 16. A company may amortize a premium or discount associated with serial bonds by using either the bonds outstanding method or the effective interest method.

T F 17. Because the economic substance of the issue of bonds with detachable warrants and bonds with a conversion provision is similar, the generally accepted accounting principles for recording the issuance of these types of securities is the same.

T F 18. When bonds are converted into common stock, a company may record a gain or loss on the conversion, regardless of the method used to account for the conversion, if there is a difference between the market value of the bonds and the market value of the stock on the date of conversion.

T F 19. To record the issuance of a noninterest-bearing note for cash, a company debits Cash for the value of the proceeds and credits Notes Payable for the same amount.

T F 20. When a noninterest-bearing note is exchanged for cash and special rights and privileges, the borrower's incremental borrowing rate is used to amortize any discount.

T F 21. In accounting for a troubled debt restructuring that involves an equity or asset exchange, the creditor, like the debtor, reports any loss on its income statement in income from continuing operations.

T F 22. Accounting by the creditor for a troubled debt restructuring that involves a modification of terms is the mirror image of the accounting by the debtor.

T F 23. In a troubled debt restructuring, a modification of terms will result in a recognition of gain by the debtor if the amount to be repaid is less than the current carrying value of the liability.

T F 24. FASB Statement No. 15 requires debtors entering into restructuring agreements to disclose the modifications in terms and/or major features of settlement for each restructuring agreement.

Part B Select the one best answer, and place its letter in the space provided.

d 1. Which of the following statements is not a reason why companies might prefer to issue bonds rather than other types of securities? (a) bonds may be the only source of funds because of the riskiness of the company; (b) bonds may have a lower cost to the corporation because of the lower perceived risk; (c) the interest payments made to bondholders are a tax deductible expense; (d) bondholders will dilute the vote of stockholders.

b 2. If the yield on a bond issue is greater than the contract rate, the bonds are sold at (a) a discount; (b) a premium; (c) par; (d) cost.

b 3. The book value of a bond issue sold at a premium is (a) the face value minus any unamortized premium; (b) the face value plus any unamortized premium; (c) the price minus any unamortized premium; (d) the price plus any unamortized premium.

a 4. A company uses the effective interest method of amortizing a bond discount or premium in order to (a) disclose the interest charges imposed on the company by the bondholders; (b) report a constant amount of interest expense each semiannual period; (c) simplify the process of amortizing and recording any premium or discount; (d) amortize a constant amount of premium or discount each semiannual period.

b 5. Legal fees and registration fees associated with the issuance of bonds are (a) expensed during the period in which the bonds are issued; (b) amortized to interest expense over the life of the bonds using the straight-line method; (c) amortized to interest expense over the life of the bonds using the effective interest method; (d) amortized over a period not to exceed five years.

b 6. Interest expense on zero coupon bonds is (a) the yield times the book value of the bonds at the end of the period; (b) the yield times the book value of the bonds at the beginning of the period; (c) the stated rate times the face value of the bonds at the beginning of the period; (d) the stated rate times the book value of the bonds at the end of the period.

a 7. On the bond retirement date the book value of the bonds (a) equals the face value of the bonds; (b) exceeds the face value of the bonds if the bonds were originally sold at a premium; (c) is less than the face value of the bonds if the bonds were originally sold at a discount; (d) is equal to the original selling price of the bonds.

a 8. When bonds are retired prior to maturity, a company recognizes a gain if the call price of the bonds is (a) less than the current book value of the bonds plus any unamortized bond issue costs; (b) less than the current book value of the bonds less any unamortized bond issue costs; (c) more than the current book value of the bonds plus any unamortized bond issue costs; (d) more than the current book value of the bonds less any unamortized bond issue costs.

____ 9. A company issues $100,000 of 8% bonds at par. Each bond carries 5 warrants, each of which allows the holder to acquire one share of $5 par value common stock for $30 a share. After issuance the bonds were quoted at 98 ex rights, and the warrants were quoted at $6 each. The value assigned to the bonds at issuance should be (a) $87,000; (b) $97,029.70; (c) $98,000; (d) $100,000.

d 10. A corporation has convertible bonds with a face value of $100,000, and a current book value of $101,500. Each $1,000 bond may be converted into 20 shares of $5 par value common stock. If all of the bonds are converted into stock when the market value of the stock is $52 a share, the journal entry to record the conversion using the book value method would include (a) a debit to Loss on Conversion of $2,500; (b) a credit to Gain on Conversion of $2,500; (c) a credit to Gain on Conversion of $4,700; (d) neither a gain nor a loss.

c 11. Fairco Corporation issues a 4 year, noninterest-bearing note with a face value of $10,000 and receives $5,920.80 in exchange. The journal entry to record the issuance of the note is which of the following:

(a)	Cash	5,920.80	
	Notes Payable		5,920.80
(b)	Cash	10,000	
	Notes Payable		10,000
(c)	Cash	5,920.80	
	Discount on Notes Payable	4,079.20	
	Notes Payable		10,000
(d)	Cash	10,000	
	Notes Payable		5,920.80
	Premium on Notes Payable		4,079.20

d 12. A company exchanges a $42,000 note with a stated interest rate of 9% solely for a used mini-computer. The 9% interest rate would be presumed fair unless (a) the stated rate of interest is clearly unreasonable; (b) the face value of the note is materially different from the cash price of the computer; (c) the face value of the note is materially different from the fair value of the note; (d) a, b, or c is true.

d 13. A troubled debt restructuring may include (a) reducing the stated interest rate for the remaining original life of the debt; (b) reducing the face amount of debt stated on the debt instrument; (c) transferring assets from the debtor to the creditor in satisfaction of the debt; (d) all of the above; (e) none of the above.

Part C Solve each of the following short problems.

1. On January 1, 2004, Wilson Corporation issued $200,000 of 10% bonds for $187,580.47. The bonds were issued to yield 12%, and pay interest semiannually on June 30 and December 31. The bonds are due on December 31, 2007.

 (a) Prepare the journal entry necessary to record the issuance of the bonds.

Cash	187,580.47	
discount on bonds payable	12 419.53	
1/1/04 Bonds payable		200,000
		187,580-47

 (b) Prepare a bond interest expense and discount amortization schedule using the effective interest method.

DATE	CREDIT	int exp 12% dr	Unamortized dis cr	Book value of bonds
6/30/04	10,000	11,254.83	1,254.83	188,835.30
12/31/04	10,000	11,330.12	1330.12	190,165.42
6/30/05	10,000	11,409.93	1409.93	191575.35
12/31/05	10,000	11,494.52	1494.52	193,069.87
6/30/06	10,000	11,584.19	1584.19	194,654.06
12/31/06	10,000	11,679.24	1679.24	196,333.30
6/30/07	10,000	11 780.00	1780.00	198,113.30
12/31/07	10,000	11,886.80	1886.80	200,000

 (c) Assume that the bonds were retired on September 30, 2006, at 101. Prepare the journal entries to record the early retirement.

Interest Expense

Discount on Bonds Pay [ ] 2069.92

Interest Payable (200,000 x .12 x 1/2) 12000

2. On July 1, 2004, Lowe Corporation sold $100,000 of 10% bonds, due July 1, 2007, at 102. Each bond pays interest semiannually on December 31 and June 30, and carries 20 warrants. Each warrant allows the holder to acquire one share of $8 par common stock for $24 per share. Shortly after issuance the bonds were quoted at 98 ex rights and the warrants were quoted at $5 each.

(a) Prepare the journal entry to record the bond issue.

(b) Determine the value to be assigned to each warrant.

(c) Prepare the journal entry to record the exercise of 1,000 warrants.

(d) Prepare the journal entry to record the expiration of the remaining rights.

3. On January 1, Wisbey Company purchased used equipment by issuing a 4-year, noninterest-bearing $50,000 note in exchange. Neither the fair value of the equipment nor that of the note is determinable. Wisbey's incremental borrowing rate is 8%. The equipment has a remaining useful life of 10 years and no projected residual value.

Prepare the journal entries to record:

(a) The issuance of the note.

(b) The interest payment at the end of the first year and annual straight-line depreciation.

(c) The interest payment at the end of the second year and annual straight-line depreciation.

ANSWERS TO POST TEST

Part A

1. T	6. F	11. T	16. T	21. T
2. T	7. T	12. F	17. F	22. T
3. F	8. T	13. T	18. F	23. T
4. F	9. F	14. T	19. F	24. T
5. F	10. F	15. F	20. T	

Part B

1. d	5. b	8. a	11. c
2. a	6. b	9. b	12. d
3. b	7. a	10. d	13. d
4. a			

Part C

1.	(a)	Cash	187,580.47	
		Discount on Bonds Payable	12,419.53	
		Bonds Payable		200,000

(b)

WILSON CORPORATION
Bond Interest Expense and Discount Amortization Schedule
Effective Interest Method
10% Bonds Sold to Yield 12%

Date	Cash Credit	Interest Expense Debit	Unamortized Discount Credit	Book Value of Bonds
1/01/04				$187,580.47
6/30/04	$10,000	$11,254.83	$1,254.83	188,835.30
12/31/04	10,000	11,330.12	1,330.12	190,165.42
6/30/05	10,000	11,409.93	1,409.93	191,575.35
12/31/05	10,000	11,494.52	1,494.52	193,069.87
6/30/06	10,000	11,584.19	1,584.19	194,654.06
12/31/06	10,000	11,679.24	1,679.24	196,333.30
6/30/07	10,000	11,780.00	1,780.00	198,113.30
12/31/07	10,000	11,886.70*	1,886.70	200,000.00

*Difference due to $0.10 rounding error.

1.	(c)	Interest Expense	5,839.62	
		Discount on Bonds Payable		839.62
		Interest Payable		5,000.00
		Interest Payable	5,000.00	
		Bonds Payable	200,000.00	
		Loss on Bond Redemption	6,506.32	
		Discount on Bonds Payable		4,506.32
		Cash [(1.01 x $200,000) + $5,000]		207,000.00

2. (a)

$$\text{Value Assigned to Bonds} = \frac{\$980 \times 100}{(\$980 \times 100) + (\$5 \times 100 \times 20)} \times \$102{,}000$$

$$= \underline{\underline{\$92{,}555.56}}$$

$$\text{Value Assigned to Rights} = \frac{(\$5 \times 100 \times 20)}{(\$980 \times 100) + (\$5 \times 100 \times 20)} \times \$102{,}000$$

$$= \underline{\underline{\$9{,}444.44}}$$

Cash (100 x $1,000 x 1.02)	102,000.00	
Discount on Bonds Payable	7,444.44	
Bonds Payable		100,000.00
Common Stock Warrants		9,444.44

2. (b) $9,444.44 ÷ 2,000 = $4.722

	(c) Cash ($24 x 1,000)	24,000.00	
	Common Stock Warrants ($4.722 x 1,000)	4,722.22	
	Common Stock, $8 par		8,000.00
	Additional Paid-in Capital on Common Stock		20,722.22
	(d) Common Stock Warrants ($9,444.44 - $4,722.22)	4,722.22	
	Additional Paid-in Capital from Expired Warrants		4,722.22
3.	(a) Equipment ($50,000 x $PV_{n=4,\ i=8\%}$)	36,751.50	
	Discount on Notes Payable	13,248.50	
	Notes Payable		50,000.00
	(b) December 31, Year 1:		
	Interest Expense [($50,000 - $13,248.50) x 0.08]	2,940.12	
	Discount on Notes Payable		2,940.12
	Depreciation Expense ($36,751.50 ÷ 10)	3,675.15	
	Accumulated Depreciation		3,675.15
	(c) December 31, Year 2:		
	Interest Expense {[$50,000 - ($13,248.50 - $2,940.12)] x 0.08}	3,175.33	
	Discount on Notes Payable		3,175.33
	Depreciation Expense ($36,751.50 ÷ 10)	3,675.15	
	Accumulated Depreciation		3,675.15

14

INVESTMENTS

CHAPTER OBJECTIVES

After careful study of this chapter, you will be able to:

1. Explain the classification and valuation of investments.
2. Account for investments in debt and equity trading securities.
3. Account for investments in available-for-sale debt and equity securities.
4. Account for investments in held-to-maturity debt securities, including amortization of bond premiums and discounts.
5. Understand transfers and impairments.
6. Understand disclosures of investments.
7. Explain the conceptual issues regarding investments in marketable securities.
8. Account for investments using the equity method.
9. Describe additional issues for investments.
10. Account for derivatives of financial instruments (Appendix).

SYNOPSIS

Investments: Classification and Valuation

1. A corporation acquires securities of other corporations or of the government for several different reasons: to obtain additional income by investing excess cash, to create long-term relationships with suppliers, or to obtain significant control over related companies. Companies may invest in common stock, preferred stock, and/or bonds of other corporations as well as municipal, state, or federal bonds. Each group of such investment securities is often referred to as a portfolio of marketable securities.

2. FASB Statement No. 115 establishes generally accepted accounting principles for all investments in debt securities and those equity securities that have readily determinable fair values. A security has a readily determinable fair value if a sales price is currently available on a securities exchange registered with the SEC or in an over-the-counter market whose prices are publicly reported.

3. A company classifies investments in debt and equity "marketable" securities at acquisition, and on subsequent reporting dates, into one of the following three categories: (a) Trading Securities, debt and equity securities purchased and held principally for the purpose of selling them in the near future. (b) Available-for-Sale Securities, debt securities not classified as held to maturity, and debt and equity securities not classified as trading securities. (c) Held-to-Maturity Debt Securities, those debt securities for which the company has the "positive intent and ability to hold the securities to maturity."

4. Debt securities, which represent a creditor relationship with another entity, include U.S. treasury securities, municipal securities, corporate bonds, convertible debt, commercial paper, and preferred stocks that have a mandatory redemption feature or are redeemable at the option of the holder. Equity securities, which represent an ownership interest in another company, include common stocks, preferred stocks, preferred stocks that are redeemable at the option of the company that issued the stock, stock warrants, stock rights, and put and call options. Fair value is the amount at which a security could be exchanged in a current transaction between willing parties.

Investments in Debt and Equity Trading Securities

5. According to GAAP, investments in debt and equity securities classified as trading securities are initially recorded at cost and subsequently reported at fair value. In addition, unrealized holding gains and losses (differences between the initial cost and the fair value at the balance sheet date) are included in net income of the current period, and interest and dividend revenue, as well as realized gains and losses on sales, are included in net income of the current period.

6. Investments in debt and equity trading securities are held primarily by such institutions as banks and stockbrokers.

Investments in Available-for-Sale Debt and Equity Securities

7. The accounting principles for investments in available-for-sale debt and equity securities are: (a) the investment is initially recorded at cost, (b) it is subsequently reported at fair value, (c) unrealized holding gains and losses are reported as a component of other comprehensive income, and (d) interest and dividend revenue, as well as realized gains and losses on sales, are included in net income for the current period.

8. The initial cost of investments in available-for-sale debt and equity securities includes the market price plus any brokerage fees and taxes. When a company purchases bonds between interest dates, it must record any accrued interest paid for by the purchaser separately from the purchase price. The company records interest revenue as it is earned during the period but records dividend revenue as it is received (or declared). The initial cost of the investment is recorded in an account called Investment in Available-for-Sale Securities.

9. At the balance sheet date, a company debits (credits) any unrealized holding gain (loss) to an Allowance for Change in Value of Investment account, an adjunct/contra account to the Investment in Available-for-Sale Securities account, and credits (debits) Unrealized Increase/ Decrease in Value of Available-for-Sale Securities, an adjunct/contra stockholders' equity account. The change in this account is included in Other Comprehensive Income for the year, and its balance is included in Accumulated Other Comprehensive Income. A credit balance in the Unrealized Increase/Decrease in Value of Available-for-Sale Securities represents the cumulative net unrealized gains and a debit balance represents the cumulative net unrealized losses. Once the Allowance account has been established, the amount of the adjustment of the Unrealized Increase/Decrease in Value in a subsequent period is determined by comparing the required carrying value of the Allowance account with the previous balance in the account.

10. A company records realized gains or losses on the sale of securities in an account called Gain (Loss) on Sale of Available-for-Sale Securities which is reported in net income. The realized gain or loss is measured as the difference between the selling price and the cost (of an equity security) or the amortized cost (of a debt security). The company "reverses" out of the accounts the cumulative balance in both the Allowance account and the Unrealized Increase/Decrease account reported at the previous balance sheet date.

Investments in Held-to-Maturity Debt Securities

11. The generally accepted accounting principles for investments in held-to-maturity debt securities are: (a) the investment is initially recorded at cost, (b) it is subsequently reported at amortized cost, (c) unrealized holding gains and losses are not recorded, and (d) interest revenue and gains and losses on disposal (if any) are all included in net income.

12. Investments in bonds are accounted for similarly to bond liabilities. However, unlike debtor companies, investor companies do not use a separate valuation account to record the premiums and discounts on investments in bonds. Instead, a company records the acquisition price in the Investment in Held-to-Maturity Debt Securities account which is directly adjusted for any premium and discount amortization. Thus, the balance in this account at the balance sheet date is reported at its carrying value.

13. If between interest dates a company makes an investment in bonds that will be held to maturity, it must pay the previous owner for the interest earned since the last interest receipt. To record this payment, Interest Revenue is usually debited and Cash is credited. Then, upon receipt of the next interest payment the amount of interest received is debited to Cash and credited to Interest Revenue. The difference between the original debit to Interest Revenue and the subsequent credit to Interest Revenue reflects the correct amount of interest earned.

14. The effective interest rate associated with the bonds purchased at a premium or discount is different from the stated interest rate. Therefore, a company must amortize any premium or discount associated with these investments in bonds to interest revenue over the remaining life of the bonds in order to assign the proper amount of interest revenue to each period. To account for premiums and discounts, the company must use the effective interest method (as described in Chapter 13) unless the straight-line method does not result in a material difference in the amount of interest revenue recognized in any year. A company makes the adjustments for premium or discount amortization directly to the Investment account, which is always reported at its net carrying value on the balance sheet.

15. The amortization of a bond premium results in an effective interest rate lower than the stated rate. The company records the premium amortization when it receives interest as follows:

Cash	XXX	
Investment in Held-to-Maturity Debt Securities		XXX
Interest Revenue		XXX

The amortization of a bond discount results in an effective interest rate higher than the stated rate. A company records the discount amortization and the receipt of interest using the following journal entry:

Cash	XXX	
Investment in Held-to-Maturity Debt Securities	XXX	
Interest Revenue		XXX

16. When a company acquires held-to-maturity bonds at a premium or a discount between interest dates, it must amortize the premium or discount over the remaining life of the bonds. On the first interest date after acquisition, the company credits Interest Revenue with the sum of the amount of accrued interest paid when the bonds were purchased plus the interest earned to date. The interest earned to date using the effective interest method is equal to the yield rate times the acquisition cost times the fraction of a year from the purchase date to the first interest date. The difference between the cash received and the credit to interest revenue is the premium (discount) amortization and is credited (debited) directly to Investment in Held-to-Maturity Debt Securities.

17. The sale prior to maturity of an investment in bonds classified as being held-to-maturity should be rare. However, such a sale of appropriately classified securities may occur with certain changes of circumstances. When a company sells an investment in held-to-maturity bonds before maturity, the purchaser must pay the sale price plus any interest earned since the last interest payment date. Before a company can determine a gain or loss on the sale, it must amortize any premium or discount on the bonds from the last interest date to the sales date. Then it compares the carrying value of the

bonds with the sales price (excluding accrued interest) to determine any gain or loss. The gain or loss is normally reported as ordinary income (loss).

Transfers and Impairments

18. Although transfers between categories should generally be rare, the transfer of a security between categories is accounted for at the fair value at the time of the transfer. In the journal entry to record the transfer, the fair value is used as the "new" investment carrying value, and the "old" investment carrying value is eliminated. The accounting for any related unrealized gain or loss varies depending on the type of transfer.

19. In a transfer from the trading category, no additional accounting for the unrealized holding gain or loss is necessary because it has already been recognized in net income. For a transfer into the trading category, the previous unrealized holding gain or loss is eliminated and a gain or loss is included in net income. The gain (loss) is recorded in a Gain (Loss) on Transfer of Securities account. For a transfer into the available-for-sale category from the held-to-maturity category, an unrealized holding gain or loss is established and included in other comprehensive income. For a transfer of an available-for-sale debt security into the held-to-maturity category, the unrealized holding gain or loss on the available-for-sale security is eliminated, and an unrealized holding gain or loss on the held-to-maturity security is created for the same amount and included in other comprehensive income. This amount is amortized over the remaining life of the security as an adjustment of interest revenue by computing a new yield to maturity for that security.

20. Impairment occurs when a decline in value below the amortized cost of the debt security classified as available for sale or held to maturity is deemed to be other than temporary, and it is, therefore, probable that an investor company will be unable to collect all amounts due. In such cases the company writes down the amortized cost of the security to the fair value, and includes the amount of the write-down in net income as a realized loss. The fair value becomes the new "cost" and subsequent changes in fair value are accounted for as originally described.

Disclosures

21. FASB Statement No. 115 requires the following disclosures related to investments in securities: (a) Trading Securities: the change in the net unrealized holding gain or loss included in each income statement must be disclosed; (b) Available-for-Sale Securities includes: disclosure for each balance sheet date includes the aggregate fair value, gross unrealized holding gains and gross unrealized holding losses, amortized cost by major security type, and the contractual maturities of debt securities; and for each income statement period, the proceeds from sales and the gross realized gains and losses on those sales, the basis on which cost was determined, the gross gains and losses included in net income from transfers of securities from this category into the trading category, and the change in the net unrealized holding gain or loss included as a separate component of other comprehensive income; (c) Held-to-Maturity Debt Securities: disclosure includes, for each balance sheet date, the aggregate fair value, gross unrealized holding gains or losses, amortized cost by major security type, and contractual maturities; as well as for any sales or transfers from this category, the amortized cost, the related realized or unrealized gain or loss, and the circumstances leading to the decision to sell or transfer the security.

22. Investments in trading securities are classified as current assets. Investments in available-for-sale securities are classified as current assets if they will be sold within one year or the operating cycle, whichever is longer. Otherwise, they are noncurrent. Investments in held-to-maturity debt securities are classified as noncurrent assets unless they mature within the next year.

FASB Statement No. 115: Conceptual Evaluation

23. Prior to FASB Statement No. 115, the lower of cost or market method was used to account for investments in marketable equity securities. Most companies used the cost method to account for investments in debt securities. The lower of cost or market method was criticized for lacking relevancy, because it did not reflect the liquidity of the company (security) when the fair value exceeded the cost, and for allowing "gains trading," (i.e., sales of securities only when those securities had fair values above cost).

24. There are four major controversies related to the revised principles: (a) in an attempt to choose values that would present information that is relevant, fair value is required in the balance sheet for trading securities and available-for-sale securities, whereas amortized cost is required for held-to-maturity securities; (b) fair value is not required for certain liabilities because of the difficulty determining which liabilities should be reported this way and the difficulty obtaining a reliable value; (c) unrealized holding gains and losses are reported in net income for trading securities to provide more relevant information for investors about the results of economic events that occur in the period and the company's return on investment; but directly in other comprehensive income for available-for-sale securities in order to avoid unnecessary volatility in reported net income; and (d) the classification of securities is based on management intent and thus may result in inconsistent application of the principles, a related lack of comparability and insufficient relevance.

International Accounting Differences

25. International accounting standards use the trading, available-for-sale, and held-to-maturity categories, but apply them to all financial assets.

Equity Method

26. The equity method of accounting (a) acknowledges the existence of a material economic relationship between the investor and the investee, (b) is based upon the requirements of accrual accounting, and (c) reflects the change in stockholders' equity of the investee company. APB Opinion No. 18 stipulates that an investor use the equity method to account for an investment in equity securities if the ownership allows the investor to exercise significant influence over the operating and financial policies of an investee. Generally speaking, this presumption is made if the investment is 20% or more of the outstanding common stock. In every case, however, the degree of influence in the investee company and not the percentage ownership is the determining factor. Therefore, certain circumstances preclude the use of the method even though 20% or more of the investee's common stock is held, and other circumstances mandate the use of the method even though less than 20% of the common stock is held.

27. Under the equity method:

$$\text{Investment} = \frac{\text{Acquisition}}{\text{Cost}} + \frac{\text{Investor's Share of}}{\text{Investee Income}} - \frac{\text{Dividends}}{\text{Received}}$$

where,

$$\frac{\text{Investor's Share of}}{\text{Investee Income}} = \left(\frac{\text{Investee's}}{\text{Net Income}} \times \frac{\text{Ownership}}{\text{Percentage}}\right) - \text{Adjustments}$$

and

$$\frac{\text{Dividends}}{\text{Received}} = \frac{\text{Total Dividends}}{\text{Paid by Investee}} \times \frac{\text{Ownership}}{\text{Percentage}}$$

28. Under the equity method, a company uses the following accounting procedures:

a. The investment in common stock is originally recorded at cost.

b. Dividends paid or declared are recorded as reductions in the carrying value of the investment account by preparing the following entry:

Cash	XXX	
Investment in Stock: Company B		XXX

c. A proportionate share (based on percentage ownership) of the investee's reported net income (loss) is recognized as income by the investor. If the investee has both ordinary and extraordinary income, the investor must also account for the income using two accounts. For example, if Company A owns 40% of Company B's common stock during all of 2004, and B Company reports 2004 ordinary income of $40,000 and extraordinary income of $10,000, the following journal entry would be made by Company A on December 31, 2004:

Investment in Stock: Company B	20,000	
Investment Income: Ordinary (0.40 x $40,000)		16,000
Investment Income: Extraordinary (0.40 x $10,000)		4,000

d. In addition, the investor company makes certain adjustments on its investment income as follows: (1) The effects of any intercompany transactions on investor net income are eliminated; (2) A proportionate share of the difference between the fair values and book values of the investee depreciable assets implied by the acquisition price of the investee assets is depreciated over the remaining useful life [any purchased goodwill is <u>not</u> amortized but is reviewed for impairment and, if necessary, an impairment loss is recognized and the investment account is reduced]; and (3) Proportionate shares of investee extraordinary items, results of discontinued operations, and cumulative effects of changes in accounting principles are treated likewise by the investor. For example, assume in the example in (c) above that Company A had purchased the 40% of Company stock on January 1, 2004, for $220,000, and that the following information concerning Company B existed at the time of the acquisition:

	Balance Sheet Book Value	Fair Value
Depreciable assets (remaining life, 10 years)	$500,000	$560,000
Other nondepreciable assets	150,000	190,000
Total	$650,000	$750,000
Liabilities	$225,000	
Common Stock	300,000	
Retained Earnings	125,000	
Total	$650,000	

On December 31, 2004, in addition to the entry in (c) above, Company A would make the following journal entry to record depreciation:

Investment Income: Ordinary	2,400	
Investment in Stock: Company B [(0.40 x $60,000*) ÷ 10]		2,400

*$60,000 = $560,000 fair value - $500,000

Company A would also compute the amount of purchased goodwill (if any), as follows:

Purchase price		$220,000
Book value of net assets acquired [0.40 x ($650,000 - $225,000)]		(170,000)
Excess of purchase price over book value of net assets		$ 50,000
Adjustments		
Increase in depreciable assets acquired [($560,000 - $500,000) x 0.40]	$24,000	
Increases in other nondepreciable assets acquired [($190,000 - $150,000) x 0.40]	16,000	
Increase in liabilities [($235,000 - $225,000) x 0.40]	(4,000)	(36,000)
Purchased goodwill		$ 14,000

If the goodwill was impaired at the end of 2004 (for simplicity, it is assumed the goodwill is not impaired), the company would record an impairment loss.

29. The investor discloses the carrying value of the investment in stock account, determined by adding the investor's share of investee net income and subtracting dividends, depreciation, and any goodwill impairment in the long-term investment section of its balance sheet. The total amount of the investor's share of the investee's net income (as adjusted) is disclosed on the investor's income statement. The notes to the financial statements include a schedule reconciling the investor's share of the investee's ordinary income with the net investment income reported as Other Revenue.

30. If an investor acquires enough additional shares during a year to exercise significant influence over the investee, a change from the fair value method to the equity method is required. When the equity method is adopted, the investor restates its investment in the investee by debiting the Investment account and crediting Retained Earnings for its previous percentage of investee income (less dividends) for the period from the date of acquisition to the date it obtained significant influence. The restatement is a prior period (retroactive) adjustment. The company also eliminates any amounts included in the Allowance and Unrealized Increase/Decrease accounts that recorded these shares at fair value. Thereafter, the investor applies the equity method in the usual manner based on the current percentage ownership.

31. If the investor sells enough stock to justify switching from the equity method to the fair value method, the investor should apply the fair value method subsequent to the date of change (prospectively). Previously recorded income remains as part of the Investment account.

32. If the purchase price of an investment in common stock accounted for by the equity method is less than the proportionate fair value of the net assets acquired, the investor should record the investment at cost. The negative goodwill, the difference between the cost and the fair value of the assets, is allocated to reduce the increase in values assigned to noncurrent assets.

33. An investor recognizes declines other than temporary in the value of investments accounted for under the equity method by debiting a Loss account and crediting the Investment account for the difference between the carrying value of the investment and the fair value. The investor does not recognize recoveries.

34. If an investor using the equity method acquires control over the operations of the investee, consolidated financial statements are prepared. In preparing such statements, the investor eliminates intercompany sales and profits and does not disclose intercompany receivables and payables in the consolidated financial reports. Although there may not be legal substance to the consolidation, the economic substance necessitates the consolidated reporting.

Additional Investment Issues

35. Non-marketable securities, shares or bonds issued by privately held companies, are outside the scope of FASB Statement No. 115. Therefore there is no requirement to report them at fair value, and they are typically reported at historical cost.

36. When an investor receives additional shares of stock from either a stock dividend or a stock split, the investor's relative percentage of ownership remains the same, and it records no income. However, because the investment is now spread over a larger number of shares, a memorandum journal entry is necessary to record the new average cost per share to be used in subsequent transactions.

37. Stock warrants issued to existing stockholders allow the stockholders to purchase a specified number of additional shares of stock at a predetermined price, usually slightly less than their current market price. Because the warrants are traded on the stock market soon after issuance, the holder can either purchase additional shares of stock by exercising the warrants or sell the stock warrants. When the warrants (rights) are received, the investor assigns a part of the carrying value of the existing common stock to the rights as discussed in Chapter 13.

38. A company reports the cash surrender value of life insurance held by the company on key officers of the organization as a long-term investment on its balance sheet. The cash surrender value is that accumulated portion of the annual premium which will be returned to the company in the event of policy cancellation. The company records the portion of the annual premium that does not increase the cash surrender value as insurance expense. The insurance expense is reduced by any dividends received on the policy. In the event of death, the company reports the difference between the proceeds and the cash surrender value of the policy as an ordinary gain.

39. When a company sets aside cash and other assets to accomplish specific future objectives, it establishes a fund. The most common long-term funds are those which are established in order to retire long-term liabilities (sinking funds), to retire preferred stock (stock redemption funds), or to purchase long-term assets (plant expansion funds). A company reports its long-term funds as investments on the balance sheet. The operations of these funds include the contribution of cash to the fund, investing the fund cash, receiving revenue, paying expenses, selling investments, and using the cash in the fund to achieve the established objective (e.g., retire bonds). Accounting for long-term funds requires a separate set of accounts to record the above transactions such as Sinking Fund Cash, Sinking Fund Securities, Sinking Fund Revenues, and Sinking Fund Expenses.

Appendix: Derivatives of Financial Instruments

40. A financial instrument is cash, evidence of ownership in an entity, or a contract that both (1) imposes on one entity a contractual obligation (a) to pay cash or another financial instrument to a second entity or (b) to exchange other financial instruments or potentially unfavorable terms with the second entity, and (2) conveys to the second entity a contractual right (a) to receive cash or another financial instrument from the first entity or (b) to exchange other financial instruments on potentially favorable terms with the first entity.

41. A derivative financial instrument (derivative) derives its value from an underlying asset or index and includes futures, forward, swap, and option contracts. Derivatives are often used by companies to reduce the risk of adverse changes in interest rates, foreign currency exchange rates, and commodity prices. Financial reporting should reflect the effects of this risk management.

42. A hedge is a means of protecting against a financial loss. There are three types of hedges: (1) fair value hedges, (2) cash flow hedges, and (3) hedges of foreign currency exposures of net investments in foreign operations. FASB Statement No. 133 governs the accounting treatment for each type of hedge.

43. One type of hedge is an interest-rate swap, an agreement in which two companies agree to exchange the interest payments on debt over a specified period. The interest payments are based on a principal amount that often is referred to as a notional (e.g. imaginary) amount because the swap does not involve an exchange of principal at either inception or maturity. An example of a fair value hedge is an interest rate swap in which a company receives a fixed rate of interest and pays a variable rate. An example of a cash flow hedge is an interest rate swap in which a company receives a variable rate of interest and pays a fixed rate.

44. A fair value hedge protects against the risk from changes in value caused by fixed terms, rates, or prices. For a fair value hedge, FASB Statement No. 133 requires that a company recognize in its current net income (1) any gain or loss from a change in the fair value of the fair value hedge, and (2) any gain or loss from the change in the fair value of the financial instrument being hedged, along with any interest revenue or expense. As a result the company reports both the derivative (fair value hedge) and the financial instrument on its balance sheet at their respective fair values. Therefore, the FASB is using the fair value method in the valuation of derivatives and the related financial instruments. There is no effect from the change in the fair value of a fair value hedge on a company's income statement because the change in the fair value of the derivative (fair value hedge) is offset by the change in the fair value of the financial instrument (i.e., an effective hedge of the fixed rate debt).

45. A cash flow hedge protects against the risk caused by variable prices, costs, rates, or terms that cause future cash flows to be uncertain. For a cash flow hedge, FASB Statement No. 133 requires that a company recognize in its current other comprehensive income any gain or loss from a change in the fair value of the cash flow hedge. The company reports the derivative (cash flow hedge) at its fair value and the related accumulated other comprehensive income in its stockholders' equity on its ending balance sheet. The company does not recognize in its financial statements any change in value of the financial instrument being hedged. When the hedged forecasted transaction occurs, the company transfers the accumulated other comprehensive income to its current net income.

SELF-EVALUATION EXERCISES

Supply the words, amounts, or computations necessary to complete each of the following items.

Investments: Classification and Valuation

ICV-1. When companies invest in the securities of other corporations or of the government, each group of such securities is often referred to as a ____________ of marketable securities.

ICV-2. Generally accepted accounting principles for all investments in debt securities and investments in equity securities that have readily determinable fair values are specified in FASB ___________ ______.

ICV-3. Debt and equity securities purchased and held principally for the purpose of selling them in the near future are classified as __________ ____________; debt securities not classified as held to maturity, and debt and equity securities not classified as trading securities are classified as ____________-____________-_____ _______; and those debt securities where the company has the "positive intent and ability to hold the securities to maturity" are classified as ______-_____-______ __________ __________.

ICV-4. Securities which represent a creditor relationship with another company are ______ securities; securities which represent an ownership interest in another company are _________ securities.

ICV-5. The amount at which a security could be exchanged in a current transaction between willing parties is the ______ ________.

Investments in Debt and Equity Trading Securities

IDE-1. Investments in debt and equity securities classified as trading securities are initially recorded at ______ and subsequently reported at __________ ________________.

IDE-2. Investments in debt and equity trading securities are held primarily by such institutions as _______ and _______________.

Investments in Available-for-Sale Debt and Equity Securities

IAS-1. In accounting for investments in available-for-sale debt and equity securities, unrealized holding gains and losses are reported as a component of

_____________ _______________ _________.

IAS-2. The initial cost of investments in available-for-sale debt and equity securities includes the _________ ________ plus any ________________ ______ and ________.

IAS-3. In accounting for investments in available-for-sale debt and equity securities, any unrealized holding gain (loss) is debited (credited) to an account titled:

____.

IAS-4. A realized gain or loss on the sale of securities is recorded in an account called: ____________________________________.

IAS-5. For an equity security, a realized gain or loss on the sale of securities is measured as the difference between the _________ ________ and the _______.

Investments in Held-to-Maturity Debt Securities

IDS-1. Under generally accepted accounting principles for investments in held-to-maturity debt securities, the investment is initially recorded at

______ and subsequently reported at ____________ _______.

IDS-2. In accounting for investments in bonds, the balance at the balance sheet date in the Investment in Held-to-Maturity Debt Securities account is reported at its

__________ ________.

IDS-3. When bonds that will be held to maturity are purchased between interest dates, the payment made to the previous owner for the interest earned since the last

interest receipt is recorded by a debit to __________ _________ and a credit

to _______.

Transfers and Impairments

TI-1. The transfer of a security between categories is accounted for at

the ______ ________ at the time of transfer.

TI-2. For a transfer <u>into the trading category</u>, the previous unrealized holding gain or loss is eliminated and a gain or loss is recorded in an account titled

_____________ _____ ____________ _____ _____________.

TI-3. _____________ occurs when a decline in value below the amortized cost of the debt security classified as available for sale or held to maturity is deemed to be other than temporary, and it is, therefore, probable that an investor company will be unable to collect all amounts due.

Disclosures

D-1. For investments in trading securities, FASB Statement No. 115

requires the disclosure of ____________________________________

____.

D-2. Investments in trading securities are classified as _________

_________; if investments in available-for-sale securities will not be sold within one year or the operating cycle whichever is longer, they are classified

as ________________ _________.

Equity Method

EM-1. The equity method must be used to account for long-term investments in equity securities when the investment allows the investor to exercise

____

____________________.

EM-2. Under the equity method, the investor records the receipt of cash

dividends by a debit to ________ and a credit to ____________

______ ____________.

EM-3. Company Y owns 30% of Company Z's common stock and uses the equity method to account for the investment. If Company Z reports ordinary income of $20,000,

Company Y must debit __________ ______ ________: ______ ________

for $________ and credit __________ ________: ____________ for

$__________.

EM-4. Under the equity method, the special adjustments which are necessary in recognizing the investor's proportionate share of the investee's net income are:

(1) ____

(2) ____

(3) ____

EM-5. Under the equity method, purchased goodwill is reviewed for impairment, and if

necessary an ________________ loss is recognized.

EM-6. The journal entry made by the investor using the equity method to depreciate the increase in the recorded value of depreciable assets acquired through a long-term investment in stock includes a debit to

__________ ________: __________ and a credit to ______________

______ ________.

EM-7. Under the equity method, the investor reports its share of investee

net income on the ________ __________.

EM-8. A switch from the equity method to the fair value method requires

that the fair value method be applied ____________.

Additional Issues

AI-1. Nonmarketable securities, shares or bonds issued by privately held companies, are typically reported at ____________ ________.

AI-2. The receipt of a stock dividend or a stock split by an investor is recorded by a ____________ ______________ ____________.

AI-3. The receipt of a stock dividend or stock split lowers the ___________ ___________ _________ ______________.

AI-4. A company should classify the cash surrender value of life insurance held on key executives on the balance sheet as a ____________ - ____________ _______________.

AI-5. A company should record the portion of the annual insurance premium which does not increase the cash surrender value of the policy as ____________ ____________.

AI-6. The receipt of cash dividends on an insurance policy reduces ______________ ____________.

AI-7. When a corporation sets aside cash in order to retire bonds in the future the corporation has established a _________________ ____________.

AI-8. A stock redemption fund must be accounted for by using a ______________ ________ ______ _______________.

Derivatives of Financial Instruments (Appendix)

DFI-1. A financial instrument which derives its value from an underlying asset or index is called a ____________________.

DFI-2. An agreement in which two companies agree to exchange interest payments on debt over a specified period is called an ____________-________-________.

DFI-3. An interest rate swap in which a company receives a fixed rate of interest and pays a variable rate is an example of a ____________ ____________ hedge.

DFI-4. The use of derivatives is often an attempt on the part of a company to manage interest rate or exchange rate ________.

ANSWERS TO SELF-EVALUATION EXERCISES

ICV-1. portfolio; ICV-2. Statement No. 115; ICV-3. trading securities, available-for-sale securities, held-to-maturity debt securities; ICV-4. debt, equity; ICV-5. fair value; IDE-1. cost, fair value; IDE-2. banks, stockbrokers; IAS-1. other comprehensive income; IAS-2. market price, brokerage fees, taxes; IAS-3. Allowance for Change in Value of Investment; IAS-4. Gain (Loss) on Sale of Available-for-Sale Securities; IAS-5. selling price, cost; IDS-1. cost, amortized cost; IDS-2. carrying value; IDS-3. Interest Revenue, Cash; TI-1. fair value; TI-2. Gain (Loss) on Transfer of Securities; TI-3. Impairment; D-1. the change in the net unrealized holding gain or loss included in each income statement; D-2. current assets, non-current assets; EM-1. significant influence over the operating and financial policies of the investee; EM-2. Cash, Investment in Stock; EM-3. Investment in Stock: Company Z; $6,000, Investment Income: Ordinary, $6,000; EM-4. (1) to eliminate the effects of any intercompany transactions on investor net income; (2) to depreciate the increase in the recorded value of depreciable assets acquired; and (3) to recognize a proportionate share of investee extraordinary items, results of discontinued operations, and cumulative effects of changes in accounting principles; EM-5. impairment; EM-6. Investment Income: Ordinary, Investment in Stock; EM-7. income statement; EM-8. prospectively; AI-1. historical cost; AI-2. memorandum journal entry; AI-3. average cost per share; AI-4. long-term investment; AI-5. insurance expense; AI-6. insurance expense; AI-7. sinking fund; AI-8. separate set of accounts; DFI-1. derivative; DFI-2. interest-rate swap; DFI-3. fair value; DFI-4. risk.

POST TEST

Part A Circle T if the statement is true and F if it is false.

T F 1. A security has a readily determinable fair value if a sales price is currently available on a securities exchange registered with the SEC or in an over-the-counter market whose prices are publicly reported.

T F 2. Debt securities not classified as held to maturity are classified as Trading Securities.

T F 3. Fair value is the amount at which a security could be exchanged in a current transaction between willing parties.

T F 4. According to GAAP, unrealized holding gains and losses on investments in debt and equity securities classified as trading securities are reported as a separate component of stockholders' equity.

T F 5. According to GAAP, unrealized holding gains and losses on investments in available-for-sale debt and equity securities are included in other comprehensive income of the current period.

T F 6. According to GAAP, unrealized holding gains and losses on investments in held-to-maturity debt securities are not recorded.

T F 7. Realized gains and losses on sales of investments in available-for-sale debt and equity securities and investments in trading securities are included in net income for the current period.

T F 8. Investments in held-to-maturity debt securities are initially recorded at cost and subsequently reported at fair value.

T F 9. Like debtor companies, investor companies use a separate valuation account to record the premiums and discounts on investments in bonds.

T F 10. The amortization of a bond premium results in an effective interest rate lower than the stated rate.

T F 11. Consistent with the conservatism principle, the transfer of a security between categories is accounted for at the historical cost.

T F 12. For a transfer into the available-for-sale category from the held-to-maturity category, an unrealized holding gain or loss is established and recognized in stockholders' equity.

T F 13. For a transfer of an available-for-sale debt security into the held-to-maturity category, an unrealized holding gain or loss on the available-for-sale security is eliminated, and an unrealized holding gain or loss on the held-to-maturity security is created and included in other comprehensive income.

T F 14. When impairment occurs, the amortized cost of the security is written down to the fair value, and the amount of the writedown is included in stockholders' equity.

T F 15. Investments in held-to-maturity debt securities are always classified as noncurrent assets.

T F 16. The effect of applying <u>FASB Statement No. 115</u> is reported as a change in accounting estimate.

T F 17. Under <u>FASB Statement No. 115</u>, fair value is required in the balance sheet for trading securities and available-for-sale securities, whereas amortized cost is required for held-to-maturity securities.

T F 18. International accounting standards and FASB standards both require the use of the trading, available-for-sale, and held-to-maturity categories in accounting for all financial assets.

T F 19. Under the equity method, the receipt of cash dividends reduces the carrying value of the Investment in Stock account.

T F 20. If an investment in equity securities is accounted for using the equity method, revenue that is recorded by the investor as a result of a sales transaction between the investee and the investor must be eliminated by the investor.

T F 21. Under the equity method, the Investment in Stock account is <u>decreased</u> by a proportionate share of the investee's reported net income.

T F 22. When the method used to account for an investment in equity securities is changed from the fair value method to the equity method, retained earnings is increased by the amount of the investor's previous percentage of investee income from the original date of acquisition to the date that it obtained significant influence.

T F 23. Stock dividends and stock splits increase the value of the Investment in Stock account.

T F 24. Because stock warrants are traded on the stock market soon after issuance, the value assigned to stock warrants received by a stockholder is equal to the current market value of the warrants.

T F 25. The value assigned to stock rights may be recorded in an Investment in Stock Rights account.

T F 26. Upon the death of an insured officer, a company reports the difference between the proceeds from the life insurance policy and the cash surrender value of the policy as ordinary gain.

T F 27. A fund involves the setting aside of cash and other assets to accomplish specific objectives.

T F 28. A contract would be considered a financial instrument if it either imposed a contractual obligation on one entity to pay cash to a second entity <u>or</u> conveyed to the second entity a contractual right to receive cash from the first entity.

T F 29. A company must report any change in the fair value of a cash flow hedge and any change in value of the financial instrument being hedged in net income.

<u>Part B</u> Select the one <u>best</u> answer and place its letter in the space provided.

_____ 1. On July 1, Sada Corporation acquired 100 shares of Radon Corporation common stock at $80 per share and 200 shares of Greenco Corporation common stock at $50 a share. Six months later, on December 31, the Radon stock had a fair value of $75 a share and the Greenco Corporation stock had a fair value of $56 a share. These shares are classified as available-for-sale equity securities. In its December 31 year-end financial statements, Sada should include which of the following? (a) $700 unrealized holding gain as a component of accumulated other comprehensive income on the balance sheet; (b) $700 unrealized holding gain on the income statement; (c) $500 unrealized holding loss as a component of accumulated other comprehensive income on the balance sheet; (d) $1,200 unrealized holding gain as a component of accumulated other comprehensive income on the balance sheet.

_____ 2. Generally accepted accounting principles for investments in debt and equity securities classified as trading securities include all of the following <u>except</u>: (a) the investment is initially recorded at cost; (b) the investment is subsequently reported at fair value; (c) unrealized holding gains and losses are included in stockholders' equity; (d) interest and dividend revenue are included in income of the current period.

_____ 3. The original cost of a portfolio of available-for-sale equity securities is $25,500. On December 31, 2004, the fair value of the portfolio was $27,000 and the Allowance for Change in Value of Investment account has a debit balance of $1,500. On December 31, 2005 the fair value of the portfolio is $26,000. To record the change in value, the Allowance account should be (a) credited for $500; (b) credited for $1,000; (c) credited for $1,500; (d) credited for $2,500.

_____ 4. Penway Company had the following portfolio of available-for-sale equity securities:

Security	Cost	12/31/04 Fair Value	Cumulative Change in Fair Value
100 shares Company A stock	$2,000	$2,500	$ 500
150 shares Company B stock	1,500	2,200	700
200 shares Company C stock	4,000	3,600	(400)
	$7,500	$8,300	$ 800

If Penway sells the 150 shares of Company B stock for $2,100 during 2005, the entry to record the sale will include (a) a $600 Gain on Sale of Available-for-Sale Securities; (b) a $100 Loss on Sale of Available-for-Sale Securities; (c) a $1,300 Gain on Sale of Available-for-Sale Securities; (d) a $100 Gain on Sale of Available-for-Sale Securities.

_____ 5. FASB Statement No. 115 requires all of the following disclosures related to investments in available-for-sale securities except (a) the aggregate fair value; (b) gross unrealized holding gains and gross unrealized holding losses; (c) the circumstances leading to decisions to sell or transfer securities; (d) the change in the net unrealized holding gain or loss included as a separate component of other comprehensive income.

_____ 6. On January 1, 2004, Hudson Company acquired an investment in bonds that will be held to maturity with a face value of $100,000 for $106,046. These bonds carry a stated interest rate of 8%, payable semiannually, and mature on December 31, 2008. The bonds yield an effective interest rate of 7%. If Hudson uses the effective interest method to account for the bonds, the balance reported on the December 31, 2004 balance sheet in Investment in Held-to-Maturity Debt Securities should be: (a) $105,459.13; (b) $105,290.25; (c) $100,000; (d) $105,469.22.

_____ 7. When a bond is purchased at a discount, amortization of the discount causes periodic interest revenue to be (a) not affected; (b) decreased; (c) increased; (d) calculated by multiplying the face value times the effective interest rate.

_____ 8. On January 1, 2004, Company Y acquired 25% of Company Z's voting stock for $30,000, and uses the equity method to account for the investment. The purchase price of the shares was equal to their book value. During 2004, Company Z declares dividends of $20,000 and reports net income of $50,000. On December 31, 2004, the balance in Company Y's Investment in Stock: Company Z account will be (a) $30,000; (b) $37,500; (c) $47,500; (d) $60,000.

_____ 9. The equity method of accounting for an investment in equity securities should be used when the investment (a) includes both common and preferred stock and both types of stock have voting rights; (b) is acquired in exchange for property, goods, or services; (c) enables the investor to exercise significant influence over the operations of the investee; (d) ensures a payment of annual dividends and a share in the reported net income of the investee.

_____ 10. The investor's depreciation of the increase in the recorded value of the investee depreciable assets acquired should be recorded under the equity method as (a) a decrease in the investee reported net income that is recognized by the investor; (b) an increase in the investor's related long-term investment in equity securities account; (c) a decrease in stockholders' equity and reported in a separate section of stockholders' equity below Contributed Capital and preceding Retained Earnings; (d) an increase to the Investor's Depreciation Expense account and reported on the investor's income statement as an operating expense.

_____ 11. Staple Corporation purchases life insurance policies on its key officers. The policies have a cash surrender value clause. At the beginning of 2004, Staple paid $15,000 in insurance premiums for the year. The cash surrender value of the policies increased from $104,150 to $108,350 during 2004. For 2004, Staple would recognize insurance expense on these policies of (a) $15,000; (b) $4,200; (c) $10,800; (d) $19,200.

_____ 12. Quick Company has established a sinking fund to retire an outstanding bond issue. During 2004, Quick collected $20,000 in interest from investments in sinking fund securities. The receipt of the interest would be recorded in Quick Company's (a) Investment Revenue account; (b) Sinking Fund Revenue account; (c) Investment in Stock account; (d) Sinking Fund Securities account.

_____ 13. McGill Company has had a $1.5 million bank loan from First National Bank. Annual interest payments are made at year-end and are determined by the variable LIBOR (London Inter Bank Offering Rate) interest rate at the beginning of the year. The applicable interest rate is reset each year after the annual interest payment is made. On January 7, 2004 when the loan has 3 years remaining, McGill enters into a 3-year interest-rate swap with a $1.5 million notional amount and agrees to pay to the bank an interest rate each year that is fixed at 7%. At the beginning of 2004 the LIBOR is 6.7%. McGill will recognize total interest expense for 2004 related to the loan of (a) $105,000; (b) $100,500; (c) $4,500; (d) $109,500.

Part C Solve each of the following short problems.

1. During 2004, Pakenda Corporation began investing its idle cash in bonds. The information contained below relates to Pakenda's investment in available-for-sale securities for 2004 and 2005.

2004

April 1 Purchased $100,000 face value 12% bonds of the Altec Corporation at $107,721.71 plus accrued interest to yield 10%. Interest is payable on these bonds each July 31 and January 31. The effective interest method is used.

July 31 Received the semiannual interest on the Altec bonds.

Dec. 31 Recorded the accrued interest on the Altec bonds. On this date Altec bonds were selling at 103 plus accrued interest.

2005

Jan. 31 Received the semiannual interest on the Altec bonds.

March 1 Sold the Altec bonds at 104 plus accrued interest.

Record Pakenda's transactions in investments in available-for-sale securities for 2004 and 2005 using the fair value method.

2. The following information is available for Robbins Corporation's investment in available-for-sale securities.

	8/15/04 Cost	12/31/04 Fair Value	12/31/05 Fair Value
Corporation X Common 400 shares	$8,000	$10,000	$10,500
Corporation Y Common 600 shares	6,000	4,800	6,200
Corporation Z Common 800 shares	16,000	14,000	14,000

(a) Prepare the journal entry to record the initial acquisition and the necessary journal entries at the end of 2004 and 2005.

(b) In March 2006, Robbins sold the 600 shares of Corporation Y common stock for $5,900. Prepare the journal entry to record the sale.

3. During 2004 and 2005, the following events occurred:

(a) On January 1, 2004, Wilson Corporation acquired 3,000 of the 12,000 outstanding shares of Lowe Company common stock for $48 per share. The purchase price of the shares was equal to their book value.

(b) On June 30, 2004, Lowe Company paid a $3 per share dividend.

(c) On December 31, 2004, Lowe Company reported net income of $30,000. On this date the price of Lowe's common stock was $46 per share.

(d) On June 30, 2005, Lowe Company paid a $2 per share dividend.

(e) On December 31, 2005, Lowe Company reported net income of $26,000, and the market price per share was $47.

Prepare the journal entries to record the above events using the equity method.

4. On January 1, 2004, Jarrad Corporation acquired bonds with a face value of $300,000 for $274,848.47. The bonds have a 10% stated interest rate and a 12% yield rate. Interest is paid semiannually on June 30 and December 31, and the bonds mature on December 31, 2010. Jarrad intends to hold the bonds until maturity. Prepare the journal entries necessary to record the purchase of the bonds and the first two interest receipts using the effective interest method of amortization.

ANSWERS TO POST TEST

Part A

1. T
2. F
3. T
4. F
5. T
6. T
7. T
8. F
9. F
10. T
11. F
12. F
13. T
14. F
15. F
16. F
17. T
18. F
19. T
20. T
21. F
22. T
23. F
24. F
25. T
26. T
27. T
28. F
29. F

Part B

1. a
2. c
3. b
4. a
5. c
6. a
7. c
8. b
9. c
10. a
11. c
12. b
13. a

Part C

1\. 2004

Date		Account	Debit	Credit
April	1	Investment in Available-for-Sale Securities	107,721.71	
		Interest Revenue ($100,000 x 0.12 x 2/12)	2,000.00	
		Cash		109,721.71
July	31	Cash	6,000	
		Interest Revenue ($107,721.71 x 0.10 x 6/12)		5,386.09
		Investment in Available-for-Sale Securities		613.91
Dec.	31	Interest Receivable	5,000	
		Interest Revenue ($107,107.80 x 0.10 x 5/12)		4,462.83
		Investment in Available-for-Sale Securities		537.17
	31	Unrealized Increase/Decrease in Value of Available-for-Sale Securities	3,570.63	
		Allowance for Change in Value of Investment [($107,721.71 - ($613.91 + $537.17) - $103,000]		3,570.63
2005				
Jan.	31	Cash	6,000	
		Interest Receivable		5,000
		Interest Revenue		888.09
		Investment in Available-for-Sale Securities		111.91
Mar.	1	Cash	105,000	
		Loss on Sale of Available-for-Sale Securities	2,345.88	
		Investment in Available-for-Sale Securities		106,458.72
		Interest Revenue		887.16
		Allowance for Change in Value of Investment	3,570.63	
		Unrealized Increase/Decrease in Value of Available-for-Sale Securities		3,570.63

2\. (a) 2004

Date		Account	Debit	Credit
Aug.	15	Investment in Available-for-Sale Securities	30,000	
		Cash		30,000
		To record initial acquisition.		

Dec. 31	Unrealized Increase/Decrease in Value of Available-for-Sale Securities	1,200	
	Allowance for Change in Value of Investment		1,200
	To record an unrealized holding loss.		

2005			
Dec. 31	Allowance for Change in Value of Investment	1,900	
	Unrealized Increase/Decrease in Value of Available-for-Sale Securities		1,900
	To adjust the Allowance account to reflect a $700 cumulative unrealized increase in value.		

(b)

Cash	5,900	
Loss on Sale of Available-for-Sale Securities	100	
Investment in Available-for-Sale Securities		6,000
Unrealized Increase/Decrease in Value of Available-for-Sale Securities	200	
Allowance for Change in Value of Investment		200
To record sale of securities.		

3\. (a) To record the acquisition of the stock:

Investment in Stock: Lowe Company	144,000	
Cash		144,000

(b) To record the receipt of the $3 dividend per share in 2004:

Cash	9,000	
Investment in Stock: Lowe Company		9,000

(c) To record Wilson Corporation's share in Lowe Company's reported net income in 2004:

Investment in Stock: Lowe Company (0.25 x $30,000)	7,500	
Investment Income: Ordinary		7,500

(d) To record the receipt of the $2 dividend per share in 2005:

Cash	6,000	
Investment in Stock: Lowe Company		6,000

3. (e) To record Wilson Corporation's share in Lowe Company's reported net income in 2005:

	Debit	Credit
Investment in Stock: Lowe Company (0.25 x $26,000)	6,500	
Investment Income: Ordinary		6,500

4. To record the bond purchase:

	Debit	Credit
Investment in Debt Securities Held to Maturity	274,848.47	
Cash		274,848.47

To record the receipt of interest on June 30, 2005:

	Debit	Credit
Cash ($300,000 x 0.10 x ½)	15,000.00	
Investment in Debt Securities Held to Maturity	1,490.91	
Interest Revenue ($274,848.47 x 0.12 x ½)		16,490.91

To record the receipt of interest on December 31, 2005:

	Debit	Credit
Cash ($300,000 x 0.10 x ½)	15,000.00	
Investment in Debt Securities Held to Maturity	1,580.36	
Interest Revenue [($274,848.47 + $1,490.91) x 0.12 x ½]		16,580.36

15

CONTRIBUTED CAPITAL

CHAPTER OBJECTIVES

After careful study of this chapter, you will be able to:

1. Explain the corporate form of organization.
2. Know the rights and terms that apply to capital stock.
3. Account for the issuance of capital stock.
4. Describe a compensatory stock option plan.
5. Recognize compensation expense for a compensatory stock option plan.
6. Account for a fixed compensatory stock option plan.
7. Account for a performance-based compensatory stock option plan.
8. Understand how to use the intrinsic value method to account for a compensatory stock option plan.
9. Describe the characteristics of preferred stock.
10. Know the components of contributed capital.
11. Understand the accounting for treasury stock.

SYNOPSIS

Corporate Form of Organization

1. FASB Statement of Concepts No. 6 includes the definition of equity as one of the elements of financial statements. Equity in a company is the ownership interest in the company and may be calculated as the difference between assets and liabilities. Equity in a company is first created by owners' investments in the company. Subsequently, the value of the equity is changed by net income (loss), additional investments by owners, and distributions to owners.

2. A corporation is a legal entity, separate and distinct from its individual owners, created under the laws of a particular state. As a result, the corporation has an unlimited life, owners have limited legal liability, and ownership interests (stocks) are easily transferable. The purpose of the corporation and the rights and powers granted by the state to the corporation to engage in certain legal activities and business transactions related to those activities are stipulated in a written contract called the articles of incorporation or corporate charter. Corporations may be classified as private or public, open or closed, domestic or foreign.

Corporate Capital Structure

3. The individual owners are called stockholders whose ownership in the corporation is evidenced by a stock certificate. Each stockholder has various stockholder's rights which include (a) the right to share in profits when a dividend is declared, (b) the right to elect directors and to establish corporate policies, (c) the preemptive right to maintain a proportionate interest in the ownership of the corporation by purchasing a proportionate share of additional capital stock, if such stock is issued, and (d) the right to share in the distribution of the assets of the corporation if it is liquidated. Common stock has all of these rights; preferred stock does not, but has certain other privileges.

4. Authorized capital stock is the number of shares of capital stock which may be issued as stated in the corporate charter. Issued capital stock is the number of shares actually issued as of a specific date. Outstanding capital stock is the number of shares issued to stockholders which are still being held by them. Treasury stock is the number of shares of capital stock which were issued to stockholders and were later reacquired by the corporation but not retired. Issued shares less outstanding shares equals treasury stock. Subscribed capital stock is the number of shares of capital stock that will be issued upon completion of an installment purchase contract with an investor.

5. Stockholders have limited liability and generally cannot be held responsible for the debts of the corporation. To protect the creditors of the corporation, states limit the amount of stockholders' equity which can be distributed to the stockholders. Although the amounts vary from state to state, the amount which cannot be distributed is the legal capital. Generally the par value or stated value of the issued capital stock is some or all of the legal capital.

6. The par value of each share of a corporation's capital stock is a designated dollar amount per share established in the corporate charter. The market value is the price at which the stock is issued or sold, and has no direct relationship to par value. Stock sold at less than par value is sold at a discount (illegal in most states), and the stockholders are additionally liable for this discount.

7. To avoid the contingent liability for the discount and to indicate to investors that par value and market value are not related, a corporation may issue no-par value stock. Although such stock is without a par value, each share may be assigned a stated value. The accounting for no-par stock with a stated value parallels the accounting for par-value stock.

8. Additional paid-in capital arises in a capital stock transaction when the exchange price (market value) of the stock is higher than the par or stated value of the stock. Sound accounting practice, as well as certain state laws, requires a corporation to identify, measure, and record this excess. Alternative names for this account are Paid-in Capital in Excess of Par (or Stated) Value, Premium on Capital Stock, and Contributed Capital in Excess of Par (or Stated) Value.

9. The stockholders' equity portion of the balance sheet discloses the corporation's capital structure in three sections: (a) Contributed Capital, the total amount invested by stockholders as a result of all corporate stock transactions, (b) Retained Earnings, corporate net income reinvested in the corporation, and (c) Accumulated Other Comprehensive Income. The basic framework of this stockholders' equity section is as follows:

Stockholders' Equity

Contributed capital	
Capital stock	$XXX
Additional paid-in capital	XXX
Retained earnings	XXX
Accumulated other comprehensive income	XXX
Total stockholders' equity	$XXX

Issuance of Capital Stock

10. When only one class of capital stock is issued, it is called common stock. The common stockholders are the claimants to the residual interest in the corporation. Although most capital stock is common stock, transactions involving different classes of stock are all recorded in a similar manner with appropriate changes in terminology.

11. The authorization to issue capital stock is recorded in the form of a memorandum journal entry. When the stock is issued for cash, Cash is debited, the capital stock account (e.g., Common Stock) is credited with the par or stated value, and the Additional Paid-in Capital account is credited with the difference. A corporation records any stock issuance costs related directly to the initial issuance of stock as an expense. Costs associated with subsequent issuances of stock reduce the proceeds, and the corporation reduces (debits) Additional Paid-in Capital when it pays the costs.

12. Investors may enter into a legally binding contract to purchase a certain number of shares of capital stock at an agreed-upon price with payment spread over a specified time period. The total amount of the stock subscription is recorded by a debit to Subscriptions Receivable: Capital Stock. This account is generally listed as a current asset, although for SEC reporting it is listed as a contra-stockholders' equity

account. At the same time, Capital Stock Subscribed is credited with the par or stated value of the stock (or the entire subscription price for no-par, no stated value stock) and is included in the Contributed Capital section of stockholders' equity because the corporation has a legal contract to issue additional stock. Additional Paid-in Capital may also be credited for the difference between the subscription price and the par value of the subscribed stock. When the subscribed stock is fully paid for, the shares are issued to the stockholder, the receivable is credited, and the Capital Stock Subscribed is transferred to the Capital Stock account.

13. When a default occurs on the subscribed stock, the provisions of the contract may require that (a) the entire amount already paid in be returned to the subscriber, (b) the amount paid in less any reissuance costs be returned to the subscriber, (c) a number of shares be issued to the subscriber based on the partial amount already paid in, or (d) the amount paid in be forfeited to the corporation. If forfeiture occurs, the corporation removes all balances in accounts relating to the subscribed stock from the records, and it credits Additional Paid-in Capital from Subscription Default for the amount of money paid in.

14. When a corporation issues two or more classes of securities in a single "package" transaction, the selling price of the package may be less than what would have been received if each class of securities had been sold separately. Therefore, the corporation allocates the selling price to each class based upon the individual relative fair value of each class. For example, assume a corporation issues 100 packages of securities for $85.50 per package for a total of $8,550. Each package consists of one share of $5 par common stock having a market value of $15 per share and two shares of $20 par preferred stock having a market value of $40 per share. The corporation would calculate the aggregate fair value first as follows:

Preferred:	$40 x 2 shares x 100 packages =	$8,000
Common:	$15 x 1 share x 100 packages =	$1,500
	Aggregate fair value	$9,500

Then it would allocate the selling price to each security as follows:

Preferred stock: $\frac{\$8,000}{\$9,500} \times \$8,550 = \$7,200$

Common stock: $\frac{\$1,500}{\$9,500} \times \$8,550 = \$1,350$

If only one market value is known, the corporation assigns that value to that security and assigns the remainder of the proceeds to the other security. If no fair values are known, it may assign an arbitrary amount to each class. Adjustments may be required subsequently when fair values become known. When recording the issuance, the corporation separates the market value into the par value and additional paid-in capital.

15. A nonmonetary exchange occurs when a corporation issues stock in exchange for assets other than cash. Generally, the corporation records the transaction at the fair value of the stock issued or the asset received, whichever is more reliable. Where fair values are unknown, assigned values may be used. The corporate board of directors makes the assignment and must be careful to avoid watered stock (overstatement of assets and a corresponding overstatement of stockholders' equity) or secret reserves (understatement of assets and stockholders' equity).

16. A stock split or stock split-up may be necessary to reduce the market price of a corporation's common stock so that it falls within the "trading range" of most investors. If the stock split is proportionate, it results in a decrease in the par value per share of stock accompanied by a proportional increase in the number of shares authorized and issued and no change in total stockholders' equity. A corporation records a proportionate stock split by a memorandum entry that indicates the new par value, the total number of shares issued, and the impact on the number of authorized shares. A disproportionate stock split results in a reduction in par value that is not proportionate to the increase in the number of shares. While total stockholders' equity is not affected, the balances of the individual contributed capital accounts are changed. Therefore, a journal entry is necessary to adjust the common stock and additional paid-in capital accounts. A reverse stock split increases the par value per share and decreases the number of shares, with no effect on total stockholders' equity.

17. A corporation may issue stock rights to current stockholders to allow them to exercise their preemptive right (the opportunity to maintain their proportionate share in the corporation by purchasing additional shares before they are issued to the public) or to encourage rapid sale of a new issue. Stock rights usually allow the stock to be purchased at a price lower than the market value of the stock, thus each right acquires a value. Because the warrants (rights) are certificates that are readily transferable, they may be traded on the stock market. When a corporation issues the stock warrants it makes a memorandum entry which lists the number of additional shares that may be acquired through the exercise of the stock rights. The corporation records the exercise of the rights by the usual journal entries to record a stock issuance, while it records the expiration of any rights by another memorandum entry.

Stock Option Plans

18. Stock option plans enable corporate employees through warrants (rights) to purchase shares of stock in the corporation, frequently at a price lower than the current market price. The plan may be either a compensatory or noncompensatory stock option plan.

19. The purpose of a noncompensatory stock option plan (employee stock purchase plan) is to raise capital or to obtain more widespread employee ownership of the corporate stock. No compensation to the employees results from this type of plan. Only memorandum entries are required until the warrants are exercised, and then the usual journal entry for the issuance of capital stock in exchange for stock warrants is required at that time. A plan is considered noncompensatory if all of the following characteristics are met: (a) almost all full-time employees may participate in the plan on an equitable basis; (b) the discount from the market price does not exceed the greater of (1) a per-share discount that would be reasonable in an offer of stock to stockholders or others, or (2) the per-share amount of stock issuance costs avoided by not issuing the stock to the public (a purchase discount of up to 15% automatically complies); (c) the plan has no option features other than (1) employees are allowed no longer than 31 days from the date the purchase price is set to decide whether to enroll in the plan, and (2) the purchase price is based solely on the market price of the stock on the purchase date, and employees are permitted to cancel their participation before the purchase date and obtain a refund of any amounts previously paid.

20. A stock-based compensation plan is a compensation agreement under which employees, in exchange for their services, receive shares of stock, stock options, or other equity instruments. A compensatory stock option plan is intended to provide additional compensation to key officers and managers and is the most common type of stock-based compensation plan. A compensatory stock option plan, by definition, does not possess all three of the criteria listed above in #19. The terms are often complex and are

related to such items as the number of shares to which each employee is entitled and the option price (both of which may depend on some future event), whether cash may be received instead of shares, the period of service which the employee must complete before becoming eligible, the date when the option can first be exercised, and the date of expiration (if any). Accounting for this type of plan is more difficult because of the complexities related to the determination of the compensation cost, the accounting periods which may be affected, and proper disclosure.

21. The exercise price (or option price) is the set price at which the corporation grants employees the right to purchase shares of stock some time in the future in exchange for services. The rights are usually issued in the form of nontransferable warrants. Historically, the intrinsic value method was used to account for the granting of the rights. Under, the intrinsic value method, the total compensation cost is the amount by which the quoted market price of the stock at the measurement date exceeds the amount the employee is required to pay to purchase the specified number of shares. The measurement date is the first date on which both the number of shares and the exercise price are known. The company recognizes the total compensation cost as an expense on a straight-line basis over the service period, the years in which it receives the services of the employee. If a company uses the intrinsic value method, it must disclose in the notes to its financial statements pro forma income and earnings per share determined as if the fair value method (described below) had been used to measure compensation expense.

22. Under the intrinsic value method, if the exercise price is equal to or higher than the market price on the measurement date, the company incurs no compensation cost and recognizes no compensation expense. This has often been the case as corporations constructed plans to take advantage of favorable tax treatment for executives. To meet the criteria of qualified (incentive) stock option plans under IRS rules, the option price must be set at the market price on the grant date. Thus, this method has been criticized as lacking relevancy because the fair value of the stock option and the compensation expense were often seriously understated while net income was overstated.

23. FASB Statement No. 123 recommends use of the fair value method of accounting for compensatory stock option plans. The company estimates the fair value of a stock option on the grant date using an option pricing model and makes no subsequent adjustment. The grant date is the date on which the corporation and an employee have an agreement concerning the terms of the stock-option-based compensation award. The option pricing model must take into account six variables: (1) exercise price; (2) expected life of the option; (3) current market price of the underlying common stock; (4) expected volatility of the stock; (5) expected dividends on the stock; and (6) risk-free interest rate for the expected term of the option.

24. The total compensation cost under the fair value method is the total fair value of the stock options that actually become vested. Stock options become vested on the date the employee's right to exercise the stock options is no longer contingent on remaining in the service of the company. The company recognizes the total compensation cost as an operating expense on a straight-line basis over the service period. The service period is the years during which the employee must work for the company in exchange for the stock options. Usually the service period equals the vesting period. If a significant number of employees are expected to forfeit their nonvested options as a result of turnover, the company calculates an estimated total compensation cost, using an estimated number of stock options expected to vest.

25. In a fixed stock option plan (cliff vesting) all the terms are set (fixed) on the grant date. On the grant date, a company uses a memorandum entry to summarize the terms of the compensatory stock option plan including the number of eligible employees, the number of stock options, the exercise price per share, the vesting period, the date of expiration of the options, and the estimated fair value of the stock options expected to be exercised. The company makes journal entries annually to recognize compensation expense and the related fair value of the common stock option warrants. When an employee exercises stock options, the company debits Cash for the exercise price, debits Common Stock Option Warrants for the previously recorded value of the warrants received, and credits Common Stock and Additional Paid-in Capital for the cash received plus the fair value of the option. When stock options expire, the company transfers the amount recorded in the Common Stock Option Warrants account to Additional Paid-in Capital.

26. In a performance-based stock option plan (variable-term plan), one or more terms are not fixed at the grant date. The terms vary depending on how well the key employees perform during the service period. For example, the exercise price or the number of stock options awarded may vary with earnings or market share for the corporation's products. The estimated total fair value depends on the number of options that are expected to be earned during the vesting period. The memorandum entry and journal entries to recognize compensation expense are the same as under a fixed stock option plan.

27. A corporation may also create appreciation rights (SARs). The stock appreciation rights enable key employees to receive stock, cash, or a combination of both, at some future date. The amount of the grant is equal to the excess of the market value over a stated price for a stated number of shares of stock on the date of exercise. The measurement date is the date the rights are exercised. The intrinsic value method is used to account for the plan. Since the exercise date normally falls after the service period, the corporation (a) estimates the total compensation cost at the end of each year based on the difference between the market price of the stock at that time and the option price; (b) records compensation expense over the service period on the basis of these estimates (and any corrections of previous estimation errors); and (c) because corrections of estimates are not made retroactively, makes additional adjustments to compensation expense each year after the service period has expired up to the date of exercise. These procedures are consistent with the matching principle.

28. Accounting for a stock appreciation rights plan is different from accounting for compensatory stock option plan in two important ways. First, the annual adjustments to compensation expense after the service period has expired are based on the difference between 100% of the estimated total compensation cost and the accrued compensation expense to date. Second, the credit entry to recognize accrued compensation expense is made either to a liability account or a stockholders' equity account depending on whether the employee is expected to elect to receive cash or stock on the date of exercise.

29. A corporation must report Compensation Expense and Common Stock Option Warrants accounts in its financial statements and disclose in the notes to the financial statements the following additional items related to a compensatory stock option plan: (a) a description of the plan including vesting requirements, number of shares authorized for grants of options, and maximum term of options granted; (b) the number and weighted-average exercise prices for options granted, exercised, outstanding, forfeited, and expired during the year; (c) the weighted-average grant-date fair values of options granted during the year; and (d) a description of the method and assumptions used during the year to estimate the fair values of options.

30. Use of the fair value method of accounting for compensatory stock option plans increases the relevance by (a) reflecting the value that the stock market places on the stock options; (b) providing a better measure of return on investment because compensation expense is included in net income; (c) providing a better measure of risk associated with the exercise of the options; and (d) increasing comparability through the information provided in the notes to the financial statements. Although the fair value method is preferred, FASB Statement No. 123 still allows use of the intrinsic value method.

Preferred Stock Characteristics

31. Some investors prefer stockholders' rights which are different than the rights normally given to common stockholders. A different class of stock called preferred stock is issued to these investors, and they have certain preferential rights. Unless stipulated otherwise, the preferred stockholder has full voting rights.

32. A preference to dividends is one right preferred stockholders have. That is, preferred stockholders must receive dividends before common stockholders, but only if dividends are declared. These dividends are usually expressed as a percentage of par value or as a specified dollar amount per share.

33. Payment of dividends is never guaranteed. If a dividend on preferred stock is not declared in a particular year, but the undeclared dividends must be accumulated and paid in a later year when dividends are declared, the undeclared dividends are referred to as dividends in arrears and the stock is cumulative preferred stock. Otherwise the preferred stock is noncumulative. Preferred stockholders of cumulative preferred stock must be paid all dividends in arrears before any dividends may be paid to common stockholders. Most preferred stock is cumulative.

34. Preferred stock may also provide for preferred stockholders to share with common stockholders in any "extra" dividends that remain after dividends in arrears, preferred dividends, and common dividends at a rate per share equal to that paid on preferred stock are paid. If the extra dividends are shared proportionately (relative to the respective par values) the stock is fully participating preferred stock. If the share in extra dividends is limited to a fixed rate or amount per share, the stock is partially participating preferred stock. Both fully and partially participating preferred stock are rare.

35. Preferred stock which allows stockholders, at their option, under specified conditions, to convert their preferred stock shares into other securities (usually common shares) is called convertible preferred stock. The value of the conversion right is difficult to ascertain and is not separately recorded at the time of issuance. At issuance, a corporation accounts for the convertible preferred stock in the same way as non-convertible preferred stock. At conversion, the book value method is used to avoid recording a gain or loss on a transaction involving the company's own capital stock. When converted, the par value and additional paid-in capital of the preferred stock are eliminated and replaced with the par or stated value of the new common stock. If the total preferred contributed capital eliminated is greater than the par or stated value of the new common stock, the corporation records the difference as an increase in additional paid-in capital related to the conversion. If the total preferred contributed capital is less, the difference reduces retained earnings because it is considered to be a dividend for the preferred stockholders.

36. Corporations may also attach warrants to other securities such as long-term bonds and preferred stock. When sècurities such as preferred stock are sold with stock rights attached (detachable warrants), values must be allocated to preferred stockholders' equity and to common stockholders' equity. The allocation is based on the relative independent fair values of the two securities at the time of issuance and may be calculated using the following equations:

$$\text{Amount Assigned to Preferred Stock} = \frac{\text{Market Value of Stock Without Warrants}}{\text{Market Value of Stock Without Warrants} + \text{Market Value of Warrants}} \times \text{Issuance Price}$$

$$\text{Amount Assigned to Warrants} = \frac{\text{Market Value of Warrants}}{\text{Market Value of Stock Without Warrants} + \text{Market Value of Warrants}} \times \text{Issuance Price}$$

37. The journal entry to record the issuance of the preferred stock with detachable warrants would be:

Cash	XXX	
Preferred Stock, at Par Value		XXX
Additional Paid-in Capital on Preferred Stock		XXX
Common Stock Warrants		XXX

Prior to exercise or expiration, the Common Stock Warrants account is an element of contributed capital. The exercise of stock warrants is recorded as:

Cash	XXX	
Common Stock Warrants	XXX	
Common Stock, at Par Value		XXX
Additional Paid-in Capital on Common Stock		XXX

and any expiration is recorded as:

Common Stock Warrants	XXX	
Additional Paid-in Capital from Fxpired Warrants		XXX

38. Callable preferred stock may be issued by a corporation and may be retired (recalled) under specified conditions at the option of the corporation. When the stock is recalled, the corporation must pay dividends in arrears and eliminate the original contributed capital related to the callable stock. If the call price exceeds the original contributed capital, the difference is debited to retained earnings because it is treated as a dividend distribution. If the call price is less, the difference is credited to additional paid-in capital because it is considered an additional stockholders' contribution. The recall and retirement permanently reduces stockholders' equity.

39. Redeemable preferred stock either may be subject to mandatory redemption at a specified future maturity date for a specified price or redeemable at the option of the holder. Because of its similarity to a liability, separate disclosure in the notes to the financial statements is required by generally accepted accounting principles.

40. Preferred stockholders usually have preference in liquidation over the common stockholders (but after creditors) with respect to the corporate assets. The preference may be expressed as a percentage of (or equal to) the par value and may require the payment of dividends in arrears.

Contributed Capital Section

41. A corporation lists the results of stock transactions in a contributed capital section of stockholders' equity on the balance sheet and usually discloses the transactions in the following manner:

    Contributed capital
      Capital stock
        Par value of preferred stock
        Par value of common stock
        Common (or preferred) stock subscribed
        Stock warrants
        Stock dividends to be distributed
      Additional paid-in capital
        On preferred stock
        On common stock
        From other sources (stock splits, preferred stock conversions, treasury stock)

    Additional disclosures include the par value of each share; number of shares authorized, issued, and outstanding; preferred dividend rate; preferred stock characteristics; dividends in arrears; and any other relevant information. A corporation may present these disclosures either parenthetically or in a note to the financial statements.

Treasury Stock (Capital Stock Reacquisition)

42. Treasury stock is a corporation's own stock which has been legally issued and fully paid for by stockholders but is later reacquired by the corporation to be held for future reissuance. Treasury stock must be acquired for some legitimate corporate purpose, has no voting rights, ordinarily does not participate in dividends, and has no rights at liquidation; however, it does participate in stock splits. A corporation treats treasury stock as a reduction in stockholders' equity and accounts for it by either the cost method or par (or stated) value method.

43. The cost method of accounting for treasury stock considers the purchase (reacquisition) to be the first element of the event and the subsequent reissuance to be the last element of the same event. When reacquisition occurs, a corporation debits a temporary account entitled Treasury Stock for the cost of the shares. Upon reissuance of the treasury shares at a price greater than cost, it records the difference between the proceeds received from the reissuance and the cost of the shares when originally reacquired as Additional Paid-in Capital from Treasury Stock. If the proceeds are less than cost, it records the deficit as a reduction of Additional Paid-in Capital from Treasury Stock (of the same class). Any remainder of the deficit reduces Retained Earnings. A corporation may acquire treasury stock at different dates and at different costs. The specific identification method, or either FIFO or average costing, may be used to record the reduction in the Treasury Stock account.

44. The par-value method views the reacquisition of capital stock as an event entirely separate and independent from the reissuance of the treasury stock. When a corporation reacquires capital stock, it debits the Treasury Stock account for the par value of the stock debits and the original Additional Paid-in Capital account for a pro rata amount based on the average price received from all of the original issuances of the stock. It credits any excess that occurs because the reacquisition price is less than the original average issuance price to a new Additional Paid-in Capital from Treasury Stock account. It records any deficit which occurs because the reacquisition price is greater than the original average issuance price first as a reduction of Additional Paid-in Capital From Treasury Stock and then as a reduction of Retained Earnings. Upon reissuance, if the proceeds exceed the par value, the corporation credits Treasury Stock at par and also Additional Paid-in Capital on Common (or Preferred) Stock. If the par value exceeds the proceeds, the deficit reduces the existing Additional Paid-in Capital related to that class of stock or to Retained Earnings if none exists.

45. The following are examples of the journal entry to record the acquisition of Treasury Stock using both the cost and par-value methods. Assume that 500 shares of common stock are reacquired at $15 per share. The stock has a par value of $10 per share and was originally issued for $13 per share.

Cost Method:

Treasury Stock	7,500	
Cash		7,500

Par-Value Method:

Treasury Stock (500 shares at $10 par)	5,000	
Additional Paid-in Capital on Common Stock ($3 average excess x 500 shares)	1,500	
Retained Earnings ($2 deficit x 500 shares)	1,000	
Cash		7,500

46. The balance sheet presentation of treasury stock depends on the method used to account for the stock. If a corporation uses the cost method, it deducts the Treasury Stock account from the total of contributed capital, unrealized capital, and retained earnings. If it uses the par value method, it deducts the Treasury Stock account from the appropriate Capital Stock account. The total stockholders' equity will be the same regardless of the method used. Retained earnings will be restricted in the amount of the cost of the treasury stock.

47. In an attempt to thwart a takeover attempt, a corporation may reacquire its common stock at a price in excess of the fair value. In such a case, it records the treasury stock at its fair value, and records and reports the excess (referred to as "greenmail") as an ordinary expense. Subsequent reissuances are accounted for using either the cost or par value method.

48. Occasionally, capital stock may be donated to a corporation by its stockholders and subsequently reissued. According to FASB Statement No. 116, a corporation recognizes such a donation as a gain in the period received based on the fair value of the exchange. If the corporation uses the cost method on the date of the donation, it debits the Treasury Stock account and credits a gain for the fair value of the stock. If the corporation uses the par value method on the date of the donation, it debits the Treasury Stock account for the par value, credits a gain for the fair value, and debits (or credits) Additional Paid-in Capital for the difference between the fair value and the par value. At reissuance under either method, the transaction is recorded in the usual manner.

49. Watered stock is created when a corporation issues an excess number of shares of stock in exchange for a non-monetary asset, and a limited number of shares are donated back to the corporation and reissued at less than par. This treasury stock subterfuge is used to avoid any contingent liability for the discount, but state laws exist to prevent this subterfuge from occurring.

50. When treasury stock is retired, legal capital is reduced. Under the cost method, a corporation accounts for retirement of treasury stock by offsetting the cost of the retired shares against both the par value in the Capital Stock account and a pro rata share from the Additional Paid-in Capital account. It either debits any difference between these two accounts to Retained Earnings or credits the difference to Additional Paid-in Capital from Treasury Stock. Under the par value method, the par value of the retired shares in the Treasury Stock account is offset against the Capital Stock account.

51. While the cost method is simpler to use, the par value method is theoretically preferable. The par value method properly identifies the separate sources and amounts of corporate capital, while the cost method makes no attempt to differentiate between the stockholders before the reacquisition and those after the reissuance. However, regardless of the method of accounting used, treasury stock has the following important characteristics: (a) treasury stock is not an asset but a reduction in stockholders' equity; (b) treasury stock does not vote, has no preemptive right, ordinarily does not share in dividends, and does not participate in assets at liquidation, but does participate in stock splits; (c) no gains or losses result from treasury stock transactions; (d) retained earnings may be reduced but never increased by treasury stock transactions; (e) retained earnings must be restricted regarding dividends when treasury stock is held; and (f) total stockholders' equity is not affected by use of either the cost or the par-value treasury stock method, but both methods affect the component elements (retained earnings, treasury stock, and additional paid-in capital) differently.

SELF-EVALUATION EXERCISES

Supply the words or dollar amounts necessary to complete each of the following items.

Corporate Form of Organization

CFO-1. Changes in the equity of a company may occur as a result of changes in _______ ___________, _______________ _____________ ____ ___________, or ______________ _____ ____________.

CFO-2. Certain rights and powers given by the state to a corporation are included in a written contract called the ______________ ________ ______________ or ________________ ________________.

Corporate Capital Structure

CCS-1. Individual owners of a corporation are called ________________.

CCS-2. The four rights that a stockholder generally has are:

1. ____
2. ____
3. ____
4. ____

CCS-3. The number of shares of stock that may be issued as stated in the corporate charter is the ____________ capital stock; the number of shares actually issued is the ____________ capital stock; the number of shares issued to stockholders and still held by them is the ______________ capital stock; and the number of shares reacquired by the corporation but not retired is the ____________ ______________.

CCS-4. The amount of stockholders' equity which legally cannot be distributed to the stockholders is the __________ ______________.

CCS-5. The dollar amount of legal capital per share of capital stock designated in the corporate charter is the _____ ___________; if there is no designated amount, the stock is ___-_____ __________ stock which may be assigned a dollar amount called the ___________ ___________.

CCS-6. If the exchange price of the capital stock is higher than the par or stated value, the excess is called ____________ ______-_____ ____________.

CCS-7. On the balance sheet, Stockholders' Equity is divided into three sections: ____________ ________________, ____________ _____ ____________ ____________, and ________________ ________________.

CCS-8. The total amount invested by stockholders as a result of all corporate stock transactions is divided on the balance sheet into two sections:

___________ ___________ and _____________ _______-_________ _____________.

Issuance of Capital Stock

ICS-1. If 1,000 shares of common stock with a par value of $10 per share are issued for $11 cash per share, the correct journal entry would include a debit to

_________ for $_______, a credit to _________ _________ for $_______, and a

credit to _________________ _____-_______ _______________ for $________.

ICS-2. To record costs related to the initial issuance of stock, a debit

entry would be made to an _____________ account.

ICS-3. A legally binding contract to purchase on an installment basis a specified number

of shares of stock at a specified price is called a __________ ____________.

ICS-4. If a subscriber of common stock enters into a subscription contract to purchase 1,000 shares of $8 par common stock at a price of $15 per share, with a down payment of $4 per share and the balance due in one month, the correct journal

entry would include debits to Cash for $4,000 and to ______________

____________: _________ _______ for $________ and credits to _______

_______ _________ for $________ and ____________ _______-_____

_____________ _____ __________ ____________ for $________.

ICS-5. When a corporation issues stock in exchange for assets other than

cash, usually it records the transaction at the _________ _________ of the stock issued or the asset received, whichever is more reliable.

ICS-6. If a corporation records assets received in exchange for stock at less than their fair values resulting in a corresponding understatement of stockholders' equity,

the corporation is said to have ____________ ____________.

ICS-7. If a corporation wants to reduce the par value and the market price

of its common stock, it may declare a ____________ __________.

ICS-8. A two-for-one proportionate stock split for a corporation with 1,000 shares of

$10 par value stock would result in ___________ issued shares of $_______ par value stock.

ICS-9. In comparison to the market price of the stock, stock rights frequently enable the holder to purchase the stock at a price which is ________________.

ICS-10. The issuance of stock rights or the expiration of those rights is recorded in a __________________ ___________.

Stock Option Plans

SO-1. A program which enables corporate employees to purchase the corporation's stock at a price frequently lower than the current market price is called a ______________ _________ _____________; if the purpose of the program is to enable employees to increase ownership in the corporation the plan is ________________, but if the purpose is to provide key employees with additional compensation the plan is ____________________.

SO-2. The fair value of the stock option and the compensation expense are often understated and net income is often overstated when using the __________________ ________________ method to account for the granting of stock rights.

SO-3. The preferred method to account for compensatory stock option plans as recommended by FASB Statement No. 123 is the __________________ ____________________ method.

SO-4. A corporation estimates the fair value of a stock option on the grant date using an ________________ ______________ model.

SO-5. Using the fair value method, the total fair value of the stock options that actually become vested is equal to the _______________ __________________ cost.

SO-6. A stock option plan in which all the terms are set on the grant date is called a _______________ stock option plan; a plan where the number of stock options awarded varies with earnings is termed a _________________-____________________ stock option plan.

SO-7. Under a fixed stock option plan, credit entries to Common Stock and Additional Paid-in Capital for a total equal to the __________ received plus the ______ ________ of the options are made when the options are ________________.

SO-8. Stock rights which enable key employees to receive stock, cash, or a combination of both at some future date are called ________________ ________________ __________.

Preferred Stock Characteristics

PSC-1. With regard to the distribution of corporate earnings to owners, preferred stockholders have a preference to ________________.

PSC-2. If a corporation is responsible for future payment of undeclared prior years' dividends on preferred stock, the stock is __________ preferred stock and the dividends are in ________________.

PSC-3. If preferred stockholders and common stockholders share "extra" dividends proportionately, the stock is ________ ________________ preferred stock.

PSC-4. When preferred stockholders can, at their option under specified conditions, convert their preferred stock for common stock, the preferred stock is ____________.

PSC-5. When convertible stock is converted, the _______ ________ method is used to avoid recording a gain or loss on a transaction involving the company's own capital stock.

PSC-6. When a corporation issues securities with detachable warrants, values are assigned to each based on the relative ________ _________.

PSC-7. Preferred stock which is issued by a corporation and which may be retired under specified conditions at the option of the corporation is __________ preferred stock.

Contributed Capital Section

CCS-1. The results of stock transactions are listed on the balance sheet in the section of stockholders' equity called ____________ ____________.

CCS-2. A corporation may present disclosures related to the contributed capital section of stockholders' equity either ____________ or in a __________ to the financial statements.

Treasury Stock (Capital Stock Reacquisition)

TS-1. Treasury stock is a corporation's own stock which has been ____________ by the corporation, but not ____________.

TS-2. Under the cost method, upon reacquisition the Treasury Stock account is debited for the stock's ____________; while under the par value method the Treasury Stock account is debited for the stock's ______ __________.

TS-3. Under the cost method, when the treasury stock is reissued and the proceeds are less than cost, the corporation records the deficit as a reduction of ____________ _______ - _____ ____________ related to previous issuances or retirements of treasury stock of the same class, and charges any excess to ____________ ____________.

TS-4. Under the cost method, if treasury stock has been reacquired at different dates and at different costs and is then reissued, the three costing alternatives that a corporation may use when recording the reissuance are (a) __________ ____________, (b)_______ or (c) ____________ __________.

TS-5. Under the cost method, a corporation deducts treasury stock on the balance sheet from the sum of __________ ____________, ____________ __________, and ____________ ____________; under the par value method a corporation deducts treasury stock from the appropriate ____________ __________ account.

TS-6. If the cost method is used for treasury stock donated by stockholders, on the date of donation the corporation recognizes the fair value of the stock as a __________.

TS-7. When a corporation retires treasury stock, legal capital is ____________.

TS-8. When a corporation has issued an excess number of shares of stock in exchange for a nonmonetary asset, receives some of the shares back through donation, and then reissues that stock at less than par, the result is ____________ ____________.

TS-9. When a corporation pays "greenmail" to thwart a takeover attempt, it records the excess over the fair value of the stock reacquired as an ______________.

ANSWERS TO SELF-EVALUATION EXERCISES

CFO-1. net income, additional investments by owners, distributions to owners; CFO-2. articles of incorporation, corporate charter; CCS-1. stockholders; CCS-2. (1) the right to share in profits when a dividend is declared, (2) the right to elect directors and establish policies, (3) the preemptive right, (4) the right to share in the distribution of assets at liquidation; CCS-3. authorized, issued, outstanding, treasury stock; CCS-4. legal capital; CCS-5. par value, no-par value, stated value; CCS-6. Additional Paid-in Capital; CCS-7. contributed capital, accumulated other comprehensive income, retained earnings; CCS-8. capital stock, additional paid-in capital; ICS-1. Cash, $11,000, Common Stock, $10,000, Additional Paid-in Capital, $1,000; ICS-2. expense; ICS-3. stock subscription; ICS-4. Subscriptions Receivable: Common Stock, $11,000, Common Stock Subscribed, $8,000, Additional Paid-in Capital on Common Stock, $7,000; ICS-5. fair value; ICS-6. secret reserves; ICS-7. stock split; ICS-8. 2,000, $5; ICS-9. lower; ICS-10. memorandum entry; SO-1. stock option plan, noncompensatory, compensatory; SO-2. intrinsic value; SO-3. fair value; SO-4. option pricing; SO-5. total compensation; SO-6. fixed, performance-based; SO-7. cash, fair value, exercised; SO-8. stock appreciation rights; PSC-1. dividends; PSC-2. cumulative, arrears; PSC-3. fully participating; PSC-4. convertible; PSC-5. book value; PSC-6. fair values; PSC-7. callable; CCS-1. Contributed Capital; CCS-2. parenthetically, note; TS-1. reacquired, retired; TS-2. cost, par value; TS-3. Additional Paid-in Capital, Retained Earnings; TS-4. specific identification, FIFO, average costing; TS-5. contributed capital, unrealized capital, retained earnings, capital stock; TS-6. gain; TS-7. reduced; TS-8. watered stock; TS-9. expense.

POST TEST

Part A Circle T if the statement is true and F if it is false.

T F 1. Generally, stockholders may be held liable for the debts of the corporation.

T F 2. Par value and market value of capital stock have a direct relationship.

T F 3. A corporation records no-par stock with a stated value in a manner similar to par value stock.

T F 4. The stockholders' equity section of the balance sheet may contain three elements, Contributed Capital, Accumulated Other Comprehensive Income, and Retained Earnings.

T F 5. To satisfy the preemptive right, a corporation may issue stock warrants to each current stockholder.

T F 6. Stock warrants may be exchanged for shares of stock and usually do not expire for a long period of time.

T F 7. A corporation accounts for "stock rights" related to stock warrants and attached to preferred stock in the same manner as "stock rights" related to convertible preferred stock.

T F 8. No-par stock must always have a stated value so it can be recorded properly.

T F 9. Common stockholders have the right each year to a fair share of the corporation's profits.

T F 10. A corporation records the authorization to issue capital stock by a memorandum entry.

T F 11. After the initial issuance of stock, costs associated with subsequent issuances reduce Additional Paid-in Capital.

T F 12. Stock subscription contracts are legally binding contracts to purchase a stated number of shares at a stated price.

T F 13. Stock certificates are issued to stock subscribers when they have paid for most of the subscription.

T F 14. When a default occurs on subscribed stock, the provisions of the contract may provide for forfeiture to the corporation of amounts already paid in.

T F 15. A corporation records assets exchanged for capital stock at the par value of the capital stock.

T F 16. In a nonmonetary exchange, if the fair value of both the asset and the capital stock are not readily determinable, the corporate board of directors may assign a value.

T F 17. A corporation may issue a stock split in order to reduce the market price per share.

T F 18. Under a noncompensatory stock option plan, participation is limited to key employees and the discount from the market price may not exceed 5%.

T F 19. Under the intrinsic value method, total compensation cost is equal to the fair value of the stock options on the exercise date.

T F 20. Under both the intrinsic value and fair value methods, total compensation cost is recognized as an operating expense on a straight-line basis over the service period.

T F 21. The fair value method of accounting for compensatory stock option plans enables corporations to meet the IRS criteria of qualified (incentive) stock option plans by requiring that the option price equal the market price on the grant date.

T F 22. Preferred stock with a preference to dividends means preferred stockholders will receive a dividend every year.

T F 23. Fully participating preferred stockholders always receive the same amount of dividends as common stockholders.

T F 24. Convertible preferred stock is callable by the corporation at any time and converted into another security of the corporation.

T F 25. When preferred stock is converted, if the value of the total preferred contributed capital that is eliminated in the transaction is less than the par or stated value of the new common stock, the difference reduces retained earnings because it is comparable to a dividend to preferred stockholders.

T F 26. Treasury stock may be acquired by a corporation to enable the corporation to issue a stock dividend.

T F 27. The cost method of accounting for treasury stock considers the reacquisition and reissuance as two elements of the treasury stock "event."

T F 28. Under the par value method of accounting for treasury stock, the reacquisition is assumed to end the financial relationship with the stockholder who sold his/her stock.

T F 29. Reissuance of treasury stock under the par value method always results in an increase in additional paid-in capital unless the treasury stock is reissued at par value.

T F 30. Because various accounts are affected differently under the cost method and the par value method of accounting for treasury stock, total stockholders' equity would be different under each method.

T F 31. When a corporation reissues treasury stock at a lower cost than the reacquisition cost, it recognizes a Loss on Treasury Stock.

Part B Select the one <u>best</u> answer, and place its letter in the space provided.

_____ 1. All common stockholders have the following rights <u>except</u> (a) the right to vote; (b) the right to share in the distribution of assets upon liquidation; (c) the right to share in profits equally on a per share basis each year; (d) the right to maintain a proportionate interest in the ownership of the corporation.

_____ 2. Alternative names for the Additional Paid-in Capital account include all of the following <u>except</u> (a) Contributed Capital in Excess of Par Value; (b) Premium on Capital Stock; (c) Paid-in Capital in Excess of Par Value; (d) Contributed Surplus.

_____ 3. When an investor enters into a stock subscription contract, the journal entry for the initial transaction includes a (a) debit to Subscriptions Receivable for the par value of the stock; (b) debit to Common Stock Subscribed for the par value of the stock; (c) credit to Common Stock Subscribed for the subscription price if the stock is no-par, no stated value stock; (d) debit to Subscriptions Receivable for the subscription price less the par value of the stock.

____ 4. When accounting for two or more classes of securities issued in a single "package" transaction, the value of each class may be determined in all of the following ways <u>except</u> by (a) arbitrarily assigning a value to each class if the fair value of only one class is known; (b) allocating the selling price to each class based upon the individual relative fair value of each class; (c) assigning the known fair value to one class and the remainder of the selling price to the other security; (d) arbitrarily assigning a value to each class if no fair values are known.

____ 5. A proportionate stock split would result in all of the following <u>except</u> (a) a decrease in the par value per share of stock; (b) a proportionate change in total stockholders' equity; (c) a proportional increase in the number of shares issued; (d) a decrease in the market price per share of stock.

____ 6. All of the following are among the characteristics which must exist for a stock option plan to be classified as noncompensatory <u>except</u>: (a) a maximum 31 day enrollment period; (b) the purchase price is based solely on the market price of the stock on the purchase date; (c) employees may not cancel participation before the purchase date; (d) almost all full-time employees may participate in the plan on an equitable basis.

____ 7. All of the following are variables which an option pricing model must use in determining fair value, <u>except</u>; (a) exercise price; (b) current market price of underlying common stock; (c) expected volatility of the stock; (d) service period; (e) expected dividends on the stock.

____ 8. On January 1, 2004, Emleah Company adopts a compensatory stock option plan for 30 of its key employees. Under the plan, each executive has the right to purchase 100 shares of $5 par common stock for $25 per share after completing a 3-year service period. The fair value of each option is estimated to be $10 on the grant date. Emleah has had a 3.5% employee turnover rate each year and expects this rate to continue. On December 31, 2004, Emleah's journal entry to record compensation expense includes a debit to Compensation Expense for: (a) $8,986; (b) $26,959 (rounded); (c) $75,000; (d) $43,425.

____ 9. On January 1, 2004, Comfair Corporation grants stock appreciation rights to Victoria Fairman, its CFO. Under the plan, Fairman is entitled to receive cash equal to the difference between the quoted market price and a $15 option price for 2,000 shares of the company's stock on the date of exercise. The service period is 4 years and the rights must be exercised within 8 years. If the quoted market price per share of common stock was $15 on January 1, 2004, $19 on December 31, 2004, and $22 on December 31, 2005, the compensation expense recorded on December 31, 2004, and December 31, 2005, respectively, were (a) $8,000 and $14,000; (b) $2,000 and $5,000; (c) $2,000 and $7,000; (d) $8,000 and $7,000.

____ 10. A true statement about preferred stock is that (a) convertible preferred stockholders may exchange the dividend preferences attaching to preferred stock for the unlimited rights to earnings held by common stockholders by exchanging shares of preferred stock for shares of common stock; (b) callable preferred stock may be turned in at the option of either the corporation or the stockholder; (c) a value must be assigned and recorded for the conversion feature of convertible preferred stock; (d) upon recall, any difference between the recall price on callable preferred stock and the original issuance price is recorded as a gain or a loss.

_____ 11. Preferred and common dividends would be the same for each class of stock if there are 10,000 shares of $100 par, 6% preferred stock, and 200,000 shares of $5 par value common, and: (a) preferred stock is partially participating up to 8% and dividends declared are $170,000; (b) preferred stock is fully participating and dividends declared are $110,000; (c) preferred stock is cumulative, dividends are 5 years in arrears, and dividends declared are $160,000; (d) preferred stock is neither cumulative nor participating, and dividends declared are $120,000.

_____ 12. All of the following accounts would be included in the capital stock section of stockholders' equity in the balance sheet <u>except</u> (a) Common Stock Subscribed; (b) Preferred Stock Subscription Receivable; (c) Common Stock, $10 par value; (d) Common Stock, $10 stated value.

_____ 13. Treasury stock is acquired by a corporation for all of the following reasons <u>except</u> (a) to maintain the market price of its stock; (b) to increase the earnings per share; (c) for issuance in an employee stock option plan; (d) to reduce dividends to others and increase dividends to itself.

_____ 14. If a corporation acquires treasury stock, total stockholders' equity (a) will vary depending on the accounting method used; (b) does not change; (c) changes but the total is the same regardless of the accounting method used; (d) increases by the total par value of the stock acquired.

_____ 15. All of the following are characteristics of treasury stock <u>except</u> the statement that (a) it has no voting rights; (b) it ordinarily does not participate in dividends; (c) it has no rights at liquidation; (d) it does not participate in stock splits.

_____ 16. Which of the following statements is true concerning treasury stock and the cost method? (a) upon reissuance of treasury shares, the difference between the proceeds received and the cost of the treasury shares is treated as an adjustment of stockholders' equity; (b) if the proceeds from reissuance are less than the cost, the deficit is always charged against retained earnings; (c) treasury stock may not be reissued below par; (d) if the reacquisition cost is greater than the original average issuance price, the deficit is charged against retained earnings.

_____ 17. Assume a corporation uses the par value method for treasury stock, issued 10,000 shares of $10 par common stock at $13 a share, reacquired 1,000 shares at $15 a share, and reissued 500 shares at $14 a share. What is the total stockholders' equity after the reissuance if retained earnings was $25,000 before any of these transactions occurred? (a) $125,000; (b) $122,000; (c) $138,000; (d) $147,000.

Part C Solve each of the following short problems.

1. Hadley Corporation has been authorized to issued 30,000 shares of common stock at $25 per share. Prepare the journal entry to record the issuance of the stock under each of the following independent assumptions:

   (a) The stock has a $5 par value per share.

(b) The stock is no-par but has a stated value of $10 a share assigned to it.

(c) The stock is no-par and has no stated value assigned to it.

2. Wright Corporation is authorized to issue 40,000 shares of $10 par common stock, and 8,000 shares of 6% preferred stock with a par value of $100 per share. Prepare the journal entries to record the following chronological transactions.

(a) Wright Corporation enters into a subscription contract for 10,000 shares of common stock at $30 per share. 20% of the contracted price is paid at the time of the subscription with the balance due in one month.

(b) 5,000 shares of preferred stock are issued at $115 per share.

(c) The balance on the subscription contracts is collected and common stock is issued.

(d) Equipment is obtained in exchange for 8,000 shares of common stock. The equipment has a book value of $350,000 on the selling company's records and the common stock is currently selling at $42 per share.

(e) A two for one stock split is declared.

3. Riback Company has 40 executives for whom it adopts a fixed compensatory stock option plan on January 1, 2003. Each executive may purchase 200 shares of $10 par common stock at $35 per share after completing a 3-year service period. The fair value of each option is $15. Riback has had a low turnover rate of 2.5% each year and expects this rate to continue. At the end of 2004, Riback revises the expected annual turnover rate to 5%. At the end of 2005, 34 executives vest in the plan. On January 8, 2006, five executives exercise their options.

(a) Prepare the journal entries in 2003, 2004, and 2005 to record the compensation expense related to the plan.

(b) Prepare the journal entry to record the exercise of the options on January 8, 2006.

4. A corporation issued 2,000 shares of $100-par value preferred stock at a price of $120 a share. Each share of preferred stock had a warrant attached which allows the holder to purchase one share of $10-par common stock at $50 a share. The preferred stock sells for $110 ex rights after the issuance and the warrants sell for $15 each.

(a) Record the sale of the preferred stock.

(b) Record the exercise of the warrants. Assume all the warrants are exercised.

5. A corporation has the following transactions relating to treasury stock. Prepare the correct journal entry to record each transaction using first the cost method and then the par value method. The average original issuance price was $25 per share.

(a) 3,000 shares of $10 par common stock were reacquired at $28 a share.

(1) Cost method

(2) Par value method

(b) 1,000 shares were reissued at $31 a share.

(1) Cost method

(2) Par value method

(c) 800 shares were reissued at $26 a share.

(1) Cost method

(2) Par value method

5. (d) The remaining 1,200 shares were reissued at $25 a share.

(1) Cost method

(2) Par value method

ANSWERS TO POST TEST

Part A

1.	F	7.	F	13.	F	19.	F	25.	T
2.	F	8.	F	14.	T	20.	T	26.	T
3.	T	9.	F	15.	F	21.	F	27.	T
4.	T	10.	T	16.	T	22.	F	28.	T
5.	T	11.	T	17.	T	23.	F	29.	F
6.	F	12.	T	18.	F	24.	F	30.	F
								31.	F

Part B

1.	c	5.	b	9.	b	13.	d
2.	d	6.	c	10.	a	14.	c
3.	c	7.	d	11.	d	15.	d
4.	a	8.	a	12.	b	16.	a
						17.	d

Part C

1.	(a)	Cash	750,000	
		Common Stock, $5 par		150,000
		Additional Paid-in Capital on Common Stock		600,000
	(b)	Cash	750,000	
		Common Stock, $10 stated value		300,000
		Additional Paid-in Capital on Common Stock		450,000
	(c)	Cash 750,000		
		Common Stock, no par (30,000 shares)		750,000
2.	(a)	Cash (0.20 x $30 x 10,000)	60,000	
		Subscriptions Receivable: Common Stock	240,000	
		Common Stock Subscribed ($10 x 10,000)		100,000
		Additional Paid-in Capital on Common Stock		200,000
	(b)	Cash	575,000	
		Preferred Stock, $100 par		500,000
		Additional Paid-in Capital on Preferred Stock		75,000
	(c)	Cash ($24 x 10,000)	240,000	
		Subscriptions Receivable: Common Stock		240,000
		Common Stock Subscribed ($10 x 10,000)	100,000	
		Common Stock, $10 par		100,000
	(d)	Equipment	336,000	
		Common Stock, $10 par		80,000
		Additional Paid-in Capital on Common Stock		256,000

(e) Memorandum entry to record the two-for-one stock split which resulted in an issuance of 18,000 additional shares of stock. There are now 36,000 shares issued and outstanding. Common Stock has a par value of $5 per share after the split.

3.	(a)	<u>Dec. 31, 2003</u>		
		Compensation Expense[a]	37,074	
		Common Stock Option Warrants		37,074

[a]$15 fair value per option x (8,000 stock options x 0.975 x 0.975 x 0.975 turnover rate) x 1/3, rounded

<u>Dec. 31, 2004</u>		
Compensation Expense[b]	31,516	
Common Stock Option Warrants		31,516

[b]$15 fair value per option x (8,000 x 0.95 x 0.95 x 0.95) x 2/3) - $37,074

<u>Dec. 31, 2005</u>		
Compensation Expense[a]	33,410	
Common Stock Option Warrants		33,410

[a]$15 fair value per option x (34 x 200) - $68,590

(b)

<u>Jan. 8, 2006</u>		
Cash [(5 x 200) x $35]	35,000	
Common Stock Option Warrants (1,000 x $15)	15,000	
Common Stock, $10 par		10,000
Additional Paid-in Capital on Common Stock		40,000

4. (a) Record the sale of the preferred stock:

$$\text{Amount Assigned to Preferred Stock} = \frac{\text{Market Value of Stock Without Warrants}}{\text{Market Value of Stock Without Warrants} + \text{Market Value of Warrants}} \times \text{Issuance Price}$$

$$= \frac{\$110 \times 2{,}000}{(\$110 \times 2{,}000) + (\$15 \times 2{,}000)} \times (\$120 \times 2{,}000)$$

$$= \$211{,}200$$

4.(a)

$$\text{Amount Assigned to Rights Warrants} = \frac{\text{Market Value of Warrants}}{\text{Market Value of Stock Without Warrants} + \text{Market Value of Warrants}} \times \text{Issuance Price}$$

$$= \frac{\$30{,}000}{\$220{,}000 + \$30{,}000} \times \$240{,}000$$

$$= \$28{,}800$$

Cash ($120 x 2,000)	240,000	
Preferred Stock, $100 par ($100 x 2,000)		200,000
Additional Paid-in Capital on Preferred Stock ($211,200 - $200,000)		11,200
Common Stock Warrants		28,800

(b) Record the exercise of the warrants:

Cash ($50 x 2,000)	100,000	
Common Stock Warrants	28,800	
Common Stock, $10 par ($10 x 2,000)		20,000
Additional Paid-in Capital on Common Stock		108,800

5. (a) Record reacquisition of 3,000 shares:

(1) <u>Cost method</u>:

Treasury Stock (3,000 x $28)	84,000	
Cash		84,000

(2) <u>Par Value method</u>:

Treasury Stock (3,000 x $10)	30,000	
Additional Paid-in Capital on Common Stock ($15 average excess x 3,000)	45,000	
Retained Earnings	9,000	
Cash		84,000

(b) Record reissuance of 1,000 shares:

(1) <u>Cost method</u>:

Cash (1,000 x $31)	31,000	
Treasury Stock (1,000 x $28)		28,000
Additional Paid-in Capital from Treasury Stock		3,000

(2) <u>Par value method</u>:

Cash	31,000	
Treasury Stock (1,000 x $10)		10,000
Additional Paid-in Capital on Common Stock (1,000 x $21)		21,000

(c) Record reissuance of 800 shares:

(1) <u>Cost method</u>:

Cash (800 x $26)	20,800	
Additional Paid-in Capital from Treasury Stock	1,600	
Treasury Stock (800 x $28)		22,400

(2) <u>Par value method</u>:

Cash	20,800	
Treasury Stock (800 x $10)		8,000
Additional Paid-in Capital on Common Stock (800 x $16)		12,800

(d) Record reissuance of 1,200 shares:

(1) <u>Cost method</u>:

Cash (1,200 x $25)	30,000	
Additional Paid-in Capital from Treasury Stock	1,400	
Retained Earnings	2,200	
Treasury Stock (1,200 x $28)		33,600

(2) <u>Par value method</u>:

Cash	30,000	
Treasury Stock (1,200 x $10)		12,000
Additional Paid-in Capital on Common Stock (1,200 x $15)		18,000

16

EARNINGS PER SHARE AND RETAINED EARNINGS

CHAPTER OBJECTIVES

After careful study of this chapter, you will be able to:

1. Know the equation for computing basic earnings per share (EPS).
2. Understand how to compute the weighted average common shares for EPS.
3. Identify the potential common shares included in diluted EPS.
4. Apply the treasury stock method for including stock options and warrants in diluted EPS.
5. Calculate the impact of a convertible security on diluted EPS.
6. Compute diluted EPS.
7. Record the declaration and payment of cash dividends.
8. Account for a property dividend.
9. Explain the difference in accounting for small and large stock dividends.
10. Understand how to report accumulated other comprehensive income.
11. Prepare a statement of changes in stockholders' equity.
12. Account for a quasi-reorganization (Appendix).

SYNOPSIS

Earnings and Earnings Per Share Information

1. FASB Statement No. 128 entitled "Earnings Per Share" contains the current standards for calculating and reporting earnings per share.

2. External decision makers often consider earnings per share to be the best single measure for summarizing a corporation's performance. Earnings per share information is useful in evaluating the return on investment and risk of a company. Earnings per share can be used to predict future cash flows per share, to compare intercompany performance using the price/earnings ratio, and to indicate the potential impact of the issuance of common stock options, convertible debt, or convertible preferred stock on future earnings per share.

Basic Earnings Per Share

3. A simple capital structure consists of only common stock. For a simple capital structure, basic earnings per share is required for reporting purposes and is computed using the following equation:

$$\text{Basic Earnings per Share} = \frac{\text{Net Income - Preferred Dividends}}{\text{Weighted Average Number of Common Shares Outstanding}}$$

   Basic earnings per share is reported on a corporation's income statement directly below net income. The numerator on the right side of this equation equals only the earnings available to common stockholders. Included in the preferred dividends of the numerator are dividends on noncumulative preferred stock that have been declared, as well as the current dividends on cumulative preferred stock whether or not they have been declared.

4. The weighted average number of common shares outstanding in the denominator of the above equation is the number of common shares outstanding at the end of the accounting period if no shares have been issued or reacquired during the year. If a corporation has issued or reacquired shares of common stock, a weighted average of these shares must be calculated by (a) determining the number of shares outstanding for each portion of the year (e.g., January - March, 3,000 shares; April - May, 6,000 shares, etc.), (b) multiplying each number times the fraction of the year the shares were outstanding (e.g., January - March: 3,000 x 3/12) to get (c) the equivalent whole units of shares outstanding (e.g., 3,000 x 3/12 = 750), and (d) summing the equivalent whole units for each fraction of the year. The result is the total weighted average common shares. The weighted average number of common shares must also be adjusted for stock dividends and stock splits which are given retroactive recognition and assumed to have occurred at the beginning of the earliest comparative period. For example, if comparative information on earnings per share is being presented for 2004 and 2005, any stock split or stock dividend that occurs in 2004 or 2005 is assumed to have occurred as of the beginning of 2004. The corporation discloses the weighted average number of common shares outstanding in the notes to its financial statements.

5. A corporation reports separate earnings per share for income from continuing operations and net income. If there are any results from discontinued operations, extraordinary items, or cumulative effects of changes in accounting principles, separate earnings per share are shown for each of these items. Each component of earnings per share is based on the same weighted average number of shares. A corporation may report earnings per share for each of the aforementioned items on the income statement in a schedule directly below the net income or in the notes to the financial statements. When

reported on the income statement, the components are summed to show the contribution of each income statement item to the total earnings per share.

Diluted Earnings Per Share

6. When a corporation has a complex capital structure, basic earnings per share and diluted earnings per share must be reported on the face of the income statement. A complex capital structure includes potential common shares which can be used by the holder to acquire common stock. Potential common shares include stock options and warrants, convertible preferred stocks and bonds, participating securities and two-class stocks, and contingent shares.

7. Diluted earnings per share shows the earnings per share after including all potential common shares that would reduce earnings per share. A corporation may include a potential common share in the earnings per share calculation only when it has a dilutive effect for that particular period. In order to evaluate the dilutive effect of each security, the potential common shares must be included in the diluted earnings-per-share (DEPS) calculation in a particular order. The following sequence should be used: (a) compute the basic earnings per share; (b) include dilutive stock options and warrants, and compute a tentative DEPS; (c) develop a ranking of each convertible preferred stock and convertible bond on DEPS; (d) include each dilutive convertible security in DEPS in a sequential order based on the ranking and compute a new tentative DEPS; and (e) select as the diluted earnings per share the lowest computed tentative DEPS. Exhibit 16-4 in the main textbook provides a useful flowchart of the earnings per share computations.

8. Stock options and warrants are always considered first in the diluted earnings per share calculations and are included in diluted earnings per share only if they are dilutive. A corporation uses the treasury stock method to determine the impact of the options and warrants upon the number of common shares. It computes the impact on the assumption that the options were exercised at the beginning of the period (or at the time of the issuance, if later), and that the assumed proceeds obtained from the exercise were used to reacquire common stock at the average market price during the period. If the assumed shares issued exceed the assumed shares reacquired, the effect is a dilution of earnings per share. This occurs whenever the average market price is greater than the option price. The incremental shares resulting from the assumed exercise of the options or warrants are then added to the denominator of the basic earnings per share and used to compute diluted earnings per share. The original numerator is used. The resulting diluted earnings per share is final if no convertible securities are outstanding.

9. Convertible securities are considered for inclusion in diluted earnings per share after stock options and warrants and are included only if dilutive. A corporation evaluates convertible securities in a specified sequence to avoid including a security which is antidilutive in combination with other securities. In order to develop a ranking of the impact of each convertible security on DEPS, the if-converted method is used. Each convertible security is assumed to have been converted into common shares, and then by dividing the resulting increase in the numerator of the earnings-per-share equation by the resulting increase in the denominator, a numerical value is calculated to use in ranking the impact on diluted earnings per share. The security with the lowest numerical impact causes the greatest decrease in diluted earnings per share and is the most dilutive. Beginning with the convertible security having the lowest numerical impact on DEPS, a corporation includes each security in a tentative diluted earnings per share calculation until the tentative diluted earnings per share is less than the

numerical impact of the next convertible security in the ranking. The final diluted earnings per share is the last tentative figure.

10. The computation of earnings per share includes the current conversion ratios for convertible securities and stock options, adjusted proportionally for stock dividends or stock splits.

11. Some contingent issuances of common stock are dependent on the satisfaction of certain conditions such as attaining or maintaining a certain level of earnings. A corporation considers these shares outstanding for basic and diluted earnings per share when the conditions have been met, and if dilutive, includes them in diluted earnings per share even if the conditions are not yet met.

12. Disclosure of both basic and diluted earnings per share is required on the income statement. In addition, a schedule or note explains the bases on which both basic and diluted earnings per share are calculated, identifies all potential common shares whether included in the diluted earnings per share computation or not, identifies the amount of preferred dividends, and describes the impact on the common shares outstanding of transactions subsequent to the end of the accounting period.

Dividends

13. Retained earnings is the section of stockholders' equity that summarizes the lifetime income of the corporation that it has retained for use in the corporation and not distributed to stockholders in the form of dividends. Retained earnings link the income statement with the balance sheet. The main items affecting retained earnings are: net income, dividends, prior period adjustments, and appropriations.

14. The corporate board of directors is responsible for establishing dividend policy including the amount, timing, and type of dividends to be declared. In decisions regarding dividends, the board must take into consideration the articles of incorporation, applicable state regulations for dividends, the impact upon legal capital, any restrictions due to a contractual agreement, as well as the financial well-being of the corporation. Generally, a corporation may not declare a dividend if retained earnings has a prior deficit (a negative retained earnings balance). The types of dividends which it may declare include cash, property, scrip, stock, and liquidating dividends. Each of these types of dividends can be classified according to its impact on the corporate capital structure as follows:

    A. Cash, property, and scrip dividends decrease retained earnings (and stockholders' equity)
    B. Liquidating dividends decrease contributed capital (and stockholders' equity)
    C. Stock dividends decrease retained earnings and increase contributed capital (no change in stockholders' equity)
    D. Stock splits do not affect the balance of any element of stockholders' equity

15. Unless stated otherwise, the term "dividend" refers to a cash dividend, the most common type of dividend. Four significant dates are associated with cash dividends as well as all other types of dividends. On the date of declaration of a dividend, the board of directors creates a legal liability when it formally declares that a dividend will be paid to stockholders of record on a specific future date. To record the declaration of a cash dividend payable to both preferred stockholders and common stockholders, the corporation makes the following journal entry:

Retained Earnings	XXX	
Dividends Payable: Preferred Stock		XXX
Dividends Payable: Common Stock		XXX

Prior to payment, Dividends Payable is normally classified as a current liability on the balance sheet. Stock sold after the date of declaration sells "with dividends attached" (at a higher market price that includes the amount of the future dividend payment) until the ex-dividend date when the stock begins selling without the declared dividend. The date of record falls several days after the ex-dividend date to allow the stockholders' ledger to be updated. All stockholders listed in the ledger as of the date of record are eligible to receive the dividend. A corporation makes a memorandum entry at this time indicating that the date of record has been reached and listing the future dividend payment date. On the date of payment, the corporation issues the dividend checks, distributes them to stockholders, and makes the following journal entry:

Dividends Payable: Preferred Stock	XXX	
Dividends Payable: Common Stock	XXX	
Cash		XXX

Preferred stock may be fully participating or partially participating. Fully participating preferred stock shares equally with common stock in any extra cash dividends. The extra dividends are distributed proportionally based on the respective total par values of each class of stock. Partially participating preferred stock is limited in its participation in extra cash dividends to a fixed rate or amount per share.

16. A property dividend is payable in assets other than cash and typically takes the form of marketable securities held in other companies. This type of dividend is a nonreciprocal nonmonetary transfer to owners (a one-way nonmonetary exchange). On the date of declaration, the corporation revalues the asset to be distributed to its fair value, recognizes a gain or loss, and records the liability.

17. When a corporation has adequate retained earnings to meet the legal requirements of paying a current cash dividend but does not have sufficient funds to pay the dividend, it may issue a scrip dividend. A scrip dividend is a promissory note to pay a dividend at some future date and may include interest. The corporation records the dividend liability on the date of declaration and accrues interest expense until the date of payment. On the payment date, the corporation must record the interest paid as an expense separately from the dividend. The classification of Scrip Dividends Payable on the balance sheet is dependent upon the expected maturity date. Scrip dividends are rare.

18. A corporation may declare a stock dividend issuing shares of its own stock to the stockholders on a pro rata (proportional) basis according to the number of shares each stockholder already owns. In an ordinary stock dividend, it issues shares of the same class of stock (e.g., common stock dividend on common stock outstanding), while in a special stock dividend it issues a different class of stock (e.g., common on preferred

or preferred on common). The corporation distributes no assets in a stock dividend. Each stockholder maintains the same percentage ownership, and the only change in stockholders' equity is a rearrangement of certain stockholders' equity accounts depending on whether the stock dividend is "large" or "small." From an accounting point of view, a stock dividend is treated as a simultaneous sale of stock and payment of dividend.

19. A stock dividend that is less than 20 to 25% of the previously outstanding shares and is presumed to have no apparent effect on the market price per share is defined as a small stock dividend. When the small stock dividend, it reduces (debits) Retained Earnings by an amount equal to the fair value of the additional shares issued, increases (credits) Common Stock To Be Distributed for the par or stated value, and credits the excess of the fair value over the par (stated) value to Additional Paid-in Capital From Stock Dividend. Common Stock To Be Distributed is not a liability but a component of Contributed Capital until the corporation issues the stock dividend and eliminates the account.

20. A large stock dividend, or a stock split effected in the form of a dividend, is similar in nature to a stock split because of the resulting decrease in the market price per share. Therefore, it is recommended that only the par or stated value (the minimum amount legally required to be capitalized) be debited to Retained Earnings and credited to Common Stock To Be Distributed when the dividend is declared. While this is theoretically inconsistent with the notion that a stock dividend is a distribution of earnings and should be based on the fair value, the use of par value with large stock dividends is still a generally accepted accounting principle.

21. Liquidating dividends represent a return of contributed capital and may occur when a corporation is ceasing operations, reducing its size, or when a natural resources corporation pays a dividend based on earnings before depletion. A corporation records the normal portion of a dividend which is, in part, a liquidating dividend as a reduction in retained earnings, and records the liquidation portion as a reduction of contributed capital. The corporation should disclose the liquidiating dividend in a note to its financial statements so that stockholders realize that a portion of contributed capital is being returned.

Prior Period Adjustments (Restatements)

22. Errors in previously issued financial statements discovered in a subsequent period may arise due to mathematical errors, oversights, incorrect use of existing facts, or mistakes in the applications of accounting principles. Correction of all such material errors, as well as certain changes in accounting principles, and a change in accounting entity, are treated as prior period adjustments (restatements) of retained earnings. A corporation records a prior period adjustment (net of income taxes) as an adjustment of the beginning balance of retained earnings. If comparative financial statements are presented, the corporation makes corresponding adjustments to its net income, retained earnings, and asset or liability account balances for all the periods reported therein.

Appropriations of Retained Earnings

23. An appropriation (or restriction) of retained earnings means that a corporation's board of directors restricts retained earnings or makes a portion of retained earnings unavailable for dividends. The appropriation may be made to meet legal requirements, to meet contractual requirements, or because of discretionary actions.

24. Most corporations disclose an appropriation of retained earnings by reporting the restrictions in a note accompanying the financial statements or a parenthetical note in stockholders' equity. When a note to the financial statements is used to disclose restrictions, a clear description of the legal, contractual, or discretionary provision and the amount of the appropriation is required.

Statement of Retained Earnings

25. A corporation may report changes in retained earnings in a separate <u>statement of retained earnings</u>, in the statement of changes in stockholders' equity, or as a supporting schedule directly beneath the income statement. A retained earnings statement usually includes only adjustments to retained earnings for net income and dividends. The following format is suggested for the statement of retained earnings for a company which reports its appropriations of retained earnings in a note to the financial statements:

Statement of Retained Earnings
For Year Ended December 31, 200X

Beginning retained earnings, as previously reported, January 1, 200X
Plus (minus): Prior period adjustments (net of income tax effect)
Adjusted retained earnings, January 1, 200X
Plus (minus): Net income (loss)
Minus: Dividends (specifically identified, including per share amounts)
Reductions due to retirement or reacquisition of capital stock
Reductions due to conversion of bonds or preferred stock
Minus (plus): Adjustments due to quasi-reorganizations
Retained earnings, December 31, 200X

Accumulated Other Comprehensive Income

26. A corporation's other comprehensive income (loss) might include four items: (1) unrealized increases (gains) or decreases (losses) in the market (fair) value of investments in available-for-sale securities, (2) translation adjustments from converting the financial statements of a company's foreign operations into U.S. dollars, (3) certain gains and losses on "derivative" financial instruments, and (4) certain pension liability adjustments. A corporation includes its other comprehensive income (or loss) accumulated to date in its <u>accumulated other comprehensive income</u> (or loss) amount which it reports in the stockholders' equity section of its balance sheet.

Miscellaneous Changes in Stockholders' Equity

27. On certain occasions, a corporation may increase stockholders' equity for events not related to the issuance of stock or to retained earnings. Examples are donated capital arising from donated assets and the discovery value of previously unknown valuable natural resources.

28. A corporation discloses the changes in the different classes of common stock, additional paid-in capital, retained earnings, accumulated other comprehensive income and treasury stock in its annual report. This information helps users of financial statements in assessing financial flexibility, profitability and risk. Disclosure may be made parenthetically or in a note to the financial statements. Many corporations

satisfy the disclosure requirements by including the changes in a <u>statement of changes in stockholders' equity</u> which must be presented as a <u>major</u> financial statement when the corporation uses it to report comprehensive income. Exhibits 16-11, 16-12, 16-13, and 16-14 in the main textbook provide excellent examples of this schedule and the related stockholders' equity.

29. Under International Accounting Standards, shareholders' interest (stockholders' equity) consists of (a) share capital and (b) other equity. While most disclosures under Share Capital are the same as required under U.S. GAAP, additional disclosures include any capital not yet paid in, any restrictions on the repayment of capital, and the shares reserved for future issuance under sales contracts. In the Other Equity section, additional disclosures different from U.S. GAAP include revaluation surplus resulting from revaluation of property, plant, and equipment, and reserves. Both International Accounting Standards and U.S. GAAP require disclosures of changes in stockholders' equity.

Appendix: Quasi-reorganization

30. When a corporation has incurred net losses over an extended period of time resulting in serious financial difficulty, rather than declare bankruptcy the corporation may engage in a quasi-reorganization if future profitability seems possible. A quasi-reorganization is a set of accounting procedures, sanctioned by applicable state laws, which provides a "fresh start." The procedures usually include (a) writing assets down to their fair value with any loss debited to retained earnings, (b) increasing additional paid-in capital by decreasing the par value of the capital stock, and (c) eliminating the retained earnings deficit by reducing additional paid-in capital. Other requirements include full disclosure to the stockholders and obtaining their approval, a zero retained earnings balance, and dating retained earnings as of the readjustment date with disclosure in the financial statements until such dating loses its significance (usually 5 to 10 years).

SELF-EVALUATION EXERCISES

Supply the words or dollar amounts necessary to complete each of the following items.

Earnings Per Share

EPS-1. External decision makers consider earnings per share to be the best single measure for __________ __________ __________.

EPS-2. Earnings per share information is useful in evaluating a corporation's __________ _____ __________ and __________.

EPS-3. For earnings per share purposes, the capital structure of a corporation is classified as __________ or __________.

Basic Earnings Per Share

BEP-1. Basic earnings per share is calculated by subtracting ____________ ________________ from _______ _______________ and dividing the difference by the weighted average number of _______________ _______________ __________________.

BEP-2. In calculating earnings per share, stock dividends and stock splits are given _______________ _______________.

BEP-3. If the income statement reports several major components of net income, separate earnings per share are shown for the ___________ _________ _______________ _______________ and any _________ _____ ______________ _____________, ________________ _________, or ______________ ___________ _____ ___________ _____ _____________ ____________, as well as _____ ________.

Diluted Earnings Per Share

DEP-1. A corporation with a complex capital structure must include two earnings per share amounts; one is called _______________ ______________ ______ ________________ and the other is called ____________ __________________ ________ __________________.

DEP-2. For corporations with a complex capital structure, the earnings per share calculation which is based on the outstanding common shares and potential common shares which have a dilutive effect is called ___________________ _______________ _______ _____________.

DEP-3. In diluted earnings per share calculations, stock options, stock warrants, convertible preferred stocks, and convertible bonds are examples of ________________ _______________ __________________.

DEP-4. When calculating diluted earnings per share, a corporation would not include stock options unless they had a ______________ __________.

DEP-5. In applying the treasury stock method to determine the impact of the options and warrants on common shares, the options and warrants are dilutive if the assumed shares ______________ exceed the assumed shares ______________.

DEP-6. After options and warrants, a corporation considers ___________ _________ ___________ _____ _________ in calculating diluted earnings per share.

DEP-7. The method used to develop a ranking of the impact of each convertible security on DEPS is the _______-________________ method.

DEP-8. Disclosure of both basic and diluted earnings per share is required on the ________________ ________________.

Dividends

D-1. A corporation may <u>not</u> declare dividends under most circumstances if the balance in the Retained Earnings account is ______________.

D-2. When a corporation declares cash dividends, property dividends, or scrip dividends, total stockholders' equity is ______________.

D-3. The date on which the corporate board of directors creates a legal liability by declaring a cash dividend is called the __________ _____ _______________; and the journal entry at that time includes a debit to ____________ ________________ and a credit to _______________ ________________.

D-4. After a corporation declares a dividend, the date on which the stock once again sells <u>without</u> dividends attached is called the _____-__________________ ________________.

D-5. The only stockholders eligible to participate in a declared dividend are those listed in the stockholders' ledger as of the ___________ _____ ______________.

D-6. The journal entry on the date of payment to record the payment of a previously declared cash dividend includes a debit to _____________ _______________ and a credit to _____________.

D-7. A corporation records property dividends at their __________ __________.

D-8. A promissory note to pay a dividend at some future date is called a

__________ __________.

D-9. When a corporation declares a stock dividend, total stockholders'

equity is __________.

D-10. When a corporation declares a small stock dividend, the market price

per share of common stock is generally __________; when it declares a large stock dividend, the market price per share of common stock is generally

__________.

D-11. Liquidating dividends result in a reduction in both __________

__________ and __________ __________.

Prior Period Adjustments

PPA-1. Items which are treated as prior period adjustments include:

(a)

(b)

(c)

PPA-2. A corporation records a prior period adjustment as an adjustment to

the beginning balance of __________ __________.

Appropriations of Retained Earnings

A-1. Three reasons for appropriating retained earnings are:

1.

2.

3.

A-2. Appropriations of retained earnings may be disclosed in the following two ways:

a.

b.

Accumulated Other Comprehensive Income

AO-1. A corporation's other comprehensive income accumulated to date is included in ____________ ________ __________ ________ which is reported in the stockholders' equity section of its balance sheet.

Miscellaneous Changes in Stockholders' Equity

OCSE-1. The schedule which discloses changes in the different classes of stock, additional paid-in capital, and retained earnings is called a

________ ____ ________ _____ __________ ________.

OCSE-2. The disclosures mentioned in OCSE-1 may also be made

____________ or in a ______ to the financial statements.

OCSE-3. Under International Accounting Standards, shareholders' interest consists of ______ _______ and ______ _______.

Appendix: Quasi-reorganization

QR-1. The three accounting procedures usually required in a quasi-reorganization are:

(1)

(2)

(3)

QR-2. Immediately after a quasi-reorganization, the balance in the Retained Earnings account is __________.

ANSWERS TO SELF-EVALUATION EXERCISES

EPS-1. summarizing company performance; EPS-2. return on investment, risk; EPS-3. simple, complex; BEP-1. preferred dividends, net income, common shares outstanding; BEP-2. retroactive recognition; BEP-3. income from continuing operations, results of discontinued operations, extraordinary items, cumulative effects of changes in accounting principles, net income; DEP-1. basic earnings per share, diluted earnings per share; DEP-2. diluted earnings per share; DEP-3. potential common shares DEP-4. dilutive effect; DEP-5. issued, reacquired; DEP-6. convertible preferred stocks and bonds; DEP-7. if-converted; DEP-8. income statement; D-1. negative; D-2. decreased; D-3. date of declaration, Retained Earnings, Dividends Payable; D-4. ex-dividend date; D-5. date of record; D-6. Dividends Payable, Cash; D-7. fair value; D-8. scrip dividend; D-9. unaffected; D-10. unaffected, decreased; D-11. retained earnings, contributed capital; PPA-1. (a) corrections of errors made in prior periods, (b) certain changes in accounting principles, (c) change in accounting entity; PPA-2. retained earnings; A-1. (1) to meet legal requirements, (2) to meet contractual requirements, (3) because of discretionary actions; A-2. (a) by reporting the restrictions in a note accompanying the financial statements, (b) a parenthetical note in stockholders' equity; AO-1. accumulated other comprehensive income; OCSE-1. Statement of Changes in Stockholders' Equity; OCSE-2. parenthetically, note; OCSE-3. share capital, other equity; QR-1. (1) assets are written down to their fair value and any loss is debited to Retained Earnings; (2) additional paid-in capital is increased by decreasing the par value of capital stock; (3) retained earnings deficit is eliminated by reducing the Additional Paid-in Capital; QR-2. zero.

POST TEST

Part A Circle T if the statement is true and F if it is false.

T F 1. Earnings per share for a company with a simple capital structure is calculated by dividing net income less preferred dividends by the number of shares outstanding at year end.

T F 2. A corporation includes current dividends on cumulative preferred stock in the numerator when calculating basic earnings per share whether or not they have been declared.

T F 3. A corporation must consider the impact of all potential common shares in computing diluted earnings per share.

T F 4. Stock options are sometimes considered potential common shares.

T F 5. If a company has issued stock options, there will be no effect on the denominator when computing earnings per share if the shares assumed to be reacquired exceed the assumed shares issued.

T F 6. If the average market price is less than the option price specified in the stock warrant, the effect on earnings per share would be antidilutive.

T F 7. The convertible security with the highest numerical-value impact is considered first in computing diluted earnings per share.

T F 8. Corporations with a complex capital structures must present basic and diluted earnings per share if they have dilutive potential common shares.

T F 9. Contingent issuances of common stock which are dilutive are considered outstanding for diluted earnings per share calculations even if the conditions on which issuance are contingent have not been met to date.

T F 10. Dividend distributions are limited to the stockholders of record on the date of declaration of a dividend.

T F 11. Stocks are sold "with dividends attached" from the date of declaration until the date of record.

T F 12. A corporation records all stock dividends, like stock splits, at par value.

T F 13. Liquidating dividends are a return of capital rather than a return on capital, and therefore, total stockholders' equity is reduced.

T F 14. Dividends always affect total stockholders' equity.

T F 15. Property dividends usually result in a gain or loss for the company.

T F 16. The appropriation of retained earnings restricts the use of specific assets in the amount of the appropriation.

T F 17. An appropriation of retained earnings makes a portion of retained earnings available for dividends.

T F 18. Disclosure of changes in the elements of stockholders' equity is optional under U.S. generally accepted accounting principles but required under International Accounting Standards.

T F 19. Accumulated other comprehensive income is reported as a category of retained earnings.

T F 20. A corporation which is having financial difficulty need only obtain permission of its management to engage in a quasi-reorganization to reduce some of its outstanding debt.

T F 21. In a quasi-reorganization, legal capital is usually reduced.

Part B Select the one <u>best</u> answer, and place its letter in the space provided.

____ 1. Bright Corporation reported net income in 2004 of $34,400. The company declared dividends of $4,000 on preferred stock and $12,000 on common stock. At the beginning of 2004, there were 8,000 shares of common stock outstanding. 2,000 additional shares of common stock were issued on May 31 and again on October 31. In 2004, the basic earnings per share was (a) $2.35; (b) $3.20; (c) $1.93; (d) $3.62.

____ 2. A company had 20,000 shares of common stock outstanding on January 1; on April 29, 4,000 shares were issued; on July 17, a 20% stock dividend was issued; and on September 1, 3,000 additional shares were issued. The denominator to be used to compute earnings per share is (a) 31,800; (b) 34,560; (c) 28,200; (d) 25,267.

____ 3. A corporation has 12,000 common shares and options to purchase 1,500 common shares at $10 per share outstanding the entire year. The average market price for the common stock during the year was $15 per share. In calculating the diluted earnings per share using the treasury stock method, the stock option would (a) have an anti-dilutive impact on earnings per share because the assumed shares reacquired exceeds the assumed shares issued; (b) have an anti-dilutive impact on earnings per share because the assumed shares issued exceeds the assumed shares reacquired; (c) have a dilutive impact on earnings per share because the assumed shares issued exceeds the assumed shares reacquired; (d) have a dilutive impact on earnings per share because the assumed shares reacquired exceeds the assumed shares issued.

____ 4. The diluted earnings per share calculation includes (a) all dilutive and antidilutive potential common shares; (b) all dilutive and antidilutive convertible securities; (c) only potential common shares which are dilutive; (d) any convertible security which is antidilutive.

____ 5. ABC Corporation has a complex capital structure. Its basic earnings per share for the 2004 fiscal year was $2.03 and its diluted earnings per share was $1.98. Rules for financial statement disclosure require that (a) only the diluted earnings per share be disclosed; (b) only the basic earnings per share be disclosed; (c) both the basic and the diluted earnings per share be disclosed; (d) neither earnings per share amount be disclosed.

_____ 6. Stang Inc., which presents comparative 2003 and 2004 income statements, issued a 2-for-1 stock split on December 31, 2004 increasing the number of common shares from 5,000 to 10,000. When calculating the earnings per share for the 2004 financial statements, the stock split is assumed to have occurred on (a) January 1, 2003; (b) January 1, 2004; (c) December 31, 2003; (d) December 31, 2004.

_____ 7. Using the information in question #6 and assuming no additional shares of stock were issued in 2003 or 2004, the weighted average shares of common stock used in calculating EPS for the financial statements on December 31, 2004 would be (a) 5,000 shares for 2003, and 10,000 shares for 2004; (b) 5,000 shares for 2003, and 5,000 shares for 2004; (c) 10,000 shares for 2003, and 10,000 shares for 2004; (d) 10,000 shares for 2003, and 20,000 shares for 2004.

_____ 8. Cash dividends, property dividends, and scrip dividends are examples of dividends which (a) decrease total stockholders' equity by decreasing contributed capital; (b) have no effect on total stockholders' equity but decrease retained earnings and increase contributed capital; (c) have no effect on any element of stockholders' equity; (d) decrease total stockholders' equity by decreasing retained earnings.

_____ 9. When a corporation declares dividends, a liability is created <u>except</u> when the dividends declared are (a) stock dividends; (b) cash dividends; (c) property dividends; (d) scrip dividends.

_____ 10. A corporation issues 7,500 shares of capital stock as a dividend. Before the dividend, 50,000 shares were authorized, 40,000 shares were issued, and 15,000 shares were held in the treasury. The dividend would be accounted for as a (a) small stock dividend; (b) large stock dividend; (c) stock split; (d) property dividend.

_____ 11. A board of directors may appropriate retained earnings for all of the following reasons <u>except</u> (a) to meet legal requirements; (b) because of discretionary actions; (c) to meet contractual obligations; (d) to meet dividends on preferred stock.

_____ 12. Other comprehensive income (loss) may include all of the following <u>except</u> (a) certain pension liability adjustments; (b) a translation adjustment from converting the financial statement of a company's foreign operations into U.S. dollars; (c) unrealized gain in the fair value of investments in trading securities; (d) losses on "derivative" financial instruments.

_____ 13. Which of the following statements is <u>not</u> true concerning a quasi-reorganization? (a) assets may be written down below cost; (b) any adjustments to the accounts are debited first to additional paid-in capital; (c) new management may be selected; (d) assets may be valued at a fair but conservative value.

Part C Solve each of the following short problems.

1. Three corporations have different types of stock options outstanding. Corporation A has issued options to purchase 1,000 shares of common stock at $50 per share, Corporation B has issued options to purchase 2,000 shares of common stock at $40 per share, and Corporation C has issued options to purchase 3,000 shares of common stock at $55 per share. In 2004, the average market prices per share of the common stock for each corporation are as follows:

	Corp. A	Corp. B	Corp. C
Average market price	$54	$46	$48

Determine the change in the number of shares used to calculate the 2004 earnings per share for each of these corporations.

(a) Corporation A

(b) Corporation B

(c) Corporation C

2. Information relating to the complex capital structure of Rinehart Corporation is as follows:

2004 net income: $24,500
2004 income tax rate: 30%
Common stock: 11,000 shares outstanding
$100 par convertible preferred stock: 1,000 shares, each share convertible into two shares of common stock
7% convertible bonds: $100,000 face value (issued at par), each $1,000 bond convertible into 35 shares of common stock
9% convertible bonds: $50,000 face value (issued at par), each $1,000 bond convertible into 50 shares of common stock
2004 preferred dividends: $2.50 per share
All stocks and bonds have been outstanding for the entire year

(a) Prepare a ranking of the order in which the securities would be included in Diluted Earnings Per Share.

(b) Compute basic earnings per share.

(c) Compute diluted earnings per share.

3. Crown Corporation had the following account balances on December 31, 2004:

Common stock, $5 par, 60,000 shares issued and outstanding	$300,000
Additional paid-in capital on common stock	600,000
Retained earnings	250,000

Common stock is currently selling at $14 per share.

Prepare the appropriate journal entries for the declaration and payment of each of the following proposed dividends (treat each proposal separately).

(a) Cash dividend of $0.70 per common share.

(b) A 10% stock dividend.

(c) A 30% stock dividend.

4. In 2004, Rehmer Corporation had a beginning retained earnings balance of $150,000. Prepare a statement of retained earnings for the year ended December 31, 2004, taking into consideration the following transactions which occurred during the year:

(a) A material error in net income of a previous period was corrected resulting in an increase in retained earnings of $9,000 after related income taxes of $2,250.

(b) Net income for the year was $79,000.

(c) Cash dividends of $11,000 and stock dividends of $8,000 were declared.

(d) One thousand shares of $100 par callable preferred stock were recalled and retired at a price of $140 per share. The original issuance price was $110 per share.

5. Lee Company has 3,000 shares of 7%, $100 par preferred stock and 20,000 shares of $10 par common stock outstanding. If $80,000 is available for dividends, determine the amount of dividends to be paid to each class of stock under each of the following independent assumptions.

(a) Preferred stock is nonparticipating and noncumulative.

(b) Preferred stock is fully participating and noncumulative.

(c) Preferred stock is nonparticipating and cumulative, and preferred dividends are 2 years in arrears.

ANSWERS TO POST TEST

Part A

1. F	6. T	11. F	16. F
2. T	7. F	12. F	17. F
3. T	8. T	13. T	18. F
4. F	9. T	14. F	19. F
5. T	10. F	15. T	20. F
			21. T

Part B

1. b	4. c	7. c	10. b
2. c	5. c	8. d	11. d
3. c	6. a	9. a	12. c
			13. b

Part C

1.

	Corp. A	Corp. B
Proceeds from assumed exercise of options:[a]		
1,000 x \$50	\$50,000	
2,000 x \$40		\$80,000
Number of shares to be issued:	1,000	2,000
Less assumed reacquisition of treasury shares:		
\$50,000 ÷ \$54	(926)	
\$80,000 ÷ \$46		(1,739)
Increase in number of shares[b]	74	261

[a]The proceeds and change in the number of shares for C are not calculated because the average market price is less than the exercise price, making its stock options antidilutive.

[b]The number of shares for A would be increased by 74 shares and for B increased by 261 shares; there would be no change for C because the effect is antidilutive.

2. (a)

Security	Impact	DEPS Rank
Convertible Preferred Stock	$\$1.25 = \frac{\$2,500}{1,000 \times 2}$	1
7% Convertible Bonds	$\$2.00 = \frac{\$7,000}{100 \times 35}$	3
9% Convertible Bonds	$\$1.80 = \frac{\$4,500}{50 \times 50}$	2

(b)

$$\text{Basic Earnings Per Share} = \frac{\$24,500 - (\$2.50 \times 1,000)}{11,000 \text{ shares}} = \$2.00$$

2. (c)

	Earnings	÷	Shares	=	EPS
Basic EPS	$22,000		11,000		$2.00
DEPS earnings and shares					
Shares from preferred conversion			2,000		
Savings in dividends	2,500				
DEPS	$24,500		13,000	=	$1.88
Shares from 9% bond conversion			2,500		
Savings in interest	4,500				
DEPS	$29,000		15,500	=	$1.87*

*The 7% convertible bonds would be antidilutive because $1.87 DEPS < $2.00.

3. (a)

Retained Earnings	42,000	
Dividends Payable: Common Stock (0.70 x 60,000)		42,000
To record declaration.		
Dividends Payable: Common Stock	42,000	
Cash		42,000
To record payment.		

(b)

Retained Earnings [(0.10 x 60,000) x $14]	84,000	
Common Stock to be Distributed ($5 x 6,000)		30,000
Additional Paid-in Capital from Stock Dividend ($9 x 6,000)		54,000
To record declaration.		
Common Stock to be Distributed	30,000	
Common Stock		30,000
To record distribution.		

(c)

Retained Earnings [(0.30 x 60,000) x $5]	90,000	
Common Stock to be Distributed		90,000
To record declaration.		
Common Stock to be Distributed	90,000	
Common Stock		90,000
To record distribution.		

4.

REHMER CORPORATION
Statement of Retained Earnings
For the Year Ended December 31, 2004

Retained earnings, January 1, 2004	$150,000
Add: Prior period adjustment (net of $2,250 income taxes)	9,000
Adjusted retained earnings, January 1, 2004	$159,000
Add: Net income, 2004	79,000
	$238,000
Less: Cash dividends, common stock	(11,000)
Stock dividends	(8,000)
Retirement of 1,000 shares of $100 par callable preferred stock	(30,000)
Retained earnings, December 31, 2004	$189,000

5. (a) Nonparticipating and noncumulative:

Dividends available	$80,000
Less: Preferred dividends ($100 x 0.07 x 3,000)	(21,000)
Dividend for common stockholders	$59,000

(b) Fully participating and noncumulative:

		Preferred	Common
7% to preferred ($100 x 0.07 x 3,000		$21,000	
Equal dividend to common ($10 x 0.07 x 20,000) (equal to 7% of par)			$14,000
Extra proportionate to par values:			
Total to distribute	$80,000		
Allocated ($21,000 and $14,000)	(35,000)		
*Extra	$45,000	27,000 (60%)	18,000 (40%)
		$48,000	$32,000

*Allocated on basis of total par value of each class of stock:

Preferred (3,000 shares x $100 par)	$300,000 (60%)
Common (20,000 shares x $10 par)	200,000 (40%)
Total par value	$500,000

(c) Nonparticipating and cumulative with dividends 2 years in arrears:

Dividends available		$80,000
Less: Preferred dividends		
Dividends in arrears ($100 x 0.07 x 3,000 x 2)		$42,000
Current dividends ($100 x 0.07 x 3,000)	21,000	(63,000)
Dividends for common stockholders		$17,000

17

INCOME RECOGNITION AND MEASUREMENT OF NET ASSETS

CHAPTER OBJECTIVES

After careful study of this chapter, you will be able to:

1. Understand the revenue recognition alternatives.

2. Explain revenue recognition at the time of sale, during production, and at time of cash receipt.

3. Explain the conceptual issues regarding revenue recognition alternatives.

4. Describe the alternative revenue recognition methods.

5. Account for revenue recognition prior to the period of sale, including the percentage-of-completion and completed contract methods.

6. Account for revenue recognition after the period of sale, including the installment and cost recovery methods.

7. Account for revenue recognition delayed until a future event occurs.

8. Understand software revenue recognition, franchises, real estate sales, retail land sales, and consignment sales.

SYNOPSIS

Revenue Recognition Alternatives

1. Recognition is the process of formally recording and reporting an item in the financial statements. Realization is the process of converting noncash resources into cash or rights to cash. A company usually recognizes revenue in the period of sale, when (a) realization has taken place, and (b) the revenues have been earned. There are, however, three revenue recognition alternatives: (a) advanced recognition (e.g., during the period of production), (b) recognition at the time of sale, and (c) deferred recognition (e.g., upon receipt of cash). Advanced or deferred recognition is used to increase the usefulness of the financial statements.

2. The revenue recognition alternative used affects not only a company's income recognition on its income statement but the measurement of net assets (assets minus liabilities) on its balance sheet. Under all three revenue recognition alternatives, a company increases related assets from cost to selling price at the point at which it recognizes revenue and expenses. For example, in a manufacturing operation, when revenue recognition is at the time of sale, the company increases accounts receivable by the selling price and reduces inventory by the cost. When recognition is advanced, revenue and expense are recognized during production, and the inventory is increased from cost to selling price. When recognition is delayed, the sale is recorded in the accounts receivable at the selling price, but accounts receivable is reduced to cost by recording the expected gross profit in a Deferred Gross Profit account (a contra-account to accounts receivable). As a company receives payment, it debits Deferred Gross Profit and credits Gross Profit, thus recognizing revenue. Net assets increase by the selling price.

3. The recognition of expenses is matched against revenues and coincides with the revenue recognition alternative selected when there is a direct "association of cause and effect." For example, depreciation expense on machinery to produce a product is included in the cost of inventory and its recognition is consistent with the recognition of revenue. However, when expenses are recognized on the basis of systematic and rational allocation (depreciation on an office building for administrative purposes) or immediately (administrative salaries), the recognition of expenses is independent of the revenue recognition alternative used.

Conceptual Issues

4. The following three factors are useful in evaluating revenue recognition issues in specific business situations. The factors may help in determining whether revenue should be recognized at the time of sale, or whether recognition should be advanced or deferred.

    (a) The economic substance of the event takes precedence over the legal form of the transaction.

    Usually a company recognizes revenue at the time of the legal transaction. However, revenue recognition may be advanced or delayed if economic "reality" would otherwise be substantially distorted. An example is the recognition of gross profit on a sales-type lease by the lessor before legal title is passed.

    (b) The risks and benefits of ownership been transferred to the buyer.

If the risks and benefits have been substantially transferred, the buyer must recognize revenue. Under a sales-type lease, the lessor must recognize revenue even though no legal sale has occurred because the risks and benefits of ownership have been transferred.

(c) The collectibility of the receivable from the sale is reasonably assured.

If collectibility is not reasonably assured, revenue has not been realized and the earning process is not complete so recognition is deferred.

Alternative Revenue Recognition Methods

5. Revenue Recognition in the Period of the Sale is used because realization has occurred and revenues are earned at the time of the sale. Accrual accounting is used, expenses are matched against revenues, inventory is recorded at cost, and accounts receivable are recorded at net realizable value. This method is used most often.

6. Revenue Recognition Prior to the Period of the Sale is used to reflect economic substance over legal form. The percentage-of-completion method of accounting for long-term construction contracts and the proportional performance method of accounting for long-term service contracts are examples.

7. Revenue Recognition at the Completion of Production is used for certain precious metals and farm products which may have a fixed market price and unit interchangeability. However, this alternative is rarely used.

8. Revenue Recognition After the Period of the Sale is used when the collectibility of receivables is not reasonably assured or cannot be reliably estimated. The installment method and the cost recovery method are both used to defer revenue recognition.

9. Revenue Recognition Delayed Until a Future Event Occurs is used when there has been insignificant transfer of the risks and benefits of ownership. The deposit method of accounting is used until sufficient risks and benefits have been transferred to the buyer. Then revenue recognition may occur.

   A summary of alternative revenue recognition methods is presented in Exhibit 17-10 in the text.

Revenue Recognition Prior to the Period of Sale

10. Long-term construction contracts arise when a company agrees to construct an asset (e.g., buildings, ships, bridges) for another entity over an extended period. The buyer may provide advance payments to help finance construction, but the legal sale does not take place until the asset is complete. Two alternative revenue recognition methods are possible: (1) the percentage-of-completion method in which a company recognizes profit each period during the life of the contract in proportion to the amount of the contract completed during the period, and values its inventory at the costs incurred plus the profit recognized to date, less any partial billings; and (2) the completed-contract method in which a company recognizes profit only when the contract is complete and records inventory at cost, less any partial billings.

11. The AICPA concluded that long-term construction contracts may be considered "continuous sales" and in its Statement of Position No. 81-1 requires that a company use the percentage-of-completion method for long-term contracts when all of the following conditions are met:

    a. The company can make reasonably dependable estimates of the extent of progress toward completion, contract revenues, and contract costs.

    b. The contract clearly specifies the enforceable rights regarding goods or services to be provided and received by both the company and the buyer, the consideration to be exchanged, and the manner and terms of settlement.

    c. The buyer can be expected to satisfy its obligations under the contract.

    d. The company expects the contractor to perform its contractual obligations.

    When any of the above conditions are not met, the company uses the completed-contract method. It also uses this method on short-term contracts and when the risks of the contract are so great that reasonably dependable estimates cannot be made.

12. A company can determine the percentage completed by either "input" or "output" measures. The cost-to-cost method or efforts-expended method are two input measures. With the cost-to-cost method, the company measures the percentage of completion by comparing the cost incurred to date with the expected total costs for the contract. With the efforts-expended method, the company measures the percentage of completion by comparing the work (labor hours, labor dollars, machine hours, material quantities, etc.) performed to date with the total estimated work for the contract. Under either method, once the company determines the percentage of completion it multiplies this percentage by the total revenue on the contract to compute the revenue to be recognized to date. The revenue to date minus the revenue recognized in previous years is the revenue to recognize in the current year. The expense to be recognized is determined in the same way. Alternatively, the company can use output measures such as units produced, units delivered, value added, or other measures of production to measure the percentage of completion. The results achieved to date compared to the total expected results of the contract are used to measure percentage of completion. A company computes revenue and expense in the same way as discussed above for the input measures.

13. Under the percentage-of-completion method, a company uses an account titled Construction in Progress to record all costs incurred on the project as well as the gross profit recognized to date. It uses a Partial Billings account to record receipts paid by the buyer during construction. This account is a contra account to Construction in Progress. The company reports a net debit balance in the Construction in Progress account on its balance sheet as an asset and a net credit balance as a liability.

14. Typical journal entries for the percentage-of-completion method are shown below:

    (a) To record construction costs:

Construction in Progress	100,000	
Accounts Payable, Raw Materials Inventory, Cash, etc.		100,000

(b) To record partial billings:

Accounts Receivable	80,000	
Partial Billings		80,000

(c) To record collections:

Cash	50,000	
Accounts Receivable		50,000

(d) To record gross profit:

Construction Expense	100,000	
Construction in Progress	40,000	
Construction Revenue		140,000

With the completed-contract method, a company would also use the first three entries, but it would recognize no gross profit until the completion date.

15. The principle advantage of the completed-contract method is that the gross profit is more reliable because it is based on final results rather than on estimates. The principle disadvantage of the completed-contract method is that it is less relevant because net income is a function of the date when contracts are completed and does not reflect current performance. The percentage-of-completion method gives economic substance precedence over legal form and produces a better measure of periodic income. However, the method relies heavily on estimates.

16. Consistent with the conservatism convention, a company must record estimated losses on long-term contracts in full under both the percentage-of-completion and completed-contract methods at the time it estimates the losses. If there is a loss in the current period, but a profit on the total contract is anticipated, the loss recognized is equal to the difference between the revenue recognized for the year and the construction costs incurred for the year. However, if a company anticipates a loss on the total contract, it must remove the gross profit on the contract to date, in addition to recognizing the loss. This is done by debiting Construction Expense for the amount of the loss plus the amount needed to reduce the cumulative profit in the Construction in Progress account to zero. The provision for the loss is a contra-account to Construction in Progress.

17. There are several additional factors which affect accounting for long-term construction contracts. (a) Contract costs may include general and administrative costs which are identifiable with or allocable to the contract; (b) Accounting Research Bulletin No. 45 requires that a company classify the net amounts of Construction in Progress and Partial Billing as current assets or current liabilities; (c) Off setting of assets and liabilities is permitted when contracts are closely related; (d) Interest costs associated with the funds used in construction are capitalized and included in the Construction in Progress account; and, (e) Disclosure of the method used to account for long-term construction contracts is required in a note to the financial statements.

18. According to APB Statement No. 4, a company must recognize revenues for services rendered when the services have been performed and are billable. However, long-term service contracts can be complex, and it may be difficult to determine when "performance" has been completed. The FASB has not yet issued general standards for revenue and expense recognition for service transactions, although an Invitation to Comment has been issued. The following recommendations are based on that Invitation to Comment.

19. When more than one act is required under a long-term service contract, a company recognizes revenue by the proportional performance method. That is, the company recognizes revenue in proportion to performance of each act, as discussed below.

20. Recognition under the proportional performance method depends on the type and number of service acts:

    (a) For a specified number of similar acts, an equal amount of revenue is recognized for each act.

    (b) For a specified number of defined but not similar acts, revenue recognized for each act is based on the ratio of the direct costs (see below) of the act to the total estimated direct costs under the contract.

    (c) For an unspecified number of similar acts, revenue is recognized on a straight-line basis over the performance period.

21. Costs under a long-term service contract include (a) initial direct costs, directly associated with negotiating and signing the contract (for example, legal fees), (b) direct costs, directly related to services performed (for example, labor costs), and (c) indirect costs, not included in either of the preceding categories.

22. A company defers initial direct costs and allocates them over the performance period, in proportion to service revenues recognized. Direct costs and indirect costs are expensed as incurred.

Revenue Recognition After the Period of Sale

23. In an installment sale, a customer makes a small down payment and contracts to pay the balance over an extended period. Although the customer typically takes possession of the item, the seller retains title until payment is completed. The seller may recognize revenue at the time of the sale if collectibility is reasonably assured or, if not, recognition may be deferred. If the seller defers recognition, either the installment method or the cost recovery method may be used. It is important to distinguish between an "installment sale" (a type of legal contract) and the "installment method" of revenue recognition. Under the installment method, the seller recognizes some gross profit with each payment received from the customer. The amount recognized is determined by the gross profit ratio in the year of the sale. Under the more conservative and less common cost recovery method, the seller recognizes no gross profit until all of the cost of the merchandise is recovered.

24. APB Opinion No. 10 found that the installment and cost recovery methods are acceptable only in exceptional cases. When a customer will make payments over a long period and the collectibility of cash is not reasonably assured, the seller uses the installment method. If collectibility is extremely uncertain, or there is no reasonable basis for estimating the degree of collectibility, the cost recovery method is appropriate. Recently, an increase in complex sales transactions where the recognition of revenue at the time of sale is inappropriate has led to wider use of the two methods. The installment method is also used for income tax reporting under certain circumstances.

25. When using the installment method a company completes the following steps:

(a) <u>During the year</u> total sales, cost of goods sold, and collections are recorded in the normal way.

(b) <u>At the end of the year</u>, the sales for which the installment method is to be used are identified. The revenue and related cost of goods sold are identified and reversed and deferred gross profit is recognized using the following entry:

Sales	XXX	
Cost of Goods Sold		XXX
Deferred Gross Profit		XXX

Then the gross profit on the sales recognized under the installment method for the year is determined and recognized as follows:

$$\text{Gross Profit Rate} = \frac{\text{Deferred Gross Profit for the Year}}{\text{Installment Method Sales for the Year}}$$

$$\text{Gross Profit Realized on Installment Method Sales} = \text{Cash Collected on Installment Method Sales for the Year} \times \text{Gross Profit Rate}$$

Deferred Gross Profit	XXX	
Gross Profit Realized on Installment Method Sales		XXX

(c) In <u>future years</u>, the remaining deferred gross profit is reduced and gross profit is recognized. The amount to recognize is calculated as follows:

$$\text{Gross Profit on Installment Method Sales from Prior Years} = \text{Cash Collected in Current Year from Previous Year's Installment Method Sales} \times \text{Gross Profit Rate for the Year Installment Method Sales Made}$$

26. On the company's income statement, Gross Profit Realized on Installment Method Sales is disclosed separately. In addition, if sales recognized under the installment method are material, the sales and related cost of goods sold must also be disclosed. On the company's balance sheet, Installment Accounts Receivable less Deferred Gross Profit are usually included in current assets.

27. Several additional factors affect the company's accounting under the installment method: (a) Operating expenses under the installment method are recognized in the normal way on the accrual basis. (b) Each installment payment received is separated into two components: a reduction of the installment receivable and interest revenue. The interest revenue is recorded on the accrual basis in the normal way. (c) An allowance for doubtful accounts is appropriate if past experience indicates that the expected resale prices of repossessed items are not sufficient to cover the remaining payments on the installment sales. (d) When an item is repossessed, the inventory is recorded, and the related receivable and deferred gross profit are written off.

28. A company may use the installment method in special credit "sale" situations. In these cases, it may initially record a Deferred Gain at the time of the "sale". Then, as it collects the cash, it reduces the deferred gain and recognizes a gain based on the percentage of the total cash collected.

29. Accounting for installment sales under the cost recovery method is the same as under the installment method except under the cost recovery method, a company recognizes gross profit at the end of each year to the extent that the cash received to date exceeds the cost of the product sold. The entry used to recognize the gross profit is:

Deferred Gross Profit	XXX	
Gross Profit Realized on Cost Recovery Transactions		XXX

Revenue Recognition Delayed Until a Future Event Occurs

30. A company uses the deposit method to postpone the recognition of revenue when a sale occurs which cannot be recognized for accounting purposes because sufficient risks and benefits of ownership have not been transferred. Until the revenue is recognized in a future period, assets and liabilities which have been transferred are separately classified on the company's balance sheet (e.g., assets of business transferred under contract), depreciation continues to be recorded, and any payments are recorded as a deposit and reported as a liability (Deposit from Purchaser) on the balance sheet. When circumstances have changed and trigger the recognition of a sale, the company recognizes revenue and eliminates the deposit account.

Additional Revenue Recognition Issues

31. For software revenue recognition, if a company has an agreement to deliver software that requires significant production, modification, or customization of software, it uses contract accounting (e.g., percentage of completion) for the agreement. If a company has an agreement to deliver software that does not require significant production, modification, or customization of software, it recognizes revenue when (a) persuasive evidence of an agreement exists, (b) delivery has occurred, (c) its fee is fixed or determinable, and (d) collectibility is probable. A company separately accounts for a service element if (a) the services are not essential to the functionality of any other element of the transaction, and (b) the services are stated separately in the contract such that the total price of the agreement would be expected to vary as the result of inclusion or exclusion of the services. Software arrangements may consist of multiple elements such as additional software products, upgrades and/or enhancements, rights to exchange or return software, and customer support. If contract accounting does not apply, a company must allocate its fee to the various elements based on fair values.

32. Under a franchise agreement, a franchisor grants business rights to a franchisee who will operate the business. A franchise agreement usually involves an initial payment (initial franchise fee) by the franchisee, and ongoing payments of continuing franchise fees.

33. FASB Statement No. 45 addresses issues concerning the timing of revenue recognition by the franchisor. The FASB concluded that the franchisor should recognize the initial franchise fee as revenue after commencement of operations by the franchisee, as soon as the franchisor has performed substantially all of its related services. Until the point of recognition, the franchisor records franchise fees as a liability (unearned franchise fees). The accrual method of accounting should be used. In exceptional cases, when collection of the initial franchise fees occurs over an extended period and no reasonable basis for estimating collectibility exists, the franchisor may use either the installment or cost recovery method of revenue recognition. In addition, when an initial franchise fee involves prepayment by the franchisee for continuing services the

franchisor should record part of that initial franchise fee as a liability and amortize it over the life of the franchise.

34. When a company sells either land or a building or both, it recognizes revenue and related expenses in the period of the sale using the accrual method if all four criteria of recognition specified in FASB Statement No. 66 are met. The four criteria relate to the economic substance of the transaction, the collectibility of the receivable, and the transfer of the risks and benefits of ownership. When the earning process is not complete or realization has not occurred, alternate revenue recognition methods are appropriate depending on the circumstances.

35. Retail land sales generally involve sales of lots by a company to widely dispersed individuals through intensive marketing. Typically, the company promises large capital outlays for improvements, a low down payment from the buyer, no (or limited) credit investigation, payments by the buyer over several years, and cancellation at the buyer's option within a specified period. The company recognizes the revenue and related expenses in the period of the sale if all of the five specific conditions specified in FASB Statement No. 66 are met. The five conditions are: (1) the buyer has made the down payment and each required subsequent payment until the period of cancellation has expired; (2) the cumulative payments of principal and interest equal or exceed 10% of the contract sales price; (3) collection experience indicates that at least 90% of contracts will be collected in full. A down payment of 20% is an acceptable indication of collectibility; (4) the receivable on the sale is not subject to subordination to new loans on the property; and (5) the company (seller) is not obligated to complete improvements or construct amenities to lots sold. Otherwise revenue is recognized using an alternate revenue recognition method prescribed by the circumstances.

36. When goods are transferred from a manufacturer or wholesaler (consignor) to a dealer (consignee) for purposes of sale and the manufacturer retains the risks and benefits of ownership (as well as the legal title) to the goods, the transfer is known as a consignment. Such an arrangement constitutes neither a sale nor an acquisition of inventory. The consignor debits a Consignment-out account for the cost of the consigned inventory and related expenses. When a sale to a third party occurs, the consignee notifies the consignor, and the consignor recognizes revenue. In addition, the Consignment-out account is credited for the costs related to the sale and the appropriate expense accounts are debited. The consignee credits a Consignment-in account for the proceeds from the sale of consigned goods and debits it for costs which will be reimbursed by the consignor and for commissions earned. When payment is transferred to the consignor, the Consignment-in account is reduced. On the balance sheet date, the consignor will report the Consignment-in account as an asset (Consignment Receivable) if it has a debit balance and a liability (Consignment Obligation) if it has a credit balance.

37. International Accounting Standards and U.S. GAAP use the same basic criteria for revenue recognition even though the terminology may differ. International accounting standards also require use of the percentage-of-completion method if the outcome can be reliably estimated. If not, use of the zero-profit method (a form of cost recovery) is required.

SELF-EVALUATION EXERCISES

Supply the words necessary to complete each of the following items.

Revenue Recognition Alternatives

RR-1. The process of formally recording and reporting an item in the financial statements is termed ________________; the process of converting noncash resources into cash or rights to cash is termed ______________.

RR-2. Recognition of revenue during the period of the sale occurs when the following two conditions have been met:

(1) ____

(2) ____

RR-3. At the point at which a company recognizes revenue, the value of its related assets is increased from ____________ to ______________ ______________.

Conceptual Issues

CI-1. The recognition of gross profit on a sales-type lease before legal title is passed is an example of advanced revenue recognition due to

____________ ____________ ____________ ____________

____________ ____________ ____________.

CI-2. A company may defer the recognition of revenue if the collectibility of the receivable is not ____________ ____________.

CI-3. If the risks and benefits of ownership have been transferred, yet no legal sale has occurred, revenue must be ________________.

Alternate Revenue Recognition Methods

RM-1. A company uses accrual accounting when revenue recognition occurs ________________ the period of the sale.

RM-2. When a company uses the proportional performance method of accounting for long-term service contracts, revenue is recognized ____________ ____________ the period of the sale.

RM-3. When a company uses the installment method, revenue is recognized ____________ the period of the sale.

RM-4. A company uses the deposit method to account for revenue when recognition is __________ ________ ___ _________ _________ _________.

Revenue Recognition Prior to the Period of Sale

PR-1. When one company agrees to construct an asset for another entity over an extended period, the agreement is called a __________-__________ __________ __________.

PR-2. The accounting method used with long-term construction contracts to recognize revenue prior to the legal completion of the sale is the ______________-________-________________ method.

PR-3. The AICPA determined that under certain conditions companies may use the percentage-of-completion method to recognize revenue prior to the sale, because a long-term construction contract may be considered a ________________ ________________.

PR-4. The two input measuring methods used to determine the percentage completed are the __________-_____-_____________ method and the ______________-____________ method.

PR-5. When the risks of a long-term construction contract are so great that a company cannot make reasonably dependable estimates, the recommended accounting method is the _____________-_____________ method.

PR-6. If there is a loss for the current period on a long-term construction contract, but a profit on the total contract is anticipated, the loss recognized is equal to the difference between the ______________________________________ and the ______________________________________.

PR-7. _Accounting Research Bulletin No. 45_ requires that companies classify the net amounts of Construction in Progress and Partial Billing as __________ __________ or __________ __________.

PR-8. Under the proportional performance method of accounting for long-term service contracts, revenue recognition depends on two factors:

(1) ____________________

(2) ____________________

PR-9. Under the proportional performance method, if the acts are similar and are of a specified number, the amount of revenue recognized for each act should be

____________.

PR-10. The three types of costs associated with long-term service contracts are (1) ____________ ____________ costs, (2) ____________ costs, and (3) ____________ costs.

PR-11. When accounting for long-term service contracts, direct costs and indirect costs should be recognized as expenses when ____________.

Revenue Recognition After the Period of Sale

RA-1. A transaction in which a customer makes a small downpayment and contracts to pay the balance over an extended period is called an ____________

____________.

RA-2. The method of accounting for installment sales that recognizes some gross profit with each payment received from the customer is the ____________ method.

RA-3. The following two conditions must exist before a company may use the installment method:

(1) ____________________

(2) ____________________

RA-4. The method of accounting for installment sales that recognizes gross profit at the end of each year to the extent that the cash received to date exceeded the cost of the product sold is the ____________ ____________ method.

RA-5. When using the installment method, the gross profit rate is equal to the ____________ ____________ ____________ for the year divided by the ____________ ____________ ____________ for the year.

RA-6. Gross profit using the installment method is calculated by multiplying the gross profit rate times ________ __________ ____ ____________ ________ ________ for the year.

Revenue Recognition Delayed Until a Future Event Occurs

RD-1. When a company must delay revenue recognition because sufficient risks and benefits of ownership have not been transferred, the accounting method used is the ______________ method.

RD-2. Under the deposit method, a company classifies the Deposit from Purchaser account on the balance sheet as a ______________.

Additional Revenue Recognition Issues

AR-1. When a company has an agreement to deliver software that requires significant production, modification, or customization, it uses __________________ accounting.

AR-2. The legal document in which one party grants business rights to another party who will operate the business is called a ________________ ________________.

AR-3. When the criteria specified in FASB Statement No. 66 are met, a company accounts for real estate sales using the______________ method.

AR-4. Sales of lots by a land development company to widely dispersed individuals through intensive sales efforts are termed __________ ____________ sales.

AR-5. When goods are transferred from a manufacturer to a dealer for the purposes of sale and the manufacturer retains legal title to the goods, the transfer is called a _______________.

AR-6. Under a consignment, when a sale occurs revenue is recognized by the ______________.

ANSWERS TO SELF-EVALUATION EXERCISES

RR-1. recognition, realization; RR-2. (1) Realization has taken place; (2) Revenues have been earned; RR-3. cost, selling price; CI-1. economic substance taking precedence over legal form; CI-2. reasonably assured; CI-3. recognized; RM-1. in; RM-2. prior to; RM-3. after; RM-4. delayed until a future event occurs; PR-1. long-term construction contract; PR-2. percentage-of-completion; PR-3. continuous sale; PR-4. cost-to-cost, efforts-expended; PR-5. completed-contract; PR-6. revenue recognized for the year and the construction costs incurred for the year; PR-7. current assets, current liabilities; PR-8. (1) the type of service acts, (2) the number of service acts; PR-9. equal; PR-10. (1) initial direct, (2) direct, (3) indirect; PR-11. incurred; RA-1. installment sale; RA-2. installment; RA-3. (1) Payments are to be received over a long period of time, (2) collectibility of cash is reasonably uncertain; RA-4. cost recovery; RA-5. deferred gross profit, installment method sales; RA-6. cash collected on installment method sales; RD-1. deposit; RD-2. liability; AR-1. contract; AR-2. franchise agreement; AR-3. accrual; AR-4. retail land; AR-5. consignment; AR-6. consignor;

POST TEST

Part A Circle T if the statement is true and F if it is false.

T F 1. Revenue is usually formally recorded and reported in the financial statements when recognition has taken place and the earning process is complete.

T F 2. The recognition of revenue may be deferred or advanced in order to increase the usefulness of the accounting information.

T F 3. The period in which a company recognizes revenue determines the period in which there is a change in the related net asset valuation.

T F 4. The recognition of related expenses is dependent on the revenue recognition alternative used when there is not a direct association of cause and effect.

T F 5. When a company recognizes revenue in the period of the sale, it records accounts receivable at net realizable value and inventory at cost.

T F 6. The deposit method is used to recognize revenue prior to the period of the sale and is an example of economic substance over legal form.

T F 7. When a company uses the completed-contract method of accounting for long-term construction contracts, it recognizes profit each period during the life of the contract in proportion to the amount of contract completed during the period.

T F 8. The AICPA recommends in Statement of Position No. 81-1 the use of the percentage-of-completion method to account for long-term construction contracts in all cases where reasonably dependable estimates can be made of the revenues and expenses associated with the contract, and both the buyer and the contractor can be expected to fulfill their contractual obligations.

T F 9. The completed-contract method gives economic substance more importance than legal form and produces a better measure of periodic income and current performance.

T F 10. An expected loss on a long-term contract accounted for by the percentage-of-completion method should be recorded based on the percentage of work completed.

T F 11. A company capitalizes interest costs associated with the funds used in long-term construction.

T F 12. When using the proportional performance method to account for a long-term service contract, initial direct costs should be charged to expense as incurred, and indirect costs should be deferred and allocated over the performance period in proportion to the service revenues recognized.

T F 13. A company may only use both the installment method and the cost recovery method in exceptional circumstances where payments are to be received over a long time period, and where the collectibility of cash is uncertain, or where there is no reasonable basis for estimating the degree of collectibility.

T F 14. While both the installment method and the cost recovery method defer recognition of installment-sales revenue, the installment method recognizes some gross profit as payment is received from the customer while the cost recovery method waits until all of the cost of the merchandise is recovered.

T F 15. When accounting for the sale of software that includes upgrades and customer support, a company must allocate its fee for the various elements based on fair values if contract accounting does not apply.

T F 16. When goods are transferred as a consignment, the consignor recognizes revenue when the consignee completes a sale to a third party.

T F 17. Under a franchise agreement, if part of the initial franchise fee is prepayment by the franchisee for continuing services, the franchisor must defer recognition of that part and amortize it over the life of the franchise.

T F 18. The cost recovery method is to be used in accounting for real estate sales when the buyer's initial and continuing investment is not adequate and recovery of the cost of the property is reasonably assured.

Part B Select the one best answer, and place its letter in the space provided.

_____ 1. In 2004, Adam Company started work on a $5,000,000 long-term construction project that will take three years to complete. At the end of the first year, the accounting records showed the following data:

Construction costs incurred	$1,125,000
Estimated costs to complete the contract	3,375,000
Partial billings to customer	900,000
Collections from customer	800,000

If Adam Company uses the percentage-of-completion method, the amount of gross profit that would be recognized in 2004 would be (a) $500,000; (b) $225,000; (c) $125,000; (d) $112,500.

_____ 2. Using the data presented above in question #1, determine the balance in the Construction in Progress account at the end of the first year under both the percentage-of-completion and completed-contract methods.

	Percentage-of-Completion	Completed-Contract
(a)	$1,250,000	$1,125,000
(b)	$1,125,000	$1,250,000
(c)	$1,250,000	$1,250,000
(d)	$1,125,000	-0-

_____ 3. At the end of 2004 the accounting records of Brightwell Construction Company showed the following data relating to a three year $2,000,000 long-term construction contract:

	2003	2004
Construction costs incurred	$ 600,000	$800,000
Estimated costs to complete the contract	1,000,000	700,000
Partial billings to customer	500,000	600,000
Collections from customer	400,000	500,000

Using the completed-contract method, the loss anticipated on the contract at the end of 2004 would (a) not be recognized until realized at the completion of the contract in 2005; (b) be recognized in 2004 by debiting Construction Expense and crediting Provision for Loss on Contract each for $100,000; (c) be recognized in 2004 by debiting Construction Expense for $220,000 which includes the amount of the loss plus the amount needed to reduce the cumulative profit in the Construction in Progress account to zero; (d) be recognized in 2004 by debiting Construction Expense and crediting Construction in Progress each for $100,000.

_____ 4. The Show Time Video Company sells two year memberships to its video club. For $500 paid in advance, a member is entitled to a specified number of dissimilar services including video, video player, and cam recorder rentals, blank video tapes, and video tape developing. Show Time should recognize revenue on which of the following bases? (a) revenue of an equal amount should be recognized for each service provided; (b) revenue should be recognized for each service provided based on the ratio of the direct costs of that service to the total estimated direct costs under the contract; (c) revenue should be recognized on a straight-line method over the performance period; (d) revenue should be recognized at the end of the contract period when the benefits of ownership have been transferred and substantial performance has occurred.

_____ 5. Fairway Company uses the installment method to account for installment sales. Fairway began operations on January 1, 2004, and at the end of the year the following accounting data was available:

Total credit sales	$800,000
Installment sales (included in total credit sales)	200,000
Cost of goods sold on installment sales	120,000
Cash receipts on installment sales	70,000

The amount of gross profit related to installment sales that Fairway should recognize in 2004 is (a) $17,500; (b) $28,000; (c) $42,000; (d) $80,000.

____ 6. In 2004, Uptown Corporation had installment sales of $180,000, installment sales cost of goods sold of $135,000, and cash receipts on 2004 installment sales of $60,000. In addition, cash receipts on 2003 installment sales of $70,000 were also recorded in 2004. The gross profit rate in 2003 was 30%. Assuming that Uptown uses the installment method, the total gross profit on installment sales recognized in 2004 would be (a) $15,000; (b) $32,500; (c) $36,000; (d) $39,000.

____ 7. Adam Company used the cost recovery method for the first time to account for $60,000 in sales in 2004. Cost of goods sold related to these sales was $48,500. Related cash collections in 2004 were $20,000, in 2005 were $32,000, and in 2006 were $8,000. The amount of gross profit that Adam Company would recognize in each of the three years, respectively, is (a) $4,166; $6,667; $1,667; (b) -0-; -0-; $12,500; (c) $4,166; $4,167; $4,167; (d) -0-; $3,500; $8,000.

____ 8. Brightwell Company and Langley Company entered into a consignment agreement on January 1, 2004. Under the terms of the agreement, Langley Company (consignee) will sell the consigned merchandise at cost plus 25% and will remit payment to Brightwell within 30 days of a sale to a third party. Langley earns a commission of 10% of the sales price on each sale. Advertising is an expense of the consignor. During 2004, Brightwell shipped goods costing $15,000 to Langley. Langley made sales of $10,000 and paid $1,200 for advertising. Langley's total payment to Brightwell for the sale of the consigned goods in 2004 was (a) $7,800; (b) $9,000; (c) $10,050; (d) $15,675.

____ 9. Using the information in question #8, how much revenue related to consignment sales will Langley Company recognize on its 2004 income statement: (a) $11,000; (b) $10,000; (c) $8,800; (d) $1,000.

____ 10. Longacre Land Development Corporation has acquired a large tract of land which it intends to develop into a residential-recreational community. The land will be divided into lots and sold on the retail real estate market to individuals. Longacre will install roads and utilities, and will build a golf course, tennis courts, and a recreational center with swimming facilities. Longacre must use the accrual method to account for the land sales unless certain conditions specified in <u>FASB Statement of Financial Accounting Standards No. 66</u> are not met. All of the following are conditions <u>except</u> which one? (a) the buyer had made the downpayment and each required subsequent payment until the period of cancellation with refund has expired; (b) the cumulative payments of principal and interest equal or exceed 10% of the contract sales price; (c) collection experience for the project indicates that at least 90% of the contracts will be collected in full; (d) the seller is obligated to complete improvements of lots sold or to construct amenities or other facilities applicable to lots sold.

____ 11. Which of the following is <u>not</u> recommended by the FASB as a method for companies to use to determine the current cost of inventory and of property, plant, and equipment? (a) direct pricing; (b) management estimate; (c) functional pricing; (d) indexation.

____ 12. Faircom Software Company is negotiating an agreement to sell its bank reconciliation software to Wayback Corporation. The software does not require significant production, modification or customization. Faircom should recognize revenue on the sale when all of the following have occurred <u>except</u>:
(a) collectibility is probable; (b) its fee is fixed or determinable; (c) delivery has occurred; (d) a good faith deposit has been received;
(e) persuasive evidence on an agreement exists.

Part C Solve each of the following short problems.

1. The following information is available for Knorr Company in 2005 at the end of its second year of operations:

	2004	2005
Total credit sales	$400,000	$520,000
Total cost of goods sold	310,000	373,000
Installment method sales*	100,000	100,800
Installment method cost of goods sold*	77,500	75,600
Cash receipts on installment method sales		
2004 sales	70,000	50,000
2005 sales		60,000

*Included in total credit sales and total cost of goods sold.

(a) Assuming that Knorr Company uses the installment method to account for its installment sales because of exceptional circumstances, prepare the journal entries to record the above events for both years.

1. (b) Prepare a partial income statement and a partial balance sheet for 2004.

2. The Texas Company has contracted to build a sports complex for $500,000 which is expected to take 3 years to complete. Information relating to the performance of the contract is summarized below:

	2003	2004	2005
Construction costs incurred during year	$150,000	$110,000	$ 80,000
Estimated cost to complete (at year end)	150,000	65,000	-0-
Billings during the year	200,000	100,000	200,000
Collections during the year	180,000	110,000	210,000

(a) Compute the gross profit or loss for each year of the contract under (1) the percentage-of-completion method and (2) the completed-contract method.

(b) Compute the following as of the end of 2004:

(1) Accounts receivable

(2) Costs and recognized profit not yet billed (percentage-of-completion method)

3. The Party-Time Pizza Company sells franchises for Party-Time Pizza Restaurants. The company charges a non-refundable initial franchise fee of $48,000. The franchise agreement requires a downpayment of $12,000, with the balance covered by the issuance of a $36,000, 10% note payable by the franchisee in three equal annual installments. In addition, the franchisee must pay an annual $5,000 continuing franchise fee.

(a) Prepare the journal entry to record the initial franchise fee assuming that all material services have been substantially performed by the franchisor, the refund period has expired, and the collectibility of the note is reasonably assured.

(b) Prepare the journal entry to record the initial franchise fee assuming that the refund period has expired and the collectibility of the note is not reasonably assured, but all material services have been performed by the franchisor.

(c) Prepare the journal entry to record the continuing franchise fee.

ANSWERS TO POST TEST

Part A

1.	F	10.	F
2.	T	11.	T
3.	T	12.	F
4.	F	13.	T
5.	T	14.	T
6.	F	15.	T
7.	F	16.	T
8.	F	17.	T
9.	F	18.	F

Part B

1.	c	5.	b	9.	d
2.	a	6.	c	10.	d
3.	b	7.	d	11.	b
4.	b	8.	a	12.	d

Part C

1. (a) 2004

Accounts Receivable	400,000	
Sales		400,000
Cost of Goods Sold	310,000	
Inventory		310,000
Cash	70,000	
Accounts Receivable		70,000
Sales	100,000	
Cost of Goods Sold		77,500
Deferred Gross Profit, 2004		22,500
Deferred Gross Profit, 2004*	15,750	
Gross Profit Realized on Installment Method Sales		15,750

*Cash receipts on installment sales x Gross profit rate
Gross profit rate = 22,500/100,000 = 0.225
$70,000 x 0.225 = $15,750

Gross Profit Realized on Installment Method Sales	15,750	
Income Summary		15,750

1. (a) 2005

Accounts Receivable	520,000	
Sales		520,000
Cost of Goods Sold	373,000	
Inventory		373,000
Cash	110,000	
Accounts Receivable		110,000
Sales	100,800	
Cost of Goods Sold		75,600
Deferred Gross Profit, 2005		25,200
Deferred Gross Profit, 2004*	11,250	
Deferred Gross Profit, 2005*	15,000	
Gross Profit Realized on Installment Method Sales		26,250

*Cash receipts on installment sales x Gross profit rate
2004 Gross profit rate = 22,500/100,000 = 0.225
$50,000 x 0.225 = $11,250
2005 Gross profit rate = 25,200/100,800 = 0.25
$60,000 x 0.25 = $15,000

Gross Profit Realized on Installment Method Sales	26,250	
Income Summary		26,250

1. (b)

KNORR COMPANY
Partial Income Statement
For Year Ended December 31, 2004

Sales	$300,000
Cost of goods sold	(232,500)
Gross profit	$ 67,500
Gross profit realized on installment method sales	15,750
Total gross profit	$ 83,250

Partial Balance Sheet
December 31, 2004

Current Assets		
Accounts receivable		$300,000
Installment accounts receivable	$30,000	
Less: Deferred gross profit	(6,750)	
		23,250

2. (a) (1) Percentage-of-completion

	2003	2004	2005
Cost incurred to date	$150,000	$260,000	$340,000
Estimated cost to complete	150,000	65,000	-0-
Total estimated costs	$300,000	$325,000	$340,000
% complete (cost-to-date ÷ total estimated costs)	50%	80%	100%
Revenue to date (% complete x $500,000 contract price)	$250,000	$400,000	$500,000
Revenue to be recognized for the year (revenue to date minus revenue previously recognized)	$250,000	$150,000	$100,000
Construction cost incurred for year	(150,000)	(110,000)	(80,000)
Gross profit to be recognized	$100,000	$ 40,000	$ 20,000

(2) Completed-contract method

2003 - No gross profit recognized	
2004 - No gross profit recognized	
2005 - Contract price	$500,000
Total cost of project	(340,000)
Gross profit recognized in 2005	$160,000

(b) (1)

Accounts receivable billed ($200,000 + $100,000)	$300,000
Collections received ($180,000 + $110,000)	(290,000)
2004 year end balance	$ 10,000

(2)

Cost to 2004 year end	$260,000	
Gross profit recognized to 2004 year end	140,000	$400,000
Less: Partial billings		(300,000)
Costs and recognized profit not yet billed		$100,000

3. (a)

Cash	12,000	
Notes Receivable	36,000	
Franchise Revenue		48,000

(b)

Cash	12,000	
Notes Receivable	36,000	
Unearned Franchise Fees		36,000
Franchise Revenue		12,000

(c)

Cash	5,000	
Continuing Franchise Fee Revenue		5,000

18

ACCOUNTING FOR INCOME TAXES

CHAPTER OBJECTIVES

After careful study of this chapter, you will be able to:

1. Understand permanent and temporary differences.
2. Explain the conceptual issues regarding interperiod tax allocation.
3. Record and report deferred tax liabilities.
4. Record and report deferred tax assets.
5. Explain an operating loss carryback and carryforward.
6. Account for an operating loss carryback.
7. Account for an operating loss carryforward.
8. Apply intraperiod tax allocation.
9. Classify deferred tax liabilities and assets.
10. Discuss the additional conceptual issues concerning interperiod income tax allocation (Appendix).

SYNOPSIS

Overview and Definitions

1. Significant differences normally exist between a company's pretax financial income and taxable income because generally accepted accounting principles are used to measure pretax financial income while the Internal Revenue Code and state tax laws are used to determine taxable income for purposes of paying income taxes.

2. The differences in income stem from the differences between the objectives of generally accepted accounting principles and those of tax laws. The objective of generally accepted accounting principles is to provide information useful to present and potential users in making rational investment, credit, or similar decisions. However, the objectives of the Internal Revenue Code are to raise revenue to operate the government and to assist the government in achieving social or economic goals.

3. The following terms are critical to understanding the accounting for income taxes:

   Deductible temporary difference - temporary difference that results in deductible amounts in future years when the related asset or liability is recovered or settled, respectively.

   Deferred tax asset - the deferred tax consequences of a corporation's deductible temporary differences and operating loss carryforwards. A deferred tax asset is measured using the applicable enacted tax rate and provisions of the enacted tax law. A corporation reduces a deferred tax asset by a valuation allowance if, based on the weight of evidence available, it is more likely than not that it will not realize some portion or all of a deferred tax asset.

   Deferred tax consequences - the future effects on a corporation's income taxes, as measured by the applicable enacted tax rate and provisions of the enacted tax law, resulting from temporary differences and operating loss carryforwards at the end of the current year.

   Deferred tax expense (or benefit) - the change during the year in a corporation's deferred tax liabilities and assets.

   Deferred tax liability - The deferred tax consequence of taxable temporary differences that will result in taxable amounts in future years. A corporation measures its deferred tax liability using the applicable enacted tax rate and provisions of the enacted tax law.

   Income tax expense (or benefit) - the sum of a corporation's income tax obligation and deferred tax expense (or benefit).

   Income tax obligation (or refund) - The amount of income taxes paid or payable (or refundable) for a year, as determined by applying the provisions of the enacted tax law to a corporation's taxable income or operating loss for that year. Sometimes called current tax expense (or benefit).

   Operating loss carryback - an excess of tax deductible expenses over taxable revenues in a year that a corporation may carry back to reduce taxable income in a prior year.

Operating loss carryforward - an excess of tax deductible expenses over taxable revenues in a year that a corporation may carry forward to reduce taxable income in a future year.

Permanent Difference - a difference between a corporation's pretax financial income and taxable income in an accounting period which will never reverse in a later accounting period.

Taxable income - the excess of a corporation's taxable revenues over tax deductible expenses and exemptions for the year as defined by the governmental taxing authority.

Taxable temporary difference - temporary difference that results in taxable amounts in future years when the related asset or liability is recovered or settled, respectively.

Temporary difference - a difference between the tax basis of an asset or liability and its reported amount in the corporation's financial statements that will result in taxable or deductible amounts in future years when the reported amount of the asset is recovered or the liability is settled.

Valuation allowance - the portion of a deferred tax asset for which it is more likely than not that a corporation will not realize a tax benefit.

Interperiod Income Tax Allocation: Basic Issues

4. Differences between a corporation's pretax financial income and taxable income are a result of either permanent or temporary differences. The three types of permanent differences are: (a) revenues that are recognized for financial reporting purposes but are never taxable, such as interest received by a corporation on an investment in municipal bonds and proceeds received from death benefits of insured officers; (b) expenses that are recognized for financial reporting purposes but are never deductible in calculating taxable income, such as premium payments on officers' life insurance and fines related to the violation of a law; and (c) deductions that are allowed for taxable income but are not allowed as expenses under generally accepted accounting principles, such as percentage depletion in excess of cost depletion, and certain dividend exclusions for investments in equity securities.

5. Interperiod tax allocation procedures are not applicable to permanent differences between a corporation's taxable income and pretax financial income. Permanent differences do not have deferred tax consequences, and, therefore, affect either a corporation's reported pretax financial income or its taxable income, but not both.

6. A temporary (timing) difference is a difference between the tax basis (book value) of a corporation's asset (or liability) for income tax purposes and the reported amount (book value) of the asset (or liability) in its financial statements that will result in taxable or deductible amounts in future years when the corporation recovers the reported amount of the asset (or settles the liability). Another way of looking at temporary differences is that they are the differences in a corporation's pretax financial income and taxable income resulting from reporting revenues and expenses in one period for income tax purposes and in another period for financial reporting purposes. The temporary differences normally originate in one or more years and reverse in later years. Temporary differences in the year of origination may result in either future pretax financial income exceeding future taxable income or future taxable income exceeding future pretax financial income in the year of reversal. Examples of various types of temporary differences in these two situations are presented in

items (7) and (8). The temporary differences create the need for interperiod tax allocation.

7. The following selected examples result in temporary differences which give rise to a deferred tax liability (future taxable amounts) because a corporation's pretax financial income is greater than taxable income in the year in which the temporary difference originates. As a result, its future taxable income will be greater than future pretax financial income in the year of reversal.

Method Used for Book Purposes	Method Used for Income Taxes
Profits on installment sales are recognized at date of sale	Profits on installment sales are recognized when collected
Percentage-of-completion method used for long-term contracts in progress	Completed-contract method
Equity method of accounting for investments when equity income exceeds dividends declared	Income is recognized when cash dividends are received
Straight-line depreciation	Accelerated depreciation
Longer estimated useful life	Shorter estimated useful life
Interest and property taxes during construction are capitalized	Interest and property taxes during construction are deducted from taxable income when paid

8. A corporation's pretax financial income may be less than its taxable income if the income tax laws require that revenue received in advance of being earned must be included in taxable income when received or if the tax laws disallow the deduction of accrued expense until actually paid. The following will result in temporary differences which give rise to a deferred tax asset (future deductible amounts) because a corporation's taxable income is greater than pretax financial income in the year in which the temporary difference originates. As a result, future taxable income will be less than future pretax financial income.

Method Used for Book Purposes	Method Used for Income Taxes
Prepaid rent, interest, royalties, or other revenue received in advance included in income when earned	Prepaid rent, interest, royalties, or other revenue received in advance included in income when received
Gains on sales and leasebacks are reported over the life of the lease contract	Gains on sales and leasebacks are taxed at the date of sale
Warranty expense, bad debt expense, compensation expense for stock option	Warranty costs, bad debt expense, compensation expense for stock option

plans, and losses on inventories in a later year are estimated in the current year	plans, and losses on inventories in a later year are deducted when paid
Indirect costs of producing inventory are expensed currently	Indirect costs of producing inventory are capitalized and deducted as part of cost of goods sold
Loss contingency is recorded when a probable loss is estimated	Loss contingencies are deducted when paid

9. The current generally accepted accounting principles which relate to income taxes are contained in FASB Statement No. 109. Under the principles specified in this Statement, comprehensive interperiod income tax allocation of temporary differences using the asset/liability method is required. Therefore, a corporation uses interperiod income tax allocation to determine its deferred tax assets and liabilities for all temporary differences, based on the currently enacted income tax rates and laws that will be in existence when the temporary differences result in future taxable amounts or deductible amounts. The corporation adjusts its deferred tax assets and liabilities when changes in the income tax rates are enacted.

Interperiod Income Tax Allocation: Recording and Reporting of Current and Deferred Taxes

10. A corporation must report any deferred tax liability or deferred tax asset on its balance sheet at the end of the current year. The liability (asset) should reflect the future amount of income taxes payable (or refundable) that are a result of the deferred tax consequences of temporary differences recognized in the current or preceding years. At the end of the current year the amount of deferred tax liability (asset) must be determined. (See item 11). Then the balance in the deferred tax liability (asset) account must be adjusted by recognizing a deferred tax expense (benefit) that is equal to the change in the deferred tax liability (asset) during the year. A valuation allowance may have to be recorded (adjusted) if any tax benefits from a deferred tax asset are not expected to be realized. A corporation's income tax expense (benefit) for the current year equals the amount of income taxes payable (refundable) plus (minus) the net change in the deferred tax liability (asset) during the year plus (minus) the change (if any) in the valuation allowance. Its income taxes payable equals taxable income times the current tax rate.

11. To measure and record the amount of current and deferred income taxes a corporation must complete the following steps:

    1. Measure the income tax obligation for the year by applying the applicable tax rate to the current taxable income.

    2. Identify the temporary differences and classify as taxable or deductible temporary differences.

    3. Measure the year-end deferred tax liability for each taxable temporary difference using the applicable tax rate.

    4. Measure the year-end deferred tax asset for each deductible temporary difference using the applicable tax rate.

5. Reduce deferred tax assets by a valuation allowance if, based on available evidence, it is <u>more likely than not</u> that some or all of the year-end deferred tax assets will not be realized.

6. Record the income tax expense (including the deferred tax expense or benefit), income tax obligation, change in deferred tax liabilities and/or deferred tax assets, and change in valuation allowance (if any).

12. To illustrate the steps for a deferred tax liability, assume that the Ryan Company, at the end of its first year of operations, reported pretax financial income of $10,000 and taxable income of $9,300 because of one temporary difference. The income tax rate is 30% for the current year, but Congress has enacted a 40% rate for future years.

Step 1: The income tax obligation for the year is $2,790 ($9,300 x 0.30).

Step 2: There is one taxable temporary difference because future taxable income will be higher than pretax financial income.

Step 3: The year-end deferred tax liability is $280 [($10,000 - $9,300) x 0.40].

Step 4: There is no deferred tax asset.

Step 5: There is no valuation allowance since there is no deferred tax asset.

Step 6: The journal entry to record the income tax expense, income tax obligation, and change in deferred tax liability (since this is the first year, the ending deferred tax liability from Step 3 is also the change) is as follows:

Income Tax Expense ($280 + $2,790)	3,070	
Income Taxes Payable		2,790
Deferred Tax Liability		280

13. To illustrate the steps for a deferred tax asset, assume that at the end of the first year of operations the Green Company reported pretax financial income of $15,000 and taxable income of $16,000 because of one temporary difference. The income tax rate is 40% for the current year, but Congress has enacted a 35% rate for future years. The company expects to be profitable in future years, so that it expects to realize any tax benefits.

Step 1: The income tax obligation for the year is $6,400 ($16,000 x 0.40).

Step 2: There is one deductible temporary difference because future taxable income will be lower than pretax financial income.

Step 3: There is no deferred tax liability.

Step 4: The year-end deferred tax asset is $350 [($15,000 - $16,000) x 0.35].

Step 5: There is no valuation allowance needed because the company expects to realize the tax benefits of the deferred tax asset.

Step 6: The journal entry to record the income tax expense, income tax obligation, and change in deferred tax asset is as follows:

Income Tax Expense ($6,400 - $350)	6,050	
Deferred Tax Asset	350	
Income Taxes Payable		6,400

14. When a corporation recognizes a deferred tax asset because of a deductible temporary difference, it will realize the tax benefits only if there is sufficient future taxable income from which to subtract the deductible temporary difference. If there is enough uncertainty about a company's future taxable income, then the company must record a valuation allowance to reduce its deferred tax asset to its realizable amount. A valuation allowance is required if, based on available evidence, it is more likely than not that the deferred tax asset will not be realized. When a valuation account is recorded, the offsetting entry is to income tax expense. A valuation allowance is deducted from the deferred tax asset on the balance sheet. If in the example in item 13, the company was not certain it would realize the tax benefits from the deferred tax asset, it would make the following journal entry (in addition to the one in item 13):

Income Tax Expense	350	
Allowance to Reduce Deferred Tax Asset to Realizable Value		350

15. When a company has more than one temporary difference, it must record a deferred tax liability (or asset) for each taxable (deductible) difference. The calculations are the same as those illustrated for the single temporary differences in items 12 and 13.

16. If a company begins a year with a deferred tax liability or a deferred tax asset, the entry to record the deferred tax expense (benefit) at year end is an adjusting entry. For example, assume that at the beginning of 2000, a company has a $480 credit balance in its Deferred Tax Liability account, and it determines that the amount of deferred tax liability at the year end is $1,800. The journal entry to recognize the deferred tax expense for the year and to bring the balance of the liability account to $1,800 would include a credit to the Deferred Tax Liability account of $1,320 ($1,800 - $480).

Operating Loss Carrybacks and Carryforwards

17. The Internal Revenue Code permits a tax break for corporations that experience operating losses. A corporation can carry back operating losses 2 years in sequential order (beginning with the earliest year) and receive a tax refund for appropriate taxes paid during this period. The excess of operating losses over taxable income for the prior 2 years can be carried forward sequentially for 20 years to reduce taxable income.

18. Under FASB Statement No. 109, a corporation must recognize the tax benefit of an operating loss carryback in the period of the loss as a current receivable on its balance sheet and as a reduction of the pretax operating loss on its income statement. By recognizing that the current operating loss which creates the tax benefit, this income statement treatment is consistent with the all-inclusive concept of income.

19. Under FASB Statement No. 109, a corporation must recognize the tax benefit of an operating loss carryforward in the period of the loss as a deferred tax asset. However, it must reduce the deferred tax asset by a valuation allowance, if based on the available evidence, it is more likely than not that it will not realize some or all of the deferred tax asset. In other words, a corporation handles operating loss carryforwards in the same manner as the deductible temporary differences discussed earlier. It measures a deferred tax asset using the enacted future tax rate, and, if

necessary, it deducts a valuation allowance from the deferred tax asset to determine its net realizable value. In the year-end journal entry to record a company's current and deferred taxes, any increase (decrease) in the deferred tax asset and valuation allowance is treated as an adjustment of income tax expense (benefit).

20. When a corporation realizes the tax benefit of an operating loss carryforward in a future year as a reduction in income taxes payable, it eliminates the deferred tax asset and related valuation allowance. The effect is to reduce income tax expense.

21. A pretax operating loss for both financial reporting and income tax purposes that is carried back is successively offset against pretax income in each of the two preceding years. The tax rate in existence at each of the prior balance sheet dates is used to calculate the income tax refund. For example, a pretax operating loss in 2004 of $70,000 would be offset first against any pretax financial and taxable income in 2002, and then in 2003 as follows:

Year	Pretax Financial and Taxable Income (Loss)	Operating Loss Carryback	Tax Rate	Income Tax Refund
2002	32,000	$32,000	0.20	$ 6,400
2003	40,000	38,000	0.30	11,400
	Total Operating Loss Carryback	$70,000	Total Income Tax Refund	$17,800

Note that although the total previous pretax income was $72,000 ($32,000 + $40,000), the corporation is only entitled to a refund of taxes paid on $70,000 of pretax income because this is the amount of the pretax operating loss. The entry at the end of 2004 to record the operating loss carryback credit would be:

Income Tax Refund Receivable	17,800	
Income Tax Benefit From Operating Loss Carryback		17,800

22. To illustrate an operating loss carryforward, assume that the Brandle Company has a pretax operating loss of $35,000 in 2004 for both financial reporting and income tax purposes. Since 2004 is its first year of operations, the operating loss must be carried forward. The income tax rate is 30% for the current and future years. Based on this information, Brandle records a deferred tax asset of $10,500 ($35,000 x 0.30) at the end of 2004 as follows:

Deferred Tax Asset	10,500	
Income Tax Benefit From Operating Loss Carryforward		10,500

Since the company has insufficient evidence of future taxable income so that it is more likely than not that it will not realize the deferred tax asset, it must also record a valuation allowance as follows:

Income Tax Benefit From Operating Loss Carryforward	10,500	
Allowance to Reduce Deferred Tax Asset to Realizable Value		10,500

Intraperiod Income Tax Allocation

23. Intraperiod income tax allocation requires that a corporation must apportion its total income tax expense for the period to the appropriate sections of its income statement (and occasionally its retained earnings statement, statement of comprehensive income, or statement of changes in stockholders' equity). A separate line item is shown on the income statement for the amount of income tax expense (based on normal income tax rates) that relates to income from continuing operations. Disclosure of the related income tax expense or tax credit should be made parenthetically for extraordinary items, cumulative effects of changes in accounting principles, the income or loss from the operations of a discontinued component, the gain or loss on disposal of a discontinued component, prior period adjustments (shown on the statement of retained earnings), and any other comprehensive income items. The marginal tax rate is multiplied times each of these items in order to determine the amount of income tax expense or tax credit to apply. A corporation reports these items <u>net</u> of the related income taxes on the appropriate financial statement. Additionally, the corporation discloses any income tax effects of gains and losses included in other comprehensive income. The underlying purpose of intraperiod income tax allocation is to associate the income tax expense or credit with the item which gave rise to the tax effect.

24. A corporation debits the Income Tax Expense account to record taxes on income from continuing operations (and generally any adjustment to deferred income taxes). It debits (or credits) the income tax expense (or credit) that applies to the income statement (and retained earnings statement) items reported on a net of tax basis <u>directly</u> to the related account.

Financial Statement Presentation and Disclosures

25. A corporation reports its income taxes payable as a current liability on its balance sheet. Deferred tax liabilities and assets are reported in two classifications: a <u>net</u> current amount and a <u>net</u> noncurrent amount. To do so, a corporation must separate its deferred tax liabilities and assets into current and noncurrent groups and then combine (net) the amounts in each group. If the net amount is a <u>debit</u> balance, it is recorded as a current (noncurrent) <u>asset</u>. If the net amount is a <u>credit</u> balance, it is recorded as a current (noncurrent) <u>liability</u>.

26. In addition to the income statement disclosure described under intraperiod income tax allocation, a corporation usually uses a note to the financial statements to fulfill the disclosure requirements related to income tax expense. The note would (a) disclose the causes of the deferred tax assets and liabilities; (b) disclose the total deferred tax liabilities, total deferred tax assets, and total valuation allowance (and its net change); (c) disclose the amount of income tax expense or benefit related to continuing operations, discontinued operations, extraordinary items, the cumulative effect of accounting changes, prior period adjustments, gains and losses included in other comprehensive income; (d) identify the significant components of income tax expense related to continuing operations each year, such as current tax expense (benefit), deferred tax expense (benefit), tax credits, benefits of carryforwards, adjustments in deferred tax liability (asset) from changes in tax laws (or rates), and adjustments of valuation allowance; (e) reconcile the differences between income tax expense related to continuing operations under the rules of financial reporting and federal taxation; and (f) identify the amounts and timing of operating loss and tax credit carryforwards.

Miscellaneous Issues

27. If the income tax laws or rates used to calculate a corporation's deferred tax liability (asset) change, the corporation adjusts the deferred income tax liability (asset) for the effect of the change. The adjustment is made directly to the deferred tax liability (asset) as of the beginning of the year in which the change is made. The resulting tax effect is included in the income tax expense related to income from continuing operations. The amount of the adjustment is the difference between the deferred tax liability (asset) balance calculated using the old rate and the balance calculated using the new rate.

28. An <u>investment tax credit</u>, allowing a corporation to deduct a specified percentage of the cost of certain depreciable assets has been enacted and suspended at various times. Two methods are allowed for reporting investment tax credits: Under the <u>flow-through</u> method, a corporation recognizes the total tax benefit in the year of acquisition. Corporations that choose to account for an <u>investment tax credit</u> using the <u>deferred method</u> (which resulted in a reduction of the effective cost of the asset, causing a reduction of depreciation expense over the life of the asset) continue to experience a temporary difference for depreciation. This temporary difference is included in the deferred tax computation.

29. Under the <u>alternative minimum tax</u> (AMT) rules, a corporation pays the higher of its AMT or its regular income tax liability. Therefore, the AMT may affect the corporation's income tax obligation in a given year. The AMT also may affect the corporation's deferred tax liability. If a corporation pays the AMT, generally it can credit some or all of the amount paid against future income taxes in years when the regular tax liability exceeds the AMT. The AMT credit may not be carried back but may be carried forward indefinitely.

30. International Accounting Standards for deferred income taxes require a company to use comprehensive allocation (in most cases) of temporary differences using the "balance sheet liability method" which is similar to the asset/liability method.

Appendix: Additional Conceptual Issues Concerning Interperiod Income Tax Allocation

31. Interperiod income tax allocation has been the subject of much debate. For a number of reasons, the FASB requires allocation. Interperiod income tax allocation, versus nonallocation, is supported by the matching principle which requires that a corporation debit all significant expenses to expense in the period in which revenue is earned. It is consistent with the accrual concept which requires that expenses be reflected when incurred and not be postponed until paid. Therefore, a corporation should report income tax expense when the pretax financial income is recognized and <u>not</u> deferred to a subsequent period in which paid. Through the use of interperiod income tax allocation, a corporation's long-term earning power is more accurately reflected in net income, and periodic distortions in net income due to income tax regulations are avoided.

32. The partial and comprehensive income tax allocation methods have been suggested for determining the amount of deferred income taxes. Partial tax allocation is the allocation of only those temporary differences expected to reverse in the foreseeable future. FASB Statement No. 109 requires the comprehensive allocation approach under which the income tax expense is based on all temporary differences. Under comprehensive allocation, a corporation records the changes for each individual item (regardless of how significant or recurrent), thereby deterring management manipulation of financial statement information. This method, which is consistent with the matching principle, reports the income tax effects of temporary differences in the same period as the related transactions are included in pretax accounting income.

33. FASB Statement No. 109 requires the asset/liability method for interperiod income tax allocation. Under this method, a corporation reports deferred tax amounts which arise out of temporary differences which will reverse in the future on the balance sheet using currently enacted income tax rates and laws that will be in existence when the temporary differences reverse. Through the use of enacted future tax rates, the deferred tax amounts more accurately represent an asset (future economic benefit) or liability (future economic sacrifice) as defined in FASB Statement of Concepts No. 6. This method emphasizes the balance sheet, increases the predictive value of the financial statements, and is conceptually the most sound. The deferred method, which was required under APB Opinion No. 11, emphasizes the income statement by focusing on the matching of expenses with revenues. Under the deferred method, a corporation uses the tax rate in existence when the temporary difference originates to determine the deferred tax amounts. While such a method may increase the reliability of the accounting information by using historical rates which are verifiable, estimates are used extensively in accounting, and the use of currently enacted future tax rates creates more reliable information than, perhaps, depreciation based on estimates. The net-of-tax method is the third alternative. This method allows a corporation to calculate the deferred tax amounts by using either the deferred method or the asset/liability method. However, it treats the deferred tax assets or tax liabilities as direct adjustments to the asset or liability account which gave rise to the temporary difference. While this method records the changes in assets and liabilities arising from transactions that affect future expense recognition, it was rejected because the values of the related assets and liabilities are distorted by singling out this effect.

SELF-EVALUATION EXERCISES

Supply the words or amounts necessary to complete each of the following items.

Overview and Definitions

OD-1. Significant differences between taxable income and pretax financial income normally exist because pretax financial income is measured using

__________ __________ __________ __________ while taxable income

is determined using the __________ __________ ______ and ________ ______

________.

OD-2. Financial transactions that affect the determination of financial income in one period and taxable income in another period are examples of ____________ differences. Revenues and expenses that are reported for financial reporting purposes but which will never be reported for income tax purposes are

_____________ differences.

OD-3. The future effects on income taxes arising from temporary differences and operating loss carryforwards at the end of the year are called ________________ ____________ _______________.

Interperiod Income Tax Allocation

IITA-1. Give two examples for each of the following types of permanent differences.

(1) Revenue is recognized for financial income but never for taxable income:

(a) ____

(b) ____

(2) Expenses are recognized for financial income but are never deductible for taxable income:

(a) ____

(b) ____

(3) Deductions are allowed for income tax purposes but are not allowed as expenses for financial income:

(a) ____

(b) ____

IITA-2. Complete the table below by placing, for each of the nine items, an "X" in one of the first two columns and an "X" in one of the remaining three columns, as appropriate, to indicate whether the originating difference listed will result in:

P - Permanent difference
T - Temporary difference
FD - Deferred tax asset (future deductible amounts)
FT - Deferred tax liability (future taxable amounts)
N/A - Interperiod tax allocation not applicable

The first two questions have been completed.

P	T	FD	FT	N/A	Nature of Difference
X				X	(1) Received "tax free" interest
	X		X		(2) Straight-line depreciation used for book purposes and accelerated depreciation used for income tax purposes
					(3) Paid $2,000 premium on officers' life insurance
					(4) Received proceeds from life insurance due to death of officer
					(5) Warranty expense accrued for book purposes and deducted when paid for income tax purposes
					(6) Installment-sale method of recognizing revenue used for tax purposes and accrual used for book purposes
					(7) Loss contingency is recorded for book purposes when probable loss is estimated and deducted from taxes when paid
					(8) Percentage-of-completion method used to record long-term construction income for book purposes and completed-contract method used for tax
					(9) Prepaid rental income is deferred for book purposes and recognized as income for tax purposes

IITA-3. Temporary differences create the need for ____________ ______ ______________.

IITA-4. The comprehensive interperiod income tax allocation method required by FASB Statement No. 109 is the _______/_______________ method.

IITA-5. Pretax financial income greater than taxable income in the year in which a temporary difference originates gives rise to future ______________ amounts; pretax taxable income greater than pretax financial income in the year in which a temporary difference originates gives rise to future ______________ amounts.

IITA-6. When a company's future taxable income will be higher than its future pretax financial income as a result of differences in depreciation methods used, the result is a ________________ ___________________ ___________________.

IITA-7. The amount of taxable temporary differences times the future expected tax rate equals the ____________ _____ ________________.

IITA-8. A company has two temporary differences between pretax financial income and taxable income in 2004, the first year of operation. These differences are a taxable amount of $1,500 due to depreciation and a deductible amount of $600 due to warranty expense. The income tax rate for 2004 is 35% and no change has been enacted for future years. In 2004, the company has a deferred tax ________________ in the amount of $__________ and a deferred tax ________________ in the amount of $__________.

IITA-9. Assuming no valuation allowance, the amount of income taxes payable (refundable) plus (minus) the net change in the deferred tax liability (asset) during the year equals a company's current year _____________ ________ _____________.

IITA-10. Taxable income times the current tax rate equals a company's current year ______________ ___________ _________________.

IITA-11. To reduce a deferred tax asset to its net realizable value when there is uncertainty about the adequacy of future taxable income, the company must record a _________________ __________________.

IITA-12. Under FASB Statement No. 109, a valuation allowance is required, if based on the available evidence, the likelihood that the deferred tax asset will not be recognized is ___________ _________________ __________ _____________.

IITA-13. If a company has a credit balance of $600 in its Deferred Tax Liability account at the beginning of 2004, and determines the deferred tax obligation at year end to be $1,300, the amount of deferred tax expense for the year would be $________.

Operating Loss Carrybacks and Carryforwards

OL-1. To the extent that the operating losses will offset taxable income during the carryback period, the Internal Revenue Code permits a corporation to carry operating losses back ______________ years and receive a tax ______________.

OL-2. The excess of operating losses over taxable income for the prior two years may be carried forward ____________ years to reduce taxable income.

OL-3. A tax refund resulting from an operating loss carryback is shown on a company's income statement as a reduction of the ____________ ____________ ______________.

OL-4. The income statement treatment of the tax benefits of an operating loss carryback is consistent with the ____________-____________ concept of income.

OL-5. On the current period balance sheet, a company recognizes the tax benefit of an operating loss carryforward as a ____________ ________ __________ arising from temporary differences that will result in future taxable amounts; if there is uncertainty about future net income, the company must reduce the deferred tax asset by a ______________ ______________.

OL-6. When a company realizes the tax benefit of an operating loss carryforward in a future year as a reduction of income taxes payable, the effect is to reduce __________ _____ ________.

Intraperiod Income Tax Allocation

ITA-1. The apportionment of the total income tax expense to various sections of the income statement and retained earnings statement is called ______________ tax allocation.

ITA-2. List the sections or items on the income statement for which intraperiod income tax allocation is applicable:

(a) ____

(b) ____

(c) ____

(d) ____

ITA-3. Intraperiod tax allocation requires that the tax effect of a prior period adjustment should be disclosed on the __________ ________ statement.

Financial Statement Presentation and Disclosures

FSP-1. To fulfill the disclosure requirements related to income tax expense, a note to the financial statements should be used and contain the following information:

(a) ______________________________

____

(b) ______________________________

____

(c) ______________________________

____

(d) ______________________________

____

(e) ______________________________

____

(f) ______________________________

____

Miscellaneous Issues

MI-1. Any tax effect resulting from an adjustment to the deferred tax liability (asset) arising from a change in the tax rates is included in a company's

__________ ________ ____________ related to ____________

________ ____________ ____________.

MI-2. When reporting investment tax credits, the method which recognizes the total tax benefit in the year of acquisition is the ______-________ method.

MI-3. Under International Accounting Standards, the balance sheet liability method used for comprehensive allocation of temporary differences is similar to the __________/__________ method.

Appendix: Additional Conceptual Issues

ACI-1. The two interperiod income tax allocation techniques considered by the APB and the FASB were the __________ and ____________ allocation approaches.

ACI-2. _______________ interperiod allocation does not require deferred income taxes to be provided for those temporary differences that are expected to be postponed indefinitely. The allocation technique required by FASB Statement No. 109 is the

_______________ allocation technique which considers the impact on income tax expense of all temporary differences.

ACI-3. The three possible methods of interperiod income tax allocation are

the _______________ method, the _______________ method, and

the _______________ method.

ACI-4. The accounting concept that is used to support comprehensive interperiod tax

allocation is the _______________ principle.

ANSWERS TO SELF-EVALUATION EXERCISES

OD-1. generally accepted accounting principles, Internal Revenue Code, state tax laws; OD-2. temporary, permanent; OD-3. deferred tax consequences; IITA-1. (1) (a) interest on municipal bonds; (b) life insurance proceeds on death of insured employee; (2) (a) payments of life insurance premiums on employees; (b) fines related to the violation of a law; (3) (a) percentage depletion in excess of cost depletion; (b) special dividend deduction;

IITA-2.

	P	T	FD	FT	N/A
(1)	X				X
(2)		X		X	
(3)	X				X
(4)	X				X
(5)		X	X		
(6)		X		X	
(7)		X	X		
(8)		X		X	
(9)		X	X		

IITA-3. interperiod tax allocation; IITA-4. asset/liability; IITA-5. taxable, deductible; IITA-6. taxable temporary difference; IITA-7. deferred tax liability; IITA-8. asset, $210, liability, $525; IITA-9. income tax expense; IITA-10. income tax payable; ITA-11. valuation allowance; IITA-12. more likely than not; IITA-13. $700; OL-1. two, refund; OL-2. twenty; OL-3. pretax operating loss; OL-4. all-inclusive; OL-5. deferred tax asset, valuation allowance; OL-6. income tax expense; ITA-1. intraperiod; ITA-2. (a) income from continuing operations, (b) results from discontinued operations, (c) extraordinary items, (d) cumulative effect of change in accounting principle;

TA-3. retained earnings; FSP-1. (a) disclose the total deferred tax liabilities, total deferred tax assets, and total valuation allowance and its net change; (b) identify the significant components of income tax expense relating to continuing operations each year; (c) reconcile the differences between income tax expense for financial reporting and federal taxation, (d) identify the amounts and timing of operating loss and tax credit carryforwards, (e) disclose the amount of income tax expense or benefit related to continuing operations, discontinued operations, extraordinary items, the cumulative effect of accounting changes, prior period adjustments, and gains or losses included in other comprehensive income, (f) disclose the causes of the deferred tax assets and liabilities; MI-1. income tax expense, income from continuing operations; MI-2. flow-through; MI-3. asset/liability; ACI-1. partial, comprehensive; ACI-2. Partial, comprehensive; ACI-3. asset/liability, deferred, net-of-tax; ACI-4. matching.

POST TEST

Part A Circle T if the statement is true and F if it is false.

T F 1. All expenses recognized for financial reporting purposes are deductible for income tax purposes.

T F 2. No reversals will occur in permanent differences between pretax financial income and taxable income, but temporary differences will normally reverse necessitating interperiod tax allocation.

T F 3. A corporation may first carry operating losses back 2 years and then forward 20 years if the taxable income for the past 2 years is not large enough to offset the amount of currently reported losses.

T F 4. Permanent differences affect both reported pretax financial income and taxable income.

T F 5. <u>FASB Statement No. 109</u> requires comprehensive income tax allocation of temporary differences using the deferred method.

T F 6. Interperiod tax allocation is the apportionment of the total income tax expense for a period to the appropriate sections of the income statement and retained earnings statement.

T F 7. The asset/liability method of interperiod income tax allocation emphasizes the balance sheet and is conceptually the most sound because it increases the reliability of the accounting information by using historical, and therefore verifiable, tax rates.

T F 8. If an expense represents both an expired cost and a tax deduction for the same amount in the same period, a corporation will deduct it from revenue to arrive at both pretax financial income and taxable income.

T F 9. Pretax financial income is the financial accounting income prior to the determination of income tax expense.

T F 10. A corporation must calculate and record a deferred tax liability or asset for each temporary difference.

T F 11. A corporation uses a valuation allowance account to adjust both deferred tax asset and deferred tax liability accounts when there is uncertainty about its future taxable income.

T F 12. Rent received in advance will normally result in a temporary difference if not earned in the same period as received.

T F 13. The partial allocation technique of deferred income taxes requires an estimation of the amount of any temporary differences that will never be reversed.

T F 14. Additional depreciation taken for tax purposes that causes taxable income to be less than pretax financial income creates a deferred tax asset.

T F 15. In a given year, the consistency principle requires a corporation to use the same tax rate to calculate both the amounts of any deferred tax liability (asset) and the current income tax obligation.

T F 16. The amount of a corporation's income tax expense for a year includes the taxes on current income and any adjustment to the deferred tax asset and/or liability accounts and any change in the valuation allowance.

T F 17. Both GAAP and International Accounting Standards require the comprehensive allocation of temporary differences, and the "balance sheet liability method" required by International Standards is very similar to the asset/liability method required by GAAP.

Part B Select the one <u>best</u> answer, and place its letter in the space provided.

____ 1. Transactions affecting the determination of pretax financial income in one period and the determination of taxable income in another period create the need for: (a) operating loss carryforwards; (b) operating loss carrybacks; (c) interperiod income tax allocations; (d) intraperiod income tax allocations.

____ 2. The amount of income taxes that relates to pretax financial income from continuing operations is reported on the income statement as: (a) income taxes payable; (b) long-term deferred income taxes (credit); (c) current deferred income tax (credit); (d) income tax expense.

____ 3. The sources of differences between pretax financial income and taxable income in the current year are: (a) permanent differences and temporary differences; (b) permanent differences only; (c) temporary differences only; (d) operating loss carrybacks and carryforwards.

____ 4. Revenue recognized for financial reporting purposes that will never be taxable is: (a) a temporary difference; (b) a permanent difference; (c) either a temporary difference or a permanent difference; (d) a good example of tax fraud.

____ 5. In 2004, the first year of operations, Rowe Company reported pretax financial income of $15,000 and taxable income of $11,000. The difference was due to a difference in depreciation for financial reporting and income tax purposes. This difference will reverse in the future as taxable income exceeds financial income by $800 in 2005, $2,000 in 2006, and $1,200 in 2007. The tax rate for the current year is 30%, and no change has been enacted for future years. The amount of income tax expense and deferred tax liability at the end of 2004 is:

	Income Tax Expense	Deferred Tax Liability
(a)	$4,500	$1,200
(b)	$3,300	$4,500
(c)	$1,100	$1,200
(d)	$3,300	$4,000

____ 6. At the end of 2004, its first year of operation, the Whitner Corporation reported $45,000 taxable income and $38,000 pretax financial income as a result of a single temporary difference. Because of uncertain economic times the company believes that only 75% of the deductible temporary difference will be realized. The tax rate for 2004 is 30%, and no change has been enacted for future years. On the 2004 year-end balance sheet, the deferred tax asset will be reported at a <u>net</u> balance of (a) $8,550; (b) $10,800; (c) $2,100; (d) $1,575.

____ 7. Using the information given in problem #6 above, the amount of income tax expense reported by Whitner Corporation on its 2004 income statement would be (a) $9,825; (b) $11,925; (c) $10,500; (d) $13,500.

____ 8. Which of the following is <u>not</u> an example of a permanent difference between pretax financial income and taxable income: (a) interest earned on municipal bonds is included in pretax financial income; (b) straight-line depreciation is expensed for financial accounting purposes but accelerated depreciation is used for income tax purposes; (c) fines related to the violation of law; (d) percentage depletion in excess of cost depletion is deducted for income tax purposes.

____ 9. Which of the following would result in a future taxable amount at the time of an originating temporary difference: (a) warranty expense is estimated for pretax financial income; (b) loss on discontinued operations is estimated at the date of formal plan to discontinue operations for a segment; (c) Modified Accelerated Cost Recovery System (MACRS) depreciation is deducted for income tax purposes and the straight-line method is used for pretax financial income; (d) prepaid rental income will be included in pretax financial income when earned in a future period.

____ 10. Beware Company reported pretax taxable income in 2001 of $30,000, in 2002 of $55,000, and in 2003 of $42,000. In 2004, the company reported a pretax operating loss for both financial reporting and income tax purposes of $90,000. Assuming that the income tax rates for the previous three years and the current year were 25% in 2001, 25% in 2002, 30% in 2003, and 30% in 2004, the income tax benefit from the operating loss carryback for 2004 would be (a) $21,250; (b) $90,000; (c) $31,750; (d) $24,250.

_____ 11. When using intraperiod income tax allocation, a corporation calculates the amount of tax to be applied to each item of "noncontinuing income" (a) by multiplying the marginal tax rate times each item; (b) by multiplying the effective tax rate times each item; (c) as the difference between the amount of tax on pretax financial income and taxable income; (d) as the difference between the amount of tax computed when including the item in taxable income and when excluding it.

Part C Solve each of the following short problems.

1. The Bradley Company acquired an asset on January 1, 2004, its first year of operation. The asset cost $40,000 and has no residual value at the end of its 8-year economic life. The company uses the straight-line depreciation method for financial reporting purposes and the MACRS method (five-year life) for income tax purposes. The appropriate MACRS percentages are 20%, 32%, 19.2%, 11.5%, 11.5%, and 5.8%. Bradley reported taxable income of $30,000 at the end of 2004. Its current tax rate is 30% and no change has been enacted for future years.

   (a) Complete the following schedule that shows the amount of annual depreciation for income tax and financial reporting purposes, the annual depreciation temporary difference and the accumulated temporary difference.

Year	Annual Income Tax - Depreciation	Annual Financial = Depreciation	Annual Depreciation Temporary Difference	Accumulated Temporary Difference
2004				
2005				
2006				
2007				
2008				
2009				
2010				
2011				

1. (b) Complete the following schedule that computes the ending deferred tax liability and the change in deferred tax liability.

	Accumulated Temporary Difference	x	Income Tax Rate	=	Ending Deferred Tax Liability	-	Beginning Deferred Tax Liability	=	Change in Deferred Tax Liability
2004	______		______		______		______		______
2005	______		______		______		______		______
2006	______		______		______		______		______
2007	______		______		______		______		______
2008	______		______		______		______		______
2009	______		______		______		______		______
2010	______		______		______		______		______
2011	______		______		______		______		______

(c) Prepare the income tax journal entry at the end of 2004.

2. At the end of 2004, Keene Company reported a pretax operating loss of $46,000 for both financial reporting and income tax purposes. In each of the years since Keene began business in 2000, the company showed a profit and reported and paid taxes on the following pretax taxable income: $6,000 in 2000, $9,500 in 2001, $15,000 in 2002, and $19,000 in 2003. Keene does not have evidence that it will be profitable in the future. The tax rate was 20% in 2000, 25% in 2001 and 2002, and 30% in 2003 and 2004, and no change has been enacted for future years.

(a) Prepare the income tax journal entries of the Keene Company at the end of 2004.

(b) Prepare the lower portion of Keene's 2004 income statement.

(c) How should the operating loss carryforward be disclosed in the 2004 financial statements?

(d) Assuming that Keene Company reports pretax income of $14,000 in 2005, prepare the income tax journal entry for the company at the end of 2005. Assume a 30% income tax rate.

(e) Prepare the lower portion of Keene's 2005 income statement where the income tax expense would be reported.

3. The Kentucky Company reports the following information for the year ended December 31, 2004:

	Amount	Income Tax Expense (or Credit)
Pretax income from continuing operations	$200,000	$ 40,000
Pretax extraordinary loss on sale of investment	(40,000)	(10,000)
Pretax income from operations of discontinued Segment A	30,000	7,500
Pretax loss on disposal of Segment A	(20,000)	(5,000)
Pretax cumulative effect of change in accounting principle	10,000	2,500
Total	$180,000	$ 35,000

Required

Prepare the lower section of the Kentucky Company's income statement beginning with pretax income from continuing operations.

ANSWERS TO POST TEST

Part A

1. F	6. F	10. T	14. F
2. T	7. F	11. F	15. F
3. T	8. T	12. T	16. T
4. F	9. T	13. T	17. T
5. F			

Part B

1. c	5. a	9. c
2. d	6. d	10. d
3. a	7. b	11. a
4. b	8. b	

Part C

1. (a)

Year	Annual Income Tax Depreciation	-	Annual Financial Depreciation	=	Annual Temporary Difference	Accumulated Temporary Difference
2004	$ 8,000		$ 5,000		$ 3,000	$ 3,000
2005	12,800		5,000		7,800	10,800
2006	7,680		5,000		2,680	13,480
2007	4,600		5,000		(400)	13,080
2008	4,600		5,000		(400)	12,680
2009	2,320		5,000		(2,680)	10,000
2010	0		5,000		(5,000)	5,000
2011	0		5,000		(5,000)	0

(b)

	Accumulated Temporary Difference	x	Income Tax Rate	=	Ending Deferred Tax Liability	-	Beginning Deferred Tax Liability	=	Change in Deferred Tax Liability
2005	$ 3,000		0.30		$ 900		$ 0		$ 900
2006	10,800		0.30		3,240		900		2,340
2007	13,480		0.30		4,044		3,240		804
2008	13,080		0.30		3,924		4,044		(120)
2009	12,680		0.30		3,804		3,924		(120)
2010	10,000		0.30		3,000		3,804		(804)
2011	5,000		0.30		1,500		3,000		(1,500)
2012	0		0.30		0		1,500		(1,500)

(c)

Income Tax Expense ($9,000 + $900)	9,900	
Income Taxes Payable ($30,000 x 0.30)		9,000
Deferred Tax Liability		900

2. (a)

Income Tax Refund Receivable	11,825	
Deferred Tax Asset	750	
Income Tax Benefit From Operating Loss Carryback		11,825
Income Tax Benefit From Operating Loss Carryforward		750

2. (a)

Income Tax Refund Receivable	9,450	
Income Tax Benefit From Operating Loss Carryback		9,450
To record carryback of operating loss to 2002 and 2003.		
Deferred Tax Asset	3,600	
Income Tax Benefit From Operating Loss Carryforward		3,600
To record carryforward of 2004 operating loss.		
Income Tax Benefit From Operating Loss Carryforward	3,600	
Allowance to Reduce Deferred Tax Asset to Realizable Value		3,600
To record valuation allowance due to insufficient positive evidence of future taxable income.		

Year	Pretax Financial Income and Taxable Income Offset by Carryback	Income Tax Rate	Income Tax Refund
2002	$15,000	0.25	$3,750
2003	19,000	0.30	5,700
	$34,000		$9,450

Deferred tax asset = ($46,000 - $34,000) x 0.30 = $3,600

(b)

Pretax operating loss	$(46,000)
Less: Income tax benefit from operating loss carryback	9,450
Net loss	$(36,550)

(c) The operating loss carryforward should be disclosed in a note to the financial statements.

(d)

Allowance to Reduce Deferred Tax Asset to Realizable Value	3,600	
Income Tax Expense	600	
Income Taxes Payable [($14,000 - $12,000) x 0.30]		600
Deferred Tax Asset ($12,000 x 0.30)		3,600

(e)

Pretax operating income	$14,000
Less: Income tax expense	(600)
Net income	$13,400

3.

KENTUCKY COMPANY
Partial Income Statement
For the Year Ended December 31, 2004

Pretax income from continuing operations		$200,000
Income tax expense		(40,000)
Income from continuing operations		$160,000
Results of discontinued operations:		
Income from operations of discontinued Segment A (net of $7,500 income taxes)	$22,500	
Loss on disposal of discontinued Segment A (net of $5,000 income tax credit)	(15,000)	7,500
Income before extraordinary loss and cumulative effect of change in accounting principle		$167,500
Extraordinary loss on sale of investment (net of $10,000 income tax credit)		(30,000)
Cumulative effect of change in accounting principle (net of $2,500 income taxes)		7,500
Net income		$145,000

19

ACCOUNTING FOR POSTEMPLOYMENT BENEFITS

CHAPTER OBJECTIVES

After careful study of this chapter, you will be able to:

1. Understand the characteristics of pension plans.
2. Explain the historical perspective of accounting for pension plans.
3. Explain the accounting principles for defined benefit plans, including computing pension expense and recognizing pension liabilities and assets.
4. Account for pensions.
5. Understand disclosures of pensions.
6. Explain the conceptual issues regarding pensions.
7. Understand several additional issues related to pensions.
8. Explain other postemployment benefits (OPEBs).
9. Account for OPEBs.
10. Explain the conceptual issues regarding OPEBs.
11. Understand present value calculations for pensions (Appendix).

SYNOPSIS

Characteristics of Pension Plans

1. A pension plan requires that a company provide income to its retired employees in return for the services they provided during their employment. A defined benefit plan either specifically states the benefits to be received by employees after retirement or the methods of determining such benefits. In contrast, under a defined contribution plan, the employer's contribution is based on a formula, and future benefits are limited to an amount which the contributions and the returns earned on the investment of these contributions can provide. Defined benefit plans are the primary focus of this chapter.

2. Under a funded pension plan, the company makes periodic payments to a funding agency which is responsible for safeguarding and investing pension assets, and for making payments to retired employees. The amounts needed to fund a pension plan are determined by actuaries using compound interest techniques, projections of future events, and actuarial funding methods. Under an unfunded plan, no such periodic payments are made. Instead, the payments to retired employees are made from current resources. Although the Pension Reform Act of 1974 eliminated unfunded company plans, some company plans are still underfunded and many governmental plans are unfunded. A pension plan is contributory if employees bear part of the cost, and noncontributory if the total cost is borne by the employer. Corporate pension plans are usually noncontributory.

3. This chapter focuses on the provisions of FASB Statement No. 87 and FASB Statement No. 132 as they relate to employers' accounting and disclosures for pension plans. The operation of private retirement plans is regulated by the Employee Retirement Income Security Act of 1974 (ERISA), also called the Pension Reform Act of 1974. In addition, most companies design their plans to meet Internal Revenue Service requirements.

Accounting Principles for Defined Benefit Pension Plans

4. The pension expense (net periodic pension cost) recognized by a company includes five components:

   (a) Service cost, the actuarial present value of the benefits attributed to current-period employee services (that is, the deferred compensation for current services, to be paid to employees during their retirement).

   (b) Plus interest cost, the increase in the projected benefit obligation over time, where the projected benefit obligation is the present value of the deferred benefits earned by employees to date, taking into account estimated future levels of compensation.

   (c) Minus expected return on plan assets, the beginning fair value of the plan assets multiplied by the expected long-term rate of return on plan assets.

   (d) Plus or minus amortization of unrecognized prior service cost, the assignment of the cost associated with retroactively granted benefits based on past employee service to each future period of service of each active employee who is expected to receive the future benefits. Note that plan amendments usually increase the projected benefit obligation, so that the amortization is usually added in the computation of pension expense. However, some companies have amended their pension plans to reduce the pension benefit obligation. In those cases the amortization is subtracted.

(e) Minus or plus gain or loss, the amortized portion of any unrecognized net gain or loss from previous periods. Gains and losses result from changes in actuarial assumptions and from differences between the actual projected benefit obligation and the expected projected benefit obligation. Amortization of an unrecognized gain or loss is included in pension expense when, at the beginning of the year, the cumulative unrecognized net gain or loss from previous periods exceeds 10% of the greater of the actual projected benefit obligation or the fair value of the plan assets.

5. Prior service cost is unrecognized. That is, it is not reported on the company's balance sheet as a liability. It is, however, "recognized" by actuaries as a relevant cost, amortized in the future as a component of pension expense, and disclosed in a note to the company's financial statements on the schedule reconciling the funding of the plan with its balance sheet amounts.

6. A company calculates the amortization of the unrecognized prior service cost by assigning an equal amount to each future period of service for each active employee at the date of the amendment who is expected to receive future benefits. This is called the "years of future service" method. Alternatively, straight-line amortization over the average remaining service life of employees may be used.

7. The service cost is affected by the discount rate chosen by the company. For example, a higher discount rate decreases, and a lower rate increases, the present value of the service cost. The discount rate, defined as a settlement rate, varies with economic conditions.

8. The pension expense that a company determines under FASB Statement No. 87 may be different from the amount it funds according to the rules of ERISA. If the expense recognized to date is greater than the amount funded, the prepaid/accrued pension cost is reported as a liability on the company's balance sheet. If the expense recognized to date is less than the amount funded, the prepaid/accrued pension cost is reported as an asset on the company's balance sheet.

9. The accumulated benefit obligation is the actuarial present value of the benefits attributed to employee service prior to a specific date. Unlike the projected benefit obligation, the accumulated benefit obligation is based only on past and current compensation levels and includes no assumptions of future pay increases. The unfunded accumulated benefit obligation (the accumulated benefit obligation minus the fair value of the plan assets) is a measure of a company's legal liability, and is the minimum pension liability a company must report on its balance sheet.

10. A company reports an additional pension liability if an unfunded accumulated benefit obligation exists at the end of the period and (a) an asset has been recognized as prepaid/accrued pension cost; (b) the liability already recognized as prepaid/accrued pension cost is less than the unfunded accumulated benefit obligation; or (c) no prepaid/accrued pension cost has been recognized. This additional liability usually is recorded when a company has a large, unrecognized prior service cost, or has earned low or negative returns on its plan investments.

11. If a company recognizes an additional pension liability, it reports <u>deferred pension cost</u> in an equal amount as an intangible asset, unless the additional liability is greater than the amount of any unrecognized prior service cost. Any excess of the additional liability over the unrecognized prior service cost is reported as a component of other comprehensive income. Note that the additional liability, the intangible asset, and the accumulated other comprehensive income are <u>not</u> amortized. Rather, they are recalculated each year and reported on the balance sheet.

12. Assuming that a company has an unfunded accumulated benefit obligation of $50,000 and a prepaid/accrued pension cost liability of $40,000, the journal entry to record the additional pension liability and intangible asset is:

Deferred Pension Cost	10,000	
Additional Pension Liability		10,000

Assuming additionally that the company has unrecognized prior service cost of $8,000, the journal entry to record the additional pension liability, intangible asset, and reduction of stockholders' equity is:

Deferred Pension Cost	8,000	
Excess of Additional Pension Liability over Unrecognized Prior Service Cost	2,000	
Additional Pension Liability		10,000

13. <u>FASB Statement No. 132</u> requires a company to disclose the following information about its defined benefit pension plan(s): (a) a reconciliation of the beginning and ending balances of the projected benefit obligation, including the amounts of the service cost, interest cost, actuarial gains and losses, benefits paid, and plan amendments; (b) a reconciliation of the beginning and ending balances of the fair value of the plan assets, including the actual return on plan assets, contributions by the company, and benefits paid; (c) the funded status of the plan, the amounts not recognized on the balance sheet, the amounts recognized on the balance sheet, including the amount of any unamortized prior service cost, the amount of any unrecognized net gain or loss, the amount of any remaining unamortized, unrecognized net obligation or net asset existing at the adoption of <u>FASB Statement No. 87</u>, the net pension prepaid asset or accrued liability, and any intangible asset and the amount of accumulated other comprehensive income; (d) the amount of pension expense, including the service cost, the interest cost, the expected return on plan assets, the amortization of any unrecognized prior service cost, the amortization of any net gains or losses, and the amortization of any unrecognized transition obligation or asset; (e) the amount included within other comprehensive income from a change in the additional pension liability; (f) the discount rate, the rate of compensation increase, and the expected long-term rate of return on the plan assets; and (g) the amounts and types of securities included in the plan assets.

Example of Accounting for Pensions

14. Exhibit 19-13 in the text shows the computations of the components of pension expense for a sample company. The simple example below illustrates the adjustment of a pension liability and recording of a pension asset. The following information about Blue's pension plan is available for 2004:

Service cost	$50,000	
Interest cost on projected benefit obligation		8,000
Expected return on plan assets		5,000
Amortization of unrecognized prior service cost		4,000
Amortization of unrecognized net gain from previous periods		1,000

(a) Blue's 2004 pension expense is $56,000 [$50,000 + $8,000 - $5,000 + $4,000 - $1,000]. Assuming that Blue funded the plan in the amount of $56,000 (e.g., Pension Expense Equal to Pension Funding), the journal entry to record pension expense is:

Pension Expense	56,000	
Cash		56,000

(b) Assuming a funding amount of $51,000 (Pension Expense Greater Than Pension Funding), the journal entry to record pension expense and increase the prepaid/accrued pension cost is:

Pension Expense	56,000	
Prepaid/Accrued Pension Cost		5,000
Cash		51,000

(c) Assuming a funding amount of $59,000 (Pension Expense Less than Pension Funding), the journal entry to record pension expense and decrease the prepaid/accrued pension cost is:

Pension Expense	56,000	
Prepaid/Accrued Pension Cost	3,000	
Cash		59,000

15. Exhibit 19-8 in the text shows a worksheet to use in the calculation of the amount of a company's pension expense and the adjustment of its prepaid/accrued pension cost. The worksheet also provides much of the information about the company's projected benefit obligation and plan assets that is required to be reported in the notes to the financial statements.

Conceptual Issues Related to Defined Benefit Plans

16. The issues related to defined benefit pension plans can be placed into three general categories: (a) pension expense; (b) pension liabilities; and (c) pension assets.

17. The issue of <u>pension expense</u> involves decisions about the amount of cost to recognize and when to report that amount as pension expense.

18. Pension cost may consist of several components, including: (a) deferred compensation (service cost), payments to be made to employees in the future in return for their current services; (b) interest cost of the deferred compensation; (c) expected return on assets (generally a negative component of pension cost); (d) prior service cost, the cost of retroactive benefits granted on initiation or modification of a plan for employee services performed in previous years; and (e) gains and losses resulting from both deviations between actual experience and the assumptions used, and changes in assumptions about the future.

19. Most changes in pension plans result in increases in future benefits. Four alternative methods have been suggested to account for the prior service costs that result from pension plan modifications: (a) The first alternative (the prospective method adopted in FASB Statement No. 87) requires that these costs be expensed in the current and future periods, with no liability recorded when a cost arises. (b) Under the second alternative, the total amount is recognized as an expense in the current period, and a liability is recorded. (c) Under the third alternative, retained earnings is debited with a prior period adjustment, and a liability is recorded. (d) Using the fourth alternative, an intangible asset and a liability of equal amount are recorded.

20. Similarly, gains and losses could also be accounted for prospectively, currently, with a prior period adjustment, or as a deferred item.

21. Liabilities are probable future sacrifices of economic benefits arising from present obligations of a company to transfer assets or provide services to other entities in the future as a result of past transactions or events. In addition, a liability must be measurable to be reported on a company's balance sheet.

22. Five alternatives have been identified for meeting the above recognition and measurement criteria, and for determining the extent of a company's pension plan liability.

    (a) Amount Attributed to Employee Service to Date. This alternative reflects the concept that the pension obligation arises as the employees work, and that pension benefits are a form of deferred compensation.

    (b) Contributions Based on an Actuarial Funding Method. Under this alternative, it is argued that the employer's obligation is to contribute to the plan, rather than directly to employees. The liability is based on the actuarial cost method used for funding the plan. This approach was adopted by FASB Statement No. 87.

    (c) Termination Liability. This alternative limits the employer's obligation to the amount that is payable on termination of the plan. However, it can be argued that an assumption of termination is not appropriate for a going concern.

    (d) Amount of Vested Benefits. A benefit is vested when an employee has the right to receive that benefit regardless of future service. Under this alternative, the employer's obligation is limited to vested benefits, on the basis that nonvested benefits are contingent on and result from future services.

    (e) Amount Payable to Retirees. Under this "pay-as-you-go" alternative, a readily measurable liability is only recognized in the period in which it will be paid to employees.

23. Assets are probable future economic benefits obtained or controlled by a company as a result of past transactions or events. Two alternative viewpoints exist concerning accounting for pension plan assets. According to the first viewpoint (adopted in FASB Statement No. 87), funding discharges the pension liability. Since pension plan assets held by the funding agency are, according to this viewpoint, not assets of the employer, they should not be disclosed on the employer's balance sheet. According to the second viewpoint, the employer's pension liability is not discharged until the retiree receives the pension check. Proponents argue that the employer is at risk with regard to assets held by the funding agency, and ultimately reaps the rewards of economic ownership of those assets. Consequently, they say, plan assets should be disclosed on the employer's balance sheet.

Additional Aspects of Pension Accounting

24. FASB Statement No. 87, issued in 1985, allowed a transition period until 1989. In the period of adoption, a company compared its projected benefit obligation with the fair value of the plan assets plus (minus) any recognized prepaid/accrued pension cost liability (asset). When the projected benefit obligation was larger, an unrecognized obligation resulted. When the projected benefit obligation was smaller, an unrecognized asset resulted. This obligation or asset is amortized by the straight-line method over the remaining service life of the employees expected to receive benefits, or optionally, up to fifteen years for a company with an average remaining service period of less than fifteen years.

25. The accounting specified in FASB Statement No. 87 for defined contribution plans is straightforward. The pension expense is equal to the pension contribution required for that period. The journal entry is a debit to Pension Expense and a credit to Cash for the contribution. Additionally, the company is required to disclose (a) a description of the plan, and (b) the amount of pension expense recognized during the period.

26. Funding agencies, which administer pension plans, issue financial statements primarily to provide information about each plan's ability to pay benefits when due. FASB Statement No. 35 requires that the annual financial statements issued by a funding agency for a company's pension plan include (a) an accrual-basis financial statement presenting information about the net assets available for benefits at the end of the plan year, (b) a financial statement presenting information about the changes during the year in the net assets available for benefits, (c) information on the actuarial present value of accumulated plan benefits at either the beginning or the end of the plan year, and (d) information on the significant effects of factors affecting the year-to-year change in the actuarial present value of accumulated plan benefits.

27. The Employee Retirement Income Security Act of 1974 (ERISA) creates standards for the operation and maintenance of pension funds and attempts to protect employees covered by pension plans. The Act includes guidelines for employee participation in pension plans, vesting provisions, minimum funding requirements, financial statement disclosure, and plan administration. Annual pension plan reports must be filed with the Department of Labor.

28. FASB Statement No. 88 requires that the net gain or loss from the settlement or curtailment of a pension plan be included by the employer in the net income of the period.

29. Termination benefits are special benefits offered to induce employees to leave a company voluntarily. FASB Statement No. 88 requires that a company record a loss and a liability for termination benefits when (a) the employee accepts the termination benefit offer, and (b) the amount can be reasonably estimated.

30. International accounting standards for a company to account for its defined benefit plan are similar to U.S. standards. However, international accounting standards require that a company expense its prior period service costs immediately. Also, the company does not have to recognize a minimum liability.

Other Postemployment Benefits

31. In addition to pensions, many companies provide their employees two types of additional benefits: (a) Postemployment benefits are provided to former employees after employment but before retirement. A company accrues the cost of postemployment benefits during employment and recognizes the amount as an expense and a liability if all the criteria for the recognition of compensated absences are met. If not all of the criteria are met, the company records an expense and a liability when the liability is probable and the amount can be reasonably estimated. (b) Postretirement benefits or other postemployment benefits (OPEBs) are provided to employees after retirement. The most significant OPEB is typically health care.

32. FASB Statement No. 106 governs employers' accounting for OPEBs. The Statement requires that companies accrue the cost of OPEBs during the periods in which the employees earn the benefits. Accounting principles for OPEBs closely parallel those for pensions.

33. Three major differences exist between pensions and OPEBs (focusing on healthcare benefits): (a) The beneficiary of a pension plan is usually the retired employee, while OPEBs are usually provided to the retired employee, a spouse, and dependents; (b) A pension benefit is defined as a fixed amount, paid monthly, while postretirement healthcare benefits are paid as used, with amounts varying geographically; (c) Pension funding is legally required under ERISA, and contributions are tax deductible, while OPEBs are generally not funded, because funding is not legally required and is not tax deductible.

34. Two concepts are necessary to an understanding of accounting principles for OPEBs:

    (a) The expected postretirement benefit obligation (EPBO) is the actuarial present value on a particular date of the benefits expected to be paid under the terms of the postretirement benefit plan.

    (b) The accumulated postretirement benefit obligation (APBO) is the actuarial present value of the benefits attributed to employee service to a specific date. On or after an employee's full eligibility date, the expected and accumulated postretirement benefit obligation for that employee are the same.

35. According to the Statement, the net postretirement benefit expense includes:

    (a) Service cost, the actuarial present value of the expected postretirement benefit obligation attributed to services rendered by the employees during the current period.

    (b) Plus interest cost, the increase in the accumulated postretirement benefit obligation due to the passage of time.

(c) Minus <u>expected return on plan assets</u>, the fair value of the plan assets at the beginning of the period multiplied by the expected long-term rate of return on plan assets. Unfunded plans, of course, have no return on plan assets.

(d) Plus or minus <u>amortization of unrecognized prior service cost</u>, where prior service cost is the increase or decrease in the accumulated postretirement benefit obligation resulting from plan amendments (and the initiation of the plan) not recognized in the period granted. This cost is amortized by assigning an equal amount to each year of service remaining until full eligibility for each employee active in the plan at the date of amendment. If all or almost all plan participants are fully eligible, the prior service cost is amortized over the participants' life expectancies. The amortization is added if benefits are increased, and subtracted if benefits are decreased.

(e) Minus or plus <u>gain or loss</u>, a change in the amount of the accumulated postretirement benefit obligation due to experience different from assumptions or to changed assumptions. Gains and losses may be amortized or recognized in the current year.

(f) Plus <u>recognition of the transition obligation</u>, the obligation or asset (accumulated postretirement benefit obligation minus the fair value of the plan assets) existing at the date of the initial adoption of the <u>Statement</u>. The transition obligation may either be recognized in full as a cumulative effect adjustment in the year the <u>Statement</u> is adopted, or amortized over the greater of the average remaining service life of plan participants or 20 years.

36. The amount of the net postretirement benefit expense to date may be different than the amount funded to date. For plans which are not funded, the liability, <u>prepaid/accrued postretirement benefit cost</u>, is increased each period by an amount equal to the expense, and decreased by payments to retired employees. However, in contrast to pension accounting, <u>no</u> "additional liability" is recognized.

37. Accounting for OPEBs differs from pension accounting in the following ways:

(a) Most pension plans tie benefits to years of service and salary levels, with the date of full eligibility being the retirement date. However, for OPEBs the attribution period, which generally begins with the date of hire or the date on which credited service begins, and ends on the date of full eligibility, usually is completed before the retirement date.

(b) There is no provision for recognition of a minimum OPEB liability, or a related intangible asset or reduction in stockholders' equity.

(c) The interest component of pension expense is based on the projected benefit obligation, while the OPEB interest component is based on the accumulated postretirement benefit obligation.

(d) Two disclosures required for OPEBs by <u>FASB Statement No. 132</u> are not required for pensions: the amount of amortization (if any) of the transition obligation, and the effect of a 1% increase and a 1% decrease in the healthcare cost trend rate on the accumulated postretirement benefit obligation and on components of postretirement benefit expense.

38. Exhibit 19-11 in the text shows information for an example illustrating the basic accounting principles for OPEBs. Two journal entries related to the information are shown:

To record postretirement benefit expense for the year, and the accompanying liability for the unfunded plan:

Postretirement Benefit Expense	31,100	
Accrued Postretirement Benefit Cost		31,100

To record the payment of retirement benefits:

Accrued Postretirement Benefit Cost	1,500	
Cash		1,500

Conceptual Evaluation of Accounting for OPEBs

39. Accounting for OPEBs on the accrual basis enhances the relevance of a company's income statement. However, implementation of the Statement created controversy. Opponents argue that OPEB costs cannot be measured with sufficient reliability, and that the costs of implementation may exceed the benefits.

40. A company may recognize the OPEB transition liability either immediately or prospectively. These recognition alternatives are inconsistent with the FASB policy of requiring retroactive adjustment for a new accounting principle, and with the requirement to amortize unrecognized prior service cost for pensions. In addition, the existence of the two alternatives decreases comparability among companies.

41. The expected postretirement benefit obligation is attributed to the periods of employee service up to the date of full eligibility, while the obligation is measured to the expected retirement date. It can be argued that ending the attribution period on the date of eligibility follows legal form rather than economic substance.

42. The adoption of FASB Statement No. 106 has had two major effects. First, the income statements and balance sheets of many companies are significantly changed by the accrual of OPEBs. Second, the accrual of OPEBs may influence management decisions about the level of benefits to provide retirees.

Appendix: Illustration of Present Value Calculations for Defined Benefit Pension Plans

43. The service cost per employee is calculated using the benefit/years-of-service method. Service cost equals the present value of future pension benefits earned by employees in the current period. Consequently, service cost equals:

Annual Benefits Earned x Present Value of Annuity for Period of Retirement x Present Value of $1 for Remaining Period of Employment

Each year the service cost is recalculated, using the characteristics of current employees.

44. The projected benefit obligation is the present value of future pension benefits earned by employees to date, based on expected salary levels. Consequently, the projected benefit obligation equals:

Total Benefits Earned x Present Value of Annuity for Period of Retirement x Present Value of $1 for Remaining Period of Employment

A company's interest cost on the projected benefit obligation is computed by multiplying the projected benefit obligation at the beginning of the year by the discount rate.

45. Prior service cost is the present value of retroactive additional pension benefits granted by plan amendment or at the initial adoption of the plan. Consequently, prior service cost equals:

Additional Benefits x Present Value of Annuity for Period of Retirement x Present Value of $1 for Remaining Period of Employment

Note that the remaining period of employment at the beginning of the year is used in the calculation. Unrecognized prior service cost is amortized in the example over the average remaining service life of the employees.

SELF-EVALUATION EXERCISES

Supply the words necessary to complete each of the following items.

Characteristics of Pension Plans

CP-1. The type of pension plan in which the employer's contribution is determined by a specified formula is a __________ ______________ plan.

CP-2. The type of pension plan in which an employee's pension is specifically stated, or computed using a specified formula, is a __________ __________ plan.

CP-3. When a pension plan is _________, the company typically makes periodic payments to a __________ __________ which safeguards and invests pension assets.

CP-4. Employees bear part of the cost of a _____________ plan.

CP-5. The Federal ____________ ________________ ________________ ____________ ______ _______ ________________ (ERISA), also called the _________ ________________ _________ ______ ________________, regulates private pension plans of corporations.

Accounting Principles for Defined Benefit Pension Plans

APD-1. Pension expense includes ______________ ___________, plus

______________ __________, minus expected return on plan assets,

plus or minus amortization of ________________ __________

___________ __________, minus or plus ___________ or ___________.

APD-2. Service cost is the ____________ ________________ for current employee services.

APD-3. The present value of the deferred benefits earned by employees to date, taking

into account estimated future compensation levels, is the _____________

__________ ______________.

APD-4. Prior service cost is _______________, i.e., not reported on the balance sheet as a liability.

APD-5. The present value of the service cost is _____________ (increased, decreased)

by a higher discount rate and _____________ (increased, decreased) by a lower discount rate.

APD-6. When the pension expense recognized to date is less than the amount

funded, the ___________/___________ ___________ ________is

reported on the balance sheet as a(an) __________.

APD-7. The actuarial present value of the benefits attributed to employee service

prior to a specific date is the _______________ _________ ______________.

APD-8. The minimum pension liability that a company must report on its

balance sheet is the _______________ _________ ______________

minus the ______ ________ ___ _____ ______ _________.

APD-9. When a company recognizes an additional pension liability, it must report an

equal amount of deferred pension cost as an _____________ ________, and report any excess of the additional liability over the unrecognized prior service cost

as a reduction of ________________ _________.

APD-10. A company with an unfunded accrued benefit obligation of $60,000 and a prepaid/accrued pension cost liability of $55,000 would record a debit of

$5,000 to ___________ ___________ _______ and a credit of $5,000 to

_______________ _________ _____________.

Conceptual Issues Related to Defined Benefit Plans

CI-1. The components of pension cost may include ______________ ____________, __________ _________, ____________ __________ _____ __________, __________ ___________ _______, and _________ _____ _________.

CI-2. Pension plan modifications, which usually entail ____________ (increases/decreases) in future benefits, result in ____________ _________ _________ for the company.

CI-3. To be recognized, a liability must be ____________ and must entail a present responsibility which obligates the company as a result of a ______ ____________ ____ ________.

CI-4. When an employee's benefits are ________________, the benefits are not contingent on future service.

CI-5. According to FASB Statement No. 87, funding discharges the pension __________.

Additional Aspects of Pension Accounting

AA-1. During the transition period allowed under FASB Statement No. 87 a company must amortize any ______________ ______________ or ____________ ____________ by the straight-line method over the remaining service life of the employees expected to receive benefits or up to fifteen years.

AA-2. In accounting for a defined contribution plan, pension expense equals the pension ____________ for the period.

AA-3. FASB Statement No. 87 requires that financial statements including specified information be issued by __________ __________ which administer pension plans.

AA-4. A net gain or loss from the settlement or curtailment of a pension plan is included in the ________ ______________ of the period.

AA-5. When an employee accepts a termination benefit offer, and the amount can be reasonably estimated, the company must record a ___________ and a ____________.

AA-6. Accounting rules for defined benefit pension plans __________ (are, are not) consistent internationally.

Other Postemployment Benefits

OPB-1. Postemployment benefits are provided to former employees after ______________ but before ______________.

OPB-2. The most significant other postemployment benefit (OPEB) is _________ ________.

OPB-3. FASB Statement No. 106 requires that companies _________ the cost of OPEBS during the periods when employees earn the benefits.

OPB-4. Funding of OPEBs _____ (is/is not) legally required and ______ (is/is not) tax deductible.

OPB-5. The ___________ _______________ __________ _____________ (EPBO) is the actuarial present value on a particular date of the benefits expected to be paid under the terms of the postretirement benefit plan.

OPB-6. The _____________ ________________ __________ ______________ (APBO) is the actuarial present value of the benefits attributed to employee service to a specific date.

OPB-7. The net postretirement benefit expense includes __________ ______, plus ___________ ______, minus _________ _________ ____ _______ _________, plus or minus _______________ ____ ______________ _______ __________ ______, minus or plus ______ ____ ______, plus _____________ ___ _____ _____________ ____________.

OPB-8. The OPEB transition obligation is the ______________ _____________ __________ __________________ minus the _______ ________ of the _______ ________ on the date of adoption of the Statement.

OPB-9. For OPEBs, the attribution period generally begins with the date of ________ or the date that __________ ____________ begins, and ends on the date of _____ ______________.

OPB-10. Companies are required to disclose the amount of amortization of the OPEB ____________ _____________ and the effect of a 1% increase in the __________________ ________ _________ rate.

Conceptual Evaluation of Accounting for OPEBs

CEO-1. Using the accrual basis to account for OPEBs enhances the ___________ (relevance, reliability) of the financial statements, but it is argued that measurement of OPEB costs is not sufficiently __________.

CEO-2. The recognition alternatives for the OPEB transition liability are _____________ (consistent, inconsistent) with the accounting treatment for a new accounting principle.

CEO-3. The expected postretirement benefit obligation is attributed to the periods of ___________ __________ up to the date of full eligibility, but the obligation is measured to the _____________ ________________ date.

Illustration of Present Value Calculations for Defined Benefit Pension Plans

IP-1. The service cost per employee is calculated using the ________/_______-____-_________ method.

IP-2. The interest cost on a company's projected benefit obligation is calculated by multiplying the projected benefit obligation at the ___________ (beginning, end) of the year by the discount rate.

IP-3. Unrecognized prior service cost is amortized by assigning an equal amount to each future period of service for each active employee, or by using the straight-line method over the ___________ ____________ service life of the employees.

ANSWERS TO SELF-EVALUATION EXERCISES

CP-1. defined contribution; CP-2. defined benefit; CP-3. funded, funding agency; CP-4. contributory; CP-5. Employee Retirement Income Security Act of 1974, Pension Reform Act of 1974; APD-1. service cost, interest cost, unrecognized prior service cost, gain, loss; APD-2. deferred compensation; APD-3. projected benefit obligation; APD-4. unrecognized; APD-5. decreased, increased; APD-6. prepaid/accrued pension cost, asset; APD-7. accumulated benefit obligation; APD-8. accumulated benefit obligation, fair value of the plan assets; APD-9. intangible asset, stockholders' equity; APD-10. Deferred Pension Cost, Additional Pension Liability; CI-1. deferred compensation, interest expense, expected return on assets, prior service cost, gains and losses; CI-2. increases, prior service cost; CI-3. measurable, past transaction or event; CI-4. vested; CI-5. liability; AA-1. unrecognized obligation, unrecognized asset; AA-2. contribution; AA-3. funding agencies; AA-4. net income; AA-5. loss, liability; AA-6. are not; OPB-1. employment, retirement; OPB-2. health care; OPB-3. accrue; OPB-4. is not, is not; OPB-5. expected postretirement benefit obligation; OPB-6. accumulated postretirement benefit obligation; OPB-7. service cost, interest cost, expected return on plan assets, amortization of unrecognized prior service cost, gain or loss, recognition of the transition obligation;

OPB-8. accumulated postretirement benefit obligation, fair value, plan assets; OPB-9. hire, credited service, full eligibility; OPB-10. transition obligation, healthcare cost trend; CEO-1. relevance, reliable; CEO-2. inconsistent; CEO-3. employee service, expected retirement; IP-1. benefit/years-of-service; IP-2. beginning; IP-3. average remaining.

POST TEST

Part A Circle T if the statement is true and F if it is false.

T F 1. Gains and losses may result from changes in actuarial assumptions as to the future.

T F 2. Under a defined benefit plan, the company must make specified payments to the plan, rather than pay specified pensions to retired employees.

T F 3. Funding agencies are typically responsible for investing pension plan assets and for making payments to retired employees.

T F 4. When a pension plan is noncontributory, the total cost is borne by the employer.

T F 5. Vested benefits are not dependent on future service by the employee.

T F 6. According to FASB Statement No. 87, the pension cost for a defined benefit plan is the contribution required for the period.

T F 7. Service cost is the present value of the benefits attributed to current-period employee services.

T F 8. FASB Statement No. 87 recommends that the costs associated with retroactively granted pension benefits be amortized by assigning them to future periods of service of participating employees.

T F 9. Prior service cost is reported on the balance sheet as an accrued liability.

T F 10. The minimum pension expense required under FASB Statement No. 87 is the amount funded according to the rules of ERISA.

T F 11. If the pension expense recognized to date is less than the amount funded, the prepaid pension cost is reported as an asset.

T F 12. When an unfunded accrued pension cost is reported as a liability, deferred pension cost must be reported in an equal amount as an intangible asset.

T F 13. When a company ends its defined benefit pension plan, the net gain or loss from the settlement of the plan is included in net income for the period.

T F 14. Interest cost, a component of pension expense, is defined as the expected return on plan assets plus an amortized portion of unrecognized prior service costs.

T F 15. Service cost is typically calculated for the current year by multiplying the current salaries of participating employees by the projected interest cost of the plan.

T F 16. The cost of OPEBs is attributed by estimating total benefits and assigning the total on the straight-line basis to each year of employee service.

T F 17. Companies are not legally required to fund OPEBs, and funded amounts are not tax deductible.

T F 18. The interest component of OPEB expense is based on the accumulated postretirement benefit obligation.

T F 19. When an employee has reached the date of full eligibility for OPEBs, the expected and accumulated postretirement benefit obligation for that employee are the same.

T F 20. An OPEB transition obligation is recognized prospectively, over a period not to exceed 10 years.

T F 21. Accounting for OPEBs, like accounting for pensions, provides for recognition of a minimum OPEB liability and a related intangible asset.

T F 22. International accounting standards require that a company expense its prior period service costs immediately.

T F 23. The OPEB expected postretirement benefit obligation is measured by the periods of employee service, but attributed up to the date of full eligibility.

T F 24. The expected return on plan assets is calculated by multiplying the beginning fair value of the plan assets by the expected long-term rate of return on the assets.

T F 25. A company reports any excess of its additional pension liability over its unrecognized prior service cost as a component of other comprehensive income.

Part B Select the one best answer, and place its letter in the space provided.

_____ 1. Prior service cost of a pension plan (a) is the pension cost assigned to years preceding the beginning of a plan; (b) is the total amount already paid out to retired employees; (c) is the cost of retroactively granted benefits; (d) is recognized by a prior period adjustment at the inception of the plan.

_____ 2. Under a defined benefit plan, payments to retired employees (a) are determined by dividing available pension assets among eligible retired employees; (b) are based only on the years of service of each retired employee; (c) are made by the employer, rather than a funding agency; (d) are computed by a stated method or are specified in the pension agreement.

_____ 3. Pension plans (a) are contributory if the total costs are borne by the employers; (b) are noncontributory if the total costs are borne by the employers; (c) are regulated by the federal Securities Act of 1933; (d) are typically accounted for on a pay-as-you-go basis.

_____ 4. Which of the following does not describe a necessary characteristic of a liability? (a) a liability must entail a future responsibility to be settled by the use or transfer of present assets; (b) a liability obligates the company, leaving little or no discretion to avoid future payment; (c) a liability results from a transaction or event that has already occurred; (d) a liability must be measurable.

_____ 5. The Attilla Company provides a defined benefit pension plan for its employees. At the beginning of 2004 Attilla had a Prepaid Pension Cost of $15,000, pension plan assets of $50,000, and a projected benefit obligation of $35,000. The service cost for 2004 was $45,000, and the amount funded was $40,000. The discount rate and expected (and actual) rate of return on plan assets were 10%. At the end of 2004 Attilla reported (a) interest cost of $3,500; (b) prepaid pension cost of $15,000; (c) pension expense of $43,500; (d) prepaid/ accrued pension cost of $5,000.

_____ 6. Which of the following is not a component of pension expense? (a) amortization of an unrecognized net loss for previous periods; (b) the accumulated benefit obligation minus the fair value of the plan assets; (c) the expected return on plan assets; (d) the interest cost of the projected benefit obligation.

_____ 7. At the beginning of 2002, the Golden Company's actuary estimated the company's total unrecognized prior service cost to be $180,000. Golden expected the following numbers of years of future service from its seven employees: Adkins-2; Bedford-2; Cleek-6; Dewey-8; Everett-10; Finley-5; Goode-3. Under the years-of-future-service method, the amount of amortization of unrecognized prior service cost to be included in pension expense in 2004 is: (a) $25,714; (b) $25,000; (c) $40,200; (d) $60,000.

_____ 8. Using the information given in number 7 above, the amount of unrecognized prior service cost remaining on January 1, 2007 is: (a) $60,000; (b) $125,000; (c) $45,000; (d) $135,000.

_____ 9. At the end of 2004, the Ipswich Company's pension records showed the following:

Fair value of the plan assets	$500,000
Accumulated benefit obligation	600,000
Prepaid/accrued pension cost (liability)	25,000

Ipswich will report on its 2004 balance sheet: (a) prepaid/accrued pension cost of $25,000, projected benefit obligation of $25,000, and additional pension liability of $50,000; (b) deferred pension cost of $25,000, unrecognized prior service cost of $25,000, and unfunded accumulated benefit obligation of $50,000; (c) deferred pension cost of $25,000 and prepaid/accrued pension cost of $25,000; (d) deferred pension cost of $75,000, and additional pension liability of $75,000.

_____ 10. Bee Company provides an unfunded OPEB plan. Zee Company provides a pension plan with the expense recognized to date less than the amount funded. The companies make identical cash payments to retired employees. Which of the following statements is correct? (a) Zee Company will recognize a minimum liability, while Bee Company will not; (b) Bee Company will report OPEB expense lower than Zee Company's pension expense; (c) Zee Company will report higher income and a lower debt-to-equity ratio than Bee Company; (d) Bee Company will report lower liabilities and subtract the actual return on plan assets in determining OPEB expense.

_____ 11. Which of the following statements regarding accounting principles for pensions and OPEBs is true? (a) accounting for both pensions and OPEBs recognizes a minimum liability and a related intangible asset or reduction in stockholders' equity; (b) the expected retirement date and the date of full eligibility are the same for pensions, but often are different for OPEBs; (c) the interest component of both pension and OPEB expense is based on the accumulated postretirement benefit obligation; (d) amortization of the transition obligation is required for both pensions and OPEBs.

_____ 12. Calculation of OPEB expense would <u>not</u> include recognition of (a) a transition liability; (b) an increase in the OPEB liability, based on an actuarial funding method; (c) the present value of the expected postretirement benefit obligation attributed to current-period services; (d) the increase in the accumulated postretirement benefit obligation due to the passage of time.

Part C Solve each of the following short problems.

1. Information about the Jefferson Company's defined benefit pension plan is shown below:

	2004	2005	2006
Service cost	$490,000	$ 550,000	$ 600,000
Plan assets (beginning of year)	800,000	?	?
Amount funded (end of year)	500,000	550,000	620,000
Projected benefit obligation (beginning of year)	750,000	1,275,000	1,892,500
End-of-year payments to retired employees	40,000	60,000	100,000
Discount rate	10%	10%	10%
Expected (and actual) rate of return	10%	8%	9%
Amortization of unrecognized net loss	3,000	2,100	2,000

<u>Required</u>

Prepare the journal entries needed to record the Jefferson Company's pension expense and pension funding at the end of 2004, 2005, and 2006.

2. The Wingador Company established a defined benefit pension plan at the beginning of 2004. Prior service costs at that time were estimated to be $135,000. Information about the plan is given below.

Discount rate used by Wingador:	10%
Expected (and actual) return on plan assets:	8%

	2004	2005	2006
Service cost	$ 10,000	$ 15,000	$ 25,000
Amounts paid to funding agency at year end	50,000	50,000	40,000
Amounts paid by funding agency to employees at year end	18,500	16,000	20,000
Projected benefit obligation at beginning of year	135,000	140,000	153,000
Accumulated benefit obligation at end of year	130,000	134,500	146,950
Amortization of unrecognized prior service cost	5,000	10,000	15,000

Required

(a) Determine Wingador's pension expense for 2004.

(b) Prepare the journal entry used to record Wingador's pension expense and funding in 2005.

(c) Show any pension amounts that would be reported on Wingador's 2006 balance sheet.

3. The Wylie Company initiated a defined benefit pension plan on January 1, 2004. Unrecognized prior service cost resulting from retroactive benefits awarded to the six participating employees were determined to be $400,000 at that time. The expected years of future service of the six employees are shown below:

Employee	Expected Years of Future Service
U	6
V	6
W	5
X	4
Y	3
Z	1

Wylie will amortize the unrecognized prior service cost using the years-of-future-service method.

Required

Prepare schedules showing (a) the amortization fraction for each year and (b) the amount of amortization of prior service cost for each year.

ANSWERS TO POST TEST

Part A

1. T	6. F	11. T	16. F	21. F
2. F	7. T	12. F	17. T	22. T
3. T	8. T	13. T	18. T	23. F
4. T	9. F	14. F	19. T	24. T
5. T	10. F	15. F	20. F	25. T

Part B

1. c	4. a	7. b	10. c
2. d	5. c	8. c	11. b
3. b	6. b	9. d	12. b

Part C

1. 2004:

Pension Expense	488,000	
Prepaid/Accrued Pension Cost	12,000	
Cash		500,000

2005:

Pension Expense	572,400	
Prepaid/Accrued Pension Cost		22,400
Cash		550,000

2006:

Pension Expense	616,902	
Prepaid/Accrued Pension Cost	3,098	
Cash		620,000

	2004	2005	2006
Service cost	$490,000	$ 550,000	$ 600,000
Interest cost	75,000	127,500	189,250
Expected return on plan assets	(80,000)	(107,200)	(174,348)
Amortization of unrecognized net loss	3,000	2,100	2,000
Pension expense	$488,000	$ 572,400	$ 616,902
Plan assets (beginning of year)	$ 800,000	$1,340,000	$1,937,200
Funded (end of year)	500,000	550,000	620,000
Payments (end of year)	(40,000)	(60,000)	(100,000)
Actual return on plan assets	80,000	107,200	174,348
Plan assets (end of year)	$1,340,000	$1,937,200	$2,631,548

2. (a) 2004

Service cost	$10,000
Interest cost (0.10 x $135,000)	13,500
Amortization of unrecognized prior service cost	5,000
2004 pension expense	$28,500

2\. (b) 2005

Pension Expense	36,480*	
Prepaid/Accrued Pension Cost	13,520	
Cash		50,000

*Service cost	$15,000
Interest cost (0.10 x $140,000)	14,000
Expected return on plan assets [0.08 ($50,000 - $18,500)]	(2,520)
Amortization of unrecognized prior service cost	10,000
2005 Pension expense	$36,480

(c)

Prepaid/accrued pension cost	$ 25,162*
Additional pension liability	78,650**
Deferred pension cost (intangible asset)	78,650***

*Prepaid/accrued pension cost	
2004 ($50,000 - $28,500) =	$21,500
2005 ($50,000 - $36,480) =	13,520
2006 ($40,000 - $49,858[a]) =	(9,858)
Balance of prepaid/accrued pension cost	$25,162

[a]2006 Pension Expense:	
Service cost	$25,000
Interest cost (0.10 x $153,000)	15,300
Expected return on plan assets {0.08 x [($50,000 - $18,500) + ($50,000 - $16,000 + $2,520)]}	(5,442)
Amortization of unrecognized prior service cost	15,000
2006 Pension expense	$49,858

**Additional pension liability = Accumulated benefit obligation - Fair value of plan assets -/+ Prepaid/accrued pension cost (credit balance/debit balance) = $146,950 - $93,462[a] + $25,162 = $78,650.

[a][($50,000 - $18,500) x 1.08 + ($50,000 - $16,000)] x 1.08 + $40,000 - $20,000

***Deferred pension cost, an intangible asset, is reported on the balance sheet at an amount equal to the Additional Pension Liability.

3\. (a)

	2004		2005		2006		2007		2008		2009		
U	1		1		1		1		1		1		
V	1		1		1		1		1		1		
W	1		1		1		1		1				
X	1		1		1		1						
Y	1		1		1								
Z	1												
	6	+	5	+	5	+	4	+	3	+	2	=	25
	6/25		5/25		5/25		4/25		3/25		2/25		

3. (b)

Year	Total Unrecognized Prior Service Cost	Amortization Fraction	Amortization to Increase Pension Expense	Remaining Unrecognized Prior Service Cost
2004	$400,000	6/25	$96,000	$304,000
2005	400,000	5/25	80,000	224,000
2006	400,000	5/25	80,000	144,000
2007	400,000	4/25	64,000	80,000
2008	400,000	3/25	48,000	32,000
2009	400,000	2/25	32,000	0

20

ACCOUNTING FOR LEASES

CHAPTER OBJECTIVES

After careful study of this chapter, you will be able to:

1. Explain the advantages of leasing.
2. Understand key terms related to leasing.
3. Explain how to classify leases of personal property.
4. Account for a lessee's operating and capital leases.
5. Understand disclosures by the lessee.
6. Account for a lessor's operating, direct financing, and sales-type leases.
7. Understand disclosures by the lessor.
8. Explain the conceptual issues regarding leases.
9. Understand lease issues related to real estate, sale-leaseback issues, leveraged leases, and changes in lease provisions (Appendix).

SYNOPSIS

Advantages of Leasing

1. FASB Statement No. 13 as Amended defines a lease as "an agreement conveying the right to use property, plant, or equipment (land or depreciable assets or both) usually for a stated period of time." A lessee acquires the right to use the property, plant, or equipment. A lessor gives up that right. Other key terms from the Statement are listed in Exhibit 20-1 in the text.

2. Although leases are generally more expensive in the long run than purchases, the advantages of leases from the lessee's point of view include: (1) Financing benefits: An asset may be acquired with 100% financing, conserving cash for the lessee. A lease contract may be more flexible than other debt arrangements, and a lease creates a claim only against the leased equipment, rather than against all assets. (2) Risk benefit: The risks of obsolescence and inadequacy may be borne by the lessor. (3) Tax benefit: Tax deductions, taken over the life of the lease, may be accelerated, and the full cost of the asset, including land, may be written off. (4) Financial reporting benefit: Some key financial ratios are improved when a leased asset is not recorded as an asset and a liability by the lessee. (5) Billing benefit: The interest element in lease payments may be charged to customers under some contracts, while debt interest may not.

3. The main advantages of leases from the lessor's point of view are that leasing provides (a) a way of indirectly making a sale; and (b) another means of obtaining a profit opportunity through the transfer of an asset by the lessor under the lease agreement.

Classification of Personal Property Leases

4. FASB Statement No. 13 as Amended, based on the concept of economic substance over legal form, concluded that a lease which transfers substantially all the risks and benefits of ownership represents in substance a purchase by the lessee and a sale by the lessor of an asset. The Statement provides criteria for the classification of leases by both the lessee and the lessor. Exhibit 20-2 in the text summarizes those criteria.

5. A lessee may have two types of lease: (a) capital lease, accounted for by the capital lease method; and (b) operating lease, accounted for by the operating method.

6. A lessor may have four types of lease: (a) sales-type lease, accounted for by the sales-financing method; (b) direct financing lease, accounted for by the financing method; (c) operating lease, accounted for by the operating method; and (d) leveraged lease, discussed in the Appendix to this chapter.

Accounting and Reporting by Lessees

7. A lease which meets none of the following general classification criteria is classified as an operating lease by the lessee:

   (a) The lease transfers ownership of the property to the lessee by the end of the lease term.

(b) The lease contains a bargain purchase option [see (16) below].

(c) The lease term is equal to 75% or more of the estimated economic life of the leased property.

(d) The present value of the minimum lease payments is at least 90% of the fair value of the leased property to the lessor.

The lessee treats payments made under an operating lease as normal rental payments, and does not report an asset or liability for the lease.

8. A lease which meets one or more of the criteria in (7) above is classified as a capital lease by the lessee. The lessee records an asset and a liability equal to the sum of the present value (not the gross rental value), at the beginning of the lease term, of the minimum lease payments during the lease term.

9. Executory costs are ownership-type costs such as insurance, maintenance, and property taxes. Although these costs may be paid by either the lessee or the lessor, it is normally expected that they should be borne by the party which is in substance the owner of the asset. Executory costs paid directly by the lessee are expensed by the lessee as incurred. If executory costs are paid by the lessor, the portion of each lease payment representing a reimbursement of executory costs is excluded by the lessee from the computation of the present value of the minimum lease payments. That is, the minimum lease payments equal the lease payments minus the executory costs paid by the lessor.

10. The lessee uses the lower of the following discount rates to compute the present value of the minimum lease payments:

(a) The lessee's incremental borrowing rate, or

(b) The lessor's interest rate implicit in the lease, if it is known by the lessee, or if it is practicable for the lessee to learn it.

11. The lessee depreciates (or amortizes) the asset over the estimated economic life of the asset if the capital lease agreement (a) transfers ownership of the asset to the lessee, or (b) contains a bargain purchase option. In other cases, the lessee amortizes the asset over the life of the lease, down to the asset's guaranteed residual value, if any, to the lessee at the end of the lease term.

12. The lessee uses the effective interest method (also called the interest method), which produces a constant rate of interest on the balance of the lease obligation outstanding at the beginning of each period, to allocate lease payments between the reduction of the principal and the payment of interest expense. Other methods are acceptable if the results do not differ materially from the results of the effective interest method.

13. Below are sample journal entries for a lessee under the capital lease method, using account titles recommended by FASB Statement No. 13 as Amended.

(a) Initial recording of the capital lease at present value:

Leased Equipment Under Capital Leases	XX	
Obligation Under Capital Leases		XX

Alternatively, the lease liability may be recorded at the gross amount with a debit to an accompanying contra-liability account for the difference between the gross amount and present value.

(b) Annual payment and recognition of interest expense on the capital lease:

Interest Expense	XX	
Obligation Under Capital Leases	XX	
Cash		XX

(c) Recognition of depreciation of the leased equipment for the period:

Depreciation Expense: Leased Equipment	XX	
Accumulated Depreciation: Leased Equipment		XX

14. The timing of the lease payments and, therefore, the type of annuity must be determined before making present value and interest calculations. An <u>ordinary annuity</u> requires lease payments to be made at the <u>end</u> of each payment period. An <u>annuity due</u> requires lease payments to be made at the <u>beginning</u> of each payment period.

15. The lessee identifies its capital lease obligations on its balance sheet and classifies the obligations into current and noncurrent portions. Two approaches are used to measure the amount of the current liability portion: (a) The <u>present value of next year's payments</u> approach discounts the payment(s) to be made in the next year to the balance sheet date, producing the same current liability each year for a given lease. (b) The <u>change in present value</u> approach measures the current liability as the amount by which the total balance of the lease liability will decrease in the next year. Under both methods the remaining portion of the obligation is classified as a noncurrent liability.

16. A <u>bargain purchase option</u> extends to the lessee the right to purchase the leased property at a price so favorable that the exercise of the option appears, at the inception of the lease, to be reasonably assured. When a bargain purchase option exists, the lessee initially records the leased asset at the present value of the minimum lease payments (which includes the bargain purchase option). Subsequent accounting follows the usual pattern for capital leases.

17. A lessee may <u>guarantee the residual value</u> of an asset under capital lease, agreeing to pay the lessor the difference between a smaller actual value at the end of the lease and the guaranteed amount. In such a case, the lessee initially records the leased asset at the present value of the minimum lease payments (which includes the guaranteed residual value). Subsequent accounting follows the usual pattern for capital leases.

18. Disclosure requirements for lessees were established in <u>FASB Statement No. 13 as Amended</u>. These requirements are shown in Exhibit 20-11 in the text.

Accounting and Reporting by Lessors

19. As shown in Exhibit 20-2 in the text, the four general classification criteria listed in (7) above apply to lessors, as well as to lessees. Two additional criteria apply only to lessors:

(a) The collectibility of the minimum lease payments is reasonably assured (i.e., predictable).

(b) No important uncertainties surround the amount of unreimbursable costs yet to be incurred by the lessor under the lease.

20. A lease that does not meet any one of the general criteria in (7) above, or both of the additional criteria in (19) above, is classified as an operating lease by the lessor. Under an operating lease, the lessor retains substantially all of the risks and benefits of ownership. For accounting purposes, a lessor reports an asset leased under an operating lease on its balance sheet as an owned asset, and records depreciation on it. Even if rental receipts from an asset under an operating lease vary, generally they should be recognized by the lessor on the straight-line basis. Executory costs, normally paid by the lessor under an operating lease, are recorded as operating expenses by the lessor and matched against the gross rental revenue.

21. The lessor may incur initial direct costs, which (a) result directly from originating a lease, and (b) would not have been incurred without that leasing transaction. The lessor records the initial direct costs of an operating lease as an asset and matches this asset as an operating expense against the rental revenue over the term of the lease.

22. In a direct financing lease, the lessor "sells" the asset at a fair value equal to its cost or carrying value, and records a receivable. To be classified as a direct financing lease, a lease must meet one or more of the four general criteria in (7) above, and both the criteria in (19) above. In addition, there must be no manufacturer's or dealer's profit or loss (discussed below) in a direct financing lease. Instead, the net receivable recorded by the lessor equals the cost or carrying value of the property.

23. The gross receivable is the sum of (a) the undiscounted minimum lease payments (net of executory costs paid by the lessor), and (b) the estimated unguaranteed residual value accruing to the lessor (not discounted). The lessor records the difference between the gross receivable (the Minimum Lease Payments Receivable account) and the cost or carrying value of the asset as unearned revenue in a contra account such as Unearned Interest: Leases. The lessor's net investment in the lease at any time is the difference between the Minimum Lease Payments Receivable and the Unearned Interest accounts. The lessor recognizes interest revenue by the effective interest method, to produce a constant rate of return on the net investment. The interest rate which discounts the gross receivable to a present value equal to the net receivable is the rate implicit in the lease.

24. Below are sample journal entries for a lessor of equipment under a direct financing lease:

(a) Initial recording of the lease:

Minimum Lease Payments Receivable	XX	
Equipment		XX
Unearned Interest: Leases		XX

(Note that the effect of this transaction is to replace the equipment asset with a monetary asset of equal amount.)

(b) Collection of payment for the period:

Cash	XX	
Minimum Lease Payments Receivable		XX

(c) Recognition of interest revenue:

Unearned Interest: Leases	XX	
Interest Revenue: Leases		XX

25. According to <u>FASB Statement No. 91</u>, the <u>initial direct costs</u> of a lease include <u>incremental direct costs</u> (costs that result directly from and are essential to the leasing transaction) and <u>other direct costs</u> (such as the costs of negotiating and preparing lease documents). Accounting for initial direct costs incurred by the lessor differs for each of the main types of lease. The total initial direct costs of a direct financing lease are <u>not</u> expensed, but are deferred and a new (lower) interest rate is determined.

26. The journal entry used by a lessor to record the initial direct costs of a direct financing lease is shown below:

Unearned Interest: Leases	XX	
Cash, etc.		XX

This entry, by reducing the Unearned Interest: Leases account, increases the net investment. Since future cash flows are unchanged, the implicit interest rate is lowered, and less interest revenue is recognized each period of the lease term.

27. To be classified as a <u>sales-type lease</u>, a lease must meet <u>one or more</u> of the four general criteria in (7) above, and <u>both</u> the criteria in (19) above. In addition, a sales-type lease must involve a <u>manufacturer's or dealer's profit or loss</u>, which exists when the asset's fair value at the inception of the lease differs from its cost or carrying value. The amount of profit or loss is the difference between (a) the present value of the minimum lease payments (net of executory costs) computed at the interest rate implicit in the lease (i.e., the sales price), and (b) the cost or carrying value of the asset <u>plus any initial direct costs less the present value of the unguaranteed residual value</u> accruing to the benefit of the lessor.

28. Two major differences distinguish a sales-type lease from a direct financing lease: the presence of manufacturer's (dealer's) profit or loss and the accounting treatment for initial direct costs.

29. The initial journal entries that a lessor makes for a sales-type lease differ from the lessor's entry for a direct financing lease: For a sales-type lease the lessor records both the sales revenue and the cost of goods sold. The sales revenue is recorded at the present value of the minimum lease payments, net of executory costs. Cost of goods sold is usually recorded at the assigned inventory cost less the present value of the <u>unguaranteed</u> residual value of the leased asset accruing to the lessor. The present value of any <u>guaranteed</u> residual value is included in sales revenue, rather than subtracted from the cost of goods sold.

Minimum Lease Payments Receivable	XX	
Sales Revenue		XX
Unearned Interest: Leases		XX
Cost of Goods Sold	XX	
Merchandise Inventory (or Equipment Held for Lease)		XX

The journal entries for the collection of rent and recognition of earned interest under a sales-type lease are the same as those for a direct financing lease.

30. As with a direct financing lease, the lessor under a sales-type lease does not report the asset or record depreciation on the leased asset. The lessee typically pays and records executory costs. The lessor recognizes the initial direct costs involved in a sales-type lease as a selling expense of the period, or as a component of cost of goods sold.

31. Unguaranteed and guaranteed residual values receive different treatment under a sales-type lease, but the same gross profit results. The lessor deducts the present value of an unguaranteed residual value from the cost or carrying value of the asset when the lessor recognizes the expenses associated with the signing of the lease. The present value of an unguaranteed residual value is not included in sales revenue. In contrast, the present value of the guaranteed residual value is not deducted from the cost and is included in sales revenue.

32. Disclosure requirements for lessors were established in FASB Statement No. 13 as Amended. These requirements are shown in Exhibit 20-21 in the text.

33. A summary of the accounting for leases by the lessee and lessor is shown in Exhibit 20-22 in the text.

Evaluation of Accounting for Leases and International Accounting Differences

34. A lessee sometimes prefers to report a lease as an operating lease rather than a capital lease in order to exclude the liability from its balance sheet. The four criteria used to distinguish between capital and operating leases may be circumvented fairly easily. For example, the estimate of the asset's economic life may be made long enough that the life of the lease is less than 75% of the estimated economic life. Many users would prefer a simple rule requiring capitalization of all leases with a life of more than one year, or other specified period. In addition, FASB Statement No. 13 has been criticized for being "mechanical," leaving no room for professional judgment.

35. Accounting standards for leases are generally more comprehensive and detailed in the U.S. than internationally. International accounting standards require capitalization when substantially all the risks and rewards of ownership are transferred, as measured by four criteria. However, differences between these criteria and those used in the U.S. impair the international comparability of financial statements.

Appendix: Lease Issues Related to Real Estate

36. Exhibit 20-23 in the text summarizes the classification of leases involving real property. When land alone is leased, the lessee classifies the lease as a capital lease only if (a) the lease transfers ownership of the land to the lessee by the end of the lease term; or (b) the lease contains a bargain purchase option. In other cases, the lease is accounted for as an operating lease. The lessee does not amortize land under a capital lease.

37. The lessor of land alone accounts for the lease as an operating lease unless the lease (a) transfers ownership or contains a bargain purchase option; and (b) meets both the collectibility and uncertainty criteria discussed in the chapter. If (a) and (b) are met and there is dealer's profit or loss, the lease is a sales-type lease. If (a) and (b) are met and there is no dealer's profit or loss, the lease is a direct financing lease.

38. In a capital lease of both land and buildings that transfers ownership or contains a bargain purchase option, the lessee allocates the present value of the minimum lease payments (net of executory costs) to the land and buildings in proportion to their fair values at the inception of the lease. The lessor accounts for a lease of land and buildings together as a single unit, using one Minimum Lease Payments Receivable account.

39. If a lease of land and buildings does not transfer ownership or contain a bargain purchase option, and the fair value of the leased land is less than 25% of the total value of the leased property at the inception of the lease, both the lessee and lessor treat the land and buildings as a single unit for purposes of classifying the lease. When applying criteria 3 and 4 of column A of Exhibit 20-23, this single unit is assumed to have an economic life equal to that of the building. For a lease classified as a capital lease by the lessee or direct financing or sales-type by the lessor, the land and buildings are accounted for as a single unit.

40. If the fair value of leased land is 25% or more of the fair value of the leased property at the inception of the lease, both the lessee and lessor consider the land and buildings separately for purposes of applying the lease classification criteria and make separate lease computations for the land and the buildings. The land and building elements may be classified as different types of leases. However, if they are both classified as operating leases, they are accounted for as a single unit.

Appendix: Sale-Leaseback Issues

41. In a sale-leaseback transaction, property is sold and immediately leased back from the buyer. The sale and leaseback are considered to be a single transaction, essentially like a secured loan. In general, the seller-lessee defers and amortizes any profit or loss on the sale in proportion to the amortization of the asset under capital lease, or in proportion to the rental payments under an operating lease. However, when the fair value of the property at the time of the transaction is less than its undepreciated cost, the seller-lessee immediately recognizes a loss up to the amount of the difference between undepreciated cost and fair value.

Appendix: Leveraged Leases

42. A leveraged lease, which is always considered to be a direct financing lease, involves at least three parties: (a) the equity participant (the owner-lessor); (b) the asset user (the lessee); and (c) the debt participant (the long-term creditor who provides nonrecourse financing for the leasing transaction). Leveraged leases are designed to provide income tax benefits to all three parties. No new accounting issues are involved for the lessee. However, accounting for leveraged leases is complex from the standpoint of the lessor.

Appendix: Changes in Lease Provisions

43. Whenever changes in lease provisions result in terms which would have required different classification if they had been in effect at the beginning of the lease, the revised agreement is considered a new agreement, and is reclassified according to the criteria discussed earlier.

44. A lessor reviews the estimate of an unguaranteed residual value annually. An increase in the estimated value is ignored, but a decline is recognized as a reduction in the lessor's net investment and a loss is recorded.

45. When a lease initially recorded as a capital lease (lessee) and a direct financing lease (lessor) is renewed at the end of the lease term, any guarantee of residual value originally in the lease is cancelled. The lessee adjusts the balances of the asset and obligation by the difference between the present value of the new future minimum lease payments and the pre-renewal balance of the obligation.

46. When changes are made to the lease provisions of a sales-type or direct financing lease during the lease term, and these changes would have caused the lease to be classified as an operating lease at its inception, the lessor accounts for the changed lease as an operating lease after (a) removing the remaining net investment in the lease from its accounts; (b) replacing Minimum Lease Payments Receivable by an asset at the lowest of original cost, fair value, or the carrying amount; and (c) reporting any net adjustment as a loss from operations in the period of the change.

47. When a renewal or extension of a sales-type or direct financing lease results in a lease that qualifies as a sales-type lease, and this renewal or extension takes place <u>during the term</u> of the lease, the lease is treated as a direct financing lease. If, however, the renewal or extension occurs <u>at the end</u> of the lease term, the lease is treated as a sales-type lease.

SELF-EVALUATION EXERCISES

Supply the words necessary to complete each of the following items.

Advantages of Leasing

AL-1. <u>FASB Statement No. 13 as Amended</u> defines a __________ "as an agreement conveying the right to use property, plant, or equipment (land or depreciable assets or both) usually for a stated period of time."

AL-2. One advantage of a lease to the lessee is that the risks of obsolescence and inadequacy may be borne by the __________.

AL-3. Leasing an asset may provide tax benefits to the lessee: tax deductions may be __________, and the full cost of the asset, including __________, may be written off.

AL-4. One advantage of a lease to the lessor is that leasing is a way of indirectly making a __________.

Classification of Personal Property Leases

CL-1. FASB Statement No. 13 as Amended reasons that a lease which transfers the __________ and ______________ of property ownership represents, in substance, the purchase and sale of an asset.

CL-2. Leases are classified into two types by the lessee: ______________ leases, and ________________ leases.

CL-3. Leases are classified into four types by the lessor: ___________-__________ leases, _____________ ______________ leases, ______________ leases, and ______________ leases.

Accounting and Reporting by Lessees

AR-1. The lessee treats payments made under an operating lease as normal __________ payments.

AR-2. Ownership-type costs such as insurance, maintenance, and taxes paid by a lessee are called __________________ costs.

AR-3. The lessee records an asset under capital lease as an asset and a liability equal to the sum of the ___________ _________ at the beginning of the lease term of the ______________ ____________ _______________ during the lease term.

AR-4. If a capital lease agreement transfers ownership of the asset to the lessee or contains a bargain purchase option, the lessee depreciates the asset over the estimated ____________ ________ of the asset.

AR-5. The accounting method which is used to allocate lease payments between principal and interest expense and which produces a constant rate of interest on the balance of the lease obligation outstanding at the beginning of each period is the ________________ __________ method.

AR-6. Lease payments are made at the end of the period in an _____________ annuity.

AR-7. Capital lease obligations are classified into ___________ and _______________ portions on classified balance sheets.

AR-8. The right to purchase leased property at a highly favorable price is extended through a _____________ _____________ __________.

Accounting and Reporting by Lessors

ARL-1. A lessor treats property leased under an ____________ lease as owned property for accounting purposes.

ARL-2. Rental receipts from property under an operating lease should be recognized by the lessor on the __________-___________ basis.

ARL-3. Executory costs paid by the lessor under an operating lease are recorded by the lessor as ____________ ___________.

ARL-4. The lessor records material __________ __________ ____________ of an operating lease as a prepaid asset and matches them against rental revenue over the life of the lease.

ARL-5. In a ___________ _____________ lease, there is no dealer's profit, and the lessor records the net receivable at the cost or carrying value of the property.

ARL-6. The initial direct costs of a lease include ____________ ________ _______ and _______ ________ _______.

ARL-7. Dealer's or manufacturer's profit or loss exists in a ________-___________ lease.

ARL-8. Under a sales-type lease, the present value of a(an) ____________ (guaranteed, unguaranteed) residual value is not deducted from the cost of the leased property, and is included in sales revenue, while the present value of a(an) ____________ (guaranteed, unguaranteed) residual value is deducted from the cost or carrying value of the asset when the expenses associated with the signing of the lease are recognized.

Evaluation of Accounting for Leases and International Accounting Differences

EI 1. Circumventing the four criteria used to distinguish between capital and operating leases ________ (is, is not) fairly easy.

EI-2. Accounting standards for leases in the U.S. are generally ________ (more, less) comprehensive than internationally.

Appendix: Lease Issues Related to Real Estate

LI-1. When a lease of land alone contains a bargain purchase option, the lease is _____________ by the lessee.

LI-2. When a capital lease of land and buildings together is initiated, the lessee ____________ the present value of the minimum lease payments to the land and buildings in proportion to their _______ _________ at the inception of the lease.

LI-3. The lessor accounts for a lease of land and buildings together as a _________ ___________.

LI-4. When a lease of land and buildings does not transfer ownership or contain a bargain purchase option and the fair value of land under lease is less than ________% of the total value of the leased property at the inception of the lease, both the lessee and the lessor treat the land and buildings as a single unit.

Appendix: Sale-Leaseback Issues

SL-1. Property is sold and immediately leased back to the seller in a ________-____________ transaction.

SL-2. In a sale-leaseback, the sale and leaseback are considered to be a __________ transaction.

Appendix: Leveraged Leases

L-1. A leveraged lease is always considered to be a _________ ____________ lease.

L-2. Leveraged leases are designed to provide _________ _______ benefits to the lease participants.

Appendix: Changes in Lease Provisions

C-1. Whenever changes in lease provisions result in terms which would have required different classification if they had been in effect at the beginning of the lease, the lease agreement is considered a _____________ agreement and is ______________.

C-2. When the estimate of an unguaranteed residual value is reviewed by the lessor, an _________ is ignored but a _________ is recognized as a reduction in the lessor's net investment.

ANSWERS TO SELF-EVALUATION EXERCISES

AL-1. lease; AL-2. lessor; AL-3. accelerated, land; AL-4. sale; CL-1. risks, benefits; CL-2. capital, operating; CL-3. sales-type, direct financing, operating, leveraged; AR-1. rental; AR-2. executory; AR-3. present value, minimum lease payments; AR-4. economic life; AR-5. effective interest; AR-6. ordinary; AR-7. current, noncurrent; AR-8. bargain purchase option; ARL-1. operating; ARL-2. straight-line; ARL-3. operating expenses; ARL-4. initial direct costs; ARL-5. direct financing; ARL-6. incremental direct costs, other direct costs; ARL-7. sales-type; ARL-8. guaranteed, unguaranteed; EI-1. is; EI-2. more; LI-1. capitalized; LI-2. allocates, fair values; LI-3. single unit; LI-4. 25; SL-1. sale-leaseback; SL-2. single; L-1. direct financing; L-2. income tax; C-1. new, reclassified; C-2. increase, decline.

POST TEST

Part A Circle T if the statement is true and F if it is false.

T F 1. If a capital lease contains a bargain purchase option, the lessee depreciates the leased property over the term of the lease.

T F 2. In a direct financing lease, there is no dealer's profit or loss.

T F 3. _FASB Statement No. 13 as Amended_ bases lease accounting on conformity with the legal form of leases.

T F 4. Initial direct costs are always capitalized by the lessor and matched to lease revenue over the term of the lease.

T F 5. Executory costs are ownership-type costs such as insurance, maintenance, and taxes.

T F 6. The effective interest method produces a constant rate of interest on the balance of the obligation outstanding at the beginning of each period.

T F 7. Under an annuity due, payments must be made at the end of each period.

T F 8. The lessee uses the lower of two discount rates to compute the present value of the minimum lease payments: the lessee's incremental borrowing rate, or the lessor's interest rate implicit in the lease, if known.

T F 9. When a bargain purchase option exists, the lessee initially records the leased property at the present value of the minimum lease payments, minus the present value of the bargain purchase option.

T F 10. The lessor recognizes rental receipts under an operating lease on the straight-line basis.

T F 11. The lessor records sales revenue and the cost of goods sold in the initial journal entries for a sales-type lease.

T F 12. Under a sales-type lease, the lessor records depreciation on the leased property over the term of the lease.

T F 13. Although guaranteed and unguaranteed residual values are treated differently under sales-type lease accounting, the same gross margin results.

T F 14. The lessee amortizes the amount representing land under capital lease over the term of the lease.

T F 15. In a sale-leaseback transaction, the sale and leaseback are considered to be separate transactions. Consequently, any profit on the sale is recognized immediately.

T F 16. When a lessee guarantees the residual value of an asset under capital lease, the lessee records the asset at the sum of the present values of the minimum lease payments, which includes the guaranteed residual value.

T F 17. A leveraged lease involves at least three parties: an equity participant, an asset user, and a debt participant.

T F 18. With a direct financing lease the lessor records the difference between the gross receivable and the cost or carrying value of the asset in a contra account as unearned revenue.

T F 19. International accounting standards for the classification of leases are identical to the classification criteria in U.S. standards.

T F 20. The lessor uses one Minimum Lease Payments Receivable account to record a lease of land and buildings together.

T F 21. The lessor's journal entries for the collection of rent and the recognition of earned interest are the same for sales-type and direct financing leases.

T F 22. A lessee may have four types of lease: sales-type, direct financing, operating, or leveraged.

T F 23. When the estimated unguaranteed residual value of a leased asset declines, the lessor recognizes a loss.

Part B Select the one best answer, and place its letter in the space provided.

_____ 1. Which of the following statements concerning initial direct costs incurred by a lessor is not true? (a) material initial direct costs of an operating lease are matched by the lessor to rental revenue over the life of the lease; (b) initial direct costs of all types of lease are recorded as a prepaid asset; (c) initial direct costs of a direct financing lease are recognized as a reduction in the interest rate implicit in the lease; (d) initial direct costs of a sales-type lease are charged against income of the period.

_____ 2. If a leased asset is not recorded as an asset and liability by the lessee, (a) the current ratio and rate of return are generally lowered; (b) comparability between companies is improved; (c) the borrowing power of the lessee may be increased; (d) financial ratios are generally unaffected.

____ 3. When a lease contains a bargain purchase option, (a) the leased asset is depreciated by the lessee over the asset's estimated economic life; (b) the leased asset is depreciated by the lessor over the lease term; (c) the lease is always classified as an operating lease by the lessee; (d) the lease is always classified as a sales-type lease by the lessor.

____ 4. Which of the following statements about direct financing leases for lessors is not true? (a) cost of goods sold and sales revenue are recorded at the inception of a direct financing lease; (b) a direct financing lease does not result in a dealer's profit; (c) interest revenue under a direct financing lease is recognized by the effective interest method; (d) the Minimum Lease Payments Receivable account is recorded at the sum of the undiscounted minimum lease payments (net of executory costs paid by the lessor) and the estimated unguaranteed residual value accruing to the lessor.

____ 5. Executory costs (a) are recorded as a prepaid asset by the lessor under a capital lease; (b) are always included by the lessee in the computation of the present value of the minimum lease payments; (c) include sales commissions, legal fees, and credit investigation charges; (d) should normally be borne by the party which is, in substance, the owner of the asset.

____ 6. FASB Statement No. 13 as Amended (a) emphasizes compliance with the legal provisions of leases; (b) reasons that a lease which transfers the risks and benefits of ownership represents, in substance, a purchase and sale; (c) attempts to provide separate classification criteria for lessees and lessors; (d) requires a lessee to include an asset under an operating lease on the balance sheet as an asset and a liability.

____ 7. Which of the following items would require a lessor to classify a lease as an operating lease? (a) the lease contains a bargain purchase option; (b) ownership of the property is transferred to the lessee during the lease term; (c) the lease term is 80% of the estimated economic life of the leased property; (d) the collectibility of the minimum lease payments is highly uncertain.

____ 8. Which of the following items would require a lessee to classify a lease of equipment as a capital lease? (a) there are no important uncertainties about unreimbursable costs to be incurred by the lessor; (b) the lease does not contain a bargain purchase option; (c) the lease term is 80% of the estimated economic life of the leased property; (d) the present value of the minimum lease payments is 85% of the fair value of the leased property.

____ 9. Which of the following items would require a lessee to classify a lease of land as a capital lease? (a) the lease does not contain a bargain purchase option; (b) the present value of the minimum lease payments is 95% of the fair value of the land; (c) there are no important uncertainties regarding the amount of unreimbursable costs to be incurred by the lessor; (d) the lease transfers ownership of the land to the lessee at the end of the lease term.

____ 10. Which of the following statements related to leases of real estate is true? (a) the lessee amortizes land under a capital lease only if the lease contains a bargain purchase option; (b) in a capital lease of land and buildings that contains a bargain purchase option, the lessee accounts for the land and buildings as a single unit; (c) when the fair value of the land component is 25% or more of the fair value of leased real estate and both the land and building leases are classified as operating leases, the land and buildings are accounted for as a single unit; (d) in general the lessor in a capital lease of real estate allocates the present value of the minimum lease payments to the land and buildings in proportion to their fair values.

Part C Solve each of the following short problems.

1. On January 1, 2004, the Bow Company leased manufacturing equipment from the Stern Company. The following information about this lease is available:

Noncancelable term of the lease: 10 years, with no bargain purchase option
Economic life of equipment: 15 years
Fair value (cost to the lessor) of the equipment: $375,000
Lease payments, due at the end of each year: $55,000
Bow Company's incremental borrowing rate (The implicit rate is not known by Bow): 12%
Bow Company's depreciation method: straight-line
Present value factor for an ordinary annuity of ten years at 12%: 5.650223
Present value factor for a single sum at the end of ten years at 12%: 0.321973

(a) Based on the above information:

(1) Classify the lease from the <u>lessee's</u> viewpoint.

(2) Using a general journal format, prepare the Bow Company's journal entry for the lease for 2004.

1. (b) Assume the same facts as above, except that the amount of the yearly lease payments is $65,000 and the economic life of the equipment is 10 years.

(1) Classify the lease from the lessee's viewpoint.

(2) Using a general journal format, prepare the Bow Company's journal entries for the lease for 2004.

2. Use the same information as in part (b) of Problem 1 above. Additional information is given below.

The collectibility of the lease payments is reasonably assured.
Initial direct costs are insignificant and assumed to be zero.
There are no important uncertainties involved in the lease.

(a) Complete the following:

(1) Classify the lease from the lessor's viewpoint.

2. (a) (2) Using a general journal format, prepare the Stern Company's journal entries for the lease for 2004.

(b) Assume the same facts as above, except that the cost of the equipment to the Stern Company was $300,000 while the fair value was $375,000.

(1) Classify the lease from the lessor's viewpoint.

(2) Using a general journal format, prepare the Stern Company's initial entry to record the lease.

3. Use the original information in Problem 1 above, with the following changes:

The lease contains a bargain purchase option. Bow is expected to pay $6,000 at the end of 10 years to purchase the equipment.

The residual value of the equipment at the end of 15 years is expected to be $5,000.

Stern paid incremental direct costs of $3,000 and other direct costs of $2,000 to complete the lease transaction.

(a) Classify the lease from the lessee's standpoint.

3. (b) Using a general journal format, prepare the <u>lessee's</u> entries to record the lease on January 1 and to record depreciation at the end of the year.

(c) Using a general journal format, prepare the <u>lessor's</u> entry to record the initial direct cots.

ANSWERS TO POST TEST

Part A

1. F	7. F	13. T	19. F
2. T	8. T	14. F	20. T
3. F	9. F	15. F	21. T
4. F	10. T	16. T	22. F
5. T	11. T	17. T	23. T
6. T	12. F	18. T	

Part B

1. b	4. a	7. d	9. d
2. c	5. d	8. c	10. c
3. a	6. b		

Part C

1. (a) (1) Operating Lease

The lease does not transfer ownership. There is no bargain purchase option. The lease term is less than 75% of the economic life of the equipment. The present value of the lease payments ($55,000 x 5.650223 = $310,762.27) is less than 90% of the equipment's fair value (0.90 x $375,000 = $337,500).

(2)

Rent Expense	55,000.00	
Cash		55,000.00
To record payment of annual rent under operating lease.		

(b) (1) Capital Lease

The lease term is equal to 100% of the economic life of the equipment. Furthermore, the present value of the minimum lease payments ($65,000 x 5.650223 = $367,264.50) is greater than 90% of the fair value of the leased property.

(2)

Leased Equipment Under Capital Lease	367,264.50	
Obligation Under Capital Leases		367,264.50
To initially record the capital lease.		
Interest Expense	44,071.74	
Obligation Under Capital Leases	20,928.26	
Cash		65,000.00
To record payment of the 2004 rental and to recognize interest expense on the capital lease for 2004 (12% x $367,264.50).		
Depreciation Expense: Leased Equipment	36,726.45	
Accumulated Depreciation: Leased Equipment		36,726.45
To recognize depreciation of the leased equipment for 2004 ($367,264.50 ÷ 10).		

2. (a) (1) Direct Financing Lease

The lease term is equal to 100% of the economic life of the equipment. The present value of the minimum lease payments is greater than 90% of the fair value of the equipment. The collectibility of the lease payments is reasonably assured. There are no important uncertainties. There is no dealer's profit or loss (the fair value of the equipment = the lessor's cost).

(2)

Minimum Lease Payments Receivable	650,000.00	
Equipment		375,000.00
Unearned Interest: Leases		275,000.00
To initially record the lease as a direct financing lease.		

		Cash	65,000.00	
		Minimum Lease Payments Receivable		65,000.00
		To record collection of the 2004 payment.		
		Unearned Interest: Leases	45,000.00	
		Interest Revenue-Leases		45,000.00
		To record interest revenue on the lease [12% x ($650,000 - $275,000)].		

(b) (1) Sales-Type Lease

Dealer's profit (fair value - cost = $375,000.00 - $300,000 = $75,000.00) is present. Other conditions are the same as given for part (a).

	(2)	Minimum Lease Payments Receivable	650,000.00	
		Sales Revenue		367,264.50
		Unearned Interest: Leases		282,735.50
		To initially record the lease as a sales-type lease.		
		Cost of Goods Sold	300,000.00	
		Equipment Held for Lease		300,000.00
		To record the related cost of goods sold.		

3. (a) Capital Lease
The lease contains a bargain purchase option.

(b)	Leased Equipment Under Capital Leases	312,694.11	
	Obligation Under Capital Leases		312,694.11
	To record the lease on January 1 [$55,000 x 5.650223 + $6,000 x 0.321973]		
	Depreciation Expense: Leased Equipment	20,512.94	
	Accumulated Depreciation: Leased Equipment		20,512.94
	To record depreciation of the leased equipment for 2004 [($312,694.11 - $5,000)/15].		

(c) Since Fair Value = Cost, this is a direct financing lease to the lessor.

Unearned Interest: Leases	5,000.00	
Cash, etc.		5,000.00
To record the initial direct costs of the lease.		

21

THE STATEMENT OF CASH FLOWS

CHAPTER OBJECTIVES

After careful study of this chapter, you will be able to:

1. Define operating, investing, and financing activities.
2. Know the categories of inflows and outflows of cash.
3. Classify cash flows as operating, investing, or financing.
4. Explain the direct and indirect methods for reporting operating cash flows.
5. Prepare a simple statement of cash flows.
6. Use a worksheet for a statement of cash flows.
7. Compute and disclose interest paid and income taxes paid.
8. Identify the operating cash inflows and outflows under the direct method (Appendix).
9. Compute the operating cash flows under the direct method (Appendix).

SYNOPSIS

Need for and History of the Statement of Cash Flows

1. Users need information about the operating, investing, and financing activities of companies. Such information about a particular company relates directly or indirectly to the company's cash flows. The FASB stated that a company's financial reports should include information about cash flows and other factors affecting its liquidity or solvency.

2. Funds statements have evolved over the years from the initial, simple "where got-where gone" schedule into the current statement of cash flows. FASB Statement No. 95 requires a statement of cash flows for the accounting period along with a company's income statement and balance sheet.

Conceptual Overview and Reporting Guidelines

3. As discussed in Chapter 2, one of the specific objectives of financial reporting is to provide information about a company's cash flows. Information about a company's liquidity, financial flexibility, operating capability, and risk is related to this objective. Liquidity is the company's ability to meet its obligations as they become due. Financial flexibility is a measure of the company's ability to adapt to unexpected needs and opportunities by changing the amounts and timing of its cash flows. Operating capability is the company's ability to maintain a given physical level of operations. Risk is the uncertainty or unpredictability of the future results of the company.

4. A statement of cash flows is a financial statement that shows a company's cash inflows, cash outflows, and net change in cash from its operating, investing, and financing activities during an accounting period, in a manner that reconciles the company's beginning and ending cash balances. The statement's primary purpose is to provide relevant information about the company's cash receipts and cash payments during the accounting period, information that is useful in evaluating the company's liquidity, financial flexibility, operating capability, and risk.

5. Operating activities (i.e., the provision of services and the acquisition, sale, and delivery of goods) include all transactions and other events that are not investing and financing activities. Generating cash from operations usually is considered to be a company's most important cash flow activity.

6. Investing activities include making and collecting loans, acquiring and selling investments, and acquiring and selling property, plant, and equipment.

7. Financing activities include obtaining resources from owners (and providing a return on, and of, those resources to the owners) and obtaining and repaying resources to creditors. The issuance of securities, payment of dividends, and borrowing and repayment of money are examples of financing activities. The settlement of liabilities, such as accounts payable associated with the acquisition of inventory, is, however, an operating activity.

8. To enable external users to predict the amounts, timing, and uncertainty of future cash flows, a company's statement of cash flows should clearly show for the accounting period: (a) the cash provided by or used in its operating activities; (b) the cash provided by or used in its investing activities; (c) the cash provided by or used in its financing activities; (d) the net increase or decrease in cash; and (e) a reconciliation of a company's beginning cash balance to its ending cash balance. "Simultaneous" investing and financing activities that do not affect cash (such as the acquisition of land by the issuance of common stock) are reported in a separate schedule (or narrative explanation) accompanying the statement of cash flows.

9. Cash equivalents are short-term, highly liquid investments. When a company makes such investments and reports "Cash and Cash Equivalents" on its balance sheet, the statement of cash flows explains the change in cash and cash equivalents.

10. The following is a typical statement of cash flows, taken from Exhibit 21-1 in the text. The format includes three sections showing the results of operating, investing, and financing activities, a reconciliation of the beginning and ending cash balances, and a schedule of investing and financing activities not affecting cash.

RYAN CORPORATION
Statement of Cash Flows
For Year Ended December 31, 2004

Net Cash Flow From Operating Activities		
Net income	$ 14,000	
Adjustments for differences between income flows and cash flows from operating activities:		
Add: Depreciation expense	8,000	
Decrease in accounts receivable	2,600	
Increase in salaries payable	800	
Less: Increase in inventory	(2,000)	
Decrease in accounts payable	(7,000)	
Net cash provided by operating activities		$ 16,400
Cash Flows From Investing Activities		
Payment for purchase of building	$(28,000)	
Payment for purchase of equipment	(4,000)	
Proceeds from sale of land, at cost	10,000	
Net cash used for investing activities		(22,000)
Cash Flows From Financing Activities		
Proceeds from issuance of common stock	$ 18,000	
Proceeds from issuance of bonds	12,000	
Payment of dividends	(9,000)	
Payment of note payable	(13,000)	
Net cash provided by financing activities		8,000
Net Increase in Cash (see Schedule 1)		$ 2,400
Cash, January 1, 2004		10,900
Cash, December 31, 2004		$ 13,300
Schedule 1: Investing and Financing Activities Not Affecting Cash		
Investing Activities		
Acquisition of land by issuance of common stock		$ (6,000)
Financing Activities		
Issuance of common stock for land		6,000

Cash Inflows and Outflows

11. A company's <u>inflows</u> of (increases in) cash can be divided into three categories: decreases in assets other than cash; increases in liabilities; and increases in stockholders' equity.

12. A company's <u>outflows</u> of (decreases in) cash can be divided into three categories: increases in assets other than cash; decreases in liabilities; and decreases in stockholders' equity.

13. Operating cash inflows are increases in stockholders' equity (i.e., retained earnings) due to certain revenues, adjusted for changes in certain current assets and certain current liabilities (related to the operating cycle). Operating cash outflows are decreases in stockholders' equity (i.e., retained earnings) due to certain expenses, adjusted for changes in certain current assets and certain current liabilities (related to the operating cycle).

14. Investing cash inflows are decreases in noncurrent assets and certain current assets (e.g., notes receivable, marketable securities). Investing cash outflows are increases in noncurrent assets and certain current assets (e.g., notes receivable, temporary investments).

15. Financing cash inflows are increases in noncurrent liabilities, stockholders' equity, and certain current liabilities (e.g., notes payable related to financing activities). Financing cash outflows are decreases in noncurrent liabilities, stockholders' equity, and certain current liabilities (e.g., notes payable and dividends payable).

Net Cash Flow From Operating Activities

16. A company's operating cycle is the average time taken to spend cash for inventory, process and sell the inventory, collect the accounts receivable, and convert them back into cash. Net income and the net cash flow within the operating cycle are unlikely to be the same because of differences between when the company receives and pays cash and when it records revenues and expenses.

17. FASB Statement No. 95 allows two methods for calculating and reporting a company's net cash flow from operating activities. While both methods result in the same amount of net cash provided by operating activities, the FASB prefers the direct method. Under the direct method, a company deducts operating cash outflows from its operating cash inflows to determine the net cash flow from operating activities. The direct method does not "tie" a company's net income to the net cash provided by operating activities, or show how the changes in the company's current assets and current liabilities affected its operating cash flows. Consequently, FASB Statement No. 95 requires that a company using the direct method also include a separate schedule reconciling net income to its operating cash flows.

18. Under the indirect method a company's net income is adjusted to its net cash flow from operating activities. That is, the indirect method converts income flows from an accrual basis to a cash flow basis. Many adjustments, involving increases and decreases in current assets and liabilities as well as noncurrent accounts, may be required. According to the FASB, a company may show the reconciliation of net income to the net cash provided by (or used in) operating activities either in the statement of cash flows or in a separate schedule. Most companies are currently using the indirect method.

Preparing the Statement Using the Indirect Method

19. When the financial statements are not complex, a company may prepare the statement of cash flows by the seldom used visual inspection method. Companies use the worksheet method most often, however, because a company may document an analysis of complex transactions and events in a concise working paper. After information has been gathered from the financial statements and accounting records, all the changes in the noncash accounts are reconstructed on the worksheet to show cash inflows and outflows

for operating, investing, and financing activities. The difference between the total cash inflows and outflows recorded must equal the change in the Cash account.

20. The steps for preparation of the statement of cash flows using the worksheet method are explained in Exhibit 21-9 of the text: (a) Enter column headings and the beginning cash balance, ending cash balance, and change in cash. (b) Enter the titles of other balance sheet accounts and the beginning balance, ending balance, and change in balance of each account. Total the amount columns to verify the debit and credit balances. (c) On the lower portion of the worksheet, enter headings for Net Cash Flow From Operating Activities, Cash Flows From Investing Activities, Cash Flows From Financing Activities, and Investing and Financing Activities Not Affecting Cash. (d) Reconstruct the journal entries for all changes occurring in the current period in the noncash accounts to show the cash inflows and outflows related to operating, investing, and financing activities. Begin with net income and account for nearly all of the changes in current assets and liabilities as adjustments to net income in the Net Cash Flow From Operating Activities section of the worksheet. Then account for the changes in the noncurrent accounts, identified as operating, investing, or financing activities. An item which does not affect an operating activity or cash is a "simultaneous" financing and/or investing transaction. (e) Record the net change in cash, verifying that the change in the Cash account is equal to the difference in total cash inflows and outflows for the noncash accounts recorded in step b. (f) Prepare the statement of cash flows and accompanying schedule using the information on the lower portion of the worksheet and the beginning and ending cash balances.

21. The adjustments to net income are shown on the worksheet in Exhibit 21-11 in the text. Note that:

    Depreciation expense and amortization expense, involving no outflows of cash, are added back to net income (although depreciation and amortization are not cash inflows from operating activities). The decrease in inventories, representing a cash inflow because a company purchased less inventory than it recorded as cost of goods sold, is added to net income. The increase in income taxes and interest payable, representing cash outflows less than the expenses recorded, are added to net income. The increase in accounts receivable, representing a cash outflow because the company collected less cash than the credit sales it made, is subtracted from net income. The increase in prepaid expenses, indicating that the company paid more cash than the expense it recorded, is subtracted from net income. The decrease in accounts payable, representing a cash outflow greater than the expense recorded, is subtracted from net income. The gain on the sale of land, which does not involve an operating inflow, is subtracted from net income.

22. A company reports cash flows from extraordinary items as investing or financing activities, and does not include these in net cash flows from operating activities. When a company reports an extraordinary item, the operating activities section of its statement of cash flows begins, as usual, with net income, and the extraordinary gain (loss) is subtracted (added) like other adjustments.

Special Topics

23. When a company sells a depreciable asset, it must consider the results of the transaction when preparing the statement of cash flows. A company treats any cash that is received as a cash inflow from an investing activity and subtracts any gain (or loss) on the sale from (added to) net income to correctly show the cash provided by operating activities.

24. Companies using the indirect method must disclose interest <u>paid</u> and income tax <u>paid</u> in a separate schedule or narrative description.

25. The issuance of <u>stock dividends</u> is <u>not</u> considered a financing activity, and is not reported on the statement of cash flows.

26. Cash inflows and outflows from related investing and financing activities must be shown separately, not "netted" against each other.

27. A company may disclose simultaneous financing and investing activities involving the exchange of cash as well as a noncash exchange either by (a) reporting the cash payment on the statement of cash flows and the noncash element on the schedule of financing and investing activities not affecting cash or (b) reporting the activities in a cash flow section.

28. Because a company reports investments in "available for sale" debt and equity securities at their fair value, using an unrealized increase or decrease account, it must carefully analyze any change in the investment account to determine its impact on its statement of cash flows. A company reports an increase in the investment account due to the purchase of securities as a cash outflow from an investing activity. It does not report an increase or decrease in the investment due to revaluation to fair value on the statement of cash flows, but must account for it on the worksheet as an adjustment of the allowance and unrealized increase/ decrease accounts. A decrease in the investment account due to the sale of securities is reported as a cash inflow from an investing activity, and the worksheet entry must reconcile the changes in the investment, allowance, unrealized increase/decrease, and realized gain or loss accounts.

29. A company discloses dividends <u>paid</u> are disclosed as a cash outflow from financing activities.

30. According to <u>FASB Statement No. 102</u>, financial institutions such as banks and securities dealers should report cash flows from the purchase or sale of trading securities, as well as interest collected and paid, in the operating activities section of the statement of cash flows. Any unrealized holding loss (gain) on trading securities is then added to (deducted from) net income to adjust net income from an accrual basis to a cash flow basis.

31. A company with foreign operations must disclose the "reporting currency equivalent" of its "foreign currency" cash flows, and report the effects of exchange rate changes as a separate part of the reconciliation of the change in cash during the period.

32. The FASB has concluded that a cash flow per share amount should <u>not</u> be reported in a company's financial statements.

33. International accounting standards require companies to prepare a statement of cash flows. However, a company that uses the direct method does not have to also reconcile its net income to its operating cash flows. There is also more flexibility as to where certain cash flows (e.g., dividends paid) may be reported.

Appendix: Direct Method for Reporting Operating Cash Flows

34. FASB Statement No. 95 allows a company to use either the indirect or direct method, but encourages the use of the direct method to report the cash flows from operating activities on the statement of cash flows. As mentioned earlier, under the direct method a company deducts the operating cash outflows from the operating cash inflows to determine the net cash provided by (or used in) operating activities.

35. The indirect method, in which a company adjusts net income to reach the net cash provided by or used in operating activities, provides information about timing differences between income and operating cash flows. The direct method, which separates operating cash receipts from the operating cash payments, may be useful in estimating future cash flows.

36. The reporting of cash flows from investing and financing activities is the same under the direct and indirect methods, although there are slight differences in the preparation of the information. The primary difference is the reporting of (and preparation of information about) cash flows from operating activities.

37. Under the direct method, a company reports operating cash inflows separately from operating cash outflows. Cash inflows are reported in three categories: (a) collections from customers: sales revenue, plus decrease in accounts receivable or minus increase in accounts receivable, and plus increase in deferred revenues or minus decrease in deferred revenues; (b) interest and dividends collected: interest and dividend revenue, plus decrease in interest/dividends receivable or minus increase in interest/dividends receivable, and plus amortization of premium on investment in bonds or minus amortization of discount on investment in bonds; and (c) other operating receipts: other revenues, minus gains on disposals of assets and liabilities, and minus investment income recognized under the equity method.

38. A company reports cash outflows from operating activities in five categories: (a) payments to suppliers: cost of goods sold, plus increase in inventory or minus decrease in inventory, plus decrease in accounts payable or minus increase in accounts payable; (b) payments to employees: salaries (wages) expense, plus decrease in salaries payable or minus increase in salaries payable; (c) payments of interest: interest expense, plus decrease in interest payable or minus increase in interest payable, plus amortization of premium on bonds payable or minus amortization of discount on bonds payable; (d) other operating payments: other operating expenses, plus increase in prepaid items or minus decrease in prepaid items, minus depreciation, depletion, and amortization expense, minus losses on disposals of assets and liabilities, minus investment loss recognized under the equity method; (e) payments of income taxes: income tax expense, plus decrease in income taxes payable or minus increase in income taxes payable, plus decrease in deferred tax liability or minus increase in deferred tax liability.

39. When a company reports operating cash flows using the direct method, it also presents a separate schedule reconciling net income to the net cash provided by or used in operating activities (i.e., a schedule prepared under the indirect method), as required by FASB Statement No. 95.

40. As discussed above for the indirect method, a company may prepare the statement of cash flows using the visual inspection method (when the financial statements are not complex) or the worksheet method.

41. Exhibit 21-17 in the main text shows a worksheet prepared for a statement of cash flows using the direct method. The six steps for the direct method, using the worksheet approach, are: (a) Enter the column headings, account titles, and debit and credit amounts from the post-closing trial balance for the previous year and the adjusted trial balance for the current year on a worksheet. (b) For each account, enter the difference between the amount on the post-closing trial balance and the amount on the adjusted trial balance in a "change" column on the worksheet. (c) Below the account titles (on the lower portion of the worksheet) enter headings for cash flows from operating, investing, and financing activities, and for investing and financing activities not affecting cash. (d) Account for all the noncash account changes that occurred during the current period, starting with the routine, ongoing revenue and expense accounts (potential operating cash inflows and outflows). Reconstruct the journal entries which resulted in the changes, modifying them as necessary to show the cash flows related to operating, investing, and financing activities. Note that worksheet entries for noncash revenues and expenses (e.g., depreciation expense) are made without modifications, and that worksheet entries for gains and losses are made in conjunction with investing or financing transactions. After finishing the ongoing revenue and expense accounts, make entries for the current asset (except cash) and current liability accounts (nearly all of which are listed as adjustments of related operating cash inflows or outflows), and noncurrent accounts. An entry which does not affect an operating activity or cash is a "simultaneous" financing and/or investing transaction, which a company must disclose on a schedule accompanying the statement of cash flows. (e) Record the net change in cash with a final worksheet entry, total the debit and credit worksheet entries, and verify that the totals are equal. (f) Prepare the statement of cash flows and the accompanying schedule using the information on the lower portion of the worksheet and the beginning and ending cash balances.

SELF-EVALUATION EXERCISES

Supply the words necessary to complete each of the following items.

Need for and History of the Statement of Cash Flows

N-1. Information about the operating, investing, and financing activities of a company relates directly or indirectly to the company's _______ _______.

N-2. FASB Statement No. 95 requires a statement of cash flows be presented with a company's _______ _______ and _______ _______.

Conceptual Overview and Reporting Guidelines

CR-1. A company's ability to adapt to unexpected needs and opportunities by changing the amounts and timing of its cash flows is its _______ _______.

CR-2. A statement of cash flows provides information that is useful in evaluating a company's ___________, financial flexibility, _____________ _____________, and _______.

CR-3. A company's statement of cash flows shows the cash inflows, cash outflows, and net change in cash from its _____________, ______________, and ______________ activities.

CR-4. Owners and creditors provide resources to a company and receive a return on those resources from the company, when the company is engaging in ________________ activities.

CR-5. Short-term, highly liquid investments are called _________ ______________.

CR-6. "______________" investing and financing activities that do not affect cash are reported in a separate schedule or narrative explanation.

Cash Inflows and Outflows

C-1. Cash inflows arise from ______________ in assets other than cash, _____________ in liabilities, and increases in _________ ____________.

C-2. Cash outflows may arise from ____________ in liabilities or ___________ in stockholders' equity.

C-3. A company reports decreases in notes receivable as ____________ _______ _________.

C-4. A company reports decreases in notes payable as ____________ _______ __________.

Net Cash Flow From Operating Activities

NC-1. The average time taken to spend cash for inventory, process and sell the inventory, and convert receivables into cash is an ___________ _________.

NC-2. <u>FASB Statement No. 95</u> allows both the ____________ method and the ____________ method for reporting net cash flows from operating activities.

NC-3. The method for reporting net cash flows from operating activities that "ties" a company's net income to its net cash provided by operating activities is the

_______________ method.

Preparing the Statement Using the Indirect Method

PS-1. When preparing the statement of cash flows, a company may use the

__________ _____________ method when financial statements are simple;

however, the ______________ method is recommended for analysis of complex transactions and events.

PS-2. The difference between the total cash inflows and outflows recorded when using

the worksheet method must equal the change in the _______ account.

PS-3. When adjustments are made under the indirect method, depreciation

expense is _________ ________ to net income and any __________ in accounts payable is subtracted.

PS-4. Cash flows from extraordinary items are reported as ____________

or ____________ activities.

Special Topics

ST-1. When preparing a statement of cash flows, a company treats cash received from the

sale of a depreciable asset as a cash __________ from an _____________

activity, and any gain on the sale as ______________ from net income.

ST-2. Companies disclose interest paid and income tax paid in a separate

schedule or narrative description when using the ____________ method.

ST-3. A company accounts for an increase or decrease in available-for-sale investments due to revaluation to fair value in the worksheet as an adjustment of the

___________ and ____________ ___________/__________ accounts.

ST-4. Dividends paid are disclosed in the cash flows from ___________ activities section of the statement of cash flows.

ST-5. FASB Statement No. 102 requires that financial institutions report cash flows

from the purchase or sale of trading securities in the _____________ section of the statement of cash flows.

ST-6. Companies with foreign operations must report the effects of ______________ ________ changes as a separate part of the reconciliation of the change in cash during the period.

ST-7. A cash flow per share amount _____________ (should, should not) be reported in a company's financial statements.

Appendix: Direct Method for Reporting Operating Cash Flows

DM-1. FASB Statement No. 95 encourages companies to use the ____________ ______________ to report the cash flows from operating activities on the statement of cash flows.

DM-2. The direct method, which separates cash receipts from cash payments, may be useful in estimating future ___________ ____________.

DM-3. Under the direct method, a company should report cash inflows from operating activities in three categories: ____________ _______ _____________; ____________ and ______________ _____________; and other operating receipts.

DM-4. When a company uses the direct method, it must present the reconciliation of net income to the net cash provided by or used in operating activities in a ______________ _____________.

ANSWERS TO SELF-EVALUATION EXERCISES

N-1. cash flows; N-2. income statement, balance sheet; CR-1. financial flexibility; CR-2. liquidity, operating capability, risk; CR-3. operating, investing, financing; CR-4. financing; CR-5. cash equivalents; CR-6. simultaneous; C-1. decreases, increases, stockholders' equity; C-2. decreases, decreases; C-3. investing cash inflows; C-4. financing cash outflows; NC-1. operating cycle; NC-2. direct, indirect; NC-3. indirect; PS-1. visual inspection, worksheet; PS-2. cash; PS-3. added back, decrease; PS-4. investing, financing; ST-1. inflow, investing, subtracted; ST-2. indirect; ST-3. allowance, unrealized increase/decrease; ST-4. financing; ST-5. operating; ST-6. exchange rate; ST-7. should not; DM-1. direct method; DM-2. cash flows; DM-3. collections from customers, interest, dividends collected; DM-4. separate schedule.

POST TEST

Part A Circle T if the statement is true and F if it is false.

T F 1. The presentations of the cash flows from financing and investing activities differ under the direct and indirect methods.

T F 2. Outflows of cash may be caused by decreases in liabilities or by decreases in owners' equity.

T F 3. FASB Statement No. 95 requires a company to report its cash flow per share on the face of the statement of cash flows.

T F 4. "Financial flexibility" refers to the company's ability to meet its obligations as they come due.

T F 5. A company reports depreciation as a cash inflow from operating activities on the statement of cash flows.

T F 6. Accrual income and the net cash flow from operating activities usually vary because of differences in when a company records revenues and expenses and when it receives and pays of cash.

T F 7. Cash flows from extraordinary items are reported as cash flows from investing or financing activities, not as cash flows from operating activities.

T F 8. A company shows payments of dividends on its statement of cash flows as cash outflows from financing activities.

T F 9. A company adds an increase in salaries payable to net income, and deducts an increase in inventory from net income, when converting net income to the net cash flow from operating activities under the indirect method.

T F 10. When a company sells equipment used in its operations, it reports the proceeds as a cash inflow from operating activities.

T F 11. Usually a company reports the effects on cash of changes in current assets and current liabilities as adjustments to net income in the net cash flow from operating activities section of its statement of cash flows using the indirect method.

T F 12. The issuance of a stock dividend is reported as a financing activity on the statement of cash flows.

T F 13. The most important activity of a company is generally considered to be generating cash from operations.

T F 14. A company's cash outflows can be divided into three categories: increases in assets other than cash, decreases in liabilities, and increases in stockholders' equity.

T F 15. Net income can be defined as the net cash flow within an operating cycle.

T F 16. The indirect method converts income flows from the accrual basis to the cash basis.

T F 17. The collection of a loan and the acquisition of a building are examples of investing activities.

T F 18. Cash equivalents include notes payable and receivable, marketable securities, and trade receivables due within 30 days.

T F 19. Cash inflows from investing and financing activities are shown net of related cash outflows.

T F 20. Operating activities include all transactions and other events that are not investing and financing activities.

T F 21. Both international accounting standards and U.S. GAAP require a reconciliation of a company's net income to its operating cash flows when a cash flow statement is presented using the direct method.

Part B Select the one best answer, and place its letter in the space provided.

____ 1. Which of the following items should be shown in a separate schedule accompanying the statement of cash flows: (a) the cash provided by, or used in, investing activities; (b) the net increase or decrease in cash; (c) simultaneous investing and financing activities that do not affect cash; (d) the net increase or decrease in accounts receivable.

____ 2. The Cooper Company had net income of $20,000, an increase in accounts receivable of $2,000, depreciation expense of $5,500, a decrease in marketable securities of $750, a payment of $10,000 for new equipment, and income tax expense (no taxes payable or deferred tax) of $6,000. Cooper's net cash flow from operating activities was (a) $18,250; (b) $24,250; (c) $14,250; (d) $23,500.

____ 3. Which of the following statements regarding the direct method of reporting the cash flows from operating activities is incorrect? (a) FASB Statement No. 95 encourages the use of the direct method; (b) the direct method "ties" a company's net income, on the accrual basis, to cash flows provided by operating activities; (c) by presenting cash receipts separately from cash disbursements, the direct method may help users estimate future cash flows; (d) under the direct method a company reports its cash inflows from operating activities in three categories: collections from customers, interest and dividends collected, and other operating receipts.

____ 4. In 2004 the Hemingray Company had net income of $450,000, a decrease in income taxes payable of $30,000, an increase in accounts payable of $15,000, and an increase in inventory of $10,000. The company purchased a new factory building for $250,000, repaid a note for $75,000, and paid dividends of $50,000. Hemingray's net cash flows from operating, financing, and investing activities (in that order) were (a) $465,000; $(280,000); $0; (b) $425,000; $(125,000); $(250,000); (c) $505,000, $125,000; $(280,000); (d) $455,000; $(50,000); $(295,000).

_____ 5. During the year the Howard Company purchased a building for $800,000 and sold land for $500,000 (at a $150,000 gain). An earthquake destroyed a factory with a cost of $2,700,000 and a book value of $1,000,000. Insurance proceeds for that factory, net of tax, were $750,000. Net income reported for the year was $500,000. The Howard Company's net cash flows from operating and investing activities were (a) $(150,000); $150,000; (b) $750,000; $(800,000); (c) $300,000; $1,045,000; (d) $600,000; $450,000.

_____ 6. The Herriott Company uses the direct method to report its cash flows from operating activities. Herriott's working papers showed the following:

Cost of goods sold	$25,000
Interest expense	400
Salaries expense	10,000
Amortization of premium on bonds payable	50
Decrease in salaries payable	150
Decrease in inventories	3,000

At what amounts should Herriott report payments to suppliers, payments to employees, and payments of interest? (a) $22,000; $10,150; $450; (b) $28,000; $9,850; $450; (c) $26,950; $10,000; $350; (d) $22,000; $10,150; $400.

_____ 7. Further information from Herriott's working papers is shown below:

Other revenues	$ 4,000
Interest revenue	1,500
Sales revenue	40,000
Investment income recognized under the equity method	3,000
Decrease in accounts receivable	500
Increase in deferred revenue	400
Amortization of discount on investment in bonds	50

At what amounts should Herriott report collections from customers, interest and dividends collected, and other operating receipts? (a) $40,500; $1,450; $1,400; (b) $39,500; $1,550; $600; (c) $44,500; $1,500; $(2,600); (d) $44,900; $5,450; $3,000.

_____ 8. The 2004 statement of cash flows of the Tucson Company shows net cash provided by operating activities in the amount of $1,000,000. During the year Tucson sold a building at a net gain of $40,000. Inventory increased by $10,000. Deferred income taxes decreased by $1,000. The company paid dividends of $30,000. Tucson's net income for 2004 was (a) $1,049,000; (b) $951,000; (c) $1,051,000; (d) $951,000.

_____ 9. The Kelso Company's accounting records show the following information:

Proceeds from collection of accounts receivable	$ 40,000
Proceeds from issuance of common stock	530,000
Purchase of factory equipment	400,000
Purchase of marketable securities	100,000
Proceeds from sale of building	250,000
Gain on sale of building	60,000
Purchase of inventory	200,000
Payment of dividends on preferred stock	10,000

Kelso's net cash flows from investing and financing activities were (a) $15,000; $(80,000); (b) $(200,000); $(520,000); (c) $140,000; $565,000; (d) $(250,000); $520,000.

_____ 10. Which of the following statements regarding the statement of cash flows is correct? (a) under the indirect method, an extraordinary gain is added back to net income to determine the net cash flow from operating activities; (b) a subsidiary loss under the equity method is reported as an outflow of cash from investing activities; (c) the direct method does not show how the changes in the elements of a company's operating cycle affected its operating cash flows; (d) equity transactions, including the acquisition of treasury stock and the issuance of stock dividends, are reported as flows of cash from financing activities.

Part C Solve each of the following short problems.

1. A partially completed worksheet for the Flint Company's 2004 statement of cash flows is shown below.

Debits	Increase (Decrease)	Worksheet Entries Debit	Worksheet Entries Credit
Cash	$ 114,000		
Noncash Accounts			
Accounts receivable	$ 6,000		
Inventory	3,200		
Land	40,000		
Buildings	(350,000)		
Equipment	33,000		
Totals	$(153,800)		
Credits			
Accumulated depreciation: equipment	$ 2,000		
Accumulated depreciation: buildings	(195,000)		
Accounts payable	1,500		
Salaries payable	800		
Common stock, $100 par	31,000		
Additional paid-in capital	10,500		
Retained earnings	(4,600)		
Totals	$(153,800)		

Net Cash Flow From Operating Activities

Cash Flows From Investing Activities

Cash Flows From Financing Activities

Investing and Financing Activities not Affecting Cash

Net Increase in Cash
Totals

Supplemental information for 2004:

Flint purchased a parcel of land for $40,000. As payment the company issued 300 shares of $100 par common stock.

Flint paid for new equipment costing $48,000 and sold obsolete equipment at a gain of $6,000. The obsolete equipment had a cost of $15,000 and a book value of $11,000.

Flint paid dividends of $4,000.

The company's depreciation expense for the year was $6,000 for equipment and $5,000 for buildings.

Flint issued ten shares of $100 par common stock as a stock dividend. The market value of the stock at the date of issue was $150 per share.

A volcano destroyed a building with a cost of $350,000 and accumulated depreciation of $200,000 (an extraordinary event). Insurance proceeds for the building were $100,000.

Flint's net income for the year was $900.

Required

Complete the worksheet, using the information given.

2. The information below was taken from the records of the Walker Company for the year ended December 31, 2004.

Acquisition of building	$ 200,000
Acquisition of land	30,000
Bond payable premium amortization	3,000
Cash balance, January 1, 2004	38,000
Cash balance, December 31, 2004	113,000
Collections from customers	627,000
Common stock issued to convert bonds	50,000
Depreciation expense	25,000
Dividends declared	25,000
Extraordinary loss on building destroyed by earthquake	30,000
Gain on sale of land	15,000
Income taxes paid	55,000
Increase in income taxes payable	4,000
Increase in inventories	15,000
Decrease in prepaid expenses	4,000
Insurance proceeds from building destroyed by earthquake	115,000
Interest received on short-term investments	5,000
Miscellaneous operating expenses paid	1,500
Net income	300,000
Patent amortization expense	10,000
Payments to employees	41,000
Payments to suppliers	194,500
Payment to retire bonds	250,000
Sale of land	100,000
Sales	2,500,000

<u>Required</u>

(a) Prepare a statement of cash flows for the Walker Company, using the indirect method to present cash flows from operating activities.

(b) Prepare the cash flows from operating activities section of the statement of cash flows, using the direct method.

(c) Compute the cash flow from operations to sales ratio and the profit margin ratio for 2004.

3. The beginning balance sheet and the statement of cash flows for the Whitman Company are shown below.

WHITMAN COMPANY
Balance Sheet
January 1, 2004

Cash		$ 10,050
Accounts receivable		22,000
Land		52,000
Building	$276,000	
Less: Accumulated depreciation	(18,400)	257,600
Total assets		$341,650
Accounts payable		$ 12,200
Notes payable		100,000
Salaries payable		2,800
Common stock, $10 par		125,000
Retained earnings		101,650
Total liabilities and stockholders' equity		$341,650

WHITMAN COMPANY
Statement of Cash Flows
For Year Ended December 31, 2004

Net Cash Flow From Operating Activities		
Net income		$ 60,200
Adjustments for differences between income flows and cash flows from operating activities:		
Add: Depreciation expense		9,200
Increase in accounts payable		2,400
Decrease in accounts receivable		4,000
Less: Decrease in salaries payable		(1,000)
Net cash provided by operating activities		$ 74,800
Cash Flows From Investing Activities		
Payment for purchase of land	$(20,000)	
Payment for purchase of equipment	(38,000)	
Net cash used for investing activities		(58,000)
Cash Flows From Financing Activities		
Proceeds from issuance of common stock (1,000 shares)	$ 10,000	
Payment of note	(7,200)	
Payment of dividends	(2,000)	
Net cash provided by financing activities		800
Net Increase in Cash		$ 17,600
Cash, January 1, 2004		10,050
Cash, December 31, 2004		$ 27,650

Required

Prepare the Whitman Company's balance sheet as of December 31, 2004.

ANSWERS TO POST TEST

Part A

1. F	6. T	11. T	16. T
2. T	7. T	12. F	17. T
3. F	8. T	13. T	18. F
4. F	9. T	14. F	19. F
5. F	10. F	15. F	20. T
			21. F

Part B

1. c	4. b	7. a	9. d
2. d	5. d	8. c	10. c
3. b	6. a		

Part C

1.

FLINT COMPANY
Worksheet for Statement of Cash Flows
For Year Ended December 31, 2004

	Increase (Decrease)	Worksheet Entries Debit	Worksheet Entries Credit
Debits			
Cash	$ 114,000	(k)114,000	
Noncash Accounts			
Accounts receivable	$ 6,000	(c) 6,000	
Inventory	3,200	(e) 3,200	
Land	40,000	(i) 40,000	
Buildings	(350,000)		(m) 350,000
Equipment	33,000	(g) 48,000	(d) 15,000
Totals	$(153,800)		
Credits			
Accumulated depreciation: equipment	$ 2,000	(d) 4,000	(b) 6,000
Accumulated depreciation: buildings	(195,000)	(m)200,000	(b) 5,000
Accounts payable	1,500		(l) 1,500
Salaries payable	800		(f) 800
Common stock, $100 par	31,000		(n) 1,000 (j) 30,000
Additional paid-in capital	10,500		(j) 10,000 (n) 500
Retained earnings	(4,600)	(h) 4,000 (n) 1,500	(a) 900
Totals	$(153,800)	420,700	420,700
Net Cash Flow From Operating Activities			
Net income		(a) 900	
Add: Depreciation expense		(b) 11,000	
Increase in salaries payable		(f) 800	
Increase in accounts payable		(l) 1,500	
Extraordinary loss		(m) 50,000	
Less: Increase in accounts receivable			(c) 6,000
Gain on sale of equipment			(d) 6,000
Increase in inventory			(e) 3,200
Cash Flows From Investing Activities			
Proceeds from sale of equipment		(d) 17,000	
Payment for purchase of equipment			(g) 48,000
Proceeds from building destroyed by volcano		(m)100,000	
Cash Flows From Financing Activities			
Payment of dividends			(h) 4,000
Investing and Financing Activities Not Affecting Cash			
Acquisition of land by issuance of common stock			(i) 40,000
Issuance of common stock for land		(j) 40,000	
Net Increase in Cash			(k)114,000
Totals		221,200	221,200

2. (a)

WALKER COMPANY
Statement of Cash Flows
For Year Ended December 31, 2004

Net Cash Flow From Operating Activities		
Net income	$ 300,000	
Adjustments for differences between income flows and cash flows from operating activities:		
Add: Depreciation expense	25,000	
Increase in income taxes payable	4,000	
Extraordinary loss from earthquake	30,000	
Patent amortization expense	10,000	
Decrease in prepaid expenses	4,000	
Less: Increase in inventories	(15,000)	
Gain on sale of land	(15,000)	
Bond premium amortization	(3,000)	
Net cash provided by operating activities		$ 340,000
Cash Flows From Investing Activities		
Payment for purchase of building	$(200,000)	
Payment for purchase of land	(30,000)	
Proceeds from building destroyed by earthquake	115,000	
Proceeds from sale of land	100,000	
Net cash used for investing activities		(15,000)
Cash Flows From Financing Activities		
Payment to retire bonds	$(250,000)	
Net cash used for financing activities		(250,000)
Net Increase in Cash (see Schedule 1)		$ 75,000
Cash, January 1, 2004		38,000
Cash, December 31, 2004		$ 113,000
Schedule 1: Investing and Financing Activities Not Affecting Cash		
Financing Activities		
Conversion of bonds to common stock	$ (50,000)	
Issuance of common stock to convert bonds	50,000	

2. (b)

Cash Flows From Operating Activities		
Cash Inflows:		
Collections from customers	$ 627,000	
Interest collected	5,000	
Cash inflows from operating activities		$ 632,000
Cash Outflows:		
Payments to suppliers	$(194,500)	
Payments to employees	(41,000)	
Other operating payments	(1,500)	
Payments of income taxes	(55,000)	
Cash outflows from operating activities		(292,000)
Net cash provided by operating activities		$ 340,000

2. (c) $\frac{\text{Cash Flow from Operations}}{\text{Sales}} = \frac{\$\ 340,000}{\$2,500,000} = 13.6\%$

$\frac{\text{Net Income}}{\text{Sales}} = \frac{\$\ 300,000}{\$2,500,000} = 12\%$

3.

WHITMAN COMPANY
Balance Sheet
December 31, 2004

Cash		$ 27,650
Accounts receivable		18,000
Land		72,000
Building	$276,000	
Less: Accumulated depreciation	(27,600)	248,400
Equipment		38,000
Total assets		$404,050
Accounts payable		$ 14,600
Salaries payable		1,800
Notes payable		92,800
Common stock, $10 par		135,000
Retained earnings		159,850
Total liabilities and stockholders' equity		$404,050

22

ACCOUNTING CHANGES AND ERRORS

CHAPTER OBJECTIVES

After careful study of this chapter, you will be able to:

1. Identify the types of accounting changes.
2. Explain the methods of disclosing an accounting change.
3. Account for a change in accounting principle using the cumulative effect method.
4. Account for a change in accounting principle using a prior period restatement.
5. Account for a change in estimate.
6. Explain the conceptual issues regarding a change in accounting principle and a change in estimate.
7. Identify a change in a reporting entity.
8. Account for a correction of an error.
9. Summarize the methods for making accounting changes and correcting errors.

SYNOPSIS

Types of Accounting Changes and Methods of Disclosure

1. APB Opinion No. 20 established the generally accepted accounting principles for the following changes:

   (a) Change in Accounting Principle - A change from one generally accepted accounting principle to another one that is preferable.

   (b) Change in Accounting Estimate - A change in a prior estimate resulting from additional information, more experience, or a new event.

   (c) Change in Reporting Entity - A change in the entity being reported, such as when the subsidiaries included in the consolidated financial statements change.

   In addition to these changes, the *Opinion* also established the accounting principles for the corrections of errors.

2. The three possible methods for a company to disclose an accounting change (or error) in its financial statements include:

   (a) Restate the financial statements of prior years [retroactive (prior period) adjustment].

   (b) Include the cumulative effect of the change in the income of the current year (cumulative effect method).

   (c) Adjust for the change prospectively (prospective adjustment).

   Exhibit 22-7 and Exhibit 22-8 in the text summarize the methods to be used and the impact on the financial statements.

Accounting for a Change in Accounting Principle

3. A change in accounting principle may be a voluntary change from one generally accepted principle to another or a mandatory change because FASB had adopted a new principle. A change in accounting principle also includes a change in the procedures used to apply the accounting principles. Common changes in accounting principles include changes in inventory cost flow assumptions, depreciation methods, or revenue recognition methods. Once a company adopts an accounting principle, the principle should not be changed unless a preferable principle is adopted. The justification for the change should be clearly disclosed in the notes to the company's financial statements.

4. As a general rule, a company accounts for a change in accounting principle by the cumulative effect method. The cumulative effect of changing to the new accounting principle (net of income taxes) on the amount of retained earnings at the beginning of the period in which the change is made is included in the company's net income of the period of change. This direct effect, the amount by which the prior years' income is increased or decreased specifically as a result of the change in accounting principle, is disclosed on the company's income statement, net of the related income taxes, in a special category between extraordinary items and net income.

5. The company then uses the new accounting principle in computing its income for the current period. The effect of adopting the new principle on income before extraordinary items and net income (including per share amounts) of the current period is disclosed in the notes to the company's financial statements. However, the company presents its financial statements of prior periods, included for comparative purposes, as previously reported.

6. Pro forma disclosures of income before extraordinary items and net income (including earnings per share amounts) are shown on the face of the company's income statement (below earnings per share) for all periods presented as if the new principle had been used in the prior periods. The pro forma amounts include the combined effect of both the direct effect and the indirect effect of the change. The indirect effect is the amount by which the company's income of prior years is affected due to the impact of the change on other elements which depend on income for their calculation, such as bonus arrangements and profit sharing.

7. The cumulative effect method is consistent with the all-inclusive income concept. It has been criticized, however, for its violation of the consistency principle because the current financial statements and prior period statements reported for comparative purposes are prepared using different accounting principles.

8. The following example illustrates the application of a change in accounting principle:

Situation: A company purchased a $40,000 asset on January 1, 2003. It used straight-line depreciation (no residual value), with a 4-year life. On January 1, 2005, the company changed to the sum-of-the-years'-digits (SYD) method. The company had income after taxes (30% tax rate) of $70,000 for 2004 and $50,000 for 2005 (after switching to the SYD depreciation method). There were 10,000 shares of common stock outstanding for the entire period.

The following schedule and partial income statement show how a company should report these items on comparative its income statements.

Computation of Cumulative Effect:

	Straight-Line Depreciation	SYD Depreciation	Difference	Difference Net of Tax
2003	$10,000	$16,000	$6,000	$4,200
2004	10,000	12,000	2,000	1,400
Total on 1/1/05	$20,000	$28,000	$8,000	$5,600
2005	$10,000	$ 8,000	($2,000)	($1,400)

Partial Comparative Income Statements

	2005	2004
Income before cumulative effect of change in accounting principle	$50,000	$70,000
Cumulative effect on prior years of changing to a different depreciation method (net of $2,400 income taxes)	(5,600)	-0-
Net Income	$44,400	$70,000
Earnings per share:		
Income before cumulative effect of change in accounting principle	$ 5.00	$ 7.00
Cumulative effect on prior years of changing to a different depreciation method	(0.56)	-0-
Earnings per share	$ 4.44	$ 7.00
Pro forma amounts assuming the new depreciation method is applied retroactively:		
Net Income	$50,000	$68,600
Earnings per share	$ 5.00	6.86

Computational Note:

The pro forma income in 2005 is $50,000 because the company adopted the new method at the beginning of 2005. A note would be included in its financial statements justifying the change and identifying the $1,400 increase (net of taxes) in 2005 net income due to the difference in depreciation. The only pro forma difference would be in the 2004 income statement. In 2004, the income would be reduced by the $1,400 difference (net of taxes) between 2004 straight-line and SYD depreciation ($70,000 - $1,400 = $68,600).

9. In addition to the financial statement disclosures for a change in accounting principle, a journal entry is required to adjust the company's accounts. The company would make following journal entry at the beginning of 2005 based on the facts presented in the above example:

Loss on Cumulative Effect of a Change in Depreciation Method	5,600	
Deferred Tax Liability	2,400	
Accumulated Depreciation		8,000

Since it is assumed that the company used the Modified Accelerated Cost Recovery System (MACRS) depreciation method for income taxes in prior years creating a deferred tax liability, the use of the sum-of-the-years'-digits method in the financial statements has reduced the temporary difference. Therefore a debit to the deferred tax liability (30% x $8,000) is necessary, as discussed in Chapter 18.

10. APB Opinion No. 20 identifies the following exceptions to the use of the cumulative effect method of accounting for a change from one generally accepted accounting principle to another: (a) Adoption of a new accounting principle to account for future events while continuing to use another principle for past events requires prospective adjustment. A company discloses the nature of the change, its effect on income before extraordinary items and net income of the period of the change, and earnings per share amounts in the notes to its financial statements. (b) If the cumulative effect is not determinable due to a lack of information, a company discloses the effect of the change on the results of operations of the period of change, earnings per share amounts, and an explanation of the situation in the note to the financial statements. (c) The financial statements may also be retroactively restated when a company makes an initial public distribution of stock to the general public. The treatment of the prior period restatement is illustrated in the discussion under error corrections. (d) There are five specific changes in accounting principles that require a company to make a retroactive (prior period) restatement: (1) a change from the LIFO inventory cost flow method to another method; (2) a change in the method of accounting for long-term construction-type contracts; (3) a change to or from the "full cost" method of accounting that is used in the extractive industries; (4) a change from retirement-replacement-betterment accounting to depreciation accounting, for railroad track structures; and, (5) a change from the fair value method to the equity method for investments in common stock. (e) When new accounting standards are issued, the FASB determines the transition method to be used. Retroactive adjustment is usually required when a FASB Statement requires mandatory adoption of a new accounting principle.

11. If a company makes a change in accounting principle in the first interim period, it includes the cumulative effect on beginning retained earnings in its net income of the first interim period. If a company makes a change in accounting principle in a period other than the first interim period, it restates the prior interim periods of the current fiscal year, by applying the newly adopted accounting principle to those prechange interim periods. The company then includes the cumulative effect of the change in the net income of the first interim period regardless of the interim period in which it makes the change.

Accounting for a Change in an Estimate

12. A change in accounting estimate normally results from the development of new information that was not reasonably available when the company first made the estimate. The accounting process requires that well-informed estimates be made for bad debts, useful life of assets, warranty provisions, residual values, and similar items. Material changes in estimates are given prospective accounting treatment. That is, the company adjusts the restated revenue or expense items on the current (and future) income statement to reflect the new estimate and makes corresponding adjustments in its balance sheet. Prior years' financial statements are not adjusted for changes in accounting estimates. The prospective treatment reduces comparability because results reported in the years before the change are based on different estimates than the years after the change.

13. The following example illustrates application of the prospective treatment:

Situation: A company is depreciating a $50,000 asset with a 10-year life by the straight-line method (no residual value). At the beginning of the sixth year, the company determines that the asset life should be revised to a total of 15 years with no residual value at the end of its life.

Financial Reporting for a Change in Estimate:

No formal journal entry is needed to report a change in estimate. In the above example, the company would determine the revised depreciation expense for the current and future years as follows:

Original cost	$50,000
Accumulated depreciation (Years 1-5)	(25,000)
Book value at time of change	$25,000
Remaining life (15 total - 5 previous)	÷ 10 years
Revised annual depreciation expense	$ 2,500

In addition to including the revised annual depreciation expense in its financial statements of the current year, the company would disclose the effect of the change on income and related earnings per share amounts of the current period in a note to its financial statements.

Accounting for a Change in a Reporting Entity

14. The third type of accounting change is a change in accounting entity which occurs when: (a) a company presents consolidated or combined statements in place of financial statements for individual companies, (b) there is a change in the specific subsidiaries that make up the group of companies, and (c) the companies included in combined statements change.

15. A company discloses a change in reporting entity by retroactively restating the financial statements so that all financial statements are presented for the same entity. This approach improves consistency.

Accounting for a Correction of an Error

16. Errors include mathematical mistakes, mistakes in the application of accounting principles, oversights, or intentional misstatements of accounting records. FASB Statement No. 16 requires that a company account for the correction of material error made in previous periods as a prior period adjustment (retroactive restatement). The correction of an error (net of the related income tax effects) is reflected as an adjustment to the beginning balance of a company's retained earnings for each year of the comparative retained earnings statements affected.

17. The retroactive technique is the most difficult to apply because it requires that a company restate all its prior years' financial statements to reflect the change. Essentially, a company restates (corrects) all balance sheet, income statement, or statement of cash flow items in its published statements. The data in its historical summaries are also restated to give appropriate effect for the change. The retroactive method has a theoretical advantage because it facilitates comparison of accounting data for the same company over a series of years. However, the use of prior period restatement may reduce confidence in the accounting profession because of the apparent lack of consistency. This method is also not consistent with the all-inclusive income concept because adjustments are made directly to retained earnings and by-pass inclusion on the income statement.

18. The following example illustrates the special presentation that is required in a company's statement of retained earnings to disclose the adjustment for the cumulative effect (net of tax) of an error on the beginning retained earnings for each year in comparative financial statements:

Situation: A company did not record $10,000 depreciation expense for each of 2002, 2003, and 2004. It discovered the error at the beginning of 2005. Assume that the company's retained earnings on 1/1/2004 was $100,000 and it had reported net income of $50,000 for 2004. The net income for 2005 was properly computed at $35,000. No dividends were reported in 2004 or 2005. The company is subject to a 30% tax rate.

Comparative Statements of Retained Earnings
For the Years Ended December 31, 2004 and 2005

	2005	2004
Retained earnings as previously reported, January 1	$150,000	$100,000
Deduct retroactive adjustment for prior-year error in depreciation (net of tax)	(21,000)(b)	(14,000)(a)
Retained earnings as adjusted, January 1	$129,000	$ 86,000
Net income	35,000	43,000 (c)
Retained earnings, December 31	$164,000	$129,000

Computations:

Cumulative effect (net of income tax) on beginning retained earnings:

(a) Beginning of 2004: 2 x [$10,000 - (0.30 x $10,000)] = ($14,000)
(b) Beginning of 2005: 3 x [$10,000 - (0.30 x $10,000)] = ($21,000)
(c) Effect on 2004 income (net of taxes):
$50,000 - [$10,000 - (0.30 x $10,000)] = $43,000

In addition to the adjustment of beginning retained earnings on the company's retained earnings statements, its financial statements for 2004 included in the 2005 annual report would be restated (corrected). That is, the company would correct depreciation expense, income taxes, and the related subtotals on its 2004 income statement. It would correct accumulated depreciation, the tax liability, and retained earnings on its ending 2004 balance sheet. The effect of the change on income before extraordinary items and net income (including per share amounts) for each year is disclosed in the notes to its financial statements.

19. Errors may affect only a company's income statement or only its balance sheet, or both financial statements. Errors affecting only the classification of either income statement or balance sheet items can be corrected without a journal entry because the particular financial statement item only needs to be reclassified. Errors affecting both the income statement and the balance sheet can be classified as counterbalancing or noncounterbalancing. Counterbalancing errors are automatically corrected in the next accounting period as a natural part of the accounting process. Many of the counter-balancing errors are the result of year-end adjustment mistakes. The following table summarizes the effects of common counterbalancing errors.

Type of Adjustment Error	Net Income Current Year	Net Income Next Year
Ending inventory overstated	over	under
Ending inventory understated	under	over
Failure to accrue expense at year end	over	under
Overstatement of accrued expense at year end	under	over
Failure to accrue earned revenue at year end	under	over
Overstatement of accrued revenue at year end	over	under
Failure to expense prepaid expense at year end	over	under
Understatement of year-end prepaid expense	under	over
Understatement of year-end liability for revenue received in advance	over	under
Overstatement of year-end liability for revenue received in advance	under	over

20. The errors listed above will affect a company's net income for both the current and subsequent years. All related balance sheet accounts will be incorrect at the end of the year in which the error was made; however, the balance sheet accounts at the end of the second year will be correct because the errors have automatically counterbalanced. A correcting journal entry is necessary for any counterbalancing error which is detected before it has counterbalanced.

21. Noncounterbalancing errors are those that will not be automatically offset in the next accounting period. A good example of a noncounter-balancing error is a failure by a company to depreciate fixed assets or amortize intangible assets with a finite life. The cumulative effect of the failure to detect a depreciation or amortization error will not be corrected until the end of the asset life or until the asset is sold. A correcting journal entry is necessary for a noncounterbalancing error.

22. International Accounting Standards allow considerable flexibility in accounting for changes. While accounting for a change in estimate is the same as U.S. standards, a change in accounting principle may be accounted for as prior period restatement, cumulative effect adjustment, or in the current and future periods.

SELF-EVALUATION EXERCISES

Supply the words or amounts necessary to complete each of the following items.

Types of Accounting Changes

TA-1. A change in accounting estimate results from ____________

______________, ______ _____________, or a _____ __________.

TA-2. When subsidiaries included in the consolidated financial statements change, this is treated as a change in ____________ __________.

TA-3. The three possible methods of disclosing an accounting change or error are _____________ ______________, _____________

_________ _________, and ____________ ______________.

Accounting for a Change in Accounting Principle

CAP-1. A change in accounting principle includes the change from one accepted

______________ _____________ ____________ principle to another generally

accounting principle and a change in the _________ used to _____________ an accounting principle.

CAP-2. A company generally accounts for a change in accounting principle by

the ________________ ________________ method.

CAP-3. When using the cumulative effect method, net income of the period of the change should include the cumulative effect of changing to a new accounting principle

(net of ____________ ______________) on the amount of ______________

__________________ at the _________________ of the period in which the change is made.

CAP-4. The use of the cumulative effect adjustment is consistent with the

_______-_____________ income concept; however, the major objection to this

method is that it violates the ___________ principle.

CAP-5. In the year of change of an accounting principle, readers of financial statements can judge the impact of the change in accounting principle on the income

statement by examining the _______ __________ information on the face of the statement.

CAP-6. The Always Change Diaper Service Company decided to change from the straight-line to the double-declining-balance (DDB) depreciation method. The asset was purchased on January 1, 2003 for $40,000 and had an estimated useful life of 5 years and no residual value. The company decided to change the method of depreciation at the beginning of 2005. Assume a tax rate of 30% for all years. The company's net income for 2004 was $100,000 and its net income for 2005 would also have been $100,000 if the straight-line method of depreciation was used. Complete the following schedule:

Year	"Old" Straight-Line Depreciation	"New" DDB Depreciation	Depreciation Difference	Net of Tax Difference
2003	$8,000	$16,000	$8,000	$5,600
2004	________	________	________	________
Total	$________	$________	$________	$________
2005	________	________	________	________

CAP-7. From the data presented in question CAP-6, prepare the following section of the income statement that would properly report the change in accounting principle. Ignore earnings per share and pro forma disclosures.

	2005	2004
Income before cumulative effect of change in accounting principle		
Cumulative effect on prior years of changing to a different depreciation method (net of $________ income taxes)	________	________
Net income	________	________

CAP-8. Based on the data presented in question CAP-6, compute the net income assuming, instead, that the double-declining-balance method of depreciation had been applied retroactively:

	2005	2004
Net income	______	______

CAP-9. If a change in accounting principle is made in the third interim period, the prior interim periods of the current fiscal year are restated and the cumulative effect of the change on retained earnings at the beginning of the ________ is included in the net income of the ________ interim period.

CAP-10. The five changes in accounting principle that are required by APB Opinion No. 20 requires a company to treat as retroactive adjustments of prior-years' financial statements are:

(1) ____

(2) ____

(3) ____

(4) ____

(5) ____

Accounting for a Change in an Estimate

CE-1. APB Opinion No. 20 concluded that a company should treat a change in accounting estimate ______________, and does not require a restatement of prior periods' financial statements.

CE-2. The St. Louis Company originally estimated that the life of special equipment would be 20 years. At the beginning of the sixth year, the company revised the asset life downward to a total life of 15 years. The asset had cost $40,000 and there is not expected to be any residual value with either estimate. The company should show the depreciation expense (under the straight-line method) on the income statement for year 5 of $_________, for year 6 is $_________, and for year 7 of $_________.

CE-3. A company should report a change in accounting estimate that is related in whole or in part to a change in accounting principle as a change in ______________.

Accounting for a Change in a Reporting Entity

RE-1. Accounting for a change in a reporting entity requires that a company's financial statements be ______________ ____________.

RE-2. The method used to disclose a change in a reporting entity improves ______________.

Accounting for a Correction of an Error

EC-1.T he major argument in favor of prior period (retroactive) restatement is that all financial statements would be ____________.

EC-2. The two major disadvantages of the prior period restatement method are that __________ in the accounting profession is reduced and this method is not consistent with the ______-____________ income concept.

EC-3. When it is acceptable to use the retroactive restatement method, the ____________ effect (net of tax) on ____________ retained earnings is shown on the ____________ ____________ statement. Pro forma computations _______ (are/are not) required to be disclosed on the income statement.

EC-4. The Springfield Company overstated its December 31, 2004 inventory by $40,000. During 2005, it discovered the error after it had issued the 2004 financial statements. Assume the 2004 retained earnings statement contained the following disclosures before the correction:

	2004
Retained earnings, January 1	$120,000
Net income	80,000
Retained earnings, December 31	$200,000

Prepare the company's retained earnings statement disclosure for 2004 and 2005 assuming the Springfield Company's <u>correct</u> net income for 2005 was $70,000. The income tax rate is 30% for all years.

EC-5. A company should account for a correction of an error as a ________ ___________ adjustment, and therefore it should show the cumulative effect (net of tax) as an adjustment of beginning ___________ _______________.

EC-6. Errors that are automatically corrected over two accounting periods are called ________________ errors and will result in misstatement of earnings for _______ period(s).

EC-7. For each of the following errors indicate the effect (over, under, or no effect) on the current year's and next year's net income:

Description of Error	Net Income 2004	Net Income 2005
(a) 12/31/04 inventory overstated		
(b) 12/31/04 inventory understated		
(c) Prepaid insurance 12/31/05 overstated		
(d) Depreciation expense (straight-line) for 2004 understated		
(e) Understatement of 12/31/04 unearned revenue		
(f) Failure to accrue 12/31/04 revenue		
(g) Understatement of 12/31/04 prepaid expense		

ANSWERS TO SELF-EVALUATION EXERCISES

TA-1. additional information, more experience, new event; TA-2. reporting entity; TA-3. retroactive adjustment, cumulative effect method, prospective adjustment; CAP-1. generally accepted accounting, procedures, apply; CAP-2. cumulative effect; CAP-3. income taxes, retained earnings, beginning; CAP-4. all-inclusive, consistency; CAP-5. pro forma;

CAP.6.

Year	"Old" Straight-Line Depreciation	"New" DDB Depreciation	Depreciation Difference	Net of Tax Difference
2003	$ 8,000	$16,000	$8,000	$5,600
2004	8,000	9,600	1,600	1,120
Total	$16,000	$25,600	$9,600	$6,720
2005	$ 8,000	$ 5,760	($2,240)	($1,568)

CAP-7.

	2005	2004
Income before cumulative effect of change in accounting principle	$101,568	$100,000
Cumulative effect on prior years of of changing to a different depreciation method (net of $2,880 income taxes)	(6,720)	-0-
Net income	$ 94,848	$100,000

CAP-8.

	2005	2004
Net Income (with straight-line depreciation)	$100,000	$100,000
Net of tax (difference in depreciation)	1,568	(1,120)
Net Income (with DDB depreciation)	$101,568	$ 98,880

CAP-9. year, first; CAP-10. (1) change from LIFO to another inventory method; (2) a change in the method of accounting for long-term construction contracts; (3) a change to or from the "full cost" method in the extractive industries; (4) a change from retirement-replacement-betterment accounting to depreciation accounting for railroad track structures; and (5) a change from the fair value method to the equity method for investments in common stock; CE-1. prospectively;

CE-2. year 5 $2,000 ($40,000 ÷ 20 years)
year 6 $3,000 ($40,000 - $10,000)
year 7 $3,000 10 years

CE-3. estimate; RE-1. retroactively restated; RE-2. consistency; EC-1. comparable; EC-2. confidence, all-inclusive; EC-3. cumulative, beginning, retained earnings, are not;

EC-4.

	2004	2005
Retained earnings as previously reported, January 1	$120,000	$200,000
Less: Prior-period restatement for inventory error (net of $12,000 income taxes)		(28,000)
Adjusted retained earnings, January 1	$120,000	$172,000
Net income ($80,000 - $28,000, for 2004)	52,000	70,000
Retained earnings, December 31	$172,000	$242,000

EC-5. prior period, retained earnings; EC-6. counterbalancing, two;

EC-7.

	2004	2005
(a)	over	under
(b)	under	over
(c)	no effect	over
(d)	over	no effect
(e)	over	under
(f)	under	over
(g)	under	over

POST TEST

Part A Circle T if the statement is true and F if it is false.

T F 1. The initial adoption by a company of an accounting principle for an event or transaction occurring for the first time is not considered a change in accounting principle.

T F 2. For a change in accounting principle, a company reports the cumulative effect (net of income tax) on its income statement between "extraordinary items" and "net income."

T F 3. The mandatory adoption of a new accounting principle as a result of an <u>FASB Statement</u> always requires a prior-period adjustment.

T F 4. Counterbalancing errors never require correction by a journal entry because they correct themselves within 2 years.

T F 5. Pro forma financial statement presentations are those that a company would have reported if it had used the newly adopted principle in past periods.

T F 6. A change from the percentage-of-completion to the completed-contract method of accounting for long-term contracts is a change in accounting principle that a company should reflect currently in its income statement for the period of change.

T F 7. A change in accounting entity requires prospective treatment in the financial statements.

T F 8. A company treats a change from an unacceptable accounting principle to a generally accepted accounting principle as a change in accounting principle.

T F 9. A change <u>from</u> the LIFO to the FIFO method of inventory valuation requires cumulative treatment in the accounting records of the current year.

T F 10. A change in the estimated service life for plant assets requires prospective treatment in the accounting records of the current and future years.

T F 11. If a company overstates ending inventory in the current period, it will understate income in the following period.

T F 12. If a company expenses immediately a cost that should be capitalized and depreciated, the error is noncounterbalancing.

T F 13. A change in an estimate that was not made in good faith is treated prospectively.

T F 14. The prior-period adjustment method is consistent with the all-inclusive income concept.

T F 15. Whenever it is impossible to determine whether a change is a change in accounting principle or a change in estimate, the change should be considered a change in estimate.

T F 16. A change from the fair value method to the equity method for investments in common stock requires prospective adjustment.

<u>Part B</u> Select the one <u>best</u> answer, and place its letter in the space provided.

_____ 1. An accounting change from straight-line to accelerated depreciation is an example of: (a) a change in accounting principle; (b) a change in accounting estimate; (c) a change in a reporting entity; (d) an error correction.

_____ 2. A change in the estimated life of a depreciable asset based on newly available information is an example of: (a) a change in accounting principle; (b) a change in accounting estimate; (c) a change in a reporting entity; (d) an error correction.

_____ 3. Most changes in an accounting principle are accounted for: (a) by the cumulative effect method; (b) prospectively; (c) by a prior period restatement; (d) any of these, as long as the same method is used for all similar changes.

_____ 4. Prior-period restatement is required for all of the following accounting changes except: (a) a change from the LIFO inventory costing method to another method; (b) a change to the LIFO inventory costing method; (c) a change in the method of accounting for long-term construction-type contracts; (d) a change to or from the "full cost" method of accounting used in extractive industries.

_____ 5. Which of the following is not an example of an error correction? (a) a change from an unacceptable accounting principle to one that is generally accepted; (b) a change in an estimate when the original estimate was not made in good faith; (c) mathematical miscalculations; (d) a change in an estimate based on newly available information.

_____ 6. Which one of the following changes requires a company to disclose pro forma data on the face of its income statement? (a) the auditor uncovered a material error in the computation of last year's depreciation expense; (b) the company changed from the direct-write-off method to the allowance method of accounting for bad debts after the controller learned that the direct-write-off method was not acceptable under generally accepted accounting principles; (c) the company changed from FIFO to average cost because the average cost method provides better matching of revenue and expense; (d) the company changed the estimated life of a machine from 15 to 20 years.

_____ 7. The Dallas Company discovered the following errors affecting its financial statements issued on December 31, 2005: (1) depreciation expense of $4,000 was understated for 2005; (2) merchandise costing $8,000 was in transit (FOB shipping point) at December 31, 2005; the purchase was not recorded and the inventory was not included in the physical inventory amount; (3) prepaid expenses of $1,000 were omitted at December 31, 2005 and the cash payment during the period was recorded as an expense; and (4) the company failed to accrue $2,000 interest revenue on December 31, 2004. Assuming that no correcting entries were made, income before income taxes for 2005 was: (a) $1,000 overstated; (b) $4,000 overstated; (c) $3,000 understated; (d) $5,000 overstated; (e) none of these.

_____ 8. In 2003, Jones Company failed to include the depreciation expense for equipment acquired during the last quarter of the fiscal year. Jones discovered the error in 2005 just after publication of its 2004 financial statements. This error is (a) a counterbalancing error which corrected itself at the end of 2004 (b) a noncounterbalancing error which will never be corrected and therefore requires a correcting journal entry in 2005; (c) a noncounterbalancing error which will be corrected when the asset is sold or at the end of its useful life and therefore requires a correcting journal entry in 2005; (d) a counterbalancing error which requires a correcting journal entry in 2005.

_____ 9. Which of the following statements about International Accounting Standards in accounting for changes and errors is not true? (a) material changes in estimate are accounted for by prospective adjustment; (b) accounting for a change in estimate is consistent with U.S. GAAP; (c) a change in accounting principle may be accounted for as a prior period restatement; (d) accounting for a change in accounting principle is consistent with U.S. GAAP.

Part C Solve each of the following short problems.

1. The Al Right Company made the following errors that were discovered by the auditors in connection with preparation of the December 31, 2005 income statement. It reported net income of $70,000 for 2004 and $100,000 for 2005. Ignore income taxes.

   (1) On January 1, 2004, the company recorded the $30,000 acquisition cost of equipment with a 10-year life as maintenance expense. Straight-line depreciation is usually used and no residual value is expected at the end of the useful life.

   (2) On January 1, 2004, Al Right Company collected $10,000 for 2 years rental income in advance and failed to set up an unearned revenue account at year-end. It credited all the rent to Rent Revenue when received.

   (3) A 3-year insurance policy costing $12,000 was charged to expense when paid in advance on January 1, 2004.

   (4) Ending inventory was overstated by $7,000 on December 31, 2004 and understated by $3,000 on December 31, 2005 due to computational errors.

   (5) Accrued wages expense was omitted in the amount of $7,000 on December 31, 2004 and $8,000 on December 31, 2005.

   Prepare a schedule to show the computation of the correct income for 2004 and 2005 in the following format:

	2005	2004
Net income as reported	$100,000	$70,000
Net income as corrected		

2. The Akron Company made the following 2 changes during 2005. The income tax rate is 30% for 2004 and 2005.

(1) The auditors advised the company that generally accepted accounting principles require the company to accrue warranty expense for an estimated amount in the period of sale. The company has been expensing the warranty amount when outlays of cash or other assets were made to honor the warranty. It deducts warranty costs for income tax reporting when paid.

	Estimated Warranty Expense	Actual Outlays for Warranties
2003	$ 50,000	$ 30,000
2004	70,000	60,000
2005	60,000	40,000
	$180,000	$130,000

(2) During 2004 a $5,000 land improvement was erroneously charged to expense. An amended tax return was filed for 2004.

(a) Prepare the correcting entries at the end of 2005 to restate the company's prior years' income and its current year's income for the effect of the change in warranty method.

(b) Prepare the entry to correct the error in recording the land improvement.

3. The Washington Company decided to change from the straight-line depreciation method to double-declining balance for all of its assets at the beginning of 2005. The following data are available:

Year	Reported Net Income	Excess of Double-Declining Balance over Straight-Line Depreciation
Prior to 2003	$300,000	$60,000
2003	500,000	80,000
2004	200,000	90,000
2005	400,000	70,000

The tax rate has been 30% and the company has used the MACRS depreciation method for income taxes. It does not plan to change the method used for tax depreciation.

Required:

(a) Compute the cumulative effect (net of taxes) of changing to the new depreciation method at the beginning of 2005.

(b) Prepare the journal entry to reflect the change in depreciation method.

ANSWERS TO POST TEST

Part A

1. T	5. T	9. F	13. F
2. T	6. F	10. T	14. F
3. F	7. F	11. T	15. T
4. F	8. F	12. T	16. F

Part B

1. a	4. b	7. d
2. b	5. d	8. c
3. a	6. c	9. d

Part C

1.

	2005	2004
Net income as reported	$100,000	$70,000
Purchase of equipment erroneously recorded as expense on January 1, 2004		30,000
Depreciation on purchase of equipment	(3,000)	(3,000)
Omission of unearned rent December 31, 2004	5,000	(5,000)
Omission of prepaid insurance December 31, 2004	(4,000)	8,000
Overstatement of December 31, 2004 inventory	7,000	(7,000)
Understatement of December 31, 2005 inventory	3,000	
Failure to accrue wages expense on December 31, 2004	7,000	(7,000)
Failure to accrue wages expense on December 31, 2005	(8,000)	
Net income as corrected	$107,000	$86,000

2. (a) (These are error corrections because they are changes from unacceptable accounting principles to generally accepted accounting principles.)

To Correct Beginning Retained Earnings

Retained Earnings [0.70 x ($120,000 - $90,000)]	21,000	
Deferred Tax Asset (0.30 x $30,000)	9,000	
Estimated Liability for Warranties		30,000

To Correct Current-Year Accounts

Warranty Expense	20,000	
Deferred Tax Asset (0.30 x $20,000)	6,000	
Income Tax Expense		6,000
Estimated Liability for Warranties		20,000

(b)

Land Improvement	5,000	
Income Taxes Payable (0.30 x $5,000)		1,500
Retained Earnings		3,500

3. (a)

Cumulative effect of changing to new depreciation method as of 1/1/05	$230,000
Income taxes (0.30)	(69,000)
Cumulative effect (net of taxes)	$161,000

(b)

Loss on Cumulative Effect of Change in Depreciation Method	161,000	
Deferred Tax Liability	69,000	
Accumulated Depreciation		230,000

Appendix C

REVIEW OF THE ACCOUNTING PROCESS

APPENDIX OBJECTIVES

After careful study of this appendix, you will be able to:

1. Understand the components of an accounting system.
2. Know the major steps in the accounting cycle.
3. Prepare journal entries in the general journal.
4. Post to the general ledger and prepare a trial balance.
5. Prepare adjusting entries.
6. Prepare the financial statements.
7. Prepare closing entries.
8. Complete a worksheet.
9. Understand subsidiary ledgers.
10. Use special journals.
11. Convert cash-basis financial statements to accrual-basis.

SYNOPSIS

The Accounting System

1. An accounting system is the means by which a company records and stores the financial and managerial information from its transactions so that it can retrieve and report the information in an accounting statement.

2. A basic accounting model provides a framework for the accounting system and serves as a basis for recording transactions. This model for a corporation, called the residual equity theory model, may be expressed as an equation:

   Assets = Liabilities + Stockholders' Equity

   Assets are the corporation's economic resources. Liabilities are its obligations owed to creditors. Stockholders' equity is the owners' residual interest in the corporate assets.

3. The equation may be expanded to include other components: Contributed capital includes stockholders' investments in shares of stock sold by the corporation. Retained earnings is the lifetime amount of net income reinvested in the corporation rather than distributed to stockholders. Dividends (which are not expenses) are amounts distributed to stockholders as a return on their investment. Revenues are charges to customers for goods and services. Expenses are the costs incurred by the corporation in providing goods and services.

4. In financial accounting, a transaction involves the transfer of something of value between the company and another party. An event is a happening of consequence to the company. An event may be (a) internal, such as the use of equipment in operations, or (b) external, such as a decline in price.

5. Source documents are business documents (such as sales invoices, checks, and freight bills) which provide initial information for recording transactions or events. A company keeps its source documents to verify and substantiate the accounting records.

6. A company uses specific accounts to store the recorded monetary information from transactions and events. Accounts are organized by number in the company's chart of accounts, which is designed to arrange the accounts efficiently and to minimize recording errors. An account may be in different physical forms. It may be located on a disk in a computer system or on paper in a manual system. Under the double-entry system, the total dollar amount of the debits that a company records for each transaction or event must equal the total dollar amount of the credits it records.

7. The balance of an account at a particular time is the difference between the total debits and total credits recorded in that account. Accounts are classified as permanent (real) accounts or temporary (nominal) accounts. Permanent accounts are the asset, liability, and stockholders' equity accounts which carry balances forward from period to period. Temporary accounts are the revenue, expense, and dividend accounts which are used to determine the change in retained earnings during a given accounting period. A company does not carry temporary account balances forward from period to period.

8. A company sometimes uses a contra (negative) account to emphasize a reduction in a related account. For example, Accumulated Depreciation is used as a contra account to Buildings.

9. Financial statements derived from the accounting equation are generally prepared by a company at the end of each accounting period as summary reports of the company's accounting system. The annual set of financial statements and accompanying supporting schedules and notes with other data, distributed to external users, is called the company's annual report. Interim statements may also be prepared for shorter periods (such as three months).

10. The three major statements of a company are the income statement, balance sheet, and statement of cash flows. The income statement summarizes the results of the company's income-producing activities for the accounting period. The balance sheet summarizes the amounts of assets, liabilities, and stockholders' equity of the company on a particular date. The statement of cash flows summarizes the cash receipts and cash payments of the company during the accounting period. The income statement is tied to the balance sheet by a supporting schedule called the statement of retained earnings, which summarizes the amount of a company's net income retained in the business. That is, the income statement, statement of retained earnings, and balance sheet are articulated. The balance sheet also articulates with the statement of cash flows, which reconciles the beginning and ending cash balances.

The Accounting Cycle

11. The accounting cycle is the series of steps completed by a company during each accounting period to record, store, and report the accounting information contained in its transactions. The major steps include: (a) recording daily transactions in a journal, (b) posting the journal entries to the accounts in the ledger, (c) preparing and posting adjusting entries, (d) preparing the financial statements, and (e) preparing and posting closing entries for the revenue, expense, and dividend accounts.

12. A company's transactions and events are initially recorded in a journal or "document of original entry." A company could record all transactions in a single general journal, although many companies also use special journals for particular types of transactions. A general journal includes columns for dates, account titles, account numbers, debits, and credits. A written explanation of each recorded transaction is included below each journal entry.

13. A company using a periodic inventory system takes a physical inventory at the end of the accounting period. Cost of goods sold is then computed by subtracting the ending inventory from cost of goods available for sale (the sum of beginning inventory and purchases). In contrast, a company using a perpetual inventory system continuously updates its inventory records for goods purchased and sold.

14. A <u>general ledger</u> is composed of all of the accounts of a particular company. Physical forms of general ledgers vary. A general ledger might, for example, be written on paper, or stored on a computer disk.

15. Journal entries are transferred to accounts in the general ledger by a process called <u>posting</u>. In posting, the date and debit and credit amounts from each journal entry are transferred to the debit and credit sides of the appropriate accounts, so that the general ledger accounts contain the same information as the journal. After all journal entries for a given accounting period have been posted, the balance in each account is determined, and often a <u>trial balance</u> is prepared. The trial balance lists all of the company's general ledger accounts and their balances. It is used to verify that the total of the debit balances equals the total of the credit balances. If the total debits are not equal to the total credits, an error has been made.

16. A company using <u>accrual</u> accounting records revenues in the period when they are earned and realized (or are realizable) and records (matches) expenses in the period when they are incurred, regardless of when cash is received or paid. Accounts that are not up-to-date at the end of an accounting period must be revised by the preparation and posting of <u>adjusting entries</u>, journal entries which ensure that the company's financial statements include the correct amounts for the current period. Adjusting entries may be classified into three categories: (a) apportionment of prepaid expenses and deferred revenues, (b) recording of accrued expenses and accrued revenues, and (c) recording of estimated items.

17. A <u>prepaid expense</u> (prepaid asset) represents goods or services purchased by a company for its operations, but not fully used as of the end of the period. Examples include prepaid rent, office supplies, and prepaid insurance. The company usually records a prepaid expense initially at cost as an asset. Consequently, an adjusting entry is necessary to match the cost against current revenues by reducing the asset account balance and recording as an expense the portion of the prepaid expense which was used up during the period.

18. <u>Deferred (unearned) revenue</u> represents payments received from a customer prior to the delivery of a product or performance of a service. A company usually records a liability initially for unearned revenue, because the company is obligated to provide future goods and services. When such goods and services have been provided during the accounting period, an adjusting entry is needed to reduce the liability and to recognize revenue earned.

19. Note that a company may instead initially record a prepayment of costs as an expense and an advance receipt of revenues as revenue. Different adjusting entries than those described above would then be needed to arrive at the same ending balances.

20. <u>Accrued expenses</u> are expenses which have been incurred by a company during the accounting period, but have been neither paid nor recorded. Examples of accrued expenses include accrued salaries, interest, and income taxes. An adjusting entry is required to recognize the expense and associated liability, thereby matching the expense with related revenue of the appropriate time period.

21. <u>Accrued revenues</u> are revenues which have been earned by a company during the accounting period, but have been neither received nor recorded. An adjusting entry is necessary to recognize such revenue and the associated receivable.

22. A company also needs adjusting entries to recognize certain accounting <u>estimates</u> at the end of the accounting period. Two examples are estimation of depreciation on assets such as buildings and equipment, and estimation of uncollectible receivables arising

from credit sales. The company systematically and rationally allocates the cost of depreciable assets as an expense to each period when the assets are used. It records depreciation in a contra (negative) asset account which is subtracted from the asset account to determine the book or carrying value of an asset. The company must recognize the bad debt expense from uncollectible accounts in the period of the sale, and must reduce net receivables. Since the identities of defaulting customers are not known in the period of sale, Accounts Receivable is not directly reduced. Instead, the company deducts a contra-asset account, Allowance for Doubtful Accounts, from Accounts Receivable on the balance sheet.

23. After a company records and posts adjusting entries to the general ledger, it recomputes account balances, if necessary. Next, it may prepare an adjusted trial balance. This adjusted trial balance lists all the accounts and their balances after adjustments but before closing. It verifies that the total of the general ledger debit balances still equals the total of the credit balances, after adjustments. The adjusted trial balance checks the accuracy of the accounting process and helps in the preparation of the financial statements. The income statement, statement of retained earnings, and balance sheet are prepared directly from information on the adjusted trial balance.

24. Closing entries are journal entries made by a company at the end of the period, after preparation of the financial statements, to (a) reduce the balances in all temporary accounts (revenue, expense, and dividend accounts) to zero, and (b) update the retained earnings and inventory accounts. Each temporary income statement account is closed, that is, debited or credited for the amount which will result in a zero balance in that account. The total of the credits to these accounts is recorded as a debit to the temporary closing account Income Summary. The total of the debits to these accounts is recorded as a credit to Income Summary. Closing entries are shown in specific order in the text: (1) The temporary income statement accounts with credit balances, including all the revenue accounts and the contra-purchases accounts, are closed first. (2) The amount of the ending inventory, determined by the physical year-end count, is recorded. (3) The temporary income statement accounts with debit balances, including all the expense accounts and the contra-sales accounts are closed. (4) The amount of the beginning inventory is eliminated. A credit balance in Income Summary at this point will appear on the income statement as net income for the period, while a debit balance will appear on the income statement as a net loss. (5) Income Summary is closed to Retained Earnings. (6) The balance in the Dividends Distributed account is closed to Retained Earnings.

25. Many companies prepare a post-closing trial balance after all closing entries have been recorded. This trial balance verifies that the total of the debit balances is equal to the total of the credit balances in the permanent accounts. It checks once again the accuracy of the accounting process.

Reversing Entries

26. After closing the temporary accounts of the current period, most companies prepare reversing entries dated on the first day of the new accounting period. Each reversing entry is the exact reverse in accounts and amounts of an adjusting entry. Reversing entries are optional. Their purpose is to simplify the recording of later transactions by eliminating the need to consider previous adjusting entries. As a general guideline, a reversing entry should be made for any adjusting entry which establishes a new balance sheet account.

27. To illustrate the adjusting and reversing entry process, assume that a company accepted, on December 1, 2004, a note that is payable in three months. The note earns interest of $30 a month, all of which is payable at the time the note is collected. The company would make the following adjusting and closing entries on December 31 (the end of its fiscal year):

12/31/04	Interest Receivable	30	
	Interest Revenue		30
	To record accrued interest at year-end. (Adjusting entry)		
12/31/04	Interest Revenue	30	
	Income Summary		30
	To close Interest Revenue to Income Summary. (Closing entry)		
1/1/05	Interest Revenue	30	
	Interest Receivable		30
	To reverse the year-end adjusting entry. (Reversing entry)		
2/28/05	Cash	90	
	Interest Revenue		90
	To record collection of interest on the note. (Receipt of the principal would also be recorded at this time.)		

The Interest Revenue account at 2/28/05 now has a balance of $60 ($90 - $30), which is the amount of interest earned on the note during 2005. If the reversing entry had not been made, the entry on February 28 would have been more complicated, as follows, and recording errors would have been more likely.

2/28/05	Cash	90	
	Interest Receivable		30
	Interest Revenue		60

Worksheets, Subsidiary Ledgers, Special Journals, and Computer Software

28. A company often uses a worksheet to aid in preparation of adjusting and closing entries and financial statements. A typical manual multicolumn worksheet is prepared on accounting paper with pairs of debit/credit columns for the trial balance, adjustments, income statement, retained earnings statement, and balance sheet. The worksheet process involves five steps: (a) prepare trial balance; (b) analyze accounts and enter necessary adjustments; (c) carry over adjusted amounts of each account to the proper column of the appropriate financial statement; (d) subtotal the income statement debit and credit columns to determine pretax income, and compute income tax; (e) total the financial statement debit and credit columns in sequential order, computing net income or loss and determining that the system is in balance. For formal financial statements, amounts from the worksheet columns for each statement are simply rearranged into proper order.

29. Instead of using only a general ledger for accounts, a company may also establish subsidiary ledgers which are not part of the double-entry system. A subsidiary ledger is a group of accounts pertaining to one specific company activity. Subsidiary ledgers are usually established for accounts receivable and accounts payable. In addition, they are often maintained for property and equipment, selling expenses, and administrative expenses. A control account is maintained in the general ledger for each subsidiary ledger. The balance of a control account on any balance sheet date is equal to the total balance of its associated subsidiary ledger. For example, an accounts receivable subsidiary ledger contains the individual accounts of the company's charge customers, while the Accounts Receivable control account in the general ledger has a debit balance equal to that of the total accounts receivable subsidiary ledger.

30. In a small business, a general journal may be used for all transactions. As a business becomes larger and more complex, a more efficient means of recording common, high-volume transactions is required. Special journals are, therefore, often used to group similar transactions. The major special journals are the sales journal (used to record all sales of merchandise on account), purchases journal (used to record all purchases of merchandise on account), cash receipts journal (used to record all receipts of cash), and cash payments journal (used to record all payments of cash). A voucher system may be established to improve control over cash payments. Under this system, the purchases journal is expanded to become a voucher register. The voucher system requires that (a) a liability (Vouchers Payable) be established for each anticipated cash payment, (b) each cash payment be supported by a voucher (a written authorization) and substantiating documents, and (c) all payments be made by check. A general journal is always necessary to record adjusting, closing, and reversing entries, and certain transactions which occur infrequently, such as purchases returns and sales returns on credit.

31. Most companies use computers to process their accounting information. Software is the set of computer programs used to operate a computer. Software packages are available for the subsidiary ledgers and special journals, as well as other accounting functions such as accounts receivable, accounts payable, inventory payroll, and the general ledger. Flexible spreadsheets, or "electronic worksheets," have also been developed and serve a variety of needs.

Cash-Basis Accounting

32. A few companies (including some small retail stores and some professionals, such as doctors and dentists) use cash-basis, rather than accrual, accounting. These companies record revenues when they collect cash, record expenses when they pay cash, and compute net income as the difference between cash receipts and cash payments. Cash-basis accounting is not allowed under GAAP.

33. Sometimes companies using the cash basis must prepare accrual financial statements. The basic adjustments to cash receipts to convert them to sales revenue and to cash payments to convert them to cost of goods sold and operating expense are shown in Exhibit C-16 in the text. In addition, depreciation must be calculated and included in operating expenses. In complex situations a worksheet may be helpful.

SELF-EVALUATION EXERCISES

Supply the words necessary to complete each of the following items.

The Accounting System

AS-1. The residual equity model equation is:

_________ = ____________ + ______________ __________

AS-2. Assets are the corporation's ____________ _________________; liabilities are the corporation's _________________ owed to creditors; stockholders' equity is the owners' _______________ _________________.

AS-3. Stockholders' investments in shares of stock sold by the corporation are included in _____________ __________.

AS-4. Charges to customers for goods and services are ___________.

Costs incurred in providing goods and services are ____________.

AS-5. A ____________ involves the transfer of something of value between a company and another party.

AS-6. Business documents which provide initial information for recording transactions or events are called ___________ documents.

AS-7. Accounts are organized by number in the company's __________ _____ ___________.

AS-8. The asset, liability, and stockholders' equity accounts which carry balances forward from period to period are _____________ accounts.

AS-9. The revenue, expense, and dividend accounts used to determine the change in retained earnings during an accounting period are ___________ accounts.

AS-10. _________ accounts are used to emphasize reductions in related accounts.

AS-11. The annual set of financial statements and accompanying supporting schedules and notes is called the _________ _________.

AS-12. ___________ financial statements are statements prepared for a period shorter than one year.

AS-13. The cash receipts and cash payments of a company are summarized in the ____________ ____ __________ ______________.

AS-14. The income statement is tied to the balance sheet by the statement of retained earnings. That is, those three statements are ______________.

The Accounting Cycle

AC-1. Financial transactions and events are initially recorded in a ____________.

AC-2. A company using a periodic inventory system takes a physical inventory, then subtracts the ending inventory amount from the cost of goods available for sale to determine the ______ ____ _______ _______.

AC-3. A company using a ____________ ____________ system continuously updates its inventory records for goods purchased and sold.

AC-4. The ___________ ___________ of a company is made up of all of the company's accounts.

AC-5. _____________ is the process of transferring journal entries for a given period to appropriate accounts in the general ledger.

AC-6. To verify that the general ledger is in balance a company may prepare a __________ ____________ listing all accounts and their balances.

AC-7. ______________ __________ are used to revise accounts that are not up to date at the end of the accounting period.

AC-8. Goods or services purchased for use by a company but not fully used at the end of the period are called ___________ _________.

AC-9. A payment received from a customer before delivery of goods or performance of a service is _______________ _______________.

AC-10. Expenses which have been incurred during the period, but which have been neither paid nor recorded, are ____________ ____________.

AC-11. Revenues which have been earned during the period, but which have been neither received nor recorded, are ___________ ____________.

AC-12. Certain accounting estimates, such as estimates of depreciation on assets, are entered at the end of the period in ____________ entries.

AC-13. ______________ __________ are the journal entries made at the end of the period to reduce temporary accounts to zero and to update the retained earnings and inventory accounts.

AC-14. In the closing process, the total of the credits to the temporary accounts is recorded as a _________ to the temporary closing account ___________ ___________.

Reversing Entries

RE-1. A reversing entry is the exact ____________ in accounts and amounts of an adjusting entry.

RE-2. In general, a reversing entry should be made for any adjusting entry which establishes a new ___________ _________ account.

Worksheets, Subsidiary Ledgers, Special Journals, and Computer Software

WS-1. When a worksheet is used in the preparation of adjusting and closing entries, the first step is to set up a ________ ___________.

WS-2. A _________________ __________ is made up of a group of accounts related to one type of company activity.

WS-3. The balance of a control account on any balance sheet date is equal to the ________ balance of its associated subsidiary ledger.

WS-4. When a voucher system is established to improve control over cash, (1) a _____________ must be established for each anticipated cash payment, (2) each cash payment must be supported by a voucher (a ___________ __________________), and (3) all payments must be made by _________.

WS-5. The set of programs used to operate a computer is the computer _____________.

Cash-Basis Accounting

CBA-1. Companies on the cash basis record revenues when they ________________ cash and record expenses when they __________ cash.

CBA-2. To convert collections from customers from the cash basis to the accrual basis a company __________ ending accounts receivable and _________________ beginning accounts receivable.

ANSWERS TO SELF-EVALUATION EXERCISES

AS-1. assets, liabilities, stockholders' equity; AS-2. economic resources, obligations, residual interest; AS-3. contributed capital; AS-4. revenues, expenses; AS-5. transaction; AS-6. source; AS-7. chart of accounts; AS-8. permanent; AS-9. temporary; AS-10. contra; AS-11. annual report; AS-12. interim; AS-13. statement of cash flows; AS-14. articulated; AC-1. journal; AC-2. cost of goods sold; AC-3. perpetual inventory; AC-4. general ledger; AC-5. posting; AC-6. trial balance; AC-7. adjusting entries; AC-8. prepaid expenses; AC-9. deferred revenue; AC-10. accrued expenses; AC-11. accrued revenues; AC-12. adjusting; AC-13. closing entries; AC-14. debit, Income Summary; RE-1. opposite; RE-2. balance sheet; WS-1. trial balance; WS-2. subsidiary ledger; WS-3. total; WS-4. liability, written authorization, check; WS-5. software; CBA-1. collect, pay; CBA-2. adds, subtracts.

POST TEST

Part A Circle T if the statement is true and F if it is false.

T F 1. Posting is the process of initially recording a financial transaction or event.

T F 2. Unusual and infrequent items are recorded in the special journals.

T F 3. "Contributed capital" is the term for company earnings that are reinvested rather than distributed to stockholders.

T F 4. A decline in price is an example of an external event.

T F 5. After closing entries have been completed, the revenue, expense, and dividend accounts have a balance of zero.

T F 6. A debit balance in the Income Summary account after the temporary income statement accounts have been closed and closing entries have been made for Inventory indicates a net loss for the company.

T F 7. The purpose of a voucher system is to improve control over cash receipts.

T F 8. A reversing entry is required whenever an adjusting entry is made.

T F 9. Prepaid expenses are expenses which have been incurred during the accounting period but have been neither paid nor recorded.

T F 10. The balance of each control account in the general ledger is equal to the total balance of its associated subsidiary ledger on any balance sheet date.

T F 11. The purchases journal is used to record purchases of merchandise for cash and on account.

T F 12. "Permanent" accounts are also called "real" accounts.

T F 13. A company using a perpetual inventory system continuously updates its inventory records for goods purchased and sold.

T F 14. Bad Debts Expense is an example of a contra account.

T F 15. The balance sheet summarizes the amounts of assets, liabilities, and stockholders' equity as of a particular date.

T F 16. Adjusting, closing, and reversing entries are recorded in the general journal.

T F 17. A post-closing trial balance verifies that the total of the debit balances is equal to the total of the credit balances in the permanent accounts.

T F 18. In financial accounting an "event" always involves the transfer of something between the company and another party.

T F 19. Sales invoices and freight bills are examples of documents of original entry.

T F 20. Adjusting entries ensure that the financial statements include the correct amounts for the current period under accrual accounting.

T F 21. When converting payments for operating costs from the cash basis to the accrual basis, a company subtracts ending prepaid expenses and adds ending accrued expenses.

T F 22. When a company uses the double-entry system the total dollar amount of debits recorded for a transaction equals the total dollar amount of credits.

Part B Select the one best answer, and place its letter in the space provided.

_____ 1. Accumulated Depreciation is an example of a (a) corporate liability; (b) temporary account; (c) contra account; (d) control account.

_____ 2. The three major financial statements do not include the (a) statement of retained earnings; (b) income statement; (c) balance sheet; (d) statement of cash flows.

_____ 3. The major special journals do not include the (a) sales journal; (b) purchases journal; (c) general journal; (d) cash payments journal.

_____ 4. Which of the following is not a temporary account? (a) Sales Revenue; (b) Warranty Expense; (c) Retained Earnings; (d) Interest Expense.

_____ 5. A purpose of closing entries is not to (a) reduce all temporary accounts to zero; (b) update the Retained Earnings account; (c) update the Inventory account; (d) apportion prepaid expenses and unearned revenues to bring accounts up to date.

_____ 6. Which of the following accounts will be reduced to zero by a year-end closing entry? (a) Accumulated Depreciation: Property, Plant, and Equipment; (b) Estimated Liability Under Product Warranty; (c) Allowance for Doubtful Accounts; (d) Sales Returns and Allowances.

_____ 7. Purchase returns for credit are commonly recorded in the (a) purchases journal; (b) cash receipts journal; (c) cash payments journal; (d) general journal.

_____ 8. Stockholders' equity is (a) the amount paid by investors for stock at the time of original issuance; (b) the residual interest of owners; (c) corporate earnings reinvested in the corporation rather than distributed; (d) amounts received by stockholders as a return on investment.

_____ 9. Which of the following is a document of original entry? (a) general ledger; (b) sales invoice; (c) general journal; (d) purchase requisition.

_____ 10. Cash received from a customer prior to delivery of the product is (a) an accrued expense; (b) a deferred revenue; (c) a prepaid expense; (d) an accrued revenue.

_____ 11. The three categories of adjusting entries necessary under accrual accounting do not include (a) apportionment of prepaid expenses and deferred revenues; (b) apportionment of recorded revenues and incurred expenses; (c) recording of accrued expenses and accrued revenues; (d) recording of estimated items.

_____ 12. Which of the following statements concerning deferred revenue is true? (a) a liability is usually recorded initially for deferred revenue; (b) when accrual accounting is used, no adjusting entry is necessary for deferred revenue; (c) deferred revenue is usually recorded initially as an expense; (d) deferred revenue is revenue which has been earned during an accounting period, but has been neither received nor recorded.

_____ 13. Reversing entries (a) are generally made for adjusting entries which establish new balance sheet accounts; (b) are required under accrual accounting; (c) are dated on the last day of the accounting period; (d) make the recording of later transactions more complex.

_____ 14. Which of the following statements is true regarding prepaid expenses? (a) prepaid expenses represent payments received from customers before the delivery of products or the performance of services; (b) prepaid rent and prepaid insurance are common examples of prepaid expenses; (c) prepaid expenses are always recorded initially as expenses; (d) prepaid expenses are estimated when preparing closing entries.

_____ 15. The Vreden Company, which began business in January, 2004, reported cash-basis net income for the year 2004 of $25,000. On December 31, Vreden's accounting records showed Accounts Receivable of $2,000; Accounts Payable of $3,500; Ending Inventory of $12,300 and Prepaid Expenses of $500. What was Vreden's accrual-basis net income for 2004? (a) $36,300; (b) $35,300; (c) $31,700; (d) $29,300.

Part C Solve each of the following short problems.

1. Below are selected account balances from the 12/31/04 trial balance of the Withers Company. Inventory at 12/31/04 is $1,000. Prepare appropriate closing entries.

	Debit	Credit
Inventory (1/1/04)	1,000	
Purchases	5,000	
Selling Expenses	1,200	
Administrative Expenses	700	
Sales		12,000
Income Tax Expense	1,000	
Dividends Distributed	1,000	

2. The Post Company uses the following journals: general journal, sales journal, purchases journal, cash receipts journal, and cash payments journal. Prepare journal entries in a general journal format for the transactions given, and indicate the appropriate journal for recording each transaction.

   (a) Made cash sales of $1,000.

   (b) Purchased $6,000 of merchandise on account.

   (c) Returned $180 of defective merchandise.

2. (d) Purchased $90 of supplies for cash.

(e) Sold $2,000 of merchandise on account.

(f) Made end-of-year (December 31) adjusting entry for insurance expired. (On July 1, Prepaid Insurance was debited $1,200 for payment of one year's premium.)

3. For each item given below, prepare a year-end adjusting entry, or indicate that an adjusting entry is not necessary.

(a) On December 1, the Jay Company paid $2,400 for one year of insurance coverage. The payment was debited to Prepaid Insurance.

(b) On December 31, $3,000 of employee salaries had accrued. No entry for these salaries has been recorded.

(c) On December 15, a customer paid $900 in advance for services to be performed in January. The payment was credited to Deferred Revenue.

(d) Interest of $50 has accrued on a note receivable accepted by the company from a customer.

(e) The company credited all sales on account to Sales. On December 31, $200 of receivables are estimated to be uncollectible.

ANSWERS TO POST TEST

Part A

1. F	6. T	11. F	17. T
2. F	7. F	12. T	18. F
3. F	8. F	13. T	19. F
4. T	9. F	14. F	20. T
5. T	10. T	15. T	21. T
		16. T	22. T

Part B

1. c	5. d	9. c	13. a
2. a	6. d	10. b	14. b
3. c	7. d	11. b	15. a
4. c	8. b	12. a	

Part C

1.

Sales	12,000	
Inventory (12/31/04)	1,000	
Income Summary		13,000
To close the temporary accounts with credit balances and to record the ending inventory.		
Income Summary	8,900	
Purchases		5,000
Selling Expenses		1,200
Administrative Expenses		700
Income Tax Expense		1,000
Inventory (1/1/04)		1,000
To close the temporary accounts with debit balances and the beginning inventory.		
Income Summary	4,100	
Retained Earnings		4,100
To close Income Summary to Retained Earnings.		
Retained Earnings	1,000	
Dividends Distributed		1,000
To close the dividends to Retained Earnings.		

(a) (cash receipts journal)

Cash	1,000	
Sales		1,000

(b) (purchases journal)

Purchases (or Inventory)	6,000	
Accounts Payable		6,000

			Debit	Credit
2.	(c)	(general journal)		
		Accounts Payable	180	
		Purchase Returns and Allowances		180
	(d)	(cash payments journal)		
		Supplies	90	
		Cash		90
	(e)	(sales journal)		
		Accounts Receivable	2,000	
		Sales		2,000
	(f)	(general journal)		
		Insurance Expense	600	
		Prepaid Insurance		600
3.	(a)	Insurance Expense	200	
		Prepaid Insurance		200
		To record expiration of one month of insurance coverage purchased on December 1.		
	(b)	Salaries Expense	3,000	
		Salaries Payable		3,000
		To record salaries earned by employees but not yet paid.		
	(c)	No adjusting entry necessary.		
	(d)	Interest Receivable	50	
		Interest Revenue		50
		To record interest accumulated on the note receivable accepted from a customer.		
	(e)	Bad Debts Expense	200	
		Allowance for Doubtful Accounts		200
		To record estimated uncollectible accounts receivable.		

Appendix D

COMPOUND INTEREST

APPENDIX OBJECTIVES

After careful study of this appendix, you will be able to:

1. Understand simple interest and compound interest.
2. Compute and use the future value of a single sum.
3. Compute and use the present value of a single sum.
4. Compute and use the future value of an ordinary annuity.
5. Compute and use the future value of an annuity due.
6. Compute and use the present value of an ordinary annuity.
7. Compute and use the present value of annuity due.
8. Compute and use the present value of a deferred ordinary annuity.
9. Explain the conceptual issues regarding the use of present value in financial reporting.

SYNOPSIS

Symbols Used

1. Symbols used in all calculations are:

p	=	principal sum (present value)
$p_{n,i}$	=	present value of 1 discounted at interest rate i for n periods
n	=	number of time periods used when solving for a single sum; number of payments (cash flows) used when solving for an annuity
i	=	interest rate for each of the stated time periods (annual stated rate divided by the number of compounding periods)
f	=	future value of a single sum at compound interest rate i for n periods
C	=	amount of each cash flow
$f_{n,i}$	=	future value of a single sum of 1 at compound interest rate i for n periods
F_0	=	future value of an ordinary annuity of a series of cash flows of any amount
$F_{0_{n,i}}$	=	future value of an ordinary annuity of a series of n cash flows of 1 each at interest rate i
F_d	=	future value of an annuity due of a series of cash flows of any amount
$F_{d_{n,i}}$	=	future value of an annuity due of a series of n cash flows of 1 each at interest rate i
P_0	=	present value of an ordinary annuity of a series of cash flows of any amount
$P_{0_{n,i}}$	=	present value of an ordinary annuity of a series of n cash flows of 1 each discounted at interest rate i
P_d	=	present value of an annuity due of a series of cash flows of any amount
$P_{d_{n,i}}$	=	present value of an annuity due of a series of n cash flows of 1 each discounted at interest rate i
$P_{deferred}$	=	present value of a deferred annuity of a series of cash flows of any amount
$p_{k,i}$	=	present value of a single sum of 1 for k periods of deferment

Time Value of Money

2. Time value of money refers to the difference in worth between a dollar received or paid today and a dollar received or paid in the future. A dollar received today is worth more than a dollar received some time in the future because of interest.

3. Interest, defined as the cost for the use of money over time, is an expense to the borrower or revenue to the lender. In other words, interest is the time value of money in quantitative (dollar) terms.

4. Discounting is the method of converting a future dollar amount into its present dollar value. It is accomplished by removing the time value of money, or interest, from the amount to be received or paid in the future. Discounting enables managers to compare the value today at time period zero of amounts received or paid at different times.

5. For purposes of comparing the value of amounts received or paid at different times, dollars can also be restated to their future value by adding the time value of money, i.e., compound interest, to the principal amounts received or paid.

Simple Interest and Compound Interest

6. Simple interest is interest on only the original principal received or paid, regardless of the number of time periods that have passed or the amount of interest that has been paid or accrued in the past. The formula for calculating simple interest is

$$\text{Interest} = \text{Principal} \times \text{Rate} \times \text{Time}$$

7. Compound interest is the interest that accrues on both the principal and the past unpaid accrued interest. It is sometimes referred to as interest on interest. There are four basic types of compound interest calculations: (a) the future value (amount) of a single sum at compound interest; (b) the present value of a single sum due in the future; (c) the future value (amount) of an annuity, and (d) the present value of an annuity.

8. For compound interest problems the interest rate, i, is the rate per period. It is calculated by dividing the annual rate by the number of compounding periods per year. For example, if the annual rate is 16%, the rate per period for interest compounded quarterly is 4% or: 16%/4.

Future Value of a Single Sum at Compound Interest

9. The future value of a single sum (f) at compound interest is the original amount paid or received plus compound interest as of a specific future date. Compound interest is calculated each period on the sum of the principal plus the accrued unpaid interest from all previous periods. Therefore, the sum of the principal plus the compound interest calculated each period from time zero to some specific future date is the future value.

10. The arithmetic approach for finding the future value is the laborious method which actually calculates the interest for each period individually as described above. To reduce calculations and the time necessary to find the future value, a formula approach or table approach is used.

11. Using the formula approach, the future value can be calculated in one step. The principal or present value (p) is multiplied times the sum of one plus the interest rate per period (1+i) raised to the n power where n = number of time periods in the year multiplied by the number of years. The formula is:

$$f = p(1+i)^n$$

12. The table approach is an even easier method to use in calculating future values. The tables contain precalculations of the future value of 1 at different interest rates (i) for different time periods (n). Using the above formula, by multiplying the precalculated amount or factor ($f_{n,i}$) times the present value or principal (p), the future value (f) is found. The formula for the future value in this case is:

$f = p$ (Factor for $f_{n,i}$) where $f_{n,i} = (1+i)^n$ when p=1; that is

where $f_{n,i}$ is the value of 1 for n time periods at i interest rate per period.

13. Sometimes the interest rate or the number of periods is not given in the tables. Interpolation can be used to find the approximate interest rate or the number of periods. The interest rate or number of periods can be estimated by calculating the distance between two rates or two periods.

Present Value of a Single Sum (p)

14. The present value of a single sum in the future is the investment that must be made at time period zero to produce the known future value. In essence, it is the future amount less all of the compound interest that would have accrued at a given interest rate. Discounting is the process of converting the future value to the present value. Using the formula approach the present value is:

$$p = f\frac{1}{(1+i)^n}$$

Using the table approach the present value is:

$p = f$ (Factor for $p_{n,i}$)

where $p_{n,i}$ is the value of 1 for n time periods at i interest rate per period.

Future Value of an Ordinary Annuity (F_0)

15. An annuity is a series of equal cash flows (payments, deposits, receipts, or withdrawals), sometimes referred to as rents, made at regular intervals with interest compounded at a certain rate. The following conditions must be present for a series of cash flows to be an annuity: (a) the periodic cash flows are equal in amount, (b) the time periods between cash flows are equal, (c) the interest rate for each time period is constant, and (d) the interest is compounded at the end of each time period.

16. When the future value is calculated immediately after the last cash flow (rent), the annuity is an ordinary annuity. The last cash flow earns no interest.

17. Either the formula approach or the table approach may be used to calculate the future value of an ordinary annuity. Using either approach, it is important to remember that n now refers to the number of cash flows, not time periods. The formula approach is:

$$F_0 = C\left[\frac{(1+i)^n - 1}{i}\right]$$

The table approach is

$$F_0 = C\,(\text{Factor for } F_{0_{n,i}})$$

where $F_{0_{n,i}} = \left[\frac{(1+i)^n - 1}{i}\right]$ when $C = 1$

Future Value of an Annuity Due (F_d)

18. When the interest on the annuity continues to be earned for one period past the last cash flow, the annuity is an annuity due. The future value of an annuity due is equal to the future value of an ordinary annuity plus the interest earned on the future value from the date of the last cash flow until one period past the last cash flow.

19. To calculate the future value of an annuity due, the table for the future value of an ordinary annuity can be used.

(a) Find the value of n+1 cash flows at the known interest rate (i) in the ordinary annuity table.

(b) Subtract 1.000000.

(c) The difference is the factor for the future value of an annuity due ($F_{d_{n,i}}$).

(d) Multiply the amount of each cash flow (C) times the converted factor ($F_{d_{n,i}}$) to find the future value of an annuity due.

The solution expressed as a formula is:

$$F_d = C(F_{d_{n,i}})$$

where $F_{d_{n,i}}$ = Factor for $F_{0_{n+1,i}}$ - 1.000000

Present Value of an Annuity

20. The present value of an annuity is the present value of a series of equal cash flows made in the future at regular intervals and discounted at compound interest. It can be thought of as the amount that must be invested today and, if left to earn compound interest, will provide for payment or receipt of a series of equal cash flows at regular intervals and result in a zero balance after the last cash flow.

Present Value of an Ordinary Annuity (P_0)

21. When the present value of an annuity is calculated as of <u>one</u> period <u>before</u> the receipt or payment of the first cash flow, the annuity is <u>an ordinary annuity</u>.

22. The present value of an ordinary annuity may be found by using the present value of a single sum table and treating the present value of each individual cash flow as a single sum. The sum of the individual present values is equal to the present value of an ordinary annuity. However, the formula approach or table approach is easier and faster. Using the <u>formula approach</u> the formula is stated as:

$$P_0 = C \left[\frac{1 - \frac{1}{(1+i)^n}}{i}\right]$$

where n = number of cash flows.

The <u>table approach</u> is:

$$P_0 = C \,(\text{Factor for } P_{0_{n,i}})$$

where $P_{0_{n,i}} = \left[\frac{1 - \frac{1}{(1+i)^n}}{i}\right]$ and C = 1.

Present Value of an Annuity Due (P_d)

23. The present value of an annuity is calculated from the date of the first cash flow in the series. The present value of an annuity due is equal to the present value of an ordinary annuity for n-1 cash flows plus one, times the value of each cash flow.

24. A two-step <u>formula approach</u> can be used to calculate the present value of an annuity due when a table is not available. The formula for the present value of an annuity due of any amount is:

$$P_d = C \left[\frac{1 - \frac{1}{(1+i)^{n-1}}}{i} + 1\right]$$

First, calculate the present value of an annuity due with n cash flows of 1 each ($P_{d_{n,i}}$):

$$P_{d_{n,i}} = \left[\frac{1 - \frac{1}{(1+i)^{n-1}}}{i} + 1\right]$$

This result is then substituted in the original formula and multiplied times the number of cash flows:

$$P_d = C\,[P_{d_{n,i}}]$$

Under the <u>table approach</u>, the equation is:

$$P_d = C\ (\text{Factor for } P_{d_{n,i}})$$

25. The present value of an annuity due also can be calculated using the present value of an ordinary annuity table.

(a) Find the present value factor of n-1 cash flows at the stated interest rate.

(b) Add 1.000000.

(c) The sum is the converted factor for the present value of an annuity due ($P_{d_{n,i}}$).

(d) Multiply the value of each cash flow C times the converted table factor ($P_{d_{n,i}}$) to find the present value of an annuity due.

The solution expressed as a formula is:

$$P_d = C(P_{d_{n,i}})$$

where $P_{d_{n,i}}$ = Factor for $P_{0_{n-1,i}}$ + 1.000000

Present Value of a Deferred Ordinary Annuity ($P_{deferred}$)

26. The <u>present value of a deferred ordinary annuity</u> is the present value of a series of cash flows where the first payment or withdrawal is due two or more periods from the present.

27. The present value of a deferred ordinary annuity may be treated as a combination of the present value of an ordinary annuity (P_0) and the present value of a single sum (p). Using the table approach, this is:

$$P_{deferred} = C\ [(\text{Factor for } P_{0_{n,i}})\ (\text{Factor for } p_{k,i})]$$

where $P_{0_{n,i}}$ = present value of the ordinary annuity of n cash flows of 1 at the given interest rate i

and $p_{k,i}$ = present value of the single sum of 1 for k periods of deferment

28. Alternatively, the present value of a deferred annuity may be treated as a combination of two ordinary annuities. The present value of an ordinary annuity of k cash flows (the cash flows that would have occurred during the deferral period) is subtracted from the present value of an ordinary annuity of n+k cash flows (the total cash flows that would have been paid if the annuity began at the present). The difference is equal to a converted factor for the present value of a deferred annuity of 1. This factor is substituted in the following expression:

$$P_{deferred} = C\ (\text{Converted Factor for Present Value of Deferred Annuity of 1})$$

29. Present value techniques are used in financial reporting, but accounting principles do not include a unifying concept to determine when present value should and should not be used. The FASB has issued a FASB Statement of Concepts No. 7 which provides general principles governing the use of present value, as well as the objectives of present value accounting measurements.

30. Almost any problem involving compound interest can be solved by analyzing the problem, drawing a diagram to help visualize the sequence of events, and using the basic compound interest formula or table. Using the tables or the formulas, the interest rate or the number of time periods (number of cash flows for annuities) can be found if the formula or table factor is known. The chart on the next page will help in selecting the appropriate formula or table.

Number of Cash Flows	Time	Type of Annuity	Formula Approach	Table Approach
Single Sum	Future Value		$f = p(1+i)^n$	$f = p$ (Factor for $f_{n,i}$)
	Present Value		$p = f \frac{1}{(1+i)^n}$	$p = f$ (Factor for $p_{n,i}$)
Series of Cash Flows of Equal Value	Future Value	Determined immediately after last cash flow = Ordinary Annuity	$F_0 = C\,[\frac{(1+i)^n - 1}{i}]$	$F_0 = C$ (Factor for $F_{0_{n,i}}$)
		Determined one period after last cash flow = Annuity Due	$F_d = C\,[\frac{(1+i)^n - 1}{i}]\,[1+i]$	$F_d = C$ [Factor for $F_{0_{n+1,i}}$ -1]
	Present Value	Determined one period before first cash flow = Ordinary Annuity	$P_0 = C\,\frac{[1 - \frac{1}{(1+i)^n}]}{i}$	$P_0 = C$ (Factor for $P_{0_{n,i}}$)
		Determined at the time of the first cash flow = Annuity Due	$P_d = C\,[\frac{1 - \frac{1}{(1+i)^{n-1}}}{i} + 1]$	$P_d = C$ (Factor for $P_{d_{n,i}}$)
		Determined 2 or more periods before first cash flow = Deferred Ordinary Annuity		$P_{deferred} = C$ [(Factor) for $P_{0_{n,i}}$ (Factor) for $p_{k,i}$]

SELF-EVALUATION EXERCISES

Supply the words, phrases, symbols, or dollar amounts necessary to complete each of the following items.

Time Value of Money, Simple Interest, Compound Interest

I-1. Because of the time value of money, a dollar held today is worth

__________ than a dollar received in one year.
(more, less)

I-2. The difference in value between a dollar received today and a dollar received in one year is called __________.

I-3. Interest that is calculated on the principal only is called __________ __________ while interest that is calculated on the principal plus accrued unpaid interest to date is called __________ __________.

I-4. To convert a future dollar amount to a present dollar value, the future amount must be __________.

I-5. If the stated simple interest rate is 12%, and interest is compounded semiannually, the interest rate per period is __________.

I-6. The simple interest on $15,000 borrowed for 60 days at 10% interest is $__________.

I-7. If $300 interest is paid for borrowing $10,000 for 90 days, the annual effective interest rate is __________%.

I-8. The total compound interest on $20,000 for 2 years at 8% would be $__________.

I-9. The three approaches which may be used to solve problems involving compound interest are the __________ approach, __________ approach, and __________ approach.

Single Sum - Present Value and Future Value

SS-1. The amount that must be invested at time period zero to produce a known future value is the __________ __________.

SS-2. The sum of a single investment plus the compound interest thereon as of a specific future date is the ___________ ___________.

SS-3. The formula $f= p(1+i)^n$ is used to find the ___________ ___________ _____ _____ _________ ______, and the formula $p = f\left[\frac{1}{(1+i)^n}\right]$ is used to find the _________ ________ _____ _____ _________ _____.

SS-4. In the formula $f = p(1+i)^n$, f stands for the _______ _________ ____ ______ __________ _____, p stands for the _______ _______, i stands for the _________ _______ ______ __________, and n stands for the _________ ______ ___________.

SS-5. The factor for the present value of 1 at the compound interest rate of 8% for 8 years is ____________.

SS-6. When the interest rate or the number of periods is not given in the interest tables, ____________ is necessary.

SS-7. The factor for the present value of 1 at compound interest of 12% for 10 years is 0.321973 and the factor for the future value of 1 at 12% for 10 years is 3.105848. In order to have $100,000 ten years from now, $___________ must be deposited today if 12% interest compounded annually can be earned.

SS-8. If the going interest rate is 10% compounded semiannually, $25,000 received today will be worth $_________ in 8 years.

Future Value of an Annuity

FAA-1. An annuity is ____

____

FAA-2. When the future value is determined immediately after the last cash flow, the annuity is called an ___________ ___________ and when it is determined at the end of one period after the last cash flow, the annuity is called an ___________ _________.

FAA-3. In both the formula approach and in the table approach forcalculating the future value of an annuity, n represents the number of _____________ _____________.

FAA-4. In the formula $F_0 = C\ [\frac{(1+i)^n - 1}{i}]$

F_0 = ________ ________ ____ ____ ________ ________

C = ________ ____ ____ ________ ________

i = ________ ________ ____ ________

n = ________ ______ ________ ________.

FAA-5. Assume the following factors for the future value of an ordinary annuity:

$F_{0_{n=10,\ i=14\%}} = 19.337295$

$F_{0_{n=11,\ i=14\%}} = 23.044516$

$F_{0_{n=12,\ i=14\%}} = 27.270749$

To find the factor for the future value of an annuity due of

11 payments at 14%, 1 is ________________ the ordinary
(added to, subtracted from)

annuity factor of ____________.

FAA-6. The factor for the future value of an ordinary annuity of 12 payments at 6% is

________.

FAA-7. The factor for the future value of an annuity due of 12 payments at 6% is

________.

FAA-8 Assume an annuity of 15 yearly payments of $1,000 at 10% compounded annually. If the payments begin on January 1, 2004, the future value on January 1, 2019, one

year after the last payment, will be $________.

Present Value of an Annuity

PVA-1. Present value of an annuity problems are concerned with three

different types of annuities: (a) ________ ________,

(b) ________ ________ and (c) ________ ________ ________.

PVA-2. Assume an annuity that consists of 10 annual payments of $1,500 each for which the present value is calculated as of today. If the first payment is made today,

the annuity is an ____________ ___________; if the first payment is made two years

from today, the annuity is a ____________ ____________ ____________; and if

the first payment is made a year from today, the annuity is an ____________

____________.

PVA-3. When looking for the factor for the present value of an ordinary annuity of $200 a month for two years discounted at 12% interest compounded monthly, <u>n</u> would

equal __________, and <u>i</u> would equal ____________.

PVA-4. You wish to deposit a sum of money today that will allow you to withdraw $100 a year for five years. The going interest rate is 12% compounded annually. If the

first withdrawal will be one year from today, you must deposit $___________ today.

PVA-5. Assume you are able to make yearly payments of $1,500 a year for 6 years. The first payment will be made two years from today. The bank interest rate is 8% compounded annually. To find the amount you could borrow today, you must find the present value of an

___________ _____________ where n = ________, i = ________, and

C = _________, as well as the present value of a ____________

__________ where f = __________, n = ________, and i = ______.

PVA-6. The semiannual payments on a $10,000 loan for 5 years at 10%

interest compounded semiannually would be $_________.

ANSWERS TO SELF-EVALUATION EXERCISES

I-1. more; I-2. interest; I-3. simple interest, compound interest;
I-4. discounted; I-5. 6%.

I-6. i = Principal x Rate x Time

$$= \$15,000 \times 0.10 \times \frac{60}{360}$$

$$= \$250$$

I-7. $i = \text{Principal} \times \text{Rate} \times \text{Time}$

$$\$300 = \$10,000 \times \text{Rate} \times \frac{90}{360}$$

$$\$300 = \$\ 2,500 \times \text{Rate}$$

$$\text{Rate} = \frac{\$300}{\$2,500}$$

$$= 0.12$$

I-8. Interest for the first year:

$i = prt$
$= \$20,000 \times 0.08 \times 1$
$= \$1,600$

Interest for the second year:

$i = prt$
$= (\$20,000 + \$1,600) \times 0.08 \times 1$
$= \$1,728$

Compound interest = \$1,600 + \$1,728
= \$3,328

I-9. arithmetic, formula, table; SS-1. present value; SS-2. future value; SS-3. future value of a single sum, present value of a single sum; SS-4. future value of a single sum, present value, interest rate per period, number of periods; SS-5. 0.540269; SS-6. interpolation; SS-7. \$32,197.30; SS-8. \$54,571.88; FAA-1. a series of equal cash flows made at regular intervals with interest compounded at a certain rate; FAA-2. ordinary annuity, annuity due; FAA-3. cash flows; FAA-4. F_0 = future value of an ordinary annuity, C = amount of each cash flow, i = interest rate per period, n = number of cash flows; FAA-5. subtracted from, 27.270749; FAA-6. 16.869941;

FAA-7. The factor for an ordinary annuity can be adjusted for an annuity due by using the following steps:

Step 1.	Look up the factor for n+1 periods (13 periods) at 6%.	18.882138
Step 2.	Subtract 1	1.000000
	This is the adjusted factor	17.882138

FAA-8. \$34,949.73; PVA-1. ordinary annuity, annuity due, deferred ordinary annuity; PVA-2. annuity due, deferred ordinary annuity, ordinary annuity; PVA-3. 24, 1%; PVA-4. \$360.48; PVA-5. ordinary annuity, n=6, i=8%, R=\$1,500, single sum, f=\$6,934.32, n=1, i=8%; PVA-6. \$1,295.05.

POST TEST

Part A Circle T if the statement is true and F if it is false.

T F 1. A dollar paid out today will have a smaller present value than a dollar paid out one year from today.

T F 2. Simple interest is interest on the original principal only, regardless of the number of time periods that have passed or the amount of interest that has been paid or accrued in the past.

T F 3. A statement that the interest rate is 12% compounded quarterly means that the interest rate for each quarter is 12%.

T F 4. The present value of a dollar discounted for 4 years at 8% is less than $1.00.

T F 5. The conditions necessary for an annuity are: (1) the periodic cash flows must be equal in amount, (2) the time period between cash flows must be of the same length, (3) the interest rate is compounded at the end of each time period, and (4) the periodic cash flows must be paid at the end of each time period.

T F 6. When calculating the future value of a single sum using the arithmetic method, the amount of interest for each period will be the same.

T F 7. A future value of an annuity due problem requires interest to continue at least one period beyond the last cash flow in the series.

T F 8. The present value of an annuity due is calculated from the date of the first cash flow.

T F 9. In solving a future compound interest problem, the interest rate must always be known.

T F 10. In solving a present-value of a single sum problem, the interest rate may be found if the present value, future value, and the number of time periods are known.

T F 11. In solving an annuity due problem, if the present value is calculated one period before the first payment is made, the annuity is a deferred ordinary annuity.

T F 12. The present value of an annuity due is a combination of an ordinary annuity and the present value of a single sum.

T F 13. The symbol $f_{n,i}$ represents the future value of 1 for n periods at i interest rate, and the values for this symbol grow larger for increasing rates of interest.

T F 14. The values for $p_{n,i}$ (present value of a future value) are always greater than 1.

T F 15. The factor for the <u>present value</u> of an ordinary annuity will always be less than the number of cash flows in the annuity.

T F 16. The factor for the <u>future value</u> of an ordinary annuity is always greater than or equal to the number of cash flows in the annuity.

T F 17. In all present value and future value problems, n is equal to the number of interest periods.

T F 18. The present value of an ordinary annuity of n cash flows at interest rate i is equal to the sum of the present values of each individual payment for each of the n periods at interest rate i.

T F 19. In a compound interest problem, the compound interest rate will always be less than the annual interest rate.

Part B Select the one best answer, and place its letter in the space provided.

_____ 1. Discounting is a method (a) for converting a present dollar amount to a future dollar value; (b) for restating a simple interest rate to a compound interest rate; (c) for restating a dollar amount received in the future to its present value; (d) for comparing amounts received or paid at different times by adding the time value of money.

_____ 2. Each of the following compound interest factors has the same number of time periods and/or cash flows (n) at the same interest rate (i). Which one is the factor for the future value of a single sum? (a) 17.548735; (b) 0.321973; (c) 3.105848; (d) 5.650223.

_____ 3. The time value of money refers to the concept that: (a) one hundred dollars deposited in a savings account today is worth more than one hundred dollars deposited in a year; (b) a dollar withdrawn in a year is worth more than a dollar withdrawn today because of interest; (c) a dollar paid today is worth less than a dollar paid in the future because of interest lost; (d) the future value of a single sum received is worth more than the present value of that amount received at a stated future date.

_____ 4. Joan Foreman wants to invest $20,000 today, at 10% interest compounded semiannually, with the hope of having enough money in 15 years to buy a retirement cottage on the beach for $80,000. To find out if she will have enough money, Joan can use a compound interest factor from (a) the present value of a single sum table; (b) the future value of a single sum table; (c) the present value of an ordinary annuity table; (d) the future value of an ordinary annuity table; (e) either a or b.

_____ 5. To calculate the present value of a single sum, you would use which of the following formulas? (a) $p(1+i)^n$; (b) $f(1+i)$;

(c) $p\frac{1}{(1+i)^n}$; (d) $f\frac{1}{(1+i)^n}$.

_____ 6. Which of the following conditions is not necessary for an ordinary annuity? (a) the time period between cash flows must be of equal length; (b) equal payments must be made annually; (c) the periodic cash flows must be equal in amount; (d) the interest rate is compounded at the end of each time period.

_____ 7. Which of the following factors would be used to calculate the present value of a single sum if the interest rate is 6% for 2 years? (a) 2.060000; (b) 0.889996; (c) 1.123600; (d) 0.003600.

____ 8. Roy Watson borrows $50,000 to purchase a house and will repay the loan in monthly payments at 12% interest for the next 25 years. Which of the following items is the unknown factor? (a) compound interest rate; (b) time periods; (c) present-value amount; (d) value of each cash flow.

____ 9. To determine the converted factor for the future value of an annuity due, one must find the factor for the future value of an ordinary annuity for (a) n cash flows and then subtract 1; (b) n-1 cash flows and then add 1; (c) n+1 cash flows and then add 1; (d) n+1 cash flows and then subtract 1.

____ 10. Assume you purchase a car for $1,000 at 14% interest and you intend to make 12 monthly payments of $95 each. This is an example of (a) simple interest; (b) compound interest; (c) ordinary annuity; (d) annuity due.

____ 11. David Wilson will deposit $1,000 a year into a savings account beginning January 1, 2004. The last payment will be made on January 1, 2013, and the total amount will be withdrawn on January 1, 2014 for a trip around the world. To find the amount available on January 1, 2014, David must determine (a) the future value of an ordinary annuity; (b) the future value of an annuity due; (c) the future value of a deferred ordinary annuity; (d) the future value of a single sum.

____ 12. The table values represented by $C\,[(P_{0_{n,i}})(p_{k,i})]$ are used to calculate the: (a) present value of an annuity due; (b) future value of a series of cash flows; (c) present value of an ordinary annuity; (d) present value of a deferred ordinary annuity.

Part C Solve each of the following short problems.

1. You have $4,000 in your savings account and you can earn 10% interest. How much money will you have 3 years from today, when you graduate, to buy a car?

   (a) Use the formula to calculate the amount.

   (b) Use the tables to calculate the amount. Is it the same amount as in (a)? Why or why not?

   (c) Suppose you estimate you will need $5,926 to buy the car you want. What interest rate must you earn?

   (d) Assume that 1 year from today you will be able to add another $1,000 to your savings account. How much money will you have 3 years from today?

2. John purchased an insurance policy several years ago which will mature in 3 years, at which time he will receive $30,000. John has decided to open his own business and needs $25,000 today to buy the necessary equipment. The insurance company will redeem the policy at a 9% discount.

(a) How much will he receive from the insurance policy today?

(1) Use the future-amount formula.

(2) Use the present-value formula.

(3) Use the present-value tables.

(b) How much more will he need to start his own business?

3. Carol Pape borrowed $60,000 from her rich uncle on January 1, 2004. She agreed to repay the principal plus interest compounded annually at 12% in 20 equal annual installments due on January 1.

(a) If the first payment is made on January 1, 2005, what would be the amount of each annual installment? Use the table approach.

(b) If the first payment is made on January 1, 2004, what would be the amount of each annual payment? Use the table approach.

(c) If Pape could afford to make 20 payments of $7,500 per year, how much should her uncle be willing to lend her at 12% interest compounded annually? Use the table approach.

3. (d) If the uncle receives $7,500 a year beginning January 1, 2004, and deposits it in an account which earns 10% interest compounded annually, how much will be in his account on January 1, 2010 after the seventh installment? Use the table approach.

ANSWERS TO POST TEST

Part A

1. F	6. F	11. F	16. T
2. T	7. T	12. F	17. F
3. F	8. T	13. T	18. T
4. T	9. F	14. F	19. F
5. F	10. T	15. T	

Part B

1. c	4. e	7. b	10. c
2. c	5. d	8. d	11. b
3. a	6. b	9. d	12. d

Part C

1. a. $f = p(1+i)^n$
$= \$4,000\ (1+0.10)^3$
$= \$5,324$

b. $f = p(f_{n,i})$ $n = 3,\ i = 0.10$
$= \$4,000\ (1.331000)$
$= \$5,324$

Yes, because the formula approach and the table approach provide the same answers except for small rounding errors.

1. c. $f = p(f_{n,i})$

$\$5,926 = \$4,000\ (f_{n=3})$

$i=?$

$(f_{n=3}) = \frac{\$5,926}{\$4,000}$

$i=?$

$= 1.4815$

1. c. Therefore i = 14%

d. $f = p(f_{n,i})$ $f = p(f_{n,i})$

$= \$4,000\ (1.331000)$ $n = 3$ $= \$1,000\ (1.21)$ $n = 2$

$= \$5,324$ $= \$1,210$

Answer: $5,324 + $1,210 = $6,534

2. a. (1) $f = p(1+i)^n$ (2) $p = f \dfrac{1}{(1+i)^n}$

$\$30,000 = p(1+0.09)^3$

$\$30,000 = p(1.295029)$

$p = \dfrac{\$30,000}{1.295029}$

$p = \$23,165.50$

$= \$30,000 \dfrac{1}{(1+0.09)^3}$

$p = \$23,165.50$

(3) $p = f(p_{n,i})$ $n = 3,\ i = 0.09$

$= \$30,000\ (0.772183)$

$p = \$23,165.49$ (rounding difference)

b. $25,000 - $23,165.50 = $1,834.50

3. a. $P_0 = C$ (Factor for $P_{0_{n,i}}$)

$\$60,000 = C\ (7.469444)$

$C = \$8,032.73$

b. $P_d = C$ [Factor for $P_{0_{n-1,i}}$ +1]

$\$60,000 = C\ (7.365777 + 1)$

$C = \$7,172.08$

c. $P_0 = C$ (Factor for $P_{0_{n,i}}$)

$P_0 = \$7,500\ (7.469444)$

$P_0 = \$56,020.83$

d. $F_0 = C$ (Factor for $F_{0_{n,i}}$)

$F_0 = \$7,500\ (9.487171)$

$F_0 = \$71,153.78$

APPENDIX E

ACCOUNTING FOR CHANGES IN PRICES

CHAPTER OBJECTIVES

After careful study of this appendix, you will be able to:

1. Understand the difference between current value and general price level adjustments.

2. Explain the three alternatives to historical cost.

3. Understand issues related to the measurement of current cost, the adjustment of historical dollars for general price-level changes, and the purchasing power gain or loss on net monetary items.

4. Explain the conceptual issues relating to the alternatives to historical cost.

5. Be aware of the disclosure requirements that have existed for alternative disclosures, including the reasons for the elimination of the required disclosures.

SYNOPSIS

Current Value and the General Price Level

1. A specific price change (current value change) is the change in the price of an individual asset or liability in response to the dynamics of the market. A general price-level change is a change in the value or purchasing power of the dollar, is known as inflation or deflation, and is caused by changes in the prices of all goods and services in the economy. Specific price changes of individual assets and liabilities may be very different from the change in the general price level.

2. Current value (generally measured by current cost) adjustments account for the changes in the values of individual assets and liabilities. They do not account for changes in the value of the dollar. Current cost is the cost in the current period of replacing (acquiring or producing) the items concerned.

3. General price-level adjustments convert dollars of different purchasing power into dollars of constant purchasing power. That is, they convert the dollar into a constant measuring unit. However, they do not account for changes in the values of individual assets and liabilities.

4. General price-level adjustments may be applied to either historical cost or current cost financial statements. Consequently, four alternative accounting methods are available.

   (a) Historical cost

   (b) Historical cost adjusted for changes in the general price level (historical cost/constant purchasing power)

   (c) Current value (current cost)

   (d) Current value adjusted for changes in the general price level (current cost/constant purchasing power)

Three Alternatives to Historical Cost

5. Holding gains and losses arise in current cost financial statements. A realized holding gain or loss is a change in the value of an asset which has been realized through a sale. An unrealized holding gain or loss is a change in the value of an asset which has not yet been sold. Some accountants advocate that a company should include unrealized holding gains and losses in income when presenting current cost financial statements. Others argue that a company should record such gains and losses directly in stockholders' equity.

6. Historical cost financial statements may compare dollars of different purchasing powers. Consequently, the statements may be misleading or not relevant to users. In contrast, historical cost/constant purchasing power financial statements adjust recorded historical costs for changes in the purchasing power of the dollar that have occurred since the historical costs were recorded.

7. Constant purchasing power accounting addresses general price-level changes, while current cost accounting addresses specific price changes. The two concepts can be combined: current cost/constant purchasing power financial statements reflect both the changing value of the dollar and the current cost of assets.

Measurement of Current Cost

8. As defined by the FASB, the current cost of inventory is the current cost of purchasing or producing the goods concerned. The current cost of property, plant, or equipment is the current cost of acquiring the same service potential.

9. Three alternatives have been suggested for measurement of the current cost of inventory and property, plant, and equipment:

   (a) Direct pricing: current invoice prices, vendors' list prices, appraisals, etc.

   (b) Functional or unit pricing: the estimation of costs per unit and multiplication of these costs by the number of units in the asset. (Functional pricing was not included in FASB Statement No. 89.)

   (c) Revision of historical acquisition cost (indexation), using externally or internally generated indexes.

   A company may choose any of the alternatives to measure any asset or liability. Generally, direct pricing is used for inventory, and functional pricing is used for buildings. Revision of the historical cost of any item is arithmetically simple using a specific price index.

10. The current cost of property, plant, and equipment may be represented by: (a) the current cost of a used asset of the same age and in the same condition as the asset owned; (b) the current cost of a new asset with the same service potential that the used asset had when new, less a deduction for depreciation; or (c) the current cost of a new asset with a different service potential, less a deduction for depreciation, and adjusted for the cost of the difference in service potential.

11. Inventory is valued on the balance sheet at its current cost at the end of the period. The cost of goods sold is reported on the income statement at the average current cost, which is measured as the units sold x [(beginning current cost per unit + ending current cost per unit) ÷ 2]. Property, plant, and equipment is valued on the balance sheet at its current cost at the end of the period. The depreciation expense reported on the income statement is based on the average current cost of the depreciable assets, which is measured as [(beginning current cost + ending current cost) ÷ 2] ÷ estimated life.

12. A general price-level index, a measure of the relationship between money and its ability to purchase a wide variety of goods and services, is used to make constant purchasing power adjustments. Historical dollars are converted to constant purchasing power dollars using a simple mathematical computation. The adjustment ratio used is the index of the current period divided by the index of the period in which the historical dollars were originally recorded:

$$\text{Constant Purchasing Power Dollars} = \text{Historical Dollars} \times \frac{\text{Current Period Price-Level Index}}{\text{Historical Price-Level Index}}$$

For the disclosures encouraged by FASB Statement No. 89 (discussed later), the average CPI-U index is used.

13. Monetary assets are money and claims to fixed sums of money in the future, such as accounts receivable and notes receivable. When a monetary asset is held during a period of inflation, a purchasing-power loss results. Monetary liabilities are obligations to repay fixed sums in the future. When a monetary liability is held during a period of inflation, a purchasing-power gain results.

14. Monetary assets and liabilities are combined to arrive at net monetary items. Purchasing-power gains and losses (monetary gains and losses, or general price-level gains and losses) are gains and losses on net monetary items from inflation and deflation. Purchasing-power gains result from holding negative net monetary items (liabilities exceed assets); purchasing-power losses result from holding positive net monetary items (assets exceed liabilities). Holders of nonmonetary assets and liabilities do not gain or lose purchasing power from general price-level changes.

Conceptual Issues Relating to Alternatives to Historical Cost

15. Income may be defined as a corporation's earnings in excess of the amount it needs to maintain the capital invested in the corporation, i.e., the return on capital. Each type of financial statement discussed (historical cost, historical cost/constant purchasing power, current cost, current cost/constant purchasing power) is based on a different capital maintenance concept. The concept of historical dollars of capital at the beginning of the year underlies historical cost statements. The concept of the purchasing power of the capital at the beginning of the year underlies historical cost/constant purchasing power statements. The concept of operating capacity (the ability to provide goods and services) at the beginning of the year measured in dollars underlies current cost statements. The concept of operating capacity measured in units of constant purchasing power underlies current cost/constant purchasing power statements. Only constant purchasing power adjusted current cost income statements report income as the excess after maintenance of capital in terms of both operating capacity and constant purchasing power.

16. Historical cost balance sheets, which report items at their exchange prices in historical dollars, may be misleading because they report amounts in dollars of varying purchasing powers. Only constant purchasing power adjusted current cost balance sheets show items at current cost (i.e., current value) and also enhance comparability over time by reporting in dollars of constant purchasing power.

17. Historical cost (and constant purchasing power adjusted historical cost) financial statements are more reliable, but less relevant, than current cost statements. Historical cost statements are more verifiable and understandable than statements based on other concepts.

18. When current cost is used in preparing financial statements, the FASB requires that current cost be measured in terms of the reproduction cost of currently owned assets. Reproduction cost is the current cost of acquiring assets identical to those owned. This measure avoids adjustments to operational expenses which might result if a measure which incorporates technological change such as replacement cost were used.

Current Exit Values

19. Historical cost, constant purchasing power, and current cost use entry values (input values). In contrast, a current exit value (net realizable value) is the net cash amount that a company would receive if it sold an item. Proponents of the use of exit values argue that the current measure of amounts to be received from future sales is relevant to financial statement users, and that exit values provide better information than input values on return on investment, liquidity, and financial flexibility.

20. When a company uses exit values, its income has two components: (a) the purchasing margin, or difference between the exit value and the acquisition cost on the date of acquisition, and (b) the holding gain or loss, or change in the exit values of the assets.

21. While generally accepted accounting principles require the use of exit values in the financial statements of a company for reporting certain investments, in some situations exit values are not relevant. For example, if a company recorded inventory at net realizable value, income would be recognized at the time of purchase, before the sale transaction. In contrast, exit values may be more relevant than input values for companies which are to be liquidated or sold.

FASB Disclosure Guidelines

22. FASB Statement No. 33 required the disclosure of the effects of changing prices as a supplement to the basic financial statements from 1979 through 1985. In 1986, FASB Statement No. 89 rescinded the disclosure requirements. FASB Statement No. 89 does, however, encourage the continued disclosure of information about the effects of changing prices, and includes guidelines for measurement and disclosure.

23. According to the FASB guidelines, the selected disclosures for the current year are: (a) income from continuing operations under the current cost basis; (b) purchasing power gain or loss on net monetary items; (c) current cost (or lower recoverable) amount of inventory and of property, plant, and equipment at the end of the current year; (d) increase or decrease in the current cost (or lower recoverable) amount of inventory and of property, plant, and equipment, before and after eliminating the effects of inflation; and (e) aggregate foreign currency translation adjustment on a current cost basis, when applicable.

24. The selected disclosures included in a 5-year summary, adjusted to average-for-the-year, end-of-year, or base-period constant purchasing power are: (a) net sales and other operating revenues; (b) income from continuing operations and related earnings per share under the current cost basis; (c) purchasing power gain or loss on net monetary items; (d) increase or decrease in the current cost (or lower recoverable amount) of inventory and of property, plant, and equipment, net of inflation; (e) aggregate foreign currency translation adjustment on a current cost basis, when applicable; (f) net assets at year-end on a current cost basis; (g) cash dividends declared per common share; and (h) market price per common share at year-end. Two additional disclosures are (1) the principal types of information used to calculate current cost, and (2) information related to calculation of current cost depreciation.

Conceptual Evaluation of the Elimination of the Required Disclosures

25. FASB Statement No. 89 eliminated the final requirements for disclosure of the effects of changing prices. A number of arguments influenced the FASB to remove the requirements. Opponents of disclosure claimed: (a) Current cost and specific price index information is not relevant, and supplementary disclosures determined by judgment and labelled as unaudited are not reliable. (b) The cost of the information exceeds its benefits. (c) The disclosures lack comparability. (d) The overly complex disclosures lack understandability. (e) In a period of low inflation, the disclosures are not needed. Inflation does, however, undeniably cause historical cost financial statements to show illusory profits and to mask the erosion of capital. Supplementary disclosures will likely be requested again if inflation increases.

International Accounting Differences

26. International Accounting Standards require a company that reports using the currency of a hyperinflationary economy to prepare its primary financial statements in terms of the currency at the balance sheet data. The company is also required to include the purchasing power gain or loss on net monetary items in its net income.

SELF-EVALUATION EXERCISES

Supply the words or amounts necessary to complete each of the following items.

Current Value and the General Price Level

CV-1. A change in the price of an individual asset in response to the dynamics of the market is a ____________ ________ __________.

CV-2. Changes in the values of individual assets are accounted for by ____________ __________ adjustments.

CV-3. Dollars of different purchasing power are converted into dollars of constant purchasing power by means of _____________ __________-________ ________________.

CV-4. General price-level adjustments ________ (do, do not) account for changes in the values of individual assets and liabilities.

Three Alternatives to Historical Cost

AH-1. An increase in the value of an asset which has not yet been sold is an ______________ _______________ __________.

AH-2. A company adjusts recorded historical costs for changes in the purchasing power of the dollar in ____________ ________/ ____________ ______________ ________ financial statements.

AH-3. Both the changing value of the dollar and the current cost of assets are reflected in __________ _________/____________ ____________ _______ financial statements.

Measurement of Current Cost

CC-1. According to the FASB, the current cost of property, plant, or equipment is the current cost of acquiring the same ____________ ______________.

CC-2. The alternatives that have been suggested for the measurement of the current cost of inventory and of property, plant, and equipment are __________ pricing, ____________ pricing, and indexation.

CC-3. Depreciation expense reported on the income statement is based on the average _____________ _____________ of the depreciable assets.

CC-4. When making constant purchasing power adjustments, historical dollars are converted to constant purchasing power dollars using a ____________ ________-________ index.

CC-5. Accounts receivable and notes receivable are examples of ____________ __________.

CC-6. Obligations to repay fixed sums of money in the future are ____________ ______________.

CC-7. In a period of inflation, purchasing power _______ result from holding negative net monetary items, while purchasing power _______ result from holding positive net monetary items.

Conceptual Issues Relating to Alternatives to Historical Cost

CIA-1. The capital maintenance concept underlying historical cost financial statements is the concept of ____________ _________ of capital at the ____________ (beginning, end) of the year.

CIA-2. Underlying current cost/constant purchasing power financial statements is the concept of ____________ __________ measured in units of ___________ _____________ ________.

CIA-3. Historical cost financial statements are considered to be more reliable and understandable, but less relevant, than _____________ _________ financial statements.

CIA-4. The ____________ __________ of an asset is the current cost of acquiring the best asset available to perform the function of the owned asset and is the measure of current cost required by FASB.

Current Exit Values

CEV-1. The net cash amount that a company would receive if it sold an item is the _____ ____________ _______ or _____________ __________.

CEV-2. The difference between the exit value and the acquisition cost on the date of acquisition, a component of income when exit values are used, is the _____________ __________.

CEV-3. A change in the exit value of an asset is a _________ _______ or _______.

FASB Disclosure Guidelines

FD-1. The selected disclosures for the current year according to the FASB guidelines include income from continuing operations under the _____________ ________ basis, and the ____________ _________ _________ ________ _________ on net monetary items.

FD-2. The selected disclosures according to the guidelines in FASB Statement No. 89 for a 5-year summary include net sales and other operating revenues adjusted to average-for-the-year, end-of-year or base-period ____________ ______________ __________.

Conceptual Evaluation of the Elimination of the Required Disclosures

EDR-1. Opponents of disclosure of the effects of changing prices claimed that current cost and specific price index information is not ___________ (reliable, relevant), and that the cost of disclosure exceeds the ___________.

International Accounting Differences

IAD-1. International Accounting Standards require that the purchasing power gain or loss on net monetary items be included in income in countries with _______________.

ANSWERS TO SELF-EVALUATION EXERCISES

CV-1. specific price change; CV-2. current value; CV-3. general price-level adjustments; CV-4. do not; AH-1. unrealized holding gain; AH-2. historical cost/constant purchasing power; AH-3. current cost/constant purchasing power; CC-1. service potential; CC-2. direct, functional; CC-3. current cost; CC-4. general price-level; CC-5. monetary assets; CC-6. monetary liabilities; CC-7. gains, losses; CIA-1. historical dollars, beginning; CIA-2. operating capacity, constant purchasing power; CIA-3. current cost; CIA-4. replacement cost; CEV-1. net realizable value, exit value; CEV-2. purchasing margin; CEV-3. holding gain, loss; FD-1. current cost, purchasing power gain or loss; FD-2. constant purchasing power; EDR-1. relevant, benefits; IAD-1. hyperinflation.

POST TEST

Part A Circle T if the statement is true and F if it is false.

T F 1. When a company is reporting on a current cost basis, inventory and property, plant, and equipment are valued on the balance sheet at current cost at the end of the period.

T F 2. Holding a monetary liability during a period of inflation results in a purchasing-power gain.

T F 3. Accumulated depreciation on a current cost basis is the sum of the current cost depreciation expenses calculated each year of the asset's life.

T F 4. The capital maintenance concept of the purchasing power of the capital at the beginning of the year underlies historical cost/constant purchasing power financial statements.

T F 5. Historical cost financial statements are considered to be more reliable, but less relevant, than current cost financial statements.

T F 6. According to <u>FASB Statement No. 89</u>, the effects of changing prices must be disclosed as an integral part of the basic financial statements.

T F 7. Current value statements account for changes in the value of the dollar.

T F 8. The FASB requires the use of the Consumer Price Index for All Urban Consumers for constant purchasing power adjustments.

T F 9. General price-level adjustments can be applied only to historical cost financial statements.

T F 10. A general price-level change is a change in the price of a specific asset in response to the dynamics of the market.

T F 11. The reproduction cost of an asset is the current cost of acquiring the best asset available to perform the function of the asset.

T F 12. Constant purchasing power adjusted current cost financial statements show items at current cost and enhance comparability over time with dollars of constant purchasing power.

T F 13. General price-level changes do not result in purchasing power gains or losses for holders of nonmonetary assets.

T F 14. An unrealized holding gain is an increase in the value of an asset which has not yet been sold.

T F 15. Exit values are more relevant for the valuation of inventory than for the valuation of fixed assets.

T F 16. International accounting standards require that countries with hyperinflation include any purchasing power gain or loss on net monetary items in net income.

T F 17. FASB Statement No. 89 eliminated the final requirements for disclosures of the effects of changing prices.

T F 18. Accounts receivable and notes receivable are examples of monetary assets.

T F 19. Purchasing-power gains and losses do not result from holding nonmonetary assets and liabilities during a period of general price-level changes.

Part B Select the one best answer, and place its letter in the space provided.

_____ 1. Which of the following statements is true? (a) historical cost financial statements are based on the capital maintenance concept of purchasing power of the capital at the beginning of the year; (b) historical cost/constant purchasing power financial statements are based on the capital maintenance concept of historical dollars of capital at the beginning of the year; (c) current cost financial statements are based on the capital maintenance concept of operating capacity at the beginning of the year measured in dollars; (d) current cost/constant purchasing power financial statements are based on the capital maintenance concept of purchasing power of the capital at the beginning of the year.

_____ 2. General price-level adjustments (a) account for changes in the value of individual assets and liabilities; (b) may be applied only to current value financial statements; (c) may be made by appraisal; (d) convert dollars of different purchasing power into dollars of constant purchasing power.

_____ 3. Unrealized holding gains (a) are increases in the value of assets which have been sold; (b) are reported as part of income from continuing operations in historical cost income statements; (c) result from constant purchasing power adjustments; (d) are increases in the value of assets which have not yet been sold.

_____ 4. The current cost of the service potential of used property, plant, or equipment may <u>not</u> be represented by (a) the book value of the asset; (b) the current cost of a used asset of the same age and in the same condition as the owned asset; (c) the current cost of a new asset with the same remaining service potential as the used asset; (d) the current cost of a new asset with a different service potential, less a deduction for depreciation, and adjusted for the cost of the difference in service potential.

_____ 5. Which of the following statements is <u>not</u> true? (a) a specific price change is a change in the price of an individual asset in response to the dynamics of the market; (b) specific price changes are caused by inflation or deflation; (c) a specific price change is also known as a current value change; (d) specific price changes of individual assets may vary greatly from changes in the general price level.

<u>Part C</u> Solve each of the following short problems.

1. On December 31, 2004, the Stoughton Company owned the following fixed assets:

Land: Purchased on January 1, 2004 for $50,000
Current cost on December 31, 2004 of $75,000

Building: Purchased on January 1, 2004 for $200,000
Current cost of $250,000 on December 31, 2004
Estimated life of 30 years
Depreciation method--straight-line, with no residual value

Equipment: Purchased on January 1, 2004 for $80,000
Current cost of $100,000 on December 31, 2004
Estimated life of 20 years
Depreciation method--straight-line, with no residual value

Compute the following 2004 disclosures for the Stoughton Company:

(a) Current cost depreciation expense

1. (b) Current cost (net) of property, plant, and equipment

2. The Washboard Company is presenting comprehensively adjusted constant purchasing power financial statements for a year when the CPI-U rose from 100 to 120. Using the information shown below, compute the Washboard Company's purchasing-power gain or loss at the average index for the year of 110. Washboard's sales, purchases, wages and salaries, interest, and income taxes are assumed to have occurred evenly throughout the year.

Account	Historical Cost
Cash (beginning balance)	$ 10,000
Accounts receivable (beginning balance)	25,000
Notes receivable (beginning balance)	75,000
Accounts payable (beginning balance)	10,000
Notes payable (beginning balance)	30,000
Sales	300,000
Interest income	5,000
Purchases	155,000
Salaries expense	80,000
Income tax expense	20,000
Dividends (paid at the end of the year)	10,000
Cash (ending balance)	30,000
Accounts receivable (ending balance)	55,000
Notes receivable (ending balance)	60,000
Accounts payable (ending balance)	20,000
Notes payable (ending balance)	15,000

ANSWERS TO POST TEST

Part A

1. T
2. T
3. F
4. T
5. T
6. F
7. F
8. T
9. F
10. F
11. F
12. T
13. T
14. T
15. F
16. T
17. T
18. T
19. T

Part B

1. c
2. d
3. d
4. a
5. b

Part C

1. (a) Current cost depreciation expense (at average current cost) = $12,000

([($200,000 + $250,000) ÷ 2] x (1/30) building) + ([($80,000 + $100,000) ÷ 2] x (1/20) equipment)

(b) Current cost (net) of property, plant, and equipment = $411,667

$75,000 land + [$250,000 - ($250,000 x 1/30)] building + [$100,000 - ($100,000 x 1/20)] equipment

2. Purchasing-power loss (at average price level): $17,000

	Historical Cost	x	Adjustment	=	Constant Purchasing Power
Beginning net monetary items[a]	$ 70,000	x	(110/100)	=	$ 77,000
Sales	$300,000	x	(110/110)	=	$300,000
Interest income	$ 5,000	x	(110/110)	=	$ 5,000
Purchases	($155,000)	x	(110/110)	=	($155,000)
Salaries expense	($ 80,000)	x	(110/110)	=	($ 80,000)
Income tax expense	($ 20,000)	x	(110/110)	=	($ 20,000)
Dividends	($ 10,000)	x	(110/120)	=	($ 9,167)
Ending net monetary items (unadjusted)[b]	$110,000				
Constant purchasing power ending balance (at average price level)					$117,833
Historical ending balance adjusted to average price level [$110,000 x (110/120)]					$100,833
Purchasing-power loss (at average price level)					$ 17,000

[a] $10,000 + $25,000 + $75,000 - $10,000 - $30,000 = $70,000

[b] $30,000 + $55,000 + $60,000 - $20,000 - $15,000 = $110,000

CHECK FIGURES for EXERCISES

INTERMEDIATE ACCOUNTING, Ninth Edition
Nikolai and Bazley

Chapter 3

E3- 1 Total current assets, $46,600
2 Total Accum. Depr., $96,800
3 Total S/H Equity, $415,600
4 No check figure
5 No check figure
6 Total Assets $112,100
7 Total Assets $238,700
8 (j) Total Assets, $149,200
9 (11) Total Assets, $140,700
10 Total Assets, $68,100
11 R/E, 12/31/04, $206,494
12 R/E, 12/31/04, $234,700

Chapter 4

E4- 1 Net Income, $16,100
2 Net Income, $16,800
3 No check figure
4 No check figure
5 Cost of Goods Sold, $122,000
6 (2) Net Income, $12,040
7 (1) Cost of Goods Sold, $101,000
8 (2) Net Income, $18,550
9 (2) R/E, 12/31/04, $54,028
10 (2) Extraord. Loss, $(2,590)
11 Net Income, 2004, $37,000
12 Gross Profit, 2005, $58,400
13 After-tax loss on write-down, $(70,000)
14 After-tax loss on write-down, $(126,000)
15 No check figure
16 Comprehensive income, $16,800
17 Net cash prov. by oper. activities, $28,400
18 Net cash prov. by oper. activities, $20,500
19 Net Increase in Cash, $7,000
20 Net Increase in Cash, $19,100

Chapter 5

E5- 1 Segment profit (B), $9,000
2 Segment profit (2), $9,000
3 Segment profit (A), $37,120
4 Segment profit (5), $3,600
5 EPS, $1.28
6 Total Assets, $130,000
7 2nd Quarter, NI, $28,200
8 (2) Est. Total Tax, 4th quarter, $21,200
9 2003 to 2005, EPS, $(0.31)
10 2005, EPS, $1.92
11 (3) 11.5% (4) 15.9%
12 (2) 8.5% (7) 4.09 times
13 No check figure

Chapter 6

E6- 1 No check figure
2 No check figure
3 1/31/04 Cash Short and Over, dr, $7.30
4 (2) Adj. Cash Bal, $987.22
5 (1) Adj. Cash Bal, $2,077.45
6 (1) Adj. Cash Bal, $18,989.20
7 (2) Adj. Cash Bal, $6,400.44
8 Receivables, cr, $44,400
9 (1) Sales, cr, $9,000
10 (2) 2/1/05, Sales, cr, $12,870
11 (2) 12/31/04, Sales Ret. & Allow, dr, $280
12 (1) Bad Debt Exp, dr, $630
13 (1) Allow. for Doubtful Accts, cr, $4,320
14 Amt. Uncoll., 30-60 days, $2,280
15 (3) Bad Debt Exp, dr, $4,165
16 Balance 12/31/00, $340,000
17 12/1/04 Cash, dr, $126,720
18 Loss from Factoring, dr, $12,800
19 9/15, Cr. Card Exp, dr, $105
20 Total Expenses, $55,100
21 (1) 2/9/05, Int. Rev, cr, $240
22 (2) Proceeds, $9,072.90
23 Loss from discounting note, Dillon, $(16.50)

Chapter 7

E7- 1 Closing Bal, Raw Mat. $40,000
2 No check figure
3 No check figure
4 Jan. Cash, dr, $27,500
5 (2) Purchases, dr, $19,600
6 (2) Purchases, dr, $49,000
7 (2) LIFO End. Inv, $1,750
8 (3) Avg. Cost End. Inv, $1,083
9 (1) FIFO, Inv. total Cost, 3/31/04, $18,000
10 LIFO - perpetual COGS, $5,660
11 $-Value LIFO, End Inv, $2,010
12 12/31/04, End. Inv, $46,000
13 $-Value LIFO, 2004, End. Inv, $255,500
14 2006 End. Inv, $349,800
15 Cost Index, 109.5628
16 (2) 2004, LIFO, Inv, $115,000
17 No check figure
18 Exchange gain, 1/30/05, $600
19 Exchange loss, 7/10/05, $250

Chapter 8

E8- 1 Product A, $66
2 Case 2, Inv. Value, $5.00
3 (2) Total Inv. Value, $4,235.50
4 12/31/05 Loss Recovery, cr, $500
5 12/31/04 Loss on Purch. Commitment, dr, $5,000
6 COGS, $450,000
7 Est. Loss of Inv., $76,000
8 No check figure
9 No check figure
10 (4) End Inv. at LCM, $40,660
11 End Inv. at Retail, $80,000
12 (3) End Inv. at LIFO Cost, $9,796
13 End. Inv. at Retail, $44,000
14 End. Inv. at Cost, $80,272
15 End. Inv. at Retail, $610,000
16 No check figure
17 NI after adj, $8,000

Chapter 9

E9- 1 No check figure
2 No check figure

E9- 3 Machine, dr, $213,000
4 (1) PV of note, $95,095.95
5 Capitalized Cost, $9,800
6 Land, $53,000
7 Cost assigned to Land, $88,000
8 No Gain Recog., Bristol
9 Denver Co., Loss, dr, $7,000
10 Denver Co., Loss, dr, $2,000
11 Harmes Co., Gain, cr, $1,000
12 Goodman Co., Gain, cr, $2,500
13 No check figure
14 Cost of Constr. Asset at full cap., $96,000
15 (2) note disclosure
16 (1) Capitalized Int, $48,000
17 Interest Rev, $330,000
18 No check figure
19 (1) (a) Expense $1,600,000

Chapter 10

E10- 1 (3) Depreciation, $44,000
2 (3) Depreciation, $50,000
3 (2) 2005 Deprec, $11,157
4 (2) (c) 2006 Deprec, $2,490
5 Net Income, Straight Line, $4,200
6 (3) x = $156,250
7 Deprec. Exp, dr, $10,000
8 Total Annual Deprec, $15,000
9 (1) Deprec. Exp, dr, $2,000
10 Total 2005 Deprec, $5,270
11 (1) $3,195 (2) $3,333
12 (2) Accum Deprec, dr, $250,000
13 Fin. Stmt Deprec, $4,500
14 (1) Accum Deprec, $123,637
15 (2) Cum. Effect on prior years, $21,000
16 Depletion Rate, $0.275/ton
17 Depletion Rate, $3.05/ton

Chapter 11

E11- 1 No check figure
2 12/31/04, Amort. Exp., $3,159
3 Book Value, 12/31/01, $26,795
4 Expense $20,000 in 2003
5 Research and Dev. Exp., $172,000
6 No check figure
7 No check figure
8 No check figure
9 Goodwill, $105,000
10 Normal Earnings 2004, $90,400
11 (2) Goodwill, $14,605
12 (1) (b) Goodwill, $90,000
13 Implied Goodwill, $260,000
14 (2) Goodwill Valuation, $10,814
15 Normal Annual Earnings, $13,750

Chapter 12

E12- 1 Discount Lost, $16,000
2 3/1/05, Int. Exp, $750
3 (3) Effective Ann. Rate, 14.51%
4 (1) 10/30/04, Mach, dr, $21,779.37
5 (2) Liab for Future Absence, $2,400
6 (2) Sales Tax Pay., cr, $15,600
7 State Un. Tax Payable, cr, $4,400
8 (1) B = $23,755.66
9 9/1/04 Prepd. Prop. Tax, dr, $4,800
10 9/10/04 Cash, cr, $24,000

E12- 11 Est. Warranty Liab, $2,100
12 (2) Unearned Warranty Rev, $6,800
13 (2) Est. Prem Claims, $135,000
14 (2) Current Liab, Est. prem. claims outstd., $20,000
15 (2) Unearned Rev, $750
16 Est. Loss from Litigation, $6,500
17 No check figure
18 2005 long-term serial bonds, $1,600,000
19 Long-Term Notes Pay, $878,550
20 C/L Notes Pay, $150,000

Chapter 13

E13- 1 6/30/04, Interest Exp, dr, $20,000
2 6/30/04, Interest Exp, dr, $59,500
3 12/31/04, Interest Exp, dr, $27,333.33
4 12/31/05, Book Value, $98,247.45
5 6/30/05, Book Value, $205,582.28
6 (2) PV of Int, $339,756.34
7 (2) Disc. on B/P, dr, $2,383.29
8 (3) Effective Int. Method, 6/30/04, Prem. on B/P, dr, $822.70
9 (3) 2/1/05, Int. Exp, dr, $485
10 (1) 8/31/05, Int. Exp, dr, $5,817.76
11 3/31/04, Int. Pay, cr, $41,250
12 Gain on Extinguishment of Debt, $92,000
13 (1)(b) Loss on Conversion, dr, $27,400
14 (2) Prem. on B/P, dr, $320,000
15 Bond Conv. Exp, dr, $20,000
16 (1) Value per Warrant, $3.89
17 B/P, cr, $3,000,000
18 (2) Int. Exp, dr, $1,077.26
19 1/1/04 Discount on N/P, dr, $27,336.15
20 (4) 12/31/06 Int. Exp, dr, $1,928.58
21 (2) 12/31/07 Int. Exp, dr, $9,090.97
22 12/31/04, Int. Exp, dr, $8,646.59
23 1/1/04 Gain on Sale, cr, $3,966.90
24 (1) 1/1/04, Disc. on N/R, cr, $5,070.15
25 (1) 1/1/04, Loss on Sale, $1,963.38
26 12/31/04, Int. Rev, cr, $1,963.38
27 2004 Income before taxes, $38,384
28 (1) Value of impaired loan, $168,335.93
29 (1) Value of impaired loan, $419,809.43
30 1/2/04 Carrying Value, $116,651
31 (1) Extraord. Gain, $16,000
32 (1) Loss on restruct. loan $(88,822.03)
33 (2) Loss on restruct. loan $(24,000)
34 1/1/06, Int. Exp, $10,600
35 (1) 12/31/05, Int. Exp, $14,639.27
36 (1) 12/31/05 PV of Int. Pmt, $42,708

Chapter 14

E14- 1 (2) Unrealized Gain, $700, on 2004 I/S
2 (2) Loss on Sale $(200), Unreal. Gain $500
3 12/31/04 Unreal. Inc/Dec in Value, dr, $1,500
4 (2) $4,000 cr bal
5 10/11/04, Allow. for Change, dr, $2,800
6 (1) 3/31/04, Invest in Debt Sec, dr, $413,800
7 (2) 6/30/04, Int. Rev, cr, $24,192.09
8 11/1/04, Gain on Sale, cr, $22,170.65
9 (3) 6/30/04, Int. Rev, cr, $11,409.92
10 (3) 6/30/04, Int. Rev, cr, $3,073.76
11 1/1/05, Loss on Sale, dr, $5,257.77
12 12/31/04, Invest in Sec, dr, $106,515.21
13 3/31/04, Invest in Stock: Crowell Co, cr, $15,000
14 12/31/04, Invest Inc, cr, $18,000
15 Purchased goodwill, $10,500

E14- 16 7/1/05, Memorandum entry
17 2/1/05, Gain on Sale, cr, $3,000
18 12/31/04, Insurance Exp, dr, $7,850
19 12/31/04, Allow for Change, dr, $3,000
20 12/31/04, Int. Rate Swap Payment, $12,000

Chapter 15

E15- 1 (2) C/S, cr, $48,000
2 (2) APIC on C/S, cr, $11,450
3 (2) Agg. FV of C/S, $13,800
4 (1)(c) Land, dr, $62,500
5 (3) Subscr. Rec, cr, $12,000
6 (2) APIC, dr, $54,000
7 1/5/07 C/S, cr, $1,500
8 (1) 2005 Current Comp. Exp, $38,734
9 (2) C/S Option Warrants, cr, $16,816
10 (2) Cash, cr, $20,000
11 (2) (b) R/E, dr, $2,700
12 (2) (a) R/E, dr, $5,000
13 (1) C/S warrants, cr, $23,579
14 (1) Cash, dr, $88,200
15 Total Contrib. Cap, $276,000
16 (3) 7/10, Treas Stock, cr, $600
17 (2) Total S/H Equity, $593,700
18 (1) (2) APIC - Treas, cr, $1,200
19 (3) Treas. Stock, dr, $6,250

Chapter 16

E16- 1 Weighted Avg, $57,218
2 (2) 2004 Basic EPS, $0.60
3 Basic EPS, $2.35
4 (1) Basic EPS, $1.60
5 (1) Impact, 11% bonds, $1.75
6 Diluted EPS, $1.17
7 Diluted EPS, $2.92
8 Basic EPS, $4.40
9 Basic EPS, $3.00
10 Diluted EPS, $2.29
11 (1)(c) Total Preferred, $44,000
12 7/6/04, R/E, dr, $48,000
13 (2) (5) $259,000
14 (1) (a), R/E, dr, $45,000
15 (1) Total S/H Equity, $2,500,000
16 (2) R/E, 12/31/04, $197,100
17 (2) (a) Fire Loss, dr, $60,000
18 R/E, 12/31/04, $169,800
19 R/E, 12/31/04, $196,400
20 S/H Equity, $757,000
21 Treas. Stock, bal, 12/31, $(3,700)
22 (2) Total Assets, $56,000
23 Total S/H Equity, $1,850,000

Chapter 17

E17- 1 No check figure
2 Total Gross Profit, $495,000
3 (1) Gross Profit, $200,000
4 2004 Profit to be recog., $300,000
5 2005 Profit to be recog., $23,333
6 (2) Gross Profit, $250,000
7 Net Income, $100,000
8 2005, Cash, dr, $172,000
9 2005, Net Income, $6,290
10 (2) Income Summary, cr, $18,000
11 (2) Total Gross Profit, $17,500

E17- 12 2005, Install. Sales, $90,000
13 Inventory, cr, $104,000
14 2006 Def. Gross Profit, dr, $20,000
15 12/31/04, Cash, dr, $15,600
16 (5) N/R, dr, $20,000
17 12/31/04 Cash, cr, $203,200
18 12/31/04 Sales, cr, $216,000

Chapter 18

E18- 1 Def. Tax Liab., cr, $560
2 Def. Tax Liab., cr, $2,100
3 Income Tax Pay., cr, $3,600
4 Income Tax Exp., dr, $13,860
5 Def. Tax Asset, dr, $1,080
6 Tax. temp. diff., 12/31/04, $3,000
7 12/31/04, Inc. Tax Pay., $22,500
8 Def. Tax Liab., cr, $51
9 (2) Net Loss, $(58,500)
10 (2) Def. Tax Asset, cr, $9,600
11 (2) Net Loss, $(81,000)
12 Inc. Tax Exp, dr, $35,000; Net Income, $143,000
13 (1) Inc. Tax Pay., cr, $28,800
14 (2) R/E, 12/31/04, $222,250
15 Noncurrent Liab, $4,900
16 (2) Def. Tax Liab., cr, $1,020

Chapter 19

E19- 1 2004 Pension Exp, $123,000
2 (1) 2004 Pension Exp, $108,000
3 (2) (a) Pension Exp, dr, $128,000
4 Cash, cr, $128,000
5 12/31/05, Pension Exp, dr, $172,800
6 Interest Cost, $72,100
7 2005, Pension Exp, $218,146
8 2004 Pension Exp, $334,500
9 2004-2006, Amort, $110,000
10 2004, Amort, $110,000
11 (1) (a) Avg. Remaining Life, 3.5
12 Net loss, $2,000
13 (2) Net gain, $2,800
14 (2) Add. Pension Liab, $181,000
15 (1) OPEB Exp, $41,000
16 2005 Pension Exp, dr, $158,211

Chapter 20

E20- 1 Operating lease
2 (2) PV = $300,000 (rounded)
3 PV = $68,036.62
4 (1) Rental Receipt, $107,785.01
5 1/2/04, Equip, cr, $60,758
6 Annual Lease Pmt, $7,665.36
7 Selling Price, $151,867.45
8 Gross Profit, $88,758.58
9 (2) PV of Lease Pmt, $60,817
10 Income before Taxes $66,059 understated
11 Income before Taxes, $40,000
12 Yearly Lease Receipt, $2,649.96
13 (2) Realized Profit on Sales, cr, $20,000

Chapter 21

E21- 1 No check figure
2 Net Cash from Oper. Act, $900
3 Net Increase in Cash, $4,500

E21- 4 Net Decrease in Cash, $(3,600)
5 (1) Net Cash from Oper. Act, $18,200
6 Machine B: Accum Deprec, dr, $4,600
7 Net Increase in Cash, $1,000
8 Net Decrease in Cash, $(2,000)
9 12/31/04, Total Assets, $23,400
10 Net cash used for Fin. Act, $(3,700)
11 Net Increase in Cash, $830
12 Total Debits, $2,830
13 Net Increase in Cash, $430
14 Interest Paid, $11,200
15 2005 Gain on sale of temp. invest., $300
16 Net cash provided by oper. act, $1,290
17 Cash outflows for oper. acct., $(69,000)
18 Net Increase in Cash, $6,400
19 Net Increase in Cash, $2,100

Chapter 22

E22- 1 No check figure
2 No check figure
3 No check figure
4 (2) 2005, Net Income, $360,000
5 (2) EPS, $2.45 (2004), $3.41 (2003)
6 (2) 2004, Pro forma Net Income, $388,500
7 No check figure
8 (3) 2004 Ending R/E, $233,100
9 R/E, end of 2003, $166,600
10 (6) R/E, dr, $15,960 or $29,960
11 No check figure
12 No check figure
13 (3) R/E, cr, $8,000
14 (1) 2004, NI, $25,800

Appendix C

EC- 1 No check figure
2 5/14, Cash, cr, $1,960
3 6/3, Gain on sale, cr, $200
4 Gross profit, $6,100
5 (5) Cost of goods sold, $111,000
6 (1) EPS, $2.10
7 Income Tax Pay., cr, $450
8 Income Tax Pay., cr, $1,056
9 Bad Debt Exp., dr, $270
10 Retained Earnings, dr, $250
11 Interest Payable, dr, $620
12 No check figure
13 (2) R/E, 12/31/04, $3,525
14 (2) R/E, 12/31/04, $11,390
15 Net income, $11,000

Appendix D

ED- 1 (2) Compound Int, $23,699.19
2 f = $31,876.96
3 (2) Present Value, $3,949.02
4 (1) F_o = $100,890.12
5 (2) P_d = $33,358.92
6 C = $3,888.22
7 (1) C = $6,935.24
8 C = $499.24
9 (2) P_o = $31,950.67
10 (2) C = $29,781.36
11 (3) p = $11,566.29
12 (1) P_o = $13,065.78
13 P_d = $12,112.05
14 P_d = $23,953.94

Appendix E

EE- 1 (2) Gross Profit, $5,000
2 C/S Constant Purch Power, $75,000
3 (2) 2002, Carrying Value, $99,200
4 (2) Ending inventory, $61,200
5 (2) Current cost (net), $174,000
6 (3) Gain on Sale of Land in 2002, $10,000

CHECK FIGURES for PROBLEMS
INTERMEDIATE ACCOUNTING, Ninth Edition
Nikolai and Bazley

Chapter 3

P3- 1 (10) X
2 No check figure
3 Total assets, $218,700
4 Total stock. equity, $58,600
5 Total assets, $264,600
6 (1) Total stock. equity, $279,900
7 (1) Total liabilities, $161,700
8 Total Assets, $184,800
9 Total assets, $166,200
10 (m) Total assets, $232,100
11 (2) Total assets, $134,900
12 Total assets, $4,944,700
13 Treas. stock, 12/31/04, $(10,400)
14 No check figure

Chapter 4

P4- 1 No check figure
2 (28) G
3 (2) Ret. earnings, 12/31/04, $297,050
4 (1) Total earnings per share, $2.60
5 (3) Ret. earnings, 12/31/04, $465,410
6 (3) Ret. earnings, 12/31/04, $181,070
7 (2) Pretax inc from cont oper, $107,500
8 (2) Net income, $9,380
9 (1) Net income, $25,970
10 (2) Inc. stmt, extraordinary item
11 (1) Pre-tax loss on write-down, $(80,000)
12 No check figure
13 Net income, $1,440,000
14 Income from cont. oper., $1,497,000
15 2004 operating income, $1,720,000
16 No check figure
17 No check figure
18 2005 tot. gross prof., $1,920,000
19 (1) Comprehensive income, $27,300
20 Net increase in cash, $11,700
21 Net increase in cash, $3,600
22 Net decrease in cash, $(2,400)
23 Total assets, $86,100

Chapter 5

P5- 1 (2) Total segment profit, $63,000
2 (2) Total segment profit, $29,880
3 (3) Retained earnings, $35,136
4 (4) Total assets, $144,675
5 No check figure
6 No check figure
7 (2) Taxable income per tax return, $665,000
8 No check figure
9 2(g) Return on total assets, 2005, 10.8%
10 2(f) Return on total assets, 2004, 13.5%
11 (1) Increase in total assets, 2003 to 2005, $92,500
12 1(e) Return on stockholders' equity, 20.7%
13 (5) Book value/share of common stk, $25.90

Chapter 6

P6- 1 Total cash on hand, $18,930
2 (1) adj. cash bal., $488.95
3 (2) unadj. cash bal., $24,781.26
4 (1) adj. cash bal., $2,994.73
5 (1) adj. bank bal., $71,867.22
6 3(a) $8,695; (b) $8,767
7 (2) Acct. Rec. end. bal., $169,800
8 May 11, Cash dr, $24,615.26
9 (2) Acct. Rec. end. bal., $177,520
10 (1a)(a) Acct. Rec, $70,000,
(1b)(a) Acct. Rec, $68,600
11 (1) Bad Debt Expense, $16,579
12 1(d) Bad Debt Expense, $16,700
13 (1) 10/15 Loss from Discount. Note, $17.10
14 (2) Accounts Receivable Assigned, $75,000
15 Cash, dr, $54,600
16 (2) Accounts Receivable Assigned, $46,900
17 (1) Customer Advances, cr, $1,746
18 (1) Allow. for Bad Accts., cr, $7,700
19 (1) Allow. for Doubtful Acct., $235,300
20 (2) Allow. for Doubtful Acct., $24,820
21 (2) Total Receivables, $430,695.05
22 7/31/04 adj. bal., $19,272.97
23 8/31/04 adj. bal., $12,751.89

Chapter 7

P7- 1 (4) excluded from inventory
2 Ending inventory, 12/31/04, $94,565
3 End. inv.: $440,000 (FIFO), $412,000 (LIFO)
4 (3) Inc. recog: $2,000 (Gross), $1,800 (Net)
5 (1) Apr. C of GS: $750(a), $850(c), $675(f)
6 (3) Ending inv.: $6,900 (FIFO); $4,655 (LIFO)
7 2004 Gross profit: $334,500 (FIFO)
8 (2) 2004 units used in prod., 15,000
9 2006 ending inventory, $58,556
10 2004 ending inventory, $9,015
11 (2) Ending Inventory Cost $374,250
12 (2) 2005 Inventory Cost $1,121,048
13 (2) 2005 Inventory Cost $652,000 (LIFO)
14 (4) Income taxes saved, $7,200
15 (1) Ending inventory, $71,264
16 (1) Corrected inventory, $61,270
17 Total Adj. to A/P, $(133,300)

Chapter 8

P8- 1 (1) LCM: $9.10(1); $7.80(2); $13.50(3)
2 (2) 2000, Loss, dr, $4,000
3 (1) when decline is temporary
4 (2)(a) 2004 Cost of goods sold, $97,000
5 Gross profit, $38,000
6 Inventory lost, $8,000
7 Inventory lost, $53,740
8 Goods in process lost, $108,000
9 WIP inv. lost, $69,000
10 Ending inv. at cost: $44,888(1); $44,020(2)
11 (1) Ending inv. at cost, $122,766
12 Est. Inv. at LCM, $37,840
13 (2) Ending inv., total cost, $33,500
14 2004 ending inv. at cost, $60,230

P8- 15 2005 ending inv. at cost, $44,963
16 9/6/05 ending inv. at cost, $52,040
17 (2) Current year: Net inc understated, $4,300
18 Adjusted amount, net sales, $8,425,000

Chapter 9

P9- 1 No check figure
2 Purch price allocation: machine, $24,000; building, $36,000
3 (6) Land, dr, $60,000; Bldgs, dr, $78,000
4 (1) Amount to capitalize, $145,815
5 (4) Record at PV of note, $8,264
6 Bal. of land, 12/31/04, $1,500,000
7 (1) Hurni: Loss of $4,000. Other: no gain
8 (3) Gain of $1,875
9 (1) Int. capitalized: $458,000 (2005)
10 (1) Capitalized Interest (2005) $1,370,000
11 Jan. 10: Acc Depr, dr, $800; Cash, cr, $800
12 (2) Mach & Equip bal, 12/31/04, $36,500
13 (3) Correction for boiler trade-in: Purch. disc, dr, $274.40; Fuel exp, dr, $741.60; Fuel inv, dr, $82.40; Acc depr, dr, $6,200; Loss, dr, $2,320; Bldg cr, $9,618.40
14 No check figure

Chapter 10

P10- 1 2004 depr.: (2) $29,250; (4) $61,905
2 2004 end book val: (2) $63,750
3 2005 depr.: (1) $11,500; (3) $22,500
4 (1) depr. rate = 50%
5 2009 depr.: (1) $1,187; (3) $1,187
6 2005 depr., $6,592
7 2004 total depr. exp., $21,933
8 (1) Dec. 31, 2007, Accum depr, cr, $15,200
9 (3) Depr exp., $14,720
10 (1) Total book value, $844,000
11 (2) 2006 Taxable income $22,334
12 (1) 2004 and 2005 depl. rate, $1.25/ton
13 (1) Total exp., $591,300
14 (1) Gain on change in acct prin, cr, $7,400
15 (1) Gain on Self-Const., dr, $1,500
16 (3) Accum depr: Bldg, 12/31/05, $5,811
17 (2) Total capitalized cost, $3,453,500
18 (14) $1,905
19 (2) Accum depr: Trucks, dr, $18,062
20 (2) Net gain on disposals, $3,300
21 (1) Auto bal, 12/31/04, $151,000
22 EPS, $3.89

Chapter 11

P11- 1 (5) Prepaid Adv., dr, $50,000
2 (3) Advertising Exp., dr, $60,000
3 Jan. 25, Adv. Exp, dr, $15,000
4 (1) R.E., dr, $50,000, Pat, cr, $50,000
5 (2) R&D Expense, dr, $55,000
6 $2,200,000
7 (5) Goodwill, dr, $90,000
8 (1) 2004 Royalty Expense, dr, $100,000
9 Total assets, $77,000
10 (1) Goodwill, $85,000
11 (2) Total intangible assets, $885,000
12 (2) Total charged against income, $740,000

P11- 13 Net income, $68,600
14 (2) Total expenses, $62,332
15 (2) Total assets, $1,496,600
16 (2) Goodwill, $790,783
17 (2) Goodwill, $375,218

Chapter 12

P12- 1 (1) 12/23/04 Accts. pay, cr, $58,800
2 1.b.(1) 12%; 1.b.(2) 13.64%
3 12/31/04 adj. entry: Int exp, dr, $520
4 (2) Liability for Employee Comp. for Future Absences, $9,000
5 (2) Sales tax payable, $56,075
6 (2) Payroll tax exp., dr, $18,904
7 (2) T = $1,401,869.16
8 (1) 10/31/04, Prop tax exp, dr, $1,317.22
9 (2) $136,700
10 Warranty expense, dr, $94,400
11 (1) Total Oct. Prem. exp, cr, $2,940
12 (1) Est. Loss from Litigation, dr, $80,000
13 (1) Mag. Subscr. Rev., cr, $600,000
14 (1) Current liability
15 $2,000,000 current liability
16 1/1 Machinery, dr, $72,597.90
17 12/31 Interest exp. on 12% note $4,000
18 12/31 Salaries Exp. (Officer's Bonus), dr, $40,412

Chapter 13

P13- 1 2006 Interest exp, dr, $12,802.81
2 12% (6/30/04, issuance)
3 (2) Ext loss on bond ret, dr, $9,084.73
4 (4) Gain: (a)$11,546.67, (b)$13,620.67
5 6/30/05, book value, $486,878.37
6 3(b) Interest exp, $34,477.51
7 (1)(c) B.V. of Bds on 6/30/05, $391,575.39
8 Prem on B. Pay, dr, $19,200 (3/1); $52,800 (9/1)
9 Value of stock warrants, $4.72 each
10 (1) Effective interest rate, 12%
11 1/1/04: Comp. equip, dr, $88,036.62
12 (2) 12/31/04 book value, $22,321.42
13 (1) 12/31/05 Int Rev, cr, $10,413.22
14 12/31/04 Int Rev, cr, $803.57
15 (3) Total gains, $87,600
16 12/31 Int. exp on 10% note payable, $6,010.50
17 (1) Effective interest rate, 5%
18 (2) 1/2/04, Loss on restruct. loan, dr, $861,666.19
19 (2) 1/2/07, Loss on restruct. loan, dr, $28,822.03
20 3(b) 6/30/05, Int Exp, dr, $26,635.69
21 (4) Prem. on Bonds Pay, dr, $8,000

Chapter 14

P14- 1 (2) Gain on sale, $300, Loss on sale, $(100), Unreal. loss on dec. in value, $(200)
2 (3) Temp inv. in trad sec (at FV), $21,450
3 (1) 3/31/04, Int. Rev, dr, $200
4 (2) First qtr. Gain on sale, $800, Div rev, $2,500
5 (1) 7/6/04, Allow for Change, dr, $975
6 (3) 6/30/04, Current assets, $69,960, Stockholders' equity, $225
7 (3) Temp invest in sec (at FV), $112,200
8 (2) Adj. cash bal, $13,194.35

P14- 9 3/31/05, Gain on Sale, cr, $1,745.97, Int. Rev, cr, $4,875
10 (2) Interest Revenue: Straight-line, $29,548.89, Effective int., $29,724.99
11 10/1/03, Int. Rev, dr, $5,250
12 2(a) '03, Int. Rev, cr, $22,334.81
2(b) '03, Int. Rev, cr, $22,549.51
13 1/1/06, Gain on Sale, cr, $4,291.67
14 2(a) Gain on Sale, cr, $2,500
2(b) Loss on Sale, dr, $2,750
15 12/31/04, Invest in Stock, cr (amort), $375
16 (2) $430,225
17 Purch. goodwill for Feeley, $8,000, for Holmes, $25,000
18 (1) 12/31/04 Unreal. inc. in value, $30,000, 12/31/04 Carrying value of invest, $630,000
19 12/31/03 Cash Surrender Value of Life Ins, dr, $672
20 12/31/04, Loss in Value of Derivative, dr, $124,342

Chapter 15

P15- 1 (3) Cash, dr, $99,000
2 (4) Retained Earnings, dr, $24,000
3 (2) 8/3/04 Subscriptions Receivable, dr, $178,200
4 10/3 Cash, dr, $47,500
5 2(b) C/S Warrants, dr, $35,580
6 (3) C/S Option Warrents, $318,505
7 (2) 1/17/07 APIC-C/S, cr, $183,750
8 (2) 12/31/05 Comp. Exp, dr, $54,330
9 (2) 12/31/07 Comp. Exp, dr, $5,000
10 1(2) Aver. issuance price, $108/sh.
11 (1) 9/22/04 Building, dr, $49,850
12 Total contri. capital, $1,491,000
13 Premium on preferred stock, $76,000
14 (g) Subscrip. Rec., cr, $190,400
15 1(b)2 Treas stock-common, dr, $5,000
16 2(a)5 Cash, cr, $19,500
17 Total Stockholders' Equity, $2,486,000

Chapter 16

P16- 1 Net Income $41,125
2 Basic EPS, 2005, $2.17
3 (1a) Basic EPS, $3.03
4 (4) Diluted EPS, $2.02
5 (2) Diluted EPS, $4.41
6 (1) Basic EPS, $3.66
7 Diluted EPS, $1.44
8 (2) Basic EPS, $2.31
9 (1) Year 2, Total Preferred, $7,000
10 Max cash distrib to common, $175,333
11 July 2, Ret. Earnings, dr, $27,440
12 (1) May 14, Ret. Earnings, dr, $84,250
13 1(5a) Gain, cr, $6,000
14 Ret. Earnings, 12/31/04, $175,600
15 (2) Ret. Earnings, 12/31/04, $262,000
16 (2) Ret. Earnings, 12/31/04, $187,900
17 (2) Tot. stock. equity, $228,600
18 (2) Tot. stock. equity, $49,540,000
19 (1) Ret. Earnings, 12/31/04, $5,515,000
20 (2) Total stockholders' eq., $694,000
21 (2) 12/31/04 Treas. stock balance, $(3,000)
P16- 22 12/31/04 Preferred stock balance $100,000,000
23 (1) Long-term liab, $8,537,640
24 (7) $934,000
25 (2) Accounts payable balance, $51,000
26 1(5) Retained Earnings, cr, $9,000

Chapter 17

P17- 1 No check figure
2 1(c) Net income, $80,000
3 (2) Total gross profit expected, $160,000
4 (1) 2006 Construction in Progress, cr, $700,000
5 (1a) 2006 Gross loss, $(200,000)
6 (1) 2005 Construction in Progress, cr, $500,000
7 (1) Revenues, 12/31/05, $416,000
8 2005, Cash, dr, $466,000
9 Income summary, cr, $28,800
10 12/31/04 Income Recognized $(65,000)
11 2005 Continuing franchise fee receivable, dr, $4,750
12 (2) 12/31 Deferred gain, dr, $7,861,862
13 (2) Consignment inventory, $123,200
14 (2) 2005 Revenues, $20,640
15 (3) 2005 Total gross profit, $515,000

Chapter 18

P18- 1 No check figure
2 (1) E, (4) H, (6) J
3 (1) 12/31/04 Income Tax Exp., dr, $900
4 (1) 12/31/04 Inc. Tax Exp., dr, $117,870
5 (2) 12/31/04 Inc. Tax Pay., cr, $15,000
6 (2) 12/31/04 Def. Tax Liab., dr, $3,300
7 (3) 12/31/04 Def Tax Liab., cr, $2,250
8 (2) 12/31/04 Inc. Tax Pay., cr, $6,000
9 (1) 12/31/04 Inc. Tax Pay., cr, $17,310
10 (4) 12/31/05 Def. Tax Asset, cr, $4,500
11 (4) 12/31/05 Def. Tax Asset, cr, $4,500
12 (3) 12/31/04 Inc. Tax Pay., cr, $25,000
13 (2) 12/31/04 Inc. Tax Pay., cr, $31,500
14 (1) 12/31/04 Inc. Tax Pay., cr, $40,500
15 (4) 12/31/04 Deferred Tax Liab, cr, $810

Chapter 19

P19- 1 2005 Pension exp, $234,000
2 (2) 12/31/04 Pension cost, cr, $24,250
3 (1) 2004 Pension exp., $345,400
4 (1) 2004 Pension exp., $670,600
5 (4) 12/31/05 Unrecog. prior ser. cost, $1,860,000
6 (2) 2005 Pension exp., $831,930
7 2006 Recognized net loss, $(200)
8 (3) Add'l pension liab, dr, $2,000
9 (e) $108,800
10 (3) Pension exp., 2004, $197,490
11 (5) 2004 Add'l pension liab, cr, $1,200
12 (1) Amort. of unrecognized prior service cost, $8,600
13 (3) $28,569

Chapter 20

P20- 1 (2) Lessee: Rent Expense, dr, $70,000
2 (2) 12/31/04 Int. Rev., cr, $21,012.70
3 (3) Interest expense, 12/31/04, $36,000
4 (1) Interest rev, 12/31/07, $36,412.35
5 (2) Interest rev, 12/31/06, $21,995.66
6 (3) 12/31/05 Int. Rev., cr, $29,270.43
7 (3) 12/31/07 Int. Rev., cr, $16,834.44
8 Lessee: 12/31/04 Int. Exp., dr, $17,681.55
9 (1a) Periodic rental receipt, $17,160.24
10 (3) Interest Revenue, cr, $2,637.47
11 (2) 12/31/04 Int. Rev., cr, $32,815.47
12 Lessee: 12/31/04 Int. Exp., dr, $30,261.66
13 Total costs and expenses, $8,420,000
14 Operating lease for both
15 Lessor: 12/31/04 Int. Rev., cr, $360,000

Chapter 21

P21- 1 No check figure
2 Net cash prov. by op. activities, $73,000
3 Net decrease in cash, $(9,600)
4 Net increase in cash, $3,400
5 (1) C/S, cr, $4,000
6 Totals, bottom of worksheet, $22,195
7 (2) Net cash used for investing activities, $(15,100)
8 (2) Net cash prov. by op. activities, $22,950
9 Extraordinary loss from tornado, dr, $2,600
10 Total assets, $125,190
11 Net increase in cash, $7,600
12 (1) Ext gain (net) from condem of land cr, $8,560
13 (2) Net increase in cash, $45,000
14 Net increase in cash, $1,000
15 Net decrease in cash, $(2,400)
16 Worksheet totals (at bottom), $2,029,000
17 (2) Net cash prov. by op. activities, $20,200
18 Totals, worksheet entries columns (at bottom), $65,420

Chapter 22

P22- 1 No check figure
2 (1) 2005 Net income, $91,000
3 (2) 2005 End. ret. earn, $12,300
4 (2) 2004 End. ret. earn, $49,000
5 (1) Loss from cum. effect of change, dr, $98,000
6 (1) 1/1/05 Ret earnings, cr, $49,000
(2) 2004 Ret earnings adj., $84,000
7 (1) Depr expense, dr, $15,000
8 Decr. in income before tax, $49,000
9 (2) Def tax liab, 12/31/05, $450,000
10 (1) 2001 Net income, $3,850
11 (1a) Interest expense, dr, $6,864
12 (1) 2004 Correct net income, $37,200
13 2004 Correct net income, $16,100
14 (4) Allow for doubt accts, cr, $8,200
15 (1) 2005 Net adjustments, $52,000
16 (2) 2005 Correct net income, $(228,400)

Appendix C

PC- 1 (3) Total debits = $318,876
2 (2) Ret. earnings, 12/31/04, $11,695
3 (3) Total stock. equity, $40,515
4 Income tax exp., dr, $1,788
5 Income tax exp., dr, $3,087
6 Rent Revenue, cr, $985 adj.
7 Accum. Depr: Del. Equip., cr, $900
8 (1) Interest Rev., dr, $42
(2) Interest Rev., cr, $84
9 (5) Net Income, 0, Tot. Assets, N
10 (1) Liab. underst. by $16,000
11 Adv. to Sales Pers., cr, $300
12 Sales Journal, total, $13,800
13 (3) Total assets, $52,155
14 (2) Ret. earnings, 12/31/04, $12,765
15 (2) Cash balance, 11/30, $12,506
16 (4) Total stock. equity, $66,140
17 (2) Net income, $22,560
18 (2) Net income, $49,475

Appendix D

PD- 1 (2) f = $18,729.81
2 (3) p = $26,695.40
3 (3) F_d = $520,788.78
4 (2) C = $6,601.38
5 (3) $P_{deferred}$ = $45,818.00
6 (2) P_d = $53,463.74
7 (3) C = $24,429.31
8 (1) C = $7,913.92
9 (4) C = $9,600.97
10 (1) 7 dep. of $4,000 + $2,960.79 dep.
11 (1) C = $727.39
12 C = $1,496.65
13 Greene's plan: P_o = $44,399.98
14 C = $56,984.16
15 PV = $15,805.22
16 Cost = $5,992.71
17 Plan 3: PV = $577,020.93
18 b(1) 6 payments of $2,500 + $1,282.10
19 (3) C = $43,434.09

Appendix E

PE- 1 (1) Gross profit, $32,500
2 (2) 2000 and 2001 Income statement, no gains or losses
3 (2) NI, $15,854
4 (2) COGS, current cost basis, $101,500